The Political Economy of Poverty, Equity, and Growth

Series editors
Deepak Lal and Hla Myint

World Bank Comparative Studies

The Political Economy of Poverty, Equity, and Growth: Malawi
and Madagascar

Frederic L. Pryor

A World Bank
Comparative Study

*The Political
Economy of Poverty,
Equity, and Growth*

*Egypt
and
Turkey*

Bent Hansen

Published for the World Bank
Oxford University Press

Oxford University Press

OXFORD NEW YORK TORONTO DELHI
BOMBAY CALCUTTA MADRAS KARACHI
PETALING JAYA SINGAPORE HONG KONG
TOKYO NAIROBI DAR ES SALAAM
CAPE TOWN MELBOURNE AUCKLAND
and associated companies in
BERLIN IBADAN

© 1991 The International Bank for
Reconstruction and Development / THE WORLD BANK
1818 H Street, N.W., Washington, D.C. 20433, U.S.A.

Manufactured in the United States of America
First printing December 1991

The findings, interpretations, and conclusions expressed in
this study are the results of research done by the World Bank,
but they are those of the author and do not necessarily
represent the views and policies of the World Bank or
its Board of Executive Directors or the countries they represent.

Library of Congress Cataloging-in-Publication Data

Hansen, Bent, 1920–
    Egypt and Turkey / Bent Hansen.
        p.   cm.—(World Bank comparative studies. The Political
    economy of poverty, equity, and growth ; 2)
    Includes bibliographical references and index.
    ISBN 0-19-520825-0
        1. Egypt—Economic conditions—1918– 2. Income distribution—
Egypt—History. 3. Poor—Egypt—History. 4. Turkey—Economic
conditions—1918–1960. 5. Turkey—Economic conditions—1960–
6. Income distribution—Turkey—History. 7. Poor—Turkey—History.
I. Title. II. Series: World Bank comparative studies. Political
economy of poverty, equity, and growth ; research paper no. 2.
HC830.H36   1991
330.9561—dc20   91-27935
                                                            CIP

Foreword

This volume is the second of several emerging from the comparative study, "The Political Economy of Poverty, Equity and Growth," sponsored by the World Bank. The study was done to provide a critical evaluation of the economic history of selected developing countries in 1950–85. It explores the *processes* that yielded different levels of growth, poverty, and equity in these countries, depending on each country's initial resource endowment and economic structure, national institutions and forms of economic organization, and economic policies (including those that might have been undertaken).

The Scope of the Comparative Study

The basic building block of the project is a coherent story of the growth and income distribution experiences of a variety of developing countries, based on the methods of what may be termed "analytical economic history" (see Collier and Lal 1986) and "political economy." Each country study provides both a historical narrative and a deeper explanation of how and why things happened. Each study also seeks to identify the role of ideology and interest groups in shaping policy.

Our comparative approach involved pairing countries whose initial conditions or policies seemed to be either significantly similar or significantly different. Although initial impressions of similarity or difference may not have been borne out on closer inspection, this binary approach offered a novel and promising way of reconciling in-depth case studies with broader comparative methods of analysis.

To provide this in-depth study of individual cases, a smaller number of countries was selected than is conventional in comparative *statistical* studies. We have serious doubts about the validity of inferences drawn from such cross-sectional regression studies about historical processes (see Hicks 1979). Therefore this project, by combining qualitative with quantitative analysis, has tried instead to interpret the nature and significance of the usual quantifiable variables for each country in its historical and institutional context.

To provide some unifying elements to the project, we presented the authors of the country studies with several provisional hypotheses to be considered in their work. These concern the determinants of growth, the importance of historical and organizational factors in finding alternative paths of growth to redress poverty, and the relative roles of ideas, interests, and ideology in decisionmaking.

Our synthesis volume in this series discusses the extent to which these hypotheses were or were not substantiated in each of the country studies. The following list of the country studies and their principal authors suggests the range of the overall comparative study:

Malawi and Madagascar	Frederic L. Pryor
Egypt and Turkey	Bent Hansen
Sri Lanka and Malaysia	Henry Bruton
Indonesia and Nigeria	David Bevan, Paul Collier, and Jan Gunning
Thailand and Ghana	Oey A. Meesook, Douglas Rimmer, and Gus Edgren
Brazil and Mexico	Angus Maddison and Associates
Costa Rica and Uruguay	Simon Rottenberg, Claudio Gonzales-Vega, and Edgardo Favaro
Colombia and Peru	Antonio Urdinola, Mauricio Carrizosa Serrano, and Richard Webb
Five Small Economies:	Ronald Findlay and Stanislaw Wellisz
Hong Kong, Singapore,	
Malta Jamaica and	
Mauritius	

Many of these volumes will be published in this series by Oxford University Press. In addition, a volume of special studies on related topics, edited by George Psacharopoulos, will also be published.

This Volume

Bent Hansen's studies of Egypt and Turkey are magisterial analytical economic histories of the two countries since their independence in the 1920s. These countries were paired because of their similar population and initial levels of income and development in the 1920s.

Both countries were also secular Islamic countries with a common history as part of the Ottoman Empire, and both became independent nations about 1923. Moreover, they have been autocracies and parliamentary democracies for roughly half of their independent histories since then, though with a different time sequence. Despite these changes in political regime both have followed an etatist development strategy based on import-substituting industrialization and a growing reliance on burgeoning public sectors, (at least until Turkey's turnabout in 1980).

Turkey grew faster than Egypt in the interwar period, but since then both have grown at about the same rate. Hansen attributes the faster rate for Turkey between wars to its higher agricultural growth rate. Turkey, unlike Egypt, which reached its land frontier in about 1900, had abundant land and expanded its cultivated area.

Since 1960 Turkey's agricultural growth was only slightly greater than Egypt's, but its industrial growth has been higher since independence. In the 1970s Egypt compensated for its lower industrial and agricultural growth with temporary growth in the petroleum sector and improvements in its terms of trade.

Hansen finds that inequality between rich and poor was greater in Turkey, and changes in equality seemed to correspond to Kuznet's U curve. Using education as an indicator of equality of opportunity, however, Hansen finds that Turkey has had more success in raising the educational level of its general population, even though it spent less than Egypt. This is in part because of the bias toward higher education in Egypt and the growing employment of graduates in a public sector in which they have a zero or negative marginal product.

Hansen blames both countries' low growth in total factor productivity on the etatist development strategy. In explaining the similar development strategy he discounts many current explanations from political economy. Instead, he emphasizes the importance of economic nationalism and the example of German industrialization influenced by List's ideas—as the dominant ideology of the interwar elites.

Hansen discusses the contrasting role of the military in the two countries and of the two leading autocrats—Atatürk in Turkey and Nasser in Egypt. He argues that although they began with a preference for market-based industrialization, they turned to etatism because of exogenously generated crises—the 1930s economic crisis in Turkey, and the 1955–56 Suez crisis in Egypt. He shows how the different nature of the military autocracies—a self-appointed Platonic Guardian role in Turkey, and a predatory spoils system in Egypt—affected economic and political evolution in the two countries.

He attempts to use the recent three-factor, factor-proportions, and trade-theoretic models to show how the evolution of real wages and, to some extent, economic policy can be explained by these deeper forces of political economy. He also provides a political economy explanation for the two countries' different agricultural price and consumer subsidy policies. Detailed discussions of land distribution, labor and product markets, and social development, for example, give the reader an up-to-date account of the economic history of the two countries.

Hansen provides an analytical account of the evolution of two economies, which takes into consideration the complex interactions between ideology and interests. This should be of wide interest—not only to economists, but also to political scientists and historians.

Deepak Lal and Hla Myint
Series editors

Contents

Preface

This book compares the political economy of growth in relation to equity and poverty in Egypt and Turkey, covering the period of modern national independence, which began in both countries in 1923. Radical stereotypes of class struggle, neocolonialism, and dependency were not useful for understanding developments. The "new" political economy, on the other hand, helps to explain, in terms of political exchange, details of politics during the period of democracy in Egypt from 1923 to 1952 and in Turkey since 1950 (with interruptions by temporary military takeovers). For the periods of dictatorship in Egypt since 1952 under Nasser, Sadat, and Mubarak, and in Turkey before 1950 under Atatürk and the Kemalists, the new political economy is less useful. While the political economy under dictatorship and military rule in Turkey may best be characterized as enlightened, platonic guardianship, in Egypt it has been a peculiar mixture of predatory rule and social compact, a solution typical of weak dictatorship with a self-serving elite, forced for its survival to placate the populace. From the outset, balanced sectoral growth was visualized in both Egypt and Turkey, but both the choice and implementation of development strategy and the institutional setting have in each country been decisively influenced by ideologies adopted by rulers and nationalistic elites.

In both countries import substitution was the chosen and, from around 1930, the implemented industrialization strategy, influenced by List's infant-industry philosophy and its apparent success in Imperial Germany. This strategy in effect still prevails in Egypt. Turkey, under pressure from international organizations oriented toward private enterprise, free trade, and market forces, shifted in 1980 to a strategy of export-led growth with structural reforms and thereby gave up the etatist ideology and institutional framework, which had been formulated and introduced by Atatürk in the early 1930s. The etatist ideology and framework, under the label of Arab socialism and with extensive nationalizations and confiscations, were imposed on Egypt by Nasser and continued, with modifications, under Sadat and Mubarak. While early etatism in Turkey may have been a rational response to the Great Depression, in postwar Egypt under the (international) great expansion it served to replace private with state ownership and modern entrepreneurship with a monstrous bureaucracy.

Agricultural strategy in the two countries was adapted to entirely different natural conditions of water supply and relative abundance of land. With the Nile the single source of water supply in Egypt, development of a modern irrigation system was initiated in the early nineteenth century and culminated under Nasser with the construction of the Aswan High Dam between 1959 and 1971. The system was enormously profitable before World War I, when the limits for economically cultivable lands were reached; returns thereafter rapidly decreased. Without the electricity it provided, the dam might not have been socially profitable. Centralized administration of irrigation gave etatism a strong role in Egyptian agriculture, that has had no counterpart in Turkey. Until the 1950s agricultural etatism in Egypt continued policies of exploiting natural advantages for exports (cotton), which on balance were unsuccessful during this century because of ecological problems. Since the 1960s, in line with basic needs philosophies, Egypt has increasingly promoted import substitution in food production. Land reforms were shallow and contributed little to equity or eradication of poverty but did extend the influence of the bureaucracy on agriculture well beyond the control of the irrigation system. Since the turn of the twentieth century, agriculture has not been a growth sector of any consequence.

Turkey until the late 1950s was essentially a frontier country (in the American sense of the word). Expansion of the transport system and the distribution of public lands made agriculture the leading growth sector with beneficial effects on equity and poverty. With the frontier conquered around 1960 Turkey fell into the same mediocre development patterns as Egypt, yet with agriculture subjected to less economic discrimination than in Egypt. Under democracy Turkish agriculture got the political clout Egyptian agriculture lost under dictatorship.

Achievements in the two countries cannot easily be tied to developments in the political economy. External shocks, wars, and violent changes in terms of trade have affected the two countries in very different ways. Migration of workers fluctuated with conditions abroad. Natural endowments such as surplus land conditioned rapid growth with improved equity in Turkey during the 1930s when land-scarce Egypt stagnated with real rents of land high and increasing. Surplus oil conditioned rapid growth with improved equity in Egypt after the mid-1970s when the oil price boosts sent Turkey's economy into recession.

Conventional stereotypes do not apply easily either. Market orientation (Egypt in the 1930s and Turkey in the 1980s) has not generally been accompanied by high growth or equity; import substitution and etatism have not generally been accompanied by low growth and improved equity. Demand management has in both countries been poor and helped to create inflation and current account deficits with soaring foreign debts. Poor management of demand more than misallocation of resources created the need for stabilization programs that led to recessions. Any beneficial effects that public expenditure programs might have had on investments and the alleviation of poverty may have been lost through effects of inflationary financing. On balance, over the six decades considered in the study, both countries achieved moderate growth and possibly some improvement in equity and alleviation of poverty. Generally, however, developments in both countries have been too complex to permit simplistic inference and conclusions about causes and effects of poverty, equity, and growth. Social relations and processes are, of course, complex and the aim of this study is to give insight into the complexities of such phenomena in Egypt and Turkey. This is the most that honest social scientists can hope for.

The study covers the period from 1923 to 1985. It is still too early to evaluate the effects of the change of strategy in Turkey in 1980 from etatist import substitution to market-oriented export-led growth. A spectacular, lasting increase in manufactured exports and in trade generally was accomplished, yet it was accompanied by high unemployment and inflation at very uneven growth rates and the result was probably an increase in inequity and poverty. A decade after the reforms were set in motion, they cannot be described as an unmixed success. Egypt has since 1982 been faced with an even stronger debt and foreign exchange crisis than the one that brought reform to Turkey. Its stagnating and inflationary economy—still without significant reforms—can safely be described as a definite failure that only profound political and institutional reform can repair.

While the topics investigated are those that I felt were appropriate, not all of them could be covered adequately because data were not always available or reliable. In recent decades, for instance, the very substantial migration abroad of workers from both countries has profoundly affected many aspects of their economies. Workers' remittances have been dealt with in the study, but the relatively rich information on Turkish workers in Europe has been largely ignored because no corresponding (reliable) information exists for Egypt. Similarly, the relatively rich information on the rural labor market in Egypt could not be fully utilized because comparable information for Turkey is missing. Such a mismatch of information has prevented a full, balanced discussion in other areas also. It is particularly regrettable, however, that a phenomenon so important as migration should suffer from this information problem.

During the almost five years that this project has been under way, I have worked along the guidelines formulated by the originators of the project, Deepak Lal and Hla Myint. Although I did not agree in all details with their approach, it was a source of inspiration that helped to bring order to my thinking about development in Egypt and Turkey, two countries I have worked on for many years. I learned much from the other participants in the project and their struggles with the countries they were comparing. I also received invaluable assistance, information, and help from a number of colleagues whom I wish to recognize individually.

Professor Şevket Pamuk of Villanova University served as consultant for the project and made important contributions to the part dealing with Turkey. His research in the history of the Ottoman Empire made him the obvious person to work out preliminary drafts of chapters 7, 8, and 9; beyond that, he invested a great deal of time in providing data and other information. He drew my attention to the national accounting estimates for 1923–48 by Bulutay, Tezel, and Yıeldırım (1974) upon which my interpretation of development under Atatürk and his followers heavily depends. I would have liked Professor Pamuk to appear as coauthor of these parts of the volume, and I wish to thank him and give him the credit he deserves.

Professor Khairy Tourk of the Illinois Institute of Technology also served as a consultant, working especially on aspects of the political economy under Nasser and Sadat. He collected interesting and not always easily accessible information about family and other relations crucial for the connections between private and public businesses under Sadat. His extensive notes on this matter served me well in drafting chapter 4. In addition he collected valuable budget data back to the early 1950s. His work for the project is greatly appreciated.

Dr. Edward F. Lucas, a specialist on index theory and computation, generously and without compensation gave his time to the project, using data from United Nations Conference on Trade and Development (UNCTAD) tapes to compute detailed trade indexes of the Fisher type for Egypt and Turkey for the period 1960 to 1985. The material is presented in chapters 1, 4, 6, and 12. An unusual piece of information, it particularly illuminates Turkey's remarkable export performance after the liberalization policies of 1980.

I also benefited greatly from statistical and econometric work on Phillips and other relations for Egypt and Turkey by Jariya Charoenwattana.

I am deeply grateful to Professors Elie Kedourie of the London School of Economics and Anne O. Krueger of Duke University for their careful reading and incisive criticism of my manuscript. Professor Kedourie raised a number of historical points related to both Turkey and Egypt. Professor Krueger, who as vice-president of the World Bank in charge of research courageously sponsored this and a number of other projects in the controversial area of political economy, prompted me specifically to question closely the overvaluation of currencies.

While working on the project I had the opportunity to discuss special problems with Professor Heba Handoussa of the American University of Cairo, Professor Şherif Mardin of Bosporus University, Dr. Karim Nashashibi of the International Monetary Fund, and Professor Robert Springborg of Macquarie University. Professor Springborg kindly let me read the manuscript of his recent study of Mubarak's style of government. At the International Labour Office, Geneva, Dr. Ralph Turvey, then chief of the ILO's statistical division, gave me access to valuable information from the Turkish labor force surveys. At the conferences of the project, members of the external review panel raised many valuable points. My almost permanent reviewer, Professor Perry Anderson of the history department at University of California at Los Angeles, gave me much criticism and encouragement in my work.

Employees in the World Bank and the Institute of International Studies at the University of California at Berkeley helped me in many ways. Among them I want especially to mention Leela Thampy and Nadine Zelinski who typed subsequent drafts of my manuscript.

Editorial work was in the hands of Alice M. Carroll. She did much to improve language and style as well as the presentation of data. It was a great pleasure to work with a craftsman of her caliber.

A very large amount of my work and time has gone into the production of this volume, and the international environment has at times been hostile. So much the more I value the practical and moral support I invariably have enjoyed from my beloved wife Soad Ibrahim Refaat.

I The Arab Republic of Egypt

1 Growth, Equity, and Poverty, 1923–85

From the time the British consolidated their power over Egypt in the 1880s to Gamal Abdel Nasser's consolidation of power in the 1950s, Egypt was characterized by private entrepreneurship and trade largely free from direct control. Its development policies consisted mainly of export promotion through public investment in agriculture and, from 1930, gentle protection through tariffs and subsidies for industry and a few agricultural products. Since the time of Nasser, public ownership in the modern sector, massive controls, and import substitution have predominated. From around 1900 to the mid-1950s the economy was stagnant, with the real national income per capita growing at an average rate of at most 0.5 percent. From 1960 to the mid-1980s the rate was 2.5–3 percent. Over these twenty-five years Egypt on balance grew at a rate not far from the rates that Japan and Sweden experienced before World War II. Available data, moreover, indicate that inequity and poverty may not have been more serious by the mid-1980s than they were when Nasser took over. Indeed, Egypt appears to be a relatively equitable society with reasonably good nutrition. Government, public enterprises, controls, and import substitution seem to have been succeeding where private enterprise and free trade with a mix of export promotion and import substitution previously failed. Many qualifications must be added to this picture of growth, equity, and poverty in Egypt, but the main record since independence is not unfavorable.

The image of Egypt as a developing country is less favorable than the record suggests. The problem is not, I think, that the record is statistically grossly misleading, although problems with national accounting and statistical indicators are disturbing. It is a fact of life that naked feet and street beggars have virtually disappeared in Egypt. But the achievements in growth, equity, and poverty in Egypt have been very uneven and their costs unnecessarily high; and yet they have to be paid.

The inefficiency of the public sector, the ineptness of government controls and policies, and the increasing corruption are indisputable. The Egyptian economy has been seriously mismanaged. However, economic inefficiency does not necessarily prevent a relatively high rate of growth with equity from prevailing. Some communist countries have, to a point at least, demonstrated this possibility. In Egypt, more could have been achieved, given the inputs—in other words, what was achieved could have been done at a lower cost.

Egypt's habit of living on the future makes the country highly vulnerable and dependent on the vagaries of international economic and political developments. Since the late 1950s when its net foreign debt was close to zero and total national expenditure almost exactly equal to national income, Egypt's expenditure has grown about 1 percent faster than its income. As a consequence Egypt has become one of the world's heavily indebted nations, with a relative public debt larger than that of Brazil or Mexico. It would take a highly efficient investment policy to justify a debt (increase) the size of Egypt's, but no such efficiency exists in Egypt. In its inability to make ends meet, moreover, Egypt has placed itself at the mercy, political designs, and calculations of donors and international financiers. Growth might stop, with unpleasant consequences for equity and wealth, the moment international aid and finance stopped, leaving Egypt politically incapable of rectifying its internal imbalances. The long period of warfare from 1963 to 1973,[1] when real growth may have been close to zero and both inequity and poverty appear to have increased, is a case in point. It seems now to be repeated. Another long period of stagnation would make Egypt's achievements since the 1950s unimpressive.

Egypt's story since the late 1950s is one of replacement of an unsuccessful private-enterprise, free-trade policy with a relatively successful, albeit inefficient and vulnerable, controlled economy with a large public sector. An imperfect democracy was replaced by autocracy. From a political economy point of view it is crucial never to forget that there were two basic institutional changes in the 1950s: the economic shift from private enterprise and free trade to heavily controlled economy with a large public sector, and the political shift from (incomplete) democracy to autocracy.[2] War and international politics interfered repeatedly, with profound effects on spending and foreign trade. The political economy of these developments is complex and analyzing them requires a flexible, pragmatic approach, using several models of political economy that can serve as a basis for analysis of the autocratic regimes that played an important role after 1952.

The Growth Record

Information on the growth of population, production, income, and expenditure between 1929 and 1986–87 is shown in Tables 1–1 and 1–2. Only crude indicators of growth exist for a few sectors before 1939; estimates of growth of gross domestic product (GDP) and gross national income (GNI) are nothing but conjectures. For 1939 to 1959–60, unofficial estimates do exist for the basic aggregates, GDP and GNI (Hansen and Marzouk 1965, statistical appendix). I believe that orders of absolute magnitude and growth rates based on these estimates may be trusted, but details may not be reliable and decimal points are deceptive. For years after 1959–60, official national accounting estimates exist. Estimates for the period 1959–60 to 1964–65, with revisions to correct obvious shortcomings, are in my view also fairly reliable (Hansen in Vatikiotis 1968).

From 1965 to fiscal 1981–82 the estimates used are those reported by the Ministry of Planning, which has always been secretive about methodology and statistical practices. My understanding is that the ministry in principle applies international standard methods of national accounting. Any shortcomings could arise from the methods themselves (use of distorted prices, or measurement of general government GDP from the input side, two problems of great importance in the context of Egypt) or from deficiencies in the data (inadequate deflators and poor data for the informal sector, also important for Egypt). These shortcomings could significantly bias the results in terms of both levels of income and growth rates. While deliberate "cooking" of statistics probably can be ruled out, the several shifts from calendar to fiscal years and vice-versa obviously had the effect of making data "opaque"—for whatever reasons. While income levels may, if anything, be underestimated and growth rates may be exaggerated, both may be used with caution as crude indicators of general welfare until the early 1980s.

The period 1981–82 to 1986–87 poses a serious dilemma, for the World Bank has published national accounting estimates for these years that deviate significantly from the estimates of the Ministry of Planning. The World Bank estimates an average rate of GDP growth of 4.1 percent annually, while the Ministry of Planning shows a rate of 6.9 percent (see table 1–1). The World Bank's estimates of real national income per capita for 1981–82 to 1986–87 show complete stagnation while the ministry's estimates point to about 3 percent growth, no different from the average for 1960 to 1981–82. Neither source has published details of the estimates and methods used. I am inclined to trust the World Bank estimates, thus concluding that Egypt from the early 1980s entered a period of stagnation. Adverse terms of trade played an important role but internal efficiency problems contributed significantly.

The periods in table 1–1 conform to the distinction between a private enterprise–free trade development period in 1929–55 (trade profoundly disturbed, of course , by World War II and its aftermath) and an etatist period in 1960–87. The quality of data available established the 1929–39 and 1939–55 periods. After 1960, the data are broken down into two high-growth periods, 1959–60 to 1964–65 and 1973 to 1981–82, and two low-growth periods, 1964–65 to 1973 and 1981–82 to 1986–87. The

Table 1-1. Growth of Population, Production, and Expenditure, Selected Periods, 1929–87

(percent p.a.)

Category	1929–39	1939–55	1959–60 to 1964–65	1964–65 to 1973	1973 to 1981–82	1959–60 to 1981–82	1981–82 to 1986–87 Ministry of Planning	1981–82 to 1986–87 World Bank
Population	1.2	2.1	2.6	2.4	2.6	2.5	2.7	2.7
Production sector								
Agriculture	1.1	0.5	3.7	1.8	2.2	2.4	3.5	2.2
Industry, petroleum, and mining	n.a.	5.6	6.6	3.3	9.3	6.4	8.4 ⎫	
Industry and mining	n.a.	n.a.	n.a.	n.a.	7.6[a]	n.a.	9.1 ⎬ 7.8	5.6
Petroleum	n.a.	n.a.	n.a.	n.a.	43.6[a]	n.a.	7.7 ⎭	
Electricity	n.a.	n.a.	14.0	15.0	11.3	13.3	13.6 ⎫	
Public utilities	n.a.	n.a.	4.8	6.4	[b]	n.a.	17.6 ⎬ 7.8	
Construction	n.a.	n.a.	16.6	1.2	5.5	6.3	3.3 ⎭	
Transport and communications	n.a.	n.a.	11.3	-2.4	22.2	10.0	7.3 ⎫	
Trade and finance	n.a.	n.a.	2.2	4.1	11.7	6.6	7.1 ⎬ 7.3	3.6
Housing	n.a.	n.a.	1.5	1.8	7.5	3.9	9.2	
Other services	n.a.	n.a.	7.6	6.1	6.1	6.4	7.5 ⎭	
Gross domestic product								
At factor cost	1.5[c]	2.5	6.1	3.1	8.1	5.8	6.9	4.1
At factor cost per capita	0.3[c]	0.4	3.5	0.7	5.5	3.3	4.2	1.4

Gross national income								
At market price	1.0[c]	3.5[c]	6.7	3.5	7.3	5.7	n.a.	2.8
At market price per capita	-0.2[c]	1.4[c]	4.1	1.1	4.7	3.2	n.a.	0.1
Total expenditure	n.a.	n.a.	6.0	4.7	8.7	6.6	n.a.	2.9
Consumption								
Total	n.a.	n.a.	6.5	4.7	7.4	6.2	7.0	5.4
Public	n.a.	n.a.	12.0	7.4	4.2	7.1	7.0	3.2
Private	n.a.	n.a.	5.1	3.8	8.6	6.0	7.4	6.2
Total investment	n.a.	n.a.	14.5	-1.8	18.4	9.6	n.a.	-5.4
National saving	n.a.	n.a.	8.1	-8.9	11.9	2.8	n.a.	-45.4
Exports[d]	0.9[e]	-1.4[e]	5.2	-0.6	12.6	5.8	n.a.	3.1
Imports[d]	-3.4[e]	2.3[e]	10.3	4.7	11.6	8.7	n.a.	0.3

Growth rates are based on various constant price estimates.

n.a. = Not available.
a. For 1974 to 1981–82.
b. Included in electricity.
c. Conjecture.
d. Goods and nonfactor services.
e. Does not include nonfactor services.

Source: Wattleworth (1975); Hansen and Marzouk (1965), statistical appendix; Ikram (1980), statistical appendix; Egypt, Ministry of Planning and International Cooporation (1987); World Bank (1988); and World Bank data.

Table 1-2. Shares of Growth, by Production Sector, 1945–82

(percent)

Category	1945 to 1952–53[a]	1952–53 to 1959–60[b]	1959–60 to 1964–65[c]	1965–66 to 1970–71[d]	1970–71 to 1974[e]	1974 to 1981–82[f]
Production sector						
Agriculture	7.7	21.6	18.1	14.2	12.3	8.2
Industry and mining	15.1[g]	25.1[g]	32.3[h]	32.8[h]	9.0[h]	14.4
Petroleum	—	—	—	—	—	13.0
Electricity and public utilities	—	—	3.5	8.3	7.1	1.5
Construction	5.2	5.9	7.6	4.4	-10.1	5.5
Transport and communications	16.3[i]	11.9[i]	16.2[i]	-15.2[i]	10.4[i]	10.0
Suez Canal	—	—	—	—	—	7.5
Trade, finance, and insurance	23.3	16.0	5.7	9.6	21.5	22.8
Housing	7.4	4.9	1.8	3.5	2.0	3.5
Other services[j]	25.1	14.6	15.0	42.4	47.9	13.5

Gross domestic product	100	100	100	100	100	100	100
Type of production							
Capital intensive	38.7	41.8	53.4	28.4	27.0	50.0	
Labor intensive	61.3	58.2	46.6	71.6	73.0	50.0	
Type of goods							
Traded	22.8[k]	46.7[k]	50.3[k]	47.0[k]	21.2[k]	44.7	
Nontraded	77.2	53.3	49.7	53.0	78.8	55.3	

Shares of growth are based on constant factor costs.
— = Not applicable.
a. Based on 1954 prices.
b. Based on 1953–54 prices.
c. Based on 1959–60 prices.
d. Based on 1964–65 prices.
e. Based on 1970 prices.
f. Based on 1975 prices.
g. Includes petroleum and electricity and public utilities.
h. Includes petroleum.
i. Includes Suez Canal.
j. Presumably includes government.
k. Does not include Suez Canal and tourism.
Source: Hansen and Marzouk (1965), statistical appendix; Hansen in Vatikiotis (1968); Ikram (1980), statistical appendix; World Bank data.

low-growth periods are the time of Egypt's involvement in open warfare in the Republic of Yemen, Sinai, and the Suez Canal Zone and the time when in the 1980s overspending with the failure of the old import-substitution strategy brought Egypt into a financial crisis that in early 1990 remained unsolved. The periodization, discussed in chapters 2 and 3, may be schematically set out as follows:

Period	Institutional setting	Basic development strategy
1929–55	Private enterprise, free trade, moderate-sized public sector (World War II)	In agriculture, mainly export promotion (public investment); in industry, import substitution (protection)
1955–60	Period of transition	Essentially unchanged
1960–65	Etatism, peace economy, strongly increasing public sectors, first five-year plan	In agriculture, export promotion and import substitution; in industry, import substitution
1965–73	Etatism, war economy, large public sectors	Subordination to military considerations
1973–	Etatism, peace economy, *infitah* (partial liberalization), large public sectors	Import substitution in agriculture and industry; in oil, Suez Canal, and tourism, promotion of export-oriented activities; migration of workers

Growth rates in table 1–1 are shown for real gross domestic product at factor cost, which is conventionally used to measure productivity, and for real gross national income at market prices, which is used as an indicator of national welfare. The difference between the two aggregates consists of indirect taxes minus subsidies (which from a national point of view is essentially a bookkeeping item) and terms of trade effects and net factor income, both items of national economic relevance. The debate about income and poverty in developing countries has paid close attention to the latter two items; some participants argue that terms of trade and net factor income explain the differences between rich and poor countries. Be that as it may, for Egypt the long-term net effects of these items have been small.

Trade indexes for Egypt go back to 1885 and some estimates of terms of trade even go back to the midnineteenth century (Hansen and Lucas 1978; Issawi 1961). The net barter terms of trade from 1885 to 1961 (annually chained Fisher indexes) shown in figure 1–1 did not move against Egypt. They fluctuated sharply for relatively short terms but their trend was favorable (if it makes sense to talk about a trend). Terms of trade deteriorated dramatically, by 31.5 percent, from 1929 to 1939. After World War II a strong recovery took place; at the peak of the Korean War boom, terms of trade were 56 percent above their 1929 level. The gain was lost

Figure 1-1. Terms of Trade, 1885-61

Index (1929 = 100)

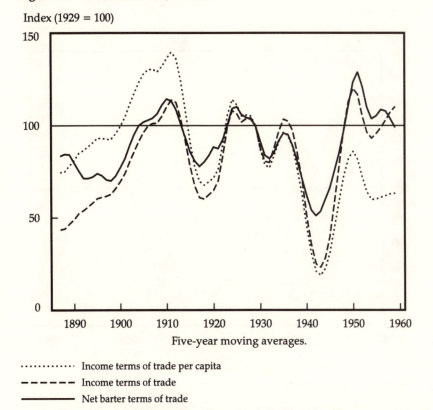

Five-year moving averages.

············ Income terms of trade per capita

－－－－－－ Income terms of trade

─────── Net barter terms of trade

Source: Hansen and Lucas (1978, p. 437).

again in 1955 and in 1960 they were about 10 percent below the 1929 level. For 1961–65 reliable indexes are not available, but terms of trade may not have changed much during this short period and may have improved slightly.

The index of net barter terms of trade in figure 1–2, based on annually chained Fisher price indexes for exports and imports in U.S. dollar values, is probably the best available for years after 1965. From the 1950s, all series are increasingly marred by the existence of multiple exchange rates or other serious trade data problems.[3] The Fisher series indicates a small improvement in 1965–74 and a decline in 1974–78 with a slightly upward trend from 1965 to 1978. There is a violent improvement, by about 80 percent, in 1978–81, followed by a slow decline to 1985. These developments are what should be expected considering Egypt's net oil trade position, changing in 1976.[4]

The World Bank series depicted in figure 1–2, covering 1966–86, seems to be based on implicit deflators (apparently the Paasche type for

Figure 1-2. Net Barter Terms of Trade, 1965-86

Index (1980 = 100)

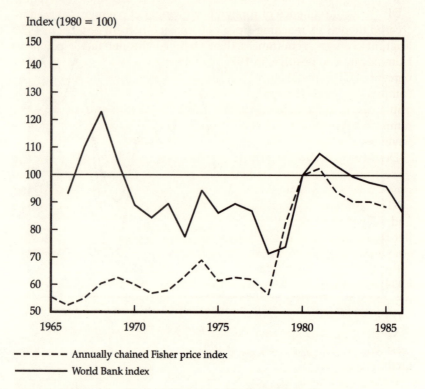

- - - - - - Annually chained Fisher price index
——————— World Bank index

Source: World Bank (1988); Fisher price indexes computed by Edward F. Lucas
from UNCTAD tape.

1966–80 and the Laspeyres type for 1980–86). Index formulas are unusually important for foreign trade in Egypt, especially for the 1970s and
1980s when relative price changes were violent (Hansen and Lucas
1978; Hansen 1983). While the Fisher index indicates a weak upward
trend in 1965–78, the World Bank index indicates the opposite tendency,
with the two indexes showing weakly correlated short-term movements.
For 1978–85 the short-term movements are quite similar although the
Fisher index indicates a stronger improvement in 1978–81 than the
World Bank index. The latter index for 1985–86 shows a violent decline
as should be expected.

The Fisher series clearly indicates a tendency to improve over the period 1965–85 but the World Bank data show no clear tendency. Thus the
trend in terms of trade from the early 1960s to the mid-1980s remains in
doubt.

Net factor payments abroad (including migrant workers' remittances)
declined strongly after World War II as a result of repayment of the pub-

lic debt during the war. During 1930–39, these may have been 2–3 percent of GDP; in the 1950s they had declined to less than 1 percent of
GDP. As a consequence of foreign borrowing, net payments abroad increased thereafter, reaching a peak of almost 3 percent of GDP in 1976.
Migrant workers' remittances then changed the net factor payments
from negative to positive; in 1979 net factor income reached a peak of 8
percent of GDP in real terms. But strongly increasing public debt and accompanying interest payments caused net factor income, including remittances, to drop below 1 percent of GDP in 1981–82. In 1985–86,
remittances appear to have been swallowed completely by interest
payments.

Despite the very strong fluctuations in both terms of trade gains (and
losses) and net factor payments (including remittances) and their, at
times, very substantial relative size, measured growth rates of GDP and
GNI in real terms do not diverge much over the long term (5.5 percent
and 5.2 percent, respectively, for 1960 to 1986–87). Terms of trade and
net factor payments together have not been important growth factors.
For shorter periods, however, the impact has been significant. The largest positive contribution to the average growth rate (1 percent) was in
1939–55, and the contributions were positive but more modest (about
0.5 percent) in 1960–65 and 1965–73. It might cause surprise that for
1973 to 1981–82 the growth rate of GNI was 0.8 percent lower than that
of GDP. The largest negative net contribution, −1.3 percent in 1981–82,
was caused by a combination of terms of trade loss and declining net
factor payments.

Population growth accelerated strongly from 1930 to 1985. From 1.2
percent for 1929–39, the growth rate increased to 2.4 percent for
1950–60 and 2.6 percent for 1960–70. After a slight decline in the late
1960s and early 1970s, the population growth rate increased further and
reached a level of 3 percent around 1980. Population growth thus absorbed increasing shares of both production and income growth from
the 1930s to the 1980s.

In comparing 1929–55, the period dominated by private enterprise,
and the etatist period beginning about 1960, the problem of the two national account estimates for 1982–83 to 1986–87 makes it best to limit
the later period to 1960 to 1981–82. Lengthening the etatist period to
1986–87 would result in a slightly better outcome using the Ministry of
Planning estimates for 1982–83 to 1986–87 and a slightly worse outcome using the World Bank estimates—in terms of the growth of GDP at
factor cost per capita (table 1–1) for 1960 to 1986–87, a rate of 3.5 percent for the former and 2.9 percent for the latter, against 3.3 percent for
1960 to 1981–82. A growth difference of 0.6 percent through a period of
twenty-six and a half years is not negligible, but for the comparison with
the 1929–55 period it makes no difference in orders of magnitude. For
evaluating the history of etatism in Egypt, on the other hand, the five

years to 1986–87 make all the difference; they are brought into the picture later.

In terms of both gross domestic product and gross national income the difference between the growth achievements during 1929–55 and 1960 to 1981–82 is striking. For the former period the average growth rate of GDP may have been about 2 percent with about 2.5 percent for GNI (0.2 percent and 0.7 percent per capita, respectively). For the latter period these growth rates were 5.8 percent and 5.7 percent, respectively (3.3 percent and 3.2 percent per capita). Although the agricultural growth rate was relatively low during 1960 to 1981–82, about 2½ percent, it was still much higher than during 1929–55 when it may have been only about 0.75 percent. Equally interesting is the fact that measured growth rates for industry and mining (not including petroleum) did not increase between 1939–55 and 1960 to 1981–82 but remained at the relatively mediocre level of 5.6–5.8 percent. The high-growth sectors during 1960 to 1981–82 were petroleum, electricity, and transport and communications, the latter carried by the Suez Canal. The nationalization of the canal took place in 1954 and canal revenues began accruing to Egypt after the Suez War. One reason for leaving the years 1955–60 out of table 1–1 is to avoid counting the nationalization act itself as a growth factor; subsequently, of course, the ownership became very important in view of the rapidly increasing tolls, paid in hard currency. The same argument holds for the Egyptianization of companies during the Suez War; while the confiscation of British and French capital would have no direct effect on GDP, it would boost GNI with the decline in factor payments abroad.

Table 1–2 throws further light on the growth process for each sector, showing contribution to total growth. It is not possible to construct this table unambiguously using data before 1945 and after 1981–82. The sectoral contributions to total GDP growth depend on both the relative size of the sector and its own growth rate. The data dictate both the periods and the sectors shown in the table. Notice that petroleum was relatively unimportant until the latest period and that the several closures and openings of the Suez Canal create special problems for transport and communications.

The contribution of agriculture to total growth has been small since World War II. Having reached a peak of 22 percent in 1952–53 to 1959–60, it declined steadily to 8 percent in 1974 to 1981–82. There is nothing here to indicate any impact from the Aswan High Dam, the monument of Nasser's development policies. The main impact of the dam shows up in electricity and public utilities from 1965–66 to 1974. The contribution from industry increased remarkably, from 15 percent in 1945 to 1952–53 (including both petroleum and electricity and public utilities) to 32–33 percent in 1959–60 to 1970–71 (including petroleum, unimportant), but it then declined to 9 percent in 1970–71 to 1974 and 14 percent in 1974 to 1981–82 (not including petroleum, now important). More-over, there are strikingly large contributions from such sectors as trade, finance, and insurance and other services (including government). The growth contributions by main sectors are summarized in table 1–3.

For 1952–53 to 1981–82 as a whole, the primary growth sector is trade, finance, and other services (including government), which gener-ated no less than 2.0 percentage points, or 39.1 percent of the total GDP growth rate of 5.1 percent. Other sectors, dominated by petroleum and the Suez Canal, generated 1.5 percentage points, or 28.8 percent of the total growth rate. Industry and agriculture were clearly secondary fac-tors, accounting for 20.2 percent and 11.7 percent, respectively, of the total growth rate from 1952–53 to 1981–82. Industry (excluding petro-leum) has not been a driving force in Egyptian growth since 1952. And agriculture's even smaller contribution points to one of the basic failures in Egyptian growth policy since 1952. The only period after 1952 in which industry dominated the picture is 1959–60 to 1964–65, the period of the first five–year plan; even then, industry and agriculture together did not generate more than half the total growth in GDP. During the other high-growth period, 1974–82, industry and agriculture together generated only 22 percent of total growth; the main contribution, about 40 percent of total growth, came from other sectors (including petro-leum and Suez Canal).

While the contributions from agriculture, industry, and other sectors (including petroleum) probably are real enough, it is the composite sec-tor of trade, finance, and other services (including government) that gives rise to suspicion about a possible upward bias in the estimates of the growth rate for total GDP. Trade and finance may include socially wasteful transaction costs (as emphasized by Douglass North) and both trade and government may include disguised unemployment. That the contributions from trade and finance should have been high after World War II (1945–53) is natural and the same may be argued for the period 1974 to 1981–82 after Sadat's *infitah* (opening, or liberalization) when private imports and capital movements increased strongly. But for the whole period, trade controls and protectionism with accompanying rent seeking may have induced significant, socially unnecessary transaction costs. Public employment expanded very strongly from 1962 to 1973 as a consequence of military build-up and from 1964 to 1987 as a conse-quence of the government's policy of automatic employment of gradu-ates from secondary and higher education and of discharged army draftees. In both cases the contribution to national welfare may be nomi-nal and even negative. To get some idea of orders of magnitude, assume that a contribution of about 1.5 percentage units from this sector would represent real growth for the years 1970–71 to 1981–82; the average growth rate of total GDP for 1945 to 1981–82 would decline by about 0.5 percentage unit from 5.1 percent to about 4.5 percent. This may have

Table 1-3. Growth Rate of Gross Domestic Product, by Main Sectors, 1945–82
(percent)

Category	1945 to 1952–53	1952–53 to 1959–60	1959–60 to 1964–65	1965–66 1970–71	1970–71 to 1974	1974 1981–82	1952–53 to 1981–82
Sector							
Agriculture	0.3	0.8	1.0	0.4	0.4	0.7	0.6
Industry	0.7[a,b]	1.0[a,b]	1.8[a]	1.0[a]	0.3[a]	1.3	1.0
Trade, finance, and other services (including government)	2.2	1.2	1.2	1.6	2.4	3.2	2.0
Other	1.3	0.8	1.6[b]	0.1[b]	0.3[b]	3.7[a,b]	1.5
Total GDP	4.5	3.8	5.6	3.1	3.4	8.9	5.1

a. Includes petroleum, which was unimportant before 1974.
b. Includes electricity and public utilities.
Source: See table 1–2.

been taken into account in the World Bank's estimates for 1981–82 to 1986–87.

Growth in Egypt has, at least since World War I, been closely associated with the foreign exchange situation. Except during World Wars I and II, when Egypt was forced by the British to help finance Allied military operations in the Middle East and thus accumulated large sterling reserves, the Egyptian pound has been overvalued, as reflected in Egypt's current account. Between the wars the public budget regularly ran substantial surpluses, yet the ample sterling reserves from World War I were drawn down steadily through current account deficits. It is not clear whether overvaluation was one of the reasons for the poor growth performance in the interwar years. After World War II overvaluation in this sense continued, but from the late 1950s increasing budget deficits also contributed to the current account deficit and the depletion of foreign exchange reserves. In the early 1960s the reserves were exhausted and Egypt became increasingly dependent on foreign financing. International complications, with the shift of Egyptian trade and aid from West to East and the emphasis on military preparedness, led to an extremely tight foreign exchange situation after 1965–66 with civilian investment the victim. With investment largely public, overvaluation ceased being a direct obstacle to growth simply because investment was no longer based on profit-maximizing considerations. Foreign exchange shortages became the direct obstacle, whether because of low exchange rates or excessive domestic demand. From 1973–74 ample supplies of foreign exchange flowed in from Arab members of the Organization of Petroleum Exporting Countries (OPEC), aid, loans, Suez Canal and petroleum revenues, and migrant workers' remittances; investment soared. Private investment once more became of some importance and low exchange rates thus again an obstacle to investment and growth.

If the two high-growth periods, 1960–65 and 1973 to 1981–82, are indicative of the growth rates Egypt can obtain under the system of etatism and with conditions of peace and a satisfactory foreign exchange situation, growth rates of 6–8 percent would apparently be feasible. To some extent, however, the 8 percent growth of GDP during 1973 to 1981–82 reflects recovery from the low growth rates during the period of open warfare in 1965–73 and replacement of capital goods destroyed during the 1967 War. Petroleum and the Suez Canal are good examples of how growth rates were affected. Generally, acts of war had a negative effect on production and capital in the canal zone. The increase in petroleum was partly a consequence of new finds of oil and gas, not to be repeated. Petroleum, however, only represented 13 percent of total growth 1974 to 1981–82. To some extent, measured high growth was a result of growth in unproductive sectors. Changes in the size of the armed forces were probably of little consequence; these forces were not cut back much from their peak of 450,000 men in 1973 and the increase in GDP in 1973 to 1981–82 was not a consequence of demobilization. The conclusion thus remains that if the foreign exchange problem could be handled, the system of etatism as such might not be an obstacle to respectable growth in Egypt.

On the expenditure side, no estimates exist for 1929–39, and those for 1939–45 are entirely unreliable; nor is the quality of data for 1945–55 satisfactory. There also are problems for years after 1960. Private consumption is always obtained as a statistical residual, compounding all errors and omissions in other items; before 1976, data on private consumption include investment in inventory. It is uncertain how military expenditures have been dealt with in the estimates of public consumption. Equipment obtained abroad may not be included. Constant price estimates are marred by the complex, multi-tiered price system prevailing in Egypt.

For the period 1960 to 1986–87 as a whole, not only total expenditure but all individual domestic expenditure categories grew faster in real terms than gross national income (table 1–1). Exports grew at the same rate as GNI. This, of course, was achieved only through the fast-growing oil exports. The gap between GNI and expenditure growth was accompanied by rapid growth of imports (discussed below). Considering the conflicting national account estimates for 1981–82 to 1986–87, I shall rather at this moment emphasize the changes in individual expenditure growth rates through the period 1960 to 1981–82. The growth rate of government consumption declined steadily from 12 percent in 1960–65 to 4.2 percent in 1973 to 1981–82. For private consumption the growth rate increased from 5.1 percent in 1960–65 to 8.6 percent in 1974 to 1981–82 after a slight decline in the intervening period; it remained at a high level of 6.2 percent during the years of stagnation in the 1980s. The present, etatist system thus started with public consumption growing faster and private consumption more slowly than both GDP and GNI. From 1973 to 1981–82 the roles were reversed (for GDP); this had a great deal to do with conditions of war and peace but may also reflect political expediency in demand management taking the upper hand after 1973. Investment grew rapidly during 1960–65 and 1973 to 1981–82—14.5 percent and 18.4 percent, respectively—but was allowed to decline during the period of war economy, 1965–73, and again during the stagnation years in the 1980s. The contrast between private consumption and investment is striking, a classical example of what has been called the social compact between ruler and people in Egypt. For 1965–73 the war may have had top priority, but to let civilians pay for the war in terms of consumption was not politically feasible. Investment and exports—in other words, future generations—had to pay. The very high rate of growth of (gross) investment after 1973 should partly be seen as replacement of capital destroyed during the war period. For

1981–82 to 1986–87, investment was sacrificed to permit a politically motivated increase in private consumption. As a result, the average growth rate of investment of 7.1 percent for the period as a whole is not impressive. Generally, the government chose the politically cheap solution in times of war and exogenous shocks to let investment serve as a buffer. The effect on growth must have been detrimental.

Growth rate differentials should result in correspondingly changing shares of production activities in GDP and of expenditure groups in GNI. Shares may be measured in nominal and real terms. Unfortunately, the base years used in constant price estimates have changed several times on both the production and the expenditure side, giving rise to inconsistencies between measured growth differentials and share changes. Thus tables 1–4 and 1–5 show the nominal value of shares, which has a more obvious economic interpretation than real value; on the other hand, it reflects the influence of price changes and government intervention in the price system. The differences between the nominal and the real value of share developments are not disturbing, however, in most cases.

On the production side the share of agriculture has been declining, as might be expected; it fell from 33 percent in 1955–56 to about 20 percent in 1986–87. It is more surprising that industry and mining, excluding petroleum, has declined from about 18 percent to 15 percent in 1983–84; including petroleum the share increased from 18 percent to 27 percent. Petroleum includes both crude oil extraction and petroleum products, but apparently manufacturing may have played a relatively declining role (see appendix 1A and table 1–3). This may be typical for mature economies but certainly not for developing countries. Both transport and communications and other services have declining shares despite the fact that the former includes the Suez Canal and the latter government, both of which have grown in relative importance. Transport and communications increased its share strongly from 1955–56 to 1965–66 when the Suez Canal was nationalized and incorporated in the national economy. With the canal closed from 1967 to 1974 the sector share declined temporarily. Construction increased its share somewhat; it remains a small sector in terms of GDP and most of the increase took place in the early 1960s with the construction of the Aswan High Dam.

Apart from petroleum, the only sector with a strongly increasing share is trade and finance, which went from 9.5 percent in 1955–56 to 20.1 percent in 1983–84. (Reclassification in 1974 shifted shares in such a way that other services fell to 20.4 percent and trade and finance rose to 15.1 percent.) The productive importance of the trade and finance sector is difficult to evaluate. It includes numerous small-scale trading establishments and petty street trading and possibly a large amount of unsocial transaction costs. Considering, on the other hand, the very strong increase in imports, the sector should tend to grow faster than the

Table 1-4. Gross Domestic Product, Current Factor Costs, by Economic Sectors, Selected Years, 1955–87
(percent)

Sector	1955–56	1965–66	1974[a]	1974[b]	1978	1983–84	1986–87
Agriculture	32.3	28.5	31.1	30.5	25.3	20.0	20.1
Industry, petroleum, and mining	17.6	21.6	20.5	20.4	21.6	26.8	28.7
Petroleum only	[c]	[c]	[c]	2.7	6.9	12.0	33.1
Electricity	[d]	1.1	1.1	1.6	1.3	1.0	
Construction	2.9	4.4	3.3	3.1	5.7	5.3	
Transport and communication	6.4	9.2	4.1	4.2	7.6	7.5	51.2
Suez Canal only	n.a.	n.a.	n.a.	-0.0	3.3	2.8	
Trade and finance	9.5	8.5	11.4	15.1	17.1	20.1	46.9
Housing	9.7	5.1	3.1	4.8	2.9	1.8	
Public utilities	[d]	0.4	0.4	[e]	[e]	[e]	
Other services	21.6	21.2	25.0	20.4	17.4	17.5	
Total GDP	100	100	100	100	100	100	100
Total value of GDP (millions of Egyptian pounds)	965	2,138	4,111	4,197	9,021	25,961	43,685

n.a. = Not available.
a. Comparable with 1955–56 and 1965–66.
b. Comparable with 1978 and 1983–84.
c. About 1.0 percent.
d. Included in industry, petroleum, and mining.
e. Included in electricity.
Source: Ikram (1980), statistical appendix, table 7; World Bank data; World Bank (1988).

Table 1-5. Gross Domestic Product, Current Market Prices, by Shares of Expenditure, Selected Years, 1952–87
(percent)

Expenditure	1952	1960	1965	1973	1976	1981–82	1986–87
Total consumption	88.1	85.8	86.4	92.0	83.3	84.4	91.4
Private consumption	71.7	68.3	66.6	63.8	58.5	63.6	72.0
Public consumption	16.4	17.5	19.8	28.2	24.8	20.8	19.4
Total investment	13.6	15.5	18.1	13.1	28.4	30.5	19.2
Exports of goods and nonfactor services	n.a.	19.2	15.3	14.0	22.3	32.0	18.0
Imports of goods and nonfactor services	n.a.	20.5	19.8	19.2	34.0	46.9	28.7
National saving	11.9[a]	14.1	13.6	14.0	19.0	15.3	6.9
Total value of GDP (millions of Egyptian pounds)[b]	868	1,459	2,459	3,806	6,727	20,171	45,182

n.a. = Not available.
a. Conjecture.
b. At current market prices.
Source: Ikram (1980), statistical appendix, table 5; World Bank (1988).

commodity-producing sectors. Nonetheless, the contrast between the possibly declining manufacturing sector and the rapidly expanding trade and finance sector indicates a basic structural weakness in the Egyptian economy. Unfortunately, official estimates of government's share in GDP do not go back many years; its relative increase adds to the structural weakness. The relative expansion of petroleum production is, on the other hand, the result of an enormously productive activity with, initially at least, very high marginal returns to inputs. But oil, in the case of Egypt, is at best a temporary solution to the country's problems since it will not last forever and may even divert attention from long-term problems.

On the expenditure side, table 1–5, the shares point immediately to another structural weakness that emerged during the years of autocracy. The share of total consumption in GNP increased strongly from 1952 to 1986–87, reaching 91 percent. Private consumption fell from about 72 percent in 1952 to about 59 percent in 1976, but increased again to 72 percent in 1986–87. The strong increase in public consumption from 1952 to 1973 followed by a steady decline to 19 percent in 1986–1987 reflects conditions of war and peace. The increase in the share of investment from 14–15 percent in 1950 and 1960 to slightly less than 31 percent in 1981–82 was matched by a strongly increasing gap between the shares of exports and imports (including nonfactor services). From levels of about 20 percent in 1960 the share of imports grew to 47 percent in 1981–82 but the share of exports only to 32 percent. The sharp decline in investment, to 19 percent in 1986–87, a decline of 11 percentage units, was accompanied by a decline of only 4 percentage units in the gap between exports and imports thanks to the increase in the share of total consumption by 7 percentage units. Squeezed between increasing popular demand for consumption and increasing difficulty with foreign financing, investment was again sacrificed, again the politically cheap solution.

The national accounts in Egypt may exaggerate the share in investment in 1981–82. Before 1976, investment in inventory was included in the residual, private consumption. On balance, investment in inventory was probably positive around 1960. In 1981–82, the share of fixed investment was 29.5 percent as compared with 30.5 percent for total investment. How development of relative prices affected the nominal shares is more uncertain. Construction costs undoubtedly increased strongly as compared with most other prices. The relatively low import duties on capital goods, measured at current market prices, may work in the opposite direction. Relative exchange rates, however, must also be taken into account. Be that as it may, the share of investment did increase strongly from 1960 to 1981–82. National saving at the same time increased only from 14 percent to 15 percent of GNI. Most of the increase in the share of investment was thus financed by loans and aid (net factor income from abroad, included in national saving, did not increase much from 1960 to 1981–82, the remittances largely being eaten up by interest payments on the foreign debt). And when the share of investment in 1986–87 fell to 19.2 percent, national saving fell to 6.9 percent so that most investment continued to be financed from abroad. Hence the increase in the national debt to about $50 billion in 1987.

There may be nothing wrong with borrowing abroad for investment purposes if the return to investment exceeds the cost of borrowing (including political strings). Here, however, a third basic weakness in Egyptian development is evident: the poor achievement in terms of total factor productivity. It is interesting, though, that this weakness is not confined to the period after 1960. Agricultural development has suffered from the same weakness since 1900.

Estimates of productivity in agriculture (in table 4–11) indicate a decline in total factor productivity by 10 percent from 1900 to 1913, with a further decline by 15 percent to the early 1920s. This decline was a consequence of poor design of the irrigation and drainage system and the emergence of cotton pests, which together cut cotton yields by about one-half. Redesign of the hydraulic system combined with new cotton varieties, improved crop rotation, increased use of chemical fertilizers, and further investment improved productivity during the 1920s, yet in 1938, total factor productivity in agriculture was almost 10 percent lower than in 1907. In the late 1950s it was still below the level of 1900. Estimates of total factor productivity in agriculture do not exist for years after 1960, but it has probably not increased.

Estimates of productivity in industry (in table 4–13) indicate increasing total factor productivity during the periods 1945–54 and 1954–62 and possibly also during World War II. For 1963–64 to 1969–70, total factor productivity declined as a result of both employment and investment policies pursued by the government after the nationalizations of 1961–62. Shortages of parts and raw materials related to the foreign exchange crisis played a role. Albeit of a rather complex nature, the radical change from increasing to declining total factor productivity in industry was partly the result of the change from private to public ownership. For the period 1973 to 1981–82 a reversal took place, with total factor productivity in industry increasing by about 5 percent annually. Availability of parts and raw materials and increased capacity utilization played a role. Since World War II, the trend seems to have been a decline in the growth of total productivity in industry. Public ownership may be the explanation.

These developments of factor productivity in agriculture and industry naturally lead to the question whether governmental intervention in Egypt should not be dated further back than 1952. With Mohammed Ali's nineteenth century policy of introducing perennial irrigation (for cotton cultivation), centralization of planning for investment in irrigation and drainage as well as for administration of the hydraulic system became a technical necessity. The new system was imposed on agriculture from above. Apart from some land reclamation and improvement and some choice in crop rotation, contributions from private entrepreneurship were modest. The failure of agricultural development from around 1900 was in that sense a failure of government intervention. But could perennial irrigation have been developed as a private business? Ultimately, complete control of the Nile from Central Africa to the Mediterranean was required. And might not the mistakes made by British engineers have been made whether the engineers were publicly or privately employed? Hydraulic technology was not well understood in the 1890s.[5] Finally, given the hydraulic system and its administration, cultivation remained a private activity until the 1960s when government-run cooperatives were given increasing power over crop rotation and the use of inputs; direct public control thus spread to agriculture.

Equity and Distribution of Income and Wealth

Little is known about income distribution before the 1950s. Uncertain estimates of functional income distribution in agriculture from 1900 to 1939 point to a shift in the distribution of agricultural factor income, more so before than after land tax, from rent of land and possibly capital to wages. Labor's share of agricultural income (including the market wages imputed to owner-cultivators) appears to have increased from about one-third in 1900 to almost one-half in 1938 while the share of land rent declined from almost one-half to almost 40 percent. No further change appears to. have taken place until the land reforms of 1952. Land-saving technological change appears to have been responsible for this development. The distribution of wealth in agriculture, skewed as it was, appears to have been unchanged from the beginning of the century to 1952, judging from Lorenz curves of size distribution of land ownership (figure 2–3). These observations do not lead to conclusions about the size distribution of agricultural income, among other things because the distribution of cultivation units (owned or rented) by size was entirely different from the distribution by ownership. Next to nothing is known about the distribution of urban income and material wealth distribution before the late 1950s. Terms of trade went against agriculture during the interwar period, but this development was reversed in the late 1940s and early 1950s. How this affected the urban-rural income distribution is difficult to say because much of urban income was generated through trade in agricultural products.

Human wealth has been very unevenly distributed and continues to be so after six decades of independence. A crude measure is the illiteracy rates shown in table 1–6. Rates were very high before independence— about 76 percent for males, 96 percent for females. One of the gravest

Table 1-6. Illiteracy Rates, Population Ten Years Old and above, Selected Years, 1907-86

(percent)

Year	Male	Female	Total
1907	87.0	98.6	92.7
1917	84.8	97.7	91.2
1927	76.1	95.6	85.9
1937	76.6	93.9	85.2
1960	56.9	84.0	70.5
1976	42.6	72.5	57.2
1986	37.8	61.8	49.4

Censuses before 1960 exclude nomads and "not stated"; they count as literates persons who are able to read but not write. Later censuses count as illiterates persons who are not able to read and write.

Source: Egypt, Ministry of Finance, *Annuaire statistique de l'Egypte*, various issues; Egypt, CAPMAS (1987).

objections to the British regime before 1923 has been its failure to develop Egypt's education system adequately. The achievements under independence have not been impressive either. In 1986 about 49 percent of the population ten years old and above were illiterate, with 38 percent of males and 62 percent of females. For young people illiteracy is obviously much lower, but in 1983 still only 84 percent of eligible children were enrolled in elementary schools—94 percent of males and 72 percent of females.

Solid information on the size distribution of income is available only from the late 1950s. In terms of both Gini and Theil coefficients for private household expenditure, estimates based on expenditure surveys for 1958–59, 1964–65, 1974–75, and 1982 point to a relatively equitable and stable distribution of disposable income in both urban and rural areas, with rural distribution appearing slightly more equitable than urban distribution. Percentages of expenditure in the lowest and highest income quintiles point in the same direction (see table 4–30).

The stability of income distribution is remarkable for a country that has experienced the external turbulence and interference in internal policy that Egypt has since the 1950s. War and peace, land reform with redistribution of land and rent control, nationalization of foreign and large-scale domestic private businesses with massive sequestration of the property of hand-picked wealthy families, government control of prices and wages, massive subsidization of basic foodstuffs, and large-scale migration of workers to Arab oil-producing countries with pay and remittances far exceeding anything available domestically, yet with a strong impact on relative, domestic wages, all appear to have left no lasting imprint on aggregative measures of income distribution. Some of these events took place before the first expenditure survey was made in 1958–59, and there are, unfortunately, no estimates of income distribution during the austerity years of war and etatism from 1965–66 to 1973 when Nasser's continued land reforms, nationalizations, sequestrations, and controls undoubtedly were biting but before the *infitah* had had an impact. Aggregative measures might have shown significantly increased equity of income distribution. In fact, both Gini and Theil coefficients for rural areas decline somewhat from 1958–59 to 1964–65 and increase then to 1974–75 and remain unchanged in 1982. But there is no such decline for urban areas and a slight improvement takes place from 1964–65 to 1974–75 with 1982 unchanged. Shares by quintile indicate a similar picture. It is a great problem how to explain the apparent robustness of the aggregative measures in view of the events. Food subsidies clearly tended to make real distribution more equitable after 1973 (Alderman and von Braun 1984; Zaitoun 1988).

The measurements of factor income shares and functional income distribution that are available suffer from serious shortcomings. Rent control in agriculture, with widespread evasion, makes it impossible to estimate functional distribution in agriculture for years after 1952. The problem of imputing wage income to the self-employed and owners is serious in both agriculture and the informal, nonagricultural sector. Moreover, in Egypt substantial amounts of property income (from the Suez Canal and the petroleum sector particularly) accrue directly to the government and should be excluded from estimates of the distribution of private income.[6] Accounting for migrant workers' remittances raises further problems. Table 1–7 shows the estimated share of wages and property income that accrued to the nonagricultural sector from 1959–60 to 1981–82, with special estimates of wage income as a percentage of GDP at factor cost and of total private income, domestically generated, excluding and including remittances. In both cases nonwage income includes rent and income from self-employment.

The estimated wage share outside of agriculture appears to have increased steadily from 1959–60 to the 1970–71 to 1974 period and then declined in 1975–76. The increase may partly have been the result of the relative increase of the government sector, in which profit by definition is nonexistent. The following decline is difficult to explain but may be a data fluke. From 1974 to 1979 wage income as a percentage of total GDP was approximately constant while wages' share in domestically generated private income increased steadily. The difference is, of course, a result of the rapid increase in canal tolls and petroleum revenue, which accrued to the government sector. Including migrant workers' remittances in private income, the wage share increases strongly from 54 percent in 1974 to 65 percent in 1979. During the 1980s the share in total GDP appears to have decreased considerably.

Table 1-7. Share of Wages in Nonagricultural Sector, GDP, and Private Income, 1959–87

(percent)

Year	Nonagricultural sector	Total GDP at factor cost	Total private income	
			Domestically generated	Including remittances
1959–60	53.7	n.a.	n.a.	n.a.
1960–61 to 1964–65	53.2	n.a.	n.a.	n.a.
1965–66 to 1966–67	54.6	n.a.	n.a.	n.a.
1967–68 to 1969–70	57.6	n.a.	n.a.	n.a.
1970–71 to 1974	60.3	n.a.	n.a.	n.a.
1975–76	52.2	n.a.	n.a.	n.a.
1974	—	42.4	52.9	54.3
1975	—	43.2	55.1	57.5
1976	—	44.7	57.4	61.3
1977	45.0	44.1	57.1	61.3
1978	—	43.0	56.5	63.1
1979	36.9	42.9	58.5	64.8
1981–82	42.1	46.3	n.a.	n.a.
1986–87	n.a.	37.6	n.a.	n.a.

n.a. = Not available.

Source: Hansen and Radwan (1982), tables 59, 60; Egypt, Ministry of Planning and International Cooperation; World Bank (1987), table 21.

Once more there is a long way from functional to size distribution of income. The size distribution (of expenditure) did not change in the aggregate from 1974–75 to 1982 despite the strong shift of distribution of private income toward wages from 1974 to 1979. The reason may be that distributions within wage income and profits dominated distribution between wages and profits. Furthermore, during the 1970s previously low-paid agricultural and construction workers experienced large relative increases in wages while the gap between the wages of public employees in higher and lower grades was compressed substantially. Finally, remittances may have been unevenly distributed over families or wage earners, classified by size of income (Adams 1988; Zaitoun 1988).

Growth probably tends, other things being equal, to generate equity to the extent that unemployment is reduced. Unfortunately, Arthur W. Lewis singled out Egypt as an example of a country with surplus labor and substantial disguised unemployment. That concept does not fit the context of Egypt. As a predominantly agricultural economy, Egypt has always suffered substantial seasonal unemployment and experienced shortages of labor at the agricultural peaks. This was particularly true under the ancient system of basin irrigation. With the gradual extension of perennial irrigation from the Nile Delta to the Valley, seasonal unemployment in the countryside may have diminished; it remained substantial, however, even after the closure of the Aswan High Dam in 1964–65 changed the seasonal pattern of cultivation. Little is known about urban unemployment before the late 1950s. During the Great Depression such unemployment appears to have been substantial. The Allied armies absorbed large numbers of Egyptian workers for military construction work during World War II. Their dismissal seems to have created employment problems in the early postwar period.

Annual unemployment statistics have been published only since the late 1950s. The unemployment count is made in May, which has become the agricultural peak season. Hence the level of measured unemployment is relatively low. On the other hand, underenumeration of females, particularly unpaid female family labor, in the labor force tends to bias the measured unemployment rates upward. It is not possible to say which of these biases dominates.

Measured unemployment, shown in figure 1–3, declined during the first high-growth period from about 5 percent of the total labor force in 1959–61 to about 2 percent in 1962–64. The labor force survey was redesigned between 1964 and 1968 and again in 1976 when data are missing and comparability is problematic. For what they are worth the data show a slight increase from 1962–64 to 1968 on the order of 1 percent. From 1968 to 1972 the unemployment rate was declining and was below the level of 1962–64. The low-growth period 1965–66 to 1973 thus did not result in higher measured unemployment. One reason may have been government employment policies of shorter work hours in all public enterprises and corresponding new hiring in 1962 and of guaranteed public employment for university and high school graduates and discharged army draftees beginning about 1964, as well as the strong increase in the size of the army during the 1960s. Civilian and military personnel in government (not including public enterprises) increased from 14 percent of the total labor force about 1965 to 20 percent in 1973. During the high-growth period after 1973 Egypt apparently became a labor-shortage economy at all levels, mainly because 10–15 percent of the labor force migrated temporarily to the Arab OPEC countries. Yet measured unemployment edged steadily upward from about 1.5 percent in 1972 to about 6 percent in 1984.[7] The increase in unemployment was confined to labor "without work experience" which probably means young people. The unemployment rate for experienced labor remained very low, declining from about 1.2 percent in 1960 to below 0.5 percent in 1984. The strongly increasing unemployment rate among young people may be related to the government policy of guaranteed public employment, with eligible candidates waiting two or three years for appointment; it may also be a reflection of expanded education and higher standards of living. Employment opportunities after 1972 certainly led

Figure 1-3. Activity Indicators, 1953-86

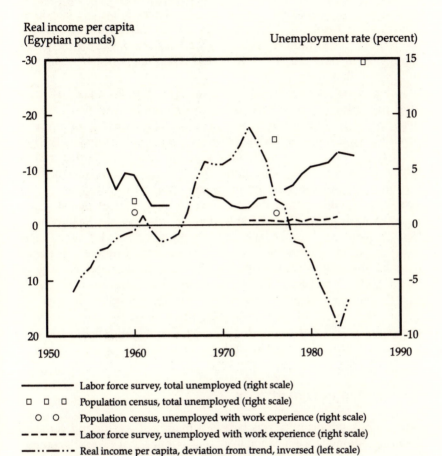

Real income per capita
(Egyptian pounds)

Unemployment rate (percent)

———— Labor force survey, total unemployed (right scale)
□ □ □ Population census, total unemployed (right scale)
○ ○ Population census, unemployed with work experience (right scale)
– – – – – Labor force survey, unemployed with work experience (right scale)
—··—··– Real income per capita, deviation from trend, inversed (left scale)

Source: Egypt, CAPMAS, *Manpower Survey by Sample*; author's calculations
from World Bank data.

to a relative improvement for important groups of low-paid workers, unskilled agricultural and construction workers and household servants,
and may have served to prevent an increase in the aggregative measures
of inequity from 1974–75 to 1982.

Comparisons of income by urban or rural location, region, and activities may be interesting in themselves and because they reveal how government policy discriminates among groups. Information on such characteristics for Egypt is given in expenditure surveys on a household basis
and is thus blurred by commuting, seasonal employment, and multiple
occupations, even for individual household members. Differences in
cost of living, externalities, public goods, economies of scale, and so

forth, further complicate the effort to arrive at comparable numbers. Quality of life indexes exist but are as always rather arbitrary. Simple comparisons of estimated average money income show urban house-holds have 2.1 times to 1.9 times as much income as rural households (Waterbury 1983, quoting Taylor and Moheieldin, p. 315) with similar figures for income per capita. To accept these numbers as measures of differences in standard of living or welfare would be naive.

Anwar Sadat, in a televised speech shortly before his assassination in 1981 proclaimed, "I am in favor of equity for both rich and poor." His remark probably confuses issues of economic equity, equal opportunity in a more general sense, and equality before the law, all of them issues that came to the fore during his tenure. The data discussed in this section refer exclusively to economic equity in the narrow sense, and the next section addresses the question of equal opportunity. The rights of the people to equality before the law were in many ways violated when Nasser was in power. The sequestrations of property were highly arbitrary, implemented on the basis of presidential decrees but often instigated by informers hoping to be appointed administrators and hence heirs of the sequestered property. The practice disappeared largely under Sadat, and sequestrations were in some cases even reversed. Sadat's remarks on equity, however, were made in a speech that served to defend the arrest of thousands of Egypt's elite whose only crime was to disagree with Sadat. Equity, in the sense of equal rights before the law, is an area in which Hosny Mubarak has made some progress; yet Egypt has still a long way to go to live up to the Helsinki standards.

Distribution of Opportunity

Before 1923, opportunity was largely a matter of wealth and connections, conditioned by education insofar as public service was concerned. Social mobility was confined mainly to the middle and upper classes; the probability that children from the lower, predominantly illiterate classes, urban or rural, should succeed in moving upward was close to zero. The situation hardly changed under the imperfectly democratic regime from 1923 to 1952.

Under Nasser things did change in some ways. Land reform, nationalizations, and sequestrations with little or no compensation cut the top of the wealth and income pyramids. The emasculation of political parties and organized pressure groups further eliminated existing ladders for upward mobility. Military connection became paramount and attachment to a military or, less importantly, civilian patron-client group (*shilla*) with absolute loyalty to the ruler became the sine qua non for a successful career. Education probably gained importance in that career became synonymous with public sector employment. Upward mobility was confined to and within the middle class. Elementary and higher education were in principle free, and both expanded considerably. Guaranteed employment of graduates of secondary schools and universities opened the public sector to children from the lower classes whose families were able to get them through higher education. However, admission to the two prestigious, high-income educations, engineering and medicine, continued to be restricted and in practice required very high grade-point averages, which depended on expensive tuition, and connections. Promotion and further career in the public sector, moreover, required connections, specifically a *shilla* attachment. Thus opportunities for lower-class children remained almost as limited as under previous regimes. The main achievement under Nasser was in trimming the top. Needless to say, women, though formally entitled to both education and public sector appointment, continued to face traditional obstacles.

Under Anwar Sadat's selective liberalization policy, the *infitah*, private sector activities once more became respectable and highly lucrative and the patron-client system lost much of its predominance. Family connections and wealth made a strong comeback as old families surfaced after the long hibernation under Nasser, and energetic and resourceful nouveaux riches began exploiting the profit opportunities that invariably sprout when a disequilibrium system with tight price controls and accompanying shortages suddenly opens up and market forces begin to function. Connections continued to play a key role in any kind of successful career but the military connection was largely replaced by the foreign connection, whether in relation to government contracts with large corporate businesses abroad or foreign companies investing directly in Egypt.

Entirely new opportunities emerged for broad groups of the population with migration of workers to Arab OPEC countries. Initially, the migrants were skilled construction workers, managers, professionals, and teachers, but from the end of the 1970s they included unskilled workers and farmers who earned ten to fifteen times more than they could in Egypt and were able to accumulate capital to invest in farming, informal manufacturing, trading, or improved housing. The continued strong expansion of the education system with guaranteed employment made access to public sector appointment a realistic proposition for a rapidly increasing number of families in the lower-income brackets, but the obstacles to promotion and career they had faced under Nasser continued. Little changed when Hosny Mubarak took power. For the large majority of the population, upward mobility through the education system still ends in the cul-de-sac of the lower-paid grades of the public sector hierarchy with little prospect of improvement. Until merit replaces connections as the principal criterion for advancement and promotion in the public sector, opportunities for lower-class children will be limited to the informal sector. It may take a sea change in social attitudes to open up the increasing opportunities in this sector to the lower classes.

Rural and Urban Poverty

Studies of rural poverty in Egypt suffer from the difficulties of delimiting the phenomenon and from its many dimensions that make simple quantification well-nigh impossible. Following the standard method of postulating a poverty line defined as the income required to finance certain food and nonfood purchases, Adams estimated the proportion of the rural population in poverty, the average poverty gap, and Sen's index of poverty for the years that expenditure surveys are available. The results, presented in table 1–8, are interesting because they tell somewhat different stories than the indicators of income distribution discussed above.

The proportion of the rural population under the poverty line declined slightly from 1958–59 to 1964–65 but then increased violently to 1974–75. An even more dramatic decline took place to 1982, with the indicator pointing to less poverty than in 1958–59. Sen's index also shows less poverty in 1982 than in 1958–59 but it records a strong increase from 1958–59 to 1964–65 and poverty remains at approximately the same level in 1974–75. With the distribution of rural population concentrated in the neighborhood of the postulated poverty line, both indicators may be oversensitive to small changes in the average level of income. The average poverty gap—which mainly indicates how poor the poor are rather than how widespread poverty is—shows a very strong increase from 1958–59 to 1964–65; it remains roughly at the same level in 1974–75 and then declines somewhat in 1982, ending up at a much higher level than in 1958–59.

The three indicators suggest that poverty was less widespread in 1982 than in 1958–59 but that it was somewhat deeper. The "poorest of the

Table 1–8. Indicators of Poverty in Rural Areas, Selected Years, 1958–82

Year	Proportion of rural population below poverty line (percent)[a]	Average poverty gap (percent)[b]	Sen's index of poverty[c]
1958–59	27	2.9	0.08
1964–65	24	9.4	0.18
1974–75	65	8.8	0.21
1982	18	6.8	0.06

a. Number of adult equivalent units in households below the chosen poverty line as a ratio of total adult equivalent units.
b. The shortfall of mean income of the poor from the poverty line.
c. Normalized, weighted sum of the income gaps of the poor.
Source: Adams (1985), table 3; Adams (1986).

poor" are disabled persons, the crippled, single persons both old and young, and sick people. When employment opportunities and pay for the employed improve, this unemployable residue may be left behind, creating the situation with less but deeper poverty. Migration of workers might have this kind of effect.

Although expenditure surveys are available for urban areas for the same years as for rural areas, studies of urban poverty in Egypt are more limited in scope and depth than those of rural poverty. Real per capita or per family income is considerably higher in urban than in rural areas and poverty in urban areas should thus be expected to be less widespread than in rural areas. Urban poverty might, nonetheless, be deeper than rural poverty.

For 1974–75 two estimates of the proportions of urban population below the poverty line result in ratios of 0.35 and 0.48, respectively, as against 0.65 for rural areas reported in table 1–8 (Waterbury 1983, 330–31). Since the rural study seems to operate with a higher poverty line than that applied in the urban studies, the difference may be a statistical artifact. An International Labour Organisation (ILO) study on the other hand, operating with a lower poverty line than any of these studies, shows only 28 percent of the population below the poverty line in rural areas (Radwan and Lee 1986). Differences between prices in rural and urban areas, availability of public services, styles of life, and so forth, add to the difficulties of comparing urban and rural poverty. Urban poverty does not appear to have been studied over time; whether the strong increase followed by the even stronger decline found for rural poverty applies to urban poverty is unknown. Neither the poverty gap nor the Sen index seems to have been computed for urban areas. If useful comparisons of urban and rural poverty are to be made, further studies are needed.

Appendix:
Composition of Industry and Mining

Before 1974, official national account estimates include petroleum in industry and mining; later estimates separate petroleum from industry and mining. Petroleum includes crude oil extraction and petroleum products. While there are good reasons for operating with an aggregate of crude oil and products to show total value added related to oil, this aggregation makes it impossible to separate out mining (including crude oil) and manufacturing industry (excluding mining but including petroleum products), a classification that is useful for many purposes (international comparisons, for instance).

For 1986–87 it is possible to come up with a complete classification, unfortunately not on the basis of ex post data but only on the basis of so-called anticipated value added. The published document (1987) presenting Egypt's second five-year plan for 1987–88 to 1991–92 includes an anticipated input-output table (table 60) for 1986–87 that makes it possible to gauge the shares in GDP of industry and mining (excluding petroleum), petroleum (crude oil and products), mining (including crude oil), and manufacturing industry (including petroleum products but excluding crude oil). This again makes it possible to gauge the error made in using industry and mining as a proxy for manufacturing industry. The results are shown in table 1A–1. Figures are from plan document tables 50 and 60. Definitionally identical figures from tables 50 (expected) and 60 (anticipated) differ significantly even though both sets are at current prices; it is not explained why. The input-output table does not appear to

Table 1A–1. Value Added in Selected Production Sectors, 1986–87

Category[a]	Expected value added[b] Millions of Egyptian pounds	Percentage of GDP	Anticipated value added[c] Thousands of Egyptian pounds	Percentage of GDP
Individual sectors				
Mines and quarries (4)	n.a.	n.a.	112,289	0.26[d]
Crude oil (5)	n.a.	n.a.	1,021,010	2.44[d]
Petroleum products (17)	n.a.	n.a.	1,006,078	2.40[d]
Aggregated sectors				
Mining (4, 5)	n.a.	n.a.	1,133,299	2.71[d]
Manufacturing industry (6–25)	n.a.	n.a.	8,826,257	21.07[d]
Industry and mining (4,6–16,18–25)	6,933.1	16.98	7,932,468	18.94[d]
Petroleum products (5,17)	1,690.1	4.14	2,027,088	4.84[d]
All production sectors (1–32)	36,232.8	88.74	37,290,328	89.02[d]
Government services	4,599.3	11.26	4,599,300[d]	10.98[d]
GDP at current factor cost	40,832.1	100	n.a.	n.a.
Indirect taxes, net	3,220.0	—	n.a.	n.a.
GDP at current market prices	44,052.1	—	41,889,600[d]	100

n.a. = Not available.
— = Not applicable.
a. Classification number of individual sectors in parentheses.
b. Based on current factor cost.
c. Presumably based on current market price.
d. Author's computations.
Source: Egypt, Ministry of Planning and International Cooperation (1987), tables 50 and 60.

include government services; hence the figure in the expected column is used in the anticipated column. Added to the anticipated value added for all production services in col. 3, GDP at current market prices in col. 3 obtain.

The share of value added in manufacturing industry is about 21 percent of GDP, both at current market prices, while the corresponding share for industry and mining is about 19 percent. The share of industry and mining is about 17 percent of GDP, both at current factor cost. These results indicate that in 1986–87 the share of manufacturing industry in GDP, both at current factor cost, may have been about 19 percent. The corresponding average for middle-income economies in 1986 was 22 percent, for lower-middle-income economies 17 percent, according to the World Bank, *World Development Report 1988*, table 3. Egypt belongs to the latter category. Thus her share of manufacturing industry is not particularly low if these computations can be trusted.

There are, unfortunately, a number of problems in the computations. First they are based on the official national account estimates that the discussion in the text for the 1980s does not rely on. The World Bank, however, does not present details in its estimates. Second, value added in petroleum products is important for the results, yet the prices at which value added in this sector has been evaluated are not known. If they are evaluated at domestic user prices for the output and at international (export) prices for the input of crude oil, value added in this sector should be very low, even negative. Value added, nonetheless, is large, even larger than in crude oil extraction which does not make sense unless input of crude oil in petroleum products has been evaluated at prices much lower than export prices. Third, the values here are expected and anticipated values for 1986–87, not actual ex post values, and the expected and anticipated values do not seem to be consistent.

For years earlier than 1986–87 there are no estimates of GDP in manufacturing industry, standard definition. Considering the expansion of both crude oil extraction and petroleum products over time, it is difficult to gauge the error involved in using estimates of industry and mining as a proxy for manufacturing industry in earlier years.

For some purposes, however, the notion of manufacturing may be of little interest. In the context of foreign trade analysis the notion of tradables is much more relevant. Shifting attention to tradables for Egypt, the problem of separating out manufacturing evaporates because the industry, mining, and petroleum sector may be a good proxy for the tradables-producing sector. The notion of tradables, however, raises other problems of classification. While under modern conditions most output from agriculture, horticulture, and fishing, as well as mining, industry, and petroleum can realistically be traded, electricity, public utilities, transport and communications, and trade and finance still raise problems.

Notes

1. Egypt was actively involved in the Yemen War from 1962. It was not until 1963–64 that the crunch on the economy really was felt.

2. The political-economic system of parliamentary democracy, predominating private entrepreneurship, and free trade in Egypt before 1952 can be characterized as pluralistic. The system that grew up under Nasser and still prevails in its main features with autocracy, a huge public sector, and pervasive government controls can be characterized as etatist (like that in Kemalist Turkey).

3. Egyptian trade indexes suffer from special index problems related to the shift of trade toward communist countries and back again and Egypt's change from a net importer to a net exporter of oil. For 1967–73 there is a huge discrepancy between customs and exchange authority statistics on imports, which may be related to Soviet and military trade.

4. Exports after 1976 increased to approximately 20 percent of GNI; a 5 percent deterioration of terms of trade corresponds then roughly to a loss of 1 percent of GNI.

5. Critical voices had been raised against the drainage designs in the 1890s before the negative effects on cotton yields appeared. There is an interesting exchange of views between Willcocks, an outstanding irrigation engineer and agronomist and the leading opponent and Major Brown, who defended the administration's choice of technology, in Willcocks (1898). The case bears a remarkable resemblance to the U.S. space shuttle disaster in 1985. Engineers with differences of opinion in technical matters which were not fully understood operated under tight budgets and strong political pressure from above (Cromer) to move ahead quickly.

6. It might be argued—correctly, in my opinion—that equity should be measured as disposable, private income, including public services. This would meet with substantial difficulties.

7. The population censuses of 1960, 1976, and 1986 enumerated unemployed and labor force. Unemployment rates thus measured are shown in figure 1–3. They show a steady increase from 2.2 percent in 1960 to 7.7 percent in 1976 and 14.7 percent in 1986. The 1960 census was taken in September, at that time the agricultural peak. The measured rate of 2.2 percent is lower than the 4.7 percent rate from the labor force survey, as should be expected considering the seasonalities at that time. The 1976 and 1986 censuses were taken in November, now the agricultural slack season. Hence, the high levels of unemployment in the censuses as compared with the labor force surveys may be a seasonal phenomenon. Be that as it may, both labor force surveys and censuses indicate roughly a doubling of the unemployment rate from the mid-1970s to the mid-1980s, possibly with an average annual unemployment rate of 5–6 percent in the mid-1970s and 10–11 percent in the mid-1980s, a substantial part of the measured unemployment being frictional and voluntary, graduates signed up for and waiting for public employment.

2 History, Background Factors, and Initial Conditions

For half of its five-thousand-year history, Egypt was ruled by foreign conquerors—Persian, Macedonian, Roman, Hellenistic, Arab, Mameluke, Ottoman, French, Albanian, and British, in that order. From the Ottoman conquest in 1517 until it was declared a sultanate under British protection in World War I, Egypt was a province in the Ottoman Empire. However, with the expulsion of Napoleon Bonaparte's expeditionary force in 1802 Mohammed Ali, an Albanian officer in the service of the Ottoman sultan, succeeded in taking power and establishing a dynasty that effectively ruled Egypt until the British occupation in 1882; he laid the foundation for modern Egypt, institutionally and economically. Politically, modern Egypt dates back to the decades before World War I when, in opposition to both the Turco-Albanian dynasty and the British occupation administration, Egyptian nationalists started the struggle for an independent, politically modernized Egypt (Vatikiotis 1969).

After a series of popular upheavals following World War I, the British unilaterally proclaimed the independence of Egypt in 1922 with concessions considered vital for the British Empire. Under a constitution promulgated in 1923, Egypt thus became a constitutional monarchy with a limited and imperfect parliamentary system. Some of the constraints on Egypt, imposed by the so-called Capitulations, expired when the underlying treaties ended. Tariff autonomy was thus obtained in 1930, the year that genuinely Egyptian development policies began. At the Montreux Conference of 1937 the Capitulary Powers finally gave up their privileges. The foreign-Egyptian Mixed Courts remained until 1949, however, and the British did not agree to leave the Suez Canal zone until 1954 and did not evacuate their forces until 1956. Not only politically but also economically, independence came about gradually but by and large was established as a result of the Anglo-Egyptian Treaty of Alliance of 1936.

Laws governing elections were modified by the king from 1928 to 1934, and elections and parliaments were manipulated throughout the period of constitutional monarchy. Disputes with the British continued. But with all its imperfections, parliamentary democracy prevailed in

Egypt, even during World War II when Allied war efforts took the upper hand, until the coup d'etat of the Free Officers in 1952. Since then, autocratic rulers—Gamal Abdel Nasser (1954–70), Anwar Sadat (1970–81), and Hosny Mubarak (since 1981)—have governed Egypt.

Basic Resources

Egypt is best characterized as a desert through which the Nile River runs. The river flows from south to north, originating in Central Africa; in prehistoric times it emptied its waters into a narrow estuary of the Mediterranean. The surrounding desert consists largely of poor soil, but the silt carried by the river mainly from Ethiopia and accumulated over time has transformed the estuary into a narrow valley and delta of extremely fertile soil. Rainfall is slight. Rainfed agriculture is possible only along a narrow coastal strip of relatively poor land, permitting cultivation of such hardy crops as barley, figs, and melons. Otherwise, agriculture is largely confined to the alluvial soil of the Delta and Valley and is entirely dependent on irrigation from the river.

Irrigation goes back to the prehistoric basin system that, in modified form (Butzer 1976), prevailed until the early nineteenth century and only disappeared completely when the Aswan High Dam was erected in the 1960s. Regular, annual floods, generated by the monsoons in Central Africa, provided water for both Valley and Delta basins that were constructed along the river, enclosed by low earth dikes with intakes and outlets for water. When the flood elevated the river level in July and August, the basins were filled. When the flood receded in October and November, the water in the basins slowly seeped into the ground and was drained away by the river. Seeds were then broadcast directly on the mud with a minimum of soil preparation and no further irrigation was required until harvest time in April. The basin system was an extremely labor- and energy-saving technology, based on gravitational forces. Its great disadvantage was that only one crop, a winter crop, could be taken annually. The rest of the year the land was fallow, a necessary condition for the restoration of fertility because fertilizers were hardly used. The standard crops were cereals and pulses. Yields were very high, even by modern standards, and large surpluses of both food and (seasonal) labor formed the basis for the civilizations of ancient Egypt but also attracted conqueror after conqueror, eager to skim off the surplus.

Perennial irrigation always existed on a small scale alongside the basin system; water was lifted from the river or pumped from under ground. These irrigation methods, however, hardly allowed for any surplus of either food or labor.

Perennial irrigation with modern technology was initiated by Mohammed Ali in the early nineteenth century. A high-yield, extra-long-staple variety of cotton was discovered by chance. Mohammed Ali, advised by French military engineers, saw the economic potentialities of this discovery. A system of deep canals was developed that permitted storage of water and irrigation throughout the year to support the cultivation of cotton, a summer crop that was mainly intended for export. To complete the system, a water distributing weir, the Delta Barrage, was constructed where the river divided at the apex of the Delta. The whole system ran into unexpected engineering problems. The barrage turned out to be structurally unstable and could not be used to full capacity so that the canals it fed tended to silt up. Cotton cultivation, nonetheless, expanded substantially but required large amounts of forced labor for cleaning the canals. It was left to British engineers with experience from Punjab and with access to new types of cement to complete the barrage in 1890 at a very low cost and to make the perennial irrigation system in the Delta work gravitationally without requiring forced labor or mechanical pumping (Willcocks 1898).[1]

During the 1890s and the first decade of the new century, cotton cultivation and exports expanded rapidly and investments were made to extend the system to Middle Egypt.[2] Egypt became a one-commodity exporter (but not a one-crop cultivator). The cultivated area reached its maximum in 1897. Then the ecological disasters began. Cotton yields started declining around 1900, cotton pests emerged and frequently decimated the crops, quality deteriorated, and bilharzia (schistosomiasis) became endemic among the rural population. All these disasters were built into the system. Drainage was badly designed, continuous cropping with clover a complementary crop to cotton gave leaf worms a chance to survive between cotton crops, and the deep canals were a hothouse for the water snails that form part of the bilharzia cycle. An international commission appointed to investigate the matter recommended restructuring the agricultural system. Improved drainage, improved water and crop rotation, control with clover cultivation, improved cotton varieties, manual pest control, increased use of chemical fertilizers, and additional investment, all began immediately but were interrupted by World War I. After the war, restructuring and expansion were continued. Around 1930 yields and quality were back to the 1900 level with cotton cultivation extended to most of Middle Egypt and the system apparently under control. This was the system as it functioned until the construction of the Aswan High Dam in the 1960s. It was a green revolution in the modern sense, but through engineering shortcomings thirty years and a large amount of capital were lost, and the bilharzia problem has not yet been solved. These mistakes were to some extent repeated by the Nasser regime after the construction of the Aswan High Dam against explicit warnings and the advice of both Soviet engineers responsible for the design, and Egyptian civil servants in ministries of Agriculture and Irrigation who had not forgotten the old lessons.

Other Natural Resources

Egypt's other major natural resource is oil, discovered at Suez before World War I. It did not become important until after World War II, when deposits were found along and under the Red Sea. Natural gas is found in the Nile Delta. Since 1976 Egypt has been an oil exporter.

Phosphate rock, sufficient for Egypt's own needs, exists in the eastern desert. Iron ore deposits of low quality exist in the western desert and at Aswan; the ore is processed in Egypt. Apart from salt and gypsum, other minerals are available only in small quantities, hardly worth exploiting. Sand and limestone are available for glass and cement production and the soil in Valley and Delta is used for making brick. The river supplies fresh water for consumption and industrial production and is the country's main sewer.

Infrastructure

The public irrigation and drainage system was the core of Egypt's infrastructure until the 1930s. Before World War I, however, Egypt had a modern, fully adequate infrastructure in transportation and communication as well as in urban public utilities. The first railroad was opened in 1852 and in 1914 the country was covered with double-track lines from Alexandria to Aswan, single-track lines from Cairo to Port Said and Suez, and a network of narrow-gauge agricultural railroads covering the countryside in the Delta and parts of Upper Egypt. Most of the railroads were, or became, publicly owned early.

The Nile has always been an important means of transportation. With the current flowing from south to north and the prevailing winds being northern, traditional river navigation required no other source of energy. Because of the peculiar geography of the country, road transportation, mainly by animals, played only a local role until the advent of the motor vehicle. Major roads were constructed in the interwar period, but the cities had been modernized (on the lines of Paris and Rome) before World War I. Telegraph and telephone systems were put in place before the end of nineteenth century.

The Suez Canal, opened in 1869 by the Companie Universelle, was mainly foreign owned but registered in Egypt. Some of the shares were held by the British government (from 1875) but most by the French petit bourgoisie. The canal company was very profitable and became a financial power in France. Egypt covered most of the costs of constructing the canal.[3] With the opening of the canal, Egypt lost the profitable overland traffic of passengers, mail, gold, and other high-value goods on the India route but gained some transit and tourist trade in the canal zone (Port Said, Ismaileya, Suez). It is difficult to say whether Egypt stood a net gain or loss until 1956 when the canal was nationalized. The canal has become a highly profitable foreign exchange earner for Egypt, even allowing for the compensation paid after nationalization of the company and the later investment to increase the capacity of the canal.

Population

In ancient times, Egypt supported a population of around 10 million people. Napoleon Bonaparte's scientific staff estimated the population in 1801 to be about 2.4 million. The first reliable census, taken in 1897, counted a population of 9.7 million. The consensus seems to be that population increased relatively rapidly throughout the nineteenth century, reflecting peaceful conditions, hygienic progress, and the increased standard of living brought about by the agricultural and urban development policies of the Turco-Albanian dynasty. Uncertain estimates indicate an increase by nine to twelve times of agricultural production during the century (O'Brien 1966). From 1897 to 1927 population increased by 1.3 percent annually to a total of 14.2 million. With high crude birth and mortality rates (42.4 percent and 27 percent, respectively, for 1917–46), life expectancy was low (35.6 years for males and 42.1 for females in 1937) and the age distribution relatively skewed in favor of the young age groups. About 14 percent lived in towns in 1897 and 17 percent in 1927 (Cleland 1936, p. 63). Urbanization was not pronounced until World War II.[4] In 1937, 69.5 percent of the labor force was recorded as agricultural, a proportion that, if anything, had been slightly increasing since 1897. The occupational distribution is difficult to trace because of the changing classifications in censuses. The economically active population appears to have been increasing relatively but the size and development of family labor, particularly from women, is a great statistical problem. The rates of illiteracy were very high (89.5 percent in 1927) and education was a privilege for those in the higher-income brackets. Public elementary education was not initiated until after independence in 1923 and progress was slow, especially in rural areas.

About 90 percent of the population was Muslim (mainly Sunni), the remainder split up in a multitude of Christian sects with the Eastern Orthodox denomination predominating, and a small Jewish group. The foreign community was numerically small, in 1927 about 226,000 or about 1.6 percent of the total population. Foreigners, however, lived mainly in urban areas and constituted a large proportion of cities' population (in Cairo 8 percent, in Alexandria 19 percent, in Port Said 20 percent). About half of them were Ottoman subjects, the remainder mostly Europeans, dominated by Italians and Greeks. The British community was small, about 24,000 of whom 14,000 were military personnel. The foreign community included all occupations from the highest to the lowest. Skilled craftsmen and professionals played an important role and so did management and white-collar workers. The resident foreign community, which went back to the time of Ismail, was relatively wealthy. Its upper layers played a key role in economic development before World War II, and its exodus or expulsion undoubtedly did harm to economic development after the war.

Under the Capitulations, foreigners had a privileged position compared to native Egyptians (and to subjects of the Ottoman Empire). Thus foreigners could not be tried in Egyptian courts. Foreigners were not, however, as is often claimed, exempted from most taxation. In fact, most taxes levied in Egypt applied in principle to all residents, without respect to nationality. Thus, foreigners were not exempted from either customs duties or land and buildings (including *ghaffir*) taxes if they actually imported goods or owned land or buildings. These were by far the most important taxes. The Capitulations prevented new taxes (such as business or general income taxes) from being imposed on subjects of the Capitulary Powers and prevented the rates of customs duties (from the 1860s fixed at 8 percent for most imports and 1 percent for exports) as well as the land and buildings taxes from being raised without their consent.[5] Since, for political reasons, the government could not increase taxes or introduce new taxes for native Egyptians when foreigners were exempted, the Capitulations effectively constrained the revenue-raising capacity of the government. This constraint was not removed until 1937 when the Anglo-Egyptian treaty took effect.

Land, Labor, and Capital Stocks

Both cultivated area and labor force and their development from around the 1890s are known but no estimate of the total stock of capital is available. Constant price estimates of capital stocks in agriculture and industry are available. Total railway track length is a good indicator of the stock of capital in transportation.[6] For urban real estate only the number of buildings paying the special buildings tax is known. All indicators of land, labor, and capital stock are presented in table 2–1.

Total population increased by 58 percent from 1902 to 1939 while the economically active population almost doubled. This should imply an increase in production and income per capita. The cultivated area, on the other hand, was almost constant and thus declined per capita and per unit of labor. This should imply a decline in production and income per capita. The stock of capital in transportation, which increased strongly per capita from 1882 to 1902, declined slightly per capita and considerably per unit of labor from 1902 to 1939. The stock of capital in agriculture, industry, and buildings, on the other hand, increased per unit of labor and per capita. Moreover, total factor productivity in agriculture declined by about 10 percent from 1900 to the 1930s (see table 4–12). Since value added in agriculture may have approached two-thirds of total GDP, it would take a considerable increase in total factor

Table 2-1. Indexes of Labor, Land, and Capital, 1882–1966
(1902=100)

Year	Population		Cultivated area	Supply of chemical fertilizers	Stock of fixed capital[a]		Railways, Track length	Number of buildings[b]
	Total	Economically active			Agriculture	Industry		
1966	287.8	284.9	—	—	582.7	643.7	—	—
1960	246.9	240.8	109.3	59,772	411.4	535.9	168.1	—
1955	219.7	226.6	107.1	39,364	369.7	446.5	173.7	—
1952	204.7	219.2	105.9	39,818	344.9	380.1	172.9	368.8
1945	175.6	203.0	108.2	13,273	324.4	210.3	167.8	283.8
1939	158.1	191.3	100.1	22,045	306.9	260.0	154.2	256.4
1934	147.3	178.3	98.2	19,182	247.0	232.1	146.4	256.1
1929	137.2	169.3	105.3	14,909	187.7	185.9	138.4	213.9
1924	131.7	158.0	97.3	—	166.8	140.3	137.1	174.5
1919	124.7	143.3	99.3	—	152.2	120.7	129.2	144.2
1914	117.6	128.7	94.2	—	148.5	147.9	130.5	141.3
1909	114.0	117.7	100.7	3,318	142.9	137.9	120.1	121.7
1902[c]	100	100	100	100	100	100	100	100
1882	75.6	n.a.	89.2	—	62.6	—	—	—

— = Not applicable.

a. At constant 1960 prices.

b. Number of buildings paying buildings tax; for 1902–29 number in Cairo and Alexandria only.

c. Based on a population of 10.5 million, of whom 3.3 million were economically active; a cultivated area of 5.3 million feddan; capital stock valued at LE156.5 million in agriculture and LE104.4 million in industry; and 3,255 kilometers of railway track.

Source: Egypt, Ministry of Finance, *Annuaire statistique de l'Egypte*, various years; Mead (1967), table 2-B-1; Crouchley (1938), table 3; El Imam (1962), 1, 2; Radwan (1974), tables A–11, 2–8, 3–3.

productivity in nonagricultural, nonservice sectors to secure increasing total factor productivity for the economy as a whole. Assume that total factor productivity for the economy as a whole was constant from 1900 to 1938. With labor and possibly capital per capita increasing and land per capita declining, it is impossible to know whether per capita income increased, declined, or remained constant.

Production, Income, and Trade

Figure 2–1 presents six well-defined and accurately measured indicators of production per capita from the 1880s to 1938. All six are increasing

Figure 2-1. Indicators of Production per capita, 1880-1938

Index (1913 = 100, log scale)

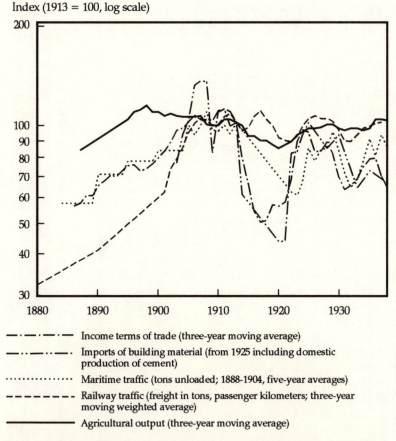

—— · — · — Income terms of trade (three-year moving average)

—— ·· — ·· — · Imports of building material (from 1925 including domestic production of cement)

················· Maritime traffic (tons unloaded; 1888-1904, five-year averages)

— — — — — — — Railway traffic (freight in tons, passenger kilometers; three-year moving weighted average)

——————— Agricultural output (three-year moving average)

Source: Wattleworth (1975); Egypt, Ministry of Finance, *Annuaire statistique de l'Egypte;* Hansen and Lucas (1978).

Figure 2-2. Indicators of Consumption (Apparent) per capita, 1880-1938

Index (1913 = 100, log scale)

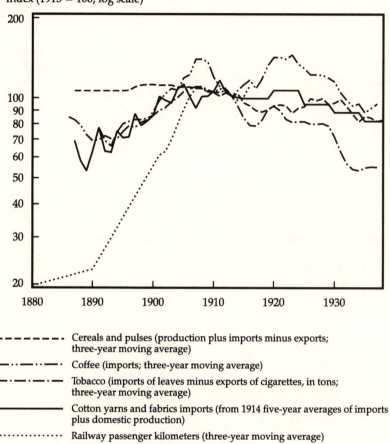

Cereals and pulses (production plus imports minus exports; three-year moving average)

Coffee (imports; three-year moving average)

Tobacco (imports of leaves minus exports of cigarettes, in tons; three-year moving average)

Cotton yarns and fabrics imports (from 1914 five-year averages of imports plus domestic production)

Railway passenger kilometers (three-year moving average)

Source: Wattleworth (1975); Egypt, Ministry of Finance, *Annuaire statistique de l'Egypte;* Hansen and Lucas (1978); Tignor (1984).

until the first decade of the new century after which the tendency is flat, if anything even declining. In 1938 all indicators are below the 1913 level and the 1928 level. Similarly, figure 2-2 shows indicators of the consumption per capita of consumer goods—cereals and pulses, coffee, tobacco, railway passenger kilometers, and cotton goods—that give the same impression: a uniform increase until the first decade of the new century and a decline thereafter. Considering relative price developments, the impression is one of increasing income per capita until 1907 followed by stagnation (Hansen 1979). These and the indicators in table

2–1 suggest that per capita production and income were roughly unchanged from 1913 to 1939.

Much the same impression is conveyed by developments of export and import volumes per capita from 1885 to 1960, shown in figure 2–3. Exports, which consist almost exclusively of cotton, including seed and seed-cake until World War II, are a component of agricultural output and thus a production indicator. Import volume is more complex, being influenced by income, relative prices, capital imports, and structural changes, particularly the shift from food to cotton cultivation; it may at most be taken as an imperfect indicator of income.[7] Considering that both Mohammed Ali and the British emphasized development of cotton for export and that thus growth in Egypt was export-led until around 1900, the twentieth century has rather been characterized by export-led shrinkage.

It is possible to gauge the level of per capita income in Egypt just before World War II and compare it with that in the United States. For

Figure 2-3. Foreign Trade Volumes per capita, 1885-1961

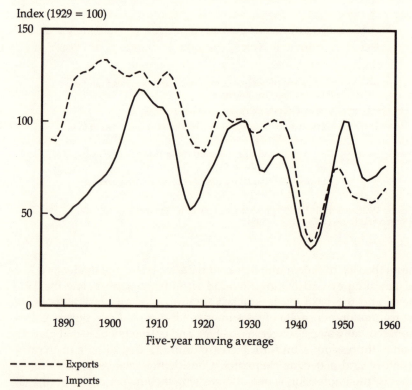

Index (1929 = 100)

Five-year moving average

- - - - - - Exports
————— Imports

Source: Hansen and Lucas (1978), p. 440.

1937–39 Anis (1950) estimates total GDP in Egypt to have been approximately LE160 million, or about LE10 (£ 10) per capita. At the then existing exchange rates that makes $50 per capita. In the United States, GNP per capita for the same years was $681 (U.S., Bureau of the Census 1975, Series F.4). Though the Egyptian pound may have been somewhat overvalued at that time, the impression is that per capita income in Egypt was about 7 percent of that in the United States. By conjecture it appears that the Egyptian per capita income at current prices in 1903–13 was about 17 percent of that in the United States. This dramatic decline in Egypt's relative position was, of course, related to the relative decline of agricultural prices, particularly of Egyptian cotton. Estimated at constant prices, Egyptian GDP per capita appears to have declined only from 9 percent to 7 percent of that in the United States, but that does not allow for the dramatic loss of about 25 percent in the terms of trade which corresponds to about 5 percent of GNP. The corresponding figure for 1984 for the United States was $15,390 against $720 for Egypt (World Bank data) with Egypt only at 4.7 percent of the United States. It would appear that for Egypt the decline in relative position is a phenomenon that goes back to the years before World War I.

Little is known about the distribution of income in Egypt before World War II. I estimate that functional distribution in agriculture may have changed somewhat in favor of labor from 1900 to 1938, the share of labor increasing from about 34 percent to 47 percent, with the share of rent (before tax) declining from 49 percent to 38 percent and the share of capital (including public investment) increasing from 7 percent to 14 percent. Very little can be inferred from functional to size distribution of income in agriculture, and nothing is known about nonagricultural income distribution.

Property and Property Law

In terms of value, land undoubtedly constituted the main form of private wealth in Egypt before World War II. Buildings, mainly located in urban areas, represented a much smaller value. The same is true of modern machinery and equipment. Mobile property, such as inventories, gold, and livestock, appears to have been more important than buildings, especially if inventories include growing crops. Financial assets and liabilities would add to and deduct from individual net wealth. The private sector as a whole became deeply indebted to foreign creditors during the two decades before World War I and, despite a dramatic reversal during World War I, probably remained a net debtor until World War II. Next to nothing is known about the distribution of private net wealth in Egypt, even today, apart from land.

Land is the only asset for which information about size distribution is available. Holdings of land ownership, on the one hand, must be carefully distinguished from holdings of units under cultivation (which may be owned or rented) on the other. The earliest years for which both distributions are available are 1950 and 1952, before land reform (Hansen and Marzouk 1965, pp. 58–60). The total number of ownerships in 1952 was 2.8 million, while the number of cultivation units in 1950 was 1.0 million; the average area per ownership was 2.1 *feddan* and per cultivation unit 6.1 *feddan*.[8] It is a common misunderstanding that land lease should diminish the average size of cultivated units. Large ownerships do tend to be broken up into smaller cultivation units, but in Egypt apparently consolidation of small ownerships (possibly within families) in larger cultivation units dominates the picture. As a consequence the distribution of cultivation units is more equitable (in terms of Gini coefficients shown in figure 2–4 and table 4–29) than the distribution of ownerships (disregarding, of course, persons [or families] without either ownership or cultivation). The distributions are crude, but judging from the Lorenz curves in figure 2–4 the distribution of ownerships is very inequitable. It remained rather stable, however, from 1910 to the time before the land reforms of 1952. The distribution in 1938 was very similar to that in 1952.

When Mohammed Ali took control of Egypt, he became the only landowner (excluding the religious endowments, the *ewkaf*) and the ownership distribution was obviously more unequal than the distribution of cultivation units. Peasants held traditional cultivation rights and were subjected to two kinds of taxation. During his lifetime, Mohammed Ali let state lands pass into (favored) private hands and by laws of 1858, 1866, and 1871 and decrees of 1880, 1891, and 1896 full private ownership of land was gradually established. By 1880 a major part of the cultivated area was privately owned, though *wakf* land and state domains continued to occupy substantial areas (Baer 1962). A new class of landowners had emerged.[9] Taxation of agricultural land was unified during the early years of the new century with a tax rate of 26 percent of the rental value as assessed by commissions headed by British administrators. Private land lease must have developed simultaneously, and peasants with traditional cultivation rights must have become owners or tenants or have lost their land altogether. This process was probably characterized by great inequity. The tenants became sharecroppers, cash tenants, or service labor on a new form of holding, the *'ezba* (Roger Owen in Udovitch 1981; Richards 1982). It has been compared with the medieval Norman manor as a relatively self-sufficient production and consumption unit, partly run by service labor. An *'ezba* worker was given a couple of *feddan* to cultivate for his own needs at a rent below the market rent but was obliged to work for the owner without compensation. The *'ezba* worker was not bonded and his position was in principle regulated by voluntary (unwritten) contract. How this form of holding worked in practice is not well un-

Figure 2-4. Distribution of Land by Ownerships and Holdings (cultivation units), 1910, 1950, and 1952

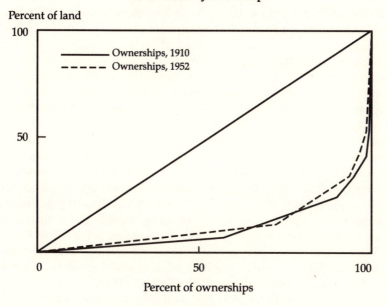

Distribution by ownerships

Percent of land

Ownerships, 1910
Ownerships, 1952

Percent of ownerships

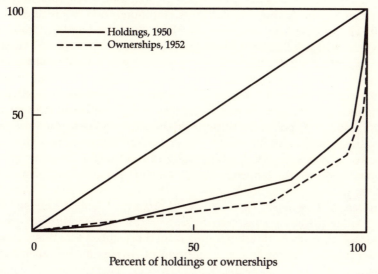

Distribution by holdings and ownerships

Percent of land

Holdings, 1950
Ownerships, 1952

Percent of holdings or ownerships

Source: Egypt, Ministry of Finance, *Annuaire statistique de l'Egypte;* Hansen and Marzouk (1965).

derstood, but the system was undoubtedly widespread and continued to exist until the land reforms of 1952.

The modern legislation regulating ownership and transfer of property dates back to 1876 when the Mixed Civil Code, to be used in the newly established Mixed Courts (1875), was promulgated (Ziadeh 1978; Forte 1978). Under the Capitulations a national of one of the Capitulary Powers who was resident in Egypt had the right to have any case in which he became involved tried at a consular court under the laws of his own country. Originally offered graciously by the then mighty Ottoman Empire as an incentive for European merchants to settle and trade in the empire, the consular courts over time had become a source of abuse in favor of foreigners (Landes [1969] vividly describes the abuses under Ismail in the 1860s). The Mixed Courts, established on Egyptian initiative in agreement with the Powers, decided all cases in which subjects of the Capitulary Powers were involved (but see below) and had a majority of foreign judges. The Mixed Civil Code, on which their decisions were based, was copied mainly from the Napoleonic Code. In 1883 National Courts were established for cases not involving foreigners, their decisions being based on a National Code modeled after the Mixed Courts and Code. Features of Islamic law were incorporated in both the Mixed and National codes, particularly in relation to land because the Napoleonic Code did not easily apply to the system of land tenure that prevailed in Egypt. Moreover, in 1889 the Mixed Courts were ordered, with the approval of the Capitulary Powers, to apply all the laws of the Egyptian government pertaining to land, embankments, and canals. An important exception was that in all cases involving the *ewkaf* (religious endowments), the Islamic *shari'a* courts continued to have jurisdiction.

In 1949 a new Civil Code replaced both the Mixed and the National Code. It integrated material from the old codes and incorporated material from the *shari'a* and from European and American codes. But it relegated the *shari'a* to third place as a general source of law and custom after explicit law and precedent and made no reference to particular schools of Islamic law. Despite the land reforms of 1952 and later, which were inspired by political philosophies alien to both Western and Islamic law, the principles of the Civil Code of 1949 still regulate real property and real rights in Egypt. Under pressure from Islamic fundamentalists some reversal of the tendency to play down the shari'a has taken place recently.

In terms of ownership and transfer of property, Islamic features of the Civil Code at some points seem to create uncertainty because on private contracts they imply different rights from those implied by Western law systems. An example is the acquisition of ownership by preemption (Ziadeh 1978, p. 255). Ownership is, however, generally protected insofar as fair compensation is prescribed when the public interest or a special private interest takes precedence over a private right of ownership.

Sequestration of property, under which "the bare title of the property remains with the owner, while the state acquires the rights of alienation and use of the property, as well as the right to income derived from it" is another matter of importance (Forte, 1978, p. 275). Originally it was used to enforce payment of taxes and thus did not require compensation. Under Nasser, however, it was used extensively against opponents of the government. Some of these sequestrations were reversed by Sadat, and in 1974 the Council of State, Egypt's highest court, declared sequestrations illegal. While Nasser's sequestrations did much to cut the top of the distributions of both income and wealth, they were a strong disincentive to and greatly distorted private investment. Nasser's use of sequestration was not based on the Civil Code, and the constitution of 1971, adopted under Sadat, explicitly states that sequestration can only be made against compensation.[10]

Mortgage legislation, copied from French law, was introduced in 1876. In 1911 the so-called Five-Feddan Law prohibited foreclosure on mortgaged lands of less than five *feddan*. This measure, introduced on the initiative of Lord Kitchener under pressure from Egyptian nationalists, was designed to help indebted small peasants. But it paralyzed the market in loans on small farms, and probably did more harm than good to the peasantry; it was definitely harmful to agricultural development.

Interest rates were regulated by law. The maximum contractual interest rate was lowered from 12 percent to 9 percent in 1882; the legal maximum (used in decisions by the Mixed Courts) in civil cases was 7 percent. In 1892 the legal rates were lowered to 5 percent in civil and 7 percent in commercial cases, and the maximum contractual rate remained unchanged at 9 percent (Hansen 1983). Although market rates in the modern financial sector declined throughout the British occupation and for loans to good customers and large real estates were lower than both maximum and legal rates (Hansen 1983), for peasant loans the legislation probably represented an element of financial repression, driving small farmers and businesses to the informal credit market where much higher rates prevailed.

The rules of succession and inheritance in the Civil Code were mainly taken over from the *shari'a*. Economically the most important implication of the Islamic law of succession, which favors males over females, is its alleged tendency to create land fragmentation in agriculture. That tendency, however, is offset by a countervailing tendency for land to consolidate within families, if not in terms of ownership, at least in terms of cultivation units.

Market Institutions

Just as Egypt's modern infrastructure was developed during the second half of the nineteenth century as a necessary condition for the expansion of cotton cultivation and export, so were modern market institutions. Modern commercial banks, some of them branches of European banks, others registered in Egypt, were established mainly to move the cotton crop and more generally to finance foreign trade. The first mortgage bank (Credit Foncier Egyptien) was established in 1880 and before World War I a modern banking system with both short- and long-term financing had been fully developed. The banks were almost exclusively foreign owned and financed.

The monetary system nevertheless remained curiously inefficient until 1914, with domestic circulation largely based on foreign gold coins (sovereigns, in particular). A note-issuing bank, the National Bank of Egypt (NBE), was founded in 1897 by Sir Ernest Cassel, with fractional gold cover modeled on the Bank of England. It did not function as a central bank, however. Its notes were not legal tender and their circulation was very limited. The NBE did not announce a discount rate, nor did it serve as a last resort for deposit banks. Private banks held their reserves in London and continued to do so until World War II. With gold imports cut off in 1914, NBE notes were made legal tender and gold conversion abrogated. Egypt went on a sterling standard with the sterling rate pegged (at the old gold parity) and the country a member of the sterling area. Until the late 1940s Egypt went on and off the gold standard with the pound sterling.

Modern banking, particularly mortgage banks, did penetrate the countryside, but local money lenders (to some extent foreigners, especially Greeks) continued to play an important role in financing the needs of small farmers. The maximum and legal rates of interest constrained the activities of modern banking in the villages, and the five-*feddan* law effectively killed the modern mortgage market for small farmers, a major setback for agricultural development that was not repaired until the early 1930s.

For the major export crops, cotton, wheat and beans, modern commodity markets were established (privately) in the 1860s during the years of the cotton famine. Formal mechanisms created for spot, forward, and futures transactions appear to have worked well (Todd 1934). Such markets emerged only for export crops and only in the major export port, Alexandria. When Egypt in the 1890s became a wheat importer, the term markets in wheat apparently disappeared. Inland, only organized spot markets apparently existed although, of course, informal term markets may have operated, perhaps as extensions of the Alexandria market. I have never discovered term quotations, even from the very large *rod el farrag* market in Cairo.

The price of Egyptian cotton in Alexandria followed closely the Liverpool quotations; in the nineteenth century, arbitrage worked effectively for cotton. The Alexandria price of Egyptian wheat was not closely geared to the Liverpool quotations for American wheat, whether because the two wheats were imperfect substitutes or because arbitrage was inefficient is unclear (Hansen 1981).

Markets for both urban real estate and agricultural land were very active; it is unclear, however, how competitive they were. The (Islamic) rules for preemptive acquisition of ownership of immobile property may have discouraged buyers from outside the extended family, village, or religious community; indeed, this may have been the rationale of the rules for preemptive acquisition. The markets consequently tended to be thin and oligopolistic. Markets for land lease were extremely active as could be expected in a country with about half the land cultivated by tenants whose leases frequently covered one crop. Again it is not clear how competitive the markets were. The tendency to exclude outsiders operated also in the lease market, although by habit only. In villages dominated by one or a few landowners, monopsonistic conditions might prevail. Nominal rents, however, appear to have been very flexible. In urban areas, rents of modern apartments did not respond immediately to the vacancies that began in 1908 after the collapse of the 1906–07 building boom (*Egyptian Gazette,* February 13, 1908) but half a year later the response was very strong, with rents falling 30 percent, 40 percent, and even 50 percent (*Egyptian Gazette,* October 14, 1908). During the interwar period, urban rents were subjected to government control and in the early 1930s, legislation was passed to bring agricultural rents down. It is not known how effective these attempts to control rent were. Agricultural rents fell very strongly in the early 1930s but considering the collapse of agricultural prices, this would probably have happened in any case.

The distance between villages in Egypt is everywhere small; both water and animal transportation has always been easy. Since the end of the nineteenth century most villages have been close to railway stations. Yet price differentials between neighboring villages could be very large, for domestic products as well as imported goods, and they tended to increase with the distance to cities and larger towns (Martin and Levi, 1910).

Official statistics for both wages and cost of living by region for 1913, presented in table 2–2, point to considerable regional differences. Wages for construction workers are broken down by skill, sex, and nationality. The cost of living index is based on twenty-three commodities, including food, coffee and alcohol, fuel, and soap, and distinguishes between low-paid civil servants' families on the one hand and workers' and government servants' (*farashin*) families on the other.

For laborers, nominal wages are clearly lower in the Delta and Middle Egypt than in the big cities, probably because agricultural workers earned only half as much as construction laborers. For skilled construction workers the tendency is the opposite, probably reflecting a smaller supply of skilled workers outside the cities. Among laborers, women are

Table 2-2. Nominal and Real Wages for Construction Workers, by Skill, Sex, Nationality, and Region, 1913

| | Wage rate (piasters per day) | | | | Cost of living index | | Index of real wage rates | | | |
| | Laborers | | Skilled males | | | Workers and govern- | Laborers[a] | | Skilled males[b] | |
Region	Male	Female	Native	Foreign	Civil servants	ment servants	Male	Female	Native	Foreign
Cairo	65	55	173	268	100	100	100	100	100	100
Alexandria[c]	68	50	186	239	99.8	119.5	87.5	76.1	107.8	89.4
Delta	55	35	190	283	89.9	94.3	89.7	67.5	122.2	117.5
Middle Egypt	50	42	175	240	98.3	93.9	78.3	81.3	102.9	91.1

a. Cost of living for workers and government servants has been applied to laborers.
b. Cost of living for civil servants has been applied to skilled males.
c. Also Port Said, Suez, Damiette.
Source: Egypt, Ministry of Finance, *Annuaire statistique de l'Egypte* (1914) pp. 376–79, (1923–24) p. 234.

everywhere paid less than men although the ratio between female and male wage rates differs greatly from region to region. Skilled, native males were paid three to four times more than the unskilled, and skilled foreigners some 50 percent more than skilled natives.

The cost of living tended to be lower in the Delta and Middle Egypt than in the big cities. Had rent and clothing been included, the difference would probably have been larger. The figures for Alexandria look a bit odd and it may be preferable to exclude this city from the real wage comparison. Real wages of laborers are considerably higher in Cairo than in the Delta and Middle Egypt but the difference might shrink if rent, transportation, and clothing were properly considered in the cost of living. Skilled workers' real wages tend to be higher in the Delta than in Cairo while Middle Egypt seems to be a mixed case. The relatively low money and real wages for foreign skilled workers in Alexandria and other ports is probably explained by the fact that these were ports of entry for such labor.

Table 2–2 does not permit simplistic statements about regional differences in prices and wages. Its main features are comprehensible in terms of demand and supply but do not permit conclusions about the efficiency of market forces in Egypt. The data in the table refer to a time, 1913, when motor traffic was still negligible but rail traffic dense.

For labor a high degree of nominal wage flexibility appears to have prevailed in both rural and urban areas. Wages in agriculture were frequently paid in kind, more so the further back in time they are. It is not known to what extent wages in kind responded to changes in productivity.

Landless labor has always existed in Egypt. Money wages appear always to have been governed by demand and supply. Slavery existed until 1895 but slave labor was mainly used for household services and in urban business. Unpaid forced labor existed until 1892 but applied only to tenants. Both slavery and the corvée were abolished on British initiative. How the open labor market was affected is not well understood. The abolition of the corvée may have increased the labor input of families on their own farms but may also have increased supply in the open market. Since the abolition of the corvée was geared to the completion of the Delta Barrage and the resulting decline in public demand for labor for canal cleaning, the net effect on the open, rural labor market may have been either way.

Seasonal unemployment in agriculture has always been massive, probably declining with the expansion of perennial irrigation. The strong seasonal fluctuations in agricultural wages raise doubts about the nature of seasonal unemployment, whether voluntary or involuntary. The existence of seasonal migration from Upper Egypt to Cairo and the Delta—from basin-irrigated areas to urban and perennially irrigated areas—may be taken to indicate that remaining seasonal unemployment in Upper Egypt was voluntary. Recent studies, however, indicating that during slack seasons actual wages exceed reservation wages, point to involuntary unemployment (Alan Richards, P. L. Martin, and R. Nagaar in Richards and Martin 1983). The phenomenon is not well understood.

The urban unemployment reported after the financial crises in 1907–08 was mainly white-collar unemployment among foreigners and may not have been typical for native Egyptians. In the early 1930s urban unemployment appears to have existed on a broader scale but quantification is impossible. In urban areas wages may not have been perfectly flexible. Unionization began before World War I among foreign workers, and during the interwar period unions were active in sugar, textiles, oil, and some craft industries. The unions' concern, however, may not have been primarily money wages (Goldberg 1986).

Foreign Capital and the National Debt

At the death of Mohammed Ali in 1849, Egypt was virtually without foreign debt. Mohammed Ali's industrial and military ventures were financed domestically and if nothing came of these ventures, at least they did not leave the country indebted. The monopolies, his major financing device, were dismantled in 1841 through British intervention and under his successors foreign borrowing accelerated until the country went bankrupt in 1876, one year after the bankruptcy of the Ottoman Empire. A great deal of money was undoubtedly wasted on "public (royal) consumption" or went into the wrong pockets (Landes 1969) but, as in Turkey, military and economic modernization efforts absorbed most of the foreign loans. That the result was bankruptcy was related partly to the inability of the rulers to raise domestic revenue, partly to adverse price developments abroad (the collapse of the cotton famine and falling sugar prices), and partly to the negative effects of the Suez Canal. The public debts were consolidated with the public finances under the supervision of the Caisse de la dette from 1876. After a brief revolt by Egypt's army under the leadership of Ahmed Arabi, the British occupied the country in 1882, one of their several motives being to secure repayment of the public debt. The policies chosen by the British represented by Lord (later the Earl of) Cromer were a tight budgetary policy, completion of Mohammed Ali's cotton cultivation and export policy, with supply economics the underlying economic philosophy, and strict adherence to the free-trade, low-tariff regime dictated by the Capitulations (particularly the treaty of 1841).

While the public debt was slowly brought down from the mid-1890s, foreign private investment accelerated, reaching almost the same size as the public debt by the outbreak of World War I. During the war Egypt in effect financed British military operations against the Ottoman Empire and through large surpluses in the current account accumulated claims in sterling on the United Kingdom that by the end of the war had almost erased the net debt. The sterling assets, mainly held by the NBE as an exchange reserve, were used to cover large current account deficits immediately after the war and Egypt again became a net debtor, on a much smaller scale than before World War I. Table 2–3 shows these developments.

In the early 1890s the national debt, almost exclusively public debt, was about one and a half times the national income; interest and dividend payments amounted to almost 7 percent of the national income and 37 percent of export revenue. Undoubtedly this was a heavy debt burden, although interest rates were low. In 1914 the national debt, half public and half private, was still larger than national income, with interest and dividends about 5 percent of national income but now absorbing less than one-quarter of export revenue. It is not possible to conjecture the size of the national income in 1919 but net interest and dividend payments had declined to (less than) 5.4 percent of export revenue. In 1934 the national debt had again increased to 30 percent of the national income with interest and dividend payments absorbing less than 2 percent of national income and less than 9 percent of export revenue. From a deeply indebted nation before World War I, Egypt before World War II

Table 2–3. National Debt, for Selected Years, 1892–1934

(millions of Egyptian pounds)

Item	1892	1914	1919	1934
Public debt held abroad	101	86	83	39
Shares and debentures held abroad	6	71	69	45
Total claims on Egypt held abroad	107	157	152	84
Foreign claims held in Egypt	—	7	150	39
Net national debt	107	150	2	45
Interest and dividends paid abroad	5.0	6.8	7.3	4.8
Interest and dividends received from abroad	n.a	0.2	n.a	2.3
Net interest and dividend payments	5.0	6.6	7.3[a]	2.5
National income[a]	75	125	n.a	150
Net national debt (percent of national income)	143	120	n.a	30
Net interest and dividend payments (percent of national income)	6.7	5.3	n.a	1.7
Net interest and dividend payments (percent of export revenue)	36.6	22.8	5.4[a]	8.6

n.a. = Not available.
— = Not applicable.
a. Conjecture.
Source: Crouchley (1936).

had become a moderately indebted country; the debt was at most a secondary problem.

In the analysis of the impact of foreign capital it is common to distinguish between portfolio and direct investment, the latter being supposed to imply foreign influence in physical investment and production decisions. The distinction is not clearcut. The public part of the national debt was of course a matter of foreign portfolio investment, but it certainly led to foreign interference with real investment and production—through the British occupation. The private part of the national debt was almost exclusively in shares and bonds issued by companies registered in Egypt and held abroad. In such companies managers and members of boards of directors typically were foreigners. However the foreign nationals involved might be resident abroad or resident in Egypt. Many managers and board members were foreigners resident in Egypt, and they might be owners of both shares and bonds (debentures). In 1883 only 20 percent of the shares and none of the bonds were held in Egypt. In 1914 half of the shares and 85 percent of the bonds were held in Egypt, and in 1934 half of the shares and 40 percent of the bonds. Though the extent of ownership of private companies by foreigners resident in Egypt is difficult to assess, it is believed that even in 1934 the lion's part of shares and bonds held in Egypt belonged to resident foreigners. This distinction is important in view of the role the resident foreigners came to play in Egyptian development policy.

A very large part of the foreign capital in the private sector was invested in financial companies, commercial banks, and finance and mortgage banks, with the mortgage banks dominating in terms of capital invested. Of a total paid-up capital of LE100 million in Egyptian companies in 1914, LE71 million was held abroad. Of the total, LE52 million was invested in financial companies and LE48 million in mortgage banks. Mortgage capital, however, is typical portfolio capital, whether in shares or bonds. Mortgage capital is lent against security in real estate (land and buildings). Once a loan is given, a mortgage company has no influence on the borrower, his investment, or his production decisions. Mortgage capital is passive capital, very different in nature from the capital of modern multinational corporations. Most of the foreign mortgage capital in Egypt was extended as agricultural loans used by landowners to purchase land from the government (which used the proceeds for repaying old foreign debts), to finance increased gold holdings (currency), and, possibly, to invest in urban real estate. Most of the foreign capital invading Egypt before World War I was therefore sucked into the country by Egyptian private demand for loans. Relatively little was pushed into the country for productive investment. Such investment was mainly in land reclamation and rural-urban development. Very little went into industry and commerce.

Government and the Public Budget

Modern government in Egypt dates back to Ismail who in the mid-nineteenth century reorganized and improved public administration along European lines. After the British occupation, British advisers were attached to all important administrations, and those were "days when advice was often tantamount to an order" (*The Times*, London, June 22, 1934). While British advisers undoubtedly increased both efficiency and honesty in public administration, they did little to improve the quality of the lower echelons.

Foreign intervention in budgetary matters after the bankruptcy, especially through the Caisse de la dette, was mainly concerned with debt service which, with tribute payments to Istanbul, absorbed more than 60 percent of public revenue in the 1880s. Budget policy became extremely conservative. Before the Anglo-French agreement of 1904, which gave the British an almost free hand in budgetary matters, substantial surpluses led to the accumulation of a reserve that in effect was a repayment of the public debt over and above scheduled debt service. After 1904 the budget ran with small deficits and most of the reserve was used up. Nonetheless, over the period 1884–1913 as a whole the budget was balanced and all public investment in irrigation and drainage and other infrastructure was financed by current revenue on the budget. This budget policy was continued by the Egyptian government after independence in 1923. With the exception of two periods with temporary deficits, large surpluses prevailed from 1914 to 1939 and, indeed, to the 1940s. The first period of deficit was during the popular upheaval after World War I when the government attempted to placate the populace through food subsidies and increased salaries for civil servants. The second period was around 1930 when the government in reality subsidized cotton growers through stockpiling in a vain attempt to stabilize Egyptian cotton prices.

The conservative budget policies should be seen against the background of the Capitulations, which until 1937 severely constrained the raising of public revenue. From the 1860s, customs duties were fixed at 8 percent for imports and 1 percent for exports with only marginal exceptions and changes until 1930 (tobacco being the only major exception), and such revenue automatically followed the value of trade. The land taxes were effectively specific taxes, frozen nominally from the early years of the twentieth century and before that, if anything, slightly lowered. The rate of taxes on buildings was frozen from the time of their introduction in the middle of the nineteenth century at one-twelfth of assessed rentals (increased to one-tenth for Cairo in 1909). Reassessments were made regularly, however, and revenue slowly followed the level of rents and the number of buildings. These were the major taxes. Income from state property (mainly land) was important and tended to fluctuate with agricultural prices. As a whole, the tax system was probably slightly progressive on income and formally equitable in the sense that equal income pays equal tax.[11]

The unnecessarily conservative budget policy under the Capitulations implied a serious constraint on expenditure, over and above debt service. Education, which had had high priority in expenditure under Ismail, had low priority under Cromer and suffered badly from the tight budgetary situation. The Capitulations did not prevent taxes from being lowered, provided that debt service was honored, and after 1923 the government came under heavy pressure from landowner groups to lower land taxes. The British had never listened to these groups. After independence land taxes became an important political issue, as did tariffs after the increases in 1930.

About 1895 the nominal debt burden began to decline steadily but the real burden fluctuated with prices. With the price level increasing from about 1897 to 1921, the real burden declined rapidly; from 1921 to 1939 it increased as the net result of repayment and falling prices.

Constitutional and Political Developments

A modest development toward representative government was made under Ismail with the establishment of an Assembly of Delegates in 1866. Election of members was indirect and the assembly had no legislative powers. Monarchy remained absolute. The assembly was transformed into a Legislative Council in 1883 and into a Legislative Assembly in 1913 with certain veto rights and investigative powers. Council and assembly never became truly legislative authorities and the assembly was abrogated from 1915.

During the public debt crisis of 1877–80, Ismail was forced to delegate responsibility to a cabinet, including Europeans. The overt interference of the European powers, when Ismail was deposed in 1879, threw Egypt into turmoil. Political opposition surfaced, ending with the Arabi revolt which provided the British with a pretext for occupation. After the occupation the system continued with a cabinet appointed by the khedive and watched by the Legislative Council. Real power, however, rested with British advisers, attached to all ministries and departments and ultimately responsible to the British consul general. Until 1904 the British were constrained by the rights of other Capitulary Powers, exercised through the Caisse, and even after the British-French agreement of 1904 the other Capitulary Powers could not be ignored.

Political activities were fostered by the assembly and later the Legislative Council but secret societies of civilians and army officers, partly based on Islamic thinking and similar to such societies in Turkey and later in Syria, played a role and became forerunners to the modern political parties formed during 1906–13. During the last two decades of the nineteenth century, Islamic sympathies prevailed and opposition was influenced by developments in Turkey. With the new century, Western philosophies predominated. Three influential Western-oriented political parties were formed: Mustapha Kamil's Nationalist party, an extremist, nationalist party (encouraged by the ruler); Ahmad Lutfi's People's party, a liberal, rationalist, and reformist group; and Ali Yusef's Constitutional Reform party, something between the other two. The most important political party, however, was the Wafd party, which began as a delegation organized by Saad Zaghloul in 1918 to present Egyptian demands for independence at the Peace Conference in London. The Wafd was mainly supported by middle-size landowners, the intellectual elite, and large Coptic landowners. Complicated triangular maneuvers and negotiations between the palace, the British, and the Wafd, interrupted by popular uprisings and demonstrations in 1919 and 1921, finally ended with Britain's unilateral recognition of Egypt's independence. Four issues were left to British discretion: the security of imperial communications in Egypt, the defense of Egypt, the protection of foreign interests in Egypt, and the future of Sudan.

A constitution was proclaimed by the king in 1923. Modeled on the Ottoman constitution of 1876, which owed much to the Belgian constitution of 1831, it gave the monarch extensive powers and did not introduce parliamentarism in the modern European sense of the word. Elections were held in 1923 and resulted in a massive victory for the Wafd. The new political system, operating as a ménage à trois with the palace, the British, and politicians as participants, proved highly unstable. Again and again the issues that caused political crises were not economic in nature, though important economic issues arose and were faced. The major controversial issues were the constitution and the relative powers of the king and parliament, on the one hand, and the continued presence of the British on the other. Profoundly controversial economic issues emerged in the late 1930s when tax reform was made possible with the abrogation of the Capitulations and land reform found supporters.

New political parties were formed during the years of parliamentary democracy, 1923–52, but the party structure did not develop along clear lines of economic interest. The Wafd became an increasingly conservative party after the formation of the Saadist party in 1938, the latter without a clear social basis. A splinter party, the Independent Wafdist Bloc, formed in 1942 by a spokesman for labor and land reform legislation, never had a large following. Small socialist and communist parties were formed but remained unimportant, but a small farmers' movement did not emerge.

Powerful organizations representing special interest groups did arise, however, foremost among them the Egyptian General Agricultural Syndicate, an association of large landowners and cotton growers, and the

Egyptian Federation of Industries, both established in the early 1920s, and various local and foreign chambers of commerce. Labor unions did exist but they were divided and their membership was small.

Everything considered, the political economy of Egypt during the period 1923–52 basically resembled that of developed countries. However, the peasants were largely politically passive and the British presence was a special feature.

Notes

1. The modern type of perennial irrigation was introduced in Fayoum in Ptolemaic times but the technology apparently fell into oblivion (Rostovtzeff 1922).

2. The seminal work on the development of cotton in the Egyptian economy until World War I is Owen (1969). The later developments are described by Brown (1955).

3. The internal rate of return on the canal itself was about 9 percent for 1859–1954. French and English shareholders obtained about that rate. Egypt's internal rate of return on her investment, allowing for the forced labor and the festivities at the opening, was about 3 percent (Hansen and Tourk 1976).

4. On the basis of the official, administrative definition of urban areas, the urban population increased from 27 percent of total population in 1927 to 28 percent in 1937 (Mead 1967, table 2–A–3).

5. Foreigners may have succeeded in evading taxation of land and buildings on a larger scale than Egyptians, thanks to the foreign consuls. But they were never exempted from these taxes payment of which was enforced from the establishment of the Mixed Courts in 1875 and the agreement of the Capitulatory Powers to impose the buildings tax on foreigners from 1883. The Capitulatory Powers never agreed to extend foreigners' tax liability to the licence (professional) tax, a kind of business tax, which Egyptians paid; for the sake of equity this tax was simply abrogated in 1895. The only taxes from which foreigners were then exempted were the stamp duties, a minor source of revenue for the government. From the early 1900s the Capitulatory Powers prevented a lowering of the land tax, important in servicing foreign debt (Milner 1904, pp. 48–51).

6. Data for rolling stock, locomotives, and passenger and freight cars exist. Track length appears to be a good indicator of the total stock of capital in railway transportation in Egypt, as I have been told it is in the United States.

7. Reasonably good estimates of import functions come out with statistically significant coefficients for these four variables for 1895–1913. For 1921–39 only income and relative prices are significant.

8. Number of ownerships exaggerates number of owners just as number of cultivation units exaggerates number of cultivators because the data were not aggregated across districts. Partnerships and delays in registration work in the other direction.

9. The khedival family with some civil servants and military dignitaries became the largest private landowners, obviously through nepotism. *'Umdas* and village sheiks became important middle-size owners, taking advantage of their local administrative powers. Wealthy urban families appear to have succeeded

in acquiring title to land through the *muqaballah* legislation of 1871, which offered full private ownership in return for payment in advance of land taxes for six years.

10. "Private ownership is safeguarded. It cannot be brought under sequestration, except in cases stipulated by law and by court order. Expropriation is only to be effected for public interest and in return for legally stipulated compensation." Article 34, quoted in Rivlin (1985), p. 48.

11. Formal equity was an important step toward economic equity in a country where favorites of the ruler, not necessarily foreigners in the sense of the Capitulations, were taxed leniently or not at all.

3 *The Failure of Democracy and Private Enterprise: Development without Growth, 1923–55*

Democracy in Egypt, as institutionalized in the Constitution of 1923, was imperfect and did not work well.[1] In the beginning, at least, the problems did not, as so often in democracies, stem from difficulty in forming majority governments. On the contrary, at the first election in 1924 the Wafd party under the leadership of Saad Zaghloul secured an overwhelming majority in both popular vote and number of seats in the parliament. The Wafd then formed the first democratically elected government in Egypt. Difficulties arose in part because the constitution did not rest on popular vote or even on popular support but had been proclaimed by the king and gave the king powers far beyond what would be compatible with parliamentary government in the European sense. "Thus the King had the right to select and appoint the Prime Minister . . . dismiss the Cabinet and dissolve Parliament . . . postpone parliamentary sessions . . . appoint the president of the senate and one-fifth of its members . . . Despite a government's majority in the Lower House, the monarch could dismiss it by decree" (Vatikiotis 1969, p. 270–71).

The king used his powers widely and frequently to promote the interests of the monarchy and the groups and parties close to the palace. The British had reserved the right to interfere whenever, according to their judgment, defense, protection of foreign interests, imperial communications, and the relations to Sudan so required. They ousted the Wafd government before the end of its first year, and when the Wafd again obtained a majority in the elections of 1926 and formed a government, they prevented Zaghloul from assuming the premiership. With the changes in its international and economic position in the 1930s, the United Kingdom's abrasive policies toward Egypt mellowed considerably. The British plan for developing the cultivation of Egyptian cotton varieties in Sudan and related hydraulic investment continued to be a controversial economic issue. On other important economic issues, however, the British were either supportive or neutral. Thus the tax reforms proposed by the Mohammed Mahmoud government (in 1928–29) met with British support and the cotton policies of 1921–32 as well as the tariff reform of 1930 were not opposed actively.

The constitution was tampered with in 1928 and a new constitution giving additional powers to the king was drafted in 1930 after the appointment of Ismail Sidqi as premier. Under Sidqi's semiautocratic government (1929–33) legislation important to economic development— tariff reform in particular—was adopted and implemented and other policies abrogated (cotton price stabilization). In 1935 the 1923 Constitution was reinstated. With the Wafd back in power in 1936, this time with the blessing of the British, the Anglo-Egyptian Treaty was negotiated, and at the Montreux Conference in 1937 the British supported and secured agreement to abolish the Capitulations. Tax reform now became possible. During World War II British intervention was heavy-handed although the constitution remained in force and parliamentary rule in principle prevailed. After World War II, Egyptianization of joint stock companies became the leading economic issue, realizing an old nationalistic dream of curbing the influence of foreign capital.

Important economic reforms were undoubtedly made under democracy; one key issue, the problem of land distribution, was not tackled. The land problem and the inability to form stable governments after World War II helped to put an end to democracy in Egypt.

Development Strategies: Philosophies and Results

There was broad consensus among political leaders, political parties, and the intellectual elite about general growth strategies, which were the basic economic issue until the end of the 1930s. When tax reform and, as a consequence of the beginning industrialization, problems of labor legislation came to the fore, opinions as could be expected were deeply divided. Land reform was another issue on which no consensus existed.

From early modern nationalism before World War I to the early years of Nasser, Egypt's growth strategy was probably much the way that Robert Tignor, the leading economic historian of the period, describes the growth policy of Ismail Sidqi: "He was an advocate of a balanced economic approach, believing that industrial and agricultural progress would be mutually reinforcing" (1984, p. 106). The notion of balanced growth remains undefined, the broadest interpretation being that neither agriculture nor industry should be ignored.

From Mohammed Ali to the end of British occupation, development policy had emphasized promotion of agricultural exports based on hydraulic investment and cultivation of cotton. The immediate purpose was to create revenue, under Mohammed Ali for financing his military ventures and the related industrialization attempts, under the British for securing debt service payments for European loans. There was little objection among Egyptian nationalists to the agricultural development measures per se. There were objections to the policy, however, on the grounds that it would make Egypt a one-commodity exporter with all the risks and dependency on the world market that involved, that agriculture would not become a sufficient employment outlet for the growing population, and that foreign economic influence should be curbed and reduced. Industrialization based on domestic capital and entrepreneurship was thought to be the answer to all these allegedly adverse aspects of the prevailing (British) policies. The successful German challenge to British hegemony, based on protection of infant industries supported by Gründer-banks (development banks), was clearly on the mind of Tala'at Harb, the most prominent nationalistic economic ideologist. He believed that the capital for such industrialization should be supplied by landowners and merchants through an industrial development bank. These ideas were elaborated by an official Commission on Commerce and Industry, appointed in 1916, in a report it submitted in 1918.

The chairman of the commission was Ismail Sidqi, Tala'at Harb was a member, and the foreign resident community was abundantly represented on it. The foreign members supported the commission's general recommendations, including the establishment of protective tariffs, an equitable tax structure, and a variety of government support measures. It was at this time that the development strategy of export promotion in agriculture combined with import substitution in industry was explicitly formulated. A limited policy of import substitution in agriculture (covering wheat and sugar) did appear during the 1930s as a response to the international agricultural crisis and the Great Depression, but by and large the dichotomous development strategy prevailed until the building of the Aswan High Dam, when both export promotion and import substitution in agriculture were stressed; finally, "basic needs" ideologies took the upper hand in the 1970s and geared both agriculture and industry completely to import substitution. The commission also recommended government support for emerging industries, but it was never a question of challenging the superiority of private entrepreneurship or recommending state ownership of industrial enterprises.

Issues of equity played a prominent role in development strategies. Egalitarianism in the sense of equal distribution of income and wealth was not a major issue, although it did emerge in the context of the tax reforms after 1937. Equity was rather a matter of the real or perceived privileges enjoyed by certain segments of the population. The privileges of the resident foreign community were perhaps the major issue. Its right to be tried by the Mixed Courts under the Mixed Code probably gave the foreign community an edge over native Egyptians in matters of business. All Egyptians supported demands for abolition of this form of extraterritoriality. Though resident foreigners were not exempt from the major taxes levied on the population, the tax system worked in their favor. The old-fashioned schedular tax system with customs duties, land tax, and buildings tax its cornerstones, did not tax business income at all, and it was in urban business that the upper layers of resident foreigners made most of their money. Replacement of the schedular tax system with a modern general income tax system thus became a leading equity issue. Opinions were divided, however, on the matter of distribution of the tax burden.

The existence of very large landed estates was another area where privileges were at issue. Once more, the issue involved not egalitarianism in land ownership but the fact that the largest estates belonged to members of the royal family and its entourage and had been obtained recently through nepotism and similar means. Moreover, many Egyptians considered the royal family to be foreigners, and the landed aristocracy in many cases were foreign nationals. Foreigners (not well defined) owned about 10 percent of registered agricultural land, mainly in relatively large estates. The growing rural population and landless rural labor made redistribution of land an emerging issue. It met, of course, with strong resistance from landowning groups and the palace and the modest proposals for land redistribution that were presented to parliament in the 1940s were mainly supported by an urban elite without much political clout.

In the late 1930s, income tax reforms were in fact instituted. While the reforms undoubtedly made taxation more equitable, they probably also made taxation less egalitarian. Land reform came in 1952 with the breakdown of democracy. The general success or failure of the growth strategy, with equal emphasis on growth in agriculture and in industry, is more difficult to evaluate. Since no indexes of industrial production before World War II are available, the evaluation of the growth policies is based here on import indexes and estimates of capital formation in agriculture and industry and on employment developments.

Figure 3–1 shows that from 1913 to 1960 the import volume per capita of capital goods fluctuated strongly. After a low during World War I, in the 1920s it exceeded slightly the level reached before the war but then fell strongly back during the 1930s. Consumer goods show a similar though less pronounced development. Materials imports increased substantially during the 1930s, led by chemical fertilizers used in agriculture. After World War II the picture changes radically, with capital goods imports increasing strongly and consumer goods imports declining. Although import licensing played a role, the effects of import-substitution policies are evident from 1945 to 1960.

The breakdown of capital goods imports in figure 3–2 shows that imports of agricultural capital goods declined drastically from the years before World War I to the 1920s and further during the 1930s. A slight recovery after World War II did not bring the level up even to that of the

Figure 3-1. Import Volume per capita: Materials, Capital Goods, and Consumer Goods for Selected Periods, 1885-1961

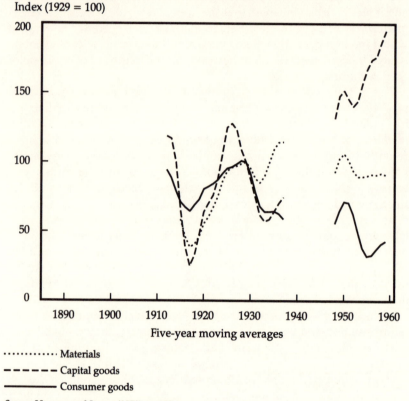

Index (1929 = 100)

Five-year moving averages

············ Materials
 ─ ─ ─ ─ ─ ─ Capital goods
 ───────── Consumer goods

Source: Hansen and Lucas (1978), p. 440.

1920s. Imports of industrial capital goods, on the other hand, increased strongly from the years before World War I to the later 1920s and fell back slightly in the 1930s but remained at a level much above that immediately before World War I. After World War II imports of both agricultural and industrial capital goods increased, the latter more than the former. The general impression is of little change in capital goods imports in the 1920s from the prewar years followed by a decline in the 1930s and a somewhat stronger increase in the 1950s with a continuous shift in the composition toward industrial capital goods.

Table 3–1 presents constant price estimates of fixed gross investment in agriculture and industry from 1903–07 to 1956–59, with a breakdown of agricultural gross investment on public (irrigation and drainage) and private (machinery, livestock, and rural dwellings). Industrial investments were largely private, at least until 1956. The upper panel shows absolute amounts. The lower panel shows normalized amounts, ad-

Figure 3-2. Import Volume per capita: Total, Industrial and Agricultural Capital Goods for Selected Periods, 1910-61

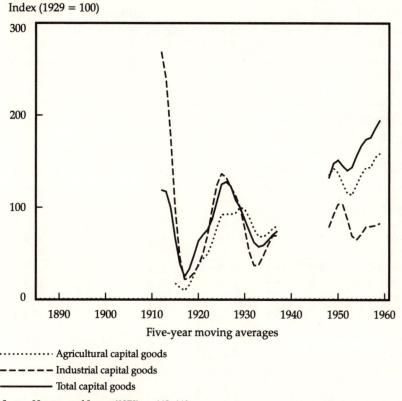

Index (1929 = 100)

Five-year moving averages

.... Agricultural capital goods

－－－－－－ Industrial capital goods

———— Total capital goods

Source: Hansen and Lucas (1978), p. 440, 441.

justed for population increase. Some form of normalization appears necessary for our purpose and since national income estimates are not available population appears a natural denominator. Similar estimates of net investment convey much the same message as the gross investment in the table. Though the estimates are uncertain and suffer from problems related to depreciation, deflation, and the like, they do make sense. The total investment for 1956–59 of LE70.7 million corresponds to about 6 percent of GDP. Total gross investment for these years ran at 15–16 percent of GDP of which 40–45 percent was in agriculture and industry (Ikram 1980, tables SA 6, 9). Thus the estimates in table 3–1 for the late 1950s tally with the official investment estimates. Assuming GDP at current prices to have been about LE100 million in 1903–07 or about LE600 million at 1960 prices, table 3–1 indicates a ratio for agriculture and industry investment in 1903–07 of about 5 percent of GDP compared with 6 percent for 1956–59. The estimates point thus to a roughly unchanged investment-GDP ratio from 1903–07 to 1956–59. This is a low gross investment-GDP ratio for agriculture and industry.

The figures on normalized investment in table 3–1 convey the same impression. Total real gross investment in agriculture and industry per capita was approximately the same during the periods 1903–07, 1930–34, 1935–39, 1946–51, 1952–55, and 1956–59. For 1908–13, 1920–24, and 1925–29 these investments were somewhat lower. The distribution

Table 3-1. Gross Fixed Investment in Agriculture and Industry, Selected Years, 1903–59

(millions of Egyptian pounds)

Period	Agriculture			Industry Private[c]	Total private investment	Total investment
	Public[a]	Private[b]	Total			
Real investment						
1903–07	6.7	6.7[d]	13.4	15.4	22.1	28.8
1908–13	5.5	1.0	6.5	10.9	11.9	17.4
1920–24	1.3	6.7	8.0	12.6	19.3	20.6
1925–29	4.6	5.6	10.2	19.3	24.9	29.5
1930–34	15.3	7.1	22.4	22.6	29.7	45.0
1935–39	16.7	6.0	22.7	21.4	27.4	44.1
1946–51	4.5	5.5	10.0	42.8	48.3	52.8
1952–55	9.2	5.8	15.0	48.2	54.0	63.2
1956–59	8.7	9.3	18.0	52.7	62.0	70.7
Normalized investment[e]						
1903–07	6.7	6.7[d]	13.4	15.4	22.1	28.8
1908–13	5.1	0.9	6.0	10.1	11.0	16.1
1920–24	1.1	5.4	6.5	10.2	15.7	16.7
1925–29	3.5	4.3	7.8	14.8	19.2	22.7
1930–34	11.1	5.1	16.2	16.4	21.5	32.6
1935–39	11.4	4.1	15.5	14.7	18.8	30.2
1946–51	2.5	3.1	5.6	23.8	26.8	29.3
1952–55	4.5	2.9	7.4	23.7	26.6	31.1
1956–59	3.9	4.2	8.1	23.6	27.8	31.7

a. Irrigation and drainage; data appear to be a mixture of gross and net figures.

b. Machinery, livestock, and dwellings; data on livestock are gross figures and seem to be slaughter figures.

c. Buildings and machinery.

d. Conjecture.

e. Real investment adjusted to reflect changes in population.

Source: Radwan (1974), tables 2–1, 2–3, 2–4, 2–5, 2–6, 3–1, 3–2.

between agriculture and industry has varied greatly over time. For 1903–07, 1930–34, and 1935–39 about one-half of gross investment was in agriculture. After World War II only one-quarter to one-third was in agriculture, with the balance in industry. It appears that while industrial gross investment was the same during the interwar years, 1925–39, as in 1903–07, for all three post–World War II periods industrial investment ran at a 50 percent higher level. Agricultural investment was more unstable. Public investment in irrigation and drainage ran (in real terms) at a level of LE6 million before World War I, dropped to low levels in the 1920s, increased to the high levels of LE11 million during the 1930s, and went back to low levels after World War II. Private agricultural investment ran at low levels during the 1930s and even more so in the 1950s. It is symptomatic that one agricultural pressure group, Union des Agriculteurs, strongly demanded lower tariffs for imported agricultural capital goods and fertilizers (*Egyptian Gazette*, February 10, 1930).

Assuming that gross investment realized per capita is a relevant indicator of the adherence to the strategy of balanced growth, it would appear that the strategy actually was followed during the 1930s while during the postwar years 1946–59 a shift toward industrialization occurred. However, had the construction of the Aswan High Dam not been delayed by obstruction from the United States, agricultural investment probably would have been much larger during the second half of the 1950s. The strong fluctuation in public investment in irrigation and drainage is, moreover, a consequence of the lumpy nature of such investment, occasionally requiring the construction of large, very expensive dams and barrages. The level of investment was never impressive. At this point the strategies were not specific, however. Explicit planning was not undertaken until the 1950s. The Commission on Commerce and Industry in 1918 did not think in terms of capital output and employment ratios or of growth rates. The Harrod-Domar model had yet to be invented. Considering the increase of population and the social consequences of a decline in the already low standard of living of the broad population—both basic considerations for the commission—zero growth per capita must have been a minimum requirement. The level of gross investment actually obtained during much of the period would hardly allow for much more than that, considering the given cultivated area and the interruption of capital formation during the two world wars.

It is perhaps surprising that the level of industrial gross investment per capita in 1925–39 after independence was no higher than during the period 1903–07 when there was no explicit industrialization policy; indeed, the British would if anything have opposed such a policy. The industrialization that nonetheless took place before World War I was initiated and mainly financed by foreign capital under booming business conditions, generated by rising cotton prices and a related local

Kuznets cycle in residential construction. Against this background it might rather be surprising that industrialization did not cease altogether during the 1930s under the impact of the international agricultural crisis and the Great Depression (this problem is discussed in the following section).

The estimates of fixed capital stock for agriculture and industry in table 2–1 are similar indicators of the balance between agricultural and industrial development efforts. The table suggests that while the economically active population grew considerably faster than total population from 1902 to 1939, from 1939 to 1960 the opposite was the case and in 1960 the economically active population was again just in line with total population as compared with 1902. This has been interpreted as indicating a decrease in surplus labor until 1939, followed by an increase to 1960. This again would seem to indicate that the development strategy was not capable of solving the employment problem although changes in age composition is part of the explanation.

The stock of fixed capital apparently grew somewhat faster in agriculture than in industry until 1939, both increasing considerably faster than total as well as active population. The faster growth of capital in agriculture may be a statistical artifact, however, since depreciation is not properly accounted for in that sector. In addition the input of chemical fertilizers grew from almost nothing to a comparatively high level. This was part of the agricultural strategy to reverse the decline in yields of cotton and should have been beneficial to agricultural employment. During the 1950s, the stock of capital in industry temporarily took the lead, with agriculture again almost catching up in 1966. The impact of the delay in the construction of the Aswan High Dam is highly visible. Taking that into account, the general picture again points to a fairly balanced development of agricultural and industrial investment.

A further indicator of the success of the strategy of balanced growth is the distribution of the economically active population by sector as enumerated by the four population censuses from 1927 to 1960. Needless to say, population censuses are a poor substitute for labor force surveys; among their serious deficiencies are under-enumeration of unpaid, female family workers. Table 3–2 shows that the only major change in the distribution of the economically active population from 1927 to 1960 was a decline in the share of agriculture by 11 percent and an increase in the share of services by 11 percent. The shares of the remaining sectors, including manufacturing, were roughly stationary. In terms of actual employment the balanced growth strategy appears thus to have been a complete failure. One of the arguments for industrialization was the belief that agriculture could not be expected to absorb the increase in the working population and that industry was needed to absorb the surplus. Of an increase by 2.6 million persons from 1937 to 1960, 0.9

Table 3-2. Economically Active Population, by Sector, 1927-60

Sector	1927 Thousands	1927 Percent of total	1937 Thousands	1937 Percent of total	1947 Thousands	1947 Percent of total	1960 Thousands	1960 Percent of total
Agriculture	3,539	67.5	4,020	69.5	4,075	61.7	4,406	56.3
Mining	10	0.2	11	0.2	13	0.2	21	0.3
Manufacturing	422	8.1	345	6.0	553	8.4	713	9.1
Electricity, gas and water	23	0.4	21	0.4	23	0.3	37	0.5
Construction	86	1.6	117	2.0	112	1.7	159	2.0
Trade and finance	459	8.7	436	7.5	588	8.9	641	8.2
Transport and communications	196	3.7	137	2.4	202	3.0	260	3.3
Services	514	9.8	696	12.0	1,046	15.8	1,595	20.3
Total	5,249	100	5,783	100	6,610	100	7,833	100
Share of total population	—	36.9	—	36.3	—	34.8	—	30.0

— = Not applicable.
Source: Population censuses, quoted in Radwan (1974).

million were absorbed by agriculture. Of the remaining 1.7 million, no less than 1.1 million were absorbed by services, only 0.3 million by manufacturing.

In sum, this and the discussion of GDP and GNI growth rates shown in table 1–1 indicate that while the investment patterns followed under democracy broadly followed the strategy of balanced growth, the efforts in terms of both capital formation and productivity were too feeble to produce anything more than token growth and in terms of employment the strategy failed completely.

Economic Policy in the Interwar Years

Like most countries, Egypt lived through much of the interwar period in the shade of the worldwide crisis in agriculture that began in the second half of the 1920s and of the Great Depression after 1929. Its development strategy was not formulated to cope with the specific problems created by these events although the measures taken were to some extent adjusted to the situation. For a fair evaluation of the strategy it is necessary to gauge the impact of both the agricultural crisis and the depression on the Egyptian economy in general and their importance for the success or failure of the development program. Asked very simply: would it be possible for a small agricultural country to grow and develop significantly during these times of crisis and depression? And, if the answer is in the affirmative, which sectors could be expected to develop?

The International Agricultural Crisis and the Great Depression

There is wide disagreement about the nature of the Great Depression, whether workers with misconceptions about present and future real wages were just taking a vacation, as some Chicago economists claim, or enterprises and labor were faced with the severe market constraints that Keynesian and so-called disequilibrium theory posit. Certainly, Egyptian exports did not face international market constraints at given, fixed prices. Egypt was a one-commodity exporter of extra-long-staple cotton, a standardized raw material that even during the Great Depression could be sold at organized commodity markets—at a price. Prices in the international commodity markets were highly flexible and would almost instantaneously adjust to demand and supply. Even without government intervention, however, prices of (nonperishable) raw materials would not fall to zero. At a sufficiently low, positive price, speculative demand from stocks would close the gap between Egyptian output of cotton and input in the world's textile mills. In this sense Egypt's export problem was a price, not a quantity, problem. What it was profitable to produce of other commodities could and would be sold domestically, possibly at the expense of imports. The combined, direct impact of agricultural crisis and Great Depression and of the accompanying foreign government interventions abroad was thus general price deflation for both exports and imports with a strong deterioration of the terms of trade; cotton prices as a matter of fact declined more than import prices and, among the latter, food prices declined more than prices for manufactured goods. Egypt had been pegged to the sterling rate since 1914. The export volume declined slightly in 1930–32, but only as the result of Egyptian policies restricting supply. When these were abrogated, the export volume returned to the level of 1927–29.

The effect on production in Egypt would thus depend entirely on the flexibility of nominal, domestic factor prices. Rent of land was probably highly flexible. Long-term rental contracts were unusual except perhaps for service labor on *'ezbas*. In sharecropping, values would adjust automatically to changes in output price. More often than not, cash rentals were negotiated for a single crop and would thus respond within six to nine months at most. Agricultural wages appear to have been highly flexible too. Money wage rates in agriculture fell by 40 percent from 1928 to 1938 when money rentals fell by 35 percent and agricultural output value by 32 percent. Little is known about urban wages. Unions did exist in several areas and industrial conflict was not unknown. But unionization was feeble and divided, and its impact on wages probably very modest. Minimum wage legislation and social security did not exist, and charitable activities were limited to *ewkaf*, mosques, and churches. Notions of *justum pretium* do not seem to exist in Islam; they would seem alien to the bargaining traditions of the Middle Eastern bazaar. Public sector wages were rigid in the short term as elsewhere, but the public sector was relatively small. As in highly developed countries, internal labor market behavior seems to be the most likely cause of urban wage rigidity. There is no reason why this factor should not have been present in the 1930s, but it might be asked how likely it is that internal labor market policy in individual enterprises should create wage rigidity in a period of general deflation (Salop 1979). With regard to rental of fixed capital (profits), it would of course be expected to be a residual in the short term; rentals of housing, however, had been regulated in law and kept at an artificially low level since World War I and thus might not go down in case of deflation. During the 1930s the legislation may, however, have become redundant. In the longer run, rent on capital would probably tend to be determined abroad, financial capital being highly mobile.

There is good reason thus to expect a relatively high degree of flexibility of domestic factor prices even in the short term. Assume then that wages and rentals of land were perfectly flexible and mobility of labor and capital within the country perfect; disregard international mobility of native, unskilled labor but assume perfect international mobility of capital (including [foreign] management and human capital, skilled labor). With the relative decline in agricultural prices, particularly cotton prices, allocation of resources would shift within agriculture from cotton to food and from agriculture to nonagricultural activities, including industry. This would happen because real wages (in terms of consumer goods) should tend to decline uniformly in agriculture (cotton and food being produced in rotation) and to increase in nonagricultural activities. And this would be the case because cotton constituted a much larger share of agricultural output than of (rural) household expenditure, and manufactured goods and services (traded or nontraded) a much larger share of nonagricultural activities than of (urban) household expenditure, food having an intermediary position. A similar argument holds for the real rental of capital. Labor and capital should thus tend to move out of agriculture into nonagricultural activities, capital possibly even going abroad (see below). With labor and capital moving out of agriculture, the marginal productivity of land would decline and on marginal land even become negative. Land would have nowhere else to go (urban development demand was probably negligible) but might go out of cultivation.

Were this model correct, the Great Depression would indeed tend to lower the growth rate in agriculture and agriculture could be expected to perform relatively poorly. Industry should perform relatively well, on the other hand. Available data do not support this neoclassical model. The cultivated area did decline by about 7 percent from 1929 to 1938 and in 1939 was still about 5 percent below 1929. Licensed motors in agriculture did decline, both in numbers and in horsepower, which would indicate a decline in pumping and the use of tractors, probably related to a decline in the cultivated area. Private investment in agriculture, both gross and net, apparently remained positive during the 1930s, however, and did not decline in comparison with 1925–29 (table 3–1). This is true even for modern machinery, except in 1933 when estimated net investment in such machinery was slightly negative (Radwan 1974, table 2–5). Active population in agriculture apparently increased from 1927 to 1937, in both absolute and relative terms (table 3–2), while active population in industry and most nontraded activities declined in both absolute and relative terms, services being the major exception. While active population in agriculture increased by 481,000, the increase in all nonagricultural activities was only 53,000 and when services are excluded, nonagricultural activities declined by 129,000. Manufacturing declined by 77,000, or by 18 percent. On balance, agriculture shifted toward cotton cultivation but that was partly related to public investment in irrigation and drainage, partly to the abrogation of supply-restricting policies prevailing in the 1920s (see below).

One case, of course, does not corroborate or refute a theory, but since in fact the neoclassical model appears to do poorly in this particular case, let us try another approach.

Fairly reliable data indicate that agriculture during the 1960s and 1970s served as an employment buffer for the Egyptian economy (Hansen and Radwan 1982, fig. 3 and pp. 154–56; Hansen 1986). During booming periods in the economy as a whole (1960–65 and 1973–84), nominal wages in agriculture appear to have increased faster than nominal value added, with a simultaneous decline in agricultural employment; in slack periods (1966–72) the opposite happened. If agriculture served in the same way as an employment buffer in the 1930s, that would indicate that the increase in agricultural employment was associated with a fall in most nonagricultural employment. This model only works, however, if there is assumed to be a lower degree of wage flexibility in nonagricultural activities than in agriculture and a certain degree of mobility of labor in response to unemployment. This also would explain why nominal wage rates in agriculture appear to have fallen more than agricultural output value. I have no difficulty in assuming a high

Figure 3-3. Import Volume per capita: Total, Industrial and Agricultural Materials for Selected Years, 1910-61

Index (1929 = 100)

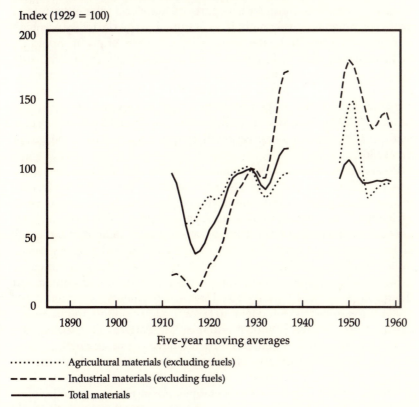

Five-year moving averages

·············· Agricultural materials (excluding fuels)

– – – – – – Industrial materials (excluding fuels)

———————— Total materials

Source: Hansen and Lucas (1978), p. 440, 441.

degree of wage flexibility in agriculture. A lower degree of wage flexibility outside agriculture could be explained by the feeble unionization, charitable activities, and internal labor market policy in nonagricultural enterprises with rigid wages in the public sector. I am not discussing flexible as opposed to rigid (fixed) nominal wages, but small differences in the degree of flexibility.

With this model, agriculture should not perform poorly as a consequence of the Great Depression, which cannot be used then as an excuse for the poor growth rate of agriculture. Industry should perform poorly—as it apparently did.

But why then did the size of the cultivated area decline despite an increase in agricultural labor and capital? The explanation may be in the decline of licensed motors and pumping. A relative increase in the price of motor oil could explain a decline in private, mechanical pumping for irrigation and drainage. It is known that the international oil companies (through Anglo-Egyptian Oil) pursued a tough monopolistic price policy in Egypt in the 1930s, with strongly increasing oil prices despite the general deflation (Tignor 1984, p. 187).

There is another problem of the effects on capital movements, which would tend to flow toward those parts of the world where the rate of profit remained relatively high. If, as assumed, wage flexibility was high in Egypt and lower in the developed world, the rate of profit should remain relatively high in Egypt and capital accordingly should move to Egypt. Downward rigidity of wages in the highly industrialized countries is one of the keys for many students to understanding the Great Depression, and even if wage flexibility in Egypt were not perfect it was certainly higher than that of countries like the United Kingdom. British textile companies actually invested in Egyptian operations at the end of the 1930s.

Presumably, savings would tend to fall because income per capita tended to fall as a consequence of the deterioration of the terms of trade. Income distribution would tend to change, presumably in favor of nonagricultural income and, thanks to the general price fall, in favor of creditors and against long-term debtors and taxpayers (land and buildings taxes being fixed in nominal terms). Owners of land and property would thus stand to lose, and mortgage loan institutions and the government to gain. Since mortgage loan institutions were mainly owned abroad and the government had to make fixed interest payments to foreign debtholders, the price fall would tend to favor foreign creditors and harm domestic debtors. Little is known about saving patterns in a society like Egypt in the interwar period. It is difficult, however, to see anything here that would induce increased domestic saving, except perhaps the increasing real rates of interest in the early 1930s.

Finally, on the problem of expectations about future prices, I would refer to standard hypotheses, with a personal preference for Keynes's "animal spirits." On balance, I believe, the relative flexibility of international factor prices would be decisive and that international capital movements might thus favor industrialization and economic development in a country like Egypt in the 1930s. Capital inflow would benefit Egypt, partly because it was a debtor country and would gain from the tendency for the rate of profit to fall as a consequence of capital inflow and partly because a transfer of technology would take place (textiles is a case in point).

Exchange Rate Policy and Overvaluation, 1913–39

Egypt was effectively put on a sterling standard in 1914 and remained a member of the sterling area until 1947. The sterling rate remained unchanged until 1962. Thus the Egyptian pound followed sterling both at the appreciation when the United Kingdom returned to the gold standard in 1925 and at the depreciation in 1931 when she left the gold standard. The exchange reserves were kept by the National Bank of Egypt which until World War II bought and sold sterling unrestricted at the official rate. During the 1930s bilateral trade agreements with special exchange arrangements became important in the world economy but Egypt entered no bilateral agreements and had no exchange controls. Perusal of the *Journal Officiel*, where any bilateral agreements should have been published by the government, reveals no such agreements between Egypt and other countries during the 1930s. Trade agreements were limited to problems of most-favored-nation status and the like. Tignor (1984, p. 158) reports that negotiations about an arrangement for bilateral quotas between Egypt and the United Kingdom, on the initiative of the latter, were well advanced at the outbreak of World War II but never materialized. In 1934 the British coerced Egypt into imposing special tariffs on cotton textiles from Japan under the pretext of dumping by the Japanese but even in this case trade remained unrestricted by quotas and licensing. Neither trade nor capital movements were subjected to government control in Egypt until World War II. During World War I Egypt ran large surpluses on current and basic account and came out of the war with very large sterling reserves, most of which had been used up by the outbreak of World War II. Egypt, however, was never short of sterling reserves during the interwar years.

During the interwar years when the sterling rate was fixed, the exchange rates of other currencies in relation to sterling, and hence to the Egyptian pound, varied considerably. Figure 3–4 traces import-weighted indexes for effective, real exchange rates for the Egyptian pound from 1913 to 1939 (1960) with 1913 as a standard of comparison to help gauge possible over- and undervaluation of the Egyptian pound. The computations are based on the nominal exchange rates for the currencies of seven important trade partners (the German mark excluded

Figure 3-4. Real Effective Exchange Rate and Fluctuations in Sterling Reserves, 1913-60

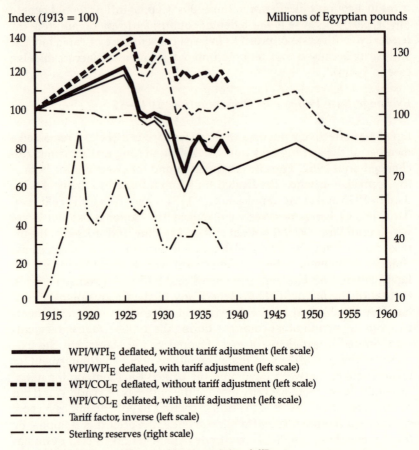

Index (1913 = 100)   Millions of Egyptian pounds

━━━━━━ WPI/WPI$_E$ deflated, without tariff adjustment (left scale)
────── WPI/WPI$_E$ deflated, with tariff adjustment (left scale)
■■■■■ WPI/COL$_E$ deflated, without tariff adjustment (left scale)
────── WPI/COL$_E$ delfated, with tariff adjustment (left scale)
─·─·─· Tariff factor, inverse (left scale)
─··─·· Sterling reserves (right scale)

Source: Egypt, Ministry of Finance, *Annuaire statistique de l'Egypte.*

1914–24) and the result is expressed in terms of foreign currency per Egyptian pound. An increase in the effective rate thus signifies appreciation of the Egyptian pound. Figure 3–4 also shows the development of the so-called factor of import tariffs (the inverse of one plus the average rate of customs duties) and the sterling reserves of the National Bank of Egypt.

The choice of deflator causes considerable difficulties. Paldam and Jorgensen (1986) argue that in computing indexes of effective, real exchange rates, deflation should ideally be performed using the cost of living (COL) index for the home country and wholesale price indexes (WPIs) for the rest of the world. The logic is that domestic costs of production (wages) probably are more closely related to the domestic COL than to the domestic WPI, while export and import prices are closely geared to the foreign WPIs. For Latin America, however, they also argue that the choice between the COL and the WPI for long-term computations is a secondary matter because the two indexes over long periods are closely correlated with no trend. That turns out not to be the case for Egypt; for the period 1938–60, the results of three deflation methods (WPI/WPI, COL/COL, and WPI/COL) prove highly sensitive to the choice of deflator. Figure 3–4 therefore shows indexes of the import-weighted real exchange rate, deflated by WPI/WPI and by WPI/COL, both with and without multiplication by the tariff factor. The difference is dramatic.[2] With WPI/WPI deflation there was some appreciation 1921–26 and strong depreciation 1932–39. With WPI/COL deflation there was an appreciation by almost 20 percent between 1921 and 1930 as compared with 1913 and about parity with 1913 from 1932 to 1939. Tignor feels that "the linking of British and Egyptian currencies had served the Egyptian economy well up until 1939" (1984, p. 197). If WPI/COL deflation provides the correct picture, the participation in the sterling area with a pegged sterling rate was harmful to the Egyptian economy, assuming, of course, that protection of industry was in fact beneficial—which some observers might deny. The important conclusion is that there was less net protection of Egyptian industry during the 1930s than would flow from tariff reform alone. The tariff reforms only compensated on average for the overvaluation of the Egyptian pound.

Quite apart from the general argument that wage cost may follow the COL more closely than the WPI, the peculiar nature of the Egyptian WPI also speaks in favor of using the COL rather than the WPI in computing effective real exchange rates. Whereas the Egyptian COL was an ordinary weighted Laspeyres index, the WPI was an unweighted, geometric mean, a so-called Jevons-Edgeworth index of the prices of twenty-six commodities, of which twenty-three were agricultural, raw, or slightly processed goods. The logic of this index is well known and not generally accepted. Both Irving Fisher (1927) and Keynes (1930) argued strongly against it in favor of weighted indexes. The Jevons-Edgeworth index, with its poor representation of industrial commodities, obviously is of limited relevance for judging urban real wages and protection of import-substituting industries.

Tariff reform had a strong upward effect on the COL. The net effect on the WPI may even have been downward because of the lower tariffs on raw materials. The argument is that the COL and urban nominal wages may have caused much of the net protection of industry to disappear. This is the rationale for using the COL in computing real effective exchange rates provided that the tariff factor is included in computing nominal depreciation. It is also the sine qua non for overvaluation. With perfectly flexible factor prices there can be no such thing as overvaluation.

A further argument in favor of the WPI/COL deflation is that it helps explain balance of payments developments during the interwar period much better than does the WPI/WPI deflation, as table 3–3 indicates. The explanatory advantage of the WPI/COL deflation is best seen for the periods 1925–29 and 1935–39. For 1925–29 the terms of trade were the same as in 1913; the WPI/WPI index was about the same and there was a strong deterioration in the balance of payments (trade as well as current account). The WPI/COL index for 1925–29 shows strong appreciation, however. For 1935–39 the WPI/COL index is at par with 1913; the strong deterioration in the terms of trade index explains the deterioration of the balance of payments. The WPI/WPI index shows a depreciation so strong that the deterioration of the balance of payments appears incomprehensible. Everything considered, for Egypt the WPI/COL deflation appears superior to the WPI/WPI deflation.

In itself the estimated real effective exchange rate does not indicate whether the currency is over- or undervalued. In 1913, Egypt was on the gold standard, but that does not exclude (short-term) over- or undervaluation. Moreover, the real effective exchange rate is at best an indicator of over- or undervaluation when the underlying disturbances are of a purely monetary nature. In Egypt there were real disturbances in the form of strong changes in the terms of trade, first deteriorating during World War I, then returning during the 1920s to the prewar level, followed by a strong deterioration in the early 1930s, after which a weak recovery took place. The fluctuations in the terms of trade do not show up in the estimated real effective exchange rates but they obviously have a systematic effect on the balance of payments. The Egyptian pound may have been overvalued throughout the 1930s, either because Egypt should have depreciated more than the United Kingdom did in 1931 or

Table 3–3. Real Effective Exchange Rate, Terms of Trade, and Balance of Payments, 1913 and 1921–39

Period	Index of import-weighted real effective exchange rate[a]		Terms of trade index[a]	Balance of payments surplus (millions of Egyptian pounds)[b]	
	WPI/COL	WPI/WPI		Trade	Current account
1913	100	100	100	5.1	−1.8
1921–24	122	103	92	−2.9	−0.2
1925–29	125	101	100	−1.2	−4.1
1930–34	106	70	78	−2.4	−5.0
1935–39	100	69	81	−0.1	−2.5[c]

a. Base year 1913.
b. Annual averages.
c. Conjecture.
Source: Hansen and Lucas (1978); Crouchley (1936), table 6; author's calculations.

because the real depreciation was very slow to work while the terms of trade deteriorated instantly.

For understanding the persistent current account deficit, it should be emphasized that the public budget, except in the years 1920 and 1930, was in the black and ran substantial surpluses. The current account deficits were thus related to an excess of investment over saving in the private sector, clearly caused by low saving rather than high investment. The public sector typically ran an excess of saving over investment. This is not a case of public deficit spending. Tignor (1984, p. 91) claims that the public surpluses were a result of underspending on new programs related to lack of experience and poor preparation. That may be true, but in any case the actual budget outcomes should tend to improve the balance of payments current account. With a balanced budget, possibly needed to boost employment, the current account deficits would have been even larger and this, of course, supports the hypothesis (discussed in chapter 4) that overvaluation is a result of several conflicting targets.

Cotton Export Policy, 1921–32

When a country is exporting along a downward-sloping foreign demand curve, possibly shifting to the right over time, its export strategy should be designed to optimize the volume of exports at any point of time and the path of export trade over time. Such optimization implies a smaller volume of exports with an improvement of the terms of trade rather than unconstrained competition. It is well known that an export tax is the appropriate policy instrument; other export-limiting devices will be less efficient. Obviously such an optimal export policy would not be in the British interest, simply because what is best for the exporting country is least good for the rest of the world. During the 1920s Egypt actually pursued a policy aimed at stabilizing the international price of Egyptian cotton. It is doubtful whether that was the most advantageous export policy for cotton. The policy operated with four different instruments. Over and above a general 1 percent ad valorem tax on exports, it included an excise tax which was levied from 1920. Since home consumption of raw cotton at that time was negligible, this tax was effectively an export tax. It was originally 35PT (piasters; LE1 = 100PT) per *kantar* (45 kilogram) but was lowered to 20 PT in 1924, to 15PT in 1930, to 10PT in 1932, and phased out in 1934. The tax never exceeded 5.9 percent ad valorem. Both the general export tax and the excise served revenue purposes but must, of course, also have tended to constrain the export of cotton.

During 1921–30 the government made advances (through the National Bank of Egypt) to cotton producers as an incentive to hold back cotton sales temporarily. This was a clear supply-limiting device. Also, from 1921 to 1933, cotton acreage restrictions became a standard policy, applied in nine years, to support the export price when foreign markets were slack. Cotton acreage restrictions had been applied in 1915 and 1918, but mainly to increase food production to alleviate shortages during the war. The restrictions in 1921–33 were applied mostly in the Delta, where extra-long-staple cotton was grown. The prescribed rate of acreage reduction was usually 20 percent but reached a maximum of 32 percent in 1932. For most years, evasion was massive (Hansen and Nashashibi 1975, p. 330).

Government purchases in spot and futures markets in Alexandria were initiated in 1921 and continued through 1923; purchases for these years were moderate. The operations were handled and financed by the NBE. In 1924–25 the accumulated stocks were sold at a profit. With cotton prices falling in late 1925 and 1926, however, purchases were resumed on a substantial scale, amounting to about 6 percent of the crop, and they continued on a massive scale when international prices crashed in 1929. Total stocks held by the government in 1930–31 amounted to about 40 percent of the crop. After the depreciation of sterling (and the Egyptian pound) in 1931, the stocks were sold abroad at prices that implied a serious loss covered from the government budget (Abdel Wahab 1930).

The cotton export policy was sponsored mainly by the General Egyptian Agricultural Syndicate, an organization founded in 1921 by large, native landowners as a counterweight to the Alexandria General Produce Association which organized the Alexandria markets and was dominated by resident foreign merchants. The Produce Association was accused of manipulating the cotton market. The accusation was to some extent based on populist ideas about middlemen and the evils of term markets and speculation, but the possibility cannot be ruled out that the market was indeed imperfect. The number of big merchant houses was small. Arbitrage with the Liverpool market where Egyptian cotton was also regularly traded appears, on the other hand, to have been rather efficient.

The Agricultural Syndicate lobbied systematically and successfully in favor of government intervention to stabilize cotton prices from 1921 to 1931. The syndicate was powerful. It appears to have had close relations with the king (*Egyptian Gazette*, January 30, 1924) and the royal family, which included some of the largest cotton growers, and it did not hesitate, at least before the declaration of independence, to contact the British authorities in Egypt for support (*Egyptian Gazette*, May 19, 1922). Before independence, it might have been necessary to refer intervention in the cotton market to "the highest British authorities" for endorsement (*Egyptian Gazette*, May 19, 1922). I have found no evidence of specific British intervention in the government's cotton market stabilization policies after 1922. Before 1922 the point of view of the British adviser to Egypt's Ministry of Finance seems partly to have been that government funds should not be wasted on purchasing cotton at higher prices than those at which the cotton could later be sold and partly that "absolutely nothing was to be gained by shifting the burden from one section of the population to another" (*Egyptian Gazette*, May 19, 1922).

Another powerful pressure group, Association des Agriculteurs, mainly consisting of expatriate landowners and land companies, does not appear to have lobbied in favor of cotton market stabilization.

Over the years the Agricultural Syndicate systematically favored price support measures in spot or futures markets, with government stockpiling and advances to growers for postponing the marketing of cotton. It also supported area restrictions limiting the cultivation of cotton. Since the end of the nineteenth century, when cotton yields began declining, a three-year rotation, with cotton limited to one-third of the acreage of each individual farm, had been recommended by government, experts, and experienced owner-growers to prevent soil exhaustion. The Agricultural Syndicate was in favor of this system, which in the long run might limit the supply of cotton to the benefit of other crops. Since large growers in any case tended to apply a three-year system, statutory adoption of the system, if at all complied with, would have limited cotton supply from small owners on two-year rotation. Small farms might have been on two-year rotation either out of ignorance or because of liquidity constraints (high loan rates). Occasionally, the Agricultural Syndicate recommended specific area restrictions to cope with short-term recessions in the international markets for Egyptian cotton. The syndicate also favored abrogation of the cotton excise tax. In 1924 it recommended that if the tax were continued its proceeds be used for financing support purchases in periods of low prices (*Egyptian Gazette*, January 26 and 30, 1924).

Apart from the cotton excise tax which it was against at any time and the three-year rotation which it favored at any time, the syndicate appears to have lobbied actively only in periods of very low cotton prices, when it seemed to ask for short-term stabilization rather than long-term limits on supply. I have never come across clear evidence that the Egyptian government or special interest groups such as the syndicate deliberately aimed at a long-term "optimal tariff" policy for cotton on the assumption that the international demand curve for Egyptian cotton was downward sloping. It was fully understood that the elasticity of foreign demand for Egyptian cotton was a crucial factor in a supply-restricting policy but the theoretical conditions for an optimal policy apparently were not fully understood. In an article in the *Egyptian Gazette* (July 6, 1926), Lackaney Bey, subcontroller in the Department of Statistics, argued that "no exact measurement is necessary. The data as they stand appear to be simple to demonstrate that the elasticity of demand for cotton is such that it does not pay the Egyptian planters to reduce by deliberate collective efforts—be it spontaneously or otherwise—their area under that crop." From his numerical examples it appears that Lackaney Bey believed that the demand elasticity was at least -2.5, hence (numerically) much higher than one. This, of course, is not the criterion for optimal supply limitation, either from a social or a group point of view. Lackaney Bey overlooked revenue from alternative crops grown on land taken out of cotton cultivation. On his assumptions and with the necessary simplifications, the socially optimal export tax would be 40 percent (about ten times the then existing cotton excise tax). That the Agricultural Syndicate should be against implementing supply limitations, whether for short- or long-term purposes, through a cotton export tax is obvious. The preferred solution from the growers' point of view would naturally be acreage restrictions with the social benefits accruing to the growers. Although the three-year rotation policy was not thought of as a long-term policy for limiting cotton supply, it might nonetheless work out that way. If so, however, it might not be an optimal policy. Since large growers in any case tended to apply a three-year rotation, possible gains from improvement of the terms of trade would—perhaps exclusively—accrue to large growers while small growers might experience losses on cotton (in the long pull they would obviously gain from the alternative crops).

When Sidqi became premier in 1929, he ordered an investigation of the problem with recommendations for a permanent cotton policy. The result was Ahmed Abdel Wahab's famous *Memorandum on the bases of a stable cotton policy, submitted to the Minister of Finance* in October 1930. Abdel Wahab argued (p. 12) that both experience and careful studies showed that the price of Egyptian cotton in the international markets was unrelated to current Egyptian supply—that, in other words, the elasticity of demand for Egyptian cotton was infinite. Elasticity of demand for Egyptian cotton was a hotly debated and controversial issue around 1930 and some of the earliest econometric studies existing were devoted to this problem, which to this day has never been given a satisfactory professional answer.[3] Sidqi had on other occasions opposed support measures in the cotton market (*Egyptian Gazette*, May 4, 1922), and earlier as president of the Federation of Industry should have tended to represent cotton textiles industry interests. Abdel Wahab's position was adopted as official policy and the advances, acreage restrictions, taxation, and stock-piling were all abrogated in the early 1930s (to be reintroduced during World War II and in the 1950s). Massive investments in the hydraulic system were undertaken to expand perennial irrigation and, among other things, cotton production to help Egyptian agriculture "produce itself through the crisis." I believe that since the elasticity of demand for Egyptian cotton at that time (or at any other time) is not known, either in the short or the long term, it is not possible to evaluate the rationale of this policy and its effects.

The Tariff Reform of 1930

The government's major instrument for industrialization was the tariff reform of 1930 with later amendments (Mabro and Radwan 1976, chapter 2). The free trade regime that the Capitulations and trade treaties with European countries imposed on Egypt set low customs duties—on imports 8 percent (with higher duties for tobacco and, after 1905, 5 percent for fuel, construction timber, livestock, and meat), on exports 1 percent. A countervailing excise on domestic cotton textile products, refunded at exports, was imposed by Cromer in 1901 (here, as so often, copying British policy in India) but abrogated in 1926. Minor tariff increases were undertaken in 1915 and 1921 with an excise of 2 percent levied on a large number of mainly imported goods. With the tariff reform of 1930 and later amendments, the level of import duties was increased substantially (see table 3–4 and figure 3–4). The tariff structure was radically changed to what was considered a scientific tariff with low rates on inputs and high rates on outputs (excepting pure revenue duties)—for example, coal, 4 percent; textile machinery, 6 percent; cotton yarn, 9–17 percent; cotton fabrics, 23–28 percent; leather, 12 percent; shoes, 36 percent. The general import duty was 1 percent from 1932. To cope with specific problems of the agricultural crisis, high flexible tariffs were placed on wheat (flour) and sugar to stabilize the prices of these two important agricultural products at a high level, possibly to compensate for the abrogation of the cotton price support policies.

Table 3–4. Foreign Trade Taxes, 1913–38
(percent)

	Imports		
Period	Merchandise[a]	Tobacco[b]	Exports[c]
1931–38	26[d]	777	3
1922–29	11[d]	392	5
1915–29	9	111	1
1913–14	7	173	1

a. Ratio of customs duties actually paid on imported and exported merchandise other than tobacco to total import value minus value of tobacco import value minus value of re-exports. The estimated rate was reduced by 1 percentage unit, which was assumed to be the collected general export tax.

b. Ratio of customs duties actually paid on tobacco imports to value of tobacco imports. It is not clear how refunding at export was accounted for.

c. Ratio of basic export tax rate of 1 percent plus cotton tax estimated as revenue from cotton tax to export value for cotton.

d. Not including the excise of 2 percent.

Source: Annuaire statistique de l'Egypte.

The tariff reform enjoyed general political support. That it should be supported by the Egyptian Federation of Industries (formed in 1922) is not surprising although the federation largely represented foreign residential business interests in Egypt. Landowners (both the Agricultural Syndicate and the Produce Association) supported the reforms because the depressed state of agriculture made wealthy landowners look for better investment outlets, because the emergence of a domestic cotton textiles industry was expected to boost the price of raw cotton (here again the idea of a sloping foreign demand curve for cotton emerges) and because protection was given to wheat and sugar. Objections came mainly from the (rudimentary) labor movement and politicians (the Wafd) concerned about the impact on the standard of living of the working classes; ironically, this was an objection to protectionism raised by Cromer before World War I and repeated by the British Chamber of Commerce in 1930. Most controversial were the duties on wheat and sugar, but even for these basic commodities the objections carried little weight. As a compensation, the Association des Agriculteurs did recommend lower tariffs on tea and coffee.

Bank Misr and Its Investment Activities

Tala'at Harb and the Commission on Commerce and Industry were fully aware that industrialization would require not only incentives in the form of protection but financing. Since foreign financing was considered undesirable, an industrial development bank, capable of raising funds in the country and investing such funds as long-term loans to new industries, had to be created. Bank Misr, founded by Tala'at Harb in 1920, became this development bank and it played a crucial role in industrialization in the 1920s and 1930s. Bank Misr raised its initial capital mainly from medium-size landowners. It became an important deposit bank, second only to the National Bank of Egypt, and handled government loans to industrial projects. It finally overextended itself and was reconstructed in 1939 under new leadership. After World War II it again played an important role as a development bank.

There is little doubt that Tala'at Harb served development well in creating a credit intermediary that specialized in channeling small, short-term loans into large-scale long-term ventures. It is questionable, however, whether he succeeded in increasing the funds available for industrial investment and whether the projects he promoted were the most profitable, either privately or socially, available. Perhaps the funds collected as share capital or deposits were in any case on the way out of agriculture. The existence of Bank Misr may have prevented their going abroad, although I think it is more likely that they would have gone into urban real estate.

Bank Misr's main projects were in cotton textiles; Misr Spinning and Weaving was to become Egypt's undisputably largest enterprise. The idea behind the establishment of a cotton textiles industry in Egypt was that since the country produced the raw material, it should also process it. Egyptian cotton, however, is an expensive, high-quality cotton that can only be used economically for producing high-quality textiles, high-count yarns, and fine fabrics. The market in Egypt for such products was extremely limited, and the industry, rather than being developed for export trade, produced low-count yarns and coarse grey cloth. Not until 1938 did Bank Misr (compromising its principle of not being involved with foreign capital), in a joint venture with a British multinational company, Bradford Dyers, turn to the production of high-quality textiles. (It would hardly have been profitable to base a domestic textiles industry on cheap cotton imported, for example, from India. The competition from India and Japan was very sharp.)[4] Imports of cotton had been banned since 1916 and it would have met with strong resistance from the landowners, Bank Misr's financial supporters, to rescind this ban.

It is not difficult to point to better investment outlets than textiles. Cement and phosphates were obvious choices. The country had a long way to go before self-sufficiency would obtain in these commodities, the raw materials existed in the country, and high transportation costs gave the country a natural advantage that should have been exploited earlier. These two industries could probably have absorbed all the funds available to Bank Misr and, as experience after World War II proved, they might even have become viable export industries along the Red Sea. A report worked out by Bank Misr in 1929 pointed to ready-made clothing, chemicals, mining, cement, leather, and glass as areas other than textiles for successful import substitution.

The Bank Misr case shows that private entrepreneurs are not always better planners than government. Tala'at Harb was a great visionary; his industrial horizon was too limited. He was a great politician but a poor businessman with an irrational faith in economies of scale in textiles and capital-intensive technology. How different were Tala'at Harb's achievements in matters of industrialization, financed with other people's money, including substantial government funds, from those of the ministers of industry under Nasser, Sadat, and Mubarak? Was Tala'at Harb Egypt's first minister of industry?

Agricultural Investment

From table 3–1 it appears that during the 1930s the government invested larger amounts in irrigation and drainage than ever before. After 1923 the Egyptian government continued the conservative British budget policy of financing both current and capital expenditures from current revenue. These investments were based on plans drawn up by British administrators (advisers) and engineers (the MacDonald report of 1920; see Tignor [1984], pp. 92–97) and, despite criticism, largely implemented by the Egyptian government after independence. The output index for agriculture indicates that returns were meager and slow to come. This is not surprising and should perhaps have been understood both by the British advisers and by Egyptian politicians. It is (at least now) well known that returns to investment in old-fashioned irrigation systems (such as canals) decline rapidly (Schultz 1964) and Egypt in 1930 may have been approaching the end of positive returns. Although new irrigation devices were constructed (Nag Hammada, Edfina) and others were expanded (the old Aswan Dam), expensive replacements (the Delta and Assiout barrages) absorbed a substantial part of Egypt's gross investment. In the meantime, large projects in Central Africa (Sennar, Gebel Auliya) helped to improve irrigation in Sudan, whose returns would not accrue to Egyptian agriculture. This raises the delicate issue of the status of Sudan and its relation to Egypt, with a history almost as old as that of Egypt, and to the British Empire.

Under Mohammed Ali and his followers Sudan was considered a natural sphere of influence, almost a province, of Egypt. After the rebellion of the Mahdi (and the seige of General Gordon at Khartoum), the British conquered and finally subdued Sudan, partly with the help of Egyptian troops and finance from the Egyptian budget, in the late 1890s. The so-called Anglo-Egyptian Condominium of 1899 virtually detached Sudan from Egypt and made it a British colony, much to the chagrin of Egyptian nationalists. Sudan and Nile control thus became "a bone of contention between Egyptian nationalists and British imperialists" (Vatikiotis 1969, p. 200). Before World War I the British initiated the Gezira project in Sudan, an irrigation project for cultivation of Egyptian extra-long-staple cotton. It was seen by the Egyptian government as a threat to the water supply for Egyptian agriculture. In 1920 promises were extracted from the British to limit the irrigated area at Gezira to 300,000 *feddan* of which only 100,000 *feddan* were to be planted with cotton (the three-year rotation system). The issue vanished during the 1930s when further Nile controls secured the Egyptian water supply. The issue seems to have been one of water supply rather than of cotton supply in the international markets (Gaitskell 1959, chap. 9; Tignor 1984, chap. 3).

Nobody has, to my knowledge, succeeded in estimating the rate of return and its development over time of investment in Egypt's hydraulic system. The effect of investment on output is gauged in table 3–5 by indexes of cultivated area, number of crops per year per acre, crop composition, and yield by crop. Only incomplete data are available, and factors such as labor input, fertilizer input, relative prices, and new plant varieties that influence the components of output are ignored.

Table 3-5. Decomposition of Agricultural Output and Capital in Irrigation and Drainage, Selected Years, 1900–59

(1900 = 100)

Year	Cultivated area	Number of crops per year per cultivated acre	Yield per crop	Crop composition plus residual[a]	Agricultural output	Fixed capital stock in irrigation and drainage
1900	100	100	100	100	100	100
1910	102.2	105.1	91.3	107.2	105.1	200.6
1920	101.4	107.3	84.7	110.1	101.5	229.7
1930	106.1	113.9	95.1	111.9	128.6	286.8
1940	102.3	115.3	108.0	113.4	144.5	511.0
1950	108.4	119.0	101.0	116.7	152.0	562.2
1959	112.1	128.2	117.8	111.0	187.9	671.2

a. Agricultural output divided by product of first three columns.

Source: Radwan (1973), tables A–10, 2–1; Wattleworth (1975), tables A–134, three-year moving averages; A–137, three-year moving averages.

The cultivated area was almost unchanged from 1900 to 1940 and grew by 10 percent from 1940 to 1959. In 1900 little reclaimable land was left for expansion of the cultivated area. Multicropping increased steadily but the increase was almost negligible in the 1930s when the stock of fixed capital in irrigation and drainage almost doubled. The ecological disaster mentioned earlier caused a sharp drop in yields. During the 1920s and 1930s a strong recovery brought yields in 1940 to a level 8 percent above 1900. In 1959 yields were only 18 percent above 1900 with a growth rate of 0.3 percent over these sixty years. The contribution from the change in composition is mainly due to the shift toward cotton, a high-value crop with a relatively high weight in the output index. The (statistical) residual is negligible.

The main long-term effects of the capital investment in irrigation and drainage after 1900 can be seen to have been multicropping and the shift in composition of output toward cotton. Figure 3–5 shows how the accelerating growth of population since 1940 has affected the per capita performance of agriculture since World War II.

Equity and Redistribution of Income

Important privileges were dismantled during the 1930s. In 1937 foreigners lost the right to be tried in the Mixed Courts under the Mixed Code. Before 1937 it was not possible to reform the tax system because neither new taxes nor higher rates on old taxes could be applied to foreigners.

Figure 3-5. Population and Agricultural Output with Decomposition, 1887-1968

Index (1887 = 100)

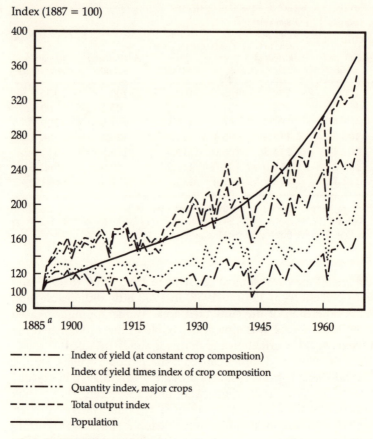

—·—·— Index of yield (at constant crop composition)
············· Index of yield times index of crop composition
—··—··· Quantity index, major crops
— — — — — Total output index
—————— Population

a. Scale for 1885-1900 is compressed
Source: Wattleworth (1975), p.A-139.

With the abolition of the Capitulations, Egypt undoubtedly became a procedurally more equitable society. Whether as a consequence of tariff and tax reforms, Egypt became a more egalitarian society in terms of real disposable income is discussed below.

THE TAX SYSTEM. The tax system began with customs duties the major indirect taxes levied and property taxes (on rural land and urban buildings) the only direct taxes. The uniform rate for taxing imports should have made the indirect taxes regressive because saving and consumption of nontraded goods and services probably increased with the size of income. On balance, the few exceptions to the 8 percent rate on imports probably worked in the opposite direction, fuel being taxed at lower rates, meat and tobacco at higher rates.

For landowners, considered in isolation, the land tax was strongly progressive, levied as a fixed, specific amount equal to 26 percent of the rental as assessed in the early years of the century. The tax was collected from the cultivators, but under competitive conditions, the incidence of a land tax will be on the owner, as is well known. Imperfect competition in rental or labor markets would not alter this conclusion since the tax was fixed. And since rentals as a share of a landowner's income would tend to increase with the size of ownership, the proportional tax on rental income would be progressive on total personal income. The very large landowner with only rental income would pay 26 percent of his total income. The very small owner-cultivator would have a tax rate on total income close to 0 percent. The same conclusion holds for the rural population as a whole, rural labor and small, informal businesses paying no income taxes.

Considering both land tax and customs duties, there is little doubt that for the rural population as a whole taxation was strongly progressive. Rural laborers, tenants, and very small owner-cultivators with (in the long term) zero saving and zero consumption of nontraded goods and services would tend to pay about 8 percent of their income as indirect taxes. The big landowner (with no other income) would pay 26 percent plus something in indirect taxation.

For the urban population the situation was different. The buildings tax, imposed at a rate of one-twelfth (or one-tenth in Cairo) of the assessed rental subject to reassessment every eighth year, would presumably in the long run be shifted onto the tenants and serve as indirect taxation. According to Engel's law, it would be a regressive tax to be superimposed on the regressive customs duties. As a whole, urban taxation was thus regressive. Most of the foreign resident population lived in urban areas and were in the same position as native landless urban residents, suffering regressive indirect taxation. Foreigners in urban areas who were big landowners would in principle be taxed like native absentee landowners.

With the tariff reform of 1930 and later amendments, customs duties probably became more regressive, particularly considering the heavy, though flexible duties on wheat and sugar. The tax reform of 1939 lowered the land tax to 16 percent of the reassessed rental. The intention was to keep the revenue from the land tax unchanged. Clearly the reform reduced the progression on total income since the maximum a landowner could pay as land tax was lowered to 16 percent of his total income. World War II delayed the next reassessment until 1949 when in view of the Korean War boom the tax rate was temporarily doubled for the years 1949–52. Three new proportional taxes were introduced in 1939—on dividends and interest (14 percent), on industrial and commercial wages and salaries, and on inheritance. The net impact on progressivity of taxation as a whole is not clear.

The consensus was that tax reform was required for equity reasons. The new taxes on dividends and interest on the one hand and wages and salaries, on the other, were nothing but extensions of the incomplete schedular income tax system, aimed at taxing all income regardless of source. Yet the reforms gave rise to great controversy, pitching landowners against urban business. Landowners strongly supported the reform and politically they had the upper hand. The tax reform of 1939 did not introduce taxation of corporate income, which only began in 1941 with an excess profits tax levied on profits of joint-stock companies in excess of their profits in previous years or 12 percent of capital invested at the beginning of 1940. It was vigorously contested by urban businesses as a disincentive to economic development. A general progressive tax on personal income, above the schedular income taxes, was not introduced until 1947–48 and did not produce revenue until 1950–51. In terms of revenue it never became an important tax. Exemptions were large and evasion massive.

THE AGRICULTURAL DEBT CRISIS. The strong decline in agricultural prices after 1929 created a crisis in Egyptian agriculture because both land tax and debt service on mortgage loans were fixed in nominal terms. Land taxes together amounted to LE6.5 million–LE7 million annually. One of the widely differing estimates of total mortgage debt was LE35 million, not including lands of less than five *feddan* which Kitchener's 5-*feddan* law exempted from foreclosure. Assuming an average rate of interest of 7 percent and the average loan to be repaid in thirty years, the annual debt service on land not exempted from foreclosure may have been about LE3.5 million annually (LE2.5 million in interest and LE1 million in amortization). Fixed tax and debt service payments would thus amount to about LE10 million annually. The main cash crop was cotton, whose value declined from LE40 million–LE45 million in the late 1920s to LE15 million–LE16 million in 1931–32 and 1932–33. Cash was, of course, obtained from crops other than cotton but part of the income from cotton on the other hand accrued to farms of less than five *feddan*. The conjectured totals indicate the depth of the liquidity crises. Heavily indebted landowners would not be able to pay both taxes and debt service and would face insolvency; even owners without mortgage debts might face liquidity problems in tax payments. Tenants would not have mortgage loans but might have personal debts, and with rents paid at the time of the harvest, they would experience a temporary squeeze. Rentals for the 1930–31 cotton crop (harvested in September–November 1930) may have been contracted at the end of 1929 before prices crashed. While owners would suffer from low prices, tenants would suffer from declining prices, assuming, realistically, that rentals adjusted with a lag to output prices and that expectations were imperfect.

Apart from the attempts to support cotton prices (discussed below), government credits were extended in 1930 for purchases of fertilizer and seed, and some tax relief was given in 1932. In 1933 mortgage debts were consolidated and subsidies provided to lower interest rates and amortizations. Further reductions of interest were made in 1935 and 1936. Mortgage companies were compensated from the budget with financing through open market sales of government securities denominated in Egyptian pounds (Egypt, National Bank of Egypt, 1948, p. 5). Rentals of land were lowered first to one-fifth, later to three-tenths, of what appears to be the assessed value (Vatikiotis 1969, p. 120). With the recovery of cotton prices after 1933–34, the situation eased somewhat and during World War II the agricultural tax–debt problem simply evaporated with inflation.

To evaluate the redistributive effects of the government measures is difficult because absentee owners, owner-cultivators, and tenants were differently affected by both price developments and policy measures. Taxes were a landowner's problem; debt might be a problem for owners and tenants. Since cotton prices declined more than other agricultural prices and cotton tended to be cultivated on large and middle-sized estates, it stands to reason that these would have been hit harder than small farms. The debt consolidation measures, which applied only to indebted owners, helped the large and middle-sized estates, not the farmers whom the Five-Feddan Law exempted from foreclosure. The relief seems on balance to have benefited those who had the largest losses, but they may also have had the broadest shoulders. There is no simple answer to this problem. The financing of the debt consolidation measures may have tightened the domestic credit market and dampened private investment activities and, hence, the industrialization process. Indeed, this may have been the most serious impact of the debt crisis.[5]

LABOR LEGISLATION. Social security and public welfare arrangements were until the 1920s either nonexistent or confined to religious endowments (*ewkaf*), mosques, churches, and other charitable institutions. The Islamic *zakat* (tithe) was always levied for charitable purposes. With industrialization, labor legislation became an issue. Such legislation as existed was rudimentary. A law of 1909, amended in 1920, protected children working in ginning, spinning, and weaving and in tobacco manufacturing. The second Wafd government drafted a labor code in 1927 that prohibited children under twelve years old from working in industry except under careful control, introduced a nine-hour day, and permitted workers to organize. The legislation floundered but a Labor Bureau was established under Sidqi and a commission was appointed to consider child and female labor conditions and workmen's compensation. A mission from the International Labor Organization (ILO) in Geneva recommended against rigid and comprehensive labor codes on Western European lines and suggested that Egypt rather should learn from Japan and India; the ILO mission considered health insurance, old-age pensions, and unemployment insurance premature. Labor laws of 1933 fixed the normal minimum work age at twelve, lowered to nine for textile factories. Children twelve to sixteen years old and women were not allowed to work more than nine hours a day. A very restrictive workmen's compensation code was made law in 1936.

World War II

Judging from available output indexes, agriculture suffered a serious setback during World War II. The problems were temporary and in large part statistical. Shortages of fertilizer and probably of labor led to a decline in yields. With international cotton markets closed or out of reach from Egypt, the Allied Middle East Supply Center forced a shift in the composition of Egypt's agricultural output from cotton toward food. Food normally has a relatively low weight in agricultural output indexes for Egypt, and the shift generated a strong decline in the index that did not take into account the (temporary) change in the relative valuation of cotton and food. If correct shadow prices were used as weights, there might be no decline in the output index. Be that as it may, when the markets became normal after the war, agricultural production recovered for both real and index reasons.

Industrial production benefited from the war. War provided natural protection against foreign competition while Allied military authorities and personnel added strongly to domestic demand. Infant industries established in the 1930s had a grace period of extended protection which apparently served them well. Despite both raw materials and replacement problems, industrial output increased substantially, possibly by 35 percent from 1939 to 1945 (Mabro and Radwan 1976).

One of the major battles of World War II was fought on Egyptian territory but the direct destruction from acts of war was marginal. Egypt was neutral until the last months of the war. Shortages of basic necessities caused by supply difficulties and the presence of large Allied military forces clearly lowered the standard of living of common people. Inflation may have worked in the same direction. The cost-of-living index, based on 1914, stood at 131 in 1939 and in 1945 had increased to 370. Employment conditions, however, improved; about 200,000 Egyptians are reported to have worked for the Allied forces. Gains and losses were probably very unevenly distributed.

Because the economy was dominated by the presence of Allied forces and their methods of financing military spending in Egypt, it is difficult to quantify developments. Clearly, however, the financial impact on

Egypt, while on a larger scale, resembles that of World War I when Egypt accumulated a large foreign exchange reserve. The Egyptian government's budget continued to show surpluses as during the interwar years, but Allied deficit spending was massive and financed through the NBE which in return collected large claims on the British government in the form of long- and short-term sterling securities, apparently at rather low interest rates (the real rate of interest was surely strongly negative). Published balance sheets of the NBE for both war and postwar years are opaque—for instance, they lump together government securities valued in British pounds and Egyptian pounds. The net foreign exchange reserve of the NBE based on these wartime claims is estimated to have been LE379 million at the end of 1945, an increase by LE345 million since 1938 (Hansen and Marzouk 1965, tables 7–9 and 7–10; Hansen and Nashashibi 1975, chapter 1, tables 3–6). The total recorded trade deficit over those years was LE97 million, indicating that Allied military spending in Egypt may have been about LE450 million. Gross domestic product, which in 1938 was about LE160 million, was about LE550 million in 1945. On an annual basis Allied military spending may have amounted to some 20 percent of GDP. Note circulation and private sector claims on the NBE increased correspondingly and inflation was severe.

Postwar Recovery and Stagnation

With conditions in agriculture returning to normal and industry continuing its wartime expansion, the growth rates for postwar years up to and including the Korean War boom, 1945–51, look impressive. In real terms GDP increased 5.4 percent a year, and gross national income, including the very large gains in terms of trade from 1947 to 1951, by 8.3 percent. Per capita the growth rates were substantial, 3.3 percent in terms of production, 6.2 percent in terms of real income. These high growth rates were transitory. Agricultural output per capita fell strongly during the war and never recovered to its prewar level. The relatively fast, but after 1950 decelerating growth of the much smaller industrial sector did not suffice to compensate for the decline in the low level of agricultural production per capita. Throughout the 1950s the picture is one of general stagnation, as table 3–6 shows.

The income growth rate of 1.4 percent from 1938 to 1950 was followed by a negative growth rate of 1.4 percent from 1950 to 1955, slightly more than compensated by a positive rate of 1.9 percent from 1955 to 1960. Per capita income in 1960 was only slightly higher than in 1950 and probably lower than in 1951. On a short-term basis, moreover, income fluctuations were disturbing. A very strong increase by 22 percent in 1948 (bumper crops plus a huge terms-of-trade gain) was followed by moderate increases of 1.6 percent to 5 percent in 1949–51. The

Table 3–6. Indexes of Production and Income per Capita, 1938–60

(1938 = 100)

Year	Agricultural output	Industrial output	GDP at constant factor cost	GNI at constant market price
1938	100	100	100	100
1945	81	118	88	86
1950	86	148	106	118
1955	81	171	107	110
1960	83	196	114	121

Source: Wattleworth (1975), table 1, p. A138; Hansen and Marzouk (1965), tables A–1, A–2, A–3; Mabro and Radwan (1976), table A–2–2.

post-Korean turnaround of the terms of trade with an accompanying temporary stagnation of industry then generated a 10 percent decline in per capita income in 1952, followed by a further 7 percent decline in 1953. Whatever the causes of the Free Officers' coup d'etat in 1952, economic developments must have been politically destabilizing. By 1952 the growth record of democracy and private enterprise must have appeared exceedingly disappointing.

The postwar years saw an intensification of Egyptian nationalism, despite Egypt's relatively early and increasing independence since 1923, in many ways no different from other anticolonial liberation movements in Asia and Africa. The continued presence of British military forces and the war in Palestine in 1947–48 added fuel to nationalism and diverted attention from economic development toward populist issues. It is not surprising that economic policy concentrated on the continued predominance of foreign capital and management in Egyptian joint stock companies and the taxation of profits and income of foreign residents rather than on general growth problems or the general problems of distribution among native Egyptians and alleviation of poverty.

General Growth Policy

A five-year plan for the years 1946–51, consisting mainly of agricultural and educational programs to be supported by the government at a total cost of LE 36 million (about 1 percent of national income annually), was little more than a paper tiger. Of the funds involved, less than one-third had been spent in 1949 and much remained unspent in 1952. The lack of ability within the administration to spend funds allocated for new programs, characteristic of the interwar years after 1923, continued to be a problem. Probably more important than the plan was the increased protection of industry provided by higher tariff rates and the foreign trade and exchange controls introduced in 1939 that continued after the war.

The tariff reform of 1930 with its amendments imposed many specific duties that declined in real terms with the wartime inflation so that protection was eroded. The duties were adjusted during and after the war, not only with the objective of reversing erosion but also of increasing protection. Moreover, duties on luxury imports were introduced and the uniform 1 percent ad valorem duty of 1932 was increased to 8 percent (with new exemptions) in 1952. A licensing fee of 7 percent was added in 1955; it was increased to 9 percent in 1958 but abolished in 1961. A statistical tax of 1 percent introduced in 1956 was increased first to 5 percent and later to 10 percent. Quayside and other duties were added. During the 1950s tariff rates thus increased considerably and the system of tariffs became increasingly complex, partly because revenue and cost-of-living considerations that entered the picture were at cross-purposes with protectionism. Thus wheat was entirely exempted from customs duties at the end of the war to alleviate the cost-of-living increase. In these developments rent seeking, certainly not absent, may have been a secondary force. In 1959 rates of effective protection ranged from about 100 percent for tobacco, textiles, and leather products to about 20 percent for food, furniture, and petroleum products, with negative protection for beverages (Mabro and Radwan 1976, pp. 50–61). Licensing, often combined with price control, seems increasingly during the 1950s to have become the major import-limiting instrument but it is not possible to quantify its effect. It stands to reason that with increased licensing and a paralysis of pluralistic political activities after the coup, rent seeking through bribery and personal corruption increased in importance, but soon increasing public ownership of modern economic activities, nationalizations, and sequestrations took the upper hand.

Foreign Exchange Rate Policy and Overvaluation

The very large sterling reserves that Egypt accumulated during World War II were blocked in London. After prolonged negotiations, with Egypt formally leaving the sterling area in 1947, a schedule was set up for slow conversion of the reserves into hard currency. Sterling reserves were in themselves of limited value since the United Kingdom was unable to deliver important commodities (grain, raw materials, capital goods) that were in short supply, and Egypt preferred to shift her trade toward hard-currency areas (Hansen and Marzouk 1965, pp. 188–90). With the nationalization of the Suez Canal and the Suez War in 1956, Egypt's sterling assets were blocked by the United Kingdom and her dollar assets by the United States, and her trade was blockaded by the United Kingdom and France. The canal did not yield net revenue for Egypt until 1960. The Soviet Union stepped in and with other communist countries became a major trade and aid partner for Egypt. Bilateral trade gained importance. Apart from a short period during the Korean War boom, Egypt was, as a consequence, relatively short of hard currency during the late 1940s and the 1950s. Licensing was introduced and a number of special foreign exchange arrangements were made— import entitlements, so-called export accounts, and export premiums. Most of these arrangements, common at that time in developing countries, were a concealed form of currency depreciation. During the war the government, as a support to agriculture, had accumulated large stocks of cotton. These stocks were slowly released and exported with export taxes, after the war, synchronized with the fluctuations of the international cotton market, apparently a return to the cotton policies of the 1920s. This confused period disrupted Egypt's foreign trade and shifted its orientation from West to East (Hansen and Nashashibi 1975, chapter 2). With all exchange reserves exhausted by 1960, and dependent on aid and loans from East and West and short-term credit from European banks, Egypt entered a period of serious foreign exchange shortages that did not definitely ease until 1974.

The exhaustion of the exchange reserves was the result of continued current account deficits which had been interrupted by a brief interlude with large surpluses during World War II. Between the two world wars the budget typically ran large surpluses but that changed after World War II when public deficit financing became the rule. In 1951 the NBE was given the powers of a central bank and with the exchange controls in Egypt (and abroad) monetary policy had a role to play despite the pegging of the sterling rate. Monetary policy during the 1950s was largely conservative, avoiding expansion of credit to the private sector. With the public deficit largely countered by foreign exchange losses, money supply expanded moderately. While there is good reason to relate the current account deficits to the public deficit financing, from a development point of view the question remains whether the Egyptian currency may be considered to have been overvalued. The evaluation of the performance of private enterprise depends partly on the answer to this question.

During the first weeks of World War II, the United Kingdom let the pound sterling float downward by about 25 percent against the U.S. dollar. In 1949 it devalued the pound by about 30 percent. In both cases Egypt kept the sterling rate unchanged (at the old gold parity). Thus, from the end of the 1930s to 1949 Egypt devalued by about 60 percent against the U.S. dollar with the sterling rate unchanged. From 1949 to 1962 official sterling and dollar rates were unchanged. Other currencies developed differently, depending on each country's policy. After 1948, moreover, Egypt had introduced special exchange arrangements.

Table 3–7 shows indexes of the trade-weighted real official and effective exchange rates for 1938–60 (based on 1938 rates) as does figure 3–4

Table 3-7. Indexes of Trade-Weighted Real Official and Effective Exchange Rates, Selected Years, 1948–60

(1938 = 100)

Deflator	Weighted by	Exchange rates	1948[a]	1952	1956	1960
WPI						
	Exports	Official	118	97	98	108
		Effective	114	104	103	97
	Imports	Official	122	100	101	109
		Effective	103	93	93	94
	Average	Official	120	99	100	109
		Effective	109	98	98	96
COL						
	Exports	Official	130	104	93	94
		Effective	125	112	97	85
	Imports	Official	137	108	96	96
		Effective	116	100	89	83
	Average	Official	133	106	94	95
		Effective	120	106	93	84
WPI and COL[b]						
	Exports	Official	106	83	78	83
		Effective	102	89	81	75
	Imports	Official	112	85	80	85
		Effective	95	79	74	74
	Average	Official	105	84	79	84
		Effective	101	84	78	75

Note: Ratio of foreign exchange per Egyptian pound to Egyptian price index over foreign price index.

a. Official exchange rates not available for Italy and the Federal Republic of Germany.

b. For Egypt, COL; for all foreign countries, WPI.

Source: Egypt, Ministry of Finance, *Annuaire statistique de l'Egypte*, various years; Mitchell (1974); Hoffmann (1965); Hansen and Nashashibi (1975), table 3–3.

for 1913–60 (based on 1913 rates). The indexes are at most informative about relative real appreciation or depreciation as compared with the base year. Whether the currency at any given time is over- or undervalued is another matter. The computations in table 3–7 are based on the same seven foreign currencies as figure 3–4 and cover 59 percent of imports and 48 percent of exports. Whether exports or imports are used in weighting does not appear important. Again, however, it does matter whether the deflation is by the WPI or the COL. The results in table 3–7 are disturbingly ambiguous. The differences between the indexes with official and with effective exchange rates, the latter with adjustment for all special exchange arrangements and changes in customs duties, are substantial and differ on the export from the import side. It is the averages at effective rates that matter here. The table suggests that there may have been a real appreciation in 1948 with clear real depreciation in 1960, the situation shifting toward real depreciation through 1952 and 1956 (in relation to 1938).

Comparisons of production costs are widely regarded as a better indicator of competitiveness than are indexes of trade-weighted real effective exchange rates (further examined in chapter 4). Insofar as wage costs are concerned, comparison with the international rate of inflation, measured by the average rate of growth of wholesale prices in countries that are members of the International Monetary Fund (IMF), indicates an improvement of the competitiveness of Egyptian manufacturing from 1945 to 1962. During 1945–52 Egyptian wage costs increased moderately by 2.8 percent annually, between 1952 and 1957 they fell strongly by 5.2 percent, and in 1957–62 they fell more slowly, by 1.3 percent. A comparison with unit costs in the United States, the United Kingdom, and the European Economic Community for 1955–61 shows similar results (Hansen and Marzouk 1965, table 6–2).

As is the case with the real effective exchange rates, the comparisons of domestic wage costs and the international rate of inflation at best reflect relative competitiveness. Other things being equal with respect to exchange rates, the relative competitiveness of Egyptian industry improved during 1945–62. In an absolute sense Egyptian industry may never have been competitive. To decide whether that is true would require comparison of absolute production costs (wage and raw material costs, and in the long term even capital costs) for individual, well-defined commodities, converted to the same currency, and taking into account trade taxes and c.i.f.–f.o.b. margins.

The Egyptianization of Joint-Stock Companies

In 1934, the last year for which reliable estimates are available, the total paid-up capital in Egyptian joint-stock companies, including all kinds of shares and debentures, amounted to LE91 million. Half of this was estimated as being held abroad and half in Egypt, depending on where coupons were cashed. "Held abroad" thus might mean that interest and dividend payments were cashed abroad by wealthy Egyptian natives living abroad, but this was probably not an important category. Held in Egypt, on the other hand, might mean that interest and dividend payments were cashed in Egypt by foreign nationals resident in Egypt; this was believed to be a very important category but the distribution between native and foreign holders was not known. Of all debentures 58 percent were held in Egypt, of all shares only 46 percent. Financing by shares and debentures varied greatly from sector to sector. Mortgage banks, for instance, relied extensively on debentures, commercial banks not at all.

The nationality of members of boards of directors, management, and other personnel is important. While native Egyptians played a slowly increasing role as owners of capital in and directors or managers of Egyptian joint-stock companies, until World War II these companies were largely dominated by foreigners and increasingly by foreigners resident in Egypt (Tignor 1984, chapter 6). Bhagwati and Brecher (1980) discuss the impact of foreign capital, foreign residents, and their capital, in terms of Heckscher-Ohlin-Samuelson theory, which is not directly applicable in the Egyptian setting with at least three factors and three commodities. Both popular and populist opinion held that foreign ownership and foreign management of Egyptian enterprises were harmful to the country, nationally as well as economically, and should be replaced by domestic ownership and management. This was the leading idea behind the creation of Bank Misr and the Misr companies during the interwar years, and after World War II it became the consensus of the native Egyptian elite and political parties of all colors. The strong tendency during the interwar years toward economic assimilation of the foreign resident community was replaced by increasing estrangement, enhanced by the creation of the state of Israel, the Palestinian war, and the 1956 Suez War.

Legislation was adopted to increase the share of native capital, management and employment in companies active in Egypt. Decrees from 1923 to 1927 required that two members of the board of directors of new companies, 25 percent of the shares, and 25 percent of the white-collar staff be Egyptian. Legislation passed in 1947 required that 40 percent of the board of directors of new companies, 51 percent of the shares, 75 percent of the white-collar staff, and 90 percent of the blue-collar staff be Egyptians and that 65 percent of salaries and 80 percent of wages go to Egyptian staff. The legislation also contained provisions against interlocking directorates and management.

Special attention was paid to foreign concessionaires who had been granted monopolies in public utilities (water, gas, and electricity), transportation (railways, tramways, the Suez Canal), oil extraction, and so forth, in many cases without controls or taxation. Typically, these concessions were renegotiated, with price controls or taxation, profit sharing, or increased royalties the result.

In an accounting sense these measures undoubtedly implied a redistribution of value added in Egyptian joint-stock companies in favor of native Egyptians. The real effect in terms of gross or net investment, employment, and productivity is difficult to appreciate. The investment data in table 3–1, employment data in table 3–2, and productivity data in table 4–14 do not give an unambiguous account. That the obsession with foreigners and foreign capital diverted attention from general growth and distribution problems seems indisputable.

The Egyptianization of the National Bank of Egypt apparently came about because the consensus was that an independent country should have a central bank worthy of the name. Until 1939 the NBE was foreign owned and managed, and resident foreigners played an important role as owners, managers, and employees. It was generally felt that the central bank should serve national interests and that foreign owners and foreign managers could not possibly do that. It was also felt that an independent country should have an independent monetary policy and that Egypt had not enjoyed such monetary policy since the monetary reform of 1885. Here the issue of who shall own and run the central bank tends to be confused with the quite different problem of which monetary policy should be pursued. It is generally acknowledged that with a pegged sterling rate and free trade and capital movements, a country cannot and will not have an independent monetary policy. Interest rates are determined abroad, money supply adjusts endogenously, and commercial banks may prefer to keep reserves abroad or domestically. Who runs and owns the system is basically irrelevant. This is the system of Bretton Woods, which Egypt essentially lived with as a member of the sterling area until 1947 and which it joined formally after the establishment of the IMF. That Egypt after 1947 was unable (and unwilling) to live up to the ideals of the Bretton Woods system is another matter. And that Egypt after the breakdown of the Bretton Woods system around 1970 opted not to go on floating rates with free trade and capital movements despite strong pressure from the IMF and the International Bank for Reconstruction and Development (IBRD) is again a different matter. Egyptian nationalists have not always understood that independence of monetary system and policy is an issue not to be confused with national independence.

Three Decades of Democracy

In his otherwise marvelous book, *Economic Development in Egypt*, Crouchley could as late as 1938 strike a note of almost Victorian optimism about the Egyptian economy. Yet it has been unmistakably clear since Issawi's early writings in the 1940s and 1950s, at least, that the half-century before 1952 was one of stagnation. Why that was so has not been equally clear. General references to imperialism, colonialism, neocolonialism, periphery-metropolis syndromes, and so on, are not helpful to economists trying to determine what were the concrete growth forces, if any, and growth impediments, if any.

Undisputably, agriculture at the turn of the century suffered an ecological disaster that made yields decline by about 15 percent from 1900 to 1920 and brought production to a standstill. With agriculture accounting for perhaps two-thirds of GDP, it would require extremely fast industrialization to produce a respectable overall growth rate. The underlying cause of the disaster was poor design of the expansion of the irrigation and drainage system accompanied by the emergence of cotton pests. Simultaneous expansion of multiple cropping and a shift in crop composition—the intended effects of the expansion of the irrigation and drainage system—served only to compensate for the unintended decline in yields. The cultivated area had reached its economical upper limit before 1900.

This would have been the historically given starting point for any Egyptian government in the early 1920s. The British had plans for repairing the damage done to yields and work began before World War I. The Egyptian government after 1923 continued to implement the British plans, scaling down projects in Central Africa. Given the circumstances, one might have expected rapid recovery—almost like the recovery after a war—with agricultural growth continuing the nineteenth century trend. That was not to happen. Agricultural output in 1920 was at the same level as in 1900; it did grow at a rate of 1.8 percent from 1920 to 1940, but with total population increasing at a rate of 1.2 percent that was not an impressive performance. Per capita agricultural output in 1940 was still more than 10 percent below the 1900 level. It is not difficult to find obstacles to fast agricultural growth. The Egyptian policy of limiting cotton supply from 1921 to 1932 obviously did harm to agricultural production; whether it improved terms of trade is not known.[6] Egyptian governments after 1923 appear to have been inefficient in preparing and implementing new projects and programs, as witnessed by underspending and budget surpluses. The very high level of illiteracy and lack of general education in the country have often been isolated as the essential obstacle to growth before 1952. Having had an extremely low priority under British rule, illiteracy was obviously an obstacle that no government could overcome within three decades. Yet, I do not think that that was a major problem for agricultural growth during the interwar period. Land was very unevenly distributed. About 12,000 persons with fifty *feddan* or more owned about 40 percent of the cultivated land. Data for 1950 and 1952 suggest that figures for ownership apply roughly to cultivation units. Despite the massive illiteracy among small and probably medium-size farmers, more than half the cultivated area may after all have been under the supervision and management of educated holders. With small farmers typically hiring out and regularly working on large farms, learning by doing may rapidly have disseminated innovations to small farms. Medium-sized farms with illiterate holders who did not hire out may have represented the most serious obstacle to technical progress. New cotton varieties proliferated during the interwar period and use of chemical fertilizers reached high levels. There is nothing to indicate that the general educational backwardness of the rural population was a serious obstacle to agricultural growth during the period. It is land reform that makes formal education for peasants a necessary condition for technical progress. The impact of the international agricultural crisis and the Great Depression is difficult to evaluate. Relative price changes worked against agriculture, and the cultivated area did decline slightly. Labor and capital input, however, increased in both relative and absolute terms. The land that went out of cultivation was, of course, marginal land and the effect on total output may have been negligible.

What, then, could have been done to increase the growth rate in agriculture, given the inexperience and inefficiency of the national government and the unfavorable international setting? In 1940 the cultivated area was still below the maximum reached in 1930 but that was a secondary problem. Multicropping and crop composition did improve, though at a slower pace than earlier; the slowdown here, however, was partly geophysically conditioned, perennial irrigation coming close to its limit. Yields nevertheless improved somewhat, at an annual rate of 1.2 percent. Could yields have been improved faster and further? I doubt it. Cotton varieties were improved very fast but the era of high-yield cereals was still to come. From 1940 to 1960 the general rate of increase in yields was a trifle, about 0.4 percent, and most of the increase took place in the late 1950s, possibly a delayed effect of investments made before the war. The three-year moving average of yields did increase another 11 percent from 1959 to 1966, mainly because of specific effects of the Aswan High Dam. There may not have been much more to be gained at that time. Egyptian yields were very high by international standards and, as Goethe knew: "Es ist dafür gesorgt dass die Bäume nicht in den Himmel wachsen."

Assuming that little more could be done to increase yields, the only form of agricultural growth available would have been to produce the same output with less labor input, which would require mechanization. Relative factor prices clearly did not speak in favor of mechanization during the interwar period, particularly the 1930s. If anything, a certain demechanization occurred, as might have been expected. Agricultural mechanization, moreover, would require that employment opportunities be opened up elsewhere in the economy. Massive industrialization in labor-intensive technologies appears to have been the only answer.

The government's industrialization policy in the 1930s took the form of protection through higher tariffs, with some subsidization through loans. Industrial gross investment per capita was no higher during 1925–39 than during the boom years 1903–07 when there was no increase in protection; employment in manufacturing was absolutely lower in 1937 than in 1927. In this sense the industrialization policy failed. Computations of real effective exchange rates unfortunately leave considerable doubt about the degree of over- and undervaluation of the Egyptian pound. Concentrating on the situation of import-substituting industries, the results depend critically on the deflators used in the computations. Available data are shown in figure 3–4 and table 3–7. With a deflator using wholesale prices both domestically (tariff adjusted) and abroad, there is on balance some real appreciation until 1926 and strong real depreciation after 1931, continuing until 1960. Were this method of deflation the appropriate one, it would be hard to understand why industrialization did not accelerate and also why the balance of current account remained in the red throughout the 1930s and after World War II. Using the cost of living domestically (tariff adjusted) and wholesale prices abroad as deflators, there is a strong appreciation until 1931 and then parity with 1913 from 1932 to 1948, with considerable depreciation from the end of the 1940s. The tariff reform of 1930 just compensated for overvaluation of the official exchange rate. Adding the de facto protection of the war years (not shown in figure 3–4), it makes sense that private industrialization should have been boosted by the war and then continued after the war. There was little net incentive, however, for industrialization before the war.

Adopting this version of the real effective exchange rate computations, it is clear that membership in the sterling area with fixed sterling rates at the old gold parity was an unfortunate policy. A strong depreciation against sterling in the early 1920s, not following sterling in 1925 when it went back on the gold standard, and thereafter possibly following sterling in 1931, 1939, and 1949 would have been an appropriate exchange policy for Egypt. It would have been feasible in the sense that it was not in principle in conflict with the Capitulations although it would clearly have been in conflict with British interests. It would have made the tariff reform of 1930 superfluous and thus have substituted a first-best for a second-best policy. Under such a policy, industrialization would have started almost a decade earlier than would otherwise have been possible, given the Capitulations. Ruling out tariff protection it is by no means obvious that the Capitulations inhibited growth before 1930. The public debt service would have increased in terms of Egyptian pounds (it was fixed in terms of sterling); since the budget typically was in surplus during the interwar years, no new taxes or increased tax rates on old taxes, impossible under the Capitulations, would have been required. The exchange reserves of the NBE would not have been used to cover current account deficits but could, to the extent they were considered excessive, have been used for paying off public debts held abroad and for improving both service balance and gross national income per capita. Finally, should during the Great Depression "animal spirits" have been flagging to such a degree that no incentive could have made industrialization move, government initiative with the establishment of industries in the public sector would have been called for. Atatürk's example would have been worth considering.

The policies against inequity that Egypt followed were mainly focused on the privileges of foreigners, and these privileges were abolished before 1952. How that affected growth is discussed below in the context of the expulsion of resident foreigners during the 1950s and 1960s.

Little is known about the distribution of income and wealth and the incidence of poverty, beyond the fact that the distribution of ownership of land was highly unequal throughout the century and did not change much until the land reform of 1952. There were essentially no policies related to distribution and poverty before the 1950s, the years when democracy and private enterprise broke down.

Notes

1. This chapter draws extensively on Tignor (1984) and Vatikiotis (1969). "Development without Growth," used in the chapter title, is borrowed from Tignor (1984, conclusion).

2. Results of computations of export-weighted indexes were similar to the results for imports.

3. Demand for Egyptian cotton was first studied econometrically by Bresciani-Turroni (1930) and Ricci (1933), and later by Nour El Din (1959), Chen (1970), and Birnberg and Resnick (1975) among others. A study by Darwish in the Ministry of Finance, which indicated high elasticity of demand and apparently played a role in decisionmaking, does not warrant serious consideration. I have tried my hand on the problem several times (1975, 1983) and have concluded that data are not available for estimating the demand side with proper specifications. These would have to take into account speculation in the short term and substitution in both textiles consumption and production as well as raw cotton supply responses from other countries in the long term. Available studies do not distinguish between short- and long-term responses and are thus of little value. In my attempts I have made this distinction but invariably have come out with higher short- than long-term elasticities. This may be related to speculation but seems to run counter to rational expectations hypotheses. But then the consensus seems to be that expectations were not "rational" at that time (Friedman and Schwartz 1982).

4. A comparison of the Egyptian and Indian cotton textiles industries is instructive. India established and developed from the 1850s, without government support and despite considerable harassment from British colonial government, a very successful cotton textiles industry that in the field of coarse yarns before the end of the nineteenth century had driven British competitors out of India, Southeast Asia, and China. The Indian cotton textiles industry was indigenously managed and financed without any kind of protection from about 1880 to World War I but did benefit temporarily from the depreciation of the silver rupee from the 1870s to 1894 when India was put on the gold standard. The key to Indian success was apparently indigenous entrepreneurship, domestic raw materials (transportation advantage), domestic markets (hand weaving), technological alertness (the ring frame), and earlier export experience (hand woven materials). Morris 1983; Metha 1953.

5. The monetary system and monetary policy in Egypt during the interwar period, with inflexible exchange rates (in the sense of a fixed, constant rate against sterling and hence fixed, not necessarily constant rates against all other

currencies) and perfectly free foreign payments, including capital transfers, would fit the modeling of Mundell (1963). He concludes that with fixed exchange rates and the interest rate determined from abroad, monetary policy—that is, open market operations in domestic securities—should have no other effects than that of substituting central bank holdings of foreign exchange (sterling-denominated claims) against domestic (Egyptian pound–denominated) claims. In particular, production (income) and its composition should be independent of monetary policy. Monetary policy thus should have no place in either short-term stabilization policy (Mundell's conclusion) or long-term growth policy. Fiscal policy with (increased) budget deficits and deficit financing in the open market, on the other hand, would in the case with idle resources have expansionary production and income effects, with current account deficits and foreign capital inflow corresponding to the budget deficit minus possible (increased) net lending (saving minus investment) in the private sector. In the case with no idle resources and hence no effects on total production and income, fiscal policy might still have an effect on consumption and saving (investment) and thus play a role in growth policy. Investment incentives from the budget, financed through a tax increase sufficient to preserve internal equilibrium despite the increase in investment and the possible decline in private saving, would clearly promote growth without effects on the current account balance. With an insufficient tax increase, private consumption would not fall sufficiently to finance the investment increase, the current account would suffer a deficit, and corresponding capital inflow would finance part of the investment increase, still with growth effects on production; income effects would depend on share of foreign financing and the difference between returns to investment and the rate of interest abroad. With idle resources both production and growth effects and possibly income effects would obtain.

The possibility of Egyptian fiscal policy financed in the open market having negative effects on investment through a tightening of the credit market clearly assumes, contrary to the Mundell modeling, that foreign and domestic claims are not perfect substitutes, a highly realistic assumption for claims on the private sector but not necessarily for the public sector, even after independence.

6. Smoot-Hawley tariff of 1930, for instance, dealt a devastating blow to Egyptian cotton, which had played an important role in American production of high-quality tires.

4 Egyptian Autocrats in Peace and War, 1952–85

Since 1952, Egypt has been ruled by a succession of autocrats, Gamal Abdel Nasser, Anwar Sadat, and Hosny Mubarak. The style of government has changed from ruler to ruler but the economic system has remained much the same. Words like Nasserism and, less frequently, Sadatism have been used to characterize the regimes. Nasserism, however, was "a political ideology constructed not by the leader himself but by theoreticians who sought to give ideological continuity to his ad hoc decisions" (Springborg 1975, pp. 86–87) while Sadat's opportunistic, erratic, and unpredictable regime hardly deserves the epithet ideology. While the label etatism has not been used to describe the Egyptian regimes since 1952, it defines what Egypt has been since Nasser consolidated his power. A mixed economy with a large, modern public enterprise sector under an autocratic ruler was what Atatürk was talking about when he coined the expression etatism. For historical and comparative reasons I prefer etatism to statism in this volume.

Nasser's was a highly centralized, military-bureaucratic regime, parliament and the single party being nothing but cosmetic devices. It effectively ended the parliamentary system that had prevailed since 1923. Political parties and organized pressure groups were destroyed or emasculated and the vacuum was filled with a network of military and civil patron-client and crony relations. Both public enterprises and public control of what remained of the private sector expanded strongly and the spoils of the system were to be had in the public sector.

Under Sadat the system was demilitarized and somewhat liberalized; family relations tended to replace the civilian patron-client system at the very top. The private sector made a comeback but despite reforms to bring about decentralization the public sector remained much the same as under Nasser. The spoils were now to be had in the relationship between the public and the private (foreign) sectors. Under Mubarak cautious political liberalization was continued but the economic system remained unchanged. Under both Nasser and Sadat, profound institutional change of significance for poverty, equity, and growth took place.

The Political Structure

After the coup of July 1952, which toppled the monarchy, a power struggle ensued between the nominal leader of the junta, General Mohammed Naguib, who wanted to restore democracy and send the army back to the barracks, and Colonel Nasser, who opposed restoration of the old regime. Nasser's aspirations were not well articulated but he clearly had the support of other members of the junta. In the struggle for power both Naguib and the majority of the junta were outmaneuvered by Nasser; supported by a group of outside loyalists, young officers, and a few civilians, Nasser with his close friend Major (later Field Marshal) Abdel Hakim Amer came out on top. Like most modern autocrats, Nasser sought to legitimate his rule through popular vote. A plebiscite in 1956 approved a new constitution and elected Nasser president for a six-year period. Later Sadat and Mubarak were each elected president through similar arrangements. All three autocrats have enjoyed unlimited power but have preferred to operate within a one-party framework until Sadat in 1978 introduced a very restricted multiparty system which continued and developed under Mubarak.

The first of the single political parties created after the coup was the Liberation Rally, established in 1953 and operated by Nasser. It was replaced in 1957 by the National Union (NU) which in turn was replaced in 1961 by the Arab Socialist Union (ASU), in 1978 reorganized as the National Democratic party (NDP). These parties were never intended to be more than an autocratic policy instrument but they have at times served as bases for power struggles among secondary actors on the political stage.

It has been shown by Binder (1978) that throughout the 1960s rural middle-class and particularly middle-size landowners and their allies tended to dominate the local committees of both the NU and the ASU in the countryside. While Binder's findings clearly indicate that with the very top eliminated, the upper layers of the landowning rural population continued to dominate the villages, it does not follow that they formed a national political basis from which the Egyptian elite was predominantly drawn and without which the autocrats could not rule. As Waterbury (1983) convincingly shows, the Egyptian elite did not predominantly originate from the rural "bourgeoisie" and did not represent the interests of the rural middle class. Even though the rural middle class "was allowed to control, directly or indirectly, much of the political infrastructure that Nasser introduced in the countryside" (Waterbury 1983, p. 277), including the cooperatives (Adams 1986), that does not mean that Nasser's single parties were politically powerful at the national level.

The plain fact that the agricultural price policies under both Nasser and Sadat discriminated against agriculture in favor of the urban population is strong circumstantial evidence that, the NU and the ASU notwithstanding, the rural middle class or the middle-size landowners never were intended or allowed to play a significant, active political role at the national level under either of the two autocrats (this is also Binder's view [1978, pp. 307, 372]). Despite minor actions in the so-called parliament under Sadat, it was pressure from international organizations and financiers, if anything, that resulted in relaxation of the discrimination against agriculture in the late 1970s and early 1980s. Binder's findings do, however, point to the importance of the distinction between national (central) and local politics and policies. Strongly centralized as Egyptian government is and has always been, certain matters are nonetheless effectively administered at the local level and influenced by local political forces. Distribution of irrigation water and certain other inputs in agriculture are good examples with income distributional consequences.

With other political parties banned and special interest groups and organizations such as the Federation of Industry, the labor unions, and the professional syndicates either destroyed or transformed into arms of the government, politics outside the official party, at least until around 1974, were limited to either illegal organizations or informal groupings. For instance, the Communist party—small, entirely unimportant, and harshly suppressed—and the Muslim Brotherhood, which is believed to have had a membership of about 1 million in 1952, were never effectively destroyed and in the 1980s the latter resurfaced as a political, moderating force. Under the Nasser regime, the *shilla*, the patron-client group, prospered and played a crucial role.

Political scientists view the family, the *dufaa*, and the *shilla* as the basic political, informal organizations in Egypt (Springborg 1975, pp. 93 ff.).[1] Before the nineteenth century the family was the overwhelmingly important organizational unit, but its policy role declined in the nineteenth and twentieth centuries (Tignor 1966). Nasser's regime, through land reform, nationalizations, and sequestrations, did much to end the dominating role of a few wealthy extended families in Egyptian politics. Whether family power dominated politics during the years of parliamentary democracy is unclear; scholars evaluate family connections for this period quite differently (Al-Sayed-Marsot 1977; Springborg 1975, 1982; Tignor 1984). Under Sadat, however, family connections again became important.

The *dufaa*, "the Egyptian equivalent of the old boy network" (Springborg 1975, p. 97), is organized around the graduating classes of secondary schools and higher educational institutions, including military schools. These groups, found all over the public sector, are intensely competitive, even hostile toward each other. Most of the Free Officers of the 1952 coup were members of the first *dufaa* of the military academy after the British-Egyptian agreement of 1936 or the 1948 *dufaa* of the staff college (Springborg 1975, p. 99). The *shilla*, a group of close acquaintances who operate together for their own benefit, often in a patron-client relationship, in public service or as a political elite, often emerges from a *dufaa*:

Since 1952 the *dufaa* has been of significance at the pinnacle of the elite. . . . The *shillas*, which were later to contend for power and influence in the elite, grew out of these [above mentioned] *dufaas*. Although the civilizing of the regime resulted in the Free Officers expanding their contacts and eventually in the formation of *shillas* and clientage networks including both officers and civilians, *dufaa* ties and inter-*dufaa* hostilities dating to the late 1930s and early 1940s are still alive. Sadat has systematically installed surviving members of his officer school *dufaa* in top command positions in the armed forces, culminating with the appointment of Ahmed Ismail as minister of war (Springborg 1975, p. 99).

Before Egypt's defeat in the 1967 War, the political system comprised two basic *shillas*, one Nasser's and the other controlled by Field Marshal Amer whom Nasser had appointed to head the armed forces. Under these two *shillas*, secondary *shillas* branched out, headed by patrons who were clients of the two primary *shillas*. Among the important patrons of the secondary *shillas* were Ali Sabri, Sayed Marei, Magdi Hassanein, Mohammed Hassanein Heikal, Sami Sharaf, and Sharawi Gomaa. Horizontal connections, friendly or hostile, as in all patron-client systems, were of great importance—so much so that some scholars call the system under Nasser a crony system (Waterbury 1983, pp. 346 ff.). Both Nasser and Amer manipulated their clients with ruthless determination as part of their own power games, and the economic policies adopted under Nasser were often the fortuitous outcome of such games at or near the top of the pyramid. With the military defeat in 1967 and Amer's death, Nasser was in full command of both civilian and military officers and the military *shillas* declined in importance.

Under Sadat, the bureaucratic empires disappeared; officers, largely depoliticized, went back to the barracks or, in quite a few cases, to jail, and two civilian clients, Sayed Marei and Aziz Sidky, rose to top positions. The intense factionalism and infighting at the top of the political elite, where the spoils were to be had under Nasser's centralized regime, changed character. Decentralization of the public enterprise sector and upgrading of the private sector under Sadat's *infitah* created new opportunities for profits and capital gains.

The canny and ambitious Egyptian no longer aspires to be a cabinet minister but instead prefers the more lucrative position . . . as "consultant". Big-time cronies are now found mutually backscratching in the interstices of the public and private sectors, while it is the smaller fry who jockey for positions within the cabinet [it being well understood that the road to consultancy goes through the cabinet]. . . . As Sadat has permitted considerable political freedom, so have virtual constituencies begun to appear. . . . The first to surface under Sadat's rise to power were the professional syndicates. . . . Since that time, loosely organized collectives . . . have sprung up and for the first time since 1952, Egyptian politics more closely resembles politics than administration (Springborg 1979, pp. 276–77).[2]

This characterization of the system under Sadat shortly before his assassination, before he purged the critical elite, carries over to the system under Mubarak where *status quo ante purgatorium*, if anything, is the leading principle. Under the ambitious chief of the armed forces, Abu Ghazala, the military did experience a certain comeback with ties to enterprises in the private (foreign) rather than the public sector (Springborg 1989, chap. 4). Abu Ghazala's resignation in the spring of 1989 left the situation less clear.

Ideological Developments

At the time of the coup, the Free Officers had no clear economic program and no conceived ideology. Political views ran from orthodox Marxism to conservative pluralism, with some members being close to the Muslim Brotherhood. For a few years private entrepreneurship was officially favored and encouraged but later a sea change was to occur in attitudes to and the position of private enterprise. International developments, the events around the Aswan Dam financing, the related nationalization of the Suez Canal, and the Suez War must have helped to bring about the change, but so did Nasser's own rise to power, as he outmaneuvered other junta members, leftists, conservatives, and Islamics. Nasser's personality was also an important factor. Nasser was a shrewd pragmatic, suspicious to the point of being paranoic, and highly emotional. He was not a great political philosopher and ideologist.[3] How much of the change in the position of private enterprise after 1956 was sheer pragmatism, how much rash emotional response, and how much a paranoic response to imagined, domestic opposition is hard to say. Little was probably due to genuine ideological change although Tito and other nonaligned leaders are known to have impressed Nasser, and rapid economic growth in the communist world with recession in the West in the 1950s may have contributed. The nationalization of the Bank Misr Group in 1960 seems thus to have been a practical move related to the unwillingness of the group to comply with the investment program of the first five-year plan (for 1960–61 to 1964–65). The massive sequestrations of November 1961, on the other hand, were apparently an irrational, angry response to the cession of Syria in September of that year.

The politics of the 1961–63 nationalizations have never been satisfactorily explained. In a conversation in 1965, Prime Minister Zakareya

Moheieldin, a senior, conservative, and pro-Western junta member, told me when I questioned him about the logic of the nationalizations: "We simply did not understand Gamal!" Loyalist officers, greedy for spoils, and Minister of Industry Sidky, anxious to expand his industrial empire, have been implicated. Peculiar ideas about hidden reserves that, if seized, might finance industrialization were officially presented by Heikal as the rationale for the nationalizations. Be that as it may, the nationalizations were poorly prepared and hastily implemented, directed by Nasser personally. Proclamation of the Charter of 1962 soon followed.

The Charter of 1962 and Arab Socialism

"Erst kommt das Fressen, dann kommt die Moral" (Brecht, *Die Dreigroschenoper*).

With the Charter of 1962, so-called Arab socialism became the official ideology of the country. Arab socialism was supposed to be distinctly different from Western and Eastern versions of socialism and also from the Syrian Baath version. In a speech in Cairo in 1962, Nasser explicitly rejected Marxism-Leninism as not recognizing religion and favoring the dictatorship of the proletariat and complete public ownership of the means of production. Yet he visualized a secular, classless, corporate society with a mixed economy tightly controlled by the government. The charter mainly post-rationalized and codified reform and institutional change actually undertaken since 1952—for whatever reason—as Arab socialism. Interestingly, it rejected concentration on heavy industry at the expense of consumer goods industries and stated: "Great concern must be directed to consumer industries. Apart from offering great possibilities of work, these industries meet an important share of consumer demands and save foreign currency. In addition, [they] offer export possibilities. . . . The mass of our people have long been deprived; to mobilize them completely for the building of heavy industry . . . is incompatible with their right to be compensated for their long deprivation." Nasser held that he was not ready to "allow mobilization for industry to delay the meeting of the people's consumer needs," it being unethical to "sacrifice the well-being of the present generation for the hypothetical happiness of future generations." The charter further emphasized "the right of each citizen to medical care, and then the right to receive education appropriate for his ability and talent. Then there is the right to an adequate job according with ability and education, together with a legally sanctioned minimum wage. And, finally, there is the right to old age benefits" (Said 1972, pp. 61, 119–20, 122). The charter thus echoed the so-called social compact to which we return below.

The 1974 October Paper and Infitah

In the 1974 October Paper Sadat outlined his policy of *infitah* (opening), which amounted to a partial liberalization of the economy with public sector enterprises and agricultural controls preserved. While Nasser in 1969 had emphasized the need for such reforms, it was left to Sadat (through his Minister of Finance, Abdel Aziz Hegazi) to formulate and implement the reforms.

The October Paper realized that higher growth rates were required and that that would necessitate both financial and technological assistance from abroad. The public sector was to continue being the primary instrument for carrying out the development plan. The public sector, however, was seen as suffering from an excess of bureaucracy and having expanded into areas that should be left to the private sector. It should in the future only undertake basic projects that other sectors would not or could not take up and provide services essential to private and foreign investment. An indicative plan for 1976–80 should be formulated, with priority given to modernized industry; labor-intensive, high-value agriculture; development of oil and energy; and tourism. Social development should at the same time take place "at compatible rates."

The *infitah* strategy was defined as a move toward a less regimented economy in which both private domestic and foreign investment were permitted to play an active and competitive role. More realistic pricing policies were a main element of the program. By 1977, all commodity imports except basic consumer goods would be paid by foreign currencies purchased through a parallel market. Greater use would be made of dual pricing for items of mass consumption and utilities. Discrimination in the distribution of subsidies would ensure that benefits would be limited to the poorer sections of the population. And in an increasing number of public sector enterprises, decisionmaking would be decentralized.

The Social Compact and la Dolce Vita

The Charter of 1962 and the October Paper of 1974 were the fundamental ideological statements under Nasser and Sadat, respectively. It has, however, been suggested by an outstanding connoisseur of the Egyptian political scene, that underlying Egyptian policy ever since 1952 there has been an unwritten, implicit social compact between ruler and ruled, and that the political economy of Egypt is best understood in terms of such a compact. His views are reported in some detail by Delwin A. Roy (1980, pp. 3–9) from whom the following quotations are taken. This social compact amounts to an "exchange of political rights for the provision of goods and services" (Roy 1980, p. 6). Obviously, this is not the kind of voluntary exchange that modern political economy visualizes as the basis for government interference (Buchanan 1987, p. 246). Egypt under autocracy is not what Buchanan calls a "liberal social order," and coercion (force) is to various degrees ever present. It is claimed that "there has for some time been a strong movement aimed at the depolitization of the Egyptian people . . . spreading to virtually all types of interest groups: students, religious, agrarian, labor and any ideologically based political parties." In return the "central government, in performance of its share of the contract, has taken on the responsibility of providing goods and services to the population at large." A dynamics of the situation (not to be confused with the conventional mechanism of "rising expectations") is, moreover, visualized in that "the *quid pro quo* of maintaining the society's apolitical character leads into constantly rising thresholds of consumption" because this "paternalistic state of affairs has on occasion led government, repeatedly unable to maintain the pace, to add new obligations as a means of evening out inefficiencies in the performance of old obligations." And "although the continuing character of the system has been clearly affected by the various *isms* of past and present leaders, it has survived them all: Egyptian nationalism (1952–60); pan-Arabian as exemplified by the formation of the United Arab Republic (UAR) (1960–62); Arab socialism (1961–71); the Corrective Revolution [the takeover by Sadat] (1971); and, now, economic liberalism. The Open Door, the closed economy, centralization, and decentralization of policy formulation and implementation are all surface, not 'core phenomena.'" It is argued that "this bargain . . . has been fairly successful in providing an atmosphere of political stability . . . although the purely economic cost involved in the performance of the contract may be viewed as inordinately high." (Roy 1980, pp. 5, 6, 9.)

These views undoubtedly capture something essential in the Egyptian political economy under Nasser and Sadat and, it could be added, Mubarak. They are based, of course, on an "as if" model. The social compact is implicit and has never been explicitly formulated and adopted as a constitution. Yet, it is possible to read it into both the charter and the October Paper. It may be questioned to what extent "the people" really are involved in the compact. It could be argued that it is essentially a compact between ruler and urban population or even, more narrowly, between ruler and elite (Springborg 1989). I am inclined to support the latter interpretation, which would be a matter of a *trahison des clercs*, the elite sacrificing political freedom in the country for la dolce vita, from the luxury life of the privileged clients to the almost free loaf of bread for the poor. The emergence of Islamic fundamentalism may have threatened the compact, but even the Muslim Brotherhood appears now to be falling in place.

Organizational Change

If ownership is defined as a set of rights or authorizations that may belong to private individuals, corporations, or the public, the nature of ownership and its distribution are crucial for economic organization. Ownership of the means of production, and with it economic organization, changed profoundly under the Nasser regime but was then largely unchanged under Sadat and Mubarak. Redistribution of ownership of old lands, distribution of ownership of newly reclaimed lands, and restriction of land ownership rights, all part of land reform, have been pursued for a variety of reasons with a variety of effects on agriculture and the rural population. Egyptianization, nationalization, sequestration, and public investment have brought large segments of the nonagricultural economy under public ownership at the same time that extended public control has restricted remaining nonagricultural, private activities.

Land Reform

Redistribution of land was initiated immediately after the coup to break the economic and political power of the royal family and big landowners and to mobilize political support for the junta among the small landowning class. Land acquired and distributed before 1969 is shown in table 4-1. The Agrarian Reform Law of September 1952 limited private landownership to a maximum of 200 *feddan* (1 *feddan* = 0.42 hectares = 1.04 acres) and set rules governing transfer to dependents. A 1958 amendment limited the maximum area owned by a person and his dependents to 300 *feddan* and a 1959 amendment limited the area operated by a person with family to 300 *feddan* with ownership per person limited to 200 *feddan*. In 1961, ownership per person was reduced to 100 *feddan*, the family maximum left at 300 *feddan*, and the maximum to be rented by one person reduced to 50 *feddan*, with landowners limited to renting only as many *feddan* as their ownership fell short of 50. In 1963 foreigners were forbidden to own land. A further reduction to 50 *feddan* of ownership per person and 100 per family, decreed in 1969, does not appear to have been fully implemented. Land owned in excess of these limits was confiscated and owners were paid far less than market value for their land.

Compensation to previous owners was to be paid in nonnegotiable government bonds, redeemable in thirty, and later forty, years with an interest of 3 percent that was later reduced to 1.5 percent. All compensations may not have been paid. Even if they had been paid, the expropriations would still have reduced the income of the old owners to about one-sixth of what they could have obtained at maximum rents from the confiscated lands.

Apart from the size limitations on ownership, full contractual freedom in sales and purchases of land continued to prevail (except in land reform areas) and land prices remained unregulated. For land lease, however, contractual freedom was significantly circumscribed. Not only were upper limits imposed on land tenure but conditions of tenure were set in favor of long-term contracts and eviction was virtually impossible. Tenure contracts must be registered with and approved by village cooperatives. In practice tenure contracts seem to be inherited now. Maximum rents were fixed in 1952 at seven times the assessment for land tax in case of cash rent and at 50 percent of output in case of sharing. During the first years after 1952 the maximum rents were by and large in line with (hypothetical) market rents. Some increase of maximum rents took place in the 1970s. With the maximum rents increasingly eroded in real terms by inflation from the 1960s onward and eviction virtually excluded, an increasing share of land rent proper must have been shifted from owner to tenant. Evasion does exist, of course, tenants being paid for giving up old contracts at the low legal rent and owners being paid for entering into new contracts at legal rents. The extent of evasion is a matter of dispute and illegal payments may be cashed by middlemen (*wakilah*) rather than by owners. Alongside the distribution of land by ownership, distribution by holdings must because of the effect of rent control and the extent of tenancy have been playing an increasingly im-

Table 4-1. Land Acquired and Distributed by Land Reform Laws, 1952-64

Action	Area (feddan)[a]		Families benefiting
	Acquired	Distributed	
Law 178, 1952; law 598, 1953[b]	450,305	356,147	146,496
Law 152, 1957; law 44, 1962[c]	148,787	189,049	78,797
Law 127, 1961	214,132	100,745	45,823
Sequestration, 1956	25,807	112,641	49,390
Law 15, 1963[d]	61,910	30,081	14,172
Law 150, 1964[e]	43,516	n.a.	n.a.
Other	n.a.	98	49
Total	944,452	797,761	334,727

n.a. = Not available
a. A total of 5,982,000 *feddan* was owned in 1952.
b. Includes confiscated estates of the royal family.
c. *Wakf* land.
d. Excludes foreigners from ownership.
e. Confiscated from persons under sequestration.
Source: M. Riad el Ghonemy in Vatikiotis (1968), p. 92; Richards (1982), table 6.3 (quoting Abdel-Fadil 1975).

portant role in income distribution in rural Egypt (Hansen and Marzouk 1965, pp. 84 ff.).

Reclamation and Distribution of Lands

"Und dann und wann ein weisser Elefant" (Rilke, "Das Karussell").

The white elephant of Egyptian planning is probably land reclamation. Almost three-quarters of all agricultural investment during the 1960s was concentrated in reclamation in the Western Desert, where 0.9 million feddan (equal to one-fifth of the total cultivated area in Egypt) were reclaimed. Less than two-thirds of this land was ever cultivated, mostly at marginal returns. It is perhaps understandable that a professional politician like Nasser let himself be carried away by the prospect of eliminating one of the most serious constraints on agricultural development and then pursued reclamation at any cost—with disastrous results. But the unconstrained spending with poor results is partly attributable to the political structure, the *shilla* system, characteristic of the Nasser regime and to the lack of clear land settlement policies, a consequence of Nasser's power games. The huge Tahrir project, particularly well researched by Robert Springborg (1975, 1979, 1982), is a classic example of political economy below the surface in a modern autocracy. This section draws heavily upon Springborg (1979) to whom this is a general reference.

In 1952, an engineer in charge of exploration in the desert west of the Delta found evidence that the area may have been cultivated in antiquity. When Magdi Hassanein, an army officer and Nasser loyalist, was informed about the discovery, he directed a unit of army engineers to investigate. The engineers, who had no experience in land reclamation, declared the land appropriate for reclamation. Hassanein then obtained Nasser's approval of a reclamation project, to be called Tahrir (Liberation) Province. In 1954, Hassanein was placed in charge of this prestigious project. It was separated from the ordinary civil service pay scale and attracted specialists with privileges and bonuses. Hassanein was aiming at creating a model state farm; he may already at that time have had leftist leanings. This, however, was strongly resisted by civilian technocrats in the Ministries of Agriculture and Irrigation who resented the military intervention in their domain. The patron of civilian agronomists and agricultural engineers was Sayed Marei, who in 1952 had been appointed chief of the Higher Committee for Agrarian Reform (HCAR), responsible for distributing land confiscated under the 1952 Agrarian Reform Law. Marei's policy in the agrarian reform areas was to combine private ownership with compulsory cooperative membership. This policy had Nasser's support and was later to be extended to all agricultural land. It being clear that Hassanein did not favor private ownership, he was called before Marei's Committee for Ownership and Exploitation of

Reformed Land. Hassanein promised the committee that the agrarian reform model would be applied to Tahrir Province, but by 1957 only a minuscule amount of land had been distributed to peasants. The rest of the reclaimed land continued to be operated as a huge state farm.

Marei's efforts were helped in 1957 when Egypt's National Assembly was convened with Latif el Baghdadi at its head. Determined to make democracy take firm root in Egypt and disliking the free-wheeling financial practices in the Tahrir project, el Baghdadi allowed the assembly to be used by Marei and other political conservatives to expose cost overruns, financial irregularities, and the poor quality of the reclamation work in Tahrir Province. The exposure led Nasser to fire Hassanein and the project was placed under the jurisdiction of Marei's Ministry of Agrarian Reform. Thus, at least for the moment, Marei became the undisputed decisionmaker in the areas of land reform and land reclamation. Wasting no time in dismantling the collective farm system, he distributed lands in the province to four hundred peasant families in July 1958. Finally, in April 1961, as minister of agriculture, he announced that private ownership would be extended to all the Tahrir lands.

Marei's ascendancy did not last long. In 1961, after the cotton worm disaster, partly caused by his negligence, Marei was dismissed as minister. In addition he was charged with lax accounting practices. This was an opportunity for the military, loyalist officers, and the chiefs of the army to reestablish control over the area's land reclamation policy.

During the 1950s, Ali Sabri, Sami Sharaf, and Abdel Mohsen Abu el Nur, all loyalist officers with an intelligence background, were gaining prominence in the regime. The officers resented Marei's rapid ascendance in the agricultural sector and worked to undermine Nasser's confidence in civilian technocrats. Their influence was restored when Nasser appointed Abu el Nur to follow Marei as minister of agriculture and land reclamation in 1961. In July 1962, Tahrir Province became a public authority independent from the Ministry of Agrarian Reform, which Marei still led.

The rise in political power of the army chief, Field Marshal Amer, was a crucial factor in development of land tenure policy. During the 1950s Amer established such firm control over the military that not even Nasser would challenge him. Amer became interested in the numerous land reclamation agencies, where well-paid positions could easily be created to which his clients could be appointed. Thus an interest group was created with Amer as its patron. The group had a strong private interest in pressing the government to reclaim ever-increasing tracts of land. The land could be turned into either private or state farms. The military chose the second alternative, not because of the ideological bent of the officers; it had everything to do with their career interest. The officers, in general, were politically conservative and some of them, including Amer, were even landowners. But if the reclaimed land had been distributed to peasant farmers, administrative authority over it would have been transferred to the Ministry of Agrarian Reform under Marei. The officers' interest in state farms emerged with the rise of Arab socialism after the July 1961 nationalization decrees and the 1962 Charter. In July 1962, an officer who was director of reclamation in Wadi el Natrun even set up a training camp to form cadres dedicated to state farming of reclaimed lands. The camp was supposed in four months to train three thousand youths who would then spread their political, social, and intellectual knowledge to all villages and farms.

A general swing to state ownership in Egypt's land tenure system did not, however, materialize—Nasser put a brake on the rapid shift to the left. Nasser had always been an enthusiastic supporter of private ownership in agriculture. Internally his policy of governing the country was based on the principle of divide and rule. To balance the increasing power of Amer and to neutralize the state ownership forces, he accepted a proposal by a conservative minister of agriculture in 1962 to set up a special ministerial committee responsible for agricultural policies, including that of reclaimed lands. Nasser thereby balanced opposing groups in the membership of the committee, and the result was a stalemate in decisions pertaining to land tenure policy. Thus, state farming after all continued on reclaimed land areas.

The conservative forces suffered a sudden eclipse when Nasser reshuffled his cabinet abruptly in March 1964. The power of the loyalist officers was now evident. Ali Sabri was made prime minister and Abu el Nur was promoted to deputy prime minister, with responsibility for agriculture, reclamation, and irrigation. A pro-Sabri leftist replaced the conservative minister of agriculture. The Syndicate of Agricultural Engineers, which had been a strong critic of the reclamation policy, was neutralized when the pro-Sabri forces succeeded in making one of their clients president of the syndicate in 1965. Professional agricultural journals were brought under the jurisdiction of the Arab Socialist Union, led by Sabri. Egypt's dependence on the Soviet Union was also on the increase. Nikita Khrushchev visited Egypt in May 1964 and, touring Tahrir Province, lectured Nasser on the advantages of setting up state farms on the reclaimed land. Soon it was announced that the Soviet Union would assist in the reclamation of ten thousand more *feddan* in the northern sector of Tahrir Province and help create a model state farm.

Just when it seemed that the private ownership proponents were on the retreat, Nasser again stepped in. General Authority for the Utilization and Development of Reclaimed Lands was created in 1966 with jurisdiction over the reclaimed land. It was headed by a civilian technocrat. The new organization enabled Nasser to control the activities of Sabri and Amer in the field of land reclamation.

The 1967 War had two effects on land reclamation. Amer was discredited and soon died and the army was reorganized, while Sabri's influence, especially in the ASU, increased. This meant again a strengthening of the pro-state voices in land reclamation policies. To counterbalance Sabri's dominance, Nasser appointed conservative ministers, including Marei, in the area of agriculture. A few days after Marei returned to the cabinet, he brought up the issue of distributing the land in South Tahrir Province to peasants. Other technocrats complained of the inefficiency of state farms, arguing that rational cost accounting and not ideology should be the basis for evaluating land tenure. Nasser took a middle-of-the-road approach; he proposed that some of the reclaimed land be distributed to peasants, some be rented to individuals and companies, and the rest be farmed by the state.

Sabri considered Nasser's proposal a sell-out and while on a trip to Moscow he voiced his criticism of Nasser to Soviet authorities. When the news of Sabri's maneuver reached Nasser, the punishment was swift. Sabri was arrested on a smuggling charge on his return and dismissed from his post in the ASU. The Soviet Union, however, demanded reinstatement of Sabri as part of the price for their involvement in Egypt's War of Attrition after 1967. Nasser gave in. Sabri was made secretary of a new foreign affairs committee in the ASU. This incident may be an indication that Nasser's ability to perform balancing acts had severely declined.

By the summer of 1970, it was rumored that state farms would be declared the sole form of cultivation on the reclaimed lands and that a new agrarian reform law would declare that all land confiscated through the three agrarian reforms since 1952 would be converted to state farms. The death of Nasser and the rise to power of Sadat brought an end to those rumors.

State ownership of land was incompatible with Sadat's declared objective of encouraging the private sector and limiting government expansion. The new president's stand in favor of the private sector won him the support of conservative landowners as well as the Syndicate of Agricultural Engineers. The syndicate enjoyed new freedom under Sadat and virtually all its members opposed state farming. They also welcomed their increasing role in decisionmaking through serving on bureaucratic and parliamentary committees but they were deeply divided on policy. Some agronomists favored the cooperative mode of the agrarian reform; a large number favored auctioning, selling, or leasing the land. One group called for an approach where scattered pieces of reclaimed land were to be sold, but large tracts of consolidated land would be offered for rent for ten or fifteen years.

In October 1971, the Ministry of Agriculture announced that the General Organization for Utilization and Development of Reclaimed Land, responsible for about 330,000 *feddan* of reclaimed land under cultivation by the state, was to be broken up into eleven independent companies. It seemed, for the moment, that the agrobusiness model had succeeded.

But powerful persons resisted, protesting against the long time lags before production could begin. The real reason for their opposition apparently was that land would not be privately sold under the agrobusiness model. Persons interested in land speculation and politically influential under Sadat suggested that the land be put to "good use" immediately.

Sadat opportunistically chose to make everybody happy. A sizable portion of the reclamation areas was distributed to pressure groups whose support Sadat needed. The Syndicate of Agricultural Engineers was rewarded with 100,000 *feddan* in South Tahrir Province and at Lake Mariot. Those who favored agrarian reform were appeased with the distribution of several large tracts of reclaimed land to peasants, each of whom received 3–5 *feddan* and the compulsory agricultural cooperative membership card. Part of the reclaimed land was sold to the highest bidders. Survivors of the 1973 War received 10,000 *feddan*. Other beneficiaries included oasis dwellers in the New Valley and residents of Wadi el Natrun. In short, the agrobusiness model did not take root and by 1975 only three of the eleven companies had been formed. Undoubtedly, the long time required for the execution of the agrobusiness model was not compatible with Sadat's political agenda. One outcome of the policy is that many of the beneficiaries (individuals and private companies) have not used their land for cultivation. The new absentee landlords have apparently kept their land for speculative purposes. Under Mubarak and the comeback of the military, land reclamation has, once more, become a favored policy, again mainly for the spoils it offers.

Agricultural Cooperatives

While financial and commercial cooperatives were not unknown in Egyptian agriculture before the coup, with the land reforms of 1952 and later, production cooperatives began to be formed. By the mid-1960s they were compulsory for all private, personal holdings in agriculture.

After the Land Reform Law of 1952, confiscated and otherwise acquired land was distributed to peasants, mostly to old tenants who now became small owners and to small holders to bring their ownership up to a minimal size. The distributed lands were sold on very favorable financial terms corresponding to the nominal compensation given to the previous owners. The land reform areas were consolidated in estates and farmers were given compulsory membership in cooperatives. The administration was from the beginning under the leadership of Sayed Marei, an important participant in the land reclamation carousel. The basic idea of the cooperatives was to enforce rational crop rotation and to combine the cooperative's economies of scale in irrigation and in soil preparation with small-scale manual- and animal-powered cultivation from sowing to harvest. The cooperative would provide seed, fertilizer, pesticides, and credit and help with marketing. This ingenious organizational form (Saab 1967), adapted from the British Gezira project at the bifurcation of the Nile in Sudan (Gaitskell 1959), appears to have been economically efficient in the areas where it was first applied under Marei's skillful leadership (Saab 1967, M. Riad el Ghonemy in Vatikiotis 1968). Encouraged by the apparent success, the government decided to expand the system to agriculture generally. Pilot projects covering two provinces were claimed also to be successful although no evidence was presented, and in 1964 the system became compulsory for all villages in Egypt.

The system has not proved successful. Administered by incompetent and unmotivated bureaucrats, and overstaffed by graduates with guaranteed employment, it has offered mechanized and extension services of poor quality and its inputs (particularly credit) have more often than not served the interests of better-off farmers (Adams 1985). Its use by the central government to enforce cultivation and delivery of crops, at unprofitable government-controlled prices, has not contributed to the popularity or the efficiency of the cooperatives. The politics surrounding the cooperatives may have been less byzantine than those of the land reclamation projects, mainly because ordinary civil servants with ordinary pay and advancement standards managed the cooperative system and it was thus not particularly attractive for clients in the military or civilian *shillas*. Yet the cooperatives have been politically controversial. Attempts to develop the system in the direction of Soviet-style collective farming have not been successful, however. The system is now mainly a public employment outlet.

Public Enterprises

From 1952 until the Suez War in 1956, industrialization policy centered on private entrepreneurship. The government invested in a few heavy industries—iron and steel, for instance—but otherwise modernization and industrialization were largely left to private enterprise under increased protection with tax and credit incentives. Foreign capital was offered more favorable treatment than under earlier Egyptianization efforts. A Production Council was set up in 1954 to appraise certain large-scale, capital-intensive industries for which joint private-government ventures were contemplated. The results were not encouraging. The recession after the Korean War boom and land reform had a negative effect on private investment and private entrepreneurs generally looked on the activities of the junta with suspicion.

That French and British interests in Egypt were sequestered during the Suez War is hardly surprising. The majority of the sequestered enterprises were banks or businesses active in finance and insurance. These enterprises were organized under a semipublic company, the Economic Organization, which also was made responsible for new projects under the first industrial five-year plan of 1957. The plan was worked out by the newly established Ministry of Industry under Aziz Sidky, a civilian loyalist and client of Nasser who played a key role in the industrialization program of the first comprehensive five-year plan for 1960–61 to 1964–65.

Sequestrations and nationalizations of the property of real or imagined political opponents of the junta did, however, take place from the very beginning of its rule. The case of Ahmed Aboud and the sugar company in 1955 is the best known example. In 1960 the Bank Misr Group, which controlled the largest industrial enterprises in the country, particularly in textiles, was nationalized. These and other enterprises were then supervised by two new government holding companies, the El Nasr and Misr organizations. About one-fifth of modern industrial output may at that time have been produced in public enterprises.

Sweeping nationalizations in July 1961 and in 1963 brought a majority of large- and medium-sized private enterprises in both manufacturing and trade under government ownership. Large-scale sequestrations in November 1961 of the property of hand-picked wealthy families completed the process, which effectively destroyed the modern entrepreneurial class. Compensations were nominal. The nationalized enterprises were consolidated into about one hundred and sixty joint stock companies (so-called *moassassa ama*) and placed under the control of eleven general organizations attached to various ministries. The Ministry of Industry controlled the major part of modern manufacturing industry. Price and wage controls combined with an employment drive converted what had been profitable industries under private ownership into loss-making public enterprises. Output targets were planned for each plant at the same time that profits and productivity were upheld as efficiency criteria. The public enterprises were thus clearly faced with contradictory objectives and saddled with rapidly growing bureaucracies. Boards of directors were filled with military clients. A series of presidential decrees completed the centralization process.

Under Sadat, decentralization of public enterprises became part of the *infitah*. The general organizations were abolished in 1976 and, in principle, managers were given greater autonomy over current production while boards of directors were given some discretion in matters related to employment, wages, and prices. Practically, little changed, however, and ultimate decisionmaking remained in the hands of the minister in charge and his bureaucracy. Under Mubarak the status quo prevailed until 1983 when a number of holding organizations (*hayaat ama*) were created to hold publicly owned equity in public enterprises. It is not clear whether this reorganization shifted decisionmaking more effectively into the hands of management.

Little is known about the details of the process of investment planning for new industrial enterprises. The Ministry of Industry under Sidky and his followers has remained a black box, from which even Nasser had great difficulty in obtaining information. The ministry has been charged with trying to please Nasser by accelerating the number of projects started—public announcements of new projects and preferably coinciding with the annual celebrations of the 1952 coup—letting unfinished projects accumulate. It has further been charged with paying little attention to economic profitability, ignoring project evaluation, disregarding problems of economies of scale, preferring capital-intensive projects, ignoring location problems, estimating import substitution on the basis of gross rather than net savings of foreign exchange, ignoring export opportunities, emphasizing consumer goods for the higher income brackets, leaving details of planning to foreign suppliers, and operating with unrealistic cost and price estimates. These are standard accusations against industrial planners in developing countries, and they may very well be justified in the case of Egypt; little concrete evidence, however, is available.

Urban Land and Real Estate

It is a peculiar feature of policy under Nasser and later leaders that urban real estate, including land, has largely remained under private ownership. In the sequestrations and nationalizations as well as in fully compensated normal expropriations for public purposes (roads and government buildings, for instance), some urban real estate must have become public property. But systematic attempts were never made to bring urban real estate under public ownership. The explanation may be the rent controls (which originated during World War I) that have kept rents of existing urban dwellings and office space at increasingly absurd low levels. When controls were introduced, urban rents were frozen at existing levels (and during the 1960s even lowered) while rents on new buildings were fixed at actual cost plus a normal (low) profit margin. With tenants protected against eviction and rental contracts automatically taken over by resident heirs, this implies a policy of virtual confiscation and redistribution of urban property rights from owners to tenants without compensation. There is no official rationing of dwellings or office space.

The effects of urban rent control have been a disastrous deterioration of repair and maintenance, often voluntarily carried out by tenants just to make apartments and office buildings habitable, and a catastrophic shortage of urban housing, with black market rentals, key money, and similar practices flourishing. Urban land values and land rents have soared, particularly in downtown areas, in accord with von Thünen's Law. There is no control on land prices (urban or rural) or on urban land rentals, and all real estate is traded freely. It is very easy (if need be through bribery) to obtain permission to add floors to buildings. Cairo and Alexandria are filled with buildings with five or six floors added on top of three to seven old floors; not infrequently, buildings collapse. Though rentals of new apartments or office space are subject to control, space may be rented furnished without controls or sold freely as condominiums. Old buildings may be converted into condominiums, if necessary with the consent of the tenant, who shares the capital gain with the owner. With urban areas expanding rapidly into agricultural and desert land, the price of such land is reflected in the rentals of new dwellings approved by the authorities, possibly through bribery. The Pyramid road in Giza is a sad example.

Urban land rentals and urban real estate values tend to lag behind hypothetical free market prices but they actually have increased rapidly. With about 45 percent of the population living in urban areas, urban land rents may now be even more important, because of their effect on technology and income distribution, than agricultural land rents. This may be why members of the old landowning classes increasingly appear among the nouveaux riches.

Even before World War I, and increasingly between the wars and during the Great Depression, big landowners shifted their wealth from rural to urban real estate. Thus they fortuitously escaped the consequences of land reforms and nationalizations (but not sequestrations, although some sequestered urban property has been handed back to the old owners under both Sadat and Mubarak).

Development Strategies and Planning

The 1918 strategy of balanced development of agriculture and industry, with export promotion in agriculture and import substitution in industry, has never explicitly been thrown out. Nevertheless, import substitution has come to dominate both agriculture and industry, and export promotion practically speaking has been limited to petroleum, the Suez Canal, and tourism. It was part and parcel of the 1918 strategy that industrialization should solve the employment problem. In the early 1960s the government apparently continued to view industrialization as the key to the employment problem but soon public employment and migration of labor became the practical solutions. With the advent of modern planning, institutionalized in the form of a Ministry of Planning and the emergence of national accounting statistics, both development targets and policies became more specific than they had been.

Formal agricultural and industrial planning was initiated in 1957 but a comprehensive five-year plan was not drawn up until 1959, for the years 1960–61 to 1964–65. The plan assumed a doubling of national income in ten years, implying a growth rate of 7.2 percent annually. An investment–GNP ratio of 18 percent was assumed, with about one-third of the investment financed from abroad on concessionary terms.

Foreign exchange shortages and the Yemen War prompted the government to cancel a second five-year plan in favor of a three-year plan mainly composed of unfinished projects from the first five-year plan. With the 1967 War, military strategy became a first priority. A ten-year plan or projection for 1972–82, again assuming a growth rate of 7.2 percent, was adopted in 1972.

Since 1973 several plans or projections have been prepared in the Ministry of Planning. Sadat's October Paper of 1974 called for a five-year plan for 1976–80. It assumed a growth rate of about 6.5 percent, with foreign financing coming to an end in 1978. These plans have hardly been more than paper tigers. Parliament under Mubarak adopted a five-year development plan for 1982–83 to 1986–87 that was considered the law of the land. It assumed a GDP growth rate of 8.1 percent, an investment rate increasing from 24 percent to 27 percent of GDP, a domestic saving rate increasing from 15 percent to 24 percent of GDP (hence the external deficit going down from 9 percent to 3 percent of GDP), and private investment increasing from about 8 percent of total investment in the mid-1970s to 15 percent in 1982–83 and 24 percent in 1986–87. Achievements fell considerably short of plans—indeed the plan was a complete failure as table 1–1 illustrates. A five-year plan for 1987–88 to 1991–92 assumed a more modest growth rate of 5.8 percent, with investment ratios of 18.5 percent in 1986–87 and 17.7 percent in 1991–92. Since this plan in considerable detail discussed reform needed in the Egyptian economy, a critical review is presented at the end of this chapter. The annual budgets, with occasional stabilization plans, have always been the main instruments of policy planning.

The centerpiece of the agricultural development strategy of the new regime was the Aswan High Dam which, with its electrical power station, also was to contribute to industrial development. The dam was the final stage in the regulation of the Nile initiated by Mohammed Ali in the first half of the nineteenth century and continued under Ismail (1861–79), the British (1882–1923), and Egyptian governments from 1923 through 1952. Thus, it did not signify new directions in Egyptian development policy. It put the final touches to a century of green revolution.

Both export promotion (cotton and rice) and import substitution (cereals and meat), as well as production of nontraded goods (electricity), were involved. Social profitability was expected to be high because of the natural advantages that could be exploited. After 1973, import substitution was stressed; by administrative order, the acreage planted in cotton was reduced and production of cereals and animal feed and products increased. This shift toward import substitution was a response to increasing domestic demand, government price policies, a hodgepodge of philosophies of self-sufficiency, and uncertainties related to international embargoes and sanctions. It was made possible by the expansion of foreign exchange earnings from petroleum, the Suez Canal, tourism, and workers' remittances. The shift toward import substitution in agriculture was not a matter of investment policy but of current production policy. Agricultural production may at any time be shifted back to socially profitable export crops, and even from a short-term point of view, there was nothing irreversible about the agricultural import substitution policy.

Industrialization (manufacturing) was to be pushed more strongly by the new regime than previously had been the case but in fact never became a primary concern. The first five-year plan 1960–61 to 1964–65 did envisage exports in case the home market was unable to absorb the full-capacity production of the planned investments but, clearly, no deliberate export promotion was involved. The basic investment criterion in industry continued to be domestic demand. Social profitability was never considered in industrial planning.

The Suez Canal, petroleum, and tourism became the big export industries after 1973. The benefits from these industries are frequently referred to as windfalls or externalities. The characterization is somewhat misleading. While, of course, the oil price increases in 1973 and 1979 were windfalls from an Egyptian point of view, considerable investments were made in exploring oil deposits, in widening and deepening the canal, and in building hotels and other tourist facilities. That these investments are socially profitable only shows that Egypt to some extent actually did invest where natural advantages existed. Oil, though, will not last forever, not even for the foreseeable future, and thus cannot be viewed as a long-term solution.

Population and Employment

The 1918 strategy acknowledged the problem of population growth; indeed, the modest growth rate of 1.2 percent was one of its major concerns. Yet no specific population policy was envisaged. Not until 1952, when the population growth rate was around 2.5 percent, was a commission formed to study the problem. In 1955 the first family planning clinics were opened, a council for family planning was formed in 1965, and from 1966 public health units in urban and rural areas distributed contraceptives. The popular response was not impressive and Islamic and Christian leaders privately advised their flocks against birth control. The population growth rate fell slightly during the war years 1967–73 but accelerated after 1973 and reached a high level of 2.9 percent in 1979. It seems that while education has tended to reduce fertility rates in the higher-income brackets, the increase in the standard of living for the uneducated, low-income classes during the 1970s has had the opposite effect. (This is what should be expected, according to the standard theory of demographic transition.)

National income growth rates increased strongly during the first decade of the Nasser regime, from the Suez War to the end of the first five-year plan, and then fell back again to very low levels during 1967–73. They surged to impressive levels in the 1970s but slowed, even stagnated in the 1980s (table 1-1). Higher population growth rates absorbed some of the increase in income growth. Per capita income growth thus rose from 1.4 percent in 1939–55 to 4.1 percent in 1960–65, fell back to 1.1 percent in 1965–73, and then accelerated to 4.7 percent in 1973 to 1981–82. It may have fallen to zero in 1982–83 to 1986–87 and even have become negative in 1986–87. Needless to say, the strong swings in the growth rate from the late 1950s to the 1980s were not the outcome of deliberate long-term growth planning and policy. Table 3–2 demonstrates how, by 1960, the 1918 strategy had to be considered a complete failure in terms of employment. In line with expectations, agricultural employment measured as a share of the labor force declined somewhat, from 67.5 percent in 1927 to 56.3 percent in 1960; employment in manufacturing during the same period increased only from 8.1 percent to 9.1 percent, while services (including government) increased from 9.8 percent to 20.3 percent. Tables 4–2 and 4–3 show a continued relative decline in agricultural employment to 43.8 percent in 1976 (population census [PC] data) and further from 54.2 percent in 1971 to 42.4 percent in 1980 (labor force survey [LFS] data), with employment in manufacturing now increasing somewhat from 8.3 percent in 1960 to 12.3 percent in 1976 (PC data) and from 12.5 percent in 1971 to 14.7 percent in 1980 (LFS data). Services declined a little from 17.0 percent in 1960 to 16.8 percent in 1976 (PC data) but then increased from 15.4 percent in 1971 to 20.2 percent in 1980 (LFS data). For the latter period, however, it should be recalled that after the oil price boost in 1973 some 10–15 percent of the labor force found employment in Arab Organization of Petroleum Exporting Countries (OPEC) countries as migrants, mostly on a temporary basis, families mainly remaining in Egypt. Those workers are not included in tables 4–2 and 4–3. Military conscripts, about 1 percent of the labor force in 1960, 4 percent after 1970, are included in table 4–2 with unknown distribution but are not included in table 4–3. Taking into account first conscripts and then migrants, we can schematically describe the development of the distribution of employed members of the labor force as follows from table 4-4.

Distinguishing between resident and total labor force, the latter including (conjectured) temporary migrants, the distributions of the resident labor force in 1960 and 1980 are based on population census and labor force surveys, respectively, which we shall assume are comparable for the present purpose. The distribution of the resident labor force in 1980 is then obtained by including the number of conscripts, included in the 1960 PC with unknown distribution but not included in the 1980 LFS. The distribution of the total labor force in 1980 is thereafter ob-

Table 4-2. Employment of Resident Labor Force, Six Years and above, by Economic Sector, 1960 and 1976

Sector	Number employed (thousands)		Annual compound growth rates (percent)	Share of total (percent)		Increase 1960-76	
	1960	1976		1960	1976	Number (thousands)	Share of total (percent)
Agriculture	4,406.3	4,881.0	0.6	56.3	43.8	474.7	14.4
Mining and quarrying	21.2	33.8	3.0	0.3	0.3	12.6	0.4
Manufacturing	647.2	1,369.5	4.7	8.3	12.3	722.3	21.9
Electricity and gas	16.9	61.8	8.3	0.2	0.6	44.9	1.4
Construction	158.9	425.1	6.3	2.0	3.8	266.2	8.1
Trade	690.8	861.3	1.4	8.8	7.7	170.5	5.2
Transport and communications	260.2	482.3	3.9	3.3	4.3	222.1	6.7
Finance	72.5	88.4	1.2	0.9	0.8	15.9	0.5
Services	1,333.3	1,868.3	2.1	17.0	16.8	535.0	16.2

Not adequately described[a]	224.7	1,060.2	10.1	2.9	9.5	835.5	25.3
Total[b]	7,832.0	11,131.7	2.2	100	100	3,299.7	100
Government portion of total[c]	(288.9)[d]	1,779.0[j]	(12.9)[f]	(3.7)[h]	16.0	(1,490.1)[d]	(45.2)
	(932.9)[e]		(6.3)[g]	(11.9)[i]		(846.1)	(25.6)

a. Includes unemployed.
b. Includes military conscripts.
c. Excludes military conscripts and public enterprise employees, both of which are reported in all sectors.
d. For 1961; comparability with 1976 figure is doubtful.
e. A special tabulation for 1976 gives a total for employees in government of 1,840,500; this figure includes a few employees in foreign embassies and enterprises and is thus not fully consistent with the figures in the table.
f. For 1961–76; at best an upper limit.
g. Based on 1961 figure.
h. For 1965–66; comparable with 1976 figure and probably higher than the unknown 1960 figure.
i. For 1965–66 to 1975; probably a lower limit.
j. Based on 1965–66 figure.
Source: Hansen and Radwan (1982), table 11.

Table 4-3. Employment of Resident Labor Force Twelve to Sixty-five Years Old, by Economic Sector, 1971 and 1980

| Sector | Number employed (thousands) | | Annual compound growth rate (percent) | Share of total (percent) | | Increase, 1971–80 | | |
	1971	1980		1971	1980	Number (thousands)	Share of total (percent)	Share of total outside agriculture (percent)
Agriculture	4,469.5	4,151.9	-0.8	54.2	42.4	-317.6	-20.5	—
Mining and quarrying	7.2	19.9	3.6	0.1	0.2	12.7	0.8	0.7
Manufacturing	1,030.2	1,439.0	3.8	12.5	14.7	409.0	26.5	21.9
Electricity and gas	25.8	83.2	13.9	0.3	0.8	57.4	3.7	3.1
Construction	193.2	425.6	9.2	2.3	4.3	232.4	15.0	12.5
Trade	797.4	884.3	1.2	9.7	9.0	86.9	5.6	4.7
Transport and communications	323.1	503.3	5.1	3.9	5.1	180.2	11.7	9.7
Finance	83.2	126.8	4.8	1.0	1.3	43.6	2.8	2.3
Services	1,268.7	1,981.8	5.1	15.4	20.2	713.1	46.1	38.3
Unspecified	54.2	183.3	14.5	0.7	1.9	129.1	8.4	6.9
Total[a]	8,252.5	9,799.1	1.9	100	100	1,546.6	100	100
Government portion of total[a,b]	1,270.5	2,489.8	7.3	15.4	25.4	1,219.3	78.8	—
Total labor force	8,405.6	10,335.0	2.3	100.0	100.0	1,929.4	100.0	—
Unemployed	153.1	535.9	14.9	1.8	5.2	382.8	19.8	—

— = Not applicable.
a. Excluding military conscripts.
b. Excluding public enterprises and authorities.
Source: Hansen and Radwan (1982) table 12; World Bank data.

Table 4-4. Distribution of Employed Labor Force, 1960 and 1980
(percent)

Category	*Employed labor force*			*Change in share of total, 1960–80*
	Total, 1960[a]	*Resident, 1980*	*Total, 1980*	
Agriculture	56.3	40.6	35.3	−21.0
Industry	8.3	14.0	12.2	3.9
Construction	2.0	4.2	3.7	1.7
Services	17.0	19.3	16.8	− 0.2
Other activities	16.4	17.4	15.1	− 1.3
Conscripts	[b]	4.4	3.8	3.8[c]
Migrants	0	0	13.0	13.0
Total	100.0	100.0	100.0	0
Government share of total[d]	11.0[e]	24.3	21.1	10.1

a. Resident labor force equals total.
b. About 1 percent, included in other sectors, distribution unknown.
c. Considering conscripts in 1960, about 2.8 percent.
d. Apparent positions or filled positions, including employees on leave for temporary migration.
e. Based on 1965–66 data; this is probably on the high side.
Source: Tables 4–2 and 4–3.

tained by assuming migrants to be 15 percent of the resident labor force. The actual distribution of the resident labor force, in 1980 does not, of course, tell us what the distribution of the total labor force would have been had no migration or increase in conscription taken place. What table 4–4 shows is that, compared with 1960, by 1980 a relative decline in agricultural employment by 21 percentage points was matched by an increase of about 16 points in migrants (13 points) and conscripts (about 3 points), 5.5 points in industry (4 points) and construction (1.5 points), with services and other activities (trade, transport, finance) declining slightly. This picture is interesting because it points to a strong decline by some 17 percentage points of employment in activities producing tradables with an almost unchanged number of points going to employment in activities producing nontradables, the difference being made up of direct export of labor—migrants. In this sense, it would thus seem that there has been no shift in employment toward production of nontradables.

The problem is, however, how we fit government employment into this picture. With migrants, government (including conscripts) has been the great employment outlet since 1960. The 10.1 percent of total employed labor force with which government has grown since 1960 is somehow included in the other sectors and we are facing a statistical puzzle. In 1960 (where conscripts are a minor problem) the services sector contained 17 percent of the total labor force while the government employed (at most) 11.0 percent. It stands to reason that most government employees were counted in the services sector. By 1980 the services sector had shrunk slightly to 16.8 percent while the government sector had increased to 21.1 percent, thus having become considerably larger than the services sector. The explanation is probably, first, that the proportion of government employees in the services sector was much larger in 1980 than in 1960. With the expansion of the public sector many services (education, health) were transferred from the private to the public sector. In addition, substantial numbers of self-employed professionals and household workers (maids, cooks, and so forth) migrated temporarily. Second, large numbers of government employees in consumer and agricultural cooperatives or in agricultural extension services may be counted in trade or agriculture. And many government employees have second jobs, for instance as farmers (Radwan and Lee 1986; Commander and Hadhoud 1986), and may be counted in the sector of the second job. Finally, substantial numbers of government employees, on leave from their permanent jobs, have migrated temporarily. Thus there may after all have been a considerable shift from employment in production of tradable goods (including direct labor export) toward production of nontradable goods. It is impossible to quantify this shift (if it really has taken place).

Shifts of employment out of agriculture are under normal circumstances an important growth factor. This has undoubtedly been the case in Egypt since 1960 if remittances from migrant workers are included in national income as income produced by Egyptians. Even assuming zero productivity in government, the productivity (from an Egyptian point of view) of migrant workers is so many times higher than that of agricultural labor that the net must have been a substantial increase in productivity per worker. Actual employment developments between 1960 and 1980 were radically at odds with employment strategies from 1918 to the first five-year plan of 1960–61 to 1964–65.

Trade

The development strategy chosen in 1918 called for trade diversification to avoid the risks and uncertainties of being a one-crop exporter, with import substitution in the form of industrialization to reduce the dependency on imports and create employment. This trade strategy survived all political developments in the interwar period and the 1950s and the overthrow of democracy by autocracy. Not even the five-year plan for 1982–83 to 1986–87 made any change in the strategy.

Diversification of exports has not been obtained, however. From being a one-crop exporter depending almost exclusively on raw cotton, Egypt has developed into another one-commodity exporter depending almost as singularly on petroleum, an exhaustible resource that will not last long and with risks and uncertainties that, if anything, exceed those related to cotton. Table 4–5 shows that raw cotton constituted 85.4 percent of total commodity exports in 1950 and petroleum 81.2 percent in 1983–84. In 1950, only 9 percent of total exports were industrial goods (petroleum export at that time being negligible); in 1983–84 the figure was the same. From the percentage distribution it might seem that considerable diversification was reached around 1970, with raw cotton accounting for 41–45 percent of total exports, petroleum 11 percent, and industrial products 30 percent. This, however, is an illusion, created by a very strong decline in raw cotton exports rather than by an increase in industrial exports. When the individual commodity groups are viewed as a percentage of GNP, raw cotton dropped from 16 percent of GNP to less than 5 percent in 1970. Industrial goods in those years were around 2 percent of GNP. In 1983–84 raw cotton had declined to less than 2 percent of GNP and petroleum was at 16 percent. Total commodity exports declined strongly in relative terms, from 19 percent of GNP in 1950 to 12 percent in 1970, and then increased to 20 percent in 1983–84. Excluding petroleum, however, the decline was dramatic, from about 19 percent in 1950 to 4 percent in 1983–84. Egypt thus reached a point where exports of commodities, agricultural and manufactured, were negligible. This development has, of course, to be judged against the background of strongly increasing service exports, Suez Canal traffic, and tourism as well as workers' remittances from abroad.

For commodity imports the strategy adopted since 1918 should in principle have implied a relative decline in processed and manufactured consumer goods with a relative increase in raw materials and capital goods. This seems to have happened since 1930 (figure 3–1 and table 4–6). Food and other consumer goods imports declined from 45 percent of total imports in 1950 to 39 percent in 1983–84, according to table 4–6, and capital goods rose from 15 percent to 26 percent. Raw materials declined from about 40 percent to 34 percent of total imports but if cereals and flour were moved from the group food to raw materials the decline would change to a slight relative increase in raw materials imports with a much stronger decline in consumer goods imports. Yet it is the relative increase in capital goods imports that dominates the picture. It occurred mainly around 1960 with the first five-year plan but accelerated somewhat in the late 1970s and the 1980s.

Measuring the absolute and relative size of total commodity imports throws up disturbing data problems. Official Egyptian trade statistics originate from two sources, the customs authority and the exchange control authority, which creates problems on both the export and the import side. For many reasons data from these two sources may differ. The differences may partly be random and tend to cancel each other

Table 4-5. Composition of Commodity Exports, Selected Years, 1950–84

Year	Cotton	Rice	Fruits and vegetables	Cotton textiles	Petroleum	Industrial goods	Total	Exports as a share of GNP
Millions of Egyptian pounds								Percent
1950	149.8	7.6	2.3	4.0	a	11.7	175.4	19.1
1955	107.4	7.3	4.5	7.4	a	11.7	138.3	13.3
1960	134.7	9.8	9.5	18.9	a	18.7	191.6	13.5
1965	146.7	19.8	12.4	47.0	a	37.6	263.1	11.3
1970	147.8	34.2	29.0	53.7	a	66.5	331.2	11.0
1970	147.8	34.3	28.3	61.7	40.0	45.2	357.4	11.9
1974	278.9	39.8	39.1	109.0	98.0	76.2	641.0	15.8
1978	131.3	19.9	67.2	138.7	493.0	133.6	983.6	9.0
1983–84	374.0	13.0	139.5	186.0	4,222.3	266.0	5,200.9	20.2

138

Percent of total

1950	85.4	4.3	1.3	2.3	a	6.7	100.0	—
1955	77.7	5.3	3.2	5.4	a	8.4	100.0	—
1960	70.3	5.1	5.0	9.9	a	9.7	100.0	—
1965	55.6	7.5	4.7	17.9	a	14.3	100.0	—
1970	44.7	10.3	8.8	16.2	a	20.1	100.0	—
1970	41.4	9.6	7.9	17.3	11.2	12.7	100.0	—
1974	43.5	6.2	6.1	17.0	15.3	11.9	100.0	—
1978	13.4	2.0	6.8	14.1	50.1	13.6	100.0	—
1983–84	7.2	0.3	2.7	3.6	81.2	5.1	100.0	—

Percent of GNP

1950	16.3	0.8	0.3	0.4	a	1.3	19.1	—
1970[b]	4.9	1.1	0.9	2.1	1.3	1.5	11.9	—
1983–84	1.5	0.1	0.5	0.7	16.4	1.0	20.2	—

— = Not applicable.

a. Included in industrial goods.

b. Based on second row of 1970 figures.

Source: Hansen and Nashashibi (1975), table 1–4; World Bank data.

Table 4-6. Composition of Commodity Imports, Selected Years, 1950–84

Year	Food	Other consumer goods	Raw materials	Capital goods	Total Imports		Total as share of GNP	
					Customs authority	Exchange authority	Customs authority	Exchange authority
							Percent	
Millions of Egyptian pounds								
1950	50.2	48.4	88.1	31.8	218.5	—	23.9	—
1955	25.0	87.4	78.8	45.2	186.4	—	17.9	—
1960	47.9	32.6	88.7	55.8	225.1	269.0	15.8	18.9
1965	110.2	45.3	155.0	95.4	400.9	417.0	17.3	18.0
1970	72.6	32.4	129.5	107.5	342.0	—	—	—
1970	66.0	42.0	154.0	80.0	342.0	517.8	11.4	17.2
1974	598.0	146.0	479.0	191.0	—	1,413.0	—	34.8
1978	490.0	370.0	733.0	750.0	—	2,343.0	—	21.5
1983–84	2,017.0	1,584.0	3,817.0	2,871.0	—	10,288.0	—	39.9

Percent of total							
1950	23.0	22.2	40.3	14.6	100.0	—	—
1955	13.4	20.1	42.3	24.3	100.0	—	—
1960	21.3	14.5	39.4	24.8	100.0	—	—
1965	27.4	11.2	38.2	23.5	100.0	—	—
1970	21.2	9.5	37.8	31.4	100.0	—	—
1970	23.0	12.3	41.3	23.4	100.0	—	—
1974	28.9	13.0	41.8	16.3	—	100.0	—
1978	25.6	12.8	27.9	33.7	—	100.0	—
1983–84	28.2	11.3	34.3	26.2	—	100.0	—
Percent of GNP							
1950	5.5	5.3	9.6	3.5	23.9	—	—
1970ᵃ	2.2	1.4	5.1	2.7	11.4	17.2	—
1983–84	7.8	6.1	14.8	11.1	—	39.9	—

— = Not applicable.

a. Based on second row of 1970 figures.

Source: For 1950 to 1970, first row, Hansen and Nashashibi (1975), table 1–5; for 1970, second row, to 1983–84, World Bank data.

out over a number of years, but systematic differences—in methods of evaluation, for instance—cannot be ruled out. Although they are disturbingly large for some years, the annual differences for exports seem actually to be random. For imports that is the case until around 1967, after which the gap grows increasingly large, with the customs authority figure for 1973 only 58 percent of the exchange control figure. No good explanation of this huge, systematic statistical difference has been offered. Table 4–6 thus includes data from both authorities until 1970. In the following years, dollar estimates of the International Monetary Fund (IMF) and the International Bank for Reconstruction and Development (IBRD), apparently based on exchange control data, are converted into Egyptian pounds through average exchange rates as indicated by the IMF-IBRD. A third set of data, from the IMF *Balance of Payments Yearbook*, which appears to be reported directly by Egyptian authorities in terms of special drawing rights and converted into Egyptian pounds and then measured as a percentage of GNP by the IMF, is shown in table 4–7. Because nobody seems to have been able to reconcile these data (perhaps military imports and payments are part of the problem[4]), comparison of the three estimates may be useful. The export data (measured on GNP) in tables 4–5 and 4–7 agree fairly well, and the import data based on exchange authority statistics in table 4–6 also agree reasonably well with those in table 4–7 except for 1983 and 1983–84 where the difference is amazing (24.7 percent against 39.9 percent of GNP). The gap between customs authority and exchange control authority data in table 4–6 for 1970 is enormous (11.4 percent and 17.3 percent of GNP). To gauge long-term trends of imports on the basis of these wildly conflicting and widely fluctuating data is difficult, and the problem of military equipment makes it more so.

In 1950 both exports and imports were relatively high compared with GNP. This was the time of the Korean War boom with exceptional export prices; and it should probably be disregarded in discussing long-term trends. From 1955 to 1965, imports ran at 16–19 percent of GNP, judging from both sets of data. For 1970 the customs authority data show a strong decline to 11 percent of GNP with the exchange control data remaining at the level from 1955–65. Casual observation points to increasing shortages of imported consumer goods, raw materials, and parts during the 1960s, reaching serious proportions around 1970, which is in full agreement with the customs authority data. The exchange control data for 1970, indicating an unchanged level of imports, do not make sense insofar as civilian imports are concerned. The violent increase in 1974 reflects a radical change in the foreign exchange situation with empty inventories being filled and pent-up consumer demand beginning to be satisfied. For 1978 imports were much lower than in 1974 but they were still high by historical standards. And for 1983 and 1983–84 there was a strong increase with a big gap between data sets.

Table 4-7. Balance of Payments as a Share of GNP, Selected Years, 1950-83

(percent)

Item	1950	1960	1970	1974	1978	1983
Exports, goods	20.8	14.3	11.8	16.1	7.0	10.3
Exports, Suez Canal dues	2.9[a]	3.5	0	0	1.8	2.7
Exports, other services	1.4[b]	—	0.1	0.2	1.0	3.2
Exports, goods and nonfactor services	25.0	17.9	12.0	16.3	11.9	16.3
Imports, goods and nonfactor services	−25.3	−19.7	−17.8	−32.1	−20.2	−24.7
Net goods and nonfactor services	−0.3	−1.8	−5.8	−15.8	−8.3	−8.4
Interest, and dividends, net	−1.2[a]	0.1	−0.9	0.1	−2.7	−3.1
Migrants' remittances	—	—	—	2.6	6.4	9.2
Current account	−1.5	−1.7	−6.7[d]	−13.1[d]	−4.6[d]	−2.2[d]
Unrequited government transfers and exceptional financing	0	0	4.4	9.6	3.6	0.2

— = Not applicable.

a. Accruing to the Suez Canal Company.

b. British Army expenditure in Egypt.

c. Including Canal dues transferred abroad by Suez Canal Company.

d. Not including unrequited government transfers and exceptional financing.

Source: Hansen and Nashashibi (1975), 1950–67 table 1–3; for 1967–83 IMF, *Balance of Payments Yearbook.* For the overlapping year 1967, the two estimates, as a percentage of GNP, agree very well. Balance of payments estimates in United States dollars by Ministry of Finance, IMF, and IBRD for 1974 to 1983 agree fairly well until 1978. For later years, the United States dollars estimate operates with large transfers of profits abroad that seem to have no counterpart in the special drawing rights estimates of the *Balance of Payments Yearbook.*

Since the 1950s, to the best of my judgment, imports have shifted somewhat away from consumer goods toward capital goods, with raw material imports relatively unchanged. Imports measured as a percentage of GNP declined somewhat during the 1960s, with serious shortages at the time of the 1973 War. From 1974 onward, imports have run at relatively high levels. Also in this regard, the 1918 strategy has failed. Egypt has if anything become more dependent on imports. The cause of this failure is probably lax demand management (discussed later) rather than structural problems.

It appears from table 4-7 that the fall in commodity exports has been partly compensated by the increase in exports of other services (including tourism) from 1.4 percent of GNP in 1950 (mainly made up of British Army expenditures) to 3.2 percent in 1983. Suez Canel dues, which strongly increased after 1975 as compared with the years of closure, 1967–74, have declined relatively as compared with 1960, from 3.5 percent to 2.7 percent of GNP. In this sense the Suez Canal has not helped to improve the balance of payments since the nationalization itself, which, of course, improved exchange earnings substantially. Remittances from migrants, reaching 9.3 percent of GNP in 1983, on the other hand, have fully made up for the decline in commodity exports from 1950 to 1983.

Direction of Trade

Trade strategies are usually concerned with the size and composition of trade by commodities but may also consider direction of trade by countries or trade areas and geographical limitations on trade laid down in bilateral agreements and the like. Such considerations did not enter the 1918 strategies, when free global trade was assumed to be the normal case. Trade constraints have, however, played an important role for Egypt since World War II. Egypt had no bilateral trade agreements before the War, its first agreements being made in 1948 with the Soviet Union and France. By the end of 1953 no less than 55 percent of all foreign transactions, covering 90.8 percent of exports and 92.1 percent of imports, were made under bilateral agreements (Hansen and Nashashibi 1975, pp. 30, 43 ff.). With the liberalization of trade in the developed world, Egypt's bilateral trade lost some of its importance during the 1950s and by 1973 it had declined to 66 percent for exports and 40 percent for imports (World Bank data). Bilateral trade with Western Europe and the United States in 1973 had almost disappeared but it remained at 100 percent for Eastern Europe and the Soviet Union.

The strong shift in trade toward the communist countries that took place from the time of the Suez War of 1956 was of great consequence, as was the equally strong reversal in the late 1970s. This radical change in trade direction was, of course, a result of the international and military complications Egypt was involved in. The reversal was related to Sadat's shift in orientation of international policy. Albeit difficult to evaluate, these changes in the trade strategy may have had more profound effects on the Egyptian economy than any other aspect of trade policy since 1952. Capital goods and technology differ greatly between communist countries and Western industrialized countries, and quality and terms of trade may differ even more.

Table 4–8 shows the distribution of trade with developed market economies, communist countries, and developing, noncommunist countries. The country classifications are arbitrary, since they are kept unchanged from 1938 through 1984. The shift toward trade with the communist countries was more pronounced for exports than for (recorded) imports. While 59 percent of Egypt's exports went to developed market economies in 1952–54 and 15 percent to communist countries, this distribution had been reversed by 1968–73 and was reversed again in 1979–84. Imports from developed market economies always outran imports from communist countries. While Egypt has been running large deficits against the developed market economies during the whole postwar period, she ran surpluses against communist countries until the late 1970s. These surpluses were probably used to pay for military equipment that did not enter the customs statistics. In 1979–84 Egypt ran deficits even against communist countries.

Table 4–9 attempts to measure terms of trade developments for Egyptian trade with developed (market) countries and centrally planned (communist) countries for the years 1965 to 1985, following roughly the same country breakdown as table 4–8. The totals show a relative improvement in the terms of trade with centrally planned countries from 1965 to 1970 and the opposite development from 1970 to 1985. It would be tempting to relate these developments to the establishment of a client relationship with the Soviet Union under Nasser and the breakdown of this relationship under Sadat. The commodity grouping, however, warns against jumping to such conclusions. During this period, commodity composition changed strongly and individual commodity groups experienced systematic differences in terms of trade developments. The chained Fisher indexes should to some extent take care of such problems; nonetheless, the possibility of a technical fluke in the index should not be excluded.

The terms of trade for finished manufactured goods show a strong relative improvement for Egypt compared to centrally planned countries throughout the period, with exactly the opposite development for the other four groups, at least after 1975. It is not obvious why that should be the case. The fact, moreover, that Egyptian exports of finished manufactured goods to developed countries were very small and specialized over the whole period and that the same was true of such exports to centrally planned countries except between 1969 and 1978, when such exports were significant, indicates the possibility of a statistical fluke. For the period as a whole, however, Egypt's terms of trade with regard to developed countries improved strongly, with a deterioration for trade with centrally planned economies. The explanation probably lies in the fact that Egypt's oil exports mainly go to developed countries.

Investment Policy

Ever since 1918, Egyptian development strategies have emphasized physical and human capital as cornerstones of development. Investments in physical capital shown in table 4–10 illustrate the differences between the preplanning period, the first five-year plan 1960–61 to

Table 4–8. Distribution of Commodity Trade by Area, Selected Years, 1938–84
(amount in millions of dollars)

Trade, by area[a]	1938		1952–54		1958–60		1961–67		1968–73		1974–78		1979–84	
	Amount	Percent	Amount	Percent	Amount	Percent	Amount	Percent	Amount	Percent	Amount	Percent	Amount	Percent
Total														
Export	151.0	100.0	408.1	100.0	487.4	100.0	533.9	100.0	815.4	100.0	1,577.5	100.0	2,932.2	100.0
Import	185.2	100.0	534.2	100.0	363.4	100.0	874.7	100.0	805.2	100.0	4,327.0	100.0	7,932.9	100.0
Balance	-34.2	—	-126.1	—	-149.0	—	-340.8	—	10.2	—	-2,749.5	—	-5,000.8	—
Developed market economies														
Export	108.9	72.1	242.0	59.3	149.9	30.8	159.0	29.8	194.7	23.8	542.9	34.4	1,582.5	54.0
Import	129.4	69.9	396.9	74.3	362.1	56.9	498.0	56.9	410.3	51.0	3,006.5	69.5	5,534.0	69.0
Balance	-20.5	—	-154.9	—	-212.2	—	-339.0	—	-215.6	—	-2,463.6	—	-3,951.5	—

Communist countries

Export	15.3	10.1	60.4	14.8	251.8	51.7	270.1	50.6	473.7	58.1	796.5	50.5	436.7	14.0
Import	18.5	10.0	42.9	8.0	202.3	31.8	237.3	27.1	269.7	33.5	727.2	16.8	799.4	10.0
Balance	-3.2	—	17.5	—	49.5	—	32.8	—	204.0	—	69.3	—	-362.8	—

Developing non-communist countries

Export	26.8	17.8	105.7	25.9	84.3	17.3	90.0	16.9	141.5	17.4	228.5	14.5	780.5	26.0
Import	37.3	20.1	94.4	17.7	71.5	11.2	120.9	13.8	118.0	14.7	519.6	12.0	1,140.5	14.0
Balance	-10.5	—	11.3	—	12.8	—	-30.9	—	23.4	—	-291.1	—	-360.0	—

Other countries

Export	0	0	0	0	1.4	0.2	14.8	2.7	5.5	0.7	9.6	0.6	132.5	4.0
Import	0	0	0	0	0.5	0.1	18.5	2.2	7.2	0.8	73.7	1.7	459.0	5.0
Balance	0	—	0	—	1.0	—	-3.7	—	-1.6	—	-64.1	—	-326.5	—

Source: Data on direction of trade from United Nations and IMF publications.
a. Exports are reported as free on board (f.o.b.), imports on cost-insurance-freight (c.i.f.) basis.

147

Table 4-9. **Terms of Trade with Developed and Centrally Planned Countries, by Commodity Groups, Selected Years, 1970–85**

(chained Fisher indexes; 1965=100)

Year	Food and food products		Agricultural raw materials		Minerals and metals		Manufactured goods		Finished manufactured goods		Total[a]		All countries
	DCs	CPCs	DCs	CPCs	DCs	CPCs	DCs	CPCs	DCs	CPCs	DCs	CPCs	
1970	146.1	132.5	113.1	121.3	104.9	90.8	97.4	104.6	88.3	181.7	109.8	112.8	108.6
1975	109.2	121.5	96.2	70.9	83.2	65.6	91.6	74.9	67.5	241.2	111.6	102.1	112.1
1980	169.1	117.2	87.5	77.3	132.6	70.7	113.6	98.2	54.1	336.5	237.5	114.2	181.2
1985	160.4	137.5	121.4	63.1	114.0	64.3	112.8	77.4	59.6	214.9	219.8	87.2	160.7

DCs = developed countries; CPCs = centrally planned countries.

a. Includes mineral fuel, which is not shown separately.

Source: Computations by Dr. Edward Lucas based on UNCTAD trade tapes with values in terms of US dollars.

1964–65, the years of open warfare on Egyptian territory with Sinai occupied and the Canal Zone in the front line, and the years of Sadat's *infitah* from 1974 onward, with 1965–66 to 1966–67 and 1974 years of transition to and from open warfare. Growth rates are clearly correlated with investment ratios, as would be expected for periods of five to ten years. The increase in the investment ratio from 14 percent in 1952–53 to 1959–60 to 17 percent in 1960–61 to 1966–67 paralleled an increase in the growth rate of GDP from 3.3 percent to 5.1 percent. The following decline in the investment ratio to about 12.5 percent in 1967–68 to 1974 was accompanied by a decline in the growth rate to 3.9 percent. The increase from 1975 to 1983–84 in the investment ratio to an average of 26.5 percent corresponds with a rise in the growth rate to 8.3 percent. For the subperiods 1975–78 and 1979 to 1983–84, however, the correlation breaks down. The fluctuations in the investment ratio were closely related to changing foreign exchange situations which again were the outcome of international conflicts and reconciliations, to factors outside the control of the Egyptian government such as the oil price shocks and demand for labor from the Arab oil-producing countries, and to demand management and other domestic policies. Neither the investment ratios nor the growth rates for 1967–68 to 1974 and 1975 to 1983–84 specify or make adjustments for the destruction of cities in the Canal Zone in the War of Attrition after 1967 and the following reconstruction.

Intersectoral Distribution of Investments

Table 4–10 shows the distribution of gross investments by the public and the private sector, the latter broken down to show foreign and domestic investments. Before 1956 about two-thirds of gross investment seems to have been private. During the first five-year plan and after the nationalizations, 1960–61 to 1973, private investment was only a small fraction of total investment. From 1974 with the *infitah*, private investment increased in importance and by 1978 to 1983–84 amounted to more than one-quarter of total investment, about half being foreign capital. Oil companies dominate as foreign investors. Private investments from other foreign sources, encouraged by law 43 of 1974 as part of the *infitah* policy opening the country to foreign capital, have never become important in the aggregate. Even at their peak in 1982–83 they amounted to little more than 2.5 percent of total investment. Despite the considerable shift of investment activities, including foreign investment, toward the private sector, the government, with three-quarters of all investments in its hands, continued to control the growth process. Foreign investments under law 43 in industry and mining and trade and finance, the sectors such capital mainly has gone into, were only an estimated 12 percent of total investments in those sectors in 1982–83.

Table 4-10. Gross Fixed Investment as a Share of Gross Domestic Product, by Sector, 1952–84
(percent)

Item	1952–53 to 1959–60	1960–61 to 1964–65	1965–66 to 1966–67	1967–68 to 1973	1974	1975 –78	1978 to 1983–84[a]
Agriculture	1.0	1.3	1.3	0.9	1.2	1.7	2.2
Irrigation and drainage[b]	0.8	2.7	2.1	1.0	4.4	5.9	6.9
Industry and mining	3.4	4.6	4.1	3.9	1.7	2.5	3.4
Petroleum	[c]	[c]	[c]	[c]	1.7	2.5	3.4
Electricity and public utilities	1.2	1.8	3.1	1.5	1.4	1.8	3.3
Construction	n.a.	0.1[d]	0.2	0.1	0.2	0.8	0.9
Transportation and communication	2.0	3.3	2.1	2.6	4.4	4.9	5.2
Suez Canal	0.2[e]	0.3	n.a.[f]	0	0	1.1	1.3
Trade and finance	n.a.	0.2[g]	0.1	0.1	0.2	0.3	0.8
Housing	4.1	1.9	1.9	1.3	1.2	2.3	2.5
Other Services[h]	1.3	1.2	0.6	0.6	1.0	1.5	2.1
Total[i]	13.9	17.4	15.6	12.1	15.8	23.0	28.5

Domestic public investment	4.8[i]	n.a.	14.1	10.7	13.7	16.2	20.4
Domestic private investment	7.7[i]	n.a.	1.5	1.5	1.1	3.9	4.6
Foreign private investment	n.a.	n.a.	n.a.	n.a.	0.9	2.3	3.4
Oil companies' investments	n.a.	n.a.	n.a.	n.a.	0.7	1.9	2.6
Law 43 investments	—	—	—	—	0.1	0.4	0.7
GDP growth rate	3.3	5.1	5.1	3.9	3.9	9.6	7.5

n.a. = Not available.
— = Not applicable.
a. Data for 1982–84 are estimates.
b. Including Aswan High Dam, except power house and lines included under electricity and public utilities.
c. Included in industry and mining.
d. Three years only.
e. From 1957 only.
f. Possibly included in transport and communications.
g. Four years only.
h. Including hotels and tourism.
i. Breakdown by public and private investment does not include land purchase.
Source: Mead (1967), table I-A-9; Hansen in Vatikiotis (1968), tables 9, 6; Ikram (1980), table 9; statistical appendix, table 9; World Bank data.

The composition of investment by sector has varied considerably over time. Table 4–11 indicates that the share of investment in sectors producing tradable goods and services moved from 37 percent before the first five-year plan to 54 percent, where it roughly remained. The shift during the first five-year plan was mainly related to the construction of the Aswan High Dam (not including the power station), initiated in 1959 and completed in 1970. At an officially estimated total cost of LE320 million (other estimates reach LE424 million, of which LE141 million is for the power station [Waterbury 1977, p. 112]) this would amount to some 1.5 percent of average GNP during the eleven years of construction with about one-third for the power station. Housing investment was cut back by more than 2 percent of GDP annually from 1960 to 1967. In this real sense the agricultural part of the project—the dam itself—was financed by a reduction of investment in housing. Cutting back on housing was considered reasonable because of the high ratio of capital to output in housing (as I recall from discussions with Dr. Nazih Deif and Dr. Mahmoud Shafei in the Ministry of Planning in 1960). Probably, after construction was speeded up after a personal decision by

Table 4-11. Gross Fixed Investment as a Share of GDP, by Tradable and Nontradable Goods and Services, 1952–84
(percent)

Sectors	1952–53 to 1959–60	1960–61 to 1966–67	1978 to 1983–84
Tradable goods and services	5.2	9.1	14.8
Export (oil, Suez Canal, tourism)	n.a.	0.7	5.7
Agriculture	1.8	3.9	2.2
Industry and mining	3.4	4.5	6.9
Nontradable goods and services	8.7	7.8	13.7
Infrastructure (electricity, utilities, transport and communications, trade, finance)	3.3	5.2	9.3
Other (construction, housing, other services)	5.4	2.6	4.4
Total	13.9	16.9	28.5
Tradable as a Share of Total	37.4	53.8	51.9

n.a. = Not available.
Source: Table 4–10.

Nasser, available building materials were absorbed by the dam project.[5] Most of the strong increase in agricultural investment before 1967 (including irrigation and drainage) was related to the dam, as was the strong increase in investment in electricity and public utilities, particularly during 1965–67. The increase in industrial investment, on the other hand, was moderate. While annual agricultural investment increased by 2.0 percent of GDP between 1952–53 to 1959–60 and 1960–61 to 1966–67, annual industrial investment increased only by 1.1 percent of GDP, investment in electricity and public utilities by 0.9 percent, and investment in transport and communications also by 0.9 percent, while investment in nontraded sectors such as construction, housing, and other services declined by about 2.5 percent of GDP. Some of the electricity, of course, would serve as input in industry, but it is not possible to characterize the first five-year plan as an industrialization plan. The Aswan Dam swamped everything in the early 1960s.

During the lean years, 1967–68 to 1973, expenditures on the dam ceased and were not replaced by any similar large investment. Investment in other sectors, including industry, held up well. For these years it is difficult to distinguish between military and civilian expenditures but this period cannot possibly be characterized as one of industrialization either.

Much the same is true for the period after 1974, with the qualification that the Aswan Dam as the major investment project was replaced by projects in the export industries: oil, Suez Canal, and tourism. Industrialization in the sense of expanding manufacturing industry did not predominate. With total annual investment running at a level of 28.5 percent of GDP during the years 1978 to 1983–84, 5.7 percent went into the three export industries; 9.3 percent into infrastructure, particularly in electricity and public utilities and in transport and communications; 4.4 percent into nontraded goods and services; only 2.2 percent into agriculture and 6.9 percent into industry and mining (excluding petroleum), of which 6.5 percent was in manufacturing, not including petroleum products. Of the total increase in investment by more than 16 percent of GNP between 1967–68 to 1973 and 1978 to 1983–84, only 3 percentage points went into manufacturing industry. Industrialization proper is today still in its infancy in Egypt after half a century of development policy proclaiming industrialization its major target. (The serious problems in defining and measuring the share of manufacturing in Egypt are discussed in appendix 1–A.)

The shift of investment toward sectors producing tradable goods and services has not been accompanied by increased exports from these sectors. On the contrary, in relation to GDP, commodity exports, apart from oil, have almost disappeared. The shares in GDP of the two major commodity-producing sectors, agriculture and industry (manufacturing), have declined strongly, the former from 32.3 percent in 1955–66 to 20.0 percent in 1983–84, the latter from 17.6 percent to 14.8 percent, respectively, and in both these activities import substitution has increasingly prevailed. The decline in the total share of agriculture and industry proper from 49.9 percent to 34.8 percent of GDP should by itself strongly tend to reduce commodity exports as a percentage of GDP. Thus import substitution within these sectors is only part of the problem.

Investment in Agriculture

Considering the very large investment in agriculture between 1961 and 1967 with the building of the Aswan High Dam, the growth rates obtained in this sector look rather disappointing, 1.8 percent during the years 1965–66 to 1973 and 2.2 percent from 1973 to 1981–82. During the first five-year plan period, before the dam had any impact on agriculture, the agricultural growth rate was 3.8 percent. The dam was expected above all to extend perennial irrigation and multicropping to substantial regions in Upper Egypt that in 1964 were still under basin irrigation; to expand the cultivation of rice, a highly profitable crop, in the northern Delta; to shift the cultivation of maize from September to December to the hot months of June to September, causing a strong increase in yields; and to increase the water supply for land reclamation in the western desert, particularly in Tahrir Province. On the first three counts, expectations were fulfilled during the first years after the closure of the coffer dam in 1964. Yields, however, were soon adversely affected by overwatering, waterlogging, and salination, the latter mainly related to poor drainage. On the fourth count, land reclamation turned out to be one of the white elephants of Egyptian planning.

When the blueprints for the final version of the dam project were drawn up by Soviet engineers, it was emphasized that extensive additional investments would have to be made in drainage to avoid a rise in the water table that would result in waterlogging and salination. This was fully understood by top civil servants in the Ministries of Agriculture and Irrigation where the lessons of the British experience before World War I had not been forgotten. Covered drains were thought to be required throughout the country, and particularly in the Delta. This part of the project was postponed year after year, obviously a consequence of war conditions and the accompanying foreign exchange shortages. With support from the World Bank, drainage projects were finally initiated in 1970. To prevent further decline in productivity, the drainage system on one million *feddan* in the Delta was to be redesigned and pumping stations were to be installed. On another half a million *feddan* in the Delta, piped drainage was planned to increase productivity. These and other drainage projects are still under construction and much output has been lost through their postponement.

Use of chemical fertilizers and pesticides was increased and improved, high-yield varieties of wheat and cotton were introduced, continuing practices promoted in Egypt since the 1890s, at least, first by the British and later by independent Egyptian governments. For wheat this policy was not successful in the 1960s. The new varieties were not pest-resistant, the short straws were not appropriate for Egyptian agricultural requirements (straw being important as fuel and animal feed), and baking qualities and taste were not congenial. For cotton, however, the policy was as successful as it had been in the interwar years. By and large, however, the vertical expansion generated by the High Dam was disappointing.

What further contributed to the poor performance of agriculture after the High Dam was the unfortunate emphasis on land reclamation. The conflict between proponents of horizontal expansion (reclamation) and vertical expansion (drainage of the old lands and improvement in planting practices)—between left-wing, Soviet-oriented army officers and junta members on one side and civil servants in the Ministries of Agriculture and Irrigation (backed until 1961 by a powerful minister of agriculture, Marei) on the other—was resolved, first by Nasser and later by Sadat, in favor of the land reclamation projects in the western desert. Of the LE675 million invested in agriculture from 1960 to 1970, no less than LE483 million is estimated to have been spent on land reclamation (Waterbury 1983, pp. 64 ff.). Soil conditions (not studied in advance) turned out to be unfavorable in part of the area and lifting water above 10–20 meters became uneconomical after the oil price increases in 1973 and 1979. In terms of output, little appears to have been achieved. Of a total of 912,000 *feddan* reclaimed since 1953, only 58–60 percent is actually cultivated, and productivity on 40 percent of this area is submarginal (Pacific Consultants 1980, p. 7a). A Soviet-financed, mechanized state farm had just been opened with great publicity as representing the future of Egyptian farming when, in 1972, work on land reclamation suddenly was virtually abrogated (Pacific Consultants 1980, pp. 297 ff.). The waxing and waning of land reclamation policies in Egypt was closely related to Nasser's internal power policy and to Soviet influence and support in Egypt. Land reclamation practically speaking came to an end as a major policy with Sadat's arrests in 1971 of Soviet-oriented politicians, the expulsion of Soviet military advisers, and the deterioration of Egypt–Soviet relations.

The poor results were very much the fault of poor management and the establishment of Soviet model state farms and graduate student farms in reclaimed areas (Springborg 1979). With other organizational forms, especially peasant settlements, run by real farmers prepared to do hard work and not by civil servants and students in three-piece suits acting as absentee landlords, returns on the reclaimed areas might have been more satisfactory and the High Dam would have appeared in a more favorable light. Without the land reclamation investments, on the other hand, funds would undoubtedly have been available throughout the 1960s for the required investment in drainage and the High Dam would again have appeared in a much more favorable light. As a balancing act, the Mubarak regime has decided to revive the old, abandoned land reclamation strategy to please the military.

There is good reason for believing that marginal value productivity of labor in agriculture is positive and in line with agricultural wages. While the agricultural labor force appears to have increased during the 1960s, agriculture has probably lost labor since 1973. Surveys of the labor force show a 7 percent decline in agricultural labor force from 1971 to 1980 (table 4–3), which by itself should point to a certain decline in agricultural production. Working hours for hired labor, moreover, declined considerably with higher real wages beginning in the second half of the 1970s (a backward bending supply curve?). The lost input may to some extent have been replaced by unpaid women and children, who are underenumerated in the surveys, and increased use of tractors and other mechanization (pumping, threshing). While this may indeed have been the case (Commander and Hadhoud 1986), the fact that the composition of production has been shifting away from some traditional female occupations (cotton picking and pest control) toward others (raising small animals, dairy products, and vegetables) makes it difficult to judge the net effect. In any case, the modest rate of growth in agriculture, at least since 1973, may partly be the result of a decline in labor input.

No complete economic evaluation of the High Dam project has, as far as I know, been made. Crude evaluations indicate that the project might break even at an interest rate of about 10 percent. However, because the project was large in relation to the existing economy and thus probably would affect shadow prices, and because it does make a great difference whether actual or optimal utilization of water and electricity is assumed, simple methods used to evaluate small projects will not suffice. Nor, on the other hand, is it feasible to use quantitative methods of analysis based on computable models. The oil price shocks of 1973 and 1979 must have improved the social profitability of the dam through the shadow price of electricity. While ecological effects may be important, opinions on them differ widely and the literature is highly emotional. Evaluating the ex post social profitability of the dam is a research project on its own, a natural task for the World Bank.

The computations of total factor productivity in agriculture in table 4–12 reveal how disastrous Egyptian agricultural developments in this century have been. With total inputs increasing at an annual rate of 1.3 percent from 1900 to 1967, total output increased by only 0.9 percent and total factor productivity thus declined by 0.4 percent annually. In other words, over two-thirds of a century the so-called residual has been negative by about half of a percent.

Table 4-12. Growth of Input, Output, and Factor Productivity in Agriculture, Selected Years, 1900–67
(percent)

Year	Input				Total output[a]	Output per unit[a]			
	Fixed capital	Labor	Land	Total[b]		Fixed capital	Labor	Land	Total input[b]
1900	1	1	1	1	1	1	1	1	1
1913	1.49	1.42	1.00	1.27	1.10	0.66	0.79	1.10	0.87
1920	1.56	1.63	1.02	1.38	1.01	0.58	0.62	0.99	0.73
1928	1.80	1.89	1.06	1.56	1.29	0.65	0.68	1.22	0.83
1938	2.96	2.16	1.00	1.83	1.51	0.46	0.70	1.51	0.83
1948	3.46	2.15	1.08	1.92	1.36	0.39	0.63	1.26	0.71
1958	3.90	2.17	1.09	2.00	1.51	0.39	0.70	1.39	0.76
1967	6.06	2.17	1.09	2.31	1.80	0.30	0.83	1.65	0.78
Annual, 1900–67	2.73	1.16	0.13	1.26	0.88	-1.78	-0.28	0.75	-0.37

a. Three-year moving average.
b. Weighted by 1938 shares of total factor income (capital 14.3 percent, labor 47.2 percent, land 38.4 percent).
Source: Radwan (1973), table 2–8; Egypt, Ministry of Finance, *Annuaire statistique de l'Egypte*, various years; Wattleworth (1975).

It is tempting to conjecture about developments since 1967. In agriculture, GDP increased in real terms by 38.3 percent from 1967 to 1981–82. Thus from 1900 to 1981–82 total output may have increased by 149 percent and grown at an annual rate of 1.13 percent. Assuming that all inputs have been unchanged since 1967, total input would have increased by 1.03 percent annually over the same period. This produces an increase of total factor productivity, a residual of 0.1 percent annually over more than eighty years. Input of land has probably been approximately constant since 1967 and input of labor may have decreased. Input of fixed capital, on the other hand, has certainly increased through investment in drainage and tractorization. It is not likely that total input should have declined. In the best of cases the residual may have been about zero over the century.

For the post-World War II period, things look a little better. The growth rates of input and output from 1948 to 1967 in table 4–13 indicate a residual of 0.5 percent, with productivity of both labor and land increasing by about 1.5 percent annually and productivity of capital declining by the same percentage. This comparison may seem overly favorable because it starts from 1948 when productivity in Egyptian agriculture still suffered from the shortage of fertilizer and the disruption of rotation during the war. By comparison, both Israel and Japan started, if not from scratch then certainly from war conditions, and both were

Table 4–13. Growth of Input, Output, and Factor Productivity in Egypt, Israel, and Japan, Selected Periods, 1948–71
(percent)

Factor	Egypt 1948–67, agriculture	Israel, 1950–65 Agriculture	Israel, 1950–65 Total economy	Japan 1952–71, total economy
Total input	1.0	5.9	7.3	4.2
Capital	3.0	9.9	13.1	9.9
Labor	0.0	4.4	5.1	2.8
Land	0.0	n.a.	n.a.	0.0
Total output	1.5	11.6	11.0	10.1
Output per unit				
Capital	–1.4	1.8	–2.1	0.1
Labor	1.5	7.2	5.9	7.3
Land	1.4	n.a.	n.a.	10.1
Total input	0.5	5.4	3.4	5.7

Note: Because of rounding and special adjustments, figures may not add to totals.
n.a. = Not available.
Source: Table 4–12; Gaathon (1971); Denison and Chung (1976).

high-growth countries for the period considered. For the years 1950–65 Israeli agriculture had a residual of 5.4 percent in agriculture with a somewhat lower 3.4 percent for the economy as a whole. For Japan the residual was 5.7 percent for the period 1952–71. By comparison, Egyptian agriculture performed poorly in the postwar period. The Aswan High Dam did not produce many agricultural benefits, considering the size of the investment, and probably did not create agricultural residual.

Investment and Industrial Growth

Investments in the oil industry mainly are undertaken by foreign companies on a sharing basis, as they are in the OPEC countries. Decisions about investments in manufacturing industries (not including petroleum products) have since the late 1950s largely been made within the Ministry of Industry. The political process by which decisionmaking in the area of industrialization passed into the hands of this ministry, under Aziz Sidky, its first minister, outside the control of the Ministries of Planning and Finance and even of the cabinet, has been told earlier. Little is known about how decisions were made and what criteria were used. Clearly, evaluations of social profitability were never made. Since, on the other hand, private profit maximization did not play a role in decisions about either investment or current operation of established public enterprises, distortions of the price system through tariffs, import and export licensing, and wage-price controls, massive though they have been since the 1950s, have probably had little bearing on the actual allocation of resources and efficiency in public enterprises. Political and bureaucratic decisionmaking has been decisive; that much is clear. In most of the industrial investment decisions made until the late 1970s, it would appear that the decisive factors were domestic demand (hitherto satisfied through imports) and foreign aid (particularly from communist countries from 1956 to 1973), subject to the preferences, prejudices, and whims of an extremely energetic and powerful minister who had little understanding of economic efficiency[6] and to the personal interests and corruption of the bureaucracy. The government set targets for levels of current production. In the late 1970s, Western donors and financiers, including international organizations such as the IMF and the IBRD, and after Camp David the U.S. government through its Agency for International Development (AID), shifted the attention of Egyptian planners, if not decisionmakers, toward efficiency or, at least, export-promotion problems. The five-year plan for 1982–83 to 1986–87 addressed those problems but obviously it will take years to change the structure of the public sector significantly, and private investments, which became more important in the 1980s than they had been, continue to respond to a highly distorted incentive system. So far, both public and private investment continue to be directed toward domestic demand (discussed below). The increased corruption since 1973 has not helped to rationalize the decision process.

It is probably fair to say that in addition to sponsoring import substitution, industrial investment has been excessively capital intensive, with obsolete technology and too much faith in large-scale economies. These prejudices that originated with Tala'at Harb in the 1930s were aggravated under Sidki and a succession of ministers after him and not made any better by Soviet aid and advice. Studies by Mabro and Radwan (1976, chap. 10) for the period up to 1970 clearly point in the direction of excessive capital intensity—among the striking examples are steel, motor cars, paper, and pharmaceutical products. Another example may be the aluminum plant at Nag Hamadi, which depends on bauxite from Australia and uses a substantial part of the electricity from the High Dam. Scale of operations is seldom optimal. The cotton textiles industry (*mahalla el kubra*) operates on too large a scale while many new industries are too small.

Economic inefficiency is, however, difficult to measure. Measurements of the degree of import substitution and export promotion as well as capital intensity in Egypt by Mabro and Radwan (1976, chaps. 10, 11, 12) do not really reveal whether allocation is efficient. Import substitutions may be highly efficient—nobody should, for instance, criticize Egypt for having practiced import substitution since 1973 in the case of oil! The bilateral expansion of exports of manufactured goods to communist countries during the 1960s and early 1970s, on the other hand, may have been highly inefficient. And the fact that housing is strongly capital intensive may be no good excuse for cutting investment in housing as Egypt did in the first five-year plan. While it probably is true that for manufacturing industry in Egypt, import substitution has been excessive, export promotion deficient, and capital intensity excessive, hard evidence is not easy to find.

Total factor productivity is one indicator, if not of efficiency in an absolute sense then possibly of the rate of change of efficiency. Table 4–14 is derived from measurements of total factor productivity in manufacturing for 1939 to 1969–70 by Mabro and Radwan (1976, chap. 11) and of the textile, food, chemical, and metallurgical and engineering industries for 1973 to 1981–82 by the Ministry of Industry.

Disregarding the period 1939–45 for which the data may not be reliable, the prenationalization period shows an annual rate of increase of 2.0 percent in total factor productivity against 1.2 percent in the postnationalization period. The expansion of public ownership seems to have been associated with a reduction of the residual factor by almost half. It is striking, though, that the period of extensive public ownership divides into one period, 1963–64 to 1969–70 when total factor productivity declined by 2.2 percent annually, and a second period, after 1973, when it increased by 5.3 percent annually. There is little doubt that the high rate

Table 4-14. Input, Output, and Factor Productivity in Manufacturing Industry, Selected Periods, 1939-82

(percent)

Period	Output	Factor input Labor	Factor input Capital	Factor input Total	Total factor productivity
1939–45	5.1	1.5	–4.0	–1.5	6.6
1945–54	7.7	2.7	5.7	6.0	1.4 ⎫ 2.0
1954–62	9.7	4.6	8.2	6.8	2.7 ⎭
1963–64 to 1969–70	2.0	8.0	0.5	3.9	–2.2 ⎫ 1.2
1973 to 1981–82	7.8[a]	3.5	2.4	2.5	5.3 ⎭

a. Value added, based on weighted average of textile, food, chemical, and metallurgical and engineering industries.

Source: Mabro and Radwan (1976), table 2–2; World Bank data.

of increase after 1973 reflects in part a recovery after the disastrous years between 1962 and 1973. Beginning about 1964, capacity utilization became low because of shortages of spare parts and raw materials related to the shortage of foreign exchange and because of tight monetary and fiscal policies. The employment drive of 1962 and the introduction of job security in public enterprises kept employment at a high level while redundancy was increasing, which would tend to make the residual small, even negative, after the nationalizations of 1961–63. The reversal of the foreign exchange situation and the improvement in supplies of spare parts and raw materials after 1973 as well as expansionary fiscal and monetary policies were bound to result in a recovery of total factor productivity, implying a high residual for at least some years after 1973. It has been argued that lax work discipline and poor management contributed seriously to the decline in total factor productivity. This, however, is a factor that should not have tended to disappear after 1973. Another factor that probably served to keep productivity down was the employment of graduates and of former employees who had been discharged from military service; the latter constituted in 1973 about 15 percent of all employees in public sector companies. Each of these factors probably contributed to the changes in total factor productivity after 1960–61, but it is not possible to quantify the contributions individually. It stands to reason, however, that the net decline in the residual after 1962 as compared with earlier years is related to the change from private to public ownership in manufacturing industry with all its ramifications, including the increased dependence on Soviet equipment and technology from 1956–58 to 1974.

For the years after 1973 an ambitious World Bank study of productivity problems in Egyptian industry presents estimates of total factor productivity in fifteen industries under the Ministry of Industry. It analyzes the residual in terms of improved efficiency, on the one hand, and technological progress, on the other. It measures productivity in 1973–79 in terms of gross output, with capital, labor, and materials as inputs, whereas the data on four industries in table 4–14 give output in terms of value added, with capital and labor the only inputs. The results of the two are thus difficult to compare. For food, chemical, and metallurgical and engineering industries the results look rather similar, but for the important textile industry the estimates in table 4–14 show much higher increases in total factor productivity than those of the World Bank study. The latter points to very large differences between industries in total factor productivity growth from 13.2 percent in the important fertilizer industry to a decrease of 2.0 percent in the even more important cotton textile industry. Eleven industries had positive growth, five even with 2 percent and above. Growth of total factor productivity contributed more than 25 percent of output growth in eight industries and contributed positively in another four. The ratio of capital to labor increased in eleven industries which thus experienced capital deepening. The data in table 4–11, however, indicate that on balance the opposite was true.

While it would thus seem that growth in total factor productivity contributed significantly to industrial growth after 1973, decomposition indicates that either increased capacity utilization or increased supply of parts and materials rather than increased efficiency in using existing technologies was the source of the strong growth in total factor productivity. This is a disappointing result. There are indications, however, that the decline in total factor productivity in 1962–69 was caused in part by stagnating demand and shortages of parts and materials, so that developments after 1973 may reflect a postwar recovery.

To measure technical efficiency, the World Bank study computes a so-called Farrell index of the difference between rates of change of total factor productivity in best-practice and average firms. The index measures the spread of the rate of change rather than the level of total factor productivity in an industry. Best-practice change in total factor productivity is taken as a standard for measuring how much the industry generally is lagging in technical progress. The index for Egypt is quite high by international standards, which only indicates that efficiency, or inefficiency, is more uniform in Egypt than in other countries for which the index has been computed. The index declined from 1973 to 1979, indicating that growth in total factor productivity had spread. The study concluded that central direction of firms in each sector kept total factor productivity growth low or negative in the 1960s but also resulted in very little dispersion of firms in terms of their relative total factor productivity levels. The 1970s in contrast were a period of rapid productivity gains but of increasing variance in total factor productivity levels as firms with greater freedom of action adjusted at varying speed to the liberalization efforts.

The degree to which technological progress has taken place seems also to vary greatly among industries. While progress by best-practice firms in industries such as edible oils, paper, transportation equipment, and electrical machinery have averaged 7–9 percent annually, an important industry such as cotton textiles has shown no progress whatsoever. It is not clear what gives rise to the large differences in technical progress. Public ownership per se apparently is not decisive, for some public industries show rapid progress. Differences in decentralization and management may play a role.

One way of assessing productive efficiency is to use resource costs as a gauge of international competitiveness. Domestic resource costs (DRCs) can be used to indicate the relative efficiency and thus to rank industries in the domestic economy. But for evaluations of absolute efficiency, comparisons must be based on adequate exchange rates and the results depend critically on possible over- or undervaluation of the domestic currency. Table 4–15 shows the ratio of domestic resource costs (based on 10 percent interest on capital) to exchange rates for several industries. For 1954, 1957, and 1960, the official exchange rates used probably exaggerate costs since the currency was probably overvalued. For 1965 the black market rate was LE0.89 per U.S. dollar against an official rate of LE0.43. It is my impression that for the whole period until the devaluation of 1979, at least, the Egyptian pound was officially overvalued. For 1965 and 1970 I have used what the IMF in 1966 in internal discussions with the Egyptian government considered a realistic rate that is, LE0.61 per U.S. dollar as opposed to the official rate of LE0.43. I believe that the overvaluation was much smaller, perhaps even negligible in 1954 but, on the other hand steadily increasing until the exchange reforms of 1973–74. These reforms are discussed below. For the years 1954, 1957, and 1960 the DRCs are thus probably increasingly exaggerated. That may not be the case for 1965 and 1970. For 1981, the free-market rate used may have been close to the equilibrium rate which is the appropriate standard for DRC comparisons.

Table 4–15 indicates that industries with natural advantages, such as a domestic supply of raw materials, have relatively low domestic resource costs and appear to have been competitive before the nationalizations. Sugar, cement, and phosphates are three such cases. Cotton textiles, using Egyptian cotton, appears not to have been competitive, even considering the possible overvaluation until 1960. That may reflect the fact that the very high quality of Egyptian cotton makes this raw material too expensive for the coarse products made for the domestic market. When the cost of foreign cotton is used as a hypothetical DRC the industry appears to be competitive. Assuming a sloping foreign demand curve for Egyptian cotton and substituting the marginal revenue at export for the full export price in the DRC estimate, the cotton textile industry would probably be competitive. Iron and steel has a very high domestic re-

Table 4-15. Ratio of Domestic Resource Costs in Eight Industries to Exchange Rate, Selected Years, 1954–81

Industry	1954[a]	1957[a]	1960[a]	1965[b]	1970[b]	1981[c]
Cotton textiles						
Egyptian cotton yarn, full export price	n.a.	1.34 [d]	1.59[d]	1.15[d,e]	1.41[d]	1.13
Foreign cotton yarn, c.i.f. price	n.a.	1.02	1.08	n.a.	0.89	n.a.
Sugar	n.a.	n.a.	0.97	n.a.	0.89	0.39
Cement	0.57[d]	0.60[d]	0.80[d]	0.51[d]	n.a.	n.a.
Fertilizers						
Phosphates	1.08	1.02	n.a.	0.54	n.a.	3.97
Nitrates	1.48	1.73	n.a.	0.85	n.a.	0.79
Tires	n.a.	n.a.	1.68	0.97	n.a.	n.a.
Paper	n.a.	n.a.	n.a.	3.41	n.a.	2.80
Iron and steel	n.a.	n.a.	n.a.	7.87	n.a.	2.01
Automobiles	n.a.	n.a.	n.a.	1.85	n.a.	−8.47[f]

n.a. = Not available.

a. At official exchange rate.

b. At realistic exchange rate as suggested by IMF officials to Egyptian government representatives in 1966.

c. At free-market exchange rate.

d. At export, f.o.b. values; all other at import, c.i.f. values.

e. Based on price of fabrics.

f. Transport equipment, negative value added at international prices.

Source: Hansen and Nashashibi (1975), tables 8–4, 10–2; World Bank data.

source cost; the low quality of the ore from Aswan and the high transportation costs to Helwan create in effect a natural disadvantage. While the industries without natural advantages—paper, iron and steel, and automobiles—have high domestic resource costs, both overvaluation and nationalization have to be taken into account.

Over time there seems in all of the industries except phosphates and automobiles to have been a tendency for domestic resource costs to decline. Considering that nationalization presumably should work in the opposite direction, the decline might be a signal that these are infant industries. Experience in Brazil, Mexico, and Turkey points in the direction of long periods of infancy and adolescence for new industries. The estimates of domestic resource costs in 1981 for a number of broadly defined industries in the public sector in table 4–16 seem to support the infant-industry argument. The old industries, particularly food, beverages, and tobacco and also cotton textiles, are competitive while the new industries typically are noncompetitive, even showing a loss in value added at international prices. The spread between best and worst plants

Table 4-16. Ratio of Domestic Resource Costs in Twelve Public Sector Industries to Shadow Exchange Rate, 1981

Industry	All plants	Best plant	Worst plant
Textiles			
Cotton	0.89[a]	0.57	2.63
Other	1.28	0.99	1.89
Food			
Oils	0.84	0.61	3.34
Other food	0.52	0.16	2.96
Alcohol, beverages, tobacco	0.56	0.42	1.45
Chemicals			
Paper	2.80	0.70	−2.90[b]
Basic chemicals	3.46	1.28	−5.70[b]
Miscellaneous	−1.16[b]	0.87	−0.83[b]
Metallurgical and engineering			
Basic metals	−45.15[b]	1.11	−0.38[b]
Transport equipment	−8.47[b]	−0.75[b]	−1.16[b]
Electrical machinery	0.80	0.34	7.29
China and glass	−5.43[b]	10.71	−1.77[b]

a. At marginal revenue for raw cotton exports.
b. Indicates negative value added at international prices.
Source: World Bank data. Capital values at replacement costs (10 percent interest rate).

was remarkable, considering that many of the industries were new. In eight out of the twelve industries the best plants were competitive; in no industry was the worst plant competitive (World Bank data).

Nontradable Goods and Services

The large increases of investment in sectors producing nontradable goods and services (for which no estimates of domestic resource costs exist) were mainly the outcome of deliberate government decisions, and although maximization of profits did not prevail in the decision process and, hence, price distortions have not directly influenced investment patterns, the latter are clearly correlated with the former, the government in both cases pursuing a common goal: to fulfill its part of the social compact, the tacit understanding between ruler and urban population whereby the ruler purchases political quiescence in return for la dolce vita. With very low prices of electricity, water, gasoline, and transport and communications services and free educational and health services goes a tremendous demand not only for these goods and services but for complementary services such as roads. Part of the explanation of the relatively high level of investment in electricity and public utilities, transport and communications, and other services is the demand for low-priced services and goods. The social compact requires not only cheap services but availability of these and related services. A telephone is worthless if few people have telephones; a motor car is of little value if there are no motor roads.

The situation in housing might seem to contradict this interpretation. Rent control keeps rents of housing unchanged at the level fixed by the authorities when the first tenants move in. Rents are therefore excessively dependent on the age of houses. Apartments in very old houses, however well kept and located, cost virtually nothing; rents on apartments in new houses are in line with current costs of construction. The dispersion of urban rents is enormous, rent controls having been in place since World War I, and the shortage of housing is serious. The implied discrimination against young people, it might be thought, would make investment in housing a first priority for a government, fearful of riots, if the idea of a social compact makes sense. As a percentage of GDP, housing investment did in fact double between 1967–68 to 1973 and 1978 to 1983–84. But while such investment was above 10 percent of total investment in the earlier period, it was only about 8 percent in the latter (and before planning began it amounted to almost 30 percent of total investment).[7] Why? First, the investment statistics may understate the investment in housing. Private investment is not well covered generally and illegal building activity is considerable. More important, perhaps, housing is de facto a rationed commodity and the majority actually occupying cheap housing has no interest in increased building activity. Economic rent on occupied apartments would decline and occupants, both parents and children, are interested in keeping alive the low legal rents on high-economic-rent apartments. Parents, moreover, are interested in keeping their adult children at home as a hedge against old age, while children are interested in taking over their parents' cheap apartments. The minority without any housing has no political clout. The situation is well known from other countries with rent control.

There has also been a strong increase in investment in construction. The construction industry, largely a private activity, has responded to the high wages of construction workers by introducing modern technology, replacing the old fashioned, very labor intensive methods with relatively capital intensive methods. The increase of high-rise buildings induced by increasing urban land prices works in the same direction.

The sharp increase, finally, of investment in trade and finance may be related to own-exchange imports and financing (discussed below), which have strongly increased trade in modern consumer goods.

Price Policy

Intervention in the price system has been extensive throughout the postwar period and undoubtedly increased greatly under the Nasser regime, then decreased again under the policy of *infitah*. The consensus is that intervention has distorted prices and, hence, both production and use—that it has led to major inefficiencies, and that it thus has been harmful to growth. Price intervention in Egypt has taken many forms and has varied considerably over time. While development strategy during the interwar years originally emphasized tariff policy, after World War II direct price control, with or without intervention in the market, has increasingly taken the upper hand. Since the 1960s direct production targets and orders have, moreover, been established for both agriculture and industry, as well as for a number of public services, and distortion and inefficiency may be the consequence of direct physical control and intervention, including export and import controls, more than of price distortions.

It is usually assumed that for tradable goods, price distortions should be measured by the deviation of domestic prices from international prices, converted to domestic currency through the application of appropriate shadow exchange rates, if need be considering sloping international demand and supply curves. For nontradable goods and services, shadow prices have to be computed by breaking down the costs of tradable goods and primary resources evaluated at their shadow prices. The tools most commonly used for such exercises are the effective rate of protection, ERP, and domestic resource costs, DRC. As substitutes for DRC, accounting ratios (AR) and socially economic returns to land (*ERL*) are used, the latter applied to agriculture only. To make judgments about the nature and extent of misallocations implied by the price distortions, effective rates of protection (*ERPs*) and DRCs for samples of commodities and services, or industries, are compared below; it is assumed that the DRC estimates (or substitutes) correctly measure social profitability, which may be a frivolous assumption. There are profound theoretical and observational problems involved in estimating and comparing these measures and the correlations based on them may be marred by both definitional problems and errors in observation.

Agriculture

For agricultural products a dual price system has been in effect since the early 1960s. Compulsory delivery at low, fixed procurement prices has been required for seed cotton, wheat, rice, beans, lentils, sesame, groundnuts, and sugarcane. The procurement quota for seed cotton has invariably been 100 percent; for other crops it has varied considerably

Table 4-17. Farmgate Prices for Fertilizer and Major Crops as a Percentage of International Prices at Black Market Exchange Rates, 1965–79

Year	Nitrogenous fertilizer	Cotton Procurement	Rice Procurement	Rice Open market	Wheat Procurement	Wheat Open market	Beans Procurement	Beans Open market	Maize Open market	Sugarcane Procurement	Sugarcane Open market
1965–69	69.5	n.a.	27.9	45.2	44.6	69.0	—	65.7	53.1	66.9	278.4
1970–74	74.9	33.7	35.6	44.7	44.8	56.8	41.1	131.0	53.1	126.3	643.7
1975–79	26.6	35.4	34.2	37.8	44.6	56.4	53.4	77.3	63.2	82.6	242.6

n.a. = Not available.
— = Not applicable.
Source: von Braun and de Haen (1983).

over time and been well below 100 percent. For rice it has been about 50 percent, for wheat it declined from 18 percent in 1965 to 7 percent in 1980, for beans it has varied between 34 percent and 12 percent, and for lentils between 91 percent and 20 percent. Goods produced in excess of the quotas may be sold at market prices, though both wholesale and retail trade in urban areas to varying degrees have been subjected to direct price controls and market prices for some commodities have been dominated by government sales at very low, subsidized prices (wheat, rice, oil, sugar). This is important from the point of view of production distortions because production is determined by the price applying at the production margin—that is (apart from seed cotton, with its 100 percent procurement quota), the market price.

Most ERP and DRC studies are based on average farmgate prices, which for all procurement crops are lower than market prices. Hence, these studies tend to exaggerate the supply-depressing effects of the system. Modern inputs (fertilizer, pesticide, seed, fuel, tractor services) and credit are supplied by government authorities, also at prices typically well below international prices. Irrigation water and drainage services have always been supplied free of charge. Table 4–17 gives an impression of input prices, procurement prices, and open market prices—converted at black market exchange rates—for important crops and inputs as compared with international prices. The gap between procurement and open market prices has tended to diminish as procurement prices edge upward to the international prices. While the relationship between procurement and market prices is independent of the conversion rate used, the relationship between all domestic and international prices depends on the conversion rate. Since the black market rate (Egyptian pound per U.S. dollar) is higher than the official rate, domestic prices look particularly low as compared with international prices. For fertilizers (as for other inputs) prices were until the early 1970s high compared with output prices, thus implying relative taxation of agriculture; since 1973 input prices have been relatively low, implying relative subsidization.

For 1981 the World Bank has estimated the *ERP* and *ERL* for fifteen crops. The latter measure is defined as total output value minus the value of all produced inputs as well as labor and capital at international prices for tradables and relevant shadow prices for nontradables, including labor and capital; produced inputs include free services such as irrigation water. Economic returns thus defined obviously measure the shadow rent of land, and land being the ultimate scarce factor of production in Egyptian agriculture, it may be argued that this may be the relevant efficiency measure for agricultural crops. Let us assume now that this is indeed the case. Statistical analysis yields the following R^2s and Spearman rank correlation coefficients, *SR*s:

1981, 15 crops
$$ERP = 87.79 - 0.05\ ERL$$
$$R^2 = 0.63$$
$$SR = -0.91\ (Z = -3.41)$$
$$ERL = 1200.49 - 12.31\ ERP$$

Estimates of effective protection rates and of domestic resource costs, DRCs, for fourteen crops for 1963 (Hansen and Nashashibi 1975, table 7–5) produce the following results:

1963, 14 crops
$$ERP = 0.09 + 0.84\ DRC$$
$$R^2 = 0.71$$
$$SR = 0.68\ (Z = 2.46)$$
$$DRC = 0.21 + 0.84\ ERP$$

Both studies indicate that effective protection of crops is inversely related to social profitability—the lower social profitability is, the higher protection.

Cuddihy (1980, statistical tables) has estimated ERP and DRC for four major crops—cotton, rice, wheat, maize—for eight years between 1965 and 1976 and meat for one year. The averages for the eight years show much the same picture as those for the fifteen crops in 1981 and the fourteen crops in 1963—higher protection goes with lower social profitability. Over time, interestingly enough, the same relationship appears in linear regressions and rank correlations for two crops, rice and wheat. For cotton and maize the relationship is the opposite, but the relationship is weak and statistically insignificant. Meat was socially very unprofitable and highly protected.

Taken together, these results unequivocally indicate, as might be expected, that both in cross section and over time, protection and social profitability of crops have been inversely related. The direction of causality, important from the point of view of political economy, is a problem. To answer it we would need access to internal information about the bureaucratic decision process.

To what extent, and in what direction, effective protection (which has mostly been negative) has affected land allocation and production is another matter. Alongside price intervention, the government has imposed area restrictions for many crops. Since the mid-1950s annual plans for area allocation have been implemented by the Ministry of Agriculture through the agricultural cooperatives. In comparing actual acreages for major crops for 1961–65 and predicted areas with actual domestic prices and hypothetical domestic prices equal to international prices, the predictions based on estimated area response functions, the ERPs fairly well explain the relative extent to which price distortions caused acreages to be off the optimum, but the ERPs were responsible for only about 25 percent of the deviations from the optimum; the dominating distorting factor was the direct, physical control imposed by the government on acreage (Hansen and Nashashibi 1975, pp. 167–94).

Industry

Since 1961 government has interfered in different ways in public and private enterprises. Until 1973 private enterprises were strongly discriminated against in many ways (import permits, investment licenses, bank credits, and so on). The situation was exactly reversed in the mid-1970s, when public enterprises were subjected to much more direct administrative interference in both inputs and outputs, prices and quantities, than private enterprises. On the input side, public enterprises have to carry out the government's policy of employing graduates and conscripts and have little possibility of dismissing employees. Wages and salaries are largely set by government decree. Imported inputs are subjected to licensing and to the official, commercial bank exchange rate. Private enterprises have full freedom in hiring labor, with somewhat limited possibilities of dismissing employees, and must comply with minimum wage legislation and collective agreements with the government-controlled unions, those agreements more often than not amounting to orders. Evasion, however, is massive. Imported inputs in principle require license, but private enterprises since 1974 have been able to participate in so-called own-exchange import arrangements, license free and subject to the free (commercial bank) exchange rate. On the output side, public enterprises are frequently faced with production targets—for example, for rationed goods sold at low prices—and most of their prices are subject to administrative approval. Private enterprises may subcontract with public enterprises and may be subject to price controls, but generally private enterprises are at liberty to produce and price their output as they see fit. Foreign-financed enterprises operating under law 43 enjoy special tax and tariff privileges not available to public and other private enterprises.

The variety of methods of interference makes measuring effective protection and price distortion difficult. Using ERPs based on tariff legislation obviously will not do. But for ERPs based on actual farm and factory prices this objection at least, is not valid. I believe that the ERPs and DRCs used below, while far from perfect, are correctly estimated.

To determine whether effective protection has served to protect inefficient industries and given incentives to generate such industries, the correlation between ERPs and DRCs can again provide suggestions. The following equations are based on a cross section sample of seventeen industries for 1981 in the World Bank study, a sample of eight industries for 1965 in Hansen and Nashashibi (1975), and the twenty-one observations for 1954–70 behind table 4–15. Computing both R^2 and Spearman rank correlation coefficient, *SR*, and as before regressing both ways (with an eye on the political economy of protection in Egypt), the results are:

1954–70, 21 observations
$$ERP = 0.67 + 0.84 \ DRC$$
$$R^2 = 0.71$$
$$SR = 0.84 \ (Z = 3.73)$$
$$DRC = -0.12 + 0.84 \ ERP$$

1965, 8 observations
$$ERP = 1.22 + 0.75 \ DRC$$
$$R^2 = 0.78$$
$$SR = 0.88 \ (Z = 2.33)$$
$$DRC = -0.81 + 1.04 \ ERP$$

1981, 17 observations
$$ERP = -93.58 + 128.66 \ DRC$$
$$R^2 = 0.73$$
$$SR = 0.82 \ (Z = 3.29)$$
$$DRC = 1.37 + 0.01 \ ERP$$

The results are remarkably consistent, much more so than I expected, and they conform to the findings for agricultural crops—the lower social profitability, the higher effective protection, and vice versa.[8] The analysis, of course, does not provide an answer to what is cause and what is effect.

For agriculture it was possible to gauge the impact of price distortions on acreage allocation through the application of estimated acreage response functions. I see no way of doing anything similar for industry but I suspect that, for public enterprises, bureaucratic decisionmaking (setting production targets for rationed goods, for instance) by the administration dominates the picture. For private enterprise, of course, price distortions are more important, at least until the establishment of the own-exchange imports and exports in 1975.

The difference in effects of protective policies on public and private enterprises comes out clearly in estimates of the contributions of border taxes (tariffs) and price controls to the effective rate of protection (table 4–18). The first column in table 4–18 shows the actual ERPs, as traditionally defined and measured (and used above). The second and third columns show hypothetical ERPs, the second column assuming all price controls removed with the border tax system intact, the third column assuming all border taxes removed and the price control system intact (the two hypothetical ERPs obviously do not add up to the actual ERP).

A large number of industries have negative effective protection. Of the twelve public industries, six suffered negative protection, among

Table 4-18. Effective Rates of Protection of Public and Private Industries, 1981

Industry[a]	Actual	Border taxes (no price controls)	Price controls (no border taxes)
		Effective rate of protection	
		Hypothetical	
Public Enterprises			
Textiles			
Cotton	−28.40[b]	−2.31	−22.43
Other	35.47	−2.62	46.13
Food			
Edible oils	−93.97	−6.31	−81.66
Manufactured foods	−69.73	−2.90	−64.29
Alcohol, beverages, tobacco	4.61	−22.27	32.46
Chemicals			
Paper	88.90	−14.06	115.80
Basic	45.35	−7.60	79.95
Miscellaneous	−3.94[b]	−1.70	−8.98
Metallurgical and engineering			
Basic metals	−2,923.73[b]	−127.46	−3,552.14
Transport equipment	354.91[b]	136.92	−226.02
Electrical machinery	9.30	−3.47	19.55
China and glass	−633.63[b]	−25.71	−656.04
Private Enterprises			
Textiles			
Spinning	42.2	−89.9	−41.7
Other	63.8	57.7	3.7
Food	−38.9	72.8	55.2
Metals, engineering	−253.8[b]	−200.2	−69.9
Building materials	95.4	96.9	0.3

a. The number of private enterprises in the sample is small and the enterprises relatively large and modern. They are in no way representative of the informal sector.
b. Negative value added at world prices.
Source: World Bank data.

them the important cotton textiles and major food industries; two out of five private industries were in the same predicament. Surprisingly, the border tax system in itself gives negative protection to eleven out of twelve public industries and two out of five private industries. By normal standards, which would assume that the rationale of the border tax system is to protect domestic activities, the Egyptian border tax system is patently absurd. That the price control system in itself should give negative protection to many industries is less surprising. The absurdity of the system from a protection point of view is related to the fact that cost-of-living effects often have been the reason for revision of the tariff system.

For most industries the impact of price controls completely dominates that of border taxes. Indeed, this is the case for all public industries. For private industries the situation is exactly the opposite. In some cases the controls have the opposite impact of the border taxes, in all cases negating the negative impact of border taxes and changing the situation into one of subsidization.

User-Price Distortion

In discussing price distortions and their possible allocative effects on agricultural and industrial production the conventional measures of effective rates of protection and domestic resource costs or economic returns to land serve reasonably well. From a welfare point of view, however, distortions in users' prices are important, consumers being the ultimate users, the purchasers of capital goods, raw materials, and other productive inputs being considered intermediate users. From this point of view, a so-called accounting ratio, AR, may be preferable. The AR, used in the World Bank study, is defined as the ratio of the shadow price of a particular, well-defined commodity or service to its market price, including net indirect taxes. The shadow price is defined as the total costs of tradable inputs evaluated at international prices and nontradable inputs estimated at international prices insofar as the tradable cost element is concerned and at shadow factor prices insofar as the primary resources element is concerned. If there is no distortion, AR = 1. The accounting ratio is in effect a gross resource cost concept, measured on output value rather than on value added content. It is not an effective protection measure showing the incentive for private producers to distort production. It is not a purchasing power parity measure, either, because it includes nontraded goods and primary resources. Rather, it indicates the distortion of final use and is thus a measure for evaluating welfare. With the free market exchange rate used to convert international prices from foreign into domestic currency, the average AR for a country should indicate the shadow exchange rate as compared with the free rate; an average AR above (or below) unity would indicate overvaluation (or undervaluation) of the currency.

To answer the question which kind of average to use for the accounting ratio, both medians and unweighted means for 130 tradable and nontradable commodities and services are presented in table 4–19.[9] In-

Table 4-19. Accounting Ratios (Shadow Price over Market Price) for Important Groups of Goods, 1979

Group (number of items)	Median	Highest	Lowest	Unweighted mean +/− standard error
Tradable manufactured, capital, and intermediary goods (38)	0.93	2.36	0.75	1.03 +/− 0.39
Agricultural inputs and outputs (13)	1.28	4.26	0.99	1.57 +/− 0.89
Petroleum products and gas (8)	5.88–6.27	15.30	1.01	7.06 +/− 5.50
Urban consumer goods (28)	0.97	5.41	0.38	1.57 +/− 1.44
Rural consumer goods (8)	1.04–1.16	2.49	0.54	1.31 +/− 0.61
Nontraded goods (34)	1.21	3.77	0.33	1.31 +/− 0.71
Total (130)	0.99	15.30	0.33	1.67 +/− 2.08
All tradable goods (96)	0.97	15.30	0.38	1.79 +/− 2.38

Source: World Bank data.

ternational prices are converted to Egyptian pounds at the free market exchange rate in 1979, which was about 10 percent higher than the official rate (in Egyptian pounds per U.S. dollar). The median ratio for all goods was 0.99, and for the tradable goods in the sample 0.97. This might indicate that the actual free (and also the official) rate in 1979 was close to the shadow rate. The unweighted mean for all goods was much higher, however—1.67—and for the tradable goods it was even as high as 1.79, implying considerable overvaluation. What correct weighting would imply is hard to say. However, a handful of twelve goods with ARs above 3.0 is responsible for increasing the mean by 0.51 units. Some of these twelve goods are quite important and might have relatively high weights. Thus it is not obvious that weighting would be a secondary matter, and the conclusion that the actual free (and the official) rate in 1979 was close to the shadow rate may not be warranted.

The spread around the average, measured by the difference between highest and lowest AR or by the standard error, is large for all groups and indicates a high degree of distortion in the economy even if the actual exchange rate should happen not to be significantly distorted in 1979. The exchange rate may even be a minor part of the problem. Comparison of groups, based on the unweighted means, indicates that prices for tradable manufactured, capital, and intermediary goods, mainly produced by public enterprises, on average may be roughly undistorted with a relatively small spread. But petroleum products and gas are grossly underpriced, and agricultural inputs and outputs and both urban and rural consumer goods are considerably underpriced. Nontraded goods appear to be less underpriced than agricultural and urban consumer goods; it is not clear, however, whether housing services are included in the sample. Housing, at least in older buildings, may be even more underpriced than petroleum products and housing has, of course, a very heavy weight. When nontraded goods are compared with all tradable goods, the nontraded are less underpriced than the tradable. This might be interpreted as evidence that the so-called Dutch disease is present, tradables being relatively cheap. The medians, unfortunately, point in the opposite direction.

Price Reform during the 1980s

The discussion so far has been based on the price system established during the 1970s. During the 1980s price reforms were undertaken in both agriculture and public enterprises, largely because of pressure from donors and international organizations to reduce price distortions and promote efficiency.

In the early 1980s, prices of export crops were revised to bring them closer to border prices. Application of the low, official exchange rate continued to keep farmgate prices for cotton and rice low; for most other crops, production quotas and compulsory delivery at low prices were phased out. Sales of subsidized food, particularly of wheat and wheat flour, however, continued to exert a downward pressure on free market prices. Transfers from agriculture through government interference (shown in table 18–4) declined from 46.2 percent of agricultural GDP (10.6 percent of total GDP) during 1974–81 to 17.6 percent of agricultural GDP (2.9 percent of total GDP) during 1982–85. Both from an incentive and from a distributive point of view, discrimination against agriculture thus diminished greatly during the first half of the 1980s.

Public sector companies in early 1989 were subject to three different output price systems (Handoussa 1988b, pp. 39 ff.). Prices for nineteen important products were centrally fixed at low levels, with only minor subsidies from the public budget, thus serving to tax the producing companies. The nineteen products included vegetable oil, milk and cheese, sugar, salt, cigarettes, soft drinks (Pepsi Cola), soap, detergents, cotton yarn, woolen yarn, refrigerators, passenger cars, pharmaceutical products, fertilizers, and reinforcing steel bars—obviously not exclusively basic needs of the poor. Also the upper layers of the bureaucracy were taken care of! Factory prices for these products had been kept virtually constant from 1970 to 1985 despite inflation. Such products amount to more than 30 percent of the total output of companies affiliated with the Ministry of Industry. For most products, prices are negotiated between the enterprise and the supervising ministry, other ministries, and possibly major customers. Prices on about nine hundred products are fixed on a cost-plus basis with markups of 5–10 percent. Slow adjustment to costs under this system has implied a deterioration in the profitability of businesses. In 1984–85, full price liberalization was introduced for selected products, and enterprises were allowed to set sales prices according to market forces. The first major group thus freed from price controls was textiles and garment products (excluding yarns).

Finally, since 1985–86 direct production subsidies to public enterprises have been gradually eliminated, either being shifted to public distribution organizations (fertilizers) or simply eliminated (popular cheap cloth is the important example). Such subsidies declined from LE323 million in 1984–85 to LE68 million in 1986–87.

The Full Employment Economy of Egyptian Etatism

After the nationalizations of 1961 and the strong expansion of government employment during the 1960s and 1970s (table 4–4) the public sector came to dominate the urban labor market and to be highly visible in rural areas. The cross classification in table 4–20 by employment status, economic activity, and urban or rural location reveals that almost one-third of the total labor force (not including unpaid family labor and the armed forces) were self-employed (one fifth) or employers (one-

Table 4-20. Distribution of Labor Force, by Employment Status and Location, 1976

Status	Percent of labor force[a]			Percent of paid employees		
	Total	Urban	Rural	Total	Urban	Rural
Employers and self-employed	31.0	21.6	38.9	—	—	—
Agriculture	19.7	2.7	32.9	—	—	—
Nonagriculture, private	11.3	18.9	6.0	—	—	—
Employees, paid	69.0	78.4	61.1	100	100	100
Public Sector	31.3	50.2	15.4	45.4	64.0	25.2
Agriculture, private	22.6	4.1	38.0	32.8	5.2	62.2
Nonagriculture, private	15.2	24.1	7.7	22.0	30.7	12.6
Total	100	100	100	—	—	—

— = Not applicable.
a. Based on population census data, not including armed forces.
Source: Hansen (1985).

tenth). About two-thirds were paid employees, almost one-half of them employed in the public sector, one-third in agriculture, and the remaining fifth in the nonagricultural, private sector, which almost coincides with the so-called informal sector. In urban areas as much as two-thirds of all paid employees were in the public sector and in rural areas a surprising one-quarter. Since 1976 the shares of employees in the public sector have almost certainly increased in both urban and rural areas and those shares would rise about 4 percent higher if they included army conscripts.

The shift toward public sector employment appears until recently to have been accompanied by low levels of unemployment. Seasonal unemployment and underemployment may have declined but are still considerable, and voluntary unemployment of educated youngsters seems to be growing rapidly. However, when unemployment is measured at the agricultural employment peak (May–June since 1964, when the maize season changed) and voluntary unemployment of educated youngsters is disregarded, unemployment seems to be negligible and to have been so since the early 1960s.

For measured unemployment, shown in figure 1–3, the evidence appears to be contradictory but careful scrutiny indicates that involuntary unemployment declined throughout the 1960s and was low throughout the 1970s and into the early 1980s.

The population censuses indicate that unemployment increased from about 2.5 percent of the total labor force in 1960 to 7.5 percent in 1976 and 14.9 percent in 1986. The censuses, while admittedly a poor source of information about unemployment, distinguish between unemployed with and without previous work experience; they report a decline in the rate of those with experience from 1.2 percent in 1960 to 0.5 percent in 1976. Since the 1960 census was taken in September, at the agricultural peak season, and the 1976 and 1986 censuses in November, a slack season in agriculture, and most of the enumerated unemployed in 1976 were children under twelve years old, it stands to reason that the increase from 1960 to 1976 was largely a matter of seasonal unemployment, cotton picking petering out in early November. The increase from 1976 to 1986 may, on the other hand, indicate a genuine increase in unemployment.

The official labor force surveys depicted in figure 1–3 report a strong decline in unemployment from 1958 to 1962 and 1964 with a slight increase in 1968, a decline to 1.5 percent in 1972 and then a slow but steady increase to 6.5 percent in 1983 and a slight decrease to 6 percent in 1984. Figure 1–3 also shows an economic activity indicator, the deviation from trend, inversed, in real income per capita. Considering the development of economic activity in the country with recessionary conditions in the late 1960s and early 1970s, strong expansion after 1973, and again recession, even stagnation after 1982, the labor force surveys' unemployment rates look a bit odd. The surveys show that from 1973, when both the surveys and the population censuses broke down the unemployed into those with and without work experience, through 1984 unemployment of workers with experience was about constant and negligible—0.2–0.5 percent. Probably that has been the case since the early 1960s, as shown by the censuses, and the fluctuations of measured total unemployment with the steady increase after 1973 is probably a matter of voluntary youth unemployment. To substantiate this interpretation we now turn to the government's military drafting and civil employment policies.

The Aswan High Dam was constructed in part by very labor intensive methods (pick, shovel, and wheelbarrow) and its demand for labor was felt everywhere in the countryside well into the mid-1960s. With the nationalizations of 1961–63, the government embarked on an urban employment drive, lowering working hours from 48 hours to 42 hours per week and forcing public enterprises to hire far more replacements than they needed. The armed forces during the 1960s were increased from about 1 percent to 4 percent of the total labor force and have remained absolutely at the same level even after 1973, thus perhaps declining in relative size to 2.5–3.0 percent. Finally, in 1964 the government instituted the right of graduates from secondary and higher schools to public sector employment after a waiting period—two years for university graduates and three years for secondary level graduates. In the early 1980s, the waiting periods were effectively increased to three and a half and six years, respectively. This policy change is clearly visible in table 4–21. Only flow data are available but given the flow and the increasing waiting periods, stocks of graduates waiting for appointment must have accelerated since the late 1970s and become large. In 1973 a similar right was given to conscripts honorably discharged from the armed forces. This veterans' policy was officially abrogated in 1976, but the military authorities appear somehow to have been able to continue it (the riot of security forces in 1986 was partly about this issue). Several attempts to abrogate or limit the policy have been thwarted by riots and other student-parent activities and it now appears to have become part and parcel of the social compact, with, however, waiting periods covertly increased as just mentioned.

Increasing numbers of graduates waiting for public employment may be responsible for the increase in enumerated unemployment from 1964 to 1968. The decline then from 1968 to 1973 may have been the consequence of heavy military drafting; after 1973, graduates again dominate the picture with a steady increase in unemployed without work experience waiting for employment in the public sector. The massive migration to Arab oil-producing countries after 1973, which obviously helped to keep unemployment down, did not to any appreciable degree absorb recently graduated students. Thus interpreted, the unemployment statistics do not contradict the characterization of autocratic Egypt as a full, or at least high, employment economy until 1984 but with substantial seasonal unemployment and permanently disguised unemployment in government and the public sector.

Standard unemployment analysis usually breaks down annual averages of monthly (or quarterly) data on frictional, seasonal, and other unemployment, the latter category obtained statistically as a residual. Such a breakdown should not be confused with the notions of voluntary versus involuntary unemployment, or with the natural rate of unemployment (Friedman 1968) and the nonaccelerating-inflation rate of unemployment, NAIRU (Coe 1985). The attempt below to make such a breakdown for 1976 and 1986 is nothing but a conjecture but may suggest orders of magnitude.

Although obviously frictional unemployment may change over time, assume that the lowest observed unemployment rates in the labor force surveys—at the agricultural peak season—are an expression of frictional unemployment. The years 1971–75 would then indicate frictional unemployment on the order of 2 percent. Accepting then both labor force survey (LFS) and population census (PC) unemployment rates at face value and assuming these to represent seasonal lows and highs, respectively, during the year, an average of LFS and PC rates for the year

Table 4-21. Waiting Periods of Graduates for Government Employment, 1973–82 and 1987

Class	Total new graduates (thousands)[a]	New diploma holders (thousands)		Government needs (thousands)[b]	Waiting period (years)	
		Graduates	Eligible applicants		University degree	Intermediary diploma
1973	n.a.	n.a.	n.a.	n.a.	2	3
1974	n.a.	n.a.	n.a.	n.a.	2	3
1975	n.a.	n.a.	n.a.	n.a.	2.5	4
1976	n.a.	n.a.	n.a.	n.a.	3	4
1977	184.7	127.2	81.7	68.2	3	4
1978	192.8	128.8	85.1	82.1	3	4
1979	207.5	143.9	82.0	75.9	3	4
1980	223.9	154.6	93.9	75.0	3	4
1981	262.8	191.0	114.0	22.4	3.5	6
1982	283.3	n.a.	n.a.	n.a.	5	6
1987	376.3	n.a.	n.a.	n.a.	5	6

n.a. = Not available.
a. University and intermediate technical schools.
b. As reported to the Ministry of Manpower for year.
Source: Handoussa (1988b, tables 2–1 to 2–4).

may then be taken to represent the annual average of monthly data (not known) for 1976 and 1986. The change in agricultural seasonalities makes the method inapplicable to 1960. Moreover because LFSs were not taken in 1976 and 1986 an average of the rates for 1975 and 1977 is used for 1976 and the LFS rate for 1984 is used for 1986. Assume, finally, that in 1976 unemployment other than seasonal was of a frictional nature. These crude methods lead to the following conjectured annual, average unemployment rates (percent):

Year	Total	Frictional	Seasonal	Other
1976	5	2	3	0
1986	10	2	3	5

This interpretation leads to the conclusion that unemployment other than frictional and seasonal did indeed increase substantially from 1976 to 1986, the bulk of it, however, probably being voluntary youth unemployment. Presumably, graduates who were not employed but had signed up for public employment with the Ministry of Manpower and had made no other effort to seek employment, preferring to wait for public appointment, would respond to the LFS interviewers as not being employed but as actively seeking jobs. The statistical authorities in Egypt, CAPMAS, are developing a new format for the survey that if sufficiently detailed may clear up these problems.

Wages and Wage Determination

Official data for agricultural, daily wage rates and weekly earnings in manufacturing, deflated by the official consumer price index, are shown in figure 4–1. Averages for wages and salaries in general government are available for the years 1945–56 and 1966 to 1984–85. They do not, however, take into account changes in the work force of general government, particularly related to the policy of graduate and veteran rights to public employment, shifting the composition of this part of the work force strongly in favor of lower age and wage grade groups.[10] Carefully weighted averages would be needed to make comparisons between general government and manufacturing wages meaningful. The establishment censuses, the main source of information for manufacturing, cover both public and private enterprises but only with ten employees and above and enumerate only so-called permanent labor, that is labor with sufficient seniority (half a year) to obtain employment security and social security benefits.

Real wages in both agriculture and manufacturing have increased steadily since World War II—3.5 percent annually in agriculture against 2.4 percent in manufacturing from 1948 to 1984. For 1960–84 the difference is even more pronounced with 4.5 percent in agriculture against 2.3

Figure 4-1. Real Wage Rates in Agriculture and Real Weekly Earnings in Manufacturing, 1948-84.

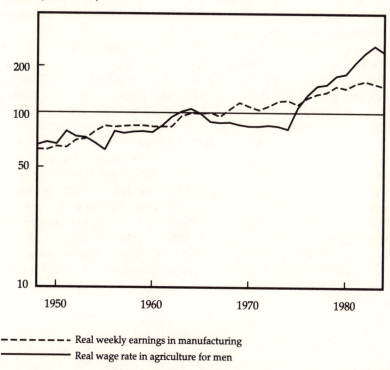

Index (1965 = 100)

- - - - - - - - Real weekly earnings in manufacturing
———————— Real wage rate in agriculture for men

Source: Data from CAPMAS and Ministry of Agriculture.

percent in manufacturing. During the same period, real gross national product per capita increased by 2.8 percent annually. In this sense agricultural labor has done much better than labor in modern industry. Relative wages have, however, developed very unevenly over the years. In the years 1964–73 manufacturing continued an upward trend while in agriculture real wages declined substantially in 1965–66 and then continued on a slightly downward path until 1973. From 1973 the roles are reversed. Manufacturing continues its upward trend, perhaps slightly accelerating during the second half of the 1970s, and the early 1980s, with agriculture shooting up, not only regaining the relative loss from 1964 to 1973 but running way ahead of manufacturing.

Agricultural wages are largely market determined, with little government intervention. Unionization is negligible. Statutory minimum wages exist but are not observed and no attempt has ever been made to enforce the legislation. In any case, since the mid-1970s current wages in agriculture have greatly exceeded the minimum wage. One single agricultural operation, manual cotton pest control, is organized by the cooperatives, which for all intents and purposes are part of the public sector. It is carried out in late May and early June by children supervised by adult women, all hired and paid by the cooperatives. For this operation, however, market wages are paid.

Studies of agricultural wages point to market clearing, at least at the peak seasons. There is considerable evidence based on surveys of employment patterns supporting the market-clearing hypothesis (Hansen 1969; Richards and Martin 1983). Whether the agricultural labor market clears outside the peak seasons is another matter. Seasonal wage flexibility is very substantial but so is measured seasonal unemployment. Information from a few villages in the Delta suggests that the market price in off-season months may exceed the reservation wage of unemployed agricultural workers who accordingly would be involuntarily unemployed (Richards and Martin 1983). If accepted at face value, this information requires that some mechanism be identified that would prevent wages from falling sufficiently to clear the labor market outside the peaks. Internal labor market theory of the efficiency variety would be a promising candidate (Hansen 1985). It is claimed (Commander and Hadhoud 1986) that long-term contracts for seasonal employment are gaining ground, but the claim is made on very uncertain ground, both empirically and theoretically.

Before World War II Egypt had free labor unions. These were small and divided, some dominated by communists (textiles, for instance), some by the Muslim Brotherhood (sugar and oil), some by the moderate Wafd party. Total membership in 1951 was about 150,000. The unions were officially recognized in 1948 when, however, in return compulsory arbitration was introduced for key industries. In 1952 compulsory arbitration was extended to all industries and the unions rapidly came under government control, the president of the unions and the Minister of Labor for a long time being the same person. The unions have had no real say in wage setting in either the private or the public sector. Public sector wages are thus one-sidedly set by the government. Since the nationalizations around 1961, a grade system has been applied to public enterprises and authorities, similar to the one applied to civil servants and employees in general government. Seniority increases are large and practically speaking mechanical. Before the nationalizations and the introduction of the grade system, piece-rate work was common in manufacturing. Since 1962 time-rate work has predominated and it is now fair to say that incentive pay is of no importance in the public sector. The grade system has been revised several times; in 1975 the number of grades was reduced and differentials between highest and lowest grades were substantially reduced for equity reasons. Over time the lowest grades have tended to get full cost-of-living compensation while the higher grades have lost considerably in real terms insofar as basic salary is concerned.

Government decisions about public enterprise wages since 1961 have in practice set minimums for large and medium-sized private, nonagricultural enterprises which also have to comply with statutory minimum wage and social security legislation. Although the real wage series for manufacturing in figure 4–1 covers both public and private enterprises above a certain size, it is a good approximation to assume that since 1961 wages in manufacturing, thus defined, have been determined by government decree.

Official annual wage data cover only establishments with ten or more (permanent) employees and do not include casual labor. For sectors other than manufacturing the official data are thus of particularly limited value. Studies of the informal sector are mostly concerned with aspects other than wages and conditions of work (Mead 1982). Information about wages for construction workers (Moheieldin 1979; Hansen and Radwan 1982, table 25) point to a very high degree of upward wage flexibility for both skilled and unskilled labor in this industry, which mostly employs casual labor. Public construction work is mostly subcontracted so that hiring and firing and negotiations about wages are in the hands of private contractors, in principle subjected to minimum wage legislation but not otherwise subordinated to the public sector wage system. Collective bargaining plays no role. Whether there would be sufficient downward wage flexibility to ensure market clearing under all circumstances is doubtful. In the late 1950s the labor force surveys showed considerable unemployment among construction workers. For unskilled building workers, who might have come from agriculture and in slack seasons and might return there, possibly on a temporary, commuter basis, the situation may be very different from that of skilled workers. The latter might attempt, as self-employed, to obtain repair and maintenance jobs for private households (thanks to rent control, repair and maintenance has become the tenant's problem). But even with the price of labor falling to nothing the demand for such work might not respond sufficiently to create full employment because materials are relatively expensive. For the rest of the informal sector, no systematic information exists about wage formation and developments. There is something to indicate that the labor market surrounding a particular small enterprise is very small (family, personal acquaintances, relatives of employees, and so forth) and for that reason tends to be imperfect (Mead 1982). It has been conjectured that internal labor market theory might apply to this sector; turnover seems to be small but some work sharing may exist that makes work time adjust to the level of activity of the enterprise, an indication that the risk-sharing variety of internal labor market theory may be relevant. For these reasons I do not believe it is reasonable to assume market clearing generally in the informal sector, but this remains a subjective conjecture.

Econometric estimates, admittedly primitive (Hansen 1986), suggest that the Phillips relation does not apply to the Egyptian labor market at all. Marginal productivity theory works fairly well for agricultural wages but not for wages in manufacturing industries, at least not for the period since the nationalizations. The relation examined here is the augmented Phillips curve in Friedman's formulation, which explains the rate of change of nominal wage rates by the level of economic activity (specifically, by the rate of unemployment) and the expected rate of price inflation (Friedman 1968). The marginal productivity theory holds that the level of nominal wage rates is determined by the value of marginal productivity, by output prices and physical (marginal) labor productivity.

Regressions of the rate of change of nominal wages in Egyptian agriculture show a strong, significant dependence on the rate of change of the consumer price index (CPI), but they show no significant impact from the unemployment rate or from other indicators of the level of activity. On the other hand, regressions of the level (not the rate of change) of agricultural wage rates on nominal value added with an employment indicator show strong, significant results, indicating that marginal productivity theory does apply to the agricultural labor market.

Regressions of the rate of change of nominal earnings in manufacturing shows, as in agriculture, a strong and significant impact of the rate of change in the CPI, while variables indicating the general level of economic activity (unemployment rate, real income per capita with a trend) contribute little or nothing to explaining wage change, and more often than not the signs go wrong. The level of wages in manufacturing turns out to be strongly related to the CPI and negatively related to productivity after 1962, but positively related to productivity with no significant impact from the CPI before 1962.

Considering that private small-scale farming has dominated agriculture and that there has been almost no government intervention in the agricultural labor market throughout the postwar period, and, on the other hand, that there have been radical institutional changes in manufacturing since 1961, the results of the econometric exercises should not be surprising. The agricultural labor market has always been and continues to be highly competitive, with probably some elements of monopsony. With market clearing, not the Phillips relation but rather the marginal productivity theory should work. For the labor market surrounding modern manufacturing, there should be a radical change in wage formation around 1961. Before 1961, with modern manufacturing dominated by powerful private entrepreneurs, weak unions subjected to arbitration, and workers typically on piece-rate work, it is natural that workers should tend to benefit from increases in productivity but not be automatically compensated when the CPI increases. Money and real wages in manufacturing since 1961 reflect the behavior of government, not of market forces. The estimated Phillips relations for manufacturing after 1961 suggest that in setting wages, the government has paid little or no attention to demand and supply in the labor market but a great deal of attention to price and real wage developments, trying at a minimum to compensate wage earners in the public sector for cost-of-living increases. This is entirely consistent with the government's concern about stabilizing the cost of living through price and rent controls, subsidization, rationing, and so on, to offset its own, at times strongly destabilizing, fiscal and monetary policies. Public sector wage and cost-of-living policies are integral parts of the social compact and thus of the government's general policy of income distribution and welfare. Thus when the coefficient for the price variable in the Phillips relation is found to be close to one, it should not be interpreted to mean that inflation is fully expected by the labor market. It reflects government behavior.

Although the inverse relation between productivity and real wages in manufacturing in 1962–70 indicates that wage determination in this sector did not conform to marginal productivity theory, it might still be argued that the government had no choice but to let manufacturing workers in the public sector enjoy the same increases in real wages as workers in the rest of the economy, lest the public sector lose labor to the private sector. In this sense, it might be claimed, public sector wages did in fact follow the market. This argument, however, overlooks the fact that agricultural real wages suffered a decline from 1964 to 1974 and in 1970 were 22 percent lower than in 1964. It seems unlikely that real wages in the informal sector should have increased substantially, given the decline of real wages in agriculture. The only way of explaining wage developments in manufacturing seems therefore to be to assume that political considerations took the upper hand—that in the public sector, wages essentially are a political price. From this point of view, it is instructive to review wage developments in manufacturing in some detail from 1961 to 1970.

After the nationalizations of 1961, real wages in manufacturing were increased strongly for two years. It was clearly a matter of demonstrating to workers and employees the blessings of Arab socialism, the newly adopted official ideology for Egypt. This is standard behavior of socialist-leaning governments after a political takeover. Allende, Mitterand, and Papandreou may stand up and be counted. In 1964 the costs of the Yemen War, with sharply deteriorating exchange reserves and foreign relations, forced the Egyptian government to adopt an austerity policy, with serious cutbacks in public investment, increases in public sector prices, and restraint in public sector wages. General budgetary considerations thus took the upper hand in the setting of public sector wages. The military defeat in 1967 then threatened the very authority of the Nasser regime. Substantial wage increases with stiffer price controls were apparently thought necessary to placate public sector workers and employees. Before his death, finally, Nasser realized how disastrous developments had become in public enterprises and the cycle of public relations in wage policy entered yet another recession; productivity and efficiency were emphasized (Waterbury 1983, p. 99) and real wages in manufacturing were cut back somewhat in 1970–71. Policy considerations of this kind are difficult to quantify. Such wage determining factors could be represented in formal regressions by dummies, but the number of dummies needed might outrun the observations; informed narrative probably handles events better.

The econometric studies of wages in manufacturing do not extend beyond 1969, and no reliable information about productivity in manufacturing is available for 1969–74. After 1974 there is no doubt that productivity in public enterprises recovered strongly from the decline in 1962–69. The period from 1974 to 1982 is too short, however, to permit systematic analysis. The upward trend in real wages in manufacturing continued, possibly somewhat accelerated. Political considerations continued to take the upper hand but the influence of the tightening labor market with surging wages in agriculture and construction, migration of workers to the Arab oil-producing countries, and increasing employment in foreign-financed, high-pay law 43 enterprises is discernible. Given these factors the government's wage policy toward public enterprises may for this period be characterized as restrained.

Wages and Competitiveness

Wages are an important cost element in both industry and agriculture and as such crucial for international competitiveness. Tables 4–22 and 4–23 compare nominal wage costs in Egypt between 1948 and 1981–82 with the trade-weighted rate of inflation of Egypt's trade partners. Estimating the rate of increase of nominal wage costs per unit of output—the difference between the rate of increase of output per worker and the rate of increase of the nominal wage rate per worker—is fraught with problems, and the results show at best orders of magnitude. The most important problems may be the omission of fringe benefits in manufacturing (there are no fringe benefits in agriculture) and the limitation of trade partners to IMF-member countries. Fringe benefits increased strongly at the time of the nationalizations and their omission may make the picture too rosy, particularly for 1962–69. Their inclusion would not, however, seriously change the picture (Hansen and Marzouk 1965, pp. 156–59); for the period 1948–82 as a whole they could at most increase the rate of increase of nominal wage costs by 0.5 percent. It is, moreover,

Table 4-22. Annual Growth in Egypt's Wage Costs and Trade Partners' Inflation, 1945–82
(percent)

Period	Manufacturing			Agriculture			Cost of living, Egypt	International inflation among trade partners[a]	
	Output per worker	Nominal wage per worker	Nominal wage cost per unit of output	Output per worker	Nominal wage per worker	Nominal wage cost per unit of output		CPI	WPI
1945–52	4.0	6.9	2.9	1.3	4.3	3.0	4.5	10.0	11.5
1952–57	8.6	3.1	-5.5	1.0	0.0	-1.9	-1.0	-0.6	-0.3
1957–62	1.0	-0.4	-1.4	1.2	4.1	2.9	-0.3	5.2	3.2
1962–69	-3.0	9.6	12.6	2.1	3.2	1.1	4.7	2.6	1.8
1969–74	n.a.	5.5	5–6[b]	1.6	6.8	5.2	4.8	9.6	10.9
1974 to 1981–82[c]	4.1	16.4	12.3	4.9	21.5	16.6	12.1	10.2	9.1
1945–81	2.3	7.5	5.2	2.2	6.5	4.3	4.4	5.7	6.0
1948–81	2.3[b]	7.7[b]	5.4[b]	1.9	7.8	5.8	n.a.	n.a	n.a.

n.a. = Not available.
a. Weighted by trade in 1948–81.
b. Conjecture.
c. For agriculture 1974–80.

Source: Author's computations based on Mabro and Radwan (1976); Egypt, CAPMAS, *Statistical Yearbook,* 1978, 1984; Radwan (1974); ILO, *Yearbook of Labor Statistics;* Wattleworth (1975); Hansen and Radwan (1982); Egypt, Ministry of Finance, *Annuaire statistique de l'Egypte;* World Bank and International Monetary Fund data.

Table 4-23. Cumulated Increase in Egypt's Wage Costs and Trade Partners' Inflation, 1948-81 (1948=100)

Year	Nominal wage costs per unit of output, Egypt		Trade partners' inflation	
	Manufacturing	Agriculture	CPI	WPI
1948	100	100	100	100
1952	110	112	146	155
1957	84	106	142	152
1962	79	122	183	179
1969	174	132	219	203
1974	227	170	347	340
1981	512	498	686	625

Source: Table 4-22.

a problem whether contributions to retirement programs and the like should be considered a social cost. The exclusion of communist countries from the trade partners is particularly serious for the years 1962–74. There is little, however, to suggest how including the communist trading partners would affect the results since the notion of competitiveness does not apply easily to such countries.

Both tables show that Egypt's relative cost developments were extremely favorable until 1962. Nominal wage costs in manufacturing fell by 1.0 percent annually and increased by a modest 0.8 percent in agriculture. Trade partners' rate of inflation was about 2.5 percent. Between 1962 and 1969 Egypt's manufacturing position deteriorated badly, but its competitiveness in agriculture was unchanged. Even so, compared with 1948 Egypt's position in both manufacturing and agriculture continued to improve. From 1969 to 1974 its position may have improved further. From 1948 to 1974, nominal wage costs increased by 3.2 percent a year in manufacturing and 2.1 percent in agriculture against a rate of inflation of 4.8–4.9 percent in trade partner countries. It is, interestingly enough, during the years of the *infitah* that Egypt's position worsened. From 1974 to 1981–82 Egypt's wage costs increased by 12.3 percent a year in manufacturing and 16.6 percent in agriculture against 9–10 percent inflation in the trade partner countries, and in 1981 Egypt's cost inflation had almost caught up with its trade partners' price inflation. The fruits of Nasser's austerity were squandered by Sadat. Yet it will be understood that relative cost developments in Egypt did not call for nominal devaluation of the Egyptian pound for 1948 to 1981–82 as a whole. This is one important piece of evidence for judging the possible over- or undervaluation of the Egyptian pound.

Fiscal and Monetary Policy—Investment and Saving

To simplify discussion of the impact of fiscal and monetary policy on inflation and the balance of payments, table 4–24 shows the difference in national saving and investment and breaks them down by public and private sector. Net borrowing or lending is used to represent deficits or surpluses; thus the external deficit—national deficit equal to national net borrowing equal to current account deficit—is equal to the difference between national gross investment and national gross saving. And the budget deficit—the public sector deficit—equals public net borrowing, the difference between public gross investment and public gross saving. Public gross saving is by definition the difference between public current revenue and expenditure—the surplus of the current budget. These notions carry over to the private sector, where the deficit or net borrowing equals the difference between private investment and saving.

Let it immediately be pointed out that the data behind table 4–24 are not entirely comparable. The estimates in table 4–24 of national saving and investment are based on national accounting estimates, official for 1974–84 but not for earlier years. The public sector estimates are based on government budget accounts, and the private sector figures are obtained as a residual. The government has never released accounts of actual expenditure and revenue for the years around the Suez War, the 1967 War, and the 1973 War. The so-called estimated budgets for the first two periods are probably misleading, and for 1973, no actual budget is available. One would, however, expect that during such emergencies both deficits and financing through the central bank would tend to increase. Monetary analysis confirms that the latter was, indeed, the case. As a substitute for the public sector deficit, public sector borrowing from the central bank is shown in table 4–24, column 5. I have measured everything as percentages of GNP at current market prices. Considering the long period covered by the table, and the relatively strong inflation in Egypt since the mid-1970s, some kind of normalization is required. The gross national product includes net factor payments to or from abroad (to the extent they are known), including interest and dividend payments and workers' remittances; these are then also taken into account in the estimates of gross saving, crucial for the years after 1973.[11]

Gross investment at the national level (discussed earlier) increased from 13–14 percent of GNP during the 1950s to 17–18 percent during the first five-year plan, fell back then to about 13 percent during the war years 1967 to 1973, and thereafter increased strongly to 28–30 percent in the early 1980s (to decline again after the mid-1980s).

Measured on GNP, the external deficit has tended to accelerate over time. Remaining at a level of 2 percent during the 1950s, with a slight increase around the Suez War, it came close to 5 percent during the first

Table 4-24. National Saving, Investment, and Borrowing by Public and Private Sectors, 1953–84
(percent of GNP at current market prices)

	National			Public sector				Private sector		
	Net borrowing	Gross saving	Gross investment	Net borrowing	Borrowing from central bank	Gross saving	Gross investment	Net borrowing	Gross[a] saving	Gross investment
1953–54 to 1955–56	1.7	13.0	14.7	2.8	4.0[b]	-0.5	2.3	-1.1	13.5	12.4
1956–57 to 1957–58	2.8	10.8	13.6	n.a.	3.3	n.a.	n.a.	n.a.	n.a.	n.a.
1958–59 to 1959–60	2.0	11.5	13.5	7.0	3.4	0.4	7.4	-5.0	11.1	6.1
1960–61 to 1964–65	4.7	12.7	17.4	13.0	3.5	2.2	15.2	-8.3	10.5	2.2
1965–66 to 1966–67	2.9	13.7	16.6	n.a.	4.3	n.a.	n.a.	n.a.	n.a.	n.a.
1967–68 to 1970–71	3.9	9.3	13.2	8.7	2.7	2.2	10.9	-4.8	7.1	2.3
1971–72 to 1973	6.7	6.3	13.0	n.a.	3.8	n.a.	n.a.	n.a.	n.a.	n.a.
1974–78	9.4	18.1	27.5	17.8	12.2	2.5	20.3	-8.4	15.6	7.2
1979 to 1983–84	12.3	17.1	29.4	14.1	7.2	7.5	21.6	-1.8	9.6	7.8

n.a. = Not available.
a. Residual—national figure minus public sector figure.
b. Conjecture; for 1955–56 only.
Source: Author's computations based on Hansen and Marzouk (1965); Hansen in Vatikiotis (1968); Ikram (1980); IMF, Government Finance Statistics Yearbook; IMF, International Financial Statistics; World Bank and IMF data.

five-year plan and then fell back to a level of 3-4 percent in 1965-70 when availability of foreign financing probably may have been the binding constraint (see below). When this constraint relaxed after 1970 through aid from Arab countries, the current account deficit soared to about 7 percent of GNP in 1971-72 to 1973 and then to 12-13 percent after 1979.

National gross saving remained roughly at the level of 12-14 percent from the early 1950s to the 1967 War. A sharp fall to 9 percent during 1967-68 to 1970-71 was mostly absorbed by a decline in investment with little impact on the external deficit. A further decline to 6 percent before 1973 was not accompanied by a further decline of investment. The full impact was now on the external deficit. After 1973 national saving soared to a level of 17-18 percent of GNP. The accompanying increase in the current account deficit reflected the even larger increase in investment.

Budget Policy

To understand deficit developments better, it is necessary to look at the public and private sectors. The public sector is defined to include public authorities and enterprises. Nationalizations and sequestrations meant that investments and savings (retained profits) in incorporated businesses were shifted from the private to the public sector during the years 1956 to 1961-63. In discussing public sector accounts—that is, fiscal policy—the distinctions are current budget ("above the line") surplus, by definition equal to public saving, and total budget, that is current plus capital budget deficit, by definition equal to net borrowing.

Ever since the Suez War, the current budget has tended to be in the black. The current surplus—public saving—increased from −0.5 percent of GNP during 1953-54 to 1955-56 to 2.2 percent during the first five-year plan years, a change that partly was related to the nationalizations and sequestrations. The current surplus then remained at that level until 1974-78, after which it increased to 7.5 percent. In this sense, budget policy has been conservative. However, both Suez Canal and oil revenues, which accrue to Egypt in foreign currency and enter the current budget as revenue (business taxes or transferred profits), have partly been absorbed by increasing subsidies on consumer goods and interest payments on public debt.

The total budget, on the other hand, has increasingly tended to be in the red. This, of course, is related to the increasing deficit on the capital budget, itself mainly a consequence of the transfer of investment activities from the private to the public sector before 1961, with the strong increase in national investment after 1973. Private sector investment declined from 12.4 percent of GNP in 1953-54 to 1955-56 to 2.2 percent during the first five-year plan years while public sector investment increased from 2.3 percent to 15.2 percent. With the accompanying increase in the public deficit (net borrowing) from 2.8 percent to 13 percent went an increase in the private sector surplus (net lending) from 1.1 percent to 8.3 percent of GNP and, consequently, only a 3 percentage-point increase in the external deficit (national net borrowing). The increase in public and unchanged private net lending (the increase in private saving largely being absorbed by increased private investment, mainly in housing) were then accompanied by a strong increase in the balance of payments deficit. The appropriateness of the budget policy has to be judged in relation to private sector developments as well as investment and balance of payments policy; the evaluation of the budget policy is postponed to the next section, where the problem of over- or undervaluation of the currency is discussed.

The figures used to represent saving in the private sector in table 4–24, obtained as residuals, should be treated with caution. However, accepting them at face value, table 4–24 shows a strong decline in private saving from 13.5 percent of GNP before the Suez War to 7.1 percent during the years 1967–68 to 1970–71. Half the decline may simply reflect the transfer to the public sector of retained profits in businesses that were nationalized and sequestered. The decline from the five-year plan period to 1967–68 to 1970–71, on the other hand, probably represents a genuine decline in the propensity to save in the private sector. Considering the uncertainties and insecurity created by nationalizations and sequestrations, this should not be surprising. To some extent, however, it may be a statistical artifact. From the 1950s, fear of confiscation prompted people to invest in assets such as jewelry, taxis, houses, inventories, and small-scale businesses. Such investments may not have been captured in the very primitive estimates of private sector investment. From the time of the first five-year plan to the mid-1970s, private investment was simply assumed in the national accounts to be about 10 percent of the total. Both private investment and, consequently, saving estimates may for that reason be biased downward for these years. Such bias does not, however, affect the estimate of net lending in the private sector, which also declined strongly from the five-year plan period to the years 1967–68 to 1970–71, a time when total investment declined by 4 percent of GNP and private saving fell by 4 percent of GNP. Disregarding the possibility of bias, the question arises whether foreign exchange (as suggested above) or private saving was the binding constraint on investment. Since there was deflation (relatively, at least) in the economy, that would indicate that foreign exchange was, indeed, the binding constraint.

With the *infitah* the investment and saving climate changed dramatically. For the years 1973 to 1983–84, estimated private saving returned almost to the level before the Suez War. Private investment only in-

creased to about half the level before the Suez War. That nationalizations and sequestrations continued to do much harm to private saving
and investment cannot be questioned. The continued policy of keeping
the nationalized enterprises in the public sector and preventing competition to these enterprises (see below) is a serious obstacle to a full comeback of the private sector on the investment side.

Inflationary Financing

For the entire postwar period, 1951–84, the growth rate of money supply (on IMF definitions) exceeded that of real gross national income
(GNI) by about 10 percent. Trade partners' trade-weighted rate of inflation during the same period was about 6 percent. Barring possible shifts
in demand for money, Egypt in that period tended to generate about 4
percent more inflation than her trade partners. Relative inflation, however, varied greatly over the years. Until 1960 Egypt had, apart from the
year of the Suez War, much less inflation than her trade partners, and if
anything, Egyptian monetary policy tended to be deflationary. From
1960 through the 1967 War, the roles were reversed, with Egypt generating domestic inflation at a rate of 9 percent against less than 1 percent
for her trade partners. Between the 1967 War and the 1973 War, Egypt
again generated less inflation than her trade partners. Finally, from 1973
and with the *infitah* euphoria, Egyptian excess money supply increased
almost two times faster than trade partners' inflation, 19–24 percent
against 11 percent.

From 1955 it is possible to show how the money supply grew through
financing of the public sector deficit by the central bank. Net borrowing
by the public sector from the central bank remained at a level of 3–4 percent of GNP throughout the postwar period until 1973, when such borrowing increased strongly (table 4–24). Table 4–25 demonstrates how, in
the international context, the budget systematically contributed to domestic inflation after the mid-1950s. The financing of the total budget
deficit was, if anything, conservative from the mid-1950s, apart from
the years of the two wars, 1956 and 1967, and the years of war and
infitah euphoria 1973–78. Column 2 shows the contribution of public
sector borrowing to the growth of money supply and column 3 the
growth rate of real GNI; the difference between the two indicates the effect of inflationary budget financing (column 5). Monetary inflation
through the budget was positive as far back as data are available (1956–
57). The inflationary impact varies, however, from about 3 percent annually during 1957–65 and 1967–72 to 22 percent during 1973–78.
Around the Suez War it was about 7 percent, around the 1967 War 11
percent, and from 1979 to 1984 a moderate 7 percent. Comparison with
international inflation as expressed by the trade-weighted average of inflation in Egypt's trade partner countries is interesting from the point of

Table 4-25. Inflationary Financing, 1951-84

Period	Growth rate of money supply[a] (1)	Increase in claims on public sector over money supply[a] (2)	Growth rate of real GNI (3)	Inflationary expansion of money supply[a]			Excessive inflation	
				Total (4)=(1-3)	Through public sector (5)=(2-3)	Trade partners' rate of inflation (6)	Total (7)=(4-6)	Through public sector (8)=(5-6)
1951–55	-1.4	—	0.9	-2.3	—	5.4	-6.8	—
1956–57	29.7	13.8	7.1	22.6	6.7	-3.7	33.4	10.1
1957–58 to 1959–60	3.4	8.1	4.3	-0.9	3.8	5.6	-6.5	-1.8
1960–61 to 1964–65	10.6	9.6	6.7	3.9	2.9	1.2	2.7	1.7
1965–66 to 1966–67	5.1	11.6	0.6	4.5	11.0	-1.2	5.7	12.2
1967–68 to 1971–72	4.7	7.7	4.8	-0.1	2.9	6.7	-6.8	-3.8
1973–78	25.3	27.9	6.3	19.0	21.6	10.6	8.4	11.0
1979 to 1983–84	30.7	13.3	6.7	24.0	6.6	11.1	12.9	-4.5
1956–57 to 1983–84	16.0	14.1	5.6	10.4	8.6	6.3	4.1	2.3

— = Not available.

a. Money supply equals money plus quasi money, IMF definitions.

Source: Author's computations based on IMF, *International Financial Statistics*; IMF and World Bank data.

view of foreign exchange policy. The theory of purchasing power parity of exchange rates would imply that with the rate of inflation in Egypt the same as among her trade partners, Egypt would have no reason for changing her (trade-weighted) nominal exchange rate. From this point of view, the budget financing may be characterized as neutral from 1957 to 1965, deflationary during the years 1967–72 and 1979–85, and (excessively) inflationary only around the Suez War and the 1967 War and during the years 1973–78.

Impact of Fiscal and Monetary Policies

Table 4–26 summarizes the impact of fiscal and monetary policies, based on the Keynesian assumption that an *increase* (or decrease) in the deficit of the total budget is expansionary (or contractionary) and on the monetarist assumption that the government always cheats and that in the short term at least an increase (or decrease) in money supply in excess of the rate of growth of GNI is expansionary (or contractionary), with expansionary (or contractionary) possibly taken to mean inflationary (or deflationary). Table 4–26 measures the fiscal impact by the increase in the budget deficit as a percentage of GNP and the monetary impact by growth of money supply over growth of real GNI. The two impacts are not additive; indeed, both are nothing but indicators (at best). The net impact is unambiguously expansionary during the five-year plan years, 1960–65, and the years of *infitah* euphoria, 1973–78; unambiguously contractionary during the years between the 1967 War and the 1973 War; and ambiguous during the short periods 1957–58 to 1959–60, 1965–66 to 1967–68, and 1979 to 1983–84.

Table 4–26. Impact of Fiscal and Monetary Policy, 1957–84

Period	Fiscal expansionary impact (percent of GNP)	Monetary impact (percent of money supply)	Net impact
1957–58 to 1959–60	4.2	−0.9	?
1960–61 to 1964–65	6.0	3.9	+
1965–66 to 1966–67	n.a.	4.5	?
1967–68 to 1971–72	−4.3	−0.1	−
1973–78	9.1	19.0	+
1979–84	−3.7	24.0	?

n.a. = Not available.
Note: Impacts not additive.
Source: Tables 4–24, 4–25.

As part of the monetary policy, interest rates have been slowly adjusted upward since the end of the 1970s to compensate for inflation (table 4–27). Even so (and despite the exemption since 1977 of deposit interest from income taxation), practically speaking all institutional, ex post real rates were negative during the years 1979–83. Ex post yields on deposits denominated in foreign currencies have at times been exceedingly high and have left no incentive for depositing in Egyptian pounds. Since liquid funds moved freely between Egyptian-pound and foreign-currency deposits, it is not clear what difference it makes except, of course, making the free market rate of the Egyptian pound highly sensitive to speculation.

Islamic investment companies attract large amounts of remittances from workers in Arab oil-producing countries, with profits rather than interest as the reward. Little is known about the activities of these companies but they seem to be investing heavily in international markets. Commercial banks have difficulty competing with the investment companies, interest rates being kept at moderate levels to avoid offending Islamic sensitivities.

Foreign Situation and Exchange Policy

The very large exchange reserve that Egypt had at the end of World War II was released by the British government only after prolonged negotiations. In 1962, nonetheless, the reserves had been used up and Egypt, under pressure from the IMF, devalued its currency by 24 percent. The devaluation was partly cosmetic because a number of special exchange rate arrangements were abrogated with the devaluation. From 1962 to 1974, Egypt operated with a unified exchange rate. Egypt appreciated against the U.S. dollar by about 10 percent in February 1973. In the general realignment of currencies under the Smithsonian agreement, the Egyptian pound was kept constant in terms of special drawing rights. This apparently was an attempt to avoid participating in the dollar's general decrease after 1970 against all major currencies, but the logic of this appreciation has never been spelled out. Cost-of-living considerations may as so often have been decisive.

From the time of the Suez War, Egypt obtained PL480 aid from the United States and loans to finance the Aswan High Dam and other projects from the Soviet Union. Nasser succeeded for some time in playing the two superpowers against one another, but Egypt came increasingly to live on short-term loans from European (particularly Italian) commercial banks at extremely high interest rates (20–25 percent), indicating a very poor credit rating for Egypt. Around 1965–66, President Lyndon Johnson and Premier Nikita Khruschev tacitily or explicitly agreed to stop the game and Egypt soon failed on its debt-service payments to Eu-

Table 4-27. **Interest Rates and Rate of Inflation, Selected Periods, 1979–83**
(percent)

Category	January 1, 1979, to April 1, 1980	April 1, 1980, to June 1, 1980	June 1, 1980, to January 1, 1981	January 1, 1981, to August 1, 1981	August 1, 1981, to July 1, 1982	July 1, 1982, to December 1, 1983	December 1, 1983, to —
Time and savings deposit							
Seven days	4.0	4.5	4.5	5.0	5.0	5.0	5.0
One month	5.5	6.0	6.5	7.5	7.5	7.5	7.5
One year	7.0	8.0	9.0	9.5	10.0	11.0	11.0
Five years	8.5	9.5	10.5	11.5	11.5	12.0	12.0
Lending							
Cotton and exports, maximum	9.5	11.0	12.0	13.0	13.0	13.0	13.0
Other, minimum	10.0	11.0	12.0	13.0	13.0	13.0	11.0
Other, maximum	12.0	13.0	14.0	15.0	15.0	15.0	15.0
Yield in Egyptian pounds, on foreign currency deposits[a]	n.a.	n.a.	n.a.	37.7	40.0	19.4	15.5
Rate of inflation (actual, average, CPI)	20.6[b]	n.a.	10.4[c]	10.4[c]	11.5	15.8	16.7

n.a. = Not available.
a. Interest rate on three-month Eurodollar deposits plus actual rate of depreciation of free market exchange rate.
b. For 1979–80.
c. For 1980–81.
Source: World Bank and IMF data.

ropean banks. The foreign exchange situation became extremely tight and investments were cut back. After the 1967 War, with the closure of the Suez Canal and the loss of the oil fields in Sinai, the exchange situation became disastrous. Financing was forthcoming mainly from the Soviet Union, not only for purchases of military equipment on a large scale but also for some development projects. Some aid in kind (oil) was obtained from Arab countries which also deposited large funds in the Central Bank of Egypt during the years before 1973.

Foreign trade and payments were subjected to direct control from the end of World War II. With the nationalizations of 1961, foreign trade—exports as well as imports—was taken over completely by government authorities and companies; legal private, international transactions virtually disappeared. The sophisticated export commodity markets in Alexandria were closed and a new system, remarkable only for its complexity and inefficiency, was adopted (Hansen and Nashashibi 1975, chap. 5). The administration of foreign trade and payments during the years 1961–74 can only be characterized as inept, the Egyptian civil servants probably being no match for the experienced and hard-nosed businessmen in Soviet trade organizations.

With the 1973 War and the oil price increase, the exchange situation changed abruptly. Arab aid; investments, grants, and loans; the flow of remittances from workers migrating to the Arab OPEC countries; the reopening of the Suez Canal; the return of the Sinai oilfields and the opening of new fields in the Red Sea that made Egypt a large-scale exporter of oil after 1976; and the increase of tourism generated a large inflow of foreign currency. Foreign trade was reoriented toward the West. The strongly expansionary domestic fiscal and monetary policies, nonetheless, generated a net outflow of foreign currency on current account, which increased from $572 million in 1973 to $3.5 billion in 1981–82, or from about 6 percent of GDP at current market prices to about 14 percent. With Camp David, Egypt's credit rating, however, changed by a stroke and the increasing deficits were easily covered, mainly from international credit markets. At the end of 1981, Egypt's foreign debt had increased to $18.3 billion, corresponding to about 106 percent of GDP. By 1983–84 the debt figure had increased to about $38 billion, not including unpaid military loans from the Soviet Union. The size of the military debt is unknown and the debt service payments appear to have been defaulted by Egypt. A rescheduling agreement based on a debt figure of the order $3.5 billion–$4 billion was finally reached in 1987 between Egypt and the Soviet Union.

With the change in the foreign exchange situation, a radical change in the trade and foreign payments system was adopted. Sadat's *infitah* gave the private sector a role to play in both exports and imports, private capital movements were legalized, and a grey foreign exchange market with an exchange rate determined by the market was allowed to develop. The key novelty here was the institution of "own-exchange" accounts and "own-exchange" imports.

Since 1974 either nationals or foreigners bringing foreign currencies into the country have been able to deposit those funds in special, dollar-denominated own-exchange accounts with commercial banks. Such funds receive Eurodollar market interest (tax exempted) and may be freely transferred abroad for any purpose, including payment for imports; hence the term own-exchange imports. Albeit limited to commodities listed by the government, these do not require import license but naturally are liable to payment of customs duties. The government's commodity lists primarily seek to shelter public enterprises against foreign competition but in fact they serve also to protect private industry in the informal sector (shoes are an example). A grey market for such funds has developed. The exchange rate in this grey market is called the free rate. The free rate has remained close to the black market rate, considerably depreciated in relation to the official rate. An increasing share of total civil imports (24.9 percent in 1983–84) is financed through own-exchange accounts. Recently, private exporters have been allowed to keep export proceeds in own-exchange accounts and use them for own-exchange imports.

The central bank does not operate in the free exchange market, from which public enterprises are excluded. Several unsuccessful attempts have been made to control the free market. Public enterprises operate through commercial banks at special rates fixed somewhere between official and free rates, with licenses required for all transactions. The commercial rates apply also to private importers with license. Government imports of basic food and agricultural chemicals and government exports of oil, rice, and cotton, along with Suez Canal and pipeline dues, continue to be settled at the official rate. This multiple, three-tiered exchange rate system, in operation since 1974, was finally replaced by a two-tier system in 1987–88 as a step toward a unified exchange rate.

Since Sadat generally pursued a policy of sheltering the domestic economy against external shock, why did he liberalize imports at free exchange rates with the repercussions that might occur on domestic prices and the cost of living? Partly the device was aimed at making repatriation of foreign exchange (remittances) more attractive for Egyptian migrant workers; but surely the avalanche of own-exchange imports and hence the downward pressure on the free market rate must have exceeded all expectations. The government may have expected that the free rate would continue to appreciate, as the black market rate actually did from 1970 to 1973. It is, moreover, important that as the system was set up, the free rate hardly affected the prices of goods or services included in the official cost-of-living indexes, which continued to be based on commodities and services with prices controlled by the government or fixed at the official exchange rate and (if need be) subsidized for imports. In this sense, the cost of living was sheltered against fluctuations in the free rate, clearly a deliberately chosen feature of the new system. Probably the fact that the own-exchange imports initially were consumer goods that had not been available for years meant that their sudden availability, at whatever prices, substantially improved the standard of living. Finally, own-exchange imports would have had no repercussion on the supply of domestic money. The commercial banks were required to keep 100 percent foreign reserves (investments in the Eurodollar market) against the own-exchange deposits.

Among the domestic areas that the institution of own-exchange imports and the development of a free rate different from the official rate might affect are employment and real wages. In a disequilibrium situation (as in 1974) with repressed inflation and considerable pent-up demand for imports, the initial impact of the new system would be a depreciation in the free exchange rate to the point where the idle funds in Egyptian pounds accumulated before 1973 equaled total own-exchange funds converted into Egyptian pounds. This should not in itself lead to a change in demand for domestic products and there should be no initial impact on demand for labor. The own-exchange imports might, however, include raw materials, spare parts, and capital goods in short supply to private enterprises and might thus generate increased production and demand for labor. This would have a downward effect on output prices from the nonagricultural, private sector and would lead to increased real wages in this sector, which would drain labor from agriculture. If own-exchange imports included agricultural machinery—especially tractors—there would be a decline in demand for labor from agriculture and an uncertain net effect on agricultural wages.

After the initial adjustment in stocks, the disequilibrium would be replaced by equilibrium with market clearing in the own-exchange commodity market. The prices of own-exchange imports in Egyptian pounds would now be determined by current flow demand for and supply of own-exchange imports. Whether the (implicit) free exchange rate would rise or fall is impossible to say, though it is clear that henceforth own-exchange imports would have a deflationary impact on the economy, assuming neutral monetary and fiscal policies. The effect of a shift in demand toward own-exchange imports would depend on which domestic sector experienced a decline in demand for its products. If demand shifted away from output of public enterprises, their sales and possibly production would decline. Under the government's employment policy there would be no layoffs, so public enterprises would suffer losses that would have to be covered from the public budget. (By and large, public enterprises have been sheltered from this possibility because their products are on the list of commodities from which own-exchange imports are not allowed.) If demand shifted away from nonagricultural, private enterprises, these enterprises would cut down on production and employment. If employment would be cut in such a way as to reduce migration to urban areas, the result would be increased employment in agriculture. Under competitive conditions, real wages in terms of output should tend to decrease in the nonagricultural, private sector and also decline in agriculture. If migration to urban areas did not decline, the result might be open unemployment. If, finally, demand shifted away from (free) agricultural products, the result would be a price fall for such products with a decline in agricultural real wages and possibly increased migration out of Egypt.

Among the other possible effects might be domestic investment of Egyptian pounds by the owners of foreign exchange. These funds would probably move toward the markets for land and real estate and drive up domestic prices. Also, the institution of own-exchange imports, with an implicit or explicit free exchange rate, could be expected to have an effect on migration and remittances. The device was intended as an incentive to repatriate migrants' earnings but it could have served also as a direct incentive to migrate and earn such funds. Assuming that earnings in the Arab OPEC countries are given in U.S. dollars or in riyals independently of the number of Egyptian workers migrating to those countries, a depreciation of the free rate would imply an increase in the earnings in Egyptian pounds and, all other things being equal, this should imply an increased number of migrants.

The official exchange rate remained unchanged from the time of the appreciation in 1973 until the beginning of 1979. Egypt then, under pressure from the IMF, devalued by 44 percent from LE0.39 per U.S. dollars to LE0.70. With the free market rate declining somewhat from 1975 to 1978 and the deficits on both budget and current account large and increasing, the IMF initially suggested that to improve the budget situation the government, among other things, cut back on food subsidies. With the riots of 1978 in mind, the government declined. The IMF then urged the government to devalue, apparently in the hope that some real reduction of the subsidies would follow somehow. The government complied—with a strong increase in the subsidies as the result. While through 1980 the free market rate remained almost unaffected by the depreciation of the official rate, from 1981 it started depreciating and by 1985 had depreciated even more than the official rate. After the decline in oil prices through 1985–86, the foreign exchange situation deteriorated rapidly despite increased American aid and in 1987 the Egyptian pound was further depreciated.

Foreign Assistance, 1952–84

From about 1960 to about 1976, Egypt was heavily dependent on foreign assistance. Before 1960, when Egypt's exchange reserves were substantial and development efforts modest, there had been little need for foreign aid. After 1976, when Egypt became an oil exporter, and particularly after the oil price increase of 1979, the dependence on foreign aid declined but was even in 1981–84 substantial. After 1984 dependence again increased strongly.

Table 4–28 shows foreign assistance as a percentage of investment, imports, and GDP. Data for 1952–59 to 1970–75 include grants plus medium- and long-term official loans from countries and concessional loans from national, regional, and international organizations. For 1974–75 to 1981–84 data are based on net official development assistance (ODA) as defined by the Organisation for Economic Co-operation and Development (OECD). Military aid is not included in the data and it is not clear to what extent aid from communist countries is covered before 1975 (the ODA data do not include such aid but it lost importance from about 1975).

Real Effective Exchange Rate, 1948–85

To a large extent, changes in Egypt's real effective exchange rate (REER) have been the fortuitous outcome of other countries' exchange rate policies and of price developments outside the control of the Egyptian government and apparently not heeded by the government. Those changes and changes in the nominal effective exchange rate (NEER) and the ratio of domestic to foreign price indexes (RPI) are shown in figure 4–2. In the computations, made on the IMF standard format, exchange rates are weighted by total trade (export plus import) with trade partners for each year. The price ratio is based on the CPI for Egypt and the WPI for partner countries, as for years before 1960 (tables 3–3 and 3–7). The twenty-

Table 4–28. Foreign Assistance as a Share of Investment, Imports, and GDP, 1952–84

(percent)

Period	Investment	Imports	GDP
1952–59	1.4	1.1	0.2
1960–64	32.0	26.1	5.6
1965–69	25.6	22.1	3.3
1970–75	34.2	24.4	4.9
1974–75	68.0	50.4	13.7
1976–80	35.2	37.8	9.0
1981–84	18.3	17.0	5.2

Source: Gouda Abdel-Khalek in Abdel-Khalek and Tignor (1982), OECD, *Development Cooperation,* various years; World Bank, *World Development Report,* 1986, 1987; IMF, *International Financial Statistics,* various years; World Bank (1988).

Figure 4-2. Egypt's Effective Exchange Rates and Relative Prices, 1948-85

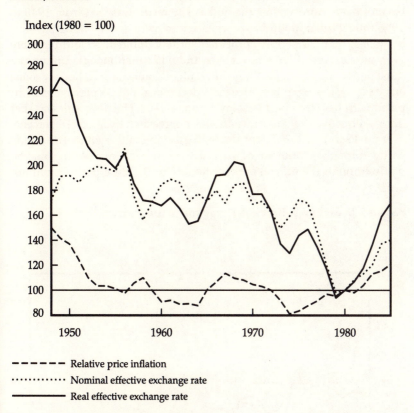

Index (1980 = 100)

- – – – – – Relative price inflation
- ·············· Nominal effective exchange rate
- ———— Real effective exchange rate

Source: IMF data; Hansen and Nashashibi (1975).

eight trade partners are all IMF-member countries; thus Rumania is the only communist country included. An increase (or decrease) in REER denotes a real appreciation (or depreciation) while an increase (or decrease) in NEER denotes a nominal appreciation (or depreciation).

In trade-weighted real terms the Egyptian pound depreciated strongly, to almost one-third its 1948 value by 1980 (figure 4–2). Thereafter an appreciation to almost two-thirds of the 1948 value took place. The real depreciation from 1948 to 1980 is surprising. For the Egyptian pound to have been overvalued in 1980 it must have been extremely overvalued in 1948. Equally surprising is the fact that the nominal effective exchange rate was almost unchanged from 1948 until 1975, when it finally began to depreciate, reaching almost one-half its 1975 value in 1980. All of this is the somewhat fortuitous outcome of relative price movements and relative depreciations of Egypt's and its trade partners' currencies against the dollar.

In 1949 Egypt followed sterling and depreciated strongly against the dollar. Her trade partners, however, as figure 4–3 shows, depreciated on balance even more against the dollar. The result was that from 1948 to 1956 the Egyptian pound appreciated nominally against trade partners by no less than 24 percent, probably entirely unintended and probably even unobserved (I have never seen the point mentioned). During the same period, however, partly as the result of domestic deflationary monetary policy, the Egyptian price level declined about 35 percent as compared with her trade partners' level (figure 4–4). The net result was that the real effective exchange rate after all depreciated by about 18 percent.

From 1956 to 1962, Egypt depreciated nominally against the dollar, partly through a number of special foreign exchange arrangements, partly through the official depreciation in 1962. Trade partners did not

Figure 4-3. Exchange Rates of Egypt and Trade Partners, 1948-85

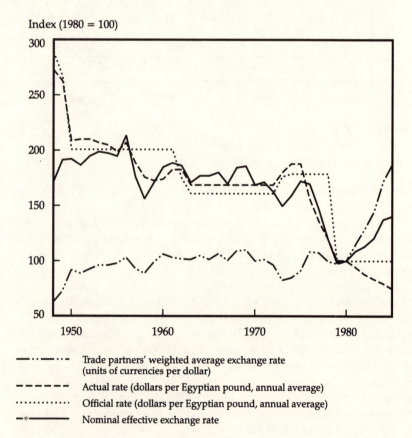

Index (1980 = 100)

——··——··· Trade partners' weighted average exchange rate
(units of currencies per dollar)

— — — — — Actual rate (dollars per Egyptian pound, annual average)

············ Official rate (dollars per Egyptian pound, annual average)

—*——— Nominal effective exchange rate

Source: IMF data.; Hansen and Nashashibi (1975).

depreciate much against the dollar during these years. In addition, some real depreciation took place because the price level in Egypt continued to be more stable and thus declined in relation to that of its trade partners. The net result was further real depreciation by 27 percent from 1956 to 1964. With real depreciation by some 40 percent from 1948 to 1964, overvaluation of the Egyptian pound in 1964 would again have implied strong overvaluation in 1948. Recall that the estimated wage costs in table 4–23 point to a strong improvement of competitiveness (at given exchange rates) from 1948 to 1962.

From 1964 to 1968 strong real appreciation took place despite no change in the official exchange rate of the Egyptian pound against the dollar. The main factor behind the real appreciation was a strong relative increase in the Egyptian CPI, part of the austerity policy embarked on when Egypt in 1966 defaulted on her short-term debts to European

Figure 4-4. Egypt's and Trade Partners' Price Inflation, 1948-85

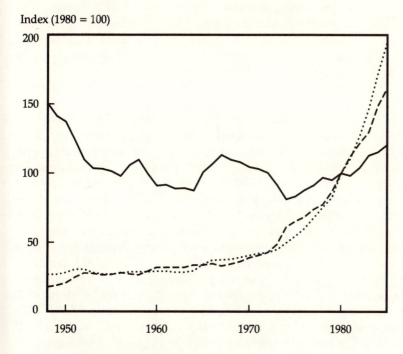

Index (1980 = 100)

- - - - - - Trade partners' weighted wholesale price index
.... Egypt, consumer price index
————— Relative price inflation

Source: IMF data.

banks and other sources of hard currency dried up. However, the relatively strong increase in the CPI was also related to the increase in wage costs and the decline in competitiveness in manufacturing in 1962–69. The following strong real effective depreciation from 1968 to 1974 was partly a reversal of the domestic CPI policy, domestic prices now being held relatively stable for political reasons. Simultaneously, however, a strong nominal effective depreciation took place, mainly through trade partners' appreciation by 22 percent against the dollar, which was counteracted in part by the Egyptian appreciation against the dollar by 10 percent in 1973.

Behind these developments is the dollar's depreciation after the breakdown of Bretton Woods and the final abandonment by the United States of the gold standard. Egypt, tying its pound to the dollar apart from the modest 10 percent appreciation in 1973, participated in its depreciation. By 1974 the real depreciation since 1948 had in this way reached 50 percent. The temporary real appreciation followed by even stronger real depreciation between 1964 and 1974 thus occurred as the joint product of domestic CPI policies, engineered through the extensive price control machinery, and the changes in the value of Egypt's trade partners' currencies against the dollar. The ups and downs of the REER during the 1960s and early 1970s are partly fictitious since Egyptian trade in those years shifted strongly toward the communist countries, which are not included in the REER estimates.

The strong real depreciation from 1974 to 1979, with a minor appreciation in 1974–76, is again the joint outcome of partly fortuitously coinciding events. Egypt did appreciate against the dollar by 10 percent in 1973 but immediately began depreciating on average against the dollar, with the movement of the free exchange rate and increased own-exchange imports, and finally with the strong official depreciation against the dollar early in 1979. The actual (average) nominal exchange rate against the dollar was stable during 1974–75 but depreciated by 46 percent in 1975–79, a nominal net depreciation against the dollar by 40 percent. The nominal trade-weighted rate against trade partners developed somewhat differently, with the 27 percent depreciation of trade partners' currencies against the dollar between 1974 and 1976, followed by a gentle 10 percent appreciation of these currencies, leaving the net depreciation 1974–79 at 14 percent. Finally, compared with its trade partners, Egypt's price level increased by 4 percent during 1973–79. The joint result of these developments was a real effective depreciation by 28 percent. The wage cost estimates in table 4–23 indicate that, at given exchange rates, competitiveness deteriorated during these years. Hence, depreciation made sense, had it been a deliberate policy.

From 1979 to 1985, with the official rate against the dollar fixed, developments were dominated by a strong depreciation—26 percent—of the Egyptian pound's average nominal rate against the dollar (through a strong depreciation of the free rate and further shift of trade to the free exchange market), and a strong depreciation of its trade partners' currencies against the dollar—92.7 percent. The result was a net appreciation of Egypt's nominal effective exchange rate against trade partners by 43 percent. Relatively strong price inflation in Egypt brought the real effective appreciation from 1979 to 1985 up to 80 percent. By the end of 1986, however, much of this appreciation had been reversed, partly through further depreciation of the free rate, partly through the decline of the dollar.

Egypt's real effective exchange rate obviously has not been a policy instrument for the Egyptian government. Had its philosophies so dictated (and had the concept been understood), the government could have computed Egypt's REER and adjusted the Egyptian pound's rates against the dollar or special drawing rights to produce the desired development of the REER. The government was not oblivious to its trade partners' exchange rate policies—Egypt devalued in 1949 when she followed her largest trade partner, the United Kingdom, and appreciated in 1973 when she reluctantly followed her trade partners more generally—but the government apparently preferred to keep the dollar rate constant for long periods and let the REER develop fortuitously. This raises two important questions. What were the effects of the policies that Egypt actually pursued—that is, the actual development of the REER—and, was the currency over- or undervalued during this long period? What were the political problems and philosophies, if any, that led the Egyptian government to pursue the policies it pursued?

Alleged Overvaluation of the Egyptian Pound

Overvaluation of the domestic currency is commonly thought to be a problem for developing countries, including Egypt. The tentative conclusion in the discussion of the interwar period in chapter 3 is that the Egyptian pound may have been overvalued during the 1920s, but that it possibly was valued at par during the 1930s in real terms, taking into account the tariff reform of 1930 and its amendments and the fact that quantitative restrictions were virtually nonexistent. Politically this was the outcome of Egypt's membership in the sterling area, which caused Egypt to go back to gold in 1925 and leave gold again in 1931 with the British. Egypt left the sterling area in 1947, paying lip service to the principles of the Bretton Woods agreement until its breakdown after 1969. Egypt adopted a unified exchange rate in 1962 and then a multiple rate policy after 1973 tied to the dollar for a major part of its international transactions but with a floating rate for a minor but rapidly increasing part. During the whole postwar period Egypt applied protectionist measures and quantitative controls to varying degrees. It has frequently been concluded that the result was endemic overvaluation.

Any attempt to judge the degree of overvaluation for a country for a specified period of time is bound to be difficult theoretically and empirically. The notion of overvaluation itself is rarely well defined. It is often described as the deviation of the actual exchange rate, possibly expressed as a weighted average, from the exchange rate in a hypothetical state of equilibrium where equilibrium as a minimum is taken to mean a balanced current account of foreign payments.

With the exchange rate defined as the price of foreign currency in terms of domestic currency and the actual exchange rate falling short of the equilibrium rate, foreign currency is underpriced and the domestic currency overvalued. Adding the elasticity approach to balance of payments theory, under well-known regularity assumptions this would imply a deficit on current account, and depreciation would be the policy to rectify the deficit. With this point of departure, a current account deficit at any time may be taken to indicate overvaluation. This, however, would among other things ignore the possibility that current account items may only respond to depreciation with a time lag, which would suggest that only averages over long periods and only persistent deficits would be considered proof of overvaluation. Egypt's balance of payments has in fact tended to run with a current account deficit ever since World War II. The conclusion would seem obvious—the Egyptian pound has been overvalued.

Even this conclusion, however, does not necessarily indicate that depreciation of the currency was warranted. Put another way, overvaluation is not necessarily a bad policy. Running a permanent, even an increasing, deficit may be a perfectly rational intertemporal policy in a growing economy if the corresponding foreign loans and assistance are invested efficiently in activities with a rate of return exceeding the rate of interest on the loans. During most of the postwar period Egypt's growing external deficit was in fact more than balanced by increasing real investment, the war years 1967–73 breaking the pattern temporarily. From the 1950s to the first five-year plan, 1960–61 to 1964–65, investment increased by 3.5 percent of GNP with the external deficit increasing only by 2.5 percent. From the first five-year plan to the years 1978 to 1983–84, investment increased by about 11 percent of GNP while the external deficit increased by only 8 percent (table 4–24). The problem has not been the volume of investment but rather its quality and composition, probably with a low rate of return if Egypt were compelled to compete in the world markets. It has, however, never been the official policy to run an external deficit over the long term. Both the first five-year plan and the early plans after 1973 targeted the external deficit to disappear at the end of the plan period. That the plans failed in this regard poses the question, what went wrong?

The real effective exchange rate, REER, depicted in figure 4–2, is frequently used as another and different indicator of possible overvaluation; appreciation of the REER is taken as indicating a tendency toward overvaluation. Behind this use of the REERs is the purchasing power parity (PPP) theory of exchange rates, a corollary of neoclassical general-equilibrium theory, although to some critics little more than the so-called law of one price applied to tradable goods under the assumption of free trade and perfect arbitrage. Apart from ignoring the problem of nontradable goods, the REER when applied as an indicator of overvaluation suffers from two weaknesses—it fails to indicate the degree of overvaluation in cases of real disturbance, and it requires an historical fixed point (with general equilibrium) from which the degree of overvaluation may be judged.

The REER estimates in figure 4–2 point to continued strong, real devaluation from 1948 with the temporary real appreciations during 1964–68 and 1980–85 partly fortuitous, not intended by the government. But for the Egyptian pound to have been overvalued in 1979–80, it would have to have been extremely overvalued immediately after World War II—which, of course, in itself proves nothing about the state of overvaluation around 1979–80. It does, however, given that the current account actually may have been close to balance in 1948–49 (Hansen and Marzouk 1965, table 7–9), suggest that there may have been little overvaluation in 1979–80.

A further problem with the REER as an indicator of overvaluation is its failure to take into account protection and controls as well as nonmonetary shocks. For the interwar period, the protection introduced by the tariff reform of 1930 is explicitly considered. It is extremely difficult to quantify the impact of protection and other controls during the postwar period. World Bank data of the net protection provided by border controls (tariffs and licensing) and price controls compounded about 1979 finds that overvaluation may have been negligible after the official devaluation in early 1979. Table 4–17 above shows that while agriculture, at least until the early 1980s, suffered substantial negative protection, tradable manufactured goods enjoyed slight positive protection, and that for all goods in the sample the strong price and quantitative distortions may on balance have been roughly neutral. The system of low agricultural procurement prices and high input prices was revised in the early 1980s but the absurd system of tariffs (frequently with negative effective rates of protection) was not rationalized (from a protection point of view) until 1986. Price controls were relaxed in 1986 and with import licensing tightening after 1985 the whole system of price and quantitative regulations may finally have become definitely protective. On balance it is not obvious, however, that at the end of the 1970s the system concealed much overvaluation of the Egyptian pound that was not disclosed by the REER. In 1948 there was, however, probably net protection.

The wage cost estimates in tables 4–22 and 4–23, serving much the same purpose as the REER, indicate increased competitiveness until 1962, a substantial decline of competitiveness in manufacturing during 1962–69 with agricultural competitiveness unchanged, possibly an improvement of both during 1969–74, with a serious decline, particularly for agriculture, from 1974 to 1981. Nonetheless, competitiveness probably on balance improved for both agriculture and manufacturing from 1948 to 1979. In itself this would again indicate that there was no need for nominal devaluation in 1979 compared with 1948.

This conclusion is supported by the fact that Egypt's inflation, measured by the rate of increase of money supply instead of by the official price indexes or wage data, was only slightly higher than that of her trading partners. Measuring potential inflation by the rate of increase of money supply is a way of getting around the downward bias in the measured REER, introduced by the massive price controls and the distorted official price indexes in Egypt. From 1955 (the first year for which data for money supply, as defined by the IMF, are available) to 1979, the Egyptian money supply increased by 12.5 percent a year while real GDP increased by 5.7 percent annually, pointing to a potential inflation rate of about 6.8 percent. Trade partners' weighted inflation rate (based on the WPI) for the same period was about 5.0 percent, which indicates excessive inflation for Egypt of about 1.8 percent annually. The NEER declined by 2.4 percent annually from 1952 to 1979. Should the Egyptian pound have been overvalued by 35 percent in 1955, that would have been taken care of in 1979.

Among the many real shocks Egypt experienced after World War II, changes in the terms of trade were not the least important. Net barter terms of trade appear (figures 4–1 and 4–2) to have been roughly the same in 1979 as in 1948. Thus there should have been no need of devaluing to compensate for the terms of trade effects on the balance of payments deficit. I do not know how to quantify the effect of the shift toward Soviet trade in the 1960s and its reversal in the 1970s.

Discussion of the possible overvaluation of the Egyptian pound since World War II has so far used 1979 as a bench mark, after the devaluation and the second oil price boost. Official, commercial, free, and black market rates were almost in line and domestic demand for goods and services may have been largely satisfied—partly of course through a large balance of payments deficit of 10–11 percent of GDP, which the indicators so far considered suggest may not have warranted a depreciation of the Egyptian pound. Few studies are available for the 1980s. The official tying of the pound to the U.S. dollar, the following strong appreciation of the dollar, and the accompanying appreciation of the REER with the collapse of oil prices in 1982 indicate that strong official depreciation may have been warranted. Free and black market dollar rates soared, with both the current account deficit and the inflation rate increasing and the investment share declining. Not until 1987 was the pound officially depreciated, certainly too late and probably too little.

The explanation of the large deficits in the balance of payments, until 1979–80 at least, may thus have to be sought not in foreign exchange rate policies but in an increasing internal macroeconomic disequilibrium with investment running ahead of domestic saving and possibly a distorted orientation of investment. Throughout the post-World War II period the budget deficit ran at increasingly high levels, reaching 25 percent of GDP in the 1980s. It may be that the huge budget deficit and budgetary policies were the villain and that a reduction of the budget deficit rather than depreciation was the policy to rectify the balance of payments deficit.

Perhaps this piecemeal analysis, jumping from one simplistic theory to another, should be replaced by a general equilibrium analysis, preferably even of the intertemporal variety "taking everything into account." Abstract general equilibrium theory, however, offers little help and computable general equilibrium (CGE) simulations without any solid empirical underpinning should not be trusted for practical purposes. Perhaps intuitive thinking along general lines can be helpful.

Generalization requires not only general theory but also simultaneous consideration of all significant policy targets of which the balance of payments is only one. The macro targets acknowledged by Egypt's second five-year plan for 1987–88 to 1991–92 (discussed below) are a balanced current account, acceptable growth with implicit investment target, full (high) employment, and price stability. Add to that a concern about income distribution and assume that the strategy of the plan is relevant for the past—that is, considering an economy in which market forces (demand and supply) determine foreign exchange rates and private sector wages as well as the rate of interest (although the plan is ambiguous here). Disregard for the moment all central bank operations, nontraded goods, migration of labor, and private capital movements, and assume public real expenditure and revenue parameters to be given. With these strong assumptions, excess demand for goods and services will be identical to excess demand for foreign exchange. Three flexible prices—the exchange rate (the price level), the domestic interest rate, and the private sector wage rate—should then, given Walras's Law and the conditions for a solution to exist, suffice for equilibrating four markets—those for goods and services (foreign exchange), domestic financing (credit), labor, and domestic money.

An important conclusion is that no matter how large the budget deficit is (more precisely, whatever the budget parameters are), there may always exist a set of prices—exchange rate, interest rate, and wage rate—

that will (temporarily) equilibrate the system; the larger the budget deficit, the higher probably the exchange rate and the interest rate and the lower the wage rate. A larger budget deficit should thus in itself in temporary equilibrium tend to increase inequity. This conclusion should not be surprising in light of the late 1980s debate about the federal budget deficit in the United States.

Assuming target investments secured by given public sector investments, fiscal policy and market forces together automatically make the macro targets of the second five-year plan materialize, while there is clearly nothing that serves to automatically balance the budget. Deficits are financed through sales of debt to the private sector (possibly via the banking system) and temporary equilibrium does not require a balanced budget in any sense. The point under discussion is, of course, neither a steady state growth equilibrium nor an ultimate stationary state, but a five-year plan. Still the distribution of income is a matter of concern, and this is where the budget deficit enters the picture.

With a balanced current account, domestic saving must equal domestic investment. Assume that domestic investment and its distribution between the public and private sectors are given—that, for instance, only the public sector invests (as was approximately the case in Egypt from the late 1950s to the mid-1970s). Private saving must then in equilibrium be larger the smaller public saving is—that is, the larger the current (and the total) budget deficit is. To put it another way, the smaller the budget deficit (current or total) is, the less private saving needs to be generated in equilibrium. Also, the larger the budget deficit, and the larger (all things being equal) the current account deficit, the more resources have to be shifted into tradable goods (exports) and, at full employment, the lower real wages have to be through higher exchange rates and lower money wages. Assume then that the higher the rate of interest is, and the more unequal income distribution is, the larger is private saving, and that in temporary equilibrium income distribution tends to be more unequal the higher the rate of interest and the lower the real wage rate are. It follows that the larger the budget deficit is, the more unequal must private income distribution be for sufficient private saving and employment to be generated in equilibrium. In this sense a budget deficit is in itself harmful to equity. For this conclusion to follow, not only need the many assumptions be fulfilled, it is also necessary that the measures taken to bring down the budget deficit not be in themselves harmful to equity. This, however, should be a matter for the details of tax subsidy and expenditure policies to ensure.

The 1979 depreciation, when the IMF urged Egypt to reduce the budget deficit and then, after the government's refusal to do so, coerced the government into depreciating, should be seen in the light of the argument above. Equilibrium might have been established either way; the IMF solution was probably the preferable one from the point of view of income distribution, given an equitable fiscal policy. The IMF is sometimes better than its reputation!

In the simplifications made so far, nontradable goods and services have been ignored. They include electricity and services such as domestic transportation and communications, mainly produced by public enterprises. If these services were available so as to satisfy demand at cost-plus prices (as recommended in the second five-year plan), no special equilibrium problems would be involved, and with public enterprise profits going into the budget, the policy would serve to diminish the deficit and increase public saving. Equilibrium for private, nontradable services, apart from housing (where rentals would have to be introduced in the analysis and standard arguments about nontradables would apply), is essentially a question of equilibrium in the private labor market. A possibly daring assumption among the other simplifications is that flexible wages in the private sector, with flexible exchange rates and interest rates, should suffice to clear the labor market with other markets.

Capital movements were also ruled out by assumption. On the other extreme, assume perfectly free movements—not very far from reality—of financial capital, that is, export and import of IOUs. With free trade, capital goods, of course, move freely. We have now to distinguish between long-term and temporary equilibrium.

With interest rates given from abroad, in the long term the net stock of IOUs in the country adjusts so that in equilibrium domestic and foreign interests are equal. The stock of IOUs, not the interest rate, is now the equilibrating variable. With IOU stock, the exchange rate, and wage rate adjusting, all markets are equilibrated at a balanced current account (including interest payments). There cannot be such a thing as under- or overvaluation of the currency.

In the short run, at a given net stock of IOUs, the net flow of IOUs in or out of the country at any moment should depend on the interest differential, assuming for the sake of simplification rational expectations (this, of course, is a point to elaborate on). Exchange rates, the wage rate, and the domestic interest rate now adjust so as to determine a temporary equilibrium with an interest differential, a certain capital inflow (IOU outflow), and current account deficit with equilibrium in goods and services (including capital services and interest), the stock of IOUs, and labor markets. It stands to reason that the foreign exchange rate will decline and compared with the initial situation (before allowing capital movements) the currency will be overvalued in the sense that there will be a current account deficit. It may be argued that it was the assumed ban on capital movements that concealed an overvaluation. In any case, the emergence of a deficit may be prevented if fiscal policy is used to run a budget surplus with increased domestic saving to replace the capital imports with equilibrium in all markets and balanced current account.

Without the budget surplus the currency would be overvalued and in this sense the lack of adequate fiscal policy could be held responsible for the overvaluation. Needless to say, without fiscal intervention the process may in the long term grind to a halt, with the net stock of IOUs reaching a stationary equilibrium. And, of course, with the rate of interest determined from abroad, the growth target may require the necessary investment to be undertaken by the public as part of the fiscal policy.

Migration of labor may, with the changes needed, be dealt with similarly. The basic difference between capital and labor movements is that while the movement of capital (sale or purchase of IOUs) itself creates a supply or demand for foreign currency, that is not the case when a worker moves out of the country (apart from transportation costs). The migrant worker is not sold for export (as a slave). The current account continues to include payments for factor services, in this case workers' remittances. In the short term, assume that net migration, the net flow of labor, depends on the differential between the given foreign wage rate and the domestic wage rate, given the stocks of national labor, domestically and abroad. Exchange rates, the domestic interest rate, and the domestic wage rate (wage differential) with equilibrium in all markets and a balanced current account (including remittances) will obtain. As the stock of migrants increases and the stock of domestic labor decreases, the temporary equilibrium will change, and only if net migration ceases will long-term equilibrium prevail. During this process there is clearly nothing that can be called overvaluation.

The conclusion to be drawn from this modest attempt at heuristic general equilibrium analysis is that when there are many targets it is the whole package of macro policies and not one aspect of the package, particularly the exchange rate policy, that is responsible for all target deviations, including the current account deficit. If a current account deficit exists, it will generally require adjustment not just of the exchange rate, but also of the interest rate, the wage rate, and fiscal policy to keep the economy on its multiple targets. It may be here that stabilization policies tend to fail, the number of instruments or their calibration, or both, being inadequate.

Finally, free markets with flexible prices has been taken to mean market clearing at competitive prices. This may be a reasonable assumption for foreign exchange markets. But it may not be justified for the domestic currency credit market and for the private sector labor market, in which case the analysis would have to be further developed in terms of involuntary unemployment and credit rationing or idle balances.

Foreign Debt

The accumulated current account deficit, prevailing since World War II, increasing to the mid-1970s and then declining (table 4–7), has become so large that Egypt now is one of the world's most heavily indebted nations (in relative terms). Estimates of Egypt's external debt encounter unusual difficulties and are surrounded by special uncertainties. Debts to communist countries, particularly those to the Soviet Union, related to deliveries of military equipment are not included in World Bank estimates. Whether Arab countries' wartime deposits in the Central Bank of Egypt should be classified as aid or loans is disputed. Table 4–29 shows three standard debt indicators: debt-GNP ratio (DOD/GNP) according to three different estimates, debt service–export earnings ratio (TDS/XGS), and interest payments–GNP ratio (INT/GNP). In addition the

Table 4-29. External Debt and Exchange Reserve Ratios, Selected Years, 1955-85

Year	DOD/GNP (percent) A	B	C	TDS/XGS (percent)	INT/GNP (percent)	RES/MGS (months)
1955	n.a.	n.a.	0ᵃ	n.a.	n.a.	15
1965	n.a.	n.a.	16	15	n.a.	3
1970	n.a.	23	26	26	n.a.	1
1971	25	n.a.	n.a.	29	0.3	1
1972	n.a.	n.a.	n.a.	31	n.a.	1
1973	23	n.a.	31	40	0.6	3
1974	n.a.	n.a.	n.a.	n.a.	n.a.	2
1975	41	n.a.	54	22	1.0	1
1976	42	48	53	18	0.8	1
1977	52	69	58	24	2.2	2
1978	61	72	66	22	2.4	2
1979	59	60	n.a.	16	1.3	2
1980	52	n.a.	n.a.	15	1.2	3
1981	56	n.a.	n.a.	21	2.0	2
1982	52	n.a.	n.a.	n.a.	1.7	2
1983	n.a.	49	n.a.	27	n.a.	2
1984	n.a.	51	73	32	n.a.	n.a.
1985	n.a.	64	82	31	n.a.	n.a.

All definitions expressed in terms of U.S. dollars.
A = From *World Debt Tables*.
B = From *World Development Report*.
C = From Ikram (1980) and the World Bank.
DOD = debt outstanding, disbursed.
GNP = gross national product.
MGS = imports of goods and services.
RES = exchange reserves.
TDS = total debt service.
XGS = exports of goods and services.
n.a. = Not available.
a. Conjecture.
Source: World Bank, *World Debt Tables*; World Bank, *World Development Report*; Ikram (1980); IMF, *International Financial Statistics*.

table shows the exchange reserves expressed as months of imports of goods and services.

Of the three estimates of the debt-GNP ratio, the one in the third column is the most complete. It includes IMF and other short-term debts and indicates an increase from virtually nothing to 31 percent of GNP in 1973, 66 percent in 1978, and 82 percent in 1985. Allowing for conjectured debts such as those to communist and Arab countries might bring the figure for 1985 up to about 100 percent. The corresponding figure for Brazil was only 48 percent. The debt-GNP ratio is dependent on the degree of overvaluation of the Egyptian currency, the conversion ratio of GNP into U.S. dollars being geared to the official exchange rate.

The ratio of debt service payments to total export earnings is often a better indicator of the dimensions of the debt problem and may be less flawed by measurement errors related to the exchange rate. Debt service payments increased from virtually nothing around 1955 to 40 percent of total export earnings in 1973, then declined to 15 percent in 1980, mainly as a consequence of the increase in the value of oil exports after 1979. In 1985 the ratio was back to 31 percent, partly because of increasing interest rates. The debt problem is most serious from an international liquidity point of view and is an obstacle to growth since imports of capital goods are limited by a shortage of foreign exchange. Egypt has on several occasions defaulted on debt service payments, including the military debts owed to the Soviet Union that were rescheduled in 1987.

In terms of interest payments, the debt burden is not excruciating. In 1978 interest payments reached 2.4 percent of GNP and they were down to 1.7 percent in 1982. A substantial part of Egypt's foreign debt is owed to foreign governments or official organizations and has for various reasons—among them international political considerations—been obtained on favorable conditions.

Distribution and Redistribution of Wealth and Income

Information on the distribution of wealth and income in Egypt is spotty and incomplete. As far as material wealth is concerned, only the distribution of land by acres, not by value, is known. Data here are from the early years of the century to the present time and are of reasonably good quality. For human wealth—capital—data on education and health are used. No national income survey is available but four national expenditure surveys of reasonable quality exist for 1957–58, 1964–65, 1974–75, and 1982.

Distribution of Land

Figure 2–3 describes land distribution before 1952 while the land reforms and the process of land redistribution since 1952 are described early in the chapter (see table 4–1). Here the discussion is limited to the distribution of holdings and ownerships of land at the beginning of the 1950s and the end of the 1970s (table 4–30). A holding is a farm, a cultivation unit. The land cultivated by a given farm may be owned by the cultivator, rented, or shared in some form of partnership. It may be consolidated or fragmented. An ownership is an aggregate consisting of all land, no matter what its location or use, and is formally or informally the property of a particular owner. In Egypt, both holdings and ownerships are registered by individuals, not by families, and statistics on distributions accordingly enumerate individuals. Statistics are compiled by agricultural districts, which creates an equalizing bias of unknown strength because owners or holders may have land in several districts. Fake contracts to evade reform laws, which are believed to be widespread, create another equalizing statistical bias of unknown strength. The difference between distribution by holding and by ownership depends, disregarding these possible biases, on the prevalence of land lease and sharing, both widespread in Egypt.

If the data are accepted at face value and the Gini coefficients are used as indicators of inequality, the distribution of holdings is more equal than the distribution of ownerships in both the 1950s and the 1970s. Lease and sharing tend to break up large estates and consolidate very small plots of land. The quintile shares, however, do not give the same picture as the Gini measures. Both the first and the fifth quintile shares are smaller for holdings than for ownership in the 1950s, the first quintile share disagreeing with the Gini. Both the quintiles and the Gini coefficients agree on a much more equal distribution for holdings than ownerships in the 1970s.

Over time, remarkably enough, there is only a slight equalization of ownership from 1952 to 1977 despite the three rounds of land reform. The Gini is down from 0.74 to 0.66, with the first quintile share up from

Table 4–30. Land Holdings and Ownerships, Early 1950s and Late 1970s

Measure	Holdings		Ownerships	
	1950	1977–78	1952	1977
First quintile (percent of total)	2	6	4	5
Second–fourth quintiles (percent of total)	25	41	18	25
Fifth quintile (percent of total)	73	53	78	70
Gini coefficient	0.68	0.48	0.74	0.66
Mean size (hectares)	2.6	0.8	0.9	0.7

Source: Egypt, Ministry of Finance, *Annuaire statistique de l'Egypte*; Egypt, Ministry of Agriculture data.

4 percent to 5 percent and the fifth down from 78 percent to 70 percent. This is hardly more than might have followed from the well-known tendency to land fragmentation, inherent in Islamic inheritance law as applied in Egypt. The large (relative) increase is in the share of middle-sized ownerships, in the second, third, and fourth quintiles. Accumulation of wealth, invested in land, appears to be the explanation. For holdings, on the other hand, there is a strong tendency toward equalization over time, the Gini declining from 0.68 to 0.48, the first quintile share increasing from 2 percent to 6 percent, the fifth falling from 73 percent to 53 percent, and the other three quintiles increasing strongly from 25 percent to 41 percent.

The development since the time of the first land reform in 1952 has thus been characterized by little change toward equalization of land ownership, strong change toward equalization of land holding (cultivation), and for both ownership and holding a tendency to concentrate in the middle. This is not really what the reforms were aiming at and it is not clear what explains this development.[12]

One should expect income distribution in rural areas to be closely related to land distribution. Much of rural income is still from ownership of land. Under perfectly competitive equilibrium, ownership and not holdings should be decisive for income distribution, rental of land being equal to marginal value productivity of land. With rent control and the possibility of the termination of rental or sharing strictly constrained by law—rental contracts can even be inherited (if not by law, certainly in practice)—distribution by holdings takes on an importance it would not otherwise have. That being the case, and with the land reforms enforced, the tendency should have been for rural income distribution to become much more equal, and to concentrate in the middle. However, no such tendencies are apparent in the data on income (expenditure) distribution in tables 4–31, 4–32, and 4–33. Distribution of nonagricultural rural income may have become more unequal.

For urban dwellings the distribution of ownership by taxes payable is known for 1959 and 1962 (Egypt, CAPMAS 1962, p. 68; 1964). The coverage of the data is not clear, however. For 1959 Alexandria is not included. For 1962 the number of owners and the total taxes payable are less than half those for 1959, so coverage must have been more limited. The tax in question is the urban buildings tax, which is collected from the tenant and not from the owner of a dwelling. The tax is a fixed percentage of the assessed rental value, which possibly may be used as an indicator of building value at the time of the assessment. What is available is thus at best a proxy, and probably not a very good one for the distribution of ownership. Gini coefficients were 0.82 for 1959 and 0.84 for 1962. These are very high Ginis compared with those for income and land ownership in Egypt (how they compare with corresponding Ginis for other countries I do not know). In any case, as indicators of material wealth they suffer from relating to gross and not net wealth, mortgage and other debts not being taken into account. This is a deficiency they have in common with those for the distribution of agricultural land as an indicator of the distribution of net wealth.

Income Distribution

Knowledge about income distribution in Egypt is limited to the period 1958-59 to 1982 and is based on inference from expenditure surveys.[13] The expenditure surveys are of reasonable quality but as indicators of income distribution they suffer from well-known shortcomings. Savings patterns are not well known and the surveys may miss the tails of the distributions. The aggregate measures of distribution in table 4-31 may thus understate the inequity of income distribution. Uncertain conjectures (Korayem 1982) suggest that the downward bias in the Gini coefficients may be on the order of 0.05. Measured Gini coefficients and Theil measures are fairly constant over the years, with rural areas slightly more equitable than urban areas. There appears to have been a temporary improvement of distribution in rural areas in 1964-65 but no such improvement occurred in urban distribution, which does show a slight permanent improvement from 1964-65 to 1974-75. The measured changes are small, however, and can hardly be considered significant.

The distribution of household expenditure by quintiles and top decile in table 4-32 gives the same impression as the distribution of aggregates. For rural areas, shares are practically speaking constant from 1958-59 to 1982. For urban areas the share of the lowest quintiles increased from 1958-59 to 1974-75 while that of the top decile declined. For 1982 only quartiles are available (table 4-33). The average for income distribution in nine other low-income countries (World Bank definitions) before 1980-81 (in most cases probably measured with large margins of error)

Table 4-31. Distribution of Expenditure by Households, Gini and Theil Measures, Selected Years, 1958-82

	Rural areas			Urban areas	Total Egypt
Year	Gini coefficient A	Gini coefficient B	Theil's measure A	Gini coefficient B	Gini coefficient B
1958-59	0.34	0.37	0.16	0.40	0.42
1964-65	0.29	0.35	0.12	0.40	0.40
1974-75	0.35	0.39	0.17	0.37	0.38
1982	0.34	n.a.	0.17	0.37	n.a.

A = From Adams.
B = From Hansen and Radwan.
n.a. = Not available.
Source: Adams (1985), table 4; Hansen and Radwan (1982), table 37; Alderman and von Braun (1984), p. 28.

Table 4–32. Distribution of Expenditure by Households in Egypt and Other Countries, by Quintile and Top Decile, Selected Years, 1958–82

(percent)

	Quintile					Top decile
	Lowest	Second	Third	Fourth	Top	
Rural Egypt						
1958–59	6.7	11.0	16.6	21.9	43.9	28.0
1964–65	7.4	11.6	16.3	22.0	42.7	27.5
1974–75	5.9	11.2	15.8	21.2	45.9	30.5
1982	6.0	11.4	16.0	22.6	44.0	28.4
Urban Egypt						
1958–59	16.4	a	14.5	n.a.	n.a.	30.4
1964–65	16.5	a	14.8	n.a.	n.a.	30.8
1974–75	18.3	a	16.1	n.a.	n.a.	27.6
1982	n.a.	n.a.	n.a.	n.a.	n.a.	n.a.
Nine other lower-middle income countries before 1980–81, average	4.3	12.4 8.1	12.6	20.0	54.9	39.1

n.a. = Not available.
a. Included in lowest quintile.
Source: Adams (1986), table 1–4; Hansen and Radwan (1982), table 58; World Bank, *World Development Report*, 1986, table 24.

though not directly comparable with the Egyptian data, make the Egyptian distribution appear relatively egalitarian. Considering differences in measurement, biases, and errors, great caution should be shown in drawing firm conclusions from these data.

Apart from other shortcomings, the expenditure distributions in nominal terms do not adequately account for the impact of price policies and rationing which have been major instruments of the government's redistributive policies since 1973. Studies of the effects of these policies are reported in the following sections.

Table 4–33. Distribution of Expenditure by Households, by Quartile, 1981–82

(percent)

	Quartile			
Area	Lowest	Second	Third	Top
Rural	12.1	20.0	27.0	40.9
Urban	11.7	18.7	25.7	43.7

Source: Zaitoun (1988).

Taxes, Subsidies, and Social Security

Table 4–34 gives an overview of public revenue and expenditure in 1983–84. As one would expect in a mixed economy with a large public sector, both total current revenue and expenditure of general government, measured as a share of GDP, are high—43 percent and 45 percent, respectively. Both social security benefits and direct subsidies are large (together about 15 percent of GDP in 1983–84); they are crucial for judging the impact of the tax-subsidy system on the distribution of government services.

Table 4–34. General Government Revenue and Expenditure, 1983–84

Category	Millions of Egyptian pounds	Percent of GDP[a]
Revenue		
Personal income tax	128.8	0.5
Social security contributions	1,436.0	5.2
Property tax	14.4	0.1
Consumer goods tax	960.3	3.5
Import duties	2,262.1	8.2
Other taxes	941.5	3.4
Total direct personal and indirect taxes	5,743.1	20.9
Company profits tax[b]	1,506.0	5.5
Total Taxes	7,249.1	26.4
Fees and miscellaneous charges	754.9	2.8
Public enterprise and authority profits after tax, transferred to budget or retained[c]	3,702.5	13.5
Total current revenue of central government	11,706.5	42.6
Total current revenue of local government	549.7	2.0
Total current revenue of general government	12,250.2	44.6
Expenditure		
Goods and services, including defense	6,100.1	22.2
Interest payments	1,111.1	4.1
Social security benefits	1,435.1	5.2
Direct price subsidies, adjusted[d]	2,802.0	10.2
Unspecified	1,005.8	3.7
Total current expenditure of general government	12,454.1	45.4
Total capital expenditure of general government	5,518.0	20.1
Total expenditure of general government	17,972.1	65.5

a. Total GDP at current factor cost amounts to LE27,461 million.
b. Oil sector and Suez Canal account for LE511.6 million.
c. Includes LE1,351 million transferred from oil sector and Suez Canal.
d. Direct subsidies plus deficit in public enterprises plus nonauthorized borrowing from the banking system by the General Agency of Supply Commodities minus losses from previous year. Direct subsidies amount to LE1,987 million.
Source: IMF, *Government Finance Statistics Yearbook* (1985); IMF data.

Table 4-35. Public Revenue, Direct Subsidies, and Social Security Benefits, 1975–84
(amount in millions of Egyptian pounds)

Year	Public revenue including social security contributions		Direct subsidies	Social security benefits	Direct subsidies plus social security benefits		
	Amount	Percent of GDP	Amount	Amount	Amount	Percent of GDP	Percent of public revenue
1975	1,793	34.4	622	229	851	16.3	47.5
1976	2,336	34.7	434	353	789	11.7	33.7
1977	3,149	37.8	650	446	1,096	13.1	35.9
1978	3,742	38.2	710	289	999	10.2	26.7
1979	4,226	33.3	1,352	378	1,730	13.6	40.9
1980–81	8,080	46.7	2,166	873	3,040	17.6	37.6
1981–82	9,282	45.9	2,192	1,219	3,411	16.9	36.8
1982–83	11,335	48.8	2,054	1,305	3,359	14.5	29.6
1983–84	11,807	43.0	2,507	1,435	3,942	14.4	33.4

Source: World Bank data; IMF, *Government Finance Statistics Yearbook* (1985).

Table 4–35 shows that direct subsidies and social security benefits since 1975 have remained at a high level, attained during a few years in the early 1970s. The subsidies in table 4–35 are called direct subsidies because they show up in the budget and appear as an expenditure for the government; in standard terminology they would be indirect subsidies because they are received by households in the form of low prices on consumer goods. Egypt also has substantial subsidies in the form of low prices that do not appear in the budget or, for that matter, in the national accounts—domestically extracted and processed oil, for example, is sold domestically at prices far below world market prices. From a social point of view, the world market prices are the true opportunity costs (shadow prices) and the difference between the world market price and the domestic sale price is socially an indirect price subsidy that does not appear anywhere in the bookkeeping system.

Considering the amounts involved, the distribution of personal (real) income might be expected to be quite different after than before taxes and subsidies. It is difficult, however, to predict the direction of the net effect. The personal income tax, which formally is highly progressive with high marginal rates, is entirely unimportant and the revenue collected amounts to only 0.5 percent of GDP. Evasion is massive and tax loopholes are enormous. Thus, income accruing in foreign currency is tax exempt; this leaves workers' remittances and salaries and fees of all kinds from foreign companies untaxed. Neither migrant workers nor consultants for foreign companies pay income tax. Personal taxes are dominated by indirect taxes (such as the consumer goods tax and import duties) and by social security contributions, which are usually considered regressive no matter whether they rest on employers or employees. Social security benefits and consumer goods subsidies should, however, tend to work the other way. Direct personal and indirect taxes, including social security contributions, amounted to 19 percent of GDP in 1983–84 while subsidies and social security benefits amounted to 15 percent. Hence, the net effect is hard to predict. In addition, company profits, taxes, and transfers raise problems; their incidence is blurred by the wide application of price controls for products sold by public enterprises.

Table 4–36 shows an attempt by M. Reda el Edel to gauge the impact on inequality of income distribution, measured by the Gini coefficient, with a distinction between indirect taxes (including employers' social security contributions and business income taxes, both assumed to be shifted on to prices), direct price subsidies, and direct taxes (including employee contributions to social security). The estimates do not appear to include social security benefits. The methodology used is not entirely transparent and the assumptions about shifting of taxes are open to doubt.

Table 4–36. Effects of Taxes and Subsidies on Income Distribution, Selected Years, 1958–75

	Gini coefficient		
Item	1958–59	1964–65	1974–75
Income before taxes and subsidies	0.4446	0.4313	0.4043
Effect of indirect taxes	−0.0044	−0.0037	−0.0058
Effect of direct price subsidies	−0.0002	−0.0019	−0.0326
Effect of direct taxes	0.0100	0.0087	0.0133
Income after taxes and subsidies	0.4300	0.4170	0.3792

Source: Adapted from M. Reda el Edel in Abdel-Khalek and Tignor (1982), p. 162.

That indirect taxes, including shifted business income taxes and social security contributions from employers, should tend to make distribution more equitable is unexpected. For Egypt, however, the result makes sense, since necessities tend to be exempted from taxation while luxury consumption carries high indirect taxes and customs duties. A carefully designed indirect tax system may be progressive. The effect is, in any case, small. Direct price subsidies were of little importance in 1958–59 and 1964–65, but during the 1970s they became the main device for redistributing income. In 1974–75 direct price subsidies alone lowered the Gini about 8 percent from 0.40 to 0.37. Direct taxes, unexpectedly, led to increased inequity. The reason must be that direct taxes, as defined in el Edel's study, include and are dominated by employee contributions to social security, a typically regressive form of direct taxation. Altogether, el Edel finds a certain improvement of income distribution over time, somewhat larger for income after than before taxes and subsidies. The tax system itself has apparently always had a positive effect on equity, which has increased over time. Had social security benefits been taken into account, the improvement would have been more pronounced, at any point of time and over time. Compared with the improvement of income distribution achieved through the tax subsidy system in some developed countries, however, the improvement in Egypt has been moderate.

Food Prices and Income Distribution

Food subsidies have been a major tool of income distribution policy since 1973. They have been a heavy burden on the budget (table 4–35) and, other things being equal, have contributed greatly to deficit financing and inflation. They have become such an integral part of the social compact that the ruler can do little to change them. Table 4–37 attempts to calculate the net transfer of income implied by both food subsidies

Table 4-37. Income per Capita Transferred through Food Subsidies and Distorted Food Prices, 1981–82

	Net transfer (Egyptian pounds)				Net transfer (percent of expenditure)			
	To consumers		For all purposes		To consumers		For all purposes	
Expenditure group	Urban	Rural	Rural	Total	Urban	Rural	Rural	Total
Household, by quartile								
Lowest	22.34	20.08	18.98	—	12.70	18.00	17.20	—
Second	19.90	21.86	20.72	—	6.40	11.90	11.40	—
Third	15.04	20.44	16.81	—	3.30	7.70	6.40	—
Highest	-4.01	25.27	18.47	—	-0.20	4.50	3.30	—
All households	13.32	21.90	18.76	—	2.80	7.80	6.70	—
Rural workers								
Small farmers	—	23.87	—	30.00	—	—	—	12.60
Large farmers	—	7.48	—	-73.16	—	—	—	-18.80
Landless farm laborers	—	24.17	—	26.56	—	—	—	14.00
Nonfarm wage laborers	—	21.36	—	22.74	—	—	—	7.50
Nonfarm self-employed	—	20.61	—	23.69	—	—	—	9.00
Urban workers								
Self-employed	6.21	—	—	6.21	—	—	—	1.10
Wage laborers	15.50	—	—	15.50	—	—	—	3.40

— = Not applicable.
Source: Alderman and von Braun (1984), tables 18–22.

and distorted food prices, measured by the difference between actual consumer price and international price. The indirect impact through deficit financing and inflation is not considered. Even so, the estimate is of considerable interest. It describes the apparent benefits from subsidies and distorted prices as people experience these, other things being equal, and helps explain the violent popular response (riots, and so on) to all attempts to abrogate, or at least reduce, the transfers.

The net transfers of income per capita are shown both in absolute terms and as a percentage of expenditure, taking into account effects through consumption and, in rural areas, agricultural production. That the effects become negative for the higher expenditure quartile in urban areas is related to purchases in the open market at high free or black market prices. The very large negative effect on large farmers arises exclusively from their production. Consumption effects, even for this group, are positive. The food price policies appear to have a strong equalizing effect, other things being equal, on income distribution and more so in rural than in urban areas. (Had the indirect effect of low prices on petroleum products after 1979 been taken into account, the equalizing effect would have been smaller, although probably not reversed.) That the transfer of income, in both absolute and relative terms, is larger in rural than in urban areas runs against the conventional view that food price policies represent exploitation by urban consumers at the expense of rural consumers and producers. From the ruler's point of view, the policy is ideal—apart from the urban upper-income brackets and large farmers, everybody wins. That the policy is popular should not be surprising. Under Mubarak the policy of exploiting agriculture seems to have been moderated and recently the food subsidies were substantially reduced (Zaitoun 1988).

Human Capital—Education and Health

The most reasonable way to examine Egypt's human capital is in the data compiled on the educational and health status of the population. Table 1–6 shows that the reduction in illiteracy from 1907 to 1986 was not impressive. The information in table 4–38 on the educational status of the labor force also indicates a slow rate of progress. The table presents both labor force and manpower data because Egyptian statistics—both population censuses and labor force surveys—grossly understate the role of unpaid female family labor and, hence, grossly exaggerate the educational status of working women.[14]

Female education, of course, improved considerably between 1960 and 1986. Yet the low rate of literacy, 30.7 percent, for females in the labor force against 54.2 percent for males in 1976 (table 4–38) clearly is a consequence of the underenumeration of unpaid female family labor. The even more remarkable difference for labor force participants with secondary education—38.8 percent for females against only 9.8 percent for males—is probably less a consequence of underenumeration of women than of the increasing tendency for women to join the paid labor force as their level of education increases. The manpower statistics give a more nearly correct picture of the educational status of the working population, particularly of people with formal education. While almost 30 percent of the males in the manpower basis had some formal education in 1976 and 32 percent in 1986, the corresponding numbers for females were 15 percent and 20 percent. It appears also that the degree of education of the Egyptian labor force, even in 1976, was very low. Data for males in the labor force, where underenumeration is not important, show only 18 percent had formal education in 1976, compared with 9 percent in 1960. The educational achievements of both the Nasser and Sadat regimes can only be characterized as unimpressive. And the achievements under independence before the autocrats took over were even less impressive. It is clear that the distribution of human wealth must have been very unequal in 1976 and continued to be so in 1986. It is equally clear that from a productivity point of view, education must have been very inadequate in 1986. The situation is much better in urban than in rural areas (table 4–39).

Enrollment ratios in Egypt have increased considerably since 1960 but are still unsatisfactory, especially for females and in rural areas. Gross enrollment ratios, as shown in table 4–40, in the second and third levels have increased strongly as a demand response to free admittance without entrance or tuition fees combined with the right to public employment for all graduates of secondary and higher education. The increase at the first level is disappointing.

The right to education was in principle extended to the entire population by the 1923 constitution. Practically, relatively little was done before 1953, especially in rural areas where many villages remained without schools. In 1953, pre-university education was reorganized at three levels: free elementary education for children six to eleven years old was made compulsory; preparatory education, for twelve- to fourteen-year-olds, and secondary education, for fifteen- to seventeen-year-olds, remained voluntary. The traditional Islamic education system under the Al Azhar establishment was coordinated with secular education. With the Charter of 1962, education fees were abolished at all levels and admittance was in principle made free. Apart from a few university departments (medicine, engineering, economics) admittance was made a right, dependent only on a diploma from the preceding level. In 1980–81 a new system, based on the Scandinavian and British models of comprehensive education which consolidate elementary and secondary education, was introduced. Both attendance and completion rates have been poor. During 1971–72 to 1976–77 only 63 percent of pupils registered for the first grade made it to the sixth grade and only 44.7 percent regis-

Table 4–38. Level of Education of Labor Force and Manpower, by Sex, 1960, 1976, and 1986

Category and educational level	1960 Males Thousands	Percent	1960 Females Thousands	Percent	1976 Males Thousands	Percent	1976 Females Thousands	Percent	1986 Males (percent)	1986 Females (percent)
Labor force[a]										
Illiterate	4,347.7	62.7	419.2	78.0	5,207.8	54.2	253.0	30.7	n.a.	n.a.
Read and write[b]	2,023.5	29.2	39.3	7.3	2,521.0	26.2	72.3	8.8	n.a.	n.a.
Primary education[c]	429.3	6.2	59.7	11.1	403.2	4.2	23.2	2.8	n.a.	n.a.
Secondary education[d]	n.a.[e]	n.a.[e]	n.a.[e]	n.a.[e]	945.5	9.8	319.9	38.8	n.a.	n.a.
University education[f]	114.8	1.7	11.9	2.2	406.6	4.2	112.8	13.7	n.a.	n.a.
Not stated	21.9	0.3	7.7	1.4	124.2	1.3	42.4	5.2	n.a.	n.a.
Total[g]	6,937.2	100.0	537.8	100.0	9,608.3	100.0	823.6	100.0	n.a.	n.a.
Manpower[h]										
Illiterate	4,904.8	56.1	7,223.7	83.7	5,405.7	41.4	8,745.1	69.9	37.8	61.8
Read and write[b]	2,861	32.8	1,089.3	12.5	3,709.5	28.4	1,667.4	13.3	30.4	18.0

Primary education[c]	793.9	9.1	299.2	3.4	1,371.1	10.5	724.8	5.8 }	26.0	17.4
Secondary education[d]	—	—	—	—	1,984.6	15.2	992.0	7.9 }		2.8
University education[f]	122.3	1.4	15.8	0.2	424.9	3.3	125.9	1.0	5.8	
Not stated	54.4	0.6	71.1	0.8	175.5	1.3	253.8	2.0	—	—
Total[g]	8,736.5	100.0	8,699.1	100.0	13,071.3	100.0	12,509.0	100.0	100.0	100.0

n.a. = Not available.
— = Not applicable.
a. Based on population censuses.
b. Without primary education certificate.
c. With primary education certificate.
d. Including university students not yet graduated.
e. Included in primary education.
f. Graduates and above.
g. Figures may not add to total because of rounding.
h. Based on population censuses, six years and above (for 1980, ten years old and above) excluding persons over sixty-five years and not working and disabled persons.

Source: Hansen and Radwan (1982), p. 68; Egypt, CAPMAS (1987).

Table 4–39. Distribution of Population, Age Ten Years and above, by Location, Sex, and Level of Education, 1960, 1976, and 1986
(percent)

Category	1960	1976	1986
Urban males	100	100	100
Illiterate	38.8	26.5	26.5
Read and write	40.2	30.4	29.7
Formal education	20.1	41.7	43.8
Not stated	0.9	1.4	—
Urban females	100	100	100
Illiterate	68.0	52.6	44.4
Read and write	22.0	19.1	22.0
Formal education	8.9	26.4	33.6
Not stated	1.1	1.9	—
Rural males	100	100	100
Illiterate	67.4	55.0	47.3
Read and write	27.6	26.2	31.1
Formal education	4.5	17.2	21.6
Not stated	0.5	1.6	—
Rural females	100	100	100
Illiterate	92.5	85.9	76.4
Read and write	6.4	7.7	14.6
Formal education	0.4	4.1	10.0
Not stated	0.7	2.3	—

— = Not applicable.
Source: Hansen and Radwan (1982), p. 70; Egypt, CAPMAS (1987).

tered for the first grade passed the final elementary school examination and obtained a diploma. The quality of education has been poor and declining at all levels because of shortages of schools, classrooms, teaching material, and qualified teachers. In rural areas, quality is particularly low. Thus, there are five thousand one-room schools. Despite a relative increase in the number of students at all levels, public expenditure on education, after increasing from 4.7 percent of GNP in 1950 to 5.2 percent in 1961, slowly declined to 4.1 percent in 1983.

Health, like education, is one of the indicators used to describe the standard of living. Nonlinearity and distribution are just two of the many limitations of such indicators. Here, certain health-related and demographic features are used as proxies for health measures.

Nutritional conditions tend to improve with increasing income, particularly at lower income levels. The decline in the intake of calories, protein, and fat from 1935–39 to 1952–54 (table 4–41) thus indicates a slight decline in per capita income. National income estimates point to a slight increase—0.8 percent annually—in per capita income for this pe-

Table 4-40. Gross Enrollment Ratios by Educational Level and Sex, 1960, 1970, and 1980

(percent of relevant age group)

Year and sex	Educational level[a] First	Second	Third
1960			
Male	80	23	8
Female	52	9	2
Total	66	16	5
1970			
Male	84	44	11
Female	53	21	4
Total	69	32	8
1980			
Male	90	65	23
Female	65	41	11
Total	78	54	18

Source: UNESCO, *Statistical Yearbook*, various years.
a. Levels as defined by UNESCO.

riod. If those two estimates are taken at face value, it might be assumed that there was an increased inequality in the distribution of income. It is doubtful, however, that anything more should be inferred than that there was little growth from the late 1930s to the early 1950s. The nutritional situation then improved somewhat to 1964–66, a period during which per capita income increased about 3 percent annually. To 1969–71 there was a slight decline in intake of both calories and proteins

Table 4-41. Nutritional Intake, Measured by Various Indicators, Selected Periods, 1935–85

Period	Calories (number)	Proteins (grams)	Fats (grams)	Calcium (milligrams)	Iron (milligrams)
1935–39	2,450	73.5	41.9	n.a.	n.a.
1952–54	2,418	70.4	37.6	n.a.	n.a.
1964–66	2,595	73.3	43.5	393	19.2
1969–71	2,564	70.2	48.8	405	19.1
1974–76	2,806	74.6	55.3	405	19.0
1979–81	3,183	81.4	64.8	425	19.4
1985	3,263	n.a.	n.a.	n.a.	n.a.

n.a. = Not available.
Source: FAO, *Production Yearbook*, various years; FAO, *Food Balance Sheet*, various years; World Bank, *World Development Report 1987*.

with a slight increase in the intake of fats and minerals showing the same mixed picture; there was little increase in per capita income from 1965 to 1970. The 1970s, on the other hand, stand out as the period when nutritional indicators for the first time since the 1930s, and probably since the early years of the century, show strong improvement; per capita income increased by close to 4 percent annually during the 1970s.

Nutritional indicators and per capita income estimates thus tend to support each other. It is particularly interesting that a comparison of the Nasser era, 1953–65, and the Sadat era, the 1970s, indicates that in terms of improved nutrition of the population the latter era as a whole appears greatly superior to the former despite the rather similar rates of increase of per capita income. It is remarkable that caloric intake, which in the late 1930s was at the same low level as that in China and India in 1985, was almost in line with that in industrialized market economies (World Bank definition) in 1985. Egypt's income per capita certainly did not increase to that extent. The explanation could be a strong equalization of income distribution but it is more likely that Sadat's food subsidization policies are responsible. Although protein and mineral intakes still leave something to be desired, the Egyptian population as a whole may be characterized as being relatively well nourished compared with the populations of other lower-middle-income countries.

Life expectancy at birth increased from forty-one years for men and forty-four years for women in the early 1950s to fifty-nine years and sixty-three years, respectively in 1985, still far below corresponding figures for industrialized market economies but above averages for the lower-middle-income countries, the group Egypt belongs to. Infant mortality has declined strongly from 172 per thousand births in 1965 to 93 in 1985 but is still relatively high by all standards and no less than ten times that in the industrialized market economies. The crude death rate fell to about half from 1965 to 1985 and was then at 10 per thousand, which is in line with that of industrial market economies.

Despite considerable improvements, health problems are still serious. Debilitating diseases, like bilharziasis (schistosomiasis) and trachoma are still chronic among large segments of the population, especially in rural areas. Health care is, in principle, free. However, the quality of public health care is low, even though the number of persons served per physician and per nurse is relatively low and has declined greatly since the 1960s.

Egypt's Second Five-Year Plan, 1987–99 to 1991–92

The numbering of Egypt's five-year plans is confusing. The first comprehensive five-year plan covered the years 1960–61 to 1964–65. A second five-year plan for 1965–66 to 1969–70 was shelved, and in effect comprehensive planning was abandoned until the early 1980s. A plan for 1982–83 to 1986–87, formally named the first five-year plan, became the law of the land, but it failed utterly. It was followed by a second five-year plan for 1987–88 to 1991–92, which was intended to overcome the difficulties the economy had run into. The document that spells out the details of the second five-year plan outlines reforms and policy changes that are designed to correct the past failures of institutions and strategies (Egypt, Ministry of Planning and International Cooperation, 1987). The document is of direct interest not for numbers but the principles for future development.

The development strategy was not radically altered. The document recommends industrialization, which Egypt has considered a cornerstone in her development strategy ever since 1930 (or even 1918). Obviously the plan is a response to the relatively low share of industry not including petroleum in GDP, which has been declining since 1965, and makes Egypt stand out among lower-middle-income countries as only moderately industrialized with limited opportunities for an immediate change in strategy toward export-led growth.[15] The plan period 1982–83 to 1986–87 had for good reasons emphasized infrastructure, which had been neglected and allowed to run down during the 1960s and 1970s. By 1987 the serious, persistent deficit in the balance of payments and Egypt's huge foreign debt made a structural change of production from nontradable toward tradable goods overdue and indispensable. The second five-year plan document proposes simultaneous expansion of production for exports and import substitution with the emphasis continuing, nonetheless, clearly to be on import substitution. It recommends (pp. 60, 62) that the policy of import substitution be extended to cover capital goods and heavy military equipment. Self-sufficiency in the area of basic needs appears to be the primary preference of the plan, though it is not clear what goods are among those serving basic needs—in some places (pp. 34, 59–60), sugar, television sets, and automobiles appear to be included. Moreover, it is not clear why the country should aim at self-sufficiency for such goods. The only rational argument, to my mind, is the risk of disruption in foreign trade, which the use of embargoes and sanctions for political purposes and the frequency of warfare in the Middle East could explain. The importance attached to self-sufficiency for basic needs goods, however, does indicate an aversion to risk bordering on isolationism, which also may be the cause of the apparent lack of sincere interest in developing exports.

Privatization—change to private ownership of public enterprises—is not part of the strategy, and the role of the bureaucracy is not reduced. It is, however, assumed that the private sector should expand as compared with the public sector. The share of private in total gross fixed investment should increase from about 25 percent in 1982–83 to 1986–87 to

40 percent in 1987–88 to 1991–92. Considering that this share may have been only about 10 percent from the time of the nationalizations in 1960–63 until the mid-1970s, this would be a large increase in the private sector over the long term, yet with the public sector continuing to dominate the economy. The plan calls for private investment to be concentrated in industry and mining, excluding petroleum (table 80), to promote efficiency in the industrialization process. Generally the plan emphasizes increased efficiency rather than physical investment as the key to growth and focuses on realignment of prices and costs to remove the striking distortions of the price structure that increasingly have characterized the whole economy since the 1950s.

In exchange rate policy, "the main thrust . . . is towards unification by gradually creating a free market where supply and demand are in equilibrium" (Egypt, Ministry of Planning and International Cooperation, 1987, p. 226). In fact the foreign exchange reform of 1987–88 was a step toward unification; a government-announced rate for banks' "free foreign exchange market" (applying to both own-exchange and licensed transactions) now coexists with a much lower official rate (applying to the government's financial transactions and trade in a few major commodities). The result is a dual system of pegged exchange rates. In 1989 there was little sign of flexibility in rate setting despite the strong swings of the U.S. dollar and increasing inflation in Egypt. With the revised and "rationalized" tariff system of 1986 in place and substantial and increasing quantitative controls, the dual system does not transfer international price relationships to domestic producers, a necessary condition for efficiency in production.

The plan for 1982–83 to 1986–87 called for "setting producer prices at levels reflecting actual costs and the addition of a profit margin guaranteeing that investment can be financed and by setting user prices at levels providing for social preference" (Egypt, Ministry of Planning and International Cooperation, 1987, p. 231). This simple mark-up rule for producer prices, with subsidies from the budget financing lower user prices for so-called essentials (including consumer durables), was carried over to the second five-year plan with some modification (p. 232). A distinction was introduced between actual costs and "economic costs and prices," the latter assuming a large number of inefficiencies—idle capacity and overstaffing, outdated technology, poor management, waste of materials, sloppy shop-floor discipline, and other practices related to the notion of X-efficiency. Again, however, "social justice must be emphasized in the pricing system through . . . subsidization of essential goods and services" (p. 234). And the plan drew a distinction between "the economic and the social price," the difference to be covered from the budget.

Under the second five-year plan the price system thus is to serve both as a mechanism for allocating resources—allegedly to ensure their efficient use in production—and a mechanism for distributing income, trading efficiency in consumption for improved income distribution. Budgetary subsidies are to be used as a wedge between producer and consumer prices to make the dual price system work. The exchange rate and foreign trade systems as outlined above and the cost-plus price system itself are unlikely to produce price signals that will lead to productive efficiency. Whether the price system will be correct from a distributive point of view depends on both the distribution generated by price formation at the production level and distribution targets to be fulfilled, the former being difficult to ascertain with any degree of precision, the latter simply not formulated precisely in the plan document.

Considerable price reform did in fact occur during the 1980s. Agricultural producer prices were adjusted in the early 1980s to conform better with border prices (see table 18–4). The process of reforming prices of industrial products that began in 1984–85 has not led to efficiency pricing, however.

The plan also recommends a dual system for factor prices. Generally it is unlikely to be conducive to productive efficiency and it could have ambiguous effects on income distribution.

The plan presumes that "private sector wages will remain subject to supply and demand considerations in the labor market" (Egypt, Ministry of Planning and International Cooperation, 1987, p. 238), which simply codifies traditional wage determination. The plan ignores the existence of minimum wage legislation and collective agreements for large private enterprises. For the public sector, a general rule with five specific principles (p. 238) implies that wages will be linked to productivity. This was clearly not the case in earlier years. Even if the rule means that nominal public enterprise wages will be linked to the marginal value of productivity, it would not imply equal wages in private and public enterprises because the government's investment policy undersupplies the private sector, particularly the informal sector, with both capital and infrastructure services.

On interest rates the plan distinguishes between domestic and international credit transactions, apparently to avoid the capital flight that the own-exchange system invites. The arguments for low interest rates on loans made in Egyptian pounds appear complex. Both private investment and cost-of-living considerations are mentioned (p. 225); Islamic religious doctrine may have played a role here.

Clearly the price policies in the second five-year plan do not guarantee efficiency in production. Market orientation of production not only requires adequate price signals but also adequate responses on the part of producers in making production decisions. This applies both to investors' decisions about capital formation and managers' decisions about current production at existing capacity. In competitive or (in the American sense) regulated markets with individual producers exerting no influence on sales prices, maximization of profit should imply efficiency in production. Nowhere does Egypt's plan spell out profit maximization as a principle of investment or production decisions. On the other hand, it contains extensive, detailed targets for physical investment and production. It sets explicit investment and production targets for forty-four budget centers in the public sector (tables 78, 87) and declares that "executive measures must be established for each unit to make sure it achieves its share of the targets set out in the plan for the various production and service budget centers. At the level of economic organization, sub-targets must be split out down to the lowest level possible and technically programmed and scheduled within the limits of available resources to spread the concept of the planning approach to economic management" (Egypt, Ministry of Planning and International Cooperation, 1987, p. 242). This is centralized planning in the most orthodox sense.

The plan does not go into detail about demand management. It does assume "self-reliance" in national financing in the sense of a balanced current account. Apart from its recommendation of flexibility in exchange rates and private sector wages and a recommendation of a balanced government budget, the plan does little to indicate how demand equilibrium at full employment can be obtained.

Notes

1. In his discussion of the patron-client system, Springborg (1975, 1979, 1983) refers to the times of Mohammed Ali, the Mamelukes, and the Ottomans. He makes no reference to the period 1923–52. Tignor (1984), the main source on the political economy of Egypt during the period of parliamentary democracy, does not mention the possible existence of a patron-client system. Historical continuity would suggest that a system so deeply rooted in Egyptian traditional society, trusting Springborg on this point, should not have disappeared completely between Mohammed Ali and World War I to suddenly reemerge after 1952. In an earlier volume, Tignor (1966) describes developments toward meritocracy under Ismail but warns against exaggerating the extent of change (p. 45). Morroe Berger, who is not explicit on this point, summarizes: "Historically, there have been ways other than those prevailing in the West today to insure high standards of performance of civil servants. These methods include sponsorship, nepotism, and personal loyalty, all of which were in harmony with the values of societies in which they were used, but which would be considered improper in the contemporary West. The special problem facing the Arab countries and Egypt is the penetration of Western notions of honesty and efficiency in government at a time when personal, familial, and communal loyalties still persist in the population being governed and from which the administrators are drawn" (1957, p. 149).

2. Waterbury (1983, pp. 135, 141, 285–86) gives two examples of genuine political activity under Sadat. Referring to law 43 of 1974 covering foreign investments, particularly joint ventures between public and foreign enterprises, the General Confederation of Labor clearly announced its dismay with foreign investments and its opposition to attempts to limit labor's rights to profit sharing and representation in company management. In 1975 the People's Assembly passed a law proposed by its agricultural committee (apparently not vetoed by the president) that in effect amounted to a strong increase in the maximum rents of land and relaxation of the rules of tenure and the eviction of tenants. Considering the composition of the assembly, this probably indicates the growing influence of the larger landowners under Sadat. However, this is legislation that would mainly affect distribution in the countryside, not between urban and rural areas; any effect in favor of urban areas would arise from absentee owners who live in urban areas.

3. Nasser does, however, seem to have had a fairly broad knowledge of political philosophy and history and of statesmen such as Bismarck, Atatürk, and Churchill (Nutting 1972, pp. 7, 13).

4. Military imports may appear in the payments statistics without having passed through the customs authorities. Data from both customs and exchange sources are not available beyond 1973, but it stands to reason that the gap should tend to disappear after 1973.

5. The Aswan Dam investments were never carefully incorporated in the first five-year plan. There were no plans for expanding the cement industry adequately and the country's substantial exports of cement ceased with the construction of the dam.

6. Sidki had a Ph.D. in regional planning from an American university but his public statements give the impression of extremely crude import-substitution thinking.

7. Official estimates of investment in housing are of poor quality; estimates of private investment are little more than guesses, having been assumed, until the early 1970s, to be about 10 percent of the total.

8. I can find only three countries with comparable DRCs and ERPs for enough industries or commodities to make similar regressions between DRC and ERP. For Ghana (Leith 1975, pp. 68–80) estimates for eleven industries yield $R^2 = 0.05$ and $SR = -0.43$; the estimates are not reliable. For Israel (Michaeli 1975, pp. 103–05) estimates for thirteen import substitutes in textiles yield $R^2 = 0.72$ and $SR = 0.79$ while for eighteen export commodities in textiles the results are $R^2 = 0.86$ and $SR = 0.69$. For Chile (Behrman 1976) estimates for eighteen tradables in 1961 yield $R^2 = 0.62$ and $SR = 0.57$, while estimates for sixteen exportables in 1968 yield $R^2 = 0.17$ and $SR = 0.34$. Estimates for India (Bhagwati and Srinivasan 1975) are in effect in both cases ERPs ($R^2 = 1.00!$).

9. UNIDO (1972) recommends excluding capital goods and using trade shares for tradable consumer goods and raw materials as weights.

10. No detailed discussion of wages and salaries in general government is ventured here. Public enterprise wages represent a "political price," and government wages and salaries even more so. Zaitoun (1988) indicates a decline in real government remuneration since the late 1970s as compared with manufactur-

ing, salaries lagging behind wages, white collar lagging behind blue collar, higher grades lagging behind lower grades, the former categories losing, the latter categories gaining in real terms. The politics behind these developments are complex but problems of social stability and equity have undoubtedly been overriding, it being understood that multiple jobs and extras are an important, not quantifiable part of the picture, presumably compensating the official losers in the higher echelons generously.

11. Fully consistent national accounts, covering domestic production, income, and expenditure formation as well as foreign income and expenditure, are not available for Egypt. The data in table 4–24 were compiled from a number of estimates, from 1974 based on official estimates from the Ministry of Planning. An attempt to check the reliability of these estimates was made by estimating national net borrowing also from the balance of payments side, adding the current account deficit and net factor payments abroad, from 1974 based on data compiled by international organizations (World Bank and IMF). The resulting tabulation is not shown here but the inconsistency in the results of the two approaches is very disturbing. It is partly related to incomplete data for international payments with evaluation problems related to the practice of multiple exchange rates. Nobody has to my knowledge ever succeeded in reconciling official national account estimates with the balance of payments estimates of the international organizations. Without doubt the margins of error of table 4–24 are large and may for some years and periods exceed 1–2 percent of GNP.

12. Information form the agricultural census of 1982, recently released (Springborg 1989b) indicates a certain, possibly rather strong reversal of the tendency for distribution by holdings to become more equal.

13. The official expenditures survey for 1981–82 is seriously flawed and appears to grossly underestimate household expenditure, presumably in the higher income brackets. The consensus seems to be that the 1981–82 survey should not be used for comparison with earlier official surveys (Korayem 1987, p. 43). The 1982 survey referred to in table 4–31 is a private one conducted by the IFPRI, Washington, D.C.

14. The underenumeration of women in the Egyptian labor force is usually ascribed to the unwillingness of male household heads, interviewed by census and survey enumerators, to admit that female family members work outside the household. The underenumeration is probably most pronounced for unpaid, female family labor, wives particularly, in rural areas. Technical and definitional matters also tend to create underenumeration in the labor force surveys (CAPMAS *Manpower Survey*, 1981, Introductory Remarks). The surveys are made in May, the seasonal peak in agriculture (since 1964, at least); but the seasonal peak for female employment in agriculture for more than a century has been the cotton harvest in September–November. Because the surveys do not include the seasonally unemployed in the labor force, female participation in the labor force and female unemployment appear low. Moreover, unpaid family members are not included in the labor force if they work less than one-third of full time (during the survey period, presumably). Peasant women who are regularly in charge of animal care and production may easily fall in this category. That the Egyptian labor force surveys (and populaton censuses) misrepresent women's participation in the labor force is apparent from the fact that special surveys regularly show a much higher share in annual agricultural labor input

than would seem possible from the labor force surveys. Commander and Hadhoud (1986) indicate that in 1984 as much as 32.9 percent of total labor input in field work was by women and children and that corresponding figure for livestock work was 40 percent, implying a share of 36 percent in total agricultural labor input. It is characteristic that for field work, female labor is almost exclusively hired labor, for animal production almost exclusively unpaid family labor.

15. On the difficult problem of measuring the share of manufacturing industry proper in Egypt, see appendix 1A.

5 The Political Economy of Egyptian Development

This chapter assesses the role of, on the one hand, institutional and organizational factors, and on the other hand, political economy factors in Egypt's story of economic growth and equity. These matters will be dealt with in sections 1 and 2. In section 3 we shall discuss some exogenous factors of particular importance in the case of Egypt.

Institutional and Organizational Developments

During the decades since Egypt gained formal independence in 1923, profound institutional and organizational change took place. After a brief interregnum, 1914–23, as a British protectorate under a nominally sovereign sultan, this previously semi-independent province of the Ottoman Empire, occupied by Britain in 1882, became a constitutional monarchy. The parliamentary democracy was somewhat imperfect, especially because of the British military presence and the right the British reserved to interfere in matters considered vital for their empire. Full independence for Egypt came about gradually with tariff autonomy from 1930, full tax autonomy from 1937, and full judiciary autonomy only in 1949. The British military presence in the Suez Canal Zone was not terminated until 1954 (56). External political constraints, which gravely limited the sovereignty of the country, set the course of economic policy and development. Thus, despite constitutional monarchy and parliamentary democracy, it was not domestic politics but rather the expiration of the Capitulations that explains the timing of the introduction of Egypt's protectionist, inward-looking strategy in 1930 and the initiation of tax reform in 1937. And British war efforts, partly administered through the Middle East Supply Centre, determined cropping, trade, and inflation policies during World War II. Despite apparently ideal free trade conditions with some protection, no development worth talking about took place before World War II.

With the Free Officers' coup of 1952, parliamentary democracy was destroyed and replaced by autocratic government. Under Nasser, Egypt

242

was transformed into a state-controlled economy, with all of its infrastructure, most of its large-scale production, foreign trade, finance, and wholesale trade, and some of its retail trade incorporated in the public sector and run by public enterprises and organizations directly under government administration. Agriculture (apart from some land reclamation areas), small-scale nonagricultural production, and most retail trade and housing were left to the private sector. The conversion of a predominantly private enterprise economy into a mixed, state-controlled economy was accomplished partly through nationalizations and sequestrations of foreign and domestic property, partly through the government's current investment policies. The share of investment in GNP probably increased with the new regime but its quality and composition may have suffered.

With public enterprises dominating so many areas, including foreign trade, and not operating on a profits maximization basis, markets were no longer competitive (if they ever had been) and thus were no longer conducive to economic efficiency. Productivity clearly suffered from the expansion of public ownership and bureaucratic interference. In addition, price controls were imposed on a large number of commodities and services, including rentals of housing and agricultural land. In the public sector (administration and services as well as enterprises) wages were set by the government, and statutory minimum wages, though widely evaded, applied to the private sector. For larger private enterprises the compulsory arbitration introduced in 1952 in practice meant that the government set wage rates while in the informal small-scale sector, including agriculture and construction, wages were left to market forces.

Price controls and licensing of foreign trade had, of course, emerged during World War II and they continued through the 1950s. Quantitative controls thus flourished before the mixed economy became an established fact in the 1960s. State controls were not invented by the Nasser regime. Between the wars, however, quantitative controls were virtually unknown and there was little direct public intervention or dominance of markets by public enterprises, public utilities being the exception. Protectionism in those years was mainly confined to tariff policy and some subsidization in the form of cheap government lending. It is difficult to say how effective and competitive markets were. The organized spot and futures markets in Alexandria for cotton and a few other export commodities, with effective arbitrage in international commodity markets (in Liverpool), were probably highly competitive. Those markets were closed in 1961 when foreign trade was taken over by public agencies. At the other end of the spectrum were the local village markets which were probably neither effective nor competitive. Price discrepancies between neighboring villages appear to have been substantial but no systematic studies of village markets are available (Martin and Levi 1910). In the middle were the urban markets, wholesale and retail, where competition appears to have been effective and keen. The advent of import licensing, price controls, and informal rationing in World War II and later the dominance by public enterprises caused the urban markets to become ineffective and imperfectly competitive.

With Sadat's *infitah*, foreign exchange markets and imports were partly liberalized. For so-called own-exchange imports—mostly nonessential consumer goods assumed not to be competing with goods produced by public enterprises—import licensing was abolished and price controls did not apply. Exchange rates for the accompanying foreign exchange transactions were free. Sadat, however, chose to preserve Nasser's Arab socialism and the nature of the economy as a mixed economy.

Much the same was true for financial markets. During the interwar period, with branches of European banks operating freely in Egypt and capital movements entirely free (insofar as the Egyptian government was concerned, though not in Europe where controls were increasing), urban credit markets were probably largely effective and competitive. The legal maximum interest of 9 percent and the lower maximum rates applied by native and mixed courts may have created some credit rationing but it was probably not important, especially in light of the low interest rates that prevailed internationally after 1929. For rural areas, the combination of maximum interest rates and Lord Kitchener's Five-Feddan Law of 1911, which banned foreclosure of farms of five *feddans* or less, virtually paralyzed the modern market for small farm mortgage loans and forced small farmers to borrow from local moneylenders, frequently of foreign origin. After 1960, with all banks and credit institutions nationalized and interest rates fixed at low levels, a situation typical of so-called financial repression prevailed; however, the gap between private saving and investment increasingly was covered by the government through inflationary financing. With Sadat's partial liberalization of the exchange market and the de facto convertibility of own-exchange accounts, capital movements were liberalized. This liberalization did not apply to public enterprises, so that in this sense they now were discriminated against.

Except in certain areas of land reclamation in the western desert, agriculture continued to be overwhelmingly dominated by private ownership. But with the land reforms of 1952 and later, agricultural cooperatives were set up to deliver certain inputs and administer crop rotation schemes, establishing, in effect, central control with cropping patterns. The intention was to combine economies of scale in irrigation and soil preparation with small-scale cultivation. By the mid-1960s such cooperatives covered the whole countryside and all farmers were forced to become members. The cooperatives monopolized the supply of such important inputs as fertilizers and pesticides, controlled both quantities and prices of credit (interest rates), and superimposed schemes of crop rotation and delivery of certain important crops, particularly export crops, at low maximum prices. The loss of half the cotton crop in 1961 stands as a monument to the Nasser regime's intervention in agriculture. The underlying strategy was one of self-sufficiency for commodities satisfying so-called basic needs. Though this strategy may have had economic motivations and have been justified as a protection against the embargo policies applied internationally on several occasions during the postwar period, it had profoundly distortive effects on agricultural production. Agricultural investment policies favored unproductive land reclamation schemes and ignored drainage of the old lands. The system vacillated between Soviet and market orientation, depending on the political power structure in the country, and around 1970 came close to Sovietizing all Egyptian agriculture. During the 1970s and 1980s the tendency turned toward increasing market orientation in agriculture.

Institutional changes in education have been important. The system of education that existed in 1923—a public university and private primary and secondary schools—had mainly been set up by and for the foreign community but to some extent served the higher-income brackets of the native population. No public elementary school system existed and the opportunities for education for the broad population, particularly in rural areas, were virtually nil. The constitution of 1923 guaranteed free compulsory education for all children seven to twelve years old. An ambitious educational program was established but progress was slow. At the time of the coup in 1952 only about half the children entitled to elementary education attended school, and attendance was strongly biased in favor of males and urban areas. In 1984 enrollments in primary schools were 94 percent for males and 72 percent for females with much lower enrollments in rural areas. With land reform and the strong shift toward small holdings, the slow progress in elementary education in rural areas has been detrimental to agricultural productivity, the more so because cooperatives were never able to deliver adequate extension services. For secondary education, progress has been faster, with 70 percent enrollment for males in 1984 against 46 percent for females. The relatively rapid growth in secondary and higher education created an employment problem after 1964 when all graduates were given the right to public employment. With the adult literacy rate estimated at only 51 percent for 1986, and much lower for females than for males and for rural than for urban areas, educational efforts since independence cannot be characterized as successful. The quality of education has been declining at all levels. Private tuition has made education at the higher levels a caricature of free education.

Economic Politics in the Period of Parliamentary Democracy

Modern political economy theory views politics and government interference as the outcome of a complex process of exchange among individuals in societies that "respect the individual value norm upon which a liberal social order is grounded" (Buchanan 1987, p. 246). In this exchange, individuals may choose to operate on their own or in groups, organizations, or parties. Egypt's parliamentary democracy from 1923 to 1952 was marked at times by heavy-handed intervention from the palace on the one hand and the British embassy on the other. Until 1930, and in some matters until 1937, the Capitulations limited the political autonomy of the country and thus the area in which politics may be seen as voluntary exchange among Egyptian individuals. The colonial order could not be described as a liberal social order, nor could the World War II setting, for Egyptian economic policy in many ways was subordinated to Allied war efforts and little choice was left to the Egyptian government. Within these constraints, a parliamentary democracy did function, and a kind of liberal social order did prevail. Political parties operated with relative freedom, and organized special-interest groups had a strong impact on economic policy. Among the latter were the Egyptian Federation of Industry, the General Egyptian Agricultural Syndicate, the Association des Agriculteurs, and a number of professional syndicates. Labor unions existed but were divided and weak; they were not recognized legally as representatives of labor in collective bargaining until after World War II when, in return, arbitration became compulsory in some areas. Thus the modern political economy models with parties, pressure groups, voters, and government as watchman appear, with some qualifications, to be applicable.

The two great issues related to growth and equity, settled through the political process during the period of parliamentary democracy, were those of development strategy and taxation, both held up by the Capitulations. The development strategy of inward-looking import substitution and infant-industry policy chosen in 1930 along with tariff reform combined with export promotion for cotton was adopted almost as a consensus, strongly influenced by the onset of the Great Depression. The strategy actually was adopted by consensus in 1918 by the members of the Commission on Commerce and Industry as a compromise among nationalistic ideologists such as Tala'at Harb, who were concerned about the problems of the economy—particularly population growth—in a future independent Egypt, and special interest groups, cotton growers and exporters, emerging industrialists and importers, and the foreign community, which operated across all these groups. That the Federation of Industry should strongly support the tariff reform of 1930 is not surprising since industry obviously would be the great beneficiary. However, the federation was dominated by the foreign business community. But the foreign community, as Tignor (1984) emphasizes, served its own "periphery" interests and not those of the "center," as so-called dependency theory would have it. Assimilation as well as political developments in Central Europe, especially in Germany, here played an important role. Support for tariff reform from the Agricultural Syndicate was related to large landowners' interest in creating domestic demand for cotton as a raw material, and the same was true for sugar. In the long run neither the cotton textile nor the sugar industry may have been viable under free trade conditions. Obviously viable industries—cement and phosphates—were ignored. Special interest groups thus distorted investment patterns. That wheat and wheat flour were given heavy protection through a strong increase in tariff rates in 1932 was, of course, attractive to agriculture. But with cotton also protected through increased subsidization (irrigation investments) the whole package began to resemble a general, albeit uneven, currency depreciation tending to favor most tradable goods and to operate against nontradables (construction and services). Depreciation perhaps was what Egypt was most in need of. Voices raised to advocate the interests of labor (the unions, the Wafd party, l'Union des Cultivateurs, the British Chamber of Commerce, among others) made little impression.

Although the development strategy almost became a consensus, the tax reforms of 1937 met with strong opposition. The issue was not primarily creating a more egalitarian distribution of income but instead the old-fashioned issue of creating equity in taxation—equal taxation of equal income. The existing tax system, built by the British around the turn of the century and within the constraints of the Capitulations, aimed at making the land tax and the urban buildings tax equitable. Among landowners and owners of urban real estate, respectively, equal, albeit different, tax rates were applied to fairly assessed land and urban real estate rental values, and Egyptians and foreigners were subjected to the same taxes. Yet, generally, income taxation was highly inequitable because income from land was taxed at very different rates than income from urban buildings while no income tax at all was applied to income from other business, capital, and labor. The so-called license tax on business was abolished in the 1890s because it proved impossible to make the Capitulary Powers agree to extend the tax to foreigners. It is characteristic of the British attitude that hard pressed as Egypt was for revenue to pay debt service on her public debt, Cromer preferred to give up the revenue from this tax completely rather than let the foreign community escape a tax that the native population paid. But the foreign community was in fact concentrated on tax-free urban business, so that the system was nonetheless highly inequitable and biased in favor of urban and foreign business. As a result, nationalists and landowners and their organizations tended to be in favor of taxation of nonagricultural business and labor income, with the Federation of Industry strongly against such income tax, partly emphasizing what is now called supply-side effects of income taxes on growth and development. A particular point of grievance of landowners was that the Capitulations prevented lowering of the assessed land taxes despite the strong decline in income derived from land during the deflation of the Great Depression. Because land-owners had the upper hand politically, the tax reforms were adopted but collection of the new income taxes did not begin until after World War II. With evasion massive, the revenue collected was minuscule and the effects on income distribution probably insignificant. In 1949, incidentally, the land taxes were reassessed and the tax rate lowered by almost half. Considering the wartime inflation, land taxes in real terms thus declined dramatically.

Growth and Equity in the Period of Autocracy

Since the coup of the Free Officers in 1952 and Nasser's rise to power, Egypt has been an autocracy, ruled by a succession of weak dictators with very different styles of government. All of them, to different degrees, violated the individual value norm and negated the liberal social order that existed before 1952. Politics as voluntary exchange has ceased functioning.

Nasser's regime banned the old political parties and replaced them with a one-party system that was little more than a cosmetic device. Organized interest groups like labor unions and the Federation of Industry were destroyed or emasculated and turned into government-controlled entities. Professional syndicates suffered the same fate. The *shilla* network with its vertical and horizontal connections and all the other characteristics of a classical patron-client system grew up. Until Egypt's defeat in the 1967 War, two patron-client systems, at times hostile and fiercely competitive, existed side by side, one with Nasser, the other with Field Marshal Amer at the top of the pyramid (Springborg 1979). Horizontal connections were, however, so important that Waterbury (1977) prefers to call it a crony system. Both Nasser and Amer, but especially Nasser, manipulated the patron-client system with ruthless determination as a means of securing and expanding their own power positions.

For the clients, a major function of such a system is distributing spoils and the systems under Nasser and Amer were no exception. With all large-scale enterprises nationalized and all foreign trade and finance handled by government agencies, the spoils were to be had in public enterprises and administration financed from the public budget, including, of course, the armed forces, and in the administration of sequestered property. The proliferation of ministers and other high administrative officers, often with salaries and perquisites above the regular scale, began under Nasser, who needed to place loyal clients, particularly officers, in lucrative positions. For some prominent second-line patrons such as Sabri, Marei, Hassanein, and Heikal, ideology with an eye on foreign connections (the Soviet Union or the United States) was an additional consideration, but ultimately even such relatively powerful figures were but clients and their ideologies but pawns in the Nasser-Amer power games.

Politics under the Nasser regime cannot be described as a system of voluntary exchange among individuals with equal rights. Within an established patron-client group an exchange might take place, loyalty being exchanged for spoils in pursuit of a common group goal, but it would not be an exchange among equals. Coercion prevailed, and any individual, whether patron or client, might at any time be deprived of civil rights by presidential decree. Moreover, entrance into such groups was not free although exit might be. The groups were mostly of such a nature that entrance tickets could not be purchased in the marketplace. The group might, for instance, consist of graduates from the military academy in a particular year. The junta itself was such a group.

Albeit peripheral to the basic issue of politics as an exchange, rent seeking has played a central role in economists' analysis of government-controlled systems. The definition of rent can be stretched to encompass any income that would not prevail in a perfectly competitive system that is in or dynamically on its way toward equilibrium (Buchanan 1987, pp. 8–14) and any effort to be in the privileged position of having the right to such income would be rent seeking. With such a broad definition the spoils of the patron-client system would be rents. On the other hand, to describe the system under Nasser as one of rent seeking would not be very informative. The previous democratic system was certainly also rent seeking. The nature of the rents depends on the institutional aspects of the system. Under parliamentary democracy, rent seeking took the form of efforts to increase tariff rates or government-subsidized loans and the rent seekers were private businesses. The spoils under Nasser were partly salaries out of proportion to merit, partly privileges of rationing. Widespread price controls, with increasing commodity shortages and informal rationing, tended to place clients, frequently officers, first in line for allocation of such things as cars, durable consumer goods, certain types of food, and telephones. Acquisition of goods in short supply—hence acquisition of rents—was closely linked to positions in the patron-client system, and entrance was not free. Much of the theory of rent seeking does not, for that reason, apply here. Two areas of particular importance with controlled prices far below potential market prices and accordingly flourishing black market trade were rentals of housing and land. Since there was no public rationing of either privately owned apartments or cultivated land, the black market trade and rentals did not represent rent seeking in the technical sense of the word.

Although there are exceptions to any rule, it would be a gross misnomer to label the clients and cronies around or, rather, under Nasser and Amer as platonic guardians. The patron-client system ruled out professional merit and detachment as the basis for career advancement in both civil administration and the armed forces and in this way did great harm to both the efficiency of the civilian bureaucracy and military capability. If ever individualism, to use a nice synonym, dominated a governmental system it was here. Nonetheless, the politics of the system cannot be described as the outcome of an exchange process in the sense of modern political economy because this was not a liberal social order. The Nasser regime was one of arbitrary dictatorship permeated by arbitrary decisionmaking and favoritism. The system led to distortions in investment no less severe than those made in favor of special interest groups under democracy—the neglect of drainage of old lands while investment funds were squandered on land reclamation is the outstanding example. And the sequestrations and administration by clients frequently amounted to little more than predatory activities, informing, embezzlement, and theft.

The question may still be asked whether the junta itself and Nasser personally could not be seen as platonic guardians operating in the service of the public interest (as perceived by themselves) in the way that the Kemalists and the military establishment in Turkey may be seen. The answer is no. Undoubtedly the junta included men of high ideals who might have deserved the epithet had they ruled the country. They were, however, with the exception of Amer, early outmaneuvered by Nasser's and Amer's power games and replaced by second-line officers and a few civilians—the cronies and clients. Nasser was himself undoubtedly a puritan of high ideals, politically and socially, but his power games always took the upper hand. Thus, important though they were from an equity point of view, land reform, nationalizations, and sequestrations were primarily actions aimed at neutralizing or destroying actual or potential, real or imagined, political opponents or power contenders. The land reforms effectively eliminated big landownership (including the royal house) as a power center, the nationalizations paralyzed the modern entrepreneurial class, and the sequestrations destroyed hand-picked wealthy, powerful families. The subordination of economic policy to power games meant that agricultural policy issues such as land reclamation settlements, agricultural cooperatives, and extension services never found consistent solutions but vacillated between Soviet-oriented and market-oriented solutions depending on the client who happened to be in favor at any particular time.

Unable to control the armed forces completely until after the defeat of 1967 and Amer's related death (which, incidentally, did much to bring an end to the patron-client system) when the armed forces lost both face and credibility, Nasser can only be characterized as a weak autocrat, and his successor Sadat as even weaker. Several commentators (Roy 1980) suggest they relied on an implicit, tacit social compact between ruler and ruled, the latter offering acquiescence and surrender of political rights in return for la dolce vita. At the penalty of riots and civil disobedience, the ruler became committed to providing an ever-increasing standard of living, a commitment that increasingly led the country into a quagmire of budget deficits, inflation, balance of payments deficits, and foreign borrowing. The process accelerated under Sadat but its first manifestations emerged under Nasser when military expenditures for the Yemen and Israeli wars were, as far as possible, financed through foreign loans and sharply reduced investment programs before private consumption was touched and after the defeat in 1967 when the populace had to be placated through increased wages and supplies of consumer goods.

Sadat's regime initially reestablished certain civil rights and partly liberalized the economy. It would be misleading, however, to claim that even the incomplete liberal social order of 1923–52 had been reestablished or that a system of voluntary political exchange now prevailed. The military went back to the barracks and the patron-client system rapidly disintegrated, but family and personal connections gained importance and corruption became rampant. Migration became a constitutional right under Sadat. With the demand for labor from Arab OPEC countries, workers' remittances became a major factor in problems of income distribution and foreign exchange. With the partial liberalization of the foreign exchange market and the emergence of own-exchange imports the private, nonagricultural sector expanded, but it was a deliberate decision of Sadat's to preserve the public sector established under Nasser. Under Sadat, political parties were permitted on a very limited scale and participated in elections. Parliament and a special council debated and passed legislation of substance, subjected, of course, to presidential approval. Professional syndicates became increasingly active. Various Islamic movements started coming out in the open, and Sadat played them against Nasserists and Marxists, with disastrous result. There was some Islamic impact on family legislation and investment (construction of mosques). It has also been claimed that labor unions regained some power—for instance, preventing mergers of public and foreign-owned enterprises. Yet Springborg (1979, pp. 276–77) is undoubtedly correct in pointing out that "for the first time since 1952, Egyptian politics more clearly resembles politics than administration." Nonetheless, Egypt continued to operate under the rules of the social compact, soaring consumer subsidies and public employment of graduates from the rapidly expanding secondary and higher education systems raised the budget deficits which were mainly financed by oil and Suez Canal revenues and by foreign borrowing. Society remained largely a spoils system, where the large spoils now obtained in contract-fixing between government and private foreign companies, contract-fixing being a specialization of so-called consultants with government connections, a development of the crony system (where old ministers play a prominent role). It was in this context that corruption and parasitic activities became rampant.

In its last phase, the Sadat regime became increasingly repressive. Sadat's actions in attempting to destroy the bar association are notorious. In the great purge in early 1981 close to two thousand members of the Egyptian elite who were critical of Sadat were thrown in prison for an indefinite period. Shortly, however, Sadat was himself destroyed by the forces he had let loose.

The Mubarak regime reversed the oppressive measures taken by the Sadat regime but otherwise continued the policies of that regime with little innovation. The electoral system has become more open, and with Islamic groups winning almost one-fifth of the popular vote in elections in the late 1980s, it seems possible that a major pressure group has emerged. But the military has begun to play an increasingly important economic role, seeking association with private domestic or foreign businesses rather than with public enterprises. Some slow rectification of the price system has occurred, mainly a result of attempts to secure foreign financing.

Assessing how the systems of political economy under Nasser, Sadat, and Mubarak affected growth and equity is an almost impossible task. Efficiency and factor productivity have suffered badly under the institutions and organizational forms favored by these regimes, and it seems clear that national saving suffered not only from the uncertainty created by nationalizations and sequestrations but also from the consumerism sponsored by the implicit social compact that has dominated the scene since the 1960s. It is not quite so obvious what the effects on fixed investment and hence on GDP growth have been. There may be no simple mechanical relation between investment and saving on the one hand and growth on the other. Still, it probably remains the case that dynamically GNP growth tends to increase with investment and GNI growth with saving. The Nasser regime was probably conducive to total investment until the mid-1960s and so was the Sadat regime from the mid-1970s. It stands to reason that the Nasser regime did much harm to private saving. What the net impact on growth of the conflicting effects on productivity, saving, and investment may have been for the entire period of government-as-dictator is difficult to say. Average growth per capita for 1960–85 was on the order of 3 percent, which compares well with the average for countries that the World Bank defines as lower middle income but it is modest compared with growth rates obtained by more successful countries. What could growth realistically have been under alternative political systems in Egypt? Parliamentary democracy did not function well during 1923–52. It is, of course, tautologically true that a better democracy would lead to better results, but democracy does not necessarily lead to efficiency in resource allocation or in public decision-making (Inman 1987, pp. 704 ff.).

Indicators of nominal income distribution and poverty in Egypt are difficult to compare internationally, but the system appears to have been relatively equitable and shows little change since the late 1950s. This is surprising considering the strong intervention in the distribution of wealth that has taken place. Land reform, nationalizations, and sequestrations together should have tended to equalize the distribution of material wealth and hence of income. Other powerful factors should have tended to operate in the same direction. The expansion and distribution of human wealth through the educational system and the equalization of the expanding public sector's wage differentials are two such factors. Migration and workers' remittances may possibly have been important, although opinions about their effect on distribution are divided. Urbanization may have worked in the opposite direction. The impact of the tax and social security systems, which, everything else being equal, have tended to improve income distribution, unfortunately cannot be separated from the impact of deficit financing via inflation. The expenditure surveys on which indicators of distribution and poverty in Egypt mainly are based do not in themselves show the impact over time of price controls and commodity subsidies, which have played a growing role in the governments' policies of income distribution and poverty. Attempts to study income distribution in real terms show, as might be expected, that such policies, everything else being equal, have had a strong equalizing effect on income distribution and alleviating effects on poverty. Once more the problem is that indirect effects through deficit financing and inflation may have tended to reverse these effects.

Exogenous Factors Influencing Growth and Equity

The exogenous factors that have profoundly affected growth and equity may conveniently be classed under war and warfare, discovery of oil, migration, and terms of trade changes. Since independence, Egypt has been involved in no less than five wars, in four of them as active belligerent. Egypt was the base of large Allied operations during World War II. Casualties and physical destruction were limited but the economy suffered a temporary setback caused by fertilizer shortages and disruption of crop rotation. Industry, on the other hand, benefited from the artificial protection the war provided and the demand from Allied forces. The economy recovered quickly after the war with the normalization of supply and the long-term effects on growth may even have been positive. The standard of living declined temporarily and it stands to reason that distribution temporarily became more unequal. A strong increase in domestic saving serves as circumstantial evidence. Poverty undoubtedly increased temporarily.

Apart from World War II, the wars afflicting the Egyptian economy can hardly be considered exogenous events. The Palestinian wars had little direct impact on the Egyptian economy; the same was the case for the Suez War of 1956 although casualties and destruction were not insignificant and the Suez Canal was closed to traffic for a short time. It was the Yemen War, 1962–67, and the Israeli wars, 1967–73, with heavy casualties, destruction, closure of the Suez Canal, and loss of the oilfields in Sinai, with soaring defense expenditures, that seriously disrupted the process of growth and possibly temporarily increased inequity and poverty. The shift of foreign trade toward communist countries may be seen as part of the cost inflicted by the series of wars from 1956 to 1973. Part of the high growth rates after 1974, may, however, be seen as recovery after the war years, with the reopening of the Suez Canal, the recovery of the Sinai oilfields, and the shift of trade back to the non-communist world. There seems, nonetheless, to be little doubt that on balance growth over the period of independence as a whole must have suffered substantially from the wars. It can hardly be claimed, on the other hand, that inequity and poverty should have increased permanently as a consequence of the wars. Disabled veterans have largely been given public employment.

The discovery of new oilfields and gas deposits, making Egypt an oil exporter after 1976, gave a strong boost to growth rates. For the period 1974 to 1981–83 about 13 percent of GDP growth (not including price effects) can be ascribed to the petroleum sector, according to the official national accounts. Price distortions for domestic sales probably imply a serious underestimation of the contribution of the petroleum sector. The direct impact of the petroleum sector, which is entirely government owned, on equity and poverty has been negligible. The indirect impact through the budget has been substantial but is difficult to separate from other budgetary policies.

Migration to Arab OPEC countries has since 1973 been massive and has alleviated both employment and foreign exchange problems and, hence, indirectly has had a positive effect on GDP growth. Remittances may or may not have tended to improve income distribution, and the effects on poverty are even less obvious.

Fluctuations in the terms of trade have been very strong since independence, with heavy losses during the Great Depression and gains during the Korean boom. For the years after 1960 conflicting evidence points to gains during the 1960s, losses around the time of the oil price increase of 1973 (when Egypt was a net oil importer), and strong gains after 1979–80 (when Egypt became an oil exporter), which were lost again after 1984. For the period since independence as a whole, Egypt has tended to gain somewhat from the terms of trade with positive effects on GNI growth and uncertain effects on equity and poverty. The impact of other countries' trade policies is a complex issue. Tendencies to trade liberalization in the highly industrialized part of the world should have benefited Egypt but she has taken little advantage of the opportunities emerging in this way. Some trade policies, particularly agricultural policies in the European Community, the United States, and Japan, have been positively harmful to the country. On balance, however, Egypt's main enemy has been Egypt.

II The Republic of Turkey

6 Growth, Equity, and Poverty, 1923–85

The Republic of Turkey was established in 1923 on the ruins of the Ottoman Empire. World War I and the War of Independence left the country economically in shambles, and the Treaty of Lausanne so constrained economic policy that the new republic did not gain full autonomy until 1929. The years 1923–29 thus became a period of institutional change, westernization, and reconstruction in which the autocratic government under Mustafa Kemal, later named Atatürk, prepared for a modern development policy with industrialization as its backbone. The Great Depression seriously compounded the country's problems. The policy that emerged after 1929 was one of the first examples among developing countries of an inward-looking, import-substitution strategy in a mixed economy with a large public enterprise sector and economic planning. After World War II it was to become the standard policy in decolonized countries. In Turkey this policy—under the name of etatism—though interrupted by World War II and a short period of liberalization in the early 1950s, and modified by the political change from autocracy to democracy in 1950, continued until 1980. Then development strategy was radically changed with liberalization of trade and export orientation. Since the introduction of democracy, the country has experienced two military takeovers, in 1960–61 and 1980–83, and a period of military interference in the democratic process in 1971–73. Each time, however, the military establishment essentially endorsed the prevailing development strategy and imposed stabilization policies. In this sense the military interventions reinforced rather than interrupted the development policies supported by Turkish democracy.

Turkey was in 1923 an agrarian economy with only rudimentary modern industry. It was also a frontier economy (in the American sense) with abundant resources of uncultivated land. Agricultural expansion therefore was as much a part of the development process as industrialization until the frontier finally was conquered in the late 1950s. Distribution of uncultivated public land, mostly to private smallholders, was a feature of development policy of no less consequence than the establish-

257

ment of the state economic enterprises that loom so large in the economic historiography of Turkey. When economic planning became a constitutional requirement in 1961, it was the exhaustion of possibilities for agricultural expansion more than anything else that directed attention toward investment and planning for industrialization and toward green revolution in agriculture.

When the inward-looking policy of import substitution finally broke down in the late 1970s, it was lax fiscal-monetary demand management as much as difficulties inherent in continued import-substitution policies that caused the radical turnaround in development strategy. The turnaround may have been long overdue, but that is another matter. Turkey did fairly well in terms of growth and probably in terms of distribution under the inward-looking development policy. Returns were rapidly decreasing, however. The achievements under the new strategy are somewhat mixed.

The Growth Record

Annual national product and expenditure estimates, at both current and constant prices, are available for Turkey since the founding of the republic in 1923. Needless to say, the older the estimates, the less reliable they are. The constant price estimates keep prices constant for extremely long periods and are based on highly distorted prices. For the interwar years and World War II they may do little more than indicate orders of magnitude. With that caveat, the estimates are taken here at face value. The growth tables in this chapter are organized to illuminate long-term developments. They single out the interwar years, 1923–25 to 1936–38; the World War II years with the following recovery, 1936–38 to 1951–53; the first decade of democratic rule which also happens to be a transformation period from the point of view of agricultural growth, 1951–53 to 1961–63; the years of systematic, inward-looking planning, 1961–63 to 1977–79; and the years of reform and export-oriented growth, 1977–79 to 1983–85. Detailed discussion of economic strategy and policy changes such as the response to the Great Depression, 1929–32, the liberalization years, 1950–53, and the stabilization efforts, 1959–60 and 1978–80, will need finer periodization. The special conditions of agricultural development and the impact of World War II make periodization necessary.

Until the second half of the 1950s, Turkey was a frontier economy with abundant uncultivated land available for extensive (horizontal) expansion of agriculture, which at that time accounted for half the economy. Capital investment in transportation (railways and roads) and mechanization (tractorization) was required to open up meadows and pastures in the interior to cultivation. The expansion of the cultivated area, however, had been interrupted by World War II, which made a big dent in the growth path of the country, especially in agriculture, and renders it difficult to separate trends and recovery around the years of the war. What further complicates the situation is the need to distinguish between trend and recovery in area and yields. Figure 6-1 illuminates the problem. It presents three-year moving averages of GDP in agriculture at constant factor costs, before 1948 at 1948 prices, after 1948 at 1968 prices, chained in 1948. Because Turkish agriculture was, and still largely is, rainfed and suffers from strong crop fluctuations related to volatile weather conditions, three-year moving averages are used to depict production. The figure also depicts the crop area—sown plus fallow land—and indicates the total cultivated area (including vineyards, vegetable gardens, orchards, and olive groves) for 1938 and selected years

Figure 6-1. Agricultural Production, Areas and Tractors, 1923-80

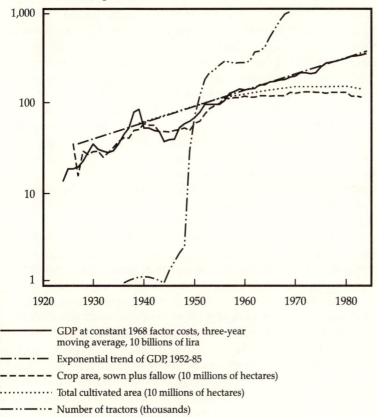

Unit of measure (log scale)

——————— GDP at constant 1968 factor costs, three-year
moving average, 10 billions of lira

— · — · — Exponential trend of GDP, 1952-85

— — — — — Crop area, sown plus fallow (10 millions of hectares)

· · · · · · · · · · · · Total cultivated area (10 millions of hectares)

— · · — · · · Number of tractors (thousands)

Source: Bulutay, Tezel, and Yıeldırım (1974); World Bank data; Turkey, SIS, *Statistical Yearbook;* Tezel (1975).

after 1955. Until recently, field crop area and total cultivated area expanded roughly proportionately; crop area is used in the discussion here because annual data are available (it is not necessary to operate with three-year averages because changes in weather conditions mainly affect the proportion between sown and fallow land, not the total crop area). Moreover, to discuss yield—here defined as GDP per hectare—under a fallow land cultivation system requires examining the total crop area, including fallow land.

Until the mid-1950s, agricultural GDP and crop area tended to move closely together, suggesting a low rate of growth of yields. (The short-term deviations between the two series would shrink if the production series were based on five-year moving averages.) From around 1956 the crop area was almost constant while production was steadily increasing. Before the second half of the 1950s, changes in production were related more to change in crop area than to change in yield, and after this time to increasing yield at, practically speaking, constant crop area. The change in the trend of yields from the second half of the 1950s might partly be the consequence of a change in agricultural policies, which in 1962 began to emphasize intensive expansion through green revolution after the cultivable frontier had been reached. It may also partly be a simple consequence of the end of the extensive expansion which pushed the cultivation margin further and further out, in terms of both fertility and location. The extensive expansion should in itself—that is, at given yields for already cultivated land—tend to reduce average yields for all lands, including new marginal lands. The change in the trend of yields, apparent in figure 6–1, thus does not imply that, all things being equal with respect to land quality (fertility and location), yields did not increase before the second half of the 1950s.

World War II led to a decline in both crop area and production with production declining more than crop area. The cause is obvious. Turkey followed a policy of neutrality during World War II and did not suffer casualties or physical destruction. The policy, however, required total mobilization with large-scale drafting of both men and animals (oxen, mainly) and imports of intermediate inputs declined. The latter was of little consequence for agriculture, which used few imported products, but the draft should obviously have led to a decline of both crop area and production. Characteristically, fallow land increased relatively during the war years with a decline in yields (as measured here). Both production and crop area, and fallow land and yields, were back to prewar levels around 1950. It might thus be tempting to date the recovery years roughly from 1945 to 1950 and consider developments thereafter as normal growth. This, however, would overlook the fact that not only did the war lead to a decline in the levels of crop area and production, but it broke the upward trends of the interwar years. It makes sense to insist that the recovery was not completed until the country was back on trend, which poses the problem of measuring the long-term trends in Turkish agriculture, in area, production, and yields.

For crop area, a natural procedure might be to fit a logistic growth trend to the data for, say, 1926–40 and 1956–85, leaving out the years 1941–55. This would, in effect, assume that the crop area was off (below) trend from 1940 to 1955. Visual inspection certainly supports the idea.

For production, the matter is more difficult. Figure 6–1 gives the impression that a log-linear, constant growth trend would nicely describe the development from 1952 to 1984. Fitting a log-linear trend to the data for 1952–85 results in a growth rate of 2.8 percent with a very good fit. When this trend is extrapolated backward from 1952, the years 1936–38 to 1938–40 are almost exactly on trend. For 1923–39 it is necessary to visualize a higher production trend growth rate. From this assumption, it follows that from a production point of view the years 1940 to 1952 were below trend.

Table 6–1 tells the long-term story by considering periods using alternative end years for the recovery after World War II, 1952 for GDP and 1956 for the crop area. The results are, unfortunately, highly sensitive to the choice of periods. For 1927–29 to 1981–83 as a whole, the growth rate is 3.5 percent for GDP in agriculture, 1.7 percent for the crop area, and 1.8 percent for yields. With the recovery period ending in 1951–53 there is a significant decline in the GDP growth rate, from 4.3 percent in 1927–29 to 1951–53 to 2.8 percent in 1951–53 to 1981–83, and the decline from 4.0 percent to 2.9 percent when the line of demarcation is 1955–57 is similar. At this point the choice of subperiod is not important.

With 1951–53 as the line of demarcation the growth rate of average yield was about 1.8 percent both before and after, with the decline in the growth of crop area, from 2.5 percent to 1.0 percent, accounting for the whole decline in GDP growth.

With 1955–57 the line of demarcation there is a strong decline in the growth rate of the crop area, from 3.1 percent to 0.2 percent, accompanied by a substantial increase in the rate of growth of yields from 0.9 percent to 2.7 percent, the decline in GDP growth now being the net of the decline in area growth and the increase in yield growth.

What makes the difference here is the period 1951–53 to 1955–57, when average yields declined by almost 20 percent. Incremental yields declined sharply, from being about 50 percent higher than average yields in 1938–40 to 1951–53 to being only one-third as high as average yields in 1951–53 to 1955–57. It is natural to link the strong decline in incremental yields to the very strong expansion in the crop area, by almost one-third, over this short period. The expansion here was intimately related to government policies of tractorization, financed by Marshall Plan aid and cheap credit, combined with distribution of pub-

Table 6-1. Agricultural Production, Area, and Yields, Selected Periods 1927–83

Period	Agricultural GDP (millions of liras)[a]	Crop area (thousands of hectares)	Yield (liras per hectare) Average	Incremental	Growth Rate (percent per year) Agricultural GDP	Crop area	Average yield
1927–29	7,559	9,506	795	1,775	6.07	3.21	2.86
1938–40	14,457	13,459	1,074	1,591	2.79	1.98	0.81
1951–53	20,666	17,361	1,190	353	2.11	6.68	−4.53
1955–57	22,463	22,453	1,000	2,193	2.90	0.19	2.71
1981–83	47,200	23,581	2,002	n.a.	n.a.	n.a.	n.a.
1927–29 to 1981–83	—	—	—	—	3.45	1.70	1.73
1951–53 recovery							
1927–29 to 1951–53	—	—	—	—	4.28	2.54	1.78
1951–53 to 1981–83	—	—	—	—	2.79	1.03	1.76
1955–57 recovery							
1927–29 to 1955–57	—	—	—	—	3.97	3.12	0.85
1955–57 to 1981–83	—	—	—	—	2.90	0.19	2.71

n.a. = Not available.
— = Not applicable.
a. In 1968 prices.
Source: Bulutay, Tezel, and Yieldırım (1974); Turkey, Statistical Yearbook; World Bank data.

lic land. This policy appears to have been relatively unproductive. Whether the blame should be put on the tractorization or the distribution of marginal land is uncertain. However, during the 1930s yields increased rapidly despite an even faster increase in area.

While thus the establishment of trends of yields across the years of World War II with recovery remains a great problem and may be intractable, it would seem that a major difference between agricultural growth before and after the second half of the 1950s is the stagnation of crop and cultivated areas, resulting in a significant decline in the growth rate of agricultural GDP. Considering the fact that agriculture produced close to half of the total GDP until the 1950s, the frontier and its conquest must have been a key factor without which long-term growth in the economy as a whole cannot be fully understood.

Since the trend of production is the product of the trends of area and yields, and since these are interrelated, a natural approach would seem to be to specify and estimate an agricultural production function. Data are not available for such an endeavor. There is no solid information about labor input in agriculture for years before 1950, and for later years the quinquennial population censuses are the basic source of data. Interpolations and conjectures about annual labor input do not suffice for this purpose.

While it is useful in discussing long-term developments to aggregate information in a few periods, Turkey's changing development strategies suggest a more detailed periodization. Table 6–2 defines the periods that are examined in chapters 8–12.

For the six decades after the founding of the republic the overall rates of growth have been 5.0 percent in terms of real GDP and 4.8 percent in terms of real gross national income (GNI) at a population growth rate of 2.2 percent. Per capita production and income thus grew annually at 2.8 percent and 2.6 percent, respectively. The slightly lower growth rate for per capita income is mainly the result of adverse terms of trade developments. Doubling of per capita product in twenty-four years is not a remarkable but certainly a respectable achievement, particularly considering the fact that the period includes about thirteen years of military mobilization for neutrality with recovery and that, as usual, the benefits of not being involved in warfare are not counted in the measure of income and, presumably, welfare.

Growth rates have varied widely, however, during this long period. Population growth accelerated from 2.1 percent during the interwar years to 2.8 percent for the 1950s and declined again to 2.1 percent in the 1980s. Growth rates of both production and income have varied even more over time with the difference between the two also varying considerably, mainly because of strong fluctuations in the terms of trade. Per capita growth rates (percent) were as follows:

Period	Production	Income
1923–25 to 1936–38	4.9	4.4
1936–38 to 1951–53	1.2	1.6
1951–53 to 1961–63	2.1	1.6
1961–63 to 1977–79	3.9	3.7
1977–79 to 1983–85	0.8	–2.1
1985–87	3.8	4.7

Per capita growth rates for both production and income were highest during the interwar years and the years of comprehensive planning, the

Table 6-2. Turkey's Development Strategy, by Period, since 1923

Period	Institutional setting	Development strategy
1923–29	Private enterprise, free trade with low tariffs (Lausanne Treaty)	Westernization, recovery, infrastructure, industrialization, tax reform
1929–39	Etatism, mixed economy with large public enterprise sector, balance of payments controls, primitive five-year planning	Inward-looking import substitution, infrastructure, industrialization
1939–46	Etatism, mixed economy, war economy for neutrality	Military considerations
1946–50	Relaxed etatism, mixed economy, controls	Recovery, increased emphasis on agriculture
1950–53	Democracy, trade liberalization, mixed economy	Agricultural expansion and mechanization
1953–59	Democracy, mixed economy, balance of payments controls	Agricultural expansion, import substitution
1959–62	Democracy replaced by military regime, etatism, mixed economy	Stabilization
1962–78	Democracy, mixed economy, comprehensive planning, labor market liberalization	Import substitution
1978–80	Same as in 1962–78	Stabilization
1980–85	Military regime followed by limited democracy, mixed economy, trade and financial liberalization, labor market repression	Stabilization, export-oriented growth
1985–	Democracy, mixed economy, trade and financial liberalization, accelerating inflation	Export-oriented growth

Source: Author.

1960s and 1970s, in this order. Both of these periods were dominated by protectionism and inward-looking import-substitution policies. Terms of trade developments were adverse and growth rates for income, accordingly, slightly lower than for production. The years of comprehensive planning, moreover, ended with stabilization policies of the kind the IMF recommends that served to keep down the per capita growth rate for this period. That the World War II years with recovery should show a low per capita growth rate is only to be expected although improving terms of trade from the 1930s to the early 1950s helped considerably in keeping the income growth rate up. The 1950s were disappointing in terms of both production and income, population growth being high and terms of trade running strongly against the country. This period also ended with IMF-type stabilization policies that served to keep down growth at the end of the period and thus for the period as a whole. The stabilization years should also here naturally be seen as part of the policies of the previous period. The apparently very poor performance in the early years of reform and export orientation in the 1980s is remarkable; moreover, terms of trade developed strongly against the country. Not until the mid-1980s did growth recover after the stabilization recession of 1978–80. Strong crop fluctuations with poor crops in 1983 and bumper crops in 1986 distort the picture. But even in 1984–86, including two average crops and one bumper crop, the average per capita rate of growth of GDP was no better than during the long period of import substitution 1961–63 to 1977–79. Terms of trade did, however, improve, and GNP growth per capita exceeded that of 1961–63 to 1977–79 by about 0.5 percent despite the possibly negative impact that the strong expansion of exports had on terms of trade.

Figure 6–2 suggests how important terms of trade developments were for Turkey's growth performance. The net barter terms of trade series for 1962 to 1984, based on annually chained Fisher indexes and computed directly from trade data in terms of U.S. dollars, is clearly the superior index from a technical point of view. When it is linked in 1962 with the series for 1923 to 1984, based on implicit national account deflators for exports and imports, the two agree fairly well (figure 6–2). The Fisher series shows slightly poorer terms of trade for the years 1965–73 and somewhat better terms of trade for years after 1973, yet the total deterioration from 1962 to 1984 for both series is about 30 percent.

The striking feature of figure 6–2 is the violent medium-term fluctuations, the terms of trade down to half from the mid-1920s to the mid-1930s, more than doubling from the end of World War II to the Korean War boom years, then down again to less than half to 1960 with a strong recovery to 1966, followed by continuous deterioration to 1982 with considerable improvement to 1985. With fluctuations that strong for prolonged periods, it may not make sense to talk about trends. Fitting, nonetheless, a linear trend for 1923–84, we find it slightly downward.

Figure 6-2. Indicators of Terms of Trade Fluctuations, 1923-84

Index (1929 = 100)

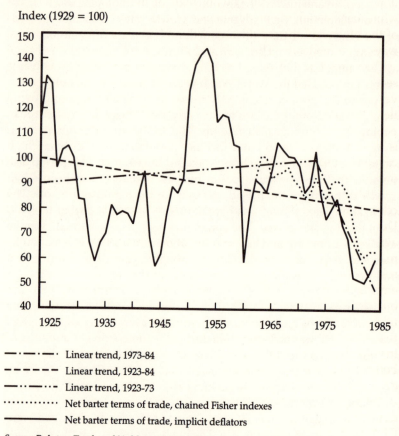

--·--·--· Linear trend, 1973-84
------- Linear trend, 1923-84
--·--··· Linear trend, 1923-73
············ Net barter terms of trade, chained Fisher indexes
————— Net barter terms of trade, implicit deflators

Source: Bulutay, Tezel, and Yıldırım (1974); World Bank data; chained Fisher indexes computed by Edward F. Lucas from UNCTAD tapes.

Modern Turkey is in this sense a country that has tended to lose on the terms of trade in the long run, but the loss has been very modest. When the oil price boost in the early 1970s is singled out as a crucial divide, the trend is slightly upward for the years 1923–73 and strongly downward thereafter. The oil price shocks in themselves did great harm to the Turkish economy and contributed strongly to the foreign exchange crisis that around 1980 led the country to radically change development strategy.

Table 6–3 shows sectoral growth, in terms of the individual sectors' own growth rates, and contributions to overall growth for the major periods since 1923. Growth rates of manufacturing are systematically high, as should be expected in a country whose main development target has been industrialization. Yet they have not been remarkably high—8–9 percent, disregarding the years of World War II with recovery and the years of export orientation after 1980 when manufacturing grew little. Mining and infrastructure sectors such as electricity, transportation, and finance showed equally high or even higher growth rates while, considering the predominance of etatist philosophies over much of the lifetime of the republic, growth in the government sector has always been moderate. The same is the case for trade and services.

Own-growth rates, however, may not be the best way of describing sectoral contributions to the growth process. A very small sector with a very high own-growth rate—finance, for example—may contribute little to total GDP growth. Therefore the GDP increase of each sector as a percentage of the total GDP increase of the economy during each period is used to measure individual sectors' contributions. These might be called the marginal GDP shares. The marginal shares depend on both own rates of growth and the size of sector shares in total GDP.

In view of the ex ante development strategies outlined in table 6–2, comparison between agriculture and industry is particularly interesting. During the interwar years when industrialization was the basic strategy, agriculture generated more than half of the increase in total GDP, with manufacturing contributing only 12 percent. Over time, however, the roles of the two sectors were reversed. Already in the 1950s, when the emphasis was on agricultural expansion, this sector generated less than one-quarter of the total increase in GDP while manufacturing was almost equally important, contributing about one-fifth. From the 1960s, the roles were reversed, manufacturing generating more of the increase in GDP than agriculture. The declining role of agriculture is the result of both declining own-growth rates, as the frontier disappeared, and the decline of the share of agriculture in total GDP.

The most expansive sector in this sense, however, was trade, which during the interwar years generated 7.5 percent of the total increase in GDP but systematically increased its share to become almost equal to that of manufacturing in the 1980s. To some extent this may reflect modernization of the economy with subsistence agriculture losing importance and commercialization gaining. But it may also reflect the increasing transactions costs of a socially unproductive nature that may be the other side of the modernization process. Or it may be an expression of disguised unemployment related to increasing open unemployment in the Turkish economy. Despite its relatively high growth rate, and despite large-scale migration of workers to Europe during the late 1960s and the early 1970s, the Turkish economy has not been able to employ its fast-growing labor force. Finally, the significance of the trade sector, at least after 1980, may be related to the strong increase in foreign trade. The increase in exports and more so in imports may show up in the trade sector which in this way may be an indicator of improved allocation of resources.

The aggregations of sectors, by capital- and labor-intensive production and tradable and nontradable goods, in table 6–3 are of consider-

Table 6-3. Growth and Shares of Growth by Production Sector, 1923–85
(percent)

Category	1923–25 to 1936–38[a]		1936–38 to 1951–53[b]		1951–53 to 1961–63[c]		1961–63 to 1977–79[c]		1977–79 to 1983–85[c]	
	Own growth rate	Share of growth	Own growth rate	Share of growth	Own growth rate	Share of growth	Own growth rate	Share of growth	Own growth rate	Share of growth
Population	2.1	—	1.8	—	2.8	—	2.5	—	2.1	—
Production sector										
Agriculture	7.4	52.2	2.7	44.3	2.7	23.7	3.0	14.0	2.3	18.0
Mining	7.7	0.9	5.6	2.6	5.0	1.7	9.4	3.2	-2.6	-2.1
Manufacturing	8.7	12.0	2.2	7.1	8.9	20.1	8.8	22.5	3.5	23.4
Electricity	14.5	0.2	7.0	1.0	11.6	1.8	10.6	2.4	5.3	3.7
Construction	7.1	3.8	3.8	8.0	5.0	6.8	6.3	6.5	1.2	2.6
Trade	6.8	7.5	4.1	10.8	6.7	12.7	8.7	16.9	4.3	22.3
Transport	7.4	4.0	5.2	8.6	7.6	10.2	8.5	11.8	1.0	3.4
Finance	10.7	1.8	2.2	1.0	9.5	3.0	8.4	2.9	—	—
Housing	2.2	4.0	2.2	5.3	3.6	4.7	5.0	4.2	2.8[d]	12.1[d]
Services	6.3	4.3	2.9	4.1	3.5	2.8	8.6	5.9	—	—

268

Government	7.4	9.4	2.4	7.4	6.5	12.7	6.1	9.7	4.7	16.7
Gross domestic product	6.8	100.0	3.0	100.0	4.9	100.0	6.4	100.0	2.9	100.0
Type of production										
Capital intensive	5.4	21.1	3.1	24.6	7.1	38.5	8.2	44.1	0.7[e]	32.4[e]
Labor intensive	7.3	78.9	2.9	75.4	4.1	61.5	5.4	55.9	3.3[e]	67.6[e]
Type of goods										
Tradable	7.6	65.1	2.7	54.0	4.0	45.5	5.2	39.7	2.6	39.3
Nontradable	5.7	34.9	3.3	46.0	6.0	54.5	7.5	60.3	3.2	60.7

— = Not applicable.
a. At constant 1948 factor cost.
b. At constant 1948 and 1968 factor cost, chained in 1948.
c. At constant 1968 factor cost.
d. Finance, housing, services.
e. For 1977–79 to 1981–83.
Source: Same as for table 6–1.

able interest. The capital-intensive sectors are mining, manufacturing, electricity, transportation, and housing; the remaining sectors are considered labor intensive. This classification is clearly rather crude. The sectors producing tradable goods are agriculture, mining, and manufacturing; the rest are assumed to produce nontradable goods and services. With both tourism and Turkish participation in international transport relatively unimportant throughout most of the period, the classification by traded and nontraded goods is fairly unproblematic.

In terms of growth contributions, capital-intensive sectors have increased strongly from 21 percent in the interwar period to 44 percent during the 1960s and 1970s with a certain decline in the 1980s, mainly because of a strong decline in the contribution from transportation. Labor-intensive sectors lost importance correspondingly. This may be a natural feature of development, with capital becoming less scarce and labor more scarce. This finding does not in itself serve as evidence for the claim that Turkey as a result of import-substitution policies and price distortions and the emphasis on state economic enterprises has tended to operate with excessively capital-intensive technologies, for table 6–3 throws no light on developments within sectors.

There is, on the other hand, a tendency for growth contributions from sectors producing tradable goods to decline strongly over time, with a corresponding increase in the importance of sectors producing nontradables. The role of agriculture is again crucial. However, policies of import substitution and protection, which tend to favor nontradables, may be at work here. And the change may reflect a tendency for the income elasticities of demand for services to be relatively high in accordance with Engel's Laws. Notice that it is the contributions of trade and transportation that have increased significantly while that of housing has remained almost constant.

Table 6–4 shows the sectoral shares in total GDP, again with aggregation according to capital and labor intensity and tradability. Here it is particularly interesting that the shares of both agriculture and manufacturing remained almost unchanged until the early 1950s, agriculture producing almost half of total GDP, manufacturing less than 10 percent. Early industrialization policies did not significantly change the structure of the economy, which by and large remained agrarian. Only after 1951–53 did the share of agriculture decline rapidly; it then fell to slightly above one-fifth of total GDP in the 1980s with industry increasing to almost one-fifth. Most of the decline in the share of agriculture was, however, matched by an increase in the shares of trade and transport; but construction also increased its share. Housing, on the other hand, fell dramatically—from a share of 16 percent in 1923–25 to 5 percent in 1977–79. Also, in terms of shares, development in sectors producing nontradable goods and services seems to be in accord with Engel's Laws.

Table 6-4. Composition of Gross Domestic Product, by Production Sector, Selected Periods, 1923–84

Category	1923–25[a]	1936–38[a]	1948A[a]	1948B[b]	1951–53[b]	1961–63[b]	1977–79[b]	1983–84[b]
Production sector (percent)								
Agriculture	46.3	49.7	48.8	48.3	47.4	38.4	23.1	22.4
Mining	0.7	0.8	1.0	1.4	1.6	1.7	2.6	1.9
Manufacturing	8.2	10.4	9.8	9.6	9.1	13.2	19.1	19.7
Electricity	0.2	0.2	0.3	0.5	0.5	1.0	1.9	2.2
Construction	3.6	3.7	3.0	4.7	6.5	6.6	6.6	6.0
Trade	7.4	7.4	7.6	7.4	8.4	10.1	14.3	15.5
Transport	3.6	3.8	4.9	5.2	5.7	7.4	10.2	9.2
Finance	0.9	1.4	1.1	1.0	1.2	1.9	2.5	—
Housing	16.1	9.2	9.9	8.2	6.8	6.0	4.9	12.4[c]
Services	4.8	4.5	4.8	4.4	4.1	3.6	5.0	—
Government	8.2	8.9	8.8	9.4	8.7	10.2	9.9	10.9
Type of production (percent)								
Capital intensive	28.8	24.4	25.9	24.9	23.7	29.3	38.7	37.9
Labor intensive	71.2	75.6	74.1	75.1	76.3	70.7	61.3	62.1
Type of goods (percent)								
Tradable	55.2	60.9	59.6	59.3	58.1	54.3	44.8	44.0
Nontradable	44.8	39.1	40.4	40.7	41.9	45.7	55.2	56.0
Value of GDP (billions of lira)	3.1	7.2	8.7	34.0	43.6	70.1	187.6	219.3

— = Not applicable.
a. At 1948 constant factor cost.
b. At 1968 constant factor cost.
c. Finance, housing, services.
Source: Same as for table 6-1.

The distribution of GDP between capital- and labor-intensive sectors and according to tradability remained roughly unchanged until 1961–63. In this sense the production structure remained unchanged. From 1961–63 to 1977–79 there was a tendency for the capital-intensive sectors to grow and the labor-intensive sectors to decline relatively, with sectors producing tradables tending to decline, sectors producing nontradables tending to increase. With the change of development strategy to export orientation after 1980, these structural changes came to a stop, but no significant reversal took place. Again, the time period may be too short for showing the effects of the change in strategy.

Table 6–5 traces the expenditure shares over time from 1923–25 to 1981–83 in terms of constant prices. For growth analysis in real terms this is the obvious way to present the expenditure side. It has, among other things, the advantage of quantifying terms of trade gains and losses, based on a year without any gain (or loss) in terms of real income. The table is converted into 1968 prices insofar as national income is concerned through chaining in 1948. The share estimates, however, are made at 1938 prices for 1923–48, and at 1968 prices for 1948–83. Hence the terms of trade gains (losses) are not directly comparable across the year 1948. The terms of trade gain (or loss) was zero in 1938 for the earlier period and zero in 1968 for the later. Turkey suffered a very large terms of trade loss of 7.6 percent of GNI from 1923–25 to 1936–38 or 1939–41 with a slight recovery to 1946–48. After 1948 there is a loss of 3.3 percent from 1951–53 to 1977–79 followed by further losses growing to 6.3 percent of GNI for 1981–83. To bridge the gap between years before and after 1948, only estimates for that year are available at both sets of constant prices. In terms of 1938 prices, 1948 showed a gain of 0.8 percent of GNI as compared with 1938. In terms of 1968 prices, 1948 showed a loss of 1.3 percent of GNI as compared with 1968. From 1938 to 1968 Turkey should thus have gained 0.8 percent + 1.3 percent = 2.1 percent of GNI. By comparison, for the whole period 1923–25 to 1981–83 there is a loss of 7.6 percent − 2.1 percent + 6.3 percent = 12.9 percent of GNI. This, of course, is but a translation into shares of GNI of what is visually clear from figure 6–2. Annually over the whole period the loss was about 0.2 percent of GNI.

In real terms the trend of the share of private consumption has been strongly but irregularly downward from 86.2 percent of GNI in 1923–25 to 69.1 percent in 1981–83 with a slightly upward trend for public consumption from 9.9 percent to 13.7 percent over the same period. Total consumption thus declined from 96.1 percent to 82.8 percent. The years 1939–41 were strongly off the trend, with private consumption down to 72.0 percent and public consumption up to 17.1 percent. This point of time has been inserted to give an impression of the costs of the mobilization for neutrality during World War II. These costs were suffered mainly

Table 6-5. Composition of National Income by Shares of Expenditures, Selected Periods, 1923–83

Category	1923–25[a]	1936–38[a]	1939–41[a]	1946–48[a]	1951–53[b]	1961–63[b]	1977–79[b]	1981–83[b]
Expenditures (percent)								
Private consumption	86.2	76.6	72.0	79.9	76.2	74.6	70.7	69.1
Public consumption	9.9	12.6	17.1	10.8	9.9	12.3	12.2	13.7
Fixed investment	8.1	10.1	9.9	9.5	16.5	15.4	22.1	18.9
Inventory investment	n.a	n.a	n.a	n.a	n.a	1.3	-1.2	1.7
Net resource gap[c]	-4.2	0.7	1.1	-0.2	-2.6	-3.6	-3.8	-3.4
National income	100	100	100	100	100	100	100	100
Exports	9.2	7.3	5.0	6.5	6.5	4.9	4.5	8.7
Imports	20.1	6.5	3.7	7.1	12.3	7.9	7.3	6.7
Terms of trade gain[d]	7.6	0.0	-0.0	0.6	3.3	-0.4	-2.5	-6.3
National saving	4.0	10.8	11.0	9.3	13.8	13.1	17.1	17.2
Total value of national income (billions of lira)	13.7	30.5	32.6	32.7	50.4	77.5	202.8	211.2

n.a. = Not available.
a. Based on constant 1938 prices.
b. Based on constant 1968 prices, chained to 1938 prices in 1948.
c. In terms of exports.
d. In terms of imports; terms of trade for 1923–48 based on 1938 = 100, for 1948–83 based on 1968 = 100.
Source: Same as for table 6–1.

in the beginning of the war; after 1942–43 public consumption was back to the prewar level. A country involved in active warfare would probably suffer the largest increase in the share of public consumption and decline in private consumption at the end of the war. It is noticeable that the temporary increase in public consumption during the first years of the war was not matched by a decline in investment. With the downward trend in total consumption, of course, there is a corresponding upward trend in national saving, which increased steadily from 4.0 percent in 1923–25 to 11.0 percent in 1939–41, 13.8 percent in 1951–53, and 17.2 percent in 1981–83.

Fixed investment remained, practically speaking, constant at about 10 percent of GNI from 1923–25 to 1946–48, after which the share jumped to 16.5 percent in 1951–53, declined slightly to 15.4 percent in 1961–63 (as a consequence of the stabilization program of 1958–60), increased strongly to 22.1 percent in 1977–79, and declined again to 18.9 percent in 1981–83 (again the consequence of a stabilization program). These figures all refer to fixed investment only; information about inventory changes is available only from around 1960.

It is interesting to compare the strongly upward trend of the share of investment with the downward trend of the GDP growth rate, apparent in table 6–3. During the interwar years a growth rate of 6.8 percent obtained at an investment share of about 9 percent. During the years of planning, 1961–63 to 1977–79, a growth rate of 6.4 percent obtained at an investment share of about 18 percent. This is another way of saying that the incremental capital-to-output ratio must have almost doubled in the long term. This should not (necessarily) be taken as an indicator of increasing inefficiency in the Turkish growth process. Most of the interwar years, 1929–39, were characterized by the same inward-looking import-substitution policy as were the years of planning, 1961–79. The change probably reflects the special role of agriculture in Turkish development and the fact that there was no longer a frontier by 1960. In her development, Turkey has for natural reasons had to rely increasingly on capital-intensive sectors, as table 6–3 shows. Efficiency problems, related to inward-looking development strategies, may be small compared with this fundamental fact of life.

The net resource gap, which equals the difference between national saving and investment (fixed plus inventory), declined only from 4.2 percent to 3.4 percent of GNI over the long term. This small decline was, however, the outcome of a radical decline from the early 1920s to the 1930s, when the resource gap actually became negative (a surplus), followed by a steady increase from a small gap of 0.2 percent in 1946–48 to a large gap of 3.8 percent in 1977–79, only slightly reduced after the change in strategy after 1980. These changes reflect political developments from the stern and austere fiscal and monetary conservatism of Atatürk and the Kemalists in the 1930s to the increasingly undisciplined and lax behavior of democratic-parliamentary Turkey after 1950; the periods of military intervention, 1960–61, 1971–73, and 1980–83, were apparently too short for definitely turning the trend back to orderly fiscal and monetary policy. Too easy access to concessionary foreign borrowing, for military-strategic and other reasons, is part of the explanation.

Table 6–5 shows the characteristic development of foreign trade of a country moving to and from inward-looking import-substitution development strategies. The export side is easier to interpret than the import side, the latter being more strongly influenced by domestic demand pressure and foreign exchange problems not directly related to the basic strategy. The share of exports declined from 9.2 percent in 1923–25 to 7.3 percent in 1936–38, the last peace years before World War II, to decline further to 5.0 percent in 1961–63 and 4.5 percent in 1977–79, finally recoiling to 8.7 percent after the change in strategy in 1980. Had data for 1983–85 been included in the table, the increase in exports would be even more pronounced. The tendency for the share of trade to decline as the result of inward-looking development strategies is probably the best macro indicator of inefficiency available.

On the import side, things were more complex and greatly influenced by both foreign supply problems and domestic demand management. The strong decline of the share of imports from 1923–25 to 1936–38 was partly related to the recovery after World War I and the following War of Independence, the country filling depleted stocks in the early 1920s. The increase in imports in 1946–48 and 1951–53 was part of the recovery process after World War II, while the decline in imports from 1977–79 to 1981–83 was related to the stabilization policies at that time.

Because table 6–5 is based on constant 1968 prices, it does not directly reflect the oil price boosts of 1973 and 1979. In real terms estimates, these show up in the terms of trade loss rather than in import developments. For balance of payments analysis, current price estimates of both exports and imports are needed (they are presented in later chapters).

Distribution of Income and Wealth

The scant information available on the distribution of income and wealth is of poor quality, in terms of both size and functional distribution. To simply conclude that there is no solid knowledge about distribution of either income or wealth at any given time or about its development over time might, however, appear to be overly pessimistic. Therefore the available findings are summarized in terms of Gini coefficients and quintile shares in tables 6–6 to 6–8 with the comments they deserve.

Results of seven studies of income distribution for various years between 1952 and 1983 are given in table 6–6. Only those covering 1968,

Table 6-6. Indicators of Income Distribution, Selected Years, 1952–83

Survey year	Gini coefficients			Lowest quintile (percent of total)			Highest quintile (percent of total)		
	National	Agri-cultural	Nonagri-cultural	National	Agri-cultural	Nonagri-cultural	National	Agri-cultural	Nonagri-cultural
1952	n.a	0.53	n.a	n.a	5.7	n.a.	n.a	60.2	n.a.
1963	0.56	0.43	0.59	4.2	6.0	3.2	61.0	49.5	65.9
1968	0.56	0.59	n.a.	3.0	3.1	n.a.	60.0	64.0	n.a.
1973	0.50	0.56	0.45	3.5	2.5	5.0	55.3	60.3	51.6
1973 adjusted	0.51	0.57	0.43	2.7	2.5	5.0	55.2	61.1	48.6
1973–74	n.a.	0.47	n.a.	n.a.	3.8	n.a.	n.a.	48.6	n.a.
1978	0.51	0.57	0.43	2.8	2.5	5.0	54.7	61.1	48.6
1978–79	n.a.	n.a.	0.40	n.a.	n.a.	6.3	n.a.	n.a.	46.4
1983	0.52	0.57	0.45	2.6	2.5	4.6	55.9	61.1	50.2

n.a. = Not available.
Source: For 1952, Hirsch (1970): 1963, Boratav (1966): 1968, Bulutay, Timur, and Ersel (1971): 1973, Kemal Derviş and Sherman Robinson, in Özbudun and Ulusan (1980); 1973, adjusted 1978, and 1983, Celasun (1986); 1973–74 and 1978–79, author's computations, based on Turkey, SIS, *Statistical Yearbook, 1981*, table 159, urban areas, 1985, tables 141, 142, national and urban areas.

Table 6–7. Distribution of Income by Region in the 1968 and 1973 Surveys

Category	Rural region[a]					Metropolitan region		
	Central[b]	North	West[c]	South	East	Ankara	Istanbul	Izmir
1968 survey								
Average household income as percent of country average	87.9	83.3	79.5	74.8	83.5	162.0	259.4	355.9[d]
Gini coefficient for the distribution within the region	0.6	0.6	0.5	0.5	0.6	0.4	0.5	0.6
1973 survey								
Average household income as percent of country average	103.1	108.7	89.3	86.7	67.5	123.5	162.7	159.9
Gini coefficient for the region	0.5	0.5	0.5	0.6	0.5	0.4	0.5	0.5
Percent of total population	18.0	15.8	20.8	13.2	9.9	5.4	13.9	3.0

a. Includes urban areas not included in metropolitan regions.
b. Excludes Ankara.
c. Excludes Istanbul and Izmir.
d. This figure is probably too high.
Source: Pamuk (1985).

278 Egypt and Turkey

Table 6-8. Indicators of Distribution of Land Holdings
and Ownerships, Selected Years, 1952-80

Survey year	Gini coefficient		Lowest quintile (percent of total)		Highest quintile (percent of total)	
	Holdings	Ownerships	Holdings	Ownerships	Holdings	Ownerships
1952	0.5	n.a.	1.8	n.a.	65.1	n.a.
1963	0.6	0.5	1.8	5.0	60.9	57.1
1970	0.6	n.a.	1.9	n.a.	63.2	n.a.
1974-75	0.4[a]	0.5[a]	n.a.	n.a.	n.a.	n.a.
1980	0.6	0.6	2.0	1.8	61.1	60.0

n.a. = Not available.
a. For selected provinces in Central Anatolia, mid-1970s; apparently not on a family basis.
Source: Hirsch (1970), author's computations from agricultural censuses; Charles K. Mann in Özbudun and Ulusan (1980), table 7-16, pp. 234-36.

1973, 1973-74, and 1978-79 are based on direct observation in the form of income surveys for the year in question. The others are estimates or projections of a more indirect and somewhat dubious nature.

The 1968 survey was flawed, among other things, because it did not include households with a male head whose wife was over forty-five years old. This shocking choice threw out 17 percent of the households and may have biased the results. Income appears, moreover, to have been underreported by no less than 38 percent. The consensus is that the survey is not up to acceptable standards. Its conclusions, however, are not entirely out of line with those of the 1973 survey. The 1973 survey suffered from a number of flaws. It imputed rent for owner-occupied buildings; remittances from migrant workers (5 percent of GNP) were not included; income in nonagricultural activities was underreported by 19.5 percent and in agriculture (after corrections) by 6.6 percent; agricultural population was underestimated; and the results for agriculture, which were deemed to be unreliable, were replaced by indirect estimates. Nevertheless this survey has—in my opinion too uncritically—been trusted and used as the basis for extensive studies of income distribution, even used in World Bank publications. The adjusted figures for 1973 (Celasun 1986) attempt to eliminate some of the flaws but the new figures are somewhat speculative.

The estimates for 1952 apply only to agriculture and were based on land distribution and information about cropping patterns and prices. The estimates for 1963 were based on a large variety of statistics whose underlying assumptions were poorly specified. It has been criticized strongly, especially because its most important conclusion—that distribution was more equitable in agriculture than elsewhere—was the result of assumptions rather than of data. The estimates for 1978 and 1983 are extrapolations of the 1973 survey results, assuming, among other things, that distribution within agriculture and nonagriculture remained unchanged from 1973, an assumption that flies in the face of available information about real wage developments and unemployment.

The computations for 1973-74 (covering rural areas only) and 1978-79 (covering urban areas only) were derived from labor force surveys reported in the *Statistical Yearbook of Turkey*. The data for rural areas were published in the 1981 yearbook, which did not give the source and the year, but since 1973-74 apparently was the only year in which a rural labor force survey was made, I assume that the data pertain to that year. For both years, published data appear to have been blown up to national totals for the areas in question. Methods of sampling and inflation are not disclosed in the source. The quality of the surveys and their presentation are not known to me but a comparison between disposable income and the accompanying expenditure data throws grave doubt on the quality of the surveys. For the 1978-79 survey the average propensity to consume by family is 0.72, which appears rather low; a simple regression across size groups yields a marginal propensity to consume out of disposable income of only 0.11 which is not credible. The Gini coefficients for that year are 0.40 for disposable income and only 0.21 for expenditure, the latter result not credible either. The expenditure data are clearly unreliable and unacceptable. If the income data are accepted, nonetheless, at face value, the disposable income Gini coefficients of 0.40 for urban areas in 1978-79 and 0.47 for rural areas in 1973-74 make sense and so do the figures for the lowest and highest quintiles. Both Gini coefficients are relatively low for Turkey, the urban coefficient lower than the rural one.

Mainly on the basis of the 1973 survey, it has become the consensus that income distribution in Turkey is relatively inequitable with a national Gini coefficient of 0.50, that distribution is more equitable in nonagriculture than in agriculture, and that regional distribution in Turkey is relatively inequitable. Given the data presented in table 6-6, all three statements are dubious, and even taken at face value, they do not provide any basis for firm conclusions about trends in income distribution. The national Gini coefficient points to a slight decline in inequity but the lowest quintile share points, if anything, in the opposite direction while the highest quintile share tends to support the national Gini coefficients.

Table 6-7 gives an impression of regional differences based on the 1968 and 1973 surveys. The difficulties in drawing firm conclusions about regional differences show up in the significant differences in the ranking of the five predominantly rural regions in 1968 and in 1973. The differences could be a consequence of differences in weather conditions between the two years, but if that were the explanation, the problem would then be one of regional differences under normal weather conditions, which is, after all, the question at issue. Moreover, the differences between 1968 and 1973 for the big cities are too large to be credible. When the 1968 and 1973 estimates are taken at face value, the ratio between the weighted average of household income for the metropolitan regions and the predominantly rural regions is 3.3 in 1968 against only 2.3 in 1973, a decline that does not seem credible in view of the fact that agricultural income was relatively low in the latter year.

Land distribution is of interest partly as an indicator of wealth distribution and partly as an indirect indicator of income distribution. The distributions by holdings and ownerships in table 6–8 are based on agricultural censuses which are not quite comparable and are ambiguous in their reporting. The reporting appears to be on a family basis (Turkey, SIS, 1980, p. 207) but the distinction between holdings and ownerships is not always clear. The results, in terms of both Gini coefficients and quintile shares, indicate a relatively equitable distribution of land in Turkey. This is what should be expected for frontier agriculture when the distribution of public land has favored small holdings, and it is one of the reasons why land reform has never become a vital issue in Turkish agricultural policy. Distributions by holdings and ownerships appear to be very similar, with the distribution by holdings slightly more inequitable than by ownership. This is unusual, because tenure normally works in the opposite direction. However, the censuses are not clear on this point. A special survey from Central Anatolia in 1974–75 (table 6–8) shows the normal result, with holdings distribution more equitable than ownership distribution. With mechanization, as tractor owners have become sharecroppers, very small ownerships have tended to be consolidated and distribution of holdings has become more equitable. The Anatolian results may be the more reliable ones. The data do not point to any significant change over time in distribution of either holdings or ownerships. If land distribution is used to infer income distribution in agriculture, the latter should be relatively equitable and relatively constant over time. This inference would partly contradict the results in table 6–6 of the 1973 survey but support those of the 1963 survey which, indeed, was partly based on land distribution data.

Land is the only form of material wealth about which distribution by size is known; distribution of land by such characteristics as owner's residence, sex, income, and education is not known. I know of no information on distribution of other forms of material wealth. The kind of information that is available on human wealth is indicators of nutritional status, life expectancy, enrollment ratios, rates of illiteracy, and years of completed formal education.

The earning capacity (productivity) of workers should tend to be positively related to their nutritional status (Leibenstein 1957), at least at low levels of nutrition. Causality also runs the other way, however, and at Turkey's level of nutrition in the early 1980s the effects of income on nutrition may dominate the picture. Table 6–9 shows that from prewar years to 1947–48, the first postwar years for which data are available, Turkey experienced a serious decline in three major nutritional indicators—intakes of calories, protein, and fat—followed by virtually complete recovery by 1950–51. This is in line with estimated changes of per capita income during this period. There was further uniform progress to 1955–56 followed, however, by some retrogression to 1961–63, probably related to the government's stabilization program and recession. During the two decades of etatist planning, the 1960s and 1970s, intakes of calories, protein, and fat increased substantially, but mineral intakes declined. During the first half of the 1980s—the new period of stabilization, recession, and reform—the picture is mixed.

Caloric intake in Turkey increased by 0.71 percent annually from 1950–51 to 1983–85, and GNP per capita increased by 3.3 percent annually during the same period. Regressions of caloric intake on per capita income in eighty-five low- and middle-income countries in 1985 (World Bank, *World Development Report 1987*, tables 1, 30) result in a low, positive income elasticity of caloric intake per capita of 0.13 ($R^2 = 0.51$). If that elasticity is applied to Turkish data, caloric intake should have increased by 0.43 percent, not 0.71 percent. Or looking at caloric intake in a different way, Turkey before World War II was at the same level as China and India were on average in 1985, while Turkey in 1985 was well above the average for upper-middle-income countries but still below that of industrial market economies, though on a level with the United Kingdom. Thus in terms of caloric intake Turkey in fifty years closed a gap equal to the distance in 1985 between China and India, on average, and the United Kingdom.

Table 6–9. Nutritional Intake, Measured by Various Indicators, Selected Periods, Prewar to 1983–85

Period	Calories	Protein (grams)	Fat (grams)	Calcium (milligrams)	Iron (milligrams)
Prewar	2,450	79	41	n.a.	n.a.
1947–48	2,120	68	37	n.a.	n.a.
1950–51	2,510	80	39	n.a.	n.a.
1955–56	2,670	88	40	n.a.	n.a.
1961–63	2,630	80	55	568	21
1969–71	2,819	80	63	523	17
1979–81	3,104	85	73	554	17
1983–85	3,180	84	77	511	18

n.a. = Not available.

Sources: Organisation for European Economic Cooperation (OEEC) (1957), table 2; FAO, *Production Yearbook*, 1986, tables 106–09.

Caloric intake in Turkey thus increased impressively during the postwar period. Fat intake increased even faster, by 0.2 percent annually. This is natural since fat has a higher income elasticity than food generally. Protein intake, on the other hand, increased by less than 0.2 percent annually and was in fact lower in 1983–85 than in 1955–56. From 1961–63 to 1983–85, mineral intakes declined. Thus, the nutritional status of the Turkish people did not improve uniformly. Its composition deteriorated, and considering the importance of protein and minerals and the dubious value of fat intake, it is by no means obvious that the Turkish nutritional status has improved since the 1950s. If nutritional status is important for productivity, it may not have been a factor helping to create a growth residual over and above factor input and it is not possible to infer from nutritional status what the distribution of income was. And the only available information from which the distribution of nutritional status could be inferred is that on income distribution which is highly unreliable.

Life expectancy in Turkey, shown in table 6–10, increased from fifty-one years in 1960 to about sixty-five years in 1985. Women, as in most countries except those in the Indian subcontinent, have longer life expectancies than men. With life expectancy, human capital per capita increases as a windfall.

Educational indicators show strong uniform improvement ever since World War II. Gross enrollment ratios, indicating investment in human capital, have increased significantly across the board, as table 6–11 shows. The ratios for the first level of education of both males and females in 1984 were above 100 percent and although for the second and third levels of education females continue to have considerably lower enrollment ratios than males, the gap has narrowed. It is believed that gross enrollment ratios are considerably lower in rural than in urban areas, but data do not seem to be available. Crude enrollment ratios are,

Table 6–10. Life Expectancy at Birth, by Sex, Selected Periods, 1960–85
(years)

Period	Male	Female	Total
1960	n.a.	n.a.	51.0
1965	52.0	55.0	n.a.
1975–80	58.3	62.8	61.0[a]
1980–85	60.0	62.3	n.a.
1985	62.0	67.0	n.a.

n.a. = Not available.
a. Data for 1978.
Source: World Bank, *World Development Report*, various years; United Nations, *Demographic Yearbook*, 1987.

Table 6-11. Gross Enrollment Ratios and Illiteracy Rates, by Age and Sex, Selected Years, 1945-84

(percent of age group)

Year and sex	Gross enrollment ratio by educational level			Illiteracy rate (age 15 and older)
	First (ages 6–10)	Second (ages 11–16)	Third (ages 20–24)	
1945				
Male	n.a.	n.a.	n.a.	55.7
Female	n.a.	n.a.	n.a.	86.5
Total	n.a.	n.a.	n.a.	71.5
1960				
Male	90	20	4.5	45.2
Female	58	8	1.2	78.9
Total	75	14	2.9	61.9
1970				
Male	124	39	9.4	30.9
Female	94	16	2.4	66.4
Total	109	28	6.1	48.7
1984				
Male	116	53[a]	11.8	14.1
Female	109	31[a]	5.8	37.5
Total	113	42[a]	8.9	25.8

n.a. = Not available.
a. For 1985.
Source: UNESCO, *Statistical Yearbook*, various years, tables 1–3 and 3–2.

however, lower in the largely rural eastern provinces than elsewhere (Selçuk Özdegiz in Özbudun and Ulusan 1980, p. 506). Illiteracy rates for the population over fifteen years old, an indicator of educational status, were down from 71.5 percent in 1945 to 25.8 percent in 1984 (table 6-11). Females, however, continued to have considerably higher illiteracy rates than males.

Table 6–12, which shows the number of years of formal education completed by workers in the various productive sectors, has several important dimensions. The level of education of workers is one of the factors generally assumed to help explain productivity of labor, and hence real earnings both in the aggregate and by economic activity. This well-known relationship has been observed for Turkey (Odekon 1977). Table 6–12 shows very large differences in educational level, ranging from 2.4 years in agriculture to 10.3 years in finance in 1980. Mining and construction are two other activities with relatively low levels of education while services (including government) and electricity are activities with relatively high educational levels. Manufacturing, trade, and transport are in between. These large differences in educational levels are partly demand induced (the high-level activities) and partly supply determined (the low-level activities).

Change in the level of education as measured by years of education is generally acknowledged as one factor that helps the rate of growth of GNP exceed that of (a weighted sum of) total factor input. A steady increase in education will create a constant residual—that is, an excess of GNP growth over factor input. The steady growth from 1970 to 1980 in the years of formal education completed from 2.6 years to 4.0 years for the average person in the total active population should be a case in point. How much residual should be expected in the Turkish case is not clear; there is little evidence available for countries at this low level of education. So much is clear, Turkey still has a lot to gain on this account, both in the aggregate and in the various economic activities. It is a problem here whether it is absolute or relative change that matters; both are shown in table 6–12. The relative increase has been relatively small in activities with relatively high numbers of years of education while the low education activities (agriculture, mining, construction) have seen

Table 6–12. Average Years of Formal Education Completed by Productive Population, Twelve Years Old and Older, 1970, 1975, and 1980

Production sector	Years of education			Increase, 1970–80	
	1970	1975	1980[a]	Years	Percent
Agriculture, fishing, forestry, and hunting	1.5	2.2	2.4	0.7	45
Mining and quarrying	3.2	3.8	4.5	1.5	48
Manufacturing	4.0	4.6	5.4	1.4	35
Electricity, gas, and water	5.3	6.2	7.4	2.4	46
Construction	3.1	3.9	4.5	1.5	49
Trade, and so forth	4.1	4.8	5.5	1.1	26
Transport, communications, and so forth	4.7	5.2	5.8	1.0	21
Finance, insurance, and so forth	9.2	9.1	10.3	1.5	17
Services[b]	6.4	7.1	8.1	1.7	27
Not defined	3.4	3.5	6.1	3.7	131
Total[c]	2.6	3.3	4.0	1.4	53

a. Excludes unemployed persons seeking jobs.
b. Includes government.
c. Does not include "graduation situation unknown" and "unknown," which are not important categories.
Source: Turkey, *Statistical Yearbook*, various years, table 43; author's computations, assuming five years in primary, three years in junior high, three years in high school, and five years in higher education.

large relative increases in education. If it is the *relative* increase in education that matters for the size of the residual, a continuation of the policy of the 1970s, then concentrating educational expansion in the low education areas should not only tend to give the highest returns nationally but should also tend to improve distribution of income.

Table 6–12 clearly shows that in rural areas, where agriculture dominates, education has been discriminated against. The agricultural population has by far the lowest educational level. It is also here the greatest potentialities are. The rural population being relatively poor, it may be that expansion of elementary education in rural areas is one of the most important examples of policies with no tradeoff between growth and equity.

Some researchers (Kemal Derviş and Sherman Robinson, in Özbudun and Ulusan, 1980; Pamuk 1985) have employed the so-called Kuznets *K* to measure the income gap between agriculture and nonagriculture as an indicator of distribution. An increase in the Kuznets *K*—the ratio between nominal gross value added per unit of labor in nonagriculture and in agriculture, respectively—indicates an increase in the per capita income gap between the two sectors and, by implication, an increase in overall inequity. The latter implication is dubious, however, if distribution is more inequitable within agriculture than within nonagriculture, as the case may be in Turkey. The estimates in table 6–13 taken at face value indicate a tendency for *K* to decline over time. (The estimates for 1927 and 1935 are little more than conjectures because the distribution of labor between agriculture and nonagriculture for those

Table 6-13. Income Distribution Indicated by the Kuznets *K*, Selected Years, 1927–84

		Change since previous reading (percent)				
Year	*Kuznets K ratio*	*Annual rate of change in K*	*Terms of trade effect*	*Total product effect, annual change*	*Migration effect*	*Average productivity effect*
1927	5.5	—	—	—	—	—
1935	7.3	3.7	2.6	1.1	—	1.1
1950	5.9	–1.4	–1.7	0.3	—	0.3
1960	4.6	–2.4	0.3	2.3	–5.0	–2.6
1970	4.5	–0.1	–0.1	4.5	–4.3	0.2
1980	4.3	–0.6	0.7	2.8	–4.1	–1.3
1984	4.6	0.4	n.a.	n.a.	n.a.	n.a.

— = Not applicable.
n.a. = Not available.
Source: Pamuk (1985), pp. 12–13.

years, which is unknown, is assumed to have been the same as in 1950.) The very high *K* for 1935 is related to the special conditions of the Great Depression. For 1950 the value is again approximately at the 1927 level, with 1960 and the following years lower and declining slightly. The table presents a decomposition (based on Derviş and Robinson, in Özbudun and Ulusan, 1980) on terms of trade effect, and average productivity effect, the latter with a breakdown on total product and migration effect. The terms of trade used here are those between nonagriculture and agriculture, measured by the ratio between the implicit value added deflators for the two sectors. This, incidentally, is not a very good proxy for the relevant terms of trade. Be that as it may, terms of trade effects appear to have been strong. The increase in *K* from 1927 to 1935 was very much the result of the relative decline of agricultural prices during the Great Depression. The decline in *K* from 1935 to 1950 reflects the reversal of relative agricultural prices from the Great Depression to the Korean War boom. After 1950, product and migration effects dominate the picture. The relative increase in productivity outside of agriculture, other things being equal, increases *K*, while outmigration from agriculture, other things being equal, has the opposite effect. The resulting development of *K* appears fortuitous and its effect on size distribution of income is ambiguous.

The estimates of the distribution of income between agriculture and nonagriculture shown in table 6–14 abstain from breaking down agricultural income. For nonagricultural income the breakdown is marred by the usual difficulties of imputing wages to owners (employers) and unpaid family labor. It is not clear whether income for the self-employed is classified as wages, nor is it clear how such income has been estimated.

The share of agriculture appears to have declined strongly to almost half from 1965 to 1985. This is, of course, the trend apparent in table

Table 6–14. Functional Distribution of Income, Selected Years, 1965–85

(percent)

| Year | Agriculture | Nonagriculture | | | National |
		Wages and salaries	Other	Total	
1965	35.8	27.0	37.2	64.2	100
1970	31.1	31.2	37.7	68.9	100
1975	30.8	31.5	37.7	69.2	100
1977	29.1	36.8	34.1	70.9	100
1980	23.9	26.7	49.4	76.1	100
1985	17.8	19.5	62.7	82.2	100

Source: Özmucur (1985–86).

6-4 where (at constant factor costs) there is a similar decline in the share of agriculture from 1961–63 to 1983–84. Deterioration of agricultural terms of trade has accelerated the decline. There is nothing controversial about this result, although its impact on overall inequity is ambiguous. Within nonagriculture, there is a certain shift in favor of wages and salaries from 1965 to 1977 and thereafter a strong decline. From about 42 percent of total nonagricultural income in 1965, wages and salaries increased to 45 percent in 1975 and then dropped to 24 percent in 1985. The decline in the share of wages and salaries from the mid-1970s is extraordinary and hardly believable. It does, however, correspond to what is known about real wage developments and also to a relatively solid estimate for manufacturing industry alone (presented in table 12–16). The latter estimate shows an increase in the share of wages and salaries from 59 percent in 1965 to 63 percent in 1975, followed by a drop to 30 percent in 1984. The increase in the share of labor from the early 1960s to the late 1970s was related to the liberalization of the labor market introduced by the 1961 constitution and followed by increasing unionization and union militancy, combined with low public enterprise prices. The very strong decline in the share of wages after 1977 was related to the reversal of government policy in 1980, with repression of the labor market and increased public enterprise prices.

Considering the change in government policy from the period of planning, 1962–79, to the reforms of 1980 and the shift in development strategy, it is easy to understand the shift in the functional distribution of nonagricultural income although the strength of the shift is surprising. With the share of both agriculture and wages and salaries declining strongly and the share of gross profits in nonagriculture increasing strongly, it stands to reason that the size distribution of income should tend to become more inequitable from the end of the 1970s although no solid evidence exists. The effects on size distribution of the changes in functional distribution from the early 1960s to the mid-1970s, on the other hand, are uncertain and may have gone either way.

Poverty

Estimates of poverty, based on the 1973 survey of income distribution, suffer, among other things, from the weaknesses of that survey. Based on a poverty line in 1973 of LT 12,000 for family income (apparently chosen as one-quarter of the GNP at current market prices for a six-person family [Celasun 1986, p. 109]), the percent of income accruing to the poor is shown in table 6–15. Because the poverty line is kept constant over time and the same for agricultural and nonagricultural families, one should already for that reason expect poverty to be more pronounced in than outside agriculture. The estimates for the 1973 survey adjusted represent an attempt by Celasun (1986) to repair some of the defects of the

Table 6-15. Indicators of Poverty, 1973, 1978, and 1983
(percent)

Category	National	Agricultural	Nonagricultural
Share of income accruing to families under poverty line			
1973 survey	38.4	49.1	29.2
1973 survey adjusted	32.0	49.9	12.9
1978 estimate	25.0	42.5	8.6
1983 estimate	29.9	51.3	12.2
Share of poor households in total number of households			
1973 survey, adjusted	32	50	n.a.
1978 estimate	25	42	n.a.
1983 estimate	30	51	n.a.

n.a. = Not available.
Source: Derviş and Robinson, in Özbudun and Ulusan (1980); Celasun (1986).

1973 survey. There is no way to know whether the adjustments are successful. Celasun extrapolated the adjusted 1973 survey to 1978 and 1983; again, it is unknown whether the extrapolations are successful. The underlying assumptions appear questionable and there is no evidence against which the results can be tested.

That poverty is more pronounced in agriculture than in nonagriculture is thus laid down in the methodology although it is probably true. More interesting is the development over time, indicating that while poverty increased somewhat after the reforms and change of development strategy in 1980, poverty seems on balance still to have been less pronounced in 1983 than in 1973. In other words, what may have been gained from 1973 to 1978 may not have been entirely lost in 1983. What allegedly led to the increase in poverty from 1978 to 1983 was the decline in real wages and the adverse price developments for agriculture. These seem to be facts of life and it stands to reason that they should lead to a certain increase in poverty. To repeat, however, the results are not a matter of observation but extrapolations based on questionable assumptions.

Distribution of Opportunity

While the Atatürk philosophies of modernization included ideas of equalization of opportunity, it is not easy to appreciate and evaluate achievements in this direction. The problem is multidimensional and has not been studied in much depth or detail. Social mobility in Turkey appears to be intimately related to migration from rural to urban areas, migration to Western Europe, and education, in this order. Education, which in industrialized societies is the main mechanism of upward mobility, is in Turkey less equally and less easily accessible than in industrial societies. Education seems in Turkey still to be a mechanism for prestige rather than for income mobility and apparently has to be enhanced by rural-urban migration or migration to Western Europe to lead to major gains in income. Migration to Western Europe, which in its early phases in the 1960s mainly was an outlet for single, skilled males from the more developed areas in western Turkey, has become increasingly accessible to the lower social strata all over Turkey, including the backward, ethnically different areas in eastern Turkey (Paine 1974).

What has made education less of an independent factor in social mobility in Turkey than elsewhere is partly the unequal geographical distribution of education facilities, with eastern Turkey and its minorities particularly disadvantaged, and partly the rationing of admission to higher (academic) education that, practically speaking, greatly favors higher social strata and upper-income brackets. In the early 1960s almost half of the elementary schools in the country were one-teacher schools, practically all located in rural areas. There are still villages in eastern Turkey without schools or easy transportation to towns; existing village schools continue frequently to be one-teacher, one-class institutions; and, perhaps most important, the parents of institutionally disadvantaged students tend themselves to be illiterate. Education is by and large tuition free. Primary education is compulsory if facilities exist but secondary education, both at lower and at higher level, both general and vocational, is voluntary; participation is obviously limited by the ability of families to keep youngsters off the labor force. Admission to higher education, including colleges, is administered centrally through highly competitive entrance tests. Of almost 300,000 applicants in 1975 only 20 percent were admitted. Residents of rural areas and women are underrepresented among the applicants and the probability of applicants from higher income brackets passing the tests has been estimated to be about three times that of applicants from the lower income brackets (Özgediz, in Özbudun and Ulusan 1980, pp. 506–07). The possibility of financing private tuition is apparently crucial for passing the test. Finally, unemployment seems to be highly, positively correlated with education.

Needless to say, many of the features of Turkish society that create inequity of opportunity are common for most developing countries, indeed for most countries in the world. To what extent they are more serious in Turkey than elsewhere is hard to say.

An important aspect of modernization and opportunity in Turkey is women's participation in the labor force and access to paid work. The problem of unpaid family labor in the measured labor force, particularly in agriculture, is again at hand; this social phenomenon may be just the opposite of modernization and emancipation. The data in table 6–16 from the labor force surveys pertain to urban areas only, except for 1985 where national and, by implication, rural data are available. For both participation rates and unemployment rates separate data are presented on the labor force including *A* and excluding *B* unpaid family workers. The difference in the results for rural areas is stunning.

For the urban labor force, table 6–16 shows that the share of females in the labor force has remained about constant at 13.4 percent in 1967–69 and 12.8 percent in 1982–85, and thus, if anything, has declined slightly if unpaid family labor is included in the labor force (*A*). When unpaid family labor is excluded from the labor force (*B*), there is a clear increase in female participation from 6.1 percent in 1967–69 to 11.9 percent in 1982–85, almost a doubling. What has happened is obviously that female participation has moved from unpaid family labor toward paid employment, presumably outside the family enterprise. Comparing female participation in urban and rural areas in 1985, everything depends on whether unpaid family labor is included in the labor force or not. With family labor included, rural areas have a participation rate of 50.3 percent against only 14.8 percent for urban areas. With unpaid labor excluded, the situation is reversed, with 13.3 percent participation in urban areas against 8.2 percent in rural areas. Even more interesting is the fact that the stabilization and liberalization policies after 1978, which among other things led to increased unemployment, hit women particularly hard. No matter which way the rate of unemployment is

Table 6–16. Labor Force Participation and Unemployment Rates of Women, Selected Years, 1967–85

(percent)

Category	Female participation		Unemployment					
			Total		Male		Female	
	A	B	A	B	A	B	A	B
Urban								
1967	13.2	7.2	2.7	2.8	2.6	2.7	3.6	3.8
1968	14.8	6.0	2.9	3.1	3.0	3.2	2.2	3.0
1969	12.3	5.0	3.3	3.5	3.4	3.6	2.5	3.4
1982	11.2	10.6	10.9	11.4	8.9	9.3	23.0	24.5
1983	11.9	11.2	12.1	12.6	10.1	10.5	24.8	26.3
1984	13.1	12.4	11.9	12.5	9.0	9.5	29.1	30.8
1985	14.8	13.3	14.8	15.6	11.7	12.2	31.1	34.7
Rural, 1985	50.3	8.2	10.3	19.1	13.2	16.6	6.0	36.7
National, 1985	33.0	10.8	12.3	17.1	12.4	14.1	12.0	35.4

A = Including unpaid family workers.
B = Excluding unpaid family workers.
Source: Turkey, *Statistical Yearbook*, various years.

measured, urban unemployment for males increased from about 3 percent in 1967–69 to about 10 percent in 1982–85—that is, more than tripled—and for females it increased from about 3 percent to 27–29 percent, almost ten times. In the late 1960s women had about the same level of open unemployment as men. By the mid-1980s women had about three times higher unemployment than men. It is women's participation in unemployment rather than in employment that has grown.

7 *The Ottoman Legacy*

At the beginning of the nineteenth century, the Ottoman central government recognized that externally it was not in a position to match the military and political power of major European countries. Internally, the central government was unable to exercise its rule over local elements in the provinces. External and internal weaknesses coupled with the demands of frequent and long-lasting military campaigns had also weakened the public finances considerably.

Throughout the nineteenth century, the central government attempted to undertake reforms to reverse the unfavorable balances of power. During the first quarter of the century the reforms aimed at modernizing the army and strengthening the central government militarily. Based on successes in these areas, the central government was able to break the power of local landlords and notables in the 1830s and 1840s, thereby achieving a considerable degree of concentration in the empire.

These developments paved the way for the reforms known as Tanzimat, proclaimed in 1839 under considerable pressure from European powers. With Tanzimat, the Ottoman government declared its intention to grant full religious and judicial equality to all citizens regardless of religion. It also announced that military service would henceforth take in all Ottoman subjects and stated that taxation would be according to financial capacity and within the limits of the law. Later, in 1856, a new proclamation was issued promising, among other things, replacement of the tax-farming system by direct collection of taxes by the government; adaptation of taxation to the conditions of production and trade; and public initiative in the development of banking and other credit institutions. Most of these attempts at reform proved to be failures. For example, the central government did not have the political and administrative strength to replace the tax-farming system. However, these attempts paved the way for more successful efforts in the twentieth century.

The period of Tanzimat paid close attention to education although the reformers' efforts concentrated mainly at the higher levels of schooling.

In addition, gradual advances were made in the codification of Ottoman law which led to the promulgation, during the midcentury, of a commercial code, a land code which recognized private property, and a commercial marine code. In general, however, the bureaucrats who instituted Tanzimat reforms had very limited visions of economic development and the role that government might play in the process. Taken together with the severe fiscal difficulties the central government faced, this meant that basic economic policy consisted of opening the empire to free trade by signing commercial treaties with all European countries (1838–41). Tariffs on imports had already been fixed at low levels during the earlier part of the century. However, exports had often been subject to restriction since the governments were concerned above all with domestic provisioning. In addition, a wave of external public borrowing that was initiated in the 1850s resulted in the default of 1875–76 and the establishment of European control over state finances. Needless to say, both the expansion of external trade and public borrowing accelerated the European penetration of the Ottoman economy.

There are many links between the Tanzimat reforms of the midcentury and the Young Turks who came to power after the Revolution of 1908, deposed Sultan Abdulhamid the next year, and established a multiparty constitutional monarchy. This new regime did not last long, however, in part because it was troubled by almost continuous war, leading to the de facto dissolution of the empire in 1918.

In comparison with the midcentury bureaucrats of Tanzimat, who were never able to do more than share power with the palace, the Young Turks with their modest middle-class origins represented a new social group in power. In contrast to the Ottoman or multi-ethnic perspective of their predecessors, they came to the conclusion after a short time in power that Turkish nationalism represented the only way of salvaging what remained of the empire in an era of Great Power politics and rivalry. Their nationalism grew stronger during the later years of their rule and particularly during World War I.

The economic outlook of the Young Turks also differed from that of their predecessors. Unlike the nineteenth-century reformers, they understood the economic foundations of national power and realized that the state, which in their opinion should have taken the lead in economic development, was in no financial position to do so. They also realized that industrial products imported from Europe had deprived local craftsmen of their livelihood. A few industrial establishments, mostly owned by foreigners or minorities, processed chiefly agricultural products and raw materials. Foreign investment in the empire went mostly into railroads, utilities, commerce, and banking.

The Young Turks began to plan and execute economic projects. To stimulate economic enterprises they passed in 1909, and revised in 1915, a Law for the Encouragement of Industry. Although the war enabled the government to increase tariffs, industrial production decreased sharply during the war. An important development during the war years was the establishment of governmental machinery for economic intervention and control, which was to become so important in the 1930s.

Although the Young Turks oversaw the disintegration of the empire, their record was not without achievements. During ten years in power they confronted a counterrevolution and four wars, responding to these challenges with strong centralized leadership. They were the first government of the Ottoman Empire to issue industrial legislation and to recognize the political importance of economic considerations. They also made the all-important decision to abandon an Ottoman-Islamic approach to politics and replace it with Turkish nationalism. Their efforts certainly made the later transition to a republic much easier. In fact, the Kemalist leadership of the republic had strong intellectual and political links with the Young Turks.

The history of the Ottoman Empire during its last century can be characterized by three trends: continued backwardness and increasing disintegration; European political, commercial, and financial penetration accompanied by Great Power rivalry between Great Britain, France, Germany, Russia, and, to a lesser extent, Austria; and attempts by the central government to reform the political, social, and economic structures.

The Economy before World War I

For the Ottoman economy, the nineteenth century was above all a period of rapid integration into world markets. Between the Napoleonic Wars and World War I, foreign trade expanded more than tenfold (Issawi 1980, chap. 3; Pamuk 1987, chap. 2). While exports of agricultural commodities expanded, traditional handicrafts declined under the onslaught of imported manufactured goods. Early import-substituting industrialization utilizing imported technology remained weak. On the eve of World War I, the Ottoman economy was overwhelmingly agrarian.

European commercial penetration was accompanied by direct investment in railroads and other infrastructure that aimed at promoting trade. Another link to Europe was financial—indiscriminate external governmental borrowing during the third quarter of the nineteenth century had led to the bankruptcy of 1875–76 and to direct European control over Ottoman finances. Throughout the nineteenth century, the standard of living remained very low, but there was some economic growth at least during the decades before World War I.

During World War I and the War of Independence that followed, Turkey suffered heavy losses in population, and both agricultural output and external trade declined. The political and economic changes of this decade may, however, have facilitated the later emergence of a national economy.

Population

During the half century preceding World War I, the population of the Ottoman Empire increased on an average by about 0.8 percent a year. As much as one-fourth of the rate of increase came from the migration of Muslims from the seceding areas of the Balkans and the Crimea to the remaining areas of the empire. By 1913 the population of the areas that later became Turkey is estimated to have approached 16 million. Regional breakdowns indicate that the mass of the population remained concentrated in coastal areas. Few data are available on the numerous nomadic populations, but there is evidence of considerable settlement during the nineteenth century in areas that had been largely barren and deserted.

Urban population grew until World War I at the same rate as total population, and no significant increase in urbanization appears to have taken place. Towns of at least 20,000 accounted for close to 20 percent of the total population throughout this period. Compared to other European countries, Turkey was relatively less urbanized in 1913 than in 1800. Istanbul was an important exception. Its population expanded rapidly until World War I, to some extent because of immigration, and in 1913 it stood close to 1.2 million, four times the population of the second largest city, İzmir. There were important shifts in the composition of urban population; that of the ports rose rapidly because of the expansion of external trade while many towns in the interior stagnated because of the decline in their handicrafts and trade. Some towns in the east actually lost population (Issawi 1980, pp. 17–19, 33–35).

During the First World War and the War of Independence (1919–22) Turkey's human losses were very large. Military casualties have been estimated at 1.8 million. Massacres, deportations, flights, and exchanges of population had reduced the population to around 14 million by 1927. The largest population exchanges took place with Greece in 1922–23; 1.2 million Greeks left and 400,000 Turks arrived from Greece and the Balkan states. These developments had profound effects on the urban population. By 1927, towns of over 20,000 had declined to only 12 percent of the total population from about 22 percent on the eve of World War I.

Another important change during the war period occurred in the ethnic composition of the population. Whereas Christians (Greeks and Armenians) made up 15–20 percent of the population of Istanbul and Anatolia before World War I, by 1927 Christians and Jews together accounted for only about 2 percent of the total population of Turkey. By the mid-1920s the non-Muslim minority population had become heavily concentrated in Istanbul (McCarthy 1983). The decline in the rural Greek and Armenian population had adverse implications for commercial agriculture. Some handicrafts and trade were also unfavorably affected.

Agriculture

Ottoman trade with Europe expanded rapidly during the nineteenth century. Exports from areas that later constituted Turkey increased almost tenfold in constant prices between 1840 and 1913. The share of agricultural commodities in exports remained high throughout the century, averaging close to 90 percent on the eve of World War I. Export expansion was probably the most important source of change in Ottoman agriculture during the period preceding World War I (Pamuk 1987, chap. 5).

Crude estimates based on official figures on tithe assessment and collection suggest that in those areas of the Ottoman Empire that were later to become Turkey, the volume of agricultural production more than doubled between the early 1860s and World War I. The increase in per capita agricultural production was, however, substantially smaller since population in those areas increased by more than 50 percent during the same period. The rate of growth of agricultural exports far exceeded the rate of growth of agricultural output, leading to a rapid rise in the share of exports in total agricultural production and in the national product until World War I.

In contrast to the export markets, the role of the domestic market in the expansion of commodity production in agriculture was rather limited during the nineteenth century. It is difficult to determine the share of domestic markets, local or otherwise, in total agricultural production, but several observations can be made. While there was some interregional trade by sea within the empire, overland domestic trade in foodstuffs remained low until the construction of railroads. Internal trade networks were, in effect, weakened by the construction of railroads, since the railroads linked agricultural areas to major ports of export and import.

Since interregional trade was not substantial, the rate of growth of the urban population and of urban markets can perhaps be taken as a rough measure of the rate of growth of agricultural commodity production for domestic markets. Data on urban population point to relatively large urban markets in the early part of the nineteenth century with rather slow rates of growth until World War I. It has been estimated that as much as three-fourths of the expansion in agricultural commodity production that took place between 1840 and 1913 within the 1911 borders of the Ottoman Empire was induced by world market demand.

Commercialization of agriculture is often accompanied by a shift in the composition of agricultural output from cereals and other subsistence crops toward industrial raw materials and other cash crops. However, since cereals were an important part of the expansion of commodity production in the Ottoman case, the shift in composition was not as pronounced as the commercialization and export orientation of agriculture. Official Ottoman statistics indicate that in 1909, cereals (wheat, barley, and others) covered 84 percent of all cultivated land and accounted for 77 percent of the value of agricultural output, excluding animal products, in the Anatolian provinces of the empire.

As for the composition of agricultural exports, Ottoman statistics indicate that during 1878–1913, no single crop dominated exports, and only rarely did the share of any single commodity exceed 12 percent of the value of total exports. The eight most important commodities—tobacco, wheat, barley, raisins, figs, raw silk, raw wool, and opium—accounted for 44 percent of the total value of exports in 1913 (Pamuk 1987, app. 1).

One of the most important developments in the early part of the nineteenth century was the rapid change in the balance of power between the central government and local elements. Sened'i İttifak, signed in 1808, represented the zenith of the power of local notables, *ayan* and *derebeys*, but it also signaled the beginning of a centralization drive by the Ottoman state. In the following decades, particularly during the 1830s, the central government moved swiftly to destroy the economic basis of provincial opposition. All forms of private de facto ownership of *miri* (state) lands were eliminated and large estates were expropriated. Lands that reverted to the central government were then leased to *mültezim*, tax farmers, for tax collection purposes. It is difficult to say to what extent these measures fulfilled the objectives of the central government, but there is evidence that even in eastern Anatolia, lands in the hands of Kurdish tribal lords were confiscated, and that some were distributed to small peasants. Later, the Land Code of 1858, enacted under pressure from the European powers, recognized private ownership of land, and in 1867 ownership of land by foreign citizens was recognized.

The long-term impact of the Land Code of 1858 on patterns of land ownership and tenure in different parts of the empire is not entirely clear. While it may have helped powerful landlords and others to register large tracts of land under their name in other parts of the empire, it appears that in Anatolia the land code, together with the strengthening of the central government, helped establish ownership of land by small peasants as an important feature of agriculture.

Another important characteristic of nineteenth century Anatolian agriculture was the relative scarcity of labor and abundance of land. The population of Anatolia began to grow in the nineteenth century with the immigration of large numbers of Muslims from the Caucasus and from the European provinces as they seceded from the empire. Throughout the nineteenth century, the Ottoman central bureaucracy was very much aware that the expansion of agricultural production, the primary source of fiscal revenue, depended critically on relieving the labor shortage and providing inexpensive means of transportation. Immigrants were settled along the Anatolian Railway in Eskişehir, Ankara, and Konya and in agronomically favorable areas of eastern Anatolia and

Antalya. In addition, attempts were made to settle the nomadic tribes in regions where labor shortage was particularly acute, such as the Çukurova Plain. Despite these policies, relative scarcity of labor, regional variations notwithstanding, continued to be an important characteristic of Ottoman agriculture until World War I.

The obverse side of the coin is the relative abundance of land. Throughout the nineteenth century, under the extensive-farming techniques employed in most parts of Thrace and Anatolia, cultivated lands were left fallow every two or three years. Uncultivated marginal lands were always available for purchase from the state at nominal prices or in return for regular payments of tithe for ten years, particularly in areas where the absence of inexpensive forms of transportation made commodity production for remote markets difficult.

In general, land prices followed the short-term and long-term fluctuations in world market conditions for agricultural commodities and for credit. Along with the expansion of world demand and of exports, land prices rose from 1840 until the early 1870s. They declined during the Great (price) Depression of 1873–96, only to rise again during the subsequent upswing, which continued until the outbreak of World War I. The availability of marginal lands meant that, despite the relative scarcity of labor and the primitive nature of agricultural implements, substantial amounts of new land could be brought under cultivation during periods of high world market prices and favorable terms of trade. If the large increases in area under cultivation and agricultural production indicated by the official Ottoman statistics for the period before World War I are to be believed, an explanation of these increases must include the availability of new land, recent immigration, and the role of the railroads.

The relative proportions of land and labor tended to favor the bargaining position of the small peasant producer. Peasants who owned or could borrow a pair of oxen and the most basic implements cultivated their own land. When marginal land was not available, peasants sharecropped for small or large landlords. Although the landlords had the right to cancel a tenancy arrangement, evictions were infrequent, indicating a shortage of labor.

Around the turn of the twentieth century, large landowners in the highly commercialized agricultural regions of Izmir-Aydin and Adana began to import implements and labor-saving machinery to reduce their dependence on relatively scarce labor. However, in an economy where marginal land was available and labor was scarce, wages were bound to remain relatively high. Large farms using year-round wage laborers could not expand at the expense of peasant households. If necessary, peasant households could exert much greater effort and accept much lower levels of consumption. Consequently, once small peasant ownership was reestablished by the central government during the early part of the century, it survived until World War I.

Another factor in the survival of simple small peasant ownership and production in Anatolia was central government policy. Throughout the century, the Ottoman state attempted to prevent the emergence of a powerful landlord class that might expand its share of the agricultural surplus at the expense of the state and even challenge the rule of the central bureaucracy.

At the same time, however, the state heavily taxed the small peasantry. Among a variety of taxes levied on the rural population the *uşr* (tithe)—a predetermined percentage of gross agricultural product—constituted the main source of revenue for the Ottoman state. After the disintegration of the feudal *timar* system, tithe revenues had been auctioned off to the *mültezim* (tax farmers), not only reducing the state's share of the taxes but increasing the rates of taxation of producers. Tax farming thus served as a primitive method of deficit financing, the tax farmers' share representing debt service. Despite the strengthening of the administration during the nineteenth century, the tax-farming system survived until World War I, even though several attempts were made to abandon it. Foreign capital was not allowed to enter this area. On the other hand, the central government was not strong enough to administer the system on its own. Locally powerful tax collectors continued to keep a large part of the tax revenues.

After the Tanzimat Decree of 1839, the tithe was fixed at 10 percent of gross agricultural output, paid mostly in kind at first but increasingly in money terms later in the century. Moreover, during the years of lower agricultural prices, the tax collectors frequently demanded and received payment in cash. The 10 percent rate was likely to increase to as much as 15 percent whenever the fiscal crisis of the state intensified. The collection of a tithe along with other forms of rural taxation such as *ağnam* (animal tax) meant that a quarter or more of agricultural production was taxed away. In addition, the taxes were highly regressive, falling mostly on the unprotected small peasantry, while the large landowners were usually underassessed.

Given the low levels of productivity, dependence of the harvest on volatile weather conditions, and heavy state taxation, both small owner-producers and tenants were permanently indebted to moneylenders at interest rates ranging from 20 percent to 120 percent. Small producers frequently had to struggle to survive from one year to the next. For these peasants, capital improvements in land and implements were unheard of. At the same time, manufacture of traditional goods in the cities declined under the competition of imported industrial products. Urban areas, therefore, offered little prospect of employment except in construction, but the availability of marginal lands prevented mass migration from rural areas.

Government attempts to improve agricultural practices and raise the quality of crops began quite early. They were not successful, however, until after the 1880s, when an agricultural bureaucracy was set up; schools and model farms were established; attempts were made to introduce new crops such as potatoes and other vegetables; and an Agricultural Bank was founded to provide credit to the producers. On the whole, however, the impact of these activities was limited.

During the nineteenth and early twentieth centuries, agriculture within the presentday borders of Turkey varied substantially by region in the proportions of land to labor, agronomical factors, composition of output, and relative importance of local urban markets. Equally important were the regional differences in proximity to major ports, availability of inexpensive forms of transportation, and the timing of the construction of railroads, as well as the degree and timing of world-market-induced commercialization.

Geographically, agriculture divided into three types of regions. The regions including Thrace, western Anatolia, the eastern Black Sea Coast, and the Adana region on the Mediterranean Coast benefited from favorable agricultural conditions and proximity to major ports. Agriculture in these coastal areas was pulled into the world trade network relatively early in the nineteenth century. On the eve of World War I, these regions were the most commercialized, most export oriented in the empire. Cash crops such as tobacco, raisins, figs, cotton, raw silk, and olive oil were their most important export commodities. In these areas, imported plows, other implements, and even agricultural machinery began to be adopted after the 1880s, and more so after the turn of the century. Large and small holdings coexisted in these regions, and sharecropping was the form of tenure most frequently adopted by large landowners. Agricultural wage laborers, mostly immigrants from other regions, were used to work crops such as cotton which demanded large amounts of seasonal labor. A considerable part of the cash crop production for external markets, however, came from peasants with medium and small holdings who cultivated their own land.

Central Anatolia was a region isolated from long-distance markets until the construction of the Anatolian Railway financed by German capital in the early 1890s. In the following two decades, peasants with small and middle-sized ownerships rapidly expanded production of wheat and barley in central Anatolia for Istanbul and European markets. The largest single investment by the government in an agricultural project was undertaken in this region. In addition the Baghdad Railway Company financed the Konya irrigation project, which was completed in 1913.

An even more isolated region encompassed eastern Anatolia with its central and southern tiers, both of which were mostly unaffected by world markets. Because there were no railroads, agricultural produce of this region could not regularly be directed toward long-distance markets. Small peasant ownership was relatively stronger in the central tier, while feudal and semifeudal relations of production dominated in southeastern Anatolia and northern Syria. Until World War I, there was virtually no improvement in the agricultural techniques and implements that had been used in the eastern Anatolian region for centuries.

Industry

Until World War I the evolution of the secondary sector in Turkey was quite similar to that in many underdeveloped countries. On the one hand, the competition of European-made industrial goods led to the decline but not the disappearance of traditional handicrafts. For example, in cotton textiles there is a good deal of evidence that while handspinning disappeared rapidly, handweaving using imported yarn managed to survive, if not flourish. On the other hand, import-substituting industrialization using imported technology did not start until the last decades of the nineteenth century and remained very weak.

The decline of traditional handicrafts accompanied the expansion of trade with Europe in the aftermath of the Napoleonic Wars. This process accelerated during the midcentury, particularly after the free trade treaties with the Capitulary Powers during 1838–41. In terms of the decline in production and loss of employment, the impact of industrial imports was most severe and most rapid in textiles, particularly in cotton spinning. A large part of this decline, it appears, was a result of the shift by peasant households from handweaving and especially spinning to commercial agricultural activities. Shortly after 1910, imports of yarn and cloth accounted for 80 percent of the total domestic consumption in cotton textiles. This is a very high figure considering that three-fourths of the population lived in rural areas. It is also an indication of the high degree of commercialization and market orientation of the rural areas on the eve of World War I.

The decline of handicrafts was less pronounced in most other branches of nonagricultural activity since costs of transportation, survival of tastes, and other factors slowed down the impact of imports.

Attempts to establish modern factories were initiated by the government in the 1830s to meet military and governmental demand. This wave of public enterprises, however, quickly ended in failure. Tanneries, textile mills, flour mills, glass works, and brick factories under private ownership began to emerge in the 1880s. It appears that they did not flourish because of the free trade treaties. In addition, they met with strong resistance from the traditional guilds and with administrative harassment by the government.

After 1900, however, and especially after the Young Turk revolution of 1908, a change is noticeable. The government began to encourage industry and exempted imports of machinery from customs duties. In addition, duties on other imports were raised to 11 percent in 1911. In response there was a considerable amount of investment, mainly by minority groups and European investors, and a number of well-equipped factories were established.

The Ottoman Industrial Census of 1913 indicates that within the borders of present day Turkey there were 560 manufacturing industry establishments employing at least 10 workers; 53 of them employed at least 100 workers. And total employment in these establishments reached 35,000. Table 7–1 summarizes the distribution by size and employment patterns in different subsectors of manufacturing industry.

Foreign Trade

On the eve of World War I, the Ottoman Empire was well integrated into world markets. Ottoman foreign trade grew relatively rapidly during the nineteenth and early twentieth centuries. The external trade of the areas that later constituted Turkey increased about tenfold in constant prices between 1840 and 1913. For the decade and a half preceding World War I, despite considerable loss of land and population during the Balkan Wars of 1911–13, the rate of growth of exports exceeded 3 percent in constant prices. Rates of growth of imports were close to 5 percent a year in constant prices during the same period (Pamuk 1987, p. 28).

Table 7–1. Distribution of Manufacturing Industries, by Size and Employment, 1913

Industry	Enterprises with 100 or more workers		Enterprises with 10 or more workers	
	Public	Private	Percent of all enterprises[a]	Percent of total employment
Textiles and clothing	20	2	25.5	45.9
Food processing and tobacco	10	1	29.7	25.3
Paper and printing	—	—	21.3	11.2
Cement and bricks	2	—	6.7	5.9
Leather works	—	1	4.6	5.3
Wood products	—	—	7.9	4.1
Chemicals	—	—	4.2	2.4
Military and shipyards	—	17	n.a.	n.a.
Total	32	21	100	100

n.a. = Not available.
— = Not applicable.
a. Based on 226 enterprises in the 1913 Ottoman industrial census.
Source: Öksün (1970).

In 1912–13, the value of Ottoman exports averaged £28.0 million per year, and imports £37.3 million. With a population of about 21.0 million in 1913, these figures correspond to per capita exports and imports of £1.3 and £1.8, respectively. As can be seen in table 7–2, these per capita export levels place the Ottoman Empire somewhere between Egypt and Iran in the Middle East, well ahead of some of the middle-sized developing countries in Asia, and behind similarly middle-sized countries in Latin America. As shown in table 7–3, more than three-fourths of Ottoman foreign trade was directed toward industrialized Europe and the United States on the eve of World War I. The rest was with countries in Southeastern Europe and the Middle East and with Russia.

One important characteristic of Ottoman exports until World War I was that they remained highly diversified. Official statistics indicate that during 1878–1913 rarely did the share of any commodity in the total value of exports exceed 12 percent. And despite the doubling of the value of total exports between 1878 and 1913, the shares of exports of the more important commodities did not change substantially. The eight largest exports accounted for 51 percent of total exports during 1878–80; by 1913 their share had declined to 44 percent, almost entirely because of a decrease in wheat exports. The fall in wheat exports (from 7 percent of the total in 1878–82 to less than 1 percent in 1911–13) occurred after

Table 7–2. Value of Exports by Various Countries on the Eve of World War I

Region and country	Population (millions)	Exports per capita (pounds)
Middle East		
Egypt	12.0	2.63
Iran	11.5	0.62
Ottoman Empire	21.0	1.33
Asia		
French Indochina	12.5	0.74
Korea	13.5	0.23
Netherlands East Indies	42.0	1.04
Philippines	9.0	1.00
Siam	8.4	0.83
Latin America		
Argentina	7.6	10.33
Brazil	24.0	2.84
Mexico	15.2	1.91
Peru	4.3	1.63

Source: Pamuk (1987), p. 138.

Table 7-3. Distribution of Ottoman Foreign Trade, by Country or Area, on the Eve of World War I

(percent)

Trading partner	Exports	Imports
Industrialized Europe and the United States	77.0	78.8
Austria	8.0	13.9
France	14.1	8.4
Germany	11.4	13.7
United Kingdom	17.9	23.9
Russia	3.9	8.7
Southeastern Europe, the Middle East, etc.	19.2	12.5
Total	100.0	100.0

Source: Pamuk (1987), pp. 31–32.

1890 when North American wheat entered world markets and world wheat prices began to fall. Only tobacco significantly increased its share in exports, rising from 6–7 percent of the total in 1878–80 to 11–12 percent by 1911–13, thereby becoming the largest export commodity. The shares of total exports by major commodity groups (table 7–4), like those of the individual commodities, did not change significantly over time.

For Ottoman imports, years 1911–13, the share of manufactured goods exceeded 50 percent, as should be expected in an underdeveloped economy. More significant, perhaps, is the large share of foodstuffs. Imports of sugar, coffee, and tea are not surprising, but by 1913 the Ottoman Empire had become a net importer of grains and flour. According to Ottoman trade statistics, imports of wheat, barley, and flour exceeded exports of those goods by an average of £1.5 million per year during 1910–13. By contrast, the same statistics indicate that in the early 1880s Ottoman exports of grain had approximately equaled imports of grain and flour. One reason for the emergence of the Ottoman Empire as a net importer of grains was its inability to protect its domestic producers. A number of European countries were able to adopt protectionist measures to support their producers after the entry of American wheat into the world market in the 1870s. The free trade treaties signed with European governments early in the century did not allow this flexibility to the Ottoman government; hence the rapid ascendancy of imported cereals in the Ottoman markets. The construction of the Anatolian Railroad linking Istanbul to the wheat-growing regions of central Anatolia did not eliminate these imports completely. Turkey became self-sufficient in cereals only in the 1920s.

Table 7-4. Ottoman Exports, by Major Commodity Groups, 1911-13
(percent)

Commodity group	Share of total
Primary products	
All foodstuffs	33–35
All raw materials (including minerals[a])	56–58
Total	89–93
Manufactured goods	
Semimanufactures (including dressed hides)	2–3
Manufactures (mostly woolen carpets)	6–7

a. Minerals accounted for 2–4 percent of all exports.
Source: Pamuk (1987), app. 1.

Table 7-5. Ottoman Imports, by Major Commodity Groups, 1911-13
(percent)

Commodity group	Share of total
Agricultural goods	
All foodstuffs (including grains, flour, rice, sugar, coffee, and tea)	32–38
Various raw materials and intermediate goods (including coal, petroleum, unworked metals, and dyes)	6–10
All yarns (mostly cotton)	4
Manufactured goods	
All manufactures of cotton, wool, silk, and linen; all clothing and apparel	36–38
Investment goods (about half of which are railroad building materials and rolling stock)	under 8
Other manufactures (including ammunition which became significant during periods of war)	8–10
Total manufactures	56–60

Source: Pamuk (1987), app. 1.

Foreign Capital

Direct foreign investment in the Ottoman Empire needs to be examined separately from foreign lending to the Ottoman government. Heavy borrowing by the Ottoman government in European financial markets during the third quarter of the nineteenth century had led to its default. With the founding of the Ottoman Public Debt Administration in 1881, European control over Ottoman finances was initiated. External borrowing continued and the public debt outstanding on the eve of World War I made up close to two-thirds of foreign capital in the Ottoman Empire (table 7–6).

More than 60 percent of foreign direct investment was concentrated in railroads. The railroads linked fertile areas of the interior to the major ports, thereby serving to facilitate external trade. From the late 1880s, railroad construction was instrumental in carving out major European powers' spheres of influence in the Ottoman Empire. French firms built railroads in Syria, the British concentrated on western Anatolia and Iraq, and German investors constructed the well-known Baghdad Railroad linking the capital to central Anatolia and later to northern Syria.

**Table 7–6. Foreign Capital per Capita Invested
in Various Countries on the Eve of World War I**
(pounds)

| Region and country | Foreign capital (pounds), per capita | | | Share of public lending in total foreign investment (percent) |
	Total	Direct investment	Investment in public debt	
Middle East				
Egypt	17.25	8.92	8.33	48
Iran	1.74	n.a.	n.a.	n.a.
Ottoman Empire	10.29	3.52	6.77	66
Asia				
French Indo-China	2.48	1.52	0.96	39
Netherlands East Indies	3.67	3.43	0.24	6
Philippines	2.56	2.34	0.22	9
Siam	1.55	0.72	0.83	46
Latin America				
Argentina	85.53	53.95	31.58	37
Brazil	18.38	12.13	6.25	34
Mexico	31.97	25.72	6.25	20
Peru	10.70	10.23	0.47	4

n.a. = Not available.
Source: Pamuk (1987), p. 145.

If the share of investment in ports and commercial companies is added to that in railroads, the share of total foreign direct investment serving to promote external trade exceeds 70 percent. In contrast, foreign investment in commodity-producing activities such as agriculture, industry, and even mining remained limited until World War I, as can be seen in table 7–7.

Another international comparison may be in order here. In 1914, foreign capital stock in the Ottoman Empire is estimated to have been £2.16 million, or approximately £10 per capita. As shown in table 7–6, this figure puts the Ottoman Empire again somewhere between Egypt and Iran in the Middle East. As in the case of per capita exports, by the end of 1913 the Ottoman Empire had received more foreign investment on a per capita basis than the medium-sized countries in Asia, but much less than the medium-sized countries in Latin America.

Estimates of National Production

Given the quality of the underlying data, it is a hazardous exercise to attempt to provide national income and production estimates for most

Table 7–7. Distribution of Foreign Capital in the Ottoman Empire, by Sector, 1913

Sector	Value (millions of pounds)[a]	Share of total (percent)
Direct investment		
Railroads	46.9	63.1
Ports	3.2	4.3
Utilities	3.8	5.1
Banking	8.9	12.0
Insurance	0.6	0.7
Commerce	4.3	5.8
Industry	4.0	5.3
Mining	2.7	3.7
Total	74.3[b]	100.0
Outstanding state debt (nominal value)	142.2	—
Total	216.5[b]	—

— = Not applicable.
a. Sum of paid-in capital and debentures.
b. Figures do not add to total because of rounding.
Source: Pamuk (1987), p. 66.

developing countries before World War I. The Ottoman case is no exception. However, the estimates in table 7–7 derived from data of questionable reliability and pockmarked by gaps in data that must be assumed away, provide a round picture of the orders of magnitude involved. On the eve of World War I, the Ottoman Empire exhibited substantial regional inequalities with respect to per capita income from Istanbul and western Anatolia to Syria and Iraq. The estimates in table 7–8 are limited to an area roughly comprising republican Turkey that could be approximated from Ottoman administrative data. In view of the major changes over time in the structure of the economy and in relative and absolute prices and the poor quality of the data underlying these estimates, intertemporal comparisons of per capita GNP pose major problems. As a rough approximation, it appears that levels of per capita income prevailing on the eve of World War I in that area were comparable to those attained in republican Turkey in the late 1920s and

Table 7–8. Estimated National Income and Production in an Area Approximating Republican Turkey, 1913

Category	Value added (millions of pounds)	Share in total NNI (percent)	Per capita (pounds)
Agriculture	70.7	50.3	4.61
Mining	1.4	1.0	0.09
Manufacturing	19.6	13.9	1.28
Construction	4.4	3.1	0.29
Transportation	5.1	3.6	0.33
Commerce	15.1	10.7	0.98
Finance	2.2	1.6	0.14
Housing	4.9	3.5	0.32
Services	7.4	5.3	0.48
Government services	12.1	8.6	0.79
Net domestic product, at factor cost	142.8	101.6	9.32
Factor income from abroad	−2.2	−1.6	−0.14
Net national income, at factor cost	140.6	100.0	9.18
Indirect taxes	6.4	—	0.41
Net national income, at market prices	147.0	—	9.59
Depreciation	6.6	—	0.43
Gross national income, at market prices	153.6	—	10.02

— = Not applicable.
Source: Eldem (1970), pp. 303–05.

early 1930s, at the end of the recovery from a decade of war and destruction.

An Extended Period of War, 1914–22

During World War I and the War of Independence, Turkey's losses were very large. Total population appears to have declined by more than 10 percent during the decade following 1914. There was a sharp decline in the urban population and in the numbers of Christian minorities.

Agriculture suffered heavily during this decade, from the wars and ethnic hostilities in western and eastern Anatolia; from the mobilization of the rural population; from the massacres, departure, and flight of Greek and Armenian peasants; and from the drastic reduction in the number of draft animals. Areas under cereals cultivation decreased by as much as 50 percent between 1913 and 1923. Cash and tree crops were also hard hit. Levels of production of tobacco, cotton, raisins, figs, silk cocoons, and all major export commodities declined dramatically during the war decade. Most branches of mining and industry were adversely affected and equipment was allowed to run down. Railways, roads, and ports were similarly affected, but some important stretches of the Baghdad railway were completed. In some branches of manufacturing the disruption of imports coupled with the rise in tariffs after 1916 encouraged the beginnings of import substitution. In the 1920s industrial production drew on this experience.

Not surprisingly, foreign trade fell sharply from its high levels in the years before World War I. In 1918 the value of exports was only 11 percent of the value in 1913 and exports 25 percent. The war also led to large government deficits and high rates of inflation. In 1920, prices of basic foodstuffs and clothing were nearly fifteen times as high as in 1914.

For the economy, then, the decade of war and hostilities brought heavy losses and a major contraction, particularly with respect to population, agriculture, and external trade. On the positive side it can be argued that wartime conditions and wartime government economic policies provided some impetus for the beginnings of import substitution and helped pave the way toward a national economy. In retrospect, the period at least until 1927 and possibly until 1929, marked by high rates of growth, should be interpreted as one of recovery and a return to prewar levels of production.

Economic Consequences of the Lausanne Treaty

After the dismemberment of the Ottoman Empire by the Allied powers and a three-year War of Independence, the Republic of Turkey was founded in 1923. It comprised a substantially smaller geographical area than the Ottoman Empire, having lost Greater Syria and Iraq, and covering only Eastern Thrace in Europe and Anatolia in Asia. The geographical boundaries of this new country and the nature of its political, economic, commercial, and financial relations with the rest of the world were codified in the Lausanne Peace Treaty of 1923 by the major powers of the time. In a number of critical areas, the Lausanne treaty represented a major break for the new republic from the agreements and international legal framework that had governed the relations of the Ottoman Empire with the European powers. Two issues that caused a great deal of disagreement and conflict in Lausanne were particularly important for the new republic.

As early as the sixteenth century, powerful Ottoman sultans had codified the favors they granted to foreigners to expand trade as a token of their generosity, or at least as an acknowledgment of their superiority in an agreement among equals. Those capitulations remained in effect only during the reign of the Ottoman ruler who had granted them. By the nineteenth century, however, in the wake of Ottoman decline, the Capitulations had changed form and were now imposed on the Ottoman government, every new sultan being forced to recognize and to renew them automatically on his accession. This capitulatory system opened the empire to arbitrary interpretations of the privileges granted to the Capitulary Powers and to penetration of foreign interest and influence in economic and political fields. Particularly in the second half of the nineteenth century, this system facilitated the penetration of foreign capital which was granted an increasing number of concessions and privileges for the establishment and operation of a variety of economic enterprises in the Ottoman Empire. Concessions for railways, public utilities, banking, and mining were especially important.

The Lausanne treaty abolished the capitulary system and all privileges provided to foreign concessionaires, to that extent restoring full sovereignty and freedom of action to the Turkish authorities. This provision made it possible for the new government at Ankara to nationalize some of the more important foreign enterprises, particularly the railways, in return for compensation.

A closely related issue concerned the right of the country to pursue independent commercial policies. The free trade treaties of 1838–41, signed first with Great Britain and later with all other European countries as an extension of the capitulatory system, ruled out government monopolies and committed the Ottoman Empire to low rates of customs duties—5 percent on imports and 12 percent on exports. Duties on exports were lowered to 1 percent ad valorem in 1861, where they remained until World War I. Ad valorem duties on imports were raised to 8 percent in 1861 and further to 11 percent in 1905. The most important aspect of the system was that tariff rates could not be changed without the agreement of the European powers. As a result, Ottoman governments were unable to pursue protectionist policies until the outbreak of World War I.

At Lausanne, tariff rates on imports were fixed at levels comparable to those established by the Ottoman tariff of 1916. After 1929, the new republic would be free to pursue independent commercial and tariff policies.

A third important issue at Lausanne was the settlement of the Ottoman debt, which had reached £142 million by 1914. After protracted negotiations, Turkey assumed responsibility for the part of this debt that corresponded to its new geographical borders. All payments on the outstanding debt including interest payments were frozen until 1929. Starting in 1929, however, this item was to become of excessive importance, partly because of the deflation in the 1930s, accounting for 13–18 percent of total budget expenditures of the republic.

It was also decided at Lausanne to eliminate all reparation payments arising from World War I and the War of Independence against Greece.

8 *Postwar Recovery, 1923–29*

The founding of the Turkish Republic in 1923—like Egypt, one of the earliest of the modern developing nation-states outside Latin America—came in the aftermath of the War of Independence. The war was fought primarily against Greece but also against the Allies, who occupied Istanbul and large parts of Anatolia after World War I and, as laid down in the 1920 Treaty of Sevres, planned to partition the country among victorious powers and national minorities. The leadership of the Turkish independence movement was in the hands of the Westernized elite of military and civilian bureaucrats and intellectuals of the Ottoman Empire. These Kemalists, followers of Mustafa Kemal, later known as Atatürk, were strongly influenced by the ideas of eighteenth century Enlightenment and the rationalist, libertarian, and egalitarian philosophies of the French Revolution. With Ziya Gökalp as leading national development ideologist, their economic development philosophies owed much to those of Friedrich List and the example set by Germany before World War I.

Clearly, this military and civilian elite could not have emerged victorious in the War of Independence without the support of broader social groups—landlords, merchants, and even religious and tribal leaders, and the Soviet Union. The Kemalist government in Ankara was not very successful, however, in obtaining the active support and participation of the peasantry during the liberation struggle. And since the country had no industrial base, there was no urban working class in the early 1920s to help establish the republic.

The government's top priorities were modernization, economic recovery, and development within the constraints of the Lausanne treaty. The Kemalists aimed at westernizing the new republic as a precondition for national and economic development. The westernization was expressed in such reforms as the replacement of Islamic law and courts by civilian, commercial, and criminal codes and a court system based on Swiss, German, and Italian models; the introduction of the Latin alphabet; a fundamental change in the position of women; establishment of a general educational system; movement of the capital from Istanbul to Ankara; reforms in clothing; and other more or less profound forms of modernization. How instrumental these reforms were in promoting economic development and equity is an open question. Certainly, legal and cultural institutions can play a crucial role in development, positively or negatively. Whether the Kemalists' reforms were instrumental in Turkey's modernization is another matter. To some extent they continued reforms initiated by the Ottoman government and in the Tanzimat, or by the Young Turks.

Economic Goals

The Kemalist leadership's strategy for economic recovery and development in the early 1920s was not well articulated. In a rank ordering of economic goals, apart from the general recovery from years of devastating wars, the most important was probably the acceleration of industrialization. The leaders decided to let industrialization be based on private entrepreneurship and to support the emerging domestic industry if need be. They also intended to accelerate the accumulation of private capital in the industrial sector with government intervention whenever necessary. Therefore, their policies even for the 1920s cannot appropriately be termed liberal. The sectors initially emphasized were sugar, textiles, and cement, which were natural areas of import substitution, partly because raw materials could be obtained domestically with advantage. Demands for founding an iron and steel complex during 1925–26 indicate that there were those within the leadership interested in a more diversified industrial structure including heavy industry even during this early period. While the government's industrialization policies in the 1920s were vague, they became more explicit and more protective after 1929 when the provisions of the Lausanne treaty expired and the Great Depression began.

Several economic provisions of the 1923 peace treaty acted as constraints on the republican government during the 1920s. The most important were related to the tariff and tax structure. The treaty froze tariffs at the level of the adjusted specific scale of 1916, which approximately corresponded to the level of nominal protection prevailing on the eve of World War I. Differential rates of excise taxes on imported and locally produced commodities were prohibited, the only significant exception being in the area of government monopolies where higher prices could be charged for revenue purposes. Under the treaty, Turkey was, moreover, obliged to eliminate existing quantitative restrictions on foreign trade and abstain from introducing new ones.

It has been suggested that the Kemalist leadership originally did not view as major concessions those provisions of the Lausanne treaty that prevented the government from pursuing autarkic policies. The leaders tended initially to favor free foreign trade and payments as long as political independence could be maintained. As a result, for example, direct investment by foreigners was encouraged, particularly in partnership with Turkish citizens, as long as the foreign investor refrained from seeking political concessions. Close to one-third of the firms established in the 1920s were joint ventures of Turkish and foreign investors. The positive attitude toward foreign capital had a counterpart in government subsidization of domestic private enterprise. The new Law for the Encouragement of Industry, passed in 1927, offered a wide variety of incentives and subsidies to new industrial establishments. Private investors also benefited from state monopoly of sugar, tobacco, oil, matches, harbors, and other business areas. The government did not directly exercise its monopoly rights but allowed them to be held by domestic or foreign firms under favorable terms. Shortages of capital for financing industrialization and mining were met by the establishment of a number of publicly owned development banks—İş Bank in 1924, and Sümer Bank and Eti Bank in the early 1930s—which extended loans to new industrial enterprises at low interest rates.

The model of industrial development being pursued by the republican governments of the 1920s thus emphasized public financing with the active participation of private local investors and capital contributions from foreign investors. In an important deviation from early modern economic development during the last decades of the Ottoman Empire, non-Muslim businesses (Greek and Armenian, in particular) were replaced by Muslim counterparts; that was fortuitous, however, rather than being a deliberate industrialization policy. Yet this new entrepreneurial element was at first weak, if it even existed. As it were, the Kemalists opted for active intervention and support for capital accumulation and entrepreneurship in the hands of Muslims and possibly favored urban over rural development.

Another apparent priority of the republican leaders was agricultural development. The aim here was both to improve the standard of living of the rural populace and to enhance the contribution of the agricultural sector to the industrialization process through supply of raw materials. The leaders were aware of the low levels of both land and labor productivity in agriculture and the potential for improvement. In the early 1920s, world market conditions were relatively favorable for exporters of primary commodities. For good economic reason, therefore, the government emphasized the increasing commercialization and export orientation of agriculture. Among the instruments of government policy were subsidies in the input markets—for example, to purchasers of tractors to alleviate the labor shortages caused by the wars of 1914–22 and the exchange of population with Greece. Most important, however, was the development of the transport network through the construction of new highways and especially railways to facilitate both the emergence of an integrated domestic market and exports of agricultural crops.

The government also changed the tax structure with the abolition of the traditional tithe (*uşr*) of about 10 percent of output in agriculture and the animal tax (*agnam*). To partially replace these sources of revenue it increased indirect taxes levied on consumer goods, with a new 10 percent tax on the value of domestic industrial products, and increased the prices of commodities such as salt, sugar, and kerosene sold by state monopolies. A first attempt to introduce income taxation was made, with agriculture exempted. The abolition of the tithe has been viewed as the most important single change in policy affecting the agricultural sector during the interwar period. In 1924 the tithe accounted for 22 percent of the central government's budget revenue and 63 percent of direct tax revenue. Since the tithe was still collected by the *mültezim*, who purchased the right at auction, actual payments by agriculture were considerably higher. Tax farming was, in effect, an old method of public borrowing (Hansen, in Udovitch 1981, pp. 502–06) and agriculture was in this way, over and above tax payments, charged with servicing the public debt. The abolition of the tithe thus involved the loss of the most important single source of public revenue and the newly instituted indirect taxes did not fully make up for the loss. As a result the overall tax payments of the agricultural population were reduced considerably during the 1920s while taxation of the urban population probably increased.

Considering the importance usually attached to the abolition of the tithe, it should be emphasized that the incentive effects and the final incidence of the tax are difficult to evaluate. First, in practice the tax may not have been levied on actual output but rather on some standardized output as negotiated between the *mültezim* and the farmer, in which case it might have had no direct effect on production. The tax may thus have tended to be a fixed tax (Hershlag 1968, p. 47, n. 4), rather unevenly distributed, depending on the bargaining powers of the two parties. Even assuming that the tax was, in effect, levied at a fixed rate on actual (expected) output, the effect on production is open to doubt. In an open economy, the tax could not be shifted on to prices and, everything else being equal, the effect should be a decline in production. The tax might, however, be shifted backward to labor. Whether this would happen depends on the elasticity of supply of labor to agriculture and the government's use of the tax revenue. If, to take an extreme case, supply of labor to agriculture were entirely inelastic, labor spent all income on tradables (food), and government spent all tax revenue on tradables (military equipment), then the incidence would be fully on labor (including subsistence farmers); landowners would pay no part of the tax as landowners, and there would be no decline in agricultural production. If, on the other hand, the government spent all revenue on hiring labor (drafting soldiers, say) and paid the same wage rate as agriculture, then the incidence would be fully on farmers (landowners) and production would decline. In the concrete case, the elasticity of supply to agriculture may have been positive. Even if the supply curve of labor for agricultural households were backward sloping, the net supply to agriculture, as a result of urban demand for labor, might have a positive elasticity. Assuming that to be the case, agricultural production was bound to go down. Even so, the government's use of revenue matters.

With the abolition of the tax came the introduction and increase of excises on various consumer goods. Levied on both domestically produced and imported commodities, thus fulfilling the provisions of the Lausanne treaty, these were undoubtedly shifted on to prices. That would tend to lower real wages everywhere and thus affect total labor supply. The effect on net supply of labor to agriculture is then open, and the impact on agricultural production might go either way. Finally, there is a problem of how the net loss of revenue was financed by the government. Deficit financing, cutbacks of purchases of tradable goods, and cutbacks in the hiring of labor would lead to entirely different effects. There is probably something to be said in favor of the conjecture that the abolition of the tithe had some positive effect on agricultural production and tended to shift income distribution in favor of land and agricultural labor but this is by no means a foregone conclusion.

In a compromise between ideology and realpolitik, Kemalist leaders thus, during the years of reconstruction, adopted a relatively free trade and finance policy. Government, to the extent possible given the external constraints, subsidized an inward-looking infant-industry strategy and an export-oriented agricultural-development strategy, shifting taxation from rural to urban population.

Recovery Achievements

The national production and income estimates summarized in tables 9–1 and 9–2 suggest that the years 1923 to 1929 were characterized by the high growth rates typical of postwar periods. Crop fluctuations caused by changing weather conditions seem to have been particularly strong during the interwar years, so three-year averages are used to eliminate the impact of fluctuations. From 1923–25 to 1927–29 the estimated growth rate for the gross domestic product was 7.5 percent. Terms of trade losses brought the rate of growth of gross national income down to 6.9 percent. The corresponding per capita growth rates were 5.4 percent and 4.8 percent, respectively. Considering that these are growth rates for a postwar reconstruction period, they are respectable but not remarkably high.

Behind the overall growth rates is an 8 percent annual increase in agriculture from 1923–25 to 1927–29; but construction and financing grew even faster, by 17 percent and 23 percent, respectively, and transport grew at a rate of 11 percent. The increase in manufacturing and in government was less than average, but what held the overall growth rate down was the very low growth in housing and services. While peace and recovery were important, it is difficult to be specific about other contributing factors. The increase in agricultural population is not known, but the exodus and exchange of population must have been a disrupting factor. Available data do not suggest any substantial increase in the cultivated area but other data for this period show violent fluctuations that may be statistical flukes. The use of modern agricultural implements and machinery began expanding during these years but data indicate a very low degree of mechanization. The unusually rapid increase in yields may be related to a return to prewar conditions and favorable weather. From a crude comparison with statistics from the Ottoman period it appears that the 1929 levels of per capita production were comparable to those prevailing in 1913–14. The relative stagnation of agricultural output in the early 1930s lends support to the argument that recovery and favorable weather conditions explain most of the high growth rate of agriculture during the 1920s. An important point that should be emphasized is the contribution of agriculture to the expansion of exports until 1929. Despite the elimination of rural Greeks and Armenians, who specialized in cash crops much more than their Muslim counterparts did, exports of tobacco, cotton, figs, raisins, and hazelnuts to Europe and the United States rose steadily. By 1929, if not earlier, volumes of exports of these cash crops from the areas within the republic's borders appear to have reached, if not surpassed, the levels of 1913.

The share of manufacturing in 1923–25 was by no means negligible, about 10 percent of total GDP. In 1927–29 the share had declined to 8–9 percent, the logical consequence of a growth rate below average. Several factors should have served as a stimulus to industrial growth but were apparently slow to work. Postwar recovery in the urban areas led to a tripling of construction activity, thus generating substantial demand for building materials, timber, brick, and cement. The high growth rate in agriculture must have generated demand for consumer goods and possibly for agricultural inputs. And investment was stimulated both by the Law for the Encouragement of Industry of 1927 and by the announcement of tariff reforms to be undertaken at the expiration of the Lausanne treaty. The rates to be introduced were not known until 1929 but preparations for the reform had begun in 1925 and the general expectation was that the new tariff would be highly protective, with high rates for commodities for final consumption and low rates for imported inputs.

Distribution, Equity, and Poverty

World War I and its aftermath, the War of Independence, inflicted suffering and misery that standard economic tools are simply not calibrated to measure. The suffering continued during the first years of the republic, partly as a consequence of the large-scale population exchange agreed at the Lausanne Conference. The main part of the exchange took place in 1923 but it was not completed until 1936. The number of people involved is roughly known, but data on the income and property lost and gained in the exchange of population are not available. And while it makes sense—too much, indeed—to talk about poverty, under the circumstances it is doubtful how to apply concepts such as distribution and equity. Equity in being drafted and sent to the battlefields? Here the poor and uneducated—rural Muslims—were always the losers (McCarthy 1983). Distribution and equity for whom? And what are the standards of comparison? Perhaps Gini coefficients based on the income of those who actually were residents at the establishment of the republic in 1923 could be compared with those of the actual residents in 1929. But what about the 1.25 million Greeks who had to leave and the 400,000 Turks who arrived? Perhaps the comparison of Gini coefficients should be for the actual residents in 1922 and a hypothetical population in 1929 that included the Greeks who left and their incomes in Greece but left out entirely the Turks who arrived. But then what about their offspring? And the dead?

The only standard indicator of distribution actually available for this period is the agricultural terms of trade. It declined, partly as a consequence of the international agricultural crisis beginning in 1925, by 18 percent from 1923 to 1925; it then improved a little in 1926–28 but by 1929 had returned to the low level of 1925. Under normal circumstances this would be taken as an indicator of a shift of income distribution against agriculture, possibly with increased inequity for the whole population as the result. Given the circumstances, however, is it possible to make such an inference?

9 The Etatist Experiment, 1929–50

The year 1929 was in several ways a turning point for economic development in Turkey. This was the year of the beginning of the Great Depression when new strategies certainly were called for. For Turkey, however, it was also the year of abolition of the Capitulations when, among other things, the country finally obtained tariff and tax autonomy. For both reasons this is the year from which new development efforts should be expected.

Since Turkey was an exporter of primary commodities, the Great Depression brought a sharp deterioration in her external terms of trade (see figure 6–2). Turkey's external terms of trade actually started to deteriorate with the international agricultural crisis of the late 1920s. After a considerable improvement in 1923–25, the external terms of trade deteriorated by 23 percent to 1929 and by another 33 percent in 1929–34. The external terms of trade were subsequently transmitted into a deterioration of the internal terms of trade against agriculture. Measured by relative GDP deflators for agricultural and industrial sectors, respectively, the internal terms of trade fell by 23 percent from 1929 to 1934. Comparisons between single years tend to exaggerate the fluctuations in the terms of trade, but even three-year averages show the changes were serious. From 1927–29 to 1931–33, internal terms of trade declined by 25 percent.

Growth rates, nonetheless, held up remarkably well. For the period 1927–29 to 1937–39—that is, the 1930s as a whole—despite the terms of trade loss the GNI growth rate was 6.3 percent, with 4.2 percent per capita growth. For the crisis years, 1927–29 to 1931–33, the GDP growth rate remained at 5.6 percent with the GNI growth rate down to 4.3 percent, the difference being caused by the terms of trade loss. After 1929 the volume of exports, overwhelmingly consisting of primary products, did not decline but continued to rise throughout the 1930s. For every year of the 1930s, exports at constant prices remained above the levels of 1926 and 1928, the best years before the Depression. Like some Asian countries (Maddison 1985), Turkey suffered from the Great Depression exclusively through the adverse terms of trade developments. The explanation lies partly in the flexibility of domestic prices (certainly as compared with highly developed countries), partly in the expansion of agriculture despite the price developments. The adoption of balance of payments controls and other forms of government intervention along with a strengthened import-substitution strategy should, however, have worked in the other direction.

The provision of the Lausanne treaty that froze Turkish tariffs at approximately the prewar levels of 11 percent was to expire in 1929 and a new tariff structure was to be implemented. The leadership was determined to use protection as an infant-industry policy when possible. The new tariff, under construction since 1925 and adopted in June 1929, provided an average nominal protection of 46 percent as compared with the previous average rate of 13 percent. The Istanbul Chamber of Commerce, dominated by importer interests, had proposed a much more moderate increase.

The year 1929 was also when the first installment of the old Ottoman debts was to be paid. Negotiations about the terms of repayment ran through the 1920s and an agreement was finally reached in 1928, with the Turkish share of the outstanding debt to be paid between 1929 and 1953. The first payments created a considerable drain on the foreign currency reserves, however, and the government suspended payments at the end of 1930, only a short time after the onset of the Great Depression. Perhaps more important, the crisis was accentuated by a sudden deterioration in the balance of trade when the announcement of the new tariff structure caused an increase in imports in 1929. The consequence was a depreciation of the (floating) Turkish lira that fortuitously initiated the balance of payments policies the government adopted. From an industrialization point of view that should have been an advantage.

After the depreciation of the lira against other currencies in the local exchange markets, however, a law was passed in February 1930 authorizing the government to intervene in these markets to stabilize the international value of the lira. In August 1930 the Turkish lira was linked to sterling, thereby linking the lira to gold. But England left the gold standard in 1931 and the Turkish government, overly concerned about maintaining the exchange rate of the lira, then linked the lira to the French franc. When the French left the gold standard in 1936, the Turkish government continued to maintain the same implicit gold parity policy, linking the lira to the Reichsmark.

The concern for maintaining the value of the currency against gold led in the 1930s to appreciation of the lira against convertible currencies such as sterling, the U.S. dollar, and the French franc (see figure 11–1). While this policy must have created difficulties for exporters, the appreciation of the lira made it relatively easy for Germany, which apparently offered favorable prices for Turkey's exports in bilateral trade, to become

Turkey's largest trading partner on the eve of World War II. Turkey was on the road to the overvaluation, which in the opinion of most observers was to be a continuing problem until 1980 when liberalization and reform finally brought an end to policies initiated in 1930.

A law passed in July 1931 gave the government the power to restrict the volume of imports. The first quota lists, announced in November 1931, left imports of agricultural and industrial machinery, raw materials, and medicine free. Imports of processed food, alcoholic beverages, clothing, shoes, leather goods, and some other consumer items were, on the other hand, eliminated completely. The volume of imports of other consumer and intermediate goods such as cement, produced domestically, was to be determined annually. Import licenses were distributed administratively. The quotas must have provided substantial economic rents to a limited number of favored importers and producers.

A leading priority of the government in the aftermath of the crisis of 1929 was to prevent another large trade deficit and, if possible, to maintain surpluses on the trade account to finance debt service. This goal was achieved from 1930. The price to be paid, however, was a severe curtailment in the volume of imports, which declined by a dramatic 60 percent from 1929 to 1933. The curtailment of imports of consumer goods conflicted with the increasing consumer demand. Concern for expanding the volume of imports without experiencing trade deficits then led the government increasingly toward bilateral trade, clearing, and barter agreements during the mid-1930s. This was in any case a worldwide trend at the time. After bilateral trade agreements with Germany, the United Kingdom, France, and Italy, 84 percent of Turkey's imports and 81 percent of its exports became part of the clearing and reciprocal quota systems between 1934 and 1939. The only important exception to the quota system was the United States. Imports from the United States were left outside the quota restrictions since Turkey maintained a trade surplus against that country throughout the 1930s.

The Policy of Etatism

Industrial output, particularly the output of manufacturing industry, registered high rates of growth after 1929. Between 1929 and 1932 the rate of growth of manufacturing industry averaged over 15 percent a year, and total industry including mining and utilities grew at annual rates exceeding 13 percent. These high rates of growth despite the temporary contraction of rural demand can only be explained by the opportunities arising from the tariff reform and the severe curtailment of imports. Clearly, import-substituting industrialization was now in progress and this can be interpreted as being in line with the broad goals of the government. Protectionism was added to the policy of subsidization begun in the 1920s.

The Kemalist leaders, however, by the end of 1930 had become increasingly dissatisfied with economic and social conditions in the country. Despite rapid growth in manufacturing output, private industry was perceived by the leaders as primitive in character and doing little more than appropriating the rents brought about by the restriction of imports and protection of the domestic market. Moreover, the private sector had been actively subsidized during the 1920s. The political leadership, in the face of widespread popular discontent brought on by the severe impact of the Great Depression on the agricultural sector, leveled charges of corruption and profiteering at private industrialists. Thus 1930 became a year of experimentation with a multiparty system. The new Liberal party, founded at the urging of Atatürk by his closest political associates, received considerable support in various parts of the country and was instrumental in the outbreak of several antigovernment demonstrations. In response, the Kemalist leadership chose to bring a rapid end to this experiment and dissolved the party by the end of the year.

It was under these conditions that a search for a new strategy for economic development and radical reorientation of economic policies began. Etatism emerged as the solution. In May 1931, the third congress of the ruling Republican People's party accepted etatism as one of its basic principles. According to this philosophy, the party would continue to recognize the importance of private enterprise, but because of international developments, the state would have to participate in economic affairs in order to raise the level of national welfare in a short time. Since there were no concrete changes in government economic policies until the second half of 1932, that year marks the beginning of the etatist period.

Basic Features of Etatism

Although the term *etatism* probably was coined in Turkey, the underlying policy was by no means unusual as a response to the Great Depression. Establishment of a mixed economy with widespread government intervention and balance of payments controls was a common approach in many countries around the world. Some Latin American countries adopted similar policies at the same time as Turkey; there were pronounced tendencies toward autarky in several European countries; and the adoption of five-year planning in the Soviet Union to replace the liberalization under the communist government's New Economic Policy attracted great attention.

Under Turkish etatism, the existing foreign trade regime was continued through the 1930s, with high tariff rates, balance of payments controls, and—perhaps most important—quantity restrictions.

The government maintained a degree of control of domestic markets. It employed direct or indirect price support policies for a number of agricultural commodities. Prices of some industrial goods were controlled, as were wages in supported industries. And interest rates in financial transactions and banking activities were fixed (in principle) by central authorities.

The most conspicuous feature of the etatist policies was the emergence of the state as a major producer and investor. During the 1930s most of the state monopolies, which had been administered by private firms, were gradually transferred back to the public sector. Foreign-owned maritime transport companies and railroads, which (with compensation) had been nationalized in the Ottoman period, were transformed into state monopolies. The state assumed an important role in large-scale investment projects and as a producer in industry and mining. State economic enterprises (SEEs) became a key factor in the development process.

Five-year industrial plans were drawn up and implemented to coordinate public activities in this area. Preparatory work on the First Five-Year Industrial Plan started in late 1932 with the help of Soviet and American advisers. The plan, adopted in 1934, was a detailed list of the investment projects the public sector intended to pursue in industry, mining, and energy, not a comprehensive exercise in planning in the modern technical sense of the term. Financing was partly obtained abroad (in the Soviet Union and the United Kingdom). Despite a number of deviations, the targets of the First Five-Year Plan were declared to have been attained by 1938. A second five-year plan, the implementation of which started in 1938, was interrupted by the war.

The emergence of the state as leading producer and investor and principal agent in the industrialization and capital accumulation process was an important aspect of government economic policies during the 1930s. This policy was not formulated as an alternative to private capitalism. In the 1920s, the Kemalist leadership had committed itself to a strategy of development based on support of private enterprise. Unfavorable external and internal conditions that, with the Great Depression, developed after 1929 led to the adoption of the new strategy. The possibility of substituting state ownership generally for private ownership did not become a topic even for discussion among the high-level Kemalist leaders during the 1930s. More radical undercurrents did exist but never gained influence at the top, and the leadership seems ultimately to have viewed etatism as a necessary policy for protecting and bolstering private ownership and private enterprise, given the unfavorable external conditions for private enterprise, rather than as a strategy designed to eliminate private activities. The leadership was clearly sincere in its plans for a mixed economy.

Table 9-1. Growth of Gross Domestic Product, by Source of Demand, 1923–38

(percent)

Period	Average annual growth rate[a]	Source of expansion			
		Domestic demand	Exports	Import substitution[b]	Total
1923–25 to 1927–29	7.5	72.7	8.8	18.5	100
1927–29 to 1931–33	5.6	32.0	10.8	57.2	100
1931–33 to 1936–38	7.0	94.9	2.1	3.0	100

a. Measured on GDP at 1938 prices.
b. Calculated on the basis of initial import propensities of each period.
Source: Chenery, Robinson, and Syrquin (1986), chap. 5.

Achievements of Etatism, 1932–39

To come to grips with the achievements of etatism, table 9–1 breaks down GDP growth by expenditure source. In the recovery period 1923–25 to 1927–29, when the GDP growth rate was 7.5 percent, export expansion contributed about 9 percent of total growth against almost 19 percent for import substitution (calculated as the impact on imports of the decline in the propensity to import). Pent-up demand and depleted inventories from the war years may be part of the explanation of the relative importance of measured import substitution in the early years of the recovery period. The residual 73 percent was then backed by domestic consumption and investment demand. In the crisis period 1927–29 to 1931–33, marked by tariff reform and quantitative trade restrictions, there is a not unexpected, very high contribution of 57 percent from import substitution. Export expansion, surprisingly, contributed slightly more to growth than it had in the recovery period. Only 32 percent of the relatively impressive average growth rate of 5.6 percent was supported by domestic demand expansion.

In the etatist period, 1931–33 to 1936–38, the contributions from both export expansion and import substitution were negligible and the expansion of domestic demand supported most of the high GDP growth rate of 7.0 percent. This is surprising because a basic idea of etatism undoubtedly was industrialization based on import substitution. Table 9–2 turns to examination of the growth of GDP by producing sectors, showing the growth rates of individual sectors. Because a high growth rate in a small sector may mean little for national growth, table 9–2 also measures (as does table 6–3) the contribution of each sector to national growth by its share of the total absolute increase in real GDP. The share of a sector thus depends both on its size and on its own growth rate. Agriculture stands out as by far the most important contributor to growth, declining from a contribution of 53 percent during the recovery period to 43 percent in the crisis period but increasing again to 57 percent during the period of etatism. The contribution of manufacturing industry increased from 7 percent during the recovery period to almost 18 percent during the crisis years and then declined to 12 percent under etatism. The contribution of government increased from 7 percent during the recovery to 20 percent during the crisis but then declined to 6 percent under etatism, which was even lower than during the recovery.

As shown in table 9–2, the share of growth in the capital-intensive sectors increased considerably from 18 percent during the recovery years to 27 percent during the crisis years, while the contributions from sectors producing tradable and nontradable goods remained unchanged between these two periods. The roles of capital- and labor-intensive industries were, however, almost the same under etatism as during reconstruction while the contribution from sectors producing tradables increased substantially. Etatism apparently did not increase import substitution beyond what had happened during the crisis years as a consequence of tariff reform and quantitative import regulations; it did not lead to growth through the expansion of capital-intensive sectors or depend on industrialization as the main growth factor. These three surprises are all related to the fact that agriculture emerged as the leading contributor to growth under etatism. The decompositions do not, however, tell anything about capital intensity within individual sectors; they do not rule out the possibility that individual public investments and public enterprises were excessively capital intensive as many observers believe they were. However, etatism did not rely on expansion of GDP in government—that is, it did not rely on government employment.

Table 9–3 shows how gross investment developed. A striking feature of table 9–3 is the low, and if anything declining, share of gross investment from recovery through crisis to etatism. It is surprising that gross investment at a level of 8–12 percent of GDP should lead to GDP growth rates of 6–7 percent. This could only happen if sectors with very low capital intensity were leading the growth process, as was the case.

The share of public investment in total gross investment increased from recovery to etatism but the increase did not suffice to compensate for the decline in private investment, which fell to almost half from the recovery years to the years of crisis and never recovered before the outbreak of World War II. It goes without saying that public investment was favored under etatism. It does not necessarily follow that private investment was positively discriminated against, and developments seem rather to indicate flagging "animal spirits." If that really were the case, Turkish private entrepreneurs would certainly be no different from entrepreneurs in the rest of the world; the elimination of Greek and Arme-

Table 9-2. Growth Rates and Shares of Growth by Production Sector, 1923–38
(percent)

Category	1923–25 to 1927–29 Own growth rate	1923–25 to 1927–29 Share of growth	1927–29 to 1931–33 Own growth rate	1927–29 to 1931–33 Share of growth	1931–33 to 1936–38 Own growth rate	1931–33 to 1936–38 Share of growth
Gross domestic product	7.3	100	5.7	100	7.2	100
Production sector						
Agriculture	8.2	52.6	5.1	42.6	8.5	56.5
Mining	12.5	1.4	2.3	0.3	8.4	0.9
Manufacturing	6.1	6.7	11.7	17.5	8.5	11.8
Electricity	7.2	0.2	12.1	0.5	0.5	0.0
Construction	16.8	9.5	-4.6	-3.5	9.6	4.7
Trade	8.4	8.5	5.3	7.1	6.9	7.1
Transport and communications	10.2	5.2	4.3	2.9	7.7	4.0

Finance	23.1	3.5	8.1	2.2	3.6	0.8
Housing	2.1	4.3	2.5	5.6	2.1	3.1
Services	2.2	1.3	6.9	4.8	9.1	5.4
Government	6.1	6.8	13.0	19.9	4.2	5.6
Type of production						
Capital intensive[a]	4.7	17.8	5.9	26.8	5.6	20.0
Labor intensive	8.3	82.2	5.7	73.2	7.7	80.0
Type of goods						
Tradable[b]	7.9	60.7	6.1	60.4	8.5	69.3
Nontradable	6.5	39.3	5.3	39.6	5.4	30.7

At constant 1948 prices.
a. Mining, manufacturing, electricity, transport and communications, housing.
b. Agriculture, mining, and manufacturing.
Source: Bulutay, Tezel, and Yieldırım (1974).

Table 9-3. Gross Investment, 1927–46

Period	Share of GDP, at current prices (percent)			Public Investment				
	Total	Public	Private	At constant 1948 prices (millions of liras)	Share of total, at current prices (percent)			
					Agriculture	Industry	Transport and communications	Health, education, etc.
1927–29	12.3	3.2	9.1	171	1.4	5.5	87.1	6.0
1931–33	8.3	3.7	4.8	197	2.7	5.7	84.6	7.0
1936–38	10.0	4.5	5.4	365	5.7	25.3	57.5	11.7
1939–46	9.5	3.7	5.7	334	6.9	17.7	61.0	14.4

Source: Tezel (1975).

Table 9-4. Saving, Investment, and External Surplus as a Share of National Income, 1923-61

(percent)

Period	National gross saving	Gross fixed investment	External surplus[a]
1923–29, average[b]	5.7	9.8	−4.1
1930–33, average[b]	10.1	9.4	0.7
1934–38, average[b]	10.7	10.2	0.5
1939–46, average[b]	10.7	9.7	1.0
1947–48, average[b]	7.0	9.5	−1.5
1948–53, average[c]	12.9	15.1	−2.2
1954–61, average[c]	12.4	15.4	−3.0

a. Difference between national gross saving and gross fixed investment.
b. At constant 1938 prices.
c. At constant 1968 prices.
Source: Same as for table 9–2.

nian business communities, well known for their "animal spirits," may, however, have contributed.

Public investment in real terms more than doubled from 1927–29 to 1936–38. Before etatism, until 1931–33, public investment was strongly concentrated on transport and communications, railways playing a dominating role. With etatism, the composition of public investment shifted somewhat away from transport and communications toward industry, education and health, and agriculture, in that order. Even so, more than half of public investment went into transport and communications. It is safe to assume that investment in transport (railroads, in particular) mainly benefited agriculture. When direct investment in agriculture is added to investment in transport, investment benefiting agriculture tended to decline somewhat. Throughout the whole interwar period, however, public investment primarily supported agriculture. Even in the last years of interwar etatism, the government allocated only about 25 percent of public investment to industry against 50 percent to agriculture and railroads. In terms of actual investment, industry was never the primary concern of the government.

While substantial financing from abroad apparently took place during the period of recovery, from 1930 to 1938 the country persistently ran small surpluses in its current account. The estimates of national saving, investment, and external surpluses shown in table 9–4 are not complete, for investment does not include inventory changes, and national saving does not take into account foreign trade in services. The change from an estimated external deficit of 4 percent of GNI in 1923–29 to a surplus of

Table 9–5. Employment in the Industrial Sector, 1913, 1927, 1938, and 1950

(thousands)

Category	1913	1927	1938	1950
Manufacturing and utilities	300	389	538	635
Public sector	n.a.	87	61[a]	82
Private sector	n.a.	[b]	486[a]	553
Large-scale enterprise	n.a.	[b]	62	89
Small-scale enterprise	n.a.	[c]	210	226
Family enterprise	n.a.	302	214	238
Mining	15	19	23	45
Public sector	n.a.	n.a.	9	41
Private sector	n.a.	n.a.	14	4
Total industrial	315	408	561	680
Public sector	n.a.	n.a.	70	123
Private sector	n.a.	n.a.	500	557

n.a. = Not available.
a. Do not add to total in manufacturing and utilities.
b. Included in public sector.
c. Included in family enterprise.
Source: Tezel (1975).

about 0.5 percent in 1930–38 is, however, so pronounced that it probably reflects realities. After 1930 the low level of investment was fully financed domestically and even accompanied by a slight net repayment of debt. Domestic monetary and budgetary policies were conservative. Substantial budgetary deficits during the first years of the republic were reduced quickly and by 1928–29 were replaced by a small surplus. The crisis years 1929–30 to 1931–32 again saw budget deficits which did not, however, exceed 1.2 percent of GDP and from 1933 deficits were negligible. Inflationary financing was never a policy of interwar etatism (Hershlag 1968, chaps. 4, 9).

Industrial Growth

The growth rate of manufacturing industry was high during the 1930s and its share in GDP increased from 8.4 percent in 1927–29 to 13.4 percent in 1937–39. The impact on employment was modest, however.

The industrial censuses show that all industries (including mining and utilities) employed 561,000 workers in 1938, or about 6 percent of the total labor force and about one-fourth of the nonagricultural labor force (table 9–5). From 1927 to 1938, the annual rate of increase in the industrial labor force was only 2.9 percent, slightly above the 2.1 percent rate of population growth. This fact implies that productivity must have increased considerably. At constant 1948 prices, GDP in total industry increased by 8.8 percent annually. Labor productivity should accordingly have increased by about 6 percent annually. In itself this looks impressive, and the increase in labor productivity may have been a consequence of high capital intensity. Government financing at low interest rates, low tariff rates for machinery and equipment, and (after 1930) possibly an overvalued currency with unrestricted imports of machinery and equipment should all have led in that direction. This may have been a rational policy for a country with an abundance of land and a relative scarcity of labor.

Small-scale and family enterprises accounted for 78 percent of all employment in manufacturing and utilities in 1927, and by 1938 for 79 percent. Employment did not grow faster in large-scale enterprises than in small-scale enterprises—the informal sector. In this sense the structure of industry did not really change as a consequence of the industrialization efforts under etatism. What happened was mainly that a larger share of large-scale enterprises was in the public sector in 1938 than in 1927. Thus it might seem that labor-intensive, private, large-scale industries were replaced by capital-intensive, public, large-scale industries, the former disappearing with the Great Depression, the latter surviving as infant industries with government financing. From a long-term point of view such a policy could have been rational.

Agriculture

The performance of agriculture during the 1930s is in a way more impressive than that of industry. The measured growth rates for 1927–29 to 1937–39 were 6.2 percent for agriculture and 10.0 percent for industry. Industry, however, was a much smaller sector than agriculture, accounting for 9.5 percent against 49.8 percent of the total GDP, and relative prices moved strongly against agriculture and in favor of industry. The terms of trade of agriculture compared to industry, measured by the ratio of the implicit deflators of agriculture and industry, deteriorated by 19 percent from 1927–29 to 1936–38 while the external terms of trade deteriorated by 23 percent (table 9–6).

To understand the relatively high growth rate obtained in agriculture despite the unfavorable relative price developments, a breakdown of agricultural growth by area and yield is illuminating. Table 9–7 indicates that while yields (measured by GDP per hectare) increased steadily by about 2.5 percent annually throughout the period, the cultivated area (sown plus fallow land) increased by 2.5 percent annually during the crisis years 1927–29 to 1931–33 and then accelerated to almost 6 percent under etatist policies in 1931–33 to 1936–38. The size of the agricultural

Table 9-6. Indexes of External and Internal Terms of Trade, Selected Periods, 1923-84

(1938 = 100)

| Period | Implicit GDP deflator | | | Foreign-trade prices[a] | | |
	Agri- culture	Manufac- turing	Ratio of agriculture to manufacturing	Export	Import	Ratio of export to import
1923-25	175.3	166.3	105.1	189.0	117.7	160.6
1927-29	188.7	158.7	117.1	170.3	131.0	130.0
1931-33	100.0	90.0	111.7	91.3	103.3	88.4
1936-38	99.3	105.2	94.6	103.7	103.3	100.4
1943-45	552.3	346.7	159.3	353.0	450.0	78.4
1948-50	501.0	419.0	119.6	434.0	346.0	125.4
1951-55	564.6	451.1	125.2	530.0	293.5	180.6
1957-59	1,104.4	838.0	131.8	472.7	346.0	136.6
1960-64	1,476.4	1,122.9	131.5	1,294.8	1,252.9	103.3
1965-69	1,863.9	1,357.6	137.3	1,435.1	1,118.9	128.3
1970-74	3,630.9	2,217.9	163.7	2,747.1	2,380.7	115.4
1975-79	11,536.1	7,111.8	162.2	7,728.5	8,263.3	93.5
1980-84	75,060.4	66,397.5	113.1	86,433.9	124,678.1	69.3

a. In lira.
Source: Bulutay, Tezel, and Yıeldırım (1974); World Bank data.

labor force and its growth rate can only be conjectured; from the end of hostilities in 1923 the share of agriculture in total employment appears to have remained roughly constant through the interwar period. If so, the agricultural labor force may have grown by slightly more than 2 percent annually during the interwar period. Productivity of labor in agriculture should thus have grown by about 3 percent annually during the crisis years and by no less than 6.5 percent under etatism, or slightly more than productivity in industry. Should wages in agriculture have increased correspondingly, that would be the rationale for increased capital intensity in industry.

There is little to explain the low but steady increase in yields. Mechanization, in any case of little importance, decreased and chemical fertilizers were hardly used until after World War II. A certain shift toward industrial cash crops—cotton and tobacco—did take place, however. Several factors, however, help to explain the strong increase in cultivated area, over and above the possible effects of the abolition of the tithe (discussed in chapter 8).

Population pressure may have forced the extensive margin of production further out on less productive lands with lower fertility or inferior

Table 9-7. Growth of Agricultural GDP, Area, and Yield, Selected Periods, 1927–83

Period	GDP[a] Index (1927–29 = 100)	GDP[a] Growth rate (percent)[c]	Crop area[d] Index (1927–29 = 100)	Crop area[d] Growth rate (percent)[c]	Sown area (percent)	Total[e] Index (1936–38 = 147.6)	Yield[b] Index (1927–29 = 100)	Yield[b] Growth rate (percent)[c]
1927–29	100	n.a.	100	n.a.	n.a.	n.a.	100	n.a.
1931–33	122.1	5.1	110.7	2.6	n.a.	n.a.	110.3	2.5
1936–38	183.5	8.5	147.6	5.9	65.9	147.6	124.3	2.4
1938–40	191.3	2.1	165.5	5.9	65.8	n.a.	115.6	−3.6
1943–45	143.7	−5.6	155.3	−1.3	63.0	n.a.	92.5	−4.4
1948–50	187.7	5.5	169.5	1.8	67.9	169.5	110.7	3.7
1951–53	244.3	9.2	209.1	7.3	68.8	206.8	116.8	1.8
1961–63	356.2	3.8	285.5	3.1	65.0	281.2	124.8	0.7
1977–79	575.8	3.0	300.9	0.3	66.9	310.3	191.4	2.7
1981–83	624.4	2.0	290.7	−0.9	71.1	300.8	214.8	2.9
1927–29 to 1961–63	—	3.8	—	3.1	—	—	—	0.7
1961–63 to 1981–83	—	2.8	—	0.1	—	—	—	2.8

n.a. = Not available.

— = Not applicable.

a. Before 1948 at constant 1948 factor costs; after 1948 at constant 1968 factor costs, chained in 1948.

b. Defined as GDP per hectare of crop area.

c. Annually, compound, since last three-year period.

d. Sown plus fallow land.

e. Including vineyards, vegetable gardens, orchards, and olive groves.

Source: Bulutay, Tezel, and Yıldırım (1974); Tezel (1975). Turkey, SIS, *Statistical Yearbook*; World Bank data.

location, as classical models suggest. This should, incidentally, tend to lower yield. Unemployed urban workers may have moved back into agriculture and accelerated the increase in the rural labor force. Agricultural labor should in that case have suffered a decline in real wages, with distribution shifted in favor of land or labor (Samuelson 1959, pp. 1–35).

While there was no redistribution of land through land reform (the change in ownership of land belonging to the rural Greek and Armenian population was a different matter about which little is known), the government distributed public, uncultivated land through grants to landless laborers and refugees and exchange population. About 6 percent of all land cultivated around 1936 had been acquired since independence by private agriculture in this way, most of it in relatively small lots (Hershlag 1968, p. 40). These land grants may have accounted for about 20 percent of the increase in the cultivated area during the 1920s and 1930s. It has been claimed that land was in this way transferred from nomadic, animal production to cultivation and thus did not fully represent a net increase in productive lands (Hirsch 1970), but quantification appears to be impossible and ecological effects may have made nomadic production positively harmful.

Perhaps most important, the transport system expanded, with government investment in roads and railways. To the extent that the expansion opened up the interior for modern commercial agriculture, investment in transport should be considered agricultural and taken into account as increased capital intensity, partly explaining the increase in yield and labor productivity.

Direct public investment in agriculture, for reclamation, irrigation, drainage, and similar purposes, was very modest. In 1936–38 it accounted for about 6 percent of all public investment (table 9–3). A special Agricultural Bank that had been established in 1899 to supply agriculture with credit at low interest rates but had made only a limited number of loans was now activated. The Agricultural Bank was used to finance government support of agricultural prices, which was provided through the Central Office of Soil Produce established in 1932. Customs duties on wheat were increased and wheat prices were supported through purchases by the Office of Soil Produce. Prices on industrial cash crops such as cotton and tobacco were supported through purchases made by state enterprises. It is not clear to what extent estimated terms of trade for agriculture take into account such price support. Price support was, however, relatively modest in the 1930s.

With population pressure a positive factor and deterioration in agricultural terms of trade a negative factor, and both of unknown effect, it is difficult to gauge the impact of government policies on the expansion of the cultivated area but probably it was considerable. Etatist development policy appears to have emphasized agriculture rather than industry and it may have brought about a net increase in real agricultural wages.

The Impact and Aftermath of World War II

Against the background of Turkey's heavy human and economic losses in World War I and its aftermath, the Kemalist leadership early decided that at all costs it should remain neutral in a future world war. Adhering to this policy, Turkey maintained its neutrality during World War II but the economic costs were high. Full-scale mobilization throughout the war required the drafting of large numbers of men from all sectors and requisition of animals from agriculture, which when combined with shortages of raw materials dramatically reduced production. From 1939 to 1945 (a very bad crop year) real value added in agriculture is estimated to have declined by 42 percent and in manufacturing by no less than 50 percent but the estimates may be biased downward (the period has not been studied in much detail). Total GDP declined somewhat less, by 37 percent. The public sector is estimated to have declined by 45 percent. This is not plausible in a country under mobilization but, under the circumstances, value added in the expanding military sector is hardly commensurate with that in civilian production. The whole notion of GDP as an aggregate indicator of welfare crumbles under conditions of war or total mobilization. The effect of the reduction of resources available for civilian production was apparently compounded by the adoption of policies that reduced incentives to produce—for example, forced delivery of agricultural products at low prices and a 10 percent tax on soil products (which, however, under the conditions of war and limited foreign trade may have been shifted on to the urban population). The infamous capital levy (*varlık*) that discriminated against non-Muslims rested mainly on urban groups (Birge 1944, p. 207).

With military considerations taking the upper hand, civilian development efforts were reduced or abrogated during the war. Estimated gross investment nonetheless held up remarkably well both as a share of GDP and in absolute, real terms (table 9–3) but it stands to reason that investment must have been somewhat reoriented to satisfy military demands. National saving increased and the country ran a substantial surplus of saving over investment with an external surplus and accumulation of foreign exchange reserves. Inventory depletions, however, have not been taken into account in the national accounts estimates. Saving was probably forced on the population partly through commodity shortages combined with price controls, partly through inflationary profits. Budget deficits were financed through the central bank, which resulted in strong inflation. From 1939 to 1945, wholesale prices increased by 327 percent and the cost of living in Istanbul by 253 percent.

With better crops, demobilization, and normalization of foreign trade, production recovered sharply in 1946 but not until 1951 did total GDP per capita reach prewar levels. The decline in cultivated area and yields in agriculture was recovered in 1948, but with a population increase of about 25 percent, real agricultural recovery did not occur until 1952. The recovery overlaps with the change of the political system from one-party rule to democracy in 1950 (discussed in chapter 10).

Distributional Consequences

Little can be said about the impact of etatism on income distribution. No information is available about either the functional or the size distribution of income during the interwar period. Nor is much known about the distribution of labor force or of population by sector, and even estimates of real income per capita by agriculture and nonagriculture are little more than conjectures. Even the choice of period is difficult. Concentrating on a single year makes results highly dependent on annual crop fluctuations and price volatility. Three-year averages circumvent this problem. Even from a distributional point of view there is much to be said in favor of operating with permanent income concepts, and a three-year average may be a reasonable proxy. With imperfect credit markets, liquidity problems may, however, be uppermost for low-income earners; for indebted small peasants, for instance, annual vagaries of crops and prices may take on crucial importance.

In a comparison of the calendar years 1929 and 1932, there was a very strong shift in distribution against agriculture. When production and price effects are combined, the annual decline in GNI per capita for the country was 3–4 percent. Agricultural production declined by about 6 percent annually and by perhaps 8 percent per capita. Adding terms of trade effects, the annual decline in real per capita income in agriculture may have been 12–13 percent. The shift against agriculture as compared to nonagriculture must have been strong.

Three-year averages for the period 1927–29 to 1931–33 indicate an increase of about 2 percent annually in GNI per capita for the country, with approximate stagnation for agriculture. Even so there must have been a substantial sectoral shift against agriculture as compared with nonagriculture.

Beyond these statements everything becomes conjecture. Assuming, for instance, that agricultural population and labor force remained a constant proportion of total population and labor force from 1927 to 1950, the first year for which the proportion is known, the Kuznets *K*s presented in table 6–13 suggest a strong relative decline in agricultural income per capita for the sectoral population, which again possibly suggests a more inequitable distribution from 1927 to 1935 with a reversal from 1935 to 1950.

Within agriculture the largest losses in relative as well as absolute terms during the Great Depression may have been suffered by large landowners producing for both the domestic and the export market. In contrast, peasants with small subsistence holdings may have seen their income increase and any losses they suffered must have been more limited since they marketed a smaller share of their output than did large landowners. As elsewhere in the world, indebted farmers (who were not necessarily small farmers) suffered badly through an increased real debt burden. With the wartime inflation the situation was sharply reversed.

In urban areas, civil servants may have gained in real income during the Great Depression but lost during wartime. For other urban groups, little solid information is available. Tax reform probably tended to make income distribution after tax more equitable. A new income tax law passed in 1934 to replace the 1925 law apparently never became effective. The law was amended in 1936–37; exemptions were lowered and progression introduced. Taxation of corporate income was widened. In view of evasion and the small amounts collected as well as the large size of the nontaxed population, the effects on distribution were probably insignificant.

10 Early Democracy and Its Failure, 1950–61

By 1946 many social groups had become dissatisfied with the Kemalist single-party regime. This was also the time when a new international order was established in the West under the leadership of the United States. Etatism came under pressure from all directions. As a result, the second half of the 1940s was characterized by a search of government and opposition alike for new economic strategies and policies.

Domestically, large segments of both the rural and the urban population had been hard hit by mobilization, the decline in production and consumption, and the redistribution of income during the years of World War II. To some extent these hardships ended when the war ended but popular dissatisfaction lingered. The political opposition to the Republican People's party, the single party in power, was mainly organized in the new Democrat party founded by former members of the Republican party (Adnan Menderes, Celal Bayār, and others) and representatives of landowners, financiers, and merchants. The Democrat party immediately gained broad popular support. Both government and organized opposition recognized that the agricultural potential of the country remained poorly utilized. In addition, powerful urban groups sought to replace etatism with policies that provided better opportunities for private entrepreneurship. A strategy emphasizing agriculture and liberalization was thus bound to become popular.

External influences were also important in shaping the new policies. Soviet threats did much to solidify public opinion in favor of the West. The aid provided by the Marshall Plan and NATO to Turkey from 1947–48 for reconstruction, development, and military purposes did not come without strings. Foreign experts and official missions arrived to express a need for liberalization. For example, a private group of American experts led by M. W. Thornburg, issued a report arguing for the dismantling of many of the etatist manufacturing establishments, among them the country's only iron and steel complex; greater emphasis on private enterprise; encouragement of foreign capital; a more liberal foreign exchange and trade regime; and greater reliance on agricultural development. The main outside impact on Turkey, however, came from the Organisation for European Economic Cooperation (OEEC) (later the OECD).

The intentions of the Kemalist leadership—now in the hands of Atatürk's old first lieutenant, İsmet İnönü—to eventually adopt a multiparty electoral system made the government both sensitive to popular demands and responsive to criticism. As a result of internal and external pressure and influence, the Kemalist government began to move in the direction of greater reliance on private initiative and agriculture, playing down the emphasis on etatism and public sector industry. A third five-year plan was prepared during the summer of 1946 but was shelved the following year. The Republican party even offered a new definition of etatism, still reserving for the public sector such activities as utilities, railroads, mining, and heavy and military industry, yet visualizing a transfer of all other public enterprises to the private sector. In 1946 the multiparty system was officially recognized and free elections were finally held in 1950.

The economic policies of Menderes's Democrat party, which came to power after the elections of 1950, aimed at carrying reform even further. Yet considering the very substantial revisions of the ideology of etatism, from a development point of view the change of regime in 1950 stands out as a matter of degree more than of kind. The Democrat party may have emphasized agricultural development more strongly, but the Kemalists had definitely been positive to agricultural development since the 1930s. The liberalization of trade with imports of large quantities of consumer goods pursued by Menderes in the early 1950s may have gone further than the Kemalists would have been prepared to go if they had been in government. Imports had, however, increased strongly before 1950 with a substantial foreign deficit the result, although the overriding reason for the increase may have been the need for filling inventories after the war. Both Kemalists and Democrats had at their disposal substantial foreign exchange reserves accumulated during the war years and the terms of trade had improved from 1947, long before unusually favorable international market conditions emerged with the Korean War boom. After the austerity years of World War II any government, backed by ample exchange reserves and faced with the need of appealing to voters, would probably have pursued a policy of trade liberalization. As a member of the OEEC, Turkey was, moreover, under obligation to liberalize foreign trade.

It should be recalled also that during the period of liberalization, 1950–53, the tariff structure that the Kemalists had set up remained unchanged and financing at low interest rates through the state banks continued. During the 1930s, import of capital goods had been outside the import license system. The main shift away from the Kemalist import-substitution system was thus the expansion of imports of consumer goods. With the simultaneous expansion of domestic demand, this may not have shifted domestic demand away from existing domestic output. When, on the other hand, at the end of 1953 exchange reserves were exhausted, import licensing was reintroduced or tightened and it soon included capital goods. Consequently, from 1954 the de facto import-substitution policy of the Democrats went beyond that of the Kemalists during the 1930s. Finally, it should be emphasized that the liberalization lasted only three years, too short a period for the productive structure of a country to be radically changed.

Comparison of Kemalist and Democrat investment policies does not indicate any dramatic change in strategy either. Public investment amounted to about half the total in both the 1930s and the 1950s after having been down to about one-third during the war years. Investment thus did not shift in favor of the private sector under Democrat rule. The share of agriculture in public investment increased from about 6 percent in 1936–38 and 7 percent during the war to about 13 percent in 1950–58, with the share of industry increasing from 25 percent to 35 percent. Investment in transport and communications declined from 57.5 percent in 1936–38 to 37 percent in 1950–58 but since during the 1930s transport investment had to a large extent favored agriculture, there is really nothing in the pattern of public investment to indicate any dramatic change in the relative emphasis on agriculture and industry. The composition of private investment in the 1930s is not known but may in the 1950s have shifted in favor of agriculture. During 1950–58 about 30 percent of private investment was in agriculture. This was partly a result of the policy of mechanization (discussed below) but was in any case a consensus policy, initiated under the Kemalists with Marshall Plan aid. The difference in emphasis on agriculture was thus in many ways little more than rhetoric aimed at the rural electorate. The most important difference may have been in agricultural price policies.

Estimates of GDP make it clear that the years from 1944–46 to 1951–53 were a period of postwar recovery of both agricultural and industrial production, like those from 1923 to 1929. After World War II, GDP increased at a rate of 8.7 percent, industry growing 9.7 percent and agriculture 9.4 percent. The recovery would probably have taken place whatever regime was in power. After 1951–53 and despite the stabilization recession during the late 1950s, industry continued growing rapidly at a rate of 8.5 percent until 1961–63; agricultural growth slowed to 2.7 percent and agriculture lost its role as a leading growth sector. It is ironical that while agriculture contributed more than half of the growth in total GDP that took place under etatism from 1931–33 to 1936–38, with industry contributing only 13 percent (table 9–2), during the period 1951–53 to 1961–63 under Menderes and the following political clean-up with the emphasis on agriculture, agriculture and industry both contributed a little less than one-quarter of total GDP growth. A careful reevaluation of agricultural growth in this period is clearly in order.

Agricultural and Development Strategy, 1946-60

The change in long-term trends in Turkish agriculture in the 1950s is difficult to define because of the impact of both World War II and fluctuating weather conditions. Figure 6-1 indicates a clear break in the growth of cultivated area around 1956. Yields (defined in terms of GDP per hectare) tended to be stagnant before the 1950s and steadily increased thereafter, but weather conditions in the 1950s make the timing of the change in the trend for yields doubtful. Turkey experienced very favorable weather in the early 1950s, then several years of mediocre weather, and favorable weather once again in 1959 and 1960. The three-year moving averages indicate a rapid increase in yields from 1944-46 to 1951-53—not surprisingly, of course, as a recovery after the war years—with a decline in yields from 1951-53 to 1955-57 and then again a rapid increase to 1958-60. Acreage and yield developments—the latter obviously dependent on the former as the cultivated margin was pushed outward—operated together to produce a constant growth trend in agricultural GDP from 1951 to 1985, with the late 1930s almost exactly on this trend.

When weather conditions and long-term trends—the former random disturbances, the latter perhaps little more than statistical artifacts—are ignored, it is clear that in the late 1940s and the 1950s strong government intervention in agriculture cut across the change of political regime. The rapid increase in crop area was partly a matter of deliberate government policy. The Land Distribution Law of 1946 which included a provision for redistribution of land from large to small owners was not used for that purpose but rather to distribute publicly owned land and communal pasture to smallholders and landless farm workers. This, in fact, was nothing but a continuation on a larger scale of etatist policy well established between the wars. From 1947 to 1954 almost 0.7 million hectares of farmland and 0.45 million hectares of communal pasture were distributed among 142,000 rural families, many of them refugees from Bulgaria. An additional 1 million hectares of public farmland and 1 million hectares of communal pastureland were distributed from 1954 to 1959. The total distributed from these sources accounts for about one-third of the increase in the cultivated area from 1947 to 1959, and it was clearly a matter of distributing small allotments to smallholders.

It is puzzling, though, that while the cultivated area stopped increasing from around 1956, at which time the area of grassland and pastures stopped declining, the distribution of both agricultural land and pastureland continued at unbroken speed until 1960, when distribution of agricultural land dropped to almost nothing and distribution of pasture-land increased. It is not obvious why the increase in crop and cultivated areas should come to a stop in 1956 while distribution continued (Hershlag 1968, table 44; Turkey, *Statistical Yearbook*).

Both the Republican and the Democrat party emphasized mechanization of agriculture and used Marshall Plan aid for financing import of agricultural machinery and tractors. The number of tractors increased from about 1,000 in 1946 to 17,000 in 1950 and almost 42,000 at the end of the 1950s. The tractors were purchased partly on favorable credit terms through the Agricultural Bank by medium and large holders who had enough collateral to expand their area under cultivation rapidly. It is estimated that while one pair of oxen could cultivate 5–10 hectares in a year, a tractor could handle 75 hectares, and it is believed that tractors were a profitable private investment. The increase in the number of tractors, however, stopped around 1957 (see figure 6–1) and then declined slightly. Not until 1963 did the number again increase strongly. Either government credit or import licensing may have influenced the extensive expansion and caused its abrupt termination in 1956. Probably the tightening of import licensing in 1957–58 was responsible.

The government thus pursued two complementary policies for extensive expansion from the end of the war to the end of the 1950s. Peasants with smallholdings benefited from the land distribution policy, and farmers with larger holdings benefited from the purchase of tractors financed by state bank credit at low interest rates. The tractors were used by owners on their own holdings and also rented to smallholders who paid for their use by crop sharing; larger holders thus emerged as share croppers for small owners and both they and smallholders benefited from the arrangement.

Population pressure and relative price developments might explain the extensive expansion of agriculture. The national labor force increased by 21 percent from 1950 to 1960, in absolute terms an increase by 2,270,000; 768,000 went into agriculture, increasing the agricultural labor force by 9 percent; the remaining 1,502,000 increased the non-agricultural labor force by 86 percent. The 1950s thus saw a large migration of rural workers to urban areas. It is not clear whether the process was dominated by push or pull factors. Tractorization did lead to substitution of capital for labor in agriculture and it is not inconceivable that part of the natural increase of the agricultural labor force was pushed into nonagricultural occupations. The consensus seems to be, however, that urban pull dominated but this remains an uncertain conjecture and push may have changed to pull with the change in import policy and the decrease in tractor purchases. No wage or unemployment data are available that might help in solving the problem.

Both external and internal terms of trade moved strongly in favor of agriculture from the interwar years to the postwar years (see table 9–6).

With the Korean War boom the external terms of trade first moved strongly in favor of and thereafter against the country. The improvement from 1948–50 to 1951–53 was 44 percent and in spite of a deterioration by 24 percent in the external terms of trade in 1957–59 they were still 9 percent above 1948–50. The internal terms of trade, when measured by the ratio between the implicit deflators for agriculture and manufacturing industry, improved by only 5 percent from 1948–50 to 1951–53, and by another 5 percent to 1957–59. The total improvement in the internal terms of trade from 1948–50 to 1957–59 amounted to 10 percent, slightly more than the improvement of the external terms of trade. It would appear then that, in terms of relative prices, agriculture did relatively well throughout the 1950s and while price developments may have served to speed up the extensive expansion during the first half of the 1950s, there is nothing here to explain why the expansion of the crop and cultivated areas suddenly stopped in 1956.

A comparison of external and internal terms of trade (table 9–6) in the 1930s with those in the postwar years indicates an interesting similarity between the two periods. From 1927–29 to 1931–33 the external terms of trade deteriorated by 32 percent, with the internal terms of trade deteriorating by only 4 percent. From 1931–33 to 1936–38 the external terms of trade improved by 14 percent, with the internal terms of trade deteriorating further by 15 percent. Thus in 1936–38 external and internal terms of trade had deteriorated by 23 percent and 19 percent, respectively, compared with 1927–29. Over the long term the internal terms of trade adjusted almost fully to the external terms of trade, both in the 1930s and in the 1950s, after lagging far behind in the short term. Is this a normal phenomenon of price rigidity or was it in both cases a consequence of government intervention, sheltering agriculture and seeking to delay domestic price adjustment?

Behind the improvement of the internal terms of trade despite the deterioration in the external terms of trade from 1951–53 to 1957–59 are the government's price support policies, particularly through purchases by the Office of Soil Produce. The government's support purchases, directly financed by the Agricultural Bank and indirectly by the central bank, thus contributed strongly to the inflation during the second half of the 1950s. In itself, however, the inflation should have been beneficial to indebted farmers, and by lowering real interest rates it should have favored investment in agriculture.

Everything considered, it would seem that while Turkey in the 1950s was beginning to approach the extensive limits of profitable cultivation, it was the foreign exchange crisis with tightening import licensing that suddenly stopped the expansion of the stock of tractors and, hence, the increase in crop area in 1956. Most probably that would have happened a few years later. In 1956, however, all other factors pointed to continued expansion of the cultivated area.

The weak point in agricultural development during the 1950s was clearly the near stagnation of yields. Changing weather conditions with the fallow land system and the expansion of the area under cultivation make it difficult to gauge the change in yields, all things being equal. From 1948–50 to 1951–53 yields measured as GDP per hectare of cultivated land increased by 0.4 percent annually. From 1951–53 to 1961–63 yields increased by 0.7 percent annually. This was poor performance. A strategy of intensive cultivation of existing farmlands to increase yields plus expansion of new areas could have made agricultural growth continue to predominate throughout the 1950s. Both Kemalists and Democrats failed to see this possibility. Fertilizer input began to increase modestly during the 1950s but green revolution continued to belong to the future, not because the technology was unknown but because politicians and administrators were committed to extensive expansion which came to an abrupt end with the foreign exchange crisis. Irrigation did not rank high on the priority list and advisers correctly tended to recommend against large-scale and for small-scale irrigation projects. Certain large irrigation projects were undertaken but returns were disappointing and slow to come.

Inflation and the Balance of Payments Crisis

The decade after the introduction of parliamentary democracy was characterized by strong inflation, leading finally to a payments crisis, a stabilization program after 1958, and military rule in 1960–61. It has been claimed that central bank financing of the deficits of state economic enterprises (SEEs), including the agricultural price support programs of the Office of Soil Produce and the cooperatives, was in the main responsible for the inflation (Fry 1972; Krueger 1974). This does not seem to be the case, however. Credit extended from the central bank to government and the SEEs (including the Soil Produce Office) did increase strongly during 1950–58 but the main culprit was credit extended from deposit banks to the private sector, including the cooperatives (see table 10–1).

Separation of government from SEE claims is a semantic or bookkeeping device. The government was clearly responsible for the operations of the SEEs. If the government and the SEE claims in table 10–1 are lumped together, the increase in the net claim of the whole banking system on the public sector contributes less than one-fifth of the increase in money supply (as defined by the IMF). Four-fifths was generated through credit extended to the private sector, including the cooperatives. Such credit would include financing of residential construction and mechanization of agriculture which appears to have dominated private fixed investment during the 1950s (Hershlag 1968, table 23).

Table 10-1. Net Changes in Assets and Liabilities of Banking System, 1950–58 and 1958–60
(billions of lira)

| | 1950–58 | | | | 1958–60 | | | |
| | Central bank | | Banking System[a] | | Central bank | | Banking System[a] | |
Changes in	Assets	Liabilities	Assets	Liabilities	Assets	Liabilities	Assets	Liabilities
Net claims on								
Rest of world		0.5		0.4	0.2		0.2	
Government	0.9		0.8		0.6		-0.4	
State economic enterprises[b]	1.3		1.3		0.0		0.0	
Banks	3.2				0.8			
Private sector		0.8	4.4			0.3	2.3	
Money and quasi money[c]		4.1[d]		6.0		1.4[d]		2.2
Total[e]	5.4	5.4	6.5	6.4	1.6	1.7	2.1	2.2

a. Included in *International Financial Statistics*, Monetary Survey, items 31n–351.
b. Including the Office of Soil Produce (cooperatives, not important, included in private sector).
c. As defined by the IMF.
d. Currency in circulation outside of banks.
e. Assets may not equal liabilities because of rounding.
Source: IMF, *International Financial Statistics*.

While expansion of credit through the banking system thus may have served to finance fixed investment and inventories in the private sector much more than price support for agricultural products and deficits in the SEEs, the result in relation to money supply and the balance of payments would have been unchanged. Thanks to the expansion of domestic demand and the deteriorating external terms of trade with liberalization of trade, exchange reserves were exhausted in 1953 and at the end of the year severe balance of payments restrictions were imposed. A vicious circle was established with price controls to keep down the cost of living, increasing agricultural support prices, increasing SEE deficits to be financed through further credit expansion with increasing inflation. With tightened licensing of both exports and imports went import surcharges and deposits and export premiums that amounted to a complex system of multiple exchange rates. Minimum export prices that exceeded world market prices frequently meant that exports could only be undertaken through the increasingly important bilateral agreements with countries that would compensate themselves through high prices on exports to Turkey and resale of the Turkish exports at world market prices to hard-currency countries. Continuous revisions, increasing complexity, and irrationality finally brought an end to the system in 1958, when foreign financing was no longer forthcoming and issuing of import licenses was abrogated (Krueger 1974, chap. 2, describes the process and its collapse).

The degree of overvaluation of the lira at the official exchange rates is indicated in the figures in chapter 11. They show how the real effective exchange rate (REER) steadily appreciated from about 1935 through World War II to 1950 and, after a short period of slight real depreciation from 1950 to 1954, entered a period of six years of accelerating appreciation. The official U.S. dollar rate was kept constant from 1948 to 1960 and the nominal effective exchange rate (NEER) was, with some fluctuations, approximately constant from 1949 to 1959. The real appreciation was entirely a consequence of the relatively strong, accelerating inflation in Turkey (figure 11–4) as compared with her trade partners. However, considering the import surcharges and export premiums, the appreciation of the lira from 1954 to 1959 was in reality less than it appears to be in figure 11–2, particularly for imports.

Devaluation and Stabilization

The depreciation, embarked on in August 1958, became in the same way a complex process, not to be finalized until 1961. The official parity rate was not altered in August 1958. An exchange tax of LT6.22 was imposed on all imports, invisibles, and capital transactions, which effectively increased the dollar rate from LT2.80 to LT9.02. On the export side no such unification of the exchange rate occurred in 1958. The premiums awarded to exports varied from LT2.10 for chrome, copper, tobacco, and opium to LT2.80 for dried fruits. The system thus continued to discriminate relatively against exports. The premiums were subsequently raised but the exchange rate did not become uniform until the official rate was increased from LT2.80 to LT9.00 per dollar in August 1960. Calculated on the official exchange rates, the depreciation of the REER from 1959 to 1961 amounted to 70.1 percent. The rationale for the gradual change of the exchange rate on the export side appears to have been the different lags in the (conjectured) supply responses for different export commodities but status considerations with political maneuvers and unwillingness to face the fact that a devaluation of the lira had in effect taken place are probably part of the explanation.

In addition to the devaluation and unification of the lira, the stabilization program included consolidation and rescheduling of Turkey's foreign debt, with Turkey agreeing not to rely on suppliers for credit. Additional massive credit came from international lenders, including the IMF and the OEEC as well as the United States; and ceilings were placed on central bank and commercial bank credit as well as on budget deficits. The program also included import liberalization, changes in the export regime, and removal of price controls and increases in SEE prices.

The stabilization measures were implemented with increasing determination, particularly after the military takeover in 1960, triggered in part by suspicion about the Democrat government's sincerity in implementing them. Table 10–1 shows how the substantial amounts of credit extended to government and the SEEs during 1951–58 were reversed during 1958–60 while credit extended to the private sector was cut substantially in real terms. The increase in money supply for the same periods was cut to about one-third, corresponding to a decline in the growth rate of money supply from 20 percent annually in 1950–59 to 9 percent during 1959–61.

The central government budget, which had been in the red during most of the 1950s, showed substantial surpluses in 1960 and 1961. As a result consumer prices, which had increased by 10 percent annually from 1950 to 1957 and accelerated to 20 percent in 1958 and 23 percent in 1959, were virtually unchanged from 1959 to 1961. That the official consumer price index underestimates the price increases during the 1950s, since it does not consider black market prices, is another matter. The price stabilization during 1960–61 is real enough. It was obtained at a high cost, however. Faced with the usual problem of crop fluctuations, the best measure of the short-term impact of the stabilization measures on economic activity may be the sum of real GDP in industry and construction, shown in table 10–2. It increased by 11 percent annually from 1950 to 1957, declined slightly in 1958, and did not increase more than 0.9 percent annually from 1957 to 1960. Not until 1961 did production in industry plus construction start growing significantly. For almost four

Table 10–2. Macroeconomic Indicators of Stabilization Program of 1958–60

Item	1950	1957	1958	1959	1960	1961
Money supply index (1950=100)[a]	100	411	433	511	556	611
Central government surplus (percent of GNI)[b]	–0.5	–0.4	–0.2	–0.2	1.0	0.5
Consumer price index (1950=100)	100	189	227	279	282	284
Index of GDP in industry and construction (1950=100)[c]	100	211.9	209.1	213.3	217.7	235.2
Balance of trade (millions of dollars)	–47.8	–51.9	–67.9	–116.2	–147.5	–160.5

a. Money and quasi money, IMF definition.
b. Not including state economic enterprises and annexed budgets.
c. At constant 1968 prices.
Source: IMF, International Financial Statistics; Krueger (1974) tables II.4 and IV.1; World Bank data.

years the economy thus plunged into recession as a consequence of the stabilization program. The deficit in the balance of trade, nonetheless, increased substantially during the years of stabilization. The stabilization program of 1958–60 thus cannot possibly be called successful.

Taxation, Social Security, and Income Distribution

One of several quantitative indicators of the distribution of income in the 1950s is the Kuznets K which declined from 5.86 in 1950 to 4.59 in 1960, mainly as a consequence of migration and productivity (table 6–13). The decline is so large that despite problems of measurement it probably expresses a real improvement in the relative position of the agricultural labor force. Terms of trade effects were not important, which is consistent with the small relative improvement in the internal terms of trade from 1948–50 to 1957–59 (table 9–6). The improvement was, it will be recalled, partly brought about by government price support policies for agriculture. Wage statistics, available from 1954 (Hershlag 1968, table 52) but of uncertain quality, when combined with the official CPI indicate strongly fluctuating real wages with no clear trend in 1954–62. Since the CPI probably underestimates the increase of prices, at least before 1959, it stands to reason that real wages may have been declining somewhat from 1954 to 1962. Salaries of civil servants and the military were certainly lagging far behind prices. Indeed, this lag was one reason for the military takeover. For agricultural income, the Gini coefficient and lowest quintile shares improved a little from 1952 to 1963 (table 6–6) but those measures are based on estimates of dubious quality. Indicators for land distribution during the same period are conflicting. The evidence is so uncertain that it is not possible to make a general judgment about the trend in the national distribution of income by size for the 1950s.

Since World War II, income distribution has been somewhat affected by tax and social security reforms. Some tax reforms took place immediately after the war. Wartime taxes on soil products and the levy on capital (*varlık*) were abrogated and the livestock tax was reduced. A new personal income tax law of 1949 instituted a progressive tax scale ranging from 15 percent to 45 percent, with relatively modest personal deductions. Income from agriculture, fishing, crafts, domestic services, and certain other activities was exempted (Hirsch and Hirsch 1966). A new corporate income tax also imposed in 1949 placed a 10 percent tax on net profits of capital associations and cooperative societies and 35 percent on other corporations. Agriculture thus became virtually free from direct taxation apart from the low property tax and possibly the tax on cooperative societies. For the urban population, and probably for the population as a whole, the tax reforms of 1949 implied a somewhat more equitable distribution of disposable income. Indirect taxation remained regressive.

Equally important, however, was the introduction in 1950 of a social security system that consisted of a retirement system for government employees and similar arrangements for other public sector employees and a partial social insurance system. Both the social reforms and labor legislation were initiated and partly implemented by the Kemalists and thus were imposed from above. Comparison with Bismarck and his political problem is by no means farfetched.

In Ottoman society, as in Islamic societies generally, social security originated with the religious practices of the *zakat*, a charitable tax on net wealth levied on all believers. A corresponding tax, *gizyah*, was levied on nonbelievers. The first modern social security organization in the Ottoman Empire was a military retirement fund set up in 1866, followed by a retirement fund for civil servants set up in 1881; both were reorganized under the Young Turks in 1909 and again under the Kemalists in 1930. The Government Employee Retirement Fund, which was established by law in 1949 and started operating in 1950, is based on employee and employer (government) contributions; its benefits are retirement, disability, and survivor pensions with certain auxiliary supplements.

Social insurance was initiated in 1946 and expanded through legislation in 1950, 1951, and 1957. Under legislation passed in 1964, the system covers old age, disability and death, sickness, maternity, and occu-

Table 10-3. Receipts and Expenditures of Social Security System, Selected Years, 1960-80

(percent of GNP)

Year	Receipts				Expenditures			
	Contributions		State and public authorities	Income from capital	Total	Benefits	Administration	Total	Surplus
	Insured persons	Employers							
1960	0.84	1.26	0.30	0.34	2.75	1.28	0.13	1.41	1.34
1965	1.00	1.40	0.16	0.56	3.12	1.58	0.14	1.72	1.40
1970	1.29	2.46	0.11	0.68	4.54	2.99	0.25	3.23	1.31
1975	2.00	3.11	0.28	0.78	6.17	2.88	0.57	3.45	2.71
1980[a]	1.44	2.57	0.59	0.56	5.16	4.15	0.20	4.34	0.81

a. Does not include public health service benefits and is not fully comparable with earlier years; for Turkey, apparently a secondary matter.
Source: ILO, The Cost of Social Security, 1978–1980, table 1; World Bank data.

pational injury and disease but not unemployment. Labor legislation requiring severance pay of fifteen days' wages for each year of employment after three years to be paid by the employer compensates to some extent for the absence of unemployment insurance. The system covers all persons employed under service contracts, excluding agricultural workers and persons who are self-employed or covered by the public sector retirement funds. A special organization, Bağ-Kur, set up in 1970 insures the self-employed, including agricultural workers, on a voluntary basis; this organization has not become important.

Employers' contributions to the insurance system add up to 14.5–20.0 percent of earnings (16.5–22.0 percent in mining), depending on risk, while employee contributions add up to 12.0 percent (13.0 percent in mining). Social insurance contributions are thus substantial and are a factor in determining the competitiveness of Turkish industry on the one hand and income distribution on the other. Receipts and expenditures of the system in 1960–80 are shown in table 10–3, which is based on a special survey conducted regularly by the International Labour Organisation. The ILO survey appears to be more comprehensive than either official statistics (*Statistical Yearbook of Turkey,* 1985 and 1979) or OECD estimates (OECD, *Economic Survey, Turkey,* 1987, statistical annex, table P). It is clear from the table that the Turkish social security system does redistribute substantial amounts of the national income and that the system systematically generates very large surpluses. About these two features all three data sets agree.

It is almost impossible to estimate the impact of the social security system on the size distribution of income, not only because pensions are distributed over time but because of the possibility that employer contributions are shifted to prices of consumer goods. Generally there should be a tendency for a shift of real income from the uninsured to the insured and within the group of insured from lower to higher income brackets. Since the uninsured to a large extent are to be found in rural areas and working in agriculture, it is difficult to say what the net effect may be.

The absence of unemployment insurance is striking and reflects on both the nature of unemployment in Turkey and the unemployment estimates. Unemployment insurance obviously cannot be the cause of unemployment in Turkey. Employers' contributions to social insurance and severance pay should, however, tend to stimulate capital-intensive technologies and thus contribute to unemployment.

11 National Planning with Etatist Orientation, 1962–79

Politically the period of parliamentary democracy from 1962 to 1979 is bracketed by military takeovers and interspersed with a few years of military monitoring. The first takeover, in 1960, set the politicoeconomic stage for the next two decades through a new constitution of 1961. The constitution imposed comprehensive development planning on the country and preserved the mixed economy with planners deliberately going for inward-looking, import-substitution policies but also liberalizing the labor market. A three-year-long incident, 1971–73, with military-sponsored governments did not in itself change basic development strategies or policies. The second takeover, in 1980, endorsed the private-enterprise and liberalization-oriented program that with the encouragement of international organizations and donors had been adopted in January 1980, shortly before the takeover. Just as the military had inaugurated the two decades of national planning with inward-looking, etatist orientation in a mixed economy, so the military effectively terminated this era, inaugurating and even implementing a strategy with market and export orientation a leading principle, but now adding a policy of labor market repression.

National Planning under the 1961 Constitution

The 1961 constitution was economically important for, among other reforms, requiring national economic planning. A law of September 30, 1960 established the State Planning Organization (SPO), which was in charge of proposing and implementing plans for economic, social, and cultural development under a High Planning Council. Long-term, prospective programming with medium-term five-year plans and detailed annual plans was required. The first three five-year plans under the new constitution covered the years 1963–67, 1968–72, and 1973–77; the fourth plan was delayed by the foreign exchange crisis of 1977–79.

Planning methodology and target setting were strongly influenced by Professor Jan Tinbergen who served as chairman of the United Nations

Development Committee in the early 1960s and became chief consultant to the SPO. In line with UN recommendations, a growth target of 7 percent was adopted, increased to 8 percent with the 1973–77 plan. Atatürk's etatist philosophy was the basic guideline. Thus it was an immutable rule, laid down by Prime Minister İnönü (as reported to the SPO staff, by its chief, Professor Besim Üstünel), that 50 percent of all fixed investment should be in the public sector. This, of course, would guarantee a continuation of the existing mixed economy. Inflationary financing of public expenditure was banned by the new constitution and budgetary policy was seen as the major policy instrument. Investment was generally oriented toward import substitution, and general exchange rate policy was not on the agenda after the strong de facto depreciation in 1958 (formalized in 1961). Foreign exchange controls with import and export licensing, tariffs, premiums, tax rebates and subsidies, and foreign aid were considered the natural instruments of balance of payments policy (Krueger 1974; World Bank 1982). An OECD consortium, formed in 1961 to institutionalize foreign borrowing on concessionary terms, carried through debt reschedulings in 1965 and 1978–80. This was, of course, the era of Bretton Woods, when the IMF frowned on any change in exchange rates that was not necessitated by a "fundamental" disequilibrium in a country's balance of payments. Exchange rate adjustments (urged by the IMF) were nonetheless undertaken in 1970 and in the second half of the 1970s as the credit policy regarding the public sector became increasingly inflationary and development policy overambitious. The tightness of the quantitative controls on foreign exchange waxed and waned with the foreign exchange situation, and the orientation of economic policy changed somewhat with the elections and changes of government in 1965, 1969, 1973, and 1977. A short liberalization period with a relatively abundant supply of foreign exchange and relaxation of controls occurred after the devaluation of 1970 and with the emergence of large remittances from migrant workers in 1969–74, but by and large principles of planning and economic policy remained unchanged until the debt crisis of 1978 (Celasun 1983). Compliance with the 1961 constitution and its spirit was carefully monitored by the military establishment.

Etatist planning and the inward-looking policy of import substitution were successful insofar as growth rates remained high, and distribution probably improved until the second half of the 1970s. The etatist-oriented policy broke down after the first increase in oil prices in 1973–74, the deterioration of the domestic political scene when domestic inflation and foreign borrowing accelerated beyond sustainable levels and foreign lending to Turkey finally dried up, the Cyprus invasion not being without importance here. One factor that tended to make the etatist policy unsustainable and contributed to its breakdown was the excessive increase in real wages, a consequence of the liberalization of the labor market and the legalization of labor unions which the 1961 constitution guaranteed. If import substitution is regarded as an infant-industry policy, it might appear successful in the sense that when, with the debt crisis, domestic demand was reduced severely, the currency was depreciated strongly, and wages were held down, industry proved capable of shifting to foreign markets and there was a remarkable increase in the export of manufactured goods. It is questionable, however, whether this should be taken to mean that infant industries had now become mature. Moreover, could not, and should not, the change in policy have happened before the first oil price increase in 1973–74 rather than after the second one in 1979–80?

Growth and Employment

The years 1961–63 to 1977–79 represent one long period of planned import substitution (with a brief relaxation of trade control in 1970–73 which was of no lasting consequence). Table 6–3 shows that compared with the period 1951–53 to 1961–63, which largely coincided with the decade of government by Menderes's Democrat party and its aftermath, there was a substantial increase in the overall growth rate. The GDP growth rate increased from 4.9 percent to 6.4 percent, with an even stronger increase (mainly because of workers' remittances) in the GNI growth rate from 4.4 percent to 6.3 percent. Since the population increase declined from 2.8 percent to 2.5 percent, GDP growth per capita increased from 2.1 percent to 3.9 percent, with GNI growth per capita increasing from 1.6 percent to 3.8 percent. Growth of per capita income thus more than doubled and the performance for the years of planning, while not remarkable, compares well with that of developing and industrialized countries. The average growth rate of GNP per capita for the period 1960–77 for middle-income countries (as defined by the World Bank) was 3.6 percent, for industrialized countries 3.4 percent, and for low-income countries 1.4 percent.

In line with conventional wisdom at that time, capital investment was viewed by Turkish planners (and their advisers) as the high road to growth and development. Fixed gross investment remained at a level of about 10 percent of GNI from the early days of the republic to 1948–50. During the 1950s the share of investment in GNI increased to 15–16 percent. Under the auspices of the SPO it was increased to about 22 percent in 1977–79.

Given factor input, factor productivity is the decisive determinant of growth. For manufacturing industries, total factor productivity has been estimated by Krueger and Tuncer (1980) to have increased by 2.1 percent annually for the period 1963–76 (table 11–1). Behind the residual of 2.1 percent is among other factors, the steady improvement of education (see table 6–12). Real output increased at a rate of 12.3 percent and total

Table 11-1. Total Factor Productivity in Manufacturing, 1963-76
(percent)

Sector	1963-67	1967-70	1970-73	1973-76	1963-76
Food processing	0.85	0.78	2.14	-4.32	-0.09
Beverages	16.32	-8.64	5.02	-1.18	3.16
Tobacco	6.68	3.02	8.50	2.93	7.44
Textiles	2.08	4.82	2.24	-4.42	1.14
Wearing apparel and footwear	2.00	6.60	5.62	-4.18	2.50
Wood and cork products	0.40	-3.13	-2.06	-1.15	-1.26
Furniture and fixtures	3.00	2.14	-10.62	9.73	-0.56
Paper and paper products	2.99	-2.82	-1.17	4.14	0.59
Fur and leather products	-2.72	4.31	-8.93	1.17	-1.17
Rubber products	11.97	-3.28	2.68	6.07	4.27
Chemicals	3.31	2.47	2.73	-1.87	1.67
Petroleum and coal	9.27	-8.30	-0.66	-7.90	0.24
Nonmetallic minerals	-1.06	2.82	3.31	-4.32	0.62
Basic metals	0.74	7.06	-1.83	-6.27	0.61
Metal products	2.23	-3.48	8.08	-0.29	2.39
Machinery	0.60	6.66	-4.96	1.46	1.02
Electrical machinery	-3.81	-3.84	6.26	7.21	1.30
Transport equipment	5.77	-6.44	9.35	3.25	1.42
Total	3.20	1.31	2.51	-1.18	2.10

Note: Compound rates, spanning initial and terminal year of each period.
Source: Krueger and Tuncer (1980).

input must thus have increased by 10.2 percent. Labor input increased by 6.3 percent and capital by 12.8 percent. Productivity of labor seems thus to have increased by 6.0 percent while productivity of capital declined at a rate of 0.5 percent. The decline in productivity of capital is not necessarily a proof of inefficiency. The residual of 2.1 percent in Turkish manufacturing for 1963–76 was by no means low as compared with the national income residuals for most developed economies (Denison and Chung 1976, table 4–8). It was in line with those for manufacturing in the United States, Israel, Hong Kong, and the Philippines but low compared with those in Norway, Japan, Italy, Singapore, South Korea, Taiwan, and China (Krueger and Tuncer 1980, pp. 24–25; Gaathon 1971, table A–13), and above average for twenty developing countries referred to by Chenery, Robinson, and Syrquin (1986, table 2–2). The residual in Turkish manufacturing seems to have been on a declining trend between 1963 and 1976, apparently fluctuating with the tightness of import controls (Krueger and Tuncer 1980, table 4). Factor productivity was found to be higher in private than in public enterprises. On the other hand, the measured residual was higher in the public than in the private sector;

Table 11-2. Total Factor Productivity, Turkey, 1958–75

	GNP, at constant 1958 prices	Capital, at constant 1958 prices	Labor force	Land	Total factor input	Total factor productivity
Index (1958 = 100)						
1958	100	100	100	100	100	100
1975	277	421	133	100	228	121
Share of factor income (percent)		0.35	0.50	0.15		

Source: Leamer (1984), table B–1; table 6–14.

Krueger and Tuncer's attempt to explain away this finding is not convincing (1980, table 3, pp. 38–42). The simple explanation may be that exchange controls favored public enterprises.

In a special study of comparative advantage, Leamer (1984, table B–1) has estimated national endowments of capital, labor, and land for Turkey (and many other countries) for 1958 and 1975. His capital estimates are crude, and his land data do not tally well with national land statistics. When his capital estimates are converted into constant 1958 lira prices, his three categories of labor are added together, and conjectured factor income shares (from table 6–14) are used as weights, we obtain table 11–2. The result, for whatever it is worth, is a modest increase of total factor productivity by 1.1 percent annually, from 1958 to 1975. With an increase of 2.1 percent in manufacturing industry, factor productivity in agriculture must have been well below 1 percent, a rather poor performance. Notice that according to this estimate the ratio of capital to labor—that is, capital intensity—increased very strongly. Considering both educational progress and structural shift from agriculture to industry, the residual is disappointing. (For the years 1973–87, see table 12–16.)

Sectoral growth rates show remarkably little change from the 1950s to the two decades of planning. The tendency of the growth rate of agriculture to decline (with the expansion toward the frontier) also shows up in the comparison of the period of planning with the 1950s; the decline, however, depends on the period of comparison chosen. A growth rate of 3.0 percent for 1961–63 to 1977–79 compares with a rate for 1948–50 to 1961–63 of 5.1 percent and a rate for 1951–53 to 1961–63 of 3.8 percent. The contribution of agriculture to total GDP growth declined even more strongly, from 23.7 percent in 1951–53 to 1961–63 to 14.0 percent in 1961–63 to 1977–79. In terms of contribution to total growth, agriculture was no longer the leading sector.

With the frontier reached in the 1950s, agricultural growth became almost exclusively dependent on increased yields (real GDP per hectare) through intensification of cultivation, decline in fallow land, improved plant varieties with increased inputs of chemicals, increased mechanization, and some expansion of irrigated lands. The intensification was partly a response to market forces from both small- and medium-sized farms but was also in many ways supported by the government's policy of subsidizing inputs through favorable exchange rates and interest rates. As a percentage of total GDP, agricultural fixed investment, however, declined from 3.5 percent during 1950–58 to about 2.5 percent during 1971–77 (table 12–15). In itself this should not be taken as an indicator of planners' neglecting agriculture in favor of industrialization. There is some doubt about the productivity of fixed capital in some forms of traditional investment in agriculture—in irrigation particularly—as compared with modern circulating capital such as fertilizers and pesticides, not included in the national account estimates of fixed gross investment.

The growth rate of manufacturing was virtually unchanged at 8.8–8.9 percent from the 1951–53 to 1961–63 period to the 1961–63 to 1977–79 period. Manufacturing now became the leading sector in terms of contribution to total growth by 22.5 percent but the increase was small, from 20.1 percent in 1951–53 to 1961–63, and did not compensate for the decline in the contribution from agriculture. This is true even when manufacturing is lumped with mining and electricity in a more broadly defined industrial group. Against the decline in the contribution of agriculture by 9.7 percentage points is an increase in the contribution of manufacturing by 2.4 percentage points and of industry in the wider sense by 4.5 percentage points. Trade is coming from behind as the big contributor, increasing from 12.7 percent in 1951–53 to 1961–63 to 16.9 percent in 1961–63 to 1977–79 with an increase of 4.2 percentage points. This trend, which continues strongly into the following period, 1977–79 to 1983–85, gives rise to a number of questions. Some are of a technical nature—how do the authorities estimate real value added in trade?—and some of an economic nature—is trade "productive" or is the value added mainly "unproductive" transaction costs, like rent seeking, as Krueger (1974a) and Douglass North argue? Krueger estimated that 15 percent of GNP went into rent seeking and similar unproductive activities. Bhagwati and Srinivasan (1975) criticize her estimates as being entirely unrealistic since they assume rent seeking to be a perfectly competitive activity. Without this assumption, the estimates would be much lower.

For both exports and imports, growth rates are relatively low and shares of foreign trade are low. Low growth rates of foreign trade (at constant prices) have been characteristic of development in Turkey since the founding of the republic and are an obvious consequence of the import-substitution policies systematically pursued since the early 1930s. A comparison between GDP and foreign trade growth rates, however, discloses a considerably higher growth of foreign trade during 1961–63 to 1977–79, relatively as well as absolutely, than during both the 1930s and the 1950s. In the policy of reducing trade relatively, Turkey resembles Latin American countries such as Argentina, Brazil, and Mexico (Chenery and Syrquin, 1975, p. 131); the resemblance extends apparently to the success in the 1980s of old import-substitution industries in the export markets.

Despite relatively high GDP growth rates and the migration (mainly to Europe) of about 4 percent of the labor force during the 1960s and 1970s, it is uncertain whether the expansion of production was sufficient to absorb the increase in the domestic labor force before 1978. Official estimates by the SPO (figure 11–1 and table 11–4) indicate an increase in unemployment (not including so-called disguised unemployment in agriculture) from 1.8 percent of the total labor force in 1962 to 7.1 percent in 1977. It is not clear how these estimates were made and they do not appear reliable. Available indicators are presented in figure 11–1 and are evaluated and analyzed in a separate study (Hansen 1989a). If anything they indicate a tendency for unemployment to decline from the late 1960s to around 1974 when it seems to have increased rapidly, probably as a consequence of the decline in labor demand from Europe and the mounting foreign exchange difficulties in combination with increasing real wage costs. Increasing unemployment may be a phenomenon that mainly belongs to the second half of the 1970s.

Detailed labor force, employment, and unemployment statistics for the years after 1962 are shown in table 11–4. As table 11–3 indicates, the trends for years after 1962 may, insofar as employment is concerned, have prevailed already during the 1950s.

Employment in agriculture seems, in absolute terms, to have declined slowly over the whole period 1962–77, with a strong decline in the share of labor employed in agriculture from 72 percent to 54 percent of the total labor force. Since the share absorbed in industry only increased from about 8 percent to 10 percent, 4 percent migrated, and unemployment increased by an estimated 5 percent, the rest was absorbed by the construction and service sectors, the total share of which increased by almost 8 percent.

Considering the probable increase in unemployment after 1974 and the possible increase of employment in low-productivity services, it would have been more appropriate then to adopt labor-intensive technologies in industry than in the 1930s. Krueger and Tuncer (1980) suggest that capital investment in manufacturing industry during 1963–76 tended to increase capital intensity rather than expanding capacity. Nationally, the tendency seems to have been the same (table 11–2). Inter-

Figure 11-1. Indicators of Change of Unemployment, for Selected Years, 1960-86

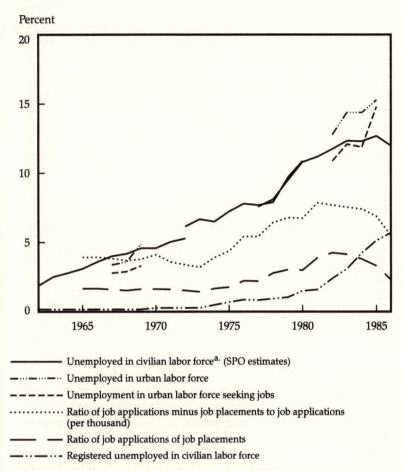

Percent

Unemployed in civilian labor force[a.] (SPO estimates)

Unemployed in urban labor force

Unemployment in urban labor force seeking jobs

Ratio of job applications minus job placements to job applications (per thousand)

Ratio of job applications of job placements

Registered unemployed in civilian labor force

a. Not including unemployed in the peak season in agriculture.
Source: Hansen (1989)

est, tariff, and exchange rate policies also worked in this direction (Krueger 1974b) and the increasing unionization with minimum wage legislation helped to increase real wages in manufacturing excessively and thus reinforced the tendency to increase capital intensity. That employment policy forced public enterprises to employ more labor than they needed may have led to X-inefficiency (in the sense of Leibenstein) and labor redundancies rather than to the adoption of labor-intensive technology. Krueger and Tuncer's finding that total productivity appears to have been lower but to have increased more in public than in private enterprises indicates that such forced hiring may have been important but may have decreased after 1963.

Table 11-3. Manpower Growth Rates and Shares, by Sector, 1955-65
(percent)

Sector	Annual growth rate, 1955-65	Share of total 1955	Share of total 1965	Total increase, 1955-65
Agriculture	0.4	77.4	71.3	24.5
Mining and quarrying	4.0[a]	0.5	0.6	1.8
Manufacturing	2.8[a]	6.0	7.1	15.0
Trade	0.7	2.7	2.6	1.5
Transport and communications, services	5.7	5.8	8.9	32.9
Not defined[b]	0.5	7.5	9.5	24.3
Total	1.2	100	100	100
Population	2.7	50.0[c]	43.3[c]	—

— = Not applicable.

a. For mining and quarrying and manufacturing the combined growth rate was 2.9 percent.

b. Includes construction, but apparently not armed forces and labor abroad.

c. Share of total manpower in the population.

Source: Hershlag (1968), table 3.

Policies of Import Substitution

Since 1929, Turkish development strategies have been dominated by import substitution with two brief periods of relaxed trade controls in 1950–53 and 1970–73. The choice of strategy was related to the political philosophies of the party in government (or the military during the takeover in 1960–61 and the interference in 1971–73) and constrained by the Bretton Woods philosophies. All along, however, the current foreign exchange situation tended to govern the degree of government intervention in and control of foreign trade and payments. At the time of the first five-year plan, elite groups and advisers, nationally and internationally, and international donors and organizations generally viewed import substitution and the nurture of infant industries as a necessary initial stage in economic development and industrialization. It is not surprising, therefore, that after the devaluation of 1958–60 both the military and the Republican party government of İnönü, taking over when parliamentary government was restored in 1962, adopted import substitution as a natural policy.

To better understand the import substitution bias in Turkish planning it may be useful to take a more technical look at the planning methodologies applied by the SPO. Investment planning, as advised by Tinbergen himself, was based on his method of planning by stages, beginning with a macroeconomic stage, followed by a sectoral (possibly also regional) stage, and concluding with a project appraisal stage in which sectoral investment targets were filled in with concrete investment projects. The macro stage used a combination of Keynesian and Harrod-Domar theory, the sectoral stage was based on Leontief's input-output model, and the project appraisal stage applied ad hoc evaluation criteria, recognizing the need to use shadow prices but with no clear conception of how to obtain such prices. During the work on preparing for the second five-year plan, thanks to emerging computerization, the macro and sectoral stages were integrated into a single stage. Investment targets continued to be determined by projected domestic sectoral demand, with export demand at most an exogenous determinant. Thus formal planning in Turkey was inward looking and tended to lead to import substitution. Problems did arise with sectors having either too many or too few projects that were acceptable according to the evaluation criterion chosen. Those problems immediately suggested the need for residual determination of both exports and imports, which resulted in Tinbergen's idea of semi-input-output planning with a sharp distinction between sectors producing traded (international) and nontraded (domestic) goods and services and calling for a completely residual determination of trade as the difference between production and domestic demand. It also became clear (Hansen 1967, pp. 2 ff.) that for traded goods the shadow prices are the relative international prices and that corresponding prices for nontraded goods and factors have to be inferred on that basis. This planning method, now known as the Little-Mirrlees method, implies that planning be oriented neither toward import substitution nor toward export promotion but toward efficiency, whatever that implies with regard to trade. Although these ideas came up in the preparations for the second plan, I do not believe they were ever applied in Turkish formal planning, which continued to be based on sectoral investment planning with subsequent filling in, sector by sector. Attempts to evaluate individual projects broke down because the staff was inexperienced, information about relevant international prices proved to be difficult to obtain, and time schedules were unrealistic. The filling in was done by authorities issuing investment and import licenses; rent-seeking activities, legal or illegal, were an important part of the process. With the election of 1965 and the emergence of the Süleyman Demirel government, the work of the SPO was reoriented toward technological planning by engineers with little sense of economic efficiency; planning became even more import-substitution oriented than it had been under İnönü.

It is symptomatic that the policy by and large was endorsed by the OECD. Since 1961 the OECD consortium has been the major financier of development in Turkey. Undoubtedly, OECD views have been important to Turkish governments as they have formulated and implemented development policies. Those views are reflected in the regularly published OECD *Economic Survey* for Turkey.

Table 11–4. Labor Force, Employment, and Unemployment, Growth Rates and Shares, 1962–84
(percent)

Category	Growth rate			Share of total labor force					Share of increase of total labor force		
					1972						
	1962–72	1972–77	1977–84	1962	A	B	1977	1984	1962–72	1972–77	1977–84
Population	2.4	2.4	2.1	43.7[a]	41.7[a]	43.5[a]	42.0[a]	40.4[a]	n.a.	n.a.	n.a.
Total labor force	2.0	1.8	1.5	100	100	100	100	100	100	100	100
Armed forces	1.0	0.0	0.0	4.5	4.1	3.3	3.0	2.7	2.3	0.0	(0.0)
Civilian labor force	2.0	1.8	1.6	95.5	95.9	96.6	97.0	97.3	97.7	100.0	100.0
Labor abroad	49.3	2.0	5.2	0.1	3.9	4.1	4.1	5.3	22.0	3.1	16.8
Domestic civilian labor force	1.6	1.8	1.4	95.5	92.0	92.6	93.0	92.0	75.7	96.8	32.7
Agriculture	-0.5	-0.1	-0.2	72.2	56.7	59.4	54.2	48.1	-16.8	-2.9	-6.4
Industry	4.3	3.6	1.3	7.8	9.8	9.3	10.2	10.0	19.3	20.2	8.4
Mining and quarrying	n.a.	4.0	-0.8	n.a.	n.a.	0.6	0.7	0.6	n.a.	1.4	-0.3

Manufacturing	n.a.	3.3	1.3	n.a.	n.a.	8.4	9.0	8.9	n.a.	16.3	7.4
Electricity	n.a.	9.9	3.5	n.a.	n.a.	0.4	0.5	0.6	n.a.	2.4	1.3
Construction	3.6	4.6	1.0	2.4	2.8	2.7	3.1	3.0	4.7	7.6	2.0
Transport and communications	5.7	5.2	1.0	2.0	2.9	2.4	2.8	2.7	7.1	7.6	1.8
Trade, finance, services	7.0	5.2	2.3	9.2	15.0	13.1	15.5	16.4	42.2	41.8	24.0
Trade	n.a.	4.3	1.8	n.a.	n.a.	3.2	3.6	3.7	n.a.	8.3	4.3
Finance	n.a.	7.5	1.8	n.a.	n.a.	0.9	1.1	1.1	n.a.	4.1	1.3
Services	n.a.	4.4	2.8	n.a.	n.a.	8.2	9.3	10.2	n.a.	21.7	17.5
Unspecified	n.a.	12.2	0.9	n.a.	n.a.	0.9	1.5	1.4	n.a.	7.7	0.9
Total employed civilians	1.2	1.5	0.6	93.6	87.2	87.0	85.9	80.2	56.7	74.2	29.7
Unemployed	12.3	6.4	9.2	1.8	4.8	5.7	7.1	11.8	19.1	22.6	53.5
Job seekers, officially listed	n.a.	n.a.	27.0	n.a.	n.a.	n.a.	0.7	3.4	n.a.	n.a.	31.2

n.a. = Not available.
A = Comparable with 1962.
B = Comparable with 1977 and 1984.
a. Share of total labor force in population.
Source: World Bank (1975), table 1–2; World Bank (1982), p. 1–2; World Bank data.

The first five-year plan was reviewed carefully in the 1963 *Survey*: Import policies will be based on the need to save foreign exchange and to protect the development of domestic industry. The liberalization of imports will not be extended to goods of which there is some domestic production or of which production in Turkey . . . could be developed in the foreseeable future. Import programmes will be established in such a way as to give priority to imports essential for the achievement of the plan, whilst imports of luxury goods will be restricted. Given the present and prospective state of the Turkish balance of payments, these policies would indeed, in general, appear necessary. (p. 24)

The 1966 *Survey* elaborated: "Whilst the inevitability of an import substitution policy was clearly recognized because of the formidable difficulties in the way of export development, doubts were expressed at that time [1963] as to the possibility of achieving so great a substitution in the first plan period" (p. 41), and "progress toward external equilibrium will require for a long time to come substitution of imports by domestic production" (p. 43). The import-substitution policy of the first plan was thus clearly endorsed by the OECD, as a temporarily necessary policy.

On the export side the 1963 *Survey* was more critical. While "the margin for [traditional] exports is probably rather limited, because the elasticity of foreign demand for them is small . . . a durable improvement of the balance of payments depends essentially on the development of new export industries. . . . A particular gap, at present, in the Five-Year Plan is that sufficiently detailed consideration seems not to have been given to this problem, except in the case of tourism" (pp. 24–25).

The 1966 *Survey* was critical of the use of licensing and other quantitative restrictions on the import side and found that "a preferable alternative might be to use the price mechanism, i.e., gradually liberalize imports and restrict import demand through higher import duties or import taxes. This would also enlarge the area over which import substitution becomes economically profitable" (p. 53). On the export side, however, "the policies directed towards increased bilateral trade and export tax rebates, debatable as they might be on other grounds, are clearly necessary in the present circumstances" (p. 44). Nowhere is the possibility of overvaluation of the lira touched on; but that would have been unusual in the Bretton Woods era, and it is a matter that a responsible international organization at that time would hesitate to discuss publicly. The OECD appeared to be prepared to throw in concessionary loans as needed (pp. 46, 50). In this sense it might thus be claimed that the lira was not overvalued.

The 1963 *Survey* was greatly concerned about the employment problem. It felt "a need to examine the possibilities of achieving a faster rate of job creation by encouraging more labour intensive industries: but it would be unwise to expect too much from this, given the need to avoid high-cost production" (p. 49). The 1967 *Survey*, however, curiously complained that "traditional light industries have tended to predominate rather more than planned while private investments in new capital-intensive ventures has fallen short of expectations" (p. 31).

The second and third five-year plans did not revise the development strategy. The only new critical comment from the OECD was a vague request for more labor-intensive technology in industry (1976 *Survey*, pp. 40, 42).

Deliberate import-substitution measures were a crucial element of Turkish development planning. To evaluate the impact of such measures, Derviş, de Melo, and Robinson (1982, chap. 11 and pp. 93–94) and Chenery, Robinson, and Syrquin (1986, pp. 129–37) examine the impact on production of four demand sources: domestic demand, export expansion, import substitution, and technological change (see table 11–5). The authors warn of definitional ambiguities involved and that their decomposition of growth may not "imply that causal relations have been established or that these proximate sources are exogenous" (Chenery, Robinson, and Syrquin 1986, p. 130). For the first three periods in table 11–5, the decomposition is essentially a matter of input-output multiplier analysis; for the last two, more advanced model simulation was applied. For all five periods the computed impacts are based on development of actual exports and change in imports and technical coefficients for whatever reason (the state of export markets abroad, for example); in particular it does not measure the impact of deliberate export-promotion or import-substitution measures. Thus, for instance, the dramatic change from 1973–77 to 1977–78 where the impact of import substitution increases from nothing (0.6 percent) to almost everything (96.6 percent) and export expansion goes from slightly negative (−1.0 percent) to very large (36.0 percent) partly reflects crop fluctuations—a very poor crop in 1977, which reduced exports and had almost no effect on imports in 1977, was followed by a bumper crop in 1978, which increased exports at a time when imports were cut severely for stabilization reasons. Similarly, in 1953–63 the impact of import substitution is small because of stabilization cutbacks in the middle of the period. The periods 1963–68 and 1968–73 are more clearly related to deliberately adopted development strategies, the import-substitution policy of the İnönü government of 1962–65 and the liberalization policy of the Demirel government of 1965–71 and of the following caretaker governments, made possible by the devaluation in 1970 and the strong inflow of workers' remittances. The computed impact of import substitution for 1963–68 was 8.3 percent of a growth rate of 6.6 percent, or about 0.5 percent growth. This is a moderate impact; export expansion during this period actually contributed half as much. For 1968–73 the export contribution was substantial, 16.3 percent of a growth rate of 6.8 percent, or about 1.1 per-

Table 11-5. Decomposition of Growth, by Source, 1953-78

(percent)

Period	Average annual growth rate	Domestic demand expansion	Export expansion	Import substitution	Change in input-output coefficient
1953-63[a]	5.3	92.3	2.5	1.8	3.3
1963-68[a]	6.6	83.6	4.9	8.3	3.2
1968-73[a]	6.8	81.8	16.3	-1.4	3.3
1973-77[b]	7.6	100.4	-1.0	0.6	n.a.
1977-78[b]	2.8	-32.6	36.0	96.6	n.a.

n.a. = Not available.
a. Based on gross output.
b. Based on GDP at constant factor cost.
Source: Derviş, de Melo, Robinson (1982), chap. 11-2, tables 11-11, and 11-12; Chenery, Robinson, and Syrquin (1986), pp. 129-37, 145-47.

cent growth, with a negative contribution from import substitution. Since this reflects a temporary relaxation of controls, it tells nothing about the long-term impact of import substitution. To clarify the impact of these alternative strategies on growth would require that the same policy be pursued systematically for prolonged periods, undisturbed by policy measures taken for other reasons and by external shocks. Turkey has experienced no such period.

Although the decomposition of growth by demand sources offers only limited guidance for evaluating the import-substitution strategy, it stands to reason that as this policy makes progress, the scope for further import substitution must diminish and returns decrease. Early import substitution may exploit natural advantages and be highly efficient, but sooner or later these advantages would be exhausted. It has been suggested that Turkey should have reached this stage in the 1970s when further import substitution largely would be limited to intermediate inputs (lignite for oil, say) and machinery and equipment at high costs. Simulation experiments and estimates of marginal capital-output ratios point in this direction (Derviş, de Melo, and Robinson 1982, table 11-13; World Bank 1982, table 1-5).

Otherwise the policies have to be evaluated on the basis of the incentives created to favor import competition and operating against exports. The exchange rate policy involved increasing appreciation of the lira throughout the period 1948-79, interrupted by major devaluations in 1958-60 and 1970. The trade incentives included multiple exchange rates, duties, taxes and subsidies, and licensing for both imports and exports. For 1953-71, Krueger (1974b) summarizes the discrimination against exports in favor of import-competing production by the ratio between average, so-called effective exchange rates for exports and imports, respectively. The effective exchange rate is here defined as the nominal exchange rate applied to a particular commodity, adjusted for duties and subsidies. This ratio remained remarkably stable at a level of 0.5 to 0.6 from 1953 to 1971, and somewhat lower during the years around the 1958 devaluation. The effective exchange rate for exports was thus only about half the rate for imports.

In the 1970s the bias against exports may have diminished somewhat in connection with tariff revisions undertaken to prepare for Turkey's eventual membership in the European Community. Changes in exchange premiums and export subsidies may, however, have worked in the opposite direction. For 1979, the World Bank (1982, table 2–24a), taking into account only nominal tariff protection and export subsidization, not including export premiums, estimated a ratio similar to the one used by Krueger to have been 0.76 for sixteen manufacturing industries. Export premiums should tend to diminish the bias if taken into account. The bias thus computed was almost unchanged through the second quarter of 1981.

To this should, however, be added the effects of import and export licensing, export price controls, and various export promotion devices. These are difficult to quantify. Krueger (1974b, p. 174) reports premiums for import licenses of eight times the parity exchange rate for 1955–58 when the lira had grossly appreciated and licensing was severely limited. With the strong devaluation of 1958–60 the premiums largely disappeared, but in 1964 they had again reached a level of 40–66 percent of the c.i.f. price, increasing to 100 percent in 1967 and 100–166 percent in 1968–69, once more largely disappearing with the devaluation of 1970. Rent seeking and corruption varied in proportion to the premiums and caused reorganizations of the distribution system, with little effect (Ayşe Öncü, in Özbudun and Ulusan 1980). Krueger's overall evaluation is that quantitative restrictions were of much greater importance than price intervention in providing incentives for import-competing production. Similar quantitative conjectures for the export side are not available. Price controls for exports, which appear to have been a real obstacle during the 1950s, appear also to have lost significance during the1960s. Throughout the period, export licenses were required for various commodities and were not granted automatically. Exchange premiums and tax rebates, which were used in the 1950s and 1960s, respectively, to promote exports, are included in the effective exchange rates reported above; at best they reduced the discrimination against exports. Other export promotion measures were minimal. With the devaluation in 1970 and the coincident rapid expansion of workers' remittances, import licensing was considerably relaxed (with tariffs unchanged) and export promotion devices were somewhat strengthened. From 1974 import controls were again tightened and with the debt crisis in 1978 became extremely severe (see below).

Throughout the period 1953–79, incentives in favor of import-substitution production and against exports were clearly substantial, even during the few years of relative relaxation of licensing in 1970–73. It stands to reason that the impact on allocation of resources may have been substantial. Krueger (1974, pp. 250–61) estimates, on the basis of highly simplifying assumptions, that while under the conditions of the second five-year plan the growth rate of manufacturing industry value added at international prices would be 10.3 percent, under more moderate import substitution this growth rate could have been 12.0 percent while under balanced import-substitution and export-promotion incentives it could have been 16.5 percent. Even assuming that these estimates are realistic, the impact on the GNP growth rate would, of course, be much smaller. With a share of industry in total gross domestic product of about one-quarter, as the case was in 1985, about 1.5 percent would be added to the GDP growth rate. It would increase the per capita growth rate of national income for 1960–62 to 1977–79 from 3.8 percent to 5.3 percent. While not revolutionary, this would certainly be a substantial improvement of per capita growth.

It should be added that the protective system also implied a certain discrimination against agriculture as compared with industry. For 1978 the average effective protection coefficient in agriculture is estimated at 1.40 compared with 1.75 (general tariff) and 1.58 (EEC tariff) for industry (World Bank 1982, p. 109). Being protected less, however, means being protected negatively, not only relatively but even absolutely (Krueger, Schiff, and Valdes 1988).

Fiscal and Monetary Policy and the Balance of Payments

Fiscal and monetary policy and balance of payments developments are examined here in the framework of a simple saving-investment analysis with a breakdown of national saving and investment in the public and private sectors. Public saving and public net borrowing are taken as indicators of fiscal policy. Theoretically, this is a primitive method of gauging the impact of fiscal policy, but the data available are not very reliable or even adequate. No breakdowns appear to be available for inventory changes in the public and private sectors. Such changes are included in private gross investment. Public gross saving is computed as current revenue minus transfers in the so-called consolidated budget minus public consumption as estimated in the national accounts. This method of estimation implies that gross saving in the public sector is net of social security funds, pension funds, and local governments' net revenue, which accordingly appears in private sector gross saving (not without some justification, incidentally), the latter obtained as the difference between national and public sector gross savings. As table 10–3 indicates, social security funds ran surpluses of 1–2 percent of GNP over the period 1960–80. Thus public saving may be underestimated, and the public deficit and private saving correspondingly overestimated. Table 11–6 may, nonetheless, show orders of magnitude and trends in saving and investment. (Estimates for 1973 to 1983 in the *OECD Economic Survey* [1984, diagram 7] give similar results; absolute figures for both private and public net lending are somewhat higher but otherwise in line with my figures.)

In principle, gross saving in the public sector equals the surplus of the current budget (not including capital transactions). The current budget shows a small surplus with a slightly falling trend from 1962–63 to 1979–80. The total budget—current plus capital budget—on the other hand, shows a large and increasing deficit from 5.1 percent of GNP in 1962–63 to 12.2 percent in 1979–80. The increase in the deficit was mainly caused by an increase in public investment from 6.8 percent of GNP in 1962–63 to 10.8 percent in 1979–80.

Investment and saving in the private sector apparently developed very differently. While private investment increased slightly from 1962–63 to 1974–78 from 8.8 percent to 11.2 percent of GNP and fell back to 9.0 percent in 1979–80, private saving increased sharply from 10.1 percent of GNP in 1962–63 to 19.5 percent in 1971–73, then fell back somewhat during 1974–78, and finally recovered slightly in 1979–80 to 17.5 percent of GNP. These developments may partly have been related to changes in workers' remittances from abroad. In any case, net lending from the private sector increased from 1.2 percent of GNP in 1962–63 to 9.4 percent in 1971–73, followed by a decline to 5.2 percent in 1974–78 and a substantial recovery to 8.5 percent in 1979–80.

During the years 1962–63 to 1971–73 the increase in net lending in the private sector more than compensated for the increase in net borrowing from the public sector and allowed national net borrowing—the current account balance—to develop from a large deficit of 3.9 percent of GNP in 1962–63 to a small surplus of 0.4 percent in 1971–73. The decline in private net lending accounts for most of the following strong increase in national net borrowing in 1974–78 to 4.5 percent of GNP. For 1979–80 a stronger increase of private net lending compensated for the increase in the public sector deficit.

Workers' remittances (shown in tables 11–6 and 12–3) probably played an important role in these developments. The decline in national net borrowing from 3.9 percent of GNP in 1962–63 to net lending by 0.4 percent in 1971–73 is accounted for almost completely by the increase in remittances from 0.1 percent to 4.5 percent of GNP during the same period while the goods and services deficit remained, practically speaking, unchanged at 3½ percent.

The following sharp increase in national borrowing to 4.5 percent of GNP in 1974–78 is accounted for by a simultaneous decline in remittances by 1.6 percent of GNP and increase of the goods and services def-

Table 11-6. Saving, Investment, and Net Borrowing, National and by Sector, 1962-84

(percent of GNP)

| | National | | | Public sector | | | |
| | | | | | Net borrowing | | |
Period	Net borrowing	Gross saving	Gross invest-ment	Total	From central bank	Gross saving	Gross invest-ment
1962–63	3.9	11.8	15.7	(5.1)	1.3	1.7	6.8
1964–70	1.4	17.2	18.6	7.9	1.4	1.1	9.0
1971–73	–0.4	18.8	18.4	9.0	2.5	–0.7	8.3
1974–78	4.5	17.2	21.7	9.8	5.3	0.7	10.5
1979–80	3.8	16.1	19.9	12.2	9.7	–1.4	10.8
1981–82	2.7	18.1	20.9	9.1	4.5	2.5	11.6
1983–84	3.1	16.5	19.6	10.0	9.8	0.6	10.6

All percentages except GNI growth rate are annual averages based on GNP at current market prices.

a. Includes all stock changes.

Source: Turkey, *Statistical Yearbook;* IMF, *International Financial Statistics;* World Bank data.

icit by 3 1/2 percent. Behind the unfavorable development in 1974–78, which led to the debt crisis, is the OPEC countries' first oil price increase in 1973–74, the expansion of fixed investment, and the inability of the Turkish authorities to cope with both problems. The loss in the terms of trade was massive (but see below). Calculated on imports and using official data, it amounted to 4 1/2 percent of GNI at factor cost from 1973 to 1975; calculated on the smaller volume of exports, it amounted to about 2 percent. The decline in remittances was induced partly by immigration restrictions in Europe and partly by uncertainty about the future of the lira and the government's foreign exchange policies. These two factors explain most or all of the reversal by 5 percent of GNP of national net borrowing; thus the deterioration in the balance of payments during the second half of the 1970s was not directly inherent in the import-substitution policies as such, but rather in the attempt to expand investment at a time when external balance of payments difficulties arose without being properly tackled (by devaluation). This may have been the time when new exchange rate policies and reforms should have been embarked on. The Turkish authorities were slow to respond to the shipwreck of Bretton Woods and face their own balance of payments problems.

Monetary expansion was increasingly inflationary from 1962–63 onward, money (money plus quasi money, as defined by the IMF) increas-

Private sector				National net borrowing			
					Related to		
						Net factor payments	
Net borrowing	Gross saving	Gross invest-ment[a]	GNI growth rate	Total	Goods and services deficit	Total	Workers' remittances
(−1.2)	(10.1)	8.8	6.9	3.9	3.6	0.3	−0.1
−6.5	16.1	9.6	6.2	1.4	1.9	−0.4	−0.8
−9.4	19.5	10.1	7.8	−0.4	3.3	−3.7	−4.5
−5.2	16.4	11.2	5.8	4.5	6.8	−2.2	−2.9
−8.5	17.5	9.0	−1.9	3.8	6.0	−2.2	−3.2
−6.4	15.6	9.3	3.4	2.7	4.7	−1.8	−4.2
−6.8	15.8	9.0	4.6	3.1	4.8	−6.7	−3.5

ing from 5.6 percent in excess of GNI growth in 1960–62 to 31.8 percent during 1975–79 (table 11–7). Apart from a brief spell during 1960–62, until 1974 monetary expansion through the public sector was in line with the growth rate of real GNI and thus, considered in isolation, cannot be considered inflationary. In this sense, monetary expansion through the private sector was the culprit during this period. From 1974, however, the picture changes radically; monetary expansion occurred exclusively through the public sector.

From the point of view of parity in purchasing power, however, monetary expansion over and above real GNI growth may not be considered excessive if it is equal to or below that of trade partners' rate of inflation. As long as monetary expansion is not excessive in this sense, no depreciation in the exchange rate would be required for reasons of monetary expansion. In this sense, monetary expansion through the budget was even deflationary from 1960–62 to 1974. From 1974 onward the situation was reversed; monetary expansion through the budget became strongly excessive. From the point of view of both internal inflation and foreign exchange rate policy, the public sector was now the culprit.

Table 11–8 gauges the net impact of Turkey's fiscal and monetary policies (as table 4–26 does for Egypt). The fiscal expansionary impact (not considering multiplier effects) is indicated by the increase in the budget deficits (as a percentage of GNP) and the monetary impact by the rate of

Table 11-7. Inflationary Financing, 1950–84

(percent)

Period	Growth rate, money supply[a]	Increase in claims on public sector over money supply[a,b]	Growth rate of real GNI[c]	Inflationary expansion of money supply[a]		Trade partners' rate of inflation	Excessive inflation	
				Total	Through public sector		Total	Through public sector
1950–59	19.9	6.7	6.4	13.5	0.3	1.4	12.1	-1.1
1960–62	9.3	9.1	3.7	5.6	5.4	2.0	3.6	3.4
1963–70	17.8	5.0	6.4	11.4	-1.4	3.2	8.2	-4.6
1971–74	27.0	8.8	7.4	19.6	1.4	10.7	8.9	-9.3
1975–79	36.1	35.1	4.3	31.8	30.8	6.6	25.2	24.2
1980–84	50.9	52.8	3.5[d]	47.4	49.3	11.8	35.6	37.5
1950–84	26.1	17.4	5.6	20.5	11.8	5.2	15.3	6.7

Annual rates.

a. Money supply equals money plus quasi money.
b. Public sector equals government plus public enterprises. IMF, *International Financial Statistics*; IMF data.
c. Author's estimates.
d. Growth rate of GNP.
Source: IMF, *International Financial Statistics*, IMF data, World Bank data.

Table 11-8. Net Impact of Fiscal and Monetary Policy, 1964-84

Period	Fiscal expansionary impact (percent of GNP)[a]	Monetary impact (percent of money supply)[b]	Direction of net impact
1964–70	+2.8	+14.0	+
1971–73	+1.1	+19.8	+
1974–78	+0.8	+23.5	+
1979–80	+2.4	+65.3	+
1981–82	−3.1	+65.7	?
1983–84	+0.9	+23.8	+

a. Fiscal expansionary impact equals increase in total public sector net borrowing.
b. Monetary impact computed as total inflationary expansion.
Source: Tables 11–6, 11–7.

change of money supply over and above the real rate of growth of GNP, thus merging Keynesian and monetarist thinking. If both fiscal and monetary indicators are positive (or negative), the net impact is expansionary (or contractionary). If the signs of the indicators differ, the sign of the net impact is unknown. Also, a positive net impact may be expansionary in a real sense with increased production or in a nominal sense with increased inflation, or possibly both. The monetary impact for all subperiods from 1964 to 1984 is positive and very strong and the fiscal impact is positive for all subperiods except 1981–82. Thus the net impact is expansionary for the whole period 1964–84, with the exception of 1981–82 where it is not possible to judge the direction of the net impact. Unemployment, however, was edging upward for the period as a whole, possibly with some decline in the early 1970s; meanwhile, inflation accelerated strongly until 1980, then decelerated under military government, and again increased from 1983 when civilian politicians took over. Increasing unionization with increasing militancy until 1980 is part of this picture but it seems likely that bottlenecks in production were another part and that these were related to shortages of foreign exchange and imports.

It is customary to accuse developing countries of overvaluing their currencies and in this way creating balance of payments problems for themselves. Figure 11-2 depicts the real effective exchange rate (REER), the nominal effective exchange rate (NEER), and the ratio of domestic to foreign price index (RPI) for Turkey and its trade partners from 1924 to 1985. Further details are shown in figures 11-3 and 11-4. The REER appreciated strongly from 1954 to 1959, mainly as a result of relatively strong inflation in Turkey. The depreciation in 1960-61 brought the REER down below its level in 1948. Most of the devaluation actually

Figure 11-2. Turkey's Effective Exchange Rates and Relative Prices, 1924-85

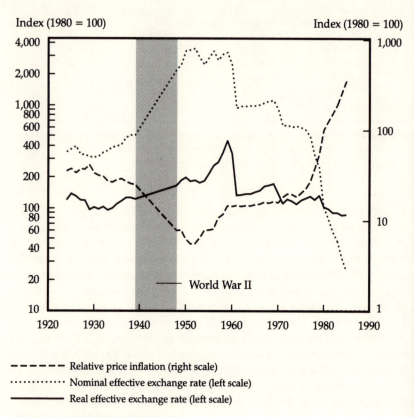

Index (1980 = 100)   Index (1980 = 100)

- - - - - - Relative price inflation (right scale)
.... Nominal effective exchange rate (left scale)
———————— Real effective exchange rate (left scale)

Note: Data not available for shaded area.
Source: IMF data.

took place in 1958–59, but the formal devaluation was postponed until 1960–61, the period used in the REER estimates. The REER then edged slowly upward by 29 percent until 1970 when a new devaluation brought it down below the level of 1961. From 1971 to 1979 the REER again slowly edged upward reaching in 1979 almost exactly the level of 1961. The slow appreciation from 1961 to 1969 was the combined result of a slight depreciation of trade partners' currencies against the dollar at a constant rate of U.S. dollar per Turkish lira (see figure 11–3) and slightly stronger inflation in Turkey than that of its trade partners (figure 11–4). The slow appreciation from 1971 to 1979 was the combined result of a slight depreciation of trade partners' currencies against the dollar at a somewhat stronger depreciation of the lira against the dollar,

Figure 11-3. Exchange Rates of Turkey and Trade Partners, 1924-85

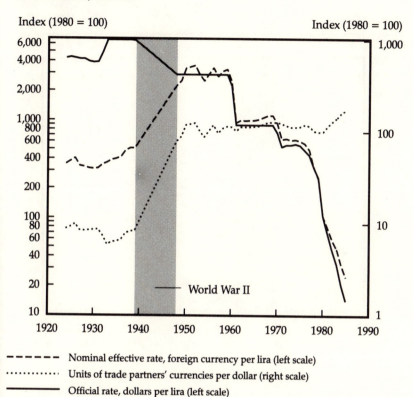

Index (1980 = 100)   Index (1980 = 100)

------ Nominal effective rate, foreign currency per lira (left scale)
············ Units of trade partners' currencies per dollar (right scale)
———— Official rate, dollars per lira (left scale)

Note: Data not available for shaded area.
Source: IMF data.

and a somewhat stronger price inflation in Turkey than among its trade partners. For the period 1961–79 as a whole it is clearly not possible to talk about increasing overvaluation in the simplistic sense of an appreciating REER. If anything, the trend for these years was toward a slight real depreciation of the Turkish lira.

The REER, however, is nothing more than an index of relative purchasing power. As such it is not informative about over- or under-valuation of the currency in any absolute sense. At best it indicates whether over- (or under-) valuation has increased or diminished. Being only an index of relative purchasing power, moreover, it at best shows the impact of monetary (cost) disturbances. It does not take into account the impact of real shocks to the economy and their effect on possible over- or undervaluation of the currency. Even if monetary policy is per-

Figure 11-4. Turkey and Trade Partners' Price Inflation, 1924-85

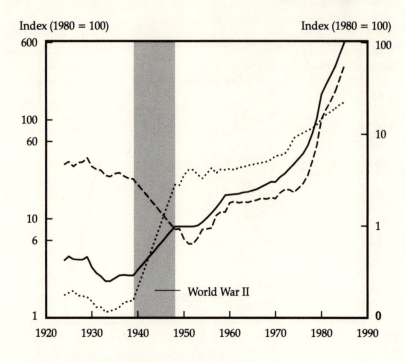

Relative price inflation (left scale)

Trade partners, wholesale price index, weighted (left scale)

Turkey, consumer price index (right scale)

Note: Data not available for shaded area.
Source: IMF data.

fectly neutral, a real adverse shock—like the oil price increases of 1973–74 and 1979–80—may create overvaluation of the currency.

The terms of trade series shown in figure 6–2 (the 1962–84 series is technically superior but it agrees fairly well with the 1923–84 series as far as it goes) indicate improvement from 1962 to 1966–67 to be lost again in 1971. After a certain improvement from 1971 to 1973–74, terms of trade deteriorated systematically and strongly, obviously dominated by the two oil price shocks of 1973–74 and 1979–80.

Using the current account (from table 12–3) as a benchmark and disregarding capital movements and the problem of their optimality as well as other possible policy targets, it might be claimed that after the devaluation of 1970 and the emergence of workers' remittances on a large scale, the lira was neither undervalued nor overvalued in 1971–73 when the current account actually was slightly in the black. (Simulations by

Derviş and Robinson [1982] and in Özbudun and Ulusan [1980, chap. 10] suggest that the lira may even have been undervalued in 1973, before the oil price increase, but this conclusion is conditioned by the authors' assumptions about capital inflows.) If so, the lira was slightly but increasingly overvalued from 1961 to 1970 and strongly overvalued from 1974 to 1979. The appreciation during the second half of the 1970s was, judging from the REER, caused by real rather than monetary disturbances—increases in the prices of oil and other imports caused the terms of trade to deteriorate while recession in Europe slowed both Turkish exports and remittances. Derviş and Robinson indicate that 45 percent of the depreciation of the nominal equilibrium exchange rate from 1973 to 1977 can be ascribed to excessive inflation, 24 percent to the oil price increase, 12 percent to higher prices for OECD countries' exports, 19 percent to decline in the remittances, and 15 percent to other factors.

Table 11–9 considers the development of foreign assistance to Turkey, with the gross inflow of aid measured by project and program credit plus grain purchases, and the net inflow by official development assistance. Even net foreign assistance is not equivalent to aid in the sense of a free lunch; more often than not it is made up of concessionary loans, and the grant element is not always easy to calculate, even disregarding such intangibles as military bases. From the early 1950s to the mid-1980s the current account deficit (net borrowing) was on average 2.5 percent of the GNP with 2.3 percent matched by gross foreign assistance.[2] For the period 1975–83, for which both sets of data are available,

Table 11–9. Foreign Assistance, 1950–83

(percent)

Period	Project and program assistance and grain aid as share of			Official development assistance as share of		
	GNP	Imports	Fixed investment	GNP	Imports	Fixed investment
1950–54	1.8	18.4	14.8	—	—	—
1955–59	2.0	31.1	12.2	—	—	—
1960–64	3.4	40.2	23.2	—	—	—
1965–69	2.1	32.5	12.0	—	—	—
1970–74	1.8	16.9	9.3	—	—	—
1975–77	1.2	9.4	5.1	0.2	2.0	1.1
1978–79	1.2	15.3	5.7	0.6	8.0	3.0
1980–83	3.1	18.8	15.6	0.9	7.7	6.5

Source: World Bank (1975), table 3–1; OECD, Economic Surveys, Turkey, 1985, table H; IMF, International Financial Statistics; OECD, Development Cooperation, various years.
— = Not applicable.

gross assistance of an average 2.0 percent of GNP implied net assistance of only 0.6 percent of GNP as compared with net borrowing of 2.0 percent. While foreign assistance has greatly helped to relieve the imbalance in Turkey's international accounts in the short term, it has not been a long-term solution. Notice that while net borrowing and foreign assistance were directly related until the mid-1970s, both reaching a peak in the early 1960s and then declining until the mid-1970s, during the second half of the 1970s net borrowing reached a new peak and foreign assistance as defined here remained at a low level. Behind this development are the strong increases in migrant workers' remittances from the mid-1960s easing the deficit in the balance of payments and then from 1973–74 a number of factors, first of course the oil price increase, leading to deterioration in the current account with deteriorating international relations (over the Cyprus dispute) which blocked foreign assistance until the debt crisis of 1978.

Finally, I remind the reader about the issue discussed at some length at the end of chapter 4. The problem of overvaluation of the domestic currency ideally should be analyzed as a multitarget, multi-instrument problem in a general equilibrium (interdependency) setting in which the current account deficit is only one of several possible targets and the exchange rate only one of several instruments, both interaction and timing being relevant.

Foreign Debt, Debt Crises, and the IMF Accord of 1978

Persistent balance of payments deficits throughout the 1960s and most of the 1970s created a debt problem that contributed to the general reconsideration of Turkey's economic policy in 1980. Table 11–10 presents three standard indicators of the foreign debt burden. The ratio of long-term external debt to GNP suffers from serious measurement problems and both the level and the rate of increase are probably biased downward. Data for years after 1980 (Kopits 1987, table 18), which are more complete than data for earlier years, indicate an underestimation of the ratio for earlier years by some 10 percent. Short-term debt, not included, has at times been important, particularly in terms of debt service. Moreover, the conversion rate between Turkish lira and U.S. dollars, hence between GNP in domestic currency and in dollars, was strongly affected by the increasing appreciation of the lira during the 1960s and the 1970s, interrupted by the strong depreciation in 1970. Both the decline of the debt ratio in 1960–67 and 1971–77 and the sudden increase in 1967–71 are for that reason statistical artifacts without real meaning. While, on the other hand, the strong increase in the debt ratio from 1977 to 1984 certainly is real enough, uncertainties about the degree of under- or overvaluation during these years of very high rates of inflation and fast depreciation make the debt ratio an equally uncertain debt indicator for these years.

Table 11-10. External Debt and Foreign Exchange Reserves, 1960-84

Year	DOD/GNP percent	TDS/XGS percent	INT/GNP percent	RES/MGS months
	(1)	(2)	(3)	(4)
1960	14	n.a.	n.a.	n.a.
1965	12	29	n.a.	3
1966	n.a.	21	n.a.	2
1967	12	16	n.a.	2
1968	n.a.	20	n.a.	2
1969	n.a.	17	n.a.	3
1970	.14	20	n.a.	5
1971	17	19	0.4	7
1972	16	20	n.a.	10
1973	13	11	0.4	11
1974	10	12	0.3	7
1975	9	13	0.3	4
1976	9	12	0.3	3
1977	9	16	0.3	2
1978	12	15	0.3	4
1979	15	21	0.3	4
1980	24	28	1.0	5
1981	24	22	1.1	3
1982	28	22	1.5	3
1983	30	29	2.3	3
1984	32	23	n.a.	2

Source: World Bank *World Debt Tables,* various years.
n.a. = Not available.
DOD = debt outstanding, disbursed.
GNP = gross national product.
INT = interest payments.
MGS = imports of goods and services.
RES = exchange reserves.
TDS = total debt service.
XGS = exports of goods and services.

Everything considered, the best debt burden indicator for Turkey is probably the ratio of debt service to export earnings. The problem of the conversion ratio here is minor because debt service and export earnings largely are negotiated and paid in foreign currency. Export earnings, however, do not include migrant workers' remittances, an omission that makes the debt service burden look somewhat high; the inclusion of re-mittances, however, would raise new problems related to foreign ex-change deposits in Turkey. This ratio, moreover, suffers from the fact that no data exist for exports of services before 1973, which explains the discontinuity between 1972 and 1973, when the ratio fell from 20 per-cent to 11 percent, exclusively because services were included in export data from 1973. After a substantial decline from 1965 to 1966 related to the rescheduling of the debt in 1965, the debt service ratio remained fairly constant at a level of about 20 percent (denominator excluding exports of services) or 12 percent (including export of services) from 1966 to 1976. Short-term debt at high and rapidly increasing interest rates now became important, but it is not taken into account. Even so, the ratio increased to a level of 28 percent. Despite continued borrowing, the strong increase in exports with a new rescheduling brought the ratio down to 23 percent in 1984. Though far from unprecedented, this is undoubtedly still a heavy debt burden.

Interest payments as a percentage of GNP remained fairly low until 1979 at a level of 0.3 percent. Here again the exclusion of short-term debt is important although both the concessionary nature of much of the debt and the low share of exports in GNP make the interest share in GNP relatively low as compared with the debt service ratio just discussed. After 1979, the interest burden increased rapidly and by 1983 had reached a level of 2.3 percent of GNP.

From 1962 to 1970, the current account deficit was largely covered by concessionary loans from the OECD consortium. The debt rescheduling in 1965 was undertaken by the consortium. During 1971–73 Turkey had, mainly as a consequence of the rapidly increasing remittances from migrant workers, a small surplus on current account and had accumulated large exchange reserves. But in 1973–74 with the oil price increase and related adverse events and much more expansionary fiscal and monetary policies, the need for foreign financing again became critical. Exchange reserves were drawn down during 1974–76, oil facility loans were obtained from the IMF and short-term loans from the Euromarkets, and exchange controls were tightened. A serious crop failure in 1977 with weak foreign markets for Turkish agricultural exports compounded the problems and in the fall of 1977 the country was unable to honor its debt service commitments. After negotiations with the IMF and the OECD consortium, a stabilization program was adopted in early 1978. The program, the IMF Accord of 1978, was intended to last two years; it included credits from the IMF and the consortium, reduction of public expenditure in real terms, higher prices on the products of state economic enterprises, import restrictions and export promotion, and devaluation of the lira, with a commitment to an incomes policy (*OECD Economic Survey, Turkey,* 1978; World Bank 1982). The impact of the program is clear from table 11–11.

The lira was devalued considerably during 1978 and 1979 (figure 11–3). With agricultural production back to normal in 1978, real exports increased vigorously but fell back strongly again in 1979. The volume of imports was reduced drastically by quantitative restrictions, and shortages of fuel, raw materials, and spare parts led to production cutbacks. Despite the recovery of agricultural production, the GDP growth rate

Table 11-11. Growth Rates of Population, Real GDP, Domestic Absorption, Foreign Trade, GNP, and GNI, 1977–86

(percent, over previous year)

Category	1977	1978	1979	1980	1981	1982	1983	1984	1985	1986
Population	2.0	2.0	2.0	2.2	2.3	2.3	2.4	2.6	2.9	2.2
GDP[a]	5.1	4.4	-0.7	-1.6	3.7	4.5	4.0	6.1	4.2	7.3
Agriculture	-1.1	2.5	2.8	1.8	0.0	6.4	-0.2	3.6	2.4	8.1
Manufacturing	7.2	3.7	-5.2	-6.3	9.2	5.5	8.5	10.3	5.5	9.7
Other industry	14.5	13.3	1.4	0.0	-3.0	-0.3	0.0	3.1	5.7	5.9
Services	5.7	3.9	-0.3	0.8	4.2	4.1	4.5	5.7	4.1	6.0
GDP per capita	3.1	2.4	-2.7	-3.8	1.4	2.2	1.6	3.5	1.3	5.1
Domestic absorption[a]	6.0	-4.4	-2.2	-0.6	0.8	1.4	4.5	7.5	4.2	10.7
Private consumption	4.9	0.4	-1.9	-4.5	-0.9	3.5	6.2	10.4	1.7	9.4
General government consumption	4.4	9.8	1.6	8.8	-0.4	1.1	2.7	0.0	4.8	12.7
Fixed gross investment	6.9	-9.8	-3.6	-9.9	2.0	3.3	2.7	0.2	16.5	12.4
Domestic absorption per capita	4.0	-6.4	-4.2	-2.8	-1.5	-0.9	2.0	4.9	1.3	8.5
Exports of goods and nonfactor services[a]	-17.7	14.1	-9.6	4.2	85.4	40.0	13.7	19.8	12.3	-2.5
Imports of goods and nonfactor services[a]	4.2	-33.5	-6.8	2.5	14.8	7.5	17.1	27.7	8.1	11.5
GNP[a]	4.7	3.2	-1.5	-1.7	3.7	4.5	3.8	5.9	5.2	7.5
GNP per capita	2.7	1.2	-3.5	-3.9	1.3	2.2	1.3	3.3	2.3	5.3
GNI[a]	3.9	2.8	-1.7	-3.0	2.7	3.4	3.3	7.7	5.5	9.9
GNI per capita	1.9	0.8	-3.7	-5.2	0.3	1.1	0.9	5.1	2.6	7.7

a. At constant 1980 prices.
Source: World Bank (1989).

was down to 4.3 percent in 1978 and became negative in 1979 and 1980. Estimated unemployment increased strongly. On the expenditure side, there were severe reductions in private, fixed investment. Private consumption fell considerably while public consumption continued to expand vigorously, with inflationary financing continuing at a high level. Inflation accelerated into hyperinflation, with a 60 percent increase in the cost of living in 1978–79, and no incomes (wage) policy was explicitly adopted. The policies of the government obviously did not support the stabilization program and when the 1979 oil price increase promised to bring a further deterioration, the Ecevit government after losing the senate elections, resigned.

Distribution and Equity

Several measures of income distribution in the 1960s and 1970s are discussed in chapter 6. Both the Gini coefficients in table 6–6 and the Kuznets K measures in table 6–13 indicate a rather stable income distribution with, perhaps, a slight tendency toward equality in this period. The functional distribution of nonagricultural income shifted somewhat in favor of wages and salaries until 1970 and was then roughly constant until about 1977 when it started moving strongly in favor of profits. All indicators thus agree that distribution became slightly more egalitarian, at least during the first part of this period.

The poverty indicators in table 6–15 do not give much information about the development of poverty during the period of parliamentary democracy. They agree on a slight decline in poverty from 1973 to 1978. The increase in unemployment (table 11–4) should, on the other hand, point to increased poverty, at the end of the period particularly since there were no public unemployment insurance programs. Little was done to reform tax and welfare systems after the reforms of the early 1950s. Attempts were made to introduce taxation of agricultural income from 1960 and taxation was established by law in 1964 but exemptions were considerable and evasion massive. The same was the case for the taxation of business. Income taxation thus continued to rest mainly on wage and salary earners who suffered strong increases in real taxation as inflation accelerated and their nominal incomes rose, pushing them into higher tax brackets. With the increase in indirect taxation in the early 1960s it is probably fair to assume that distribution of after-tax income tended to worsen during the 1970s.

12 Market Orientation and Export-Led Growth, 1980–85

The resignation in late 1979 of the coalition government under the Republican People's party (Ecevit) and its replacement by another coalition government under the Justice party (Demirel) had unexpectedly profound consequences. In January 1980 the new government surprisingly announced a radical program to break the vicious circle of hyperinflation, stagnation, and unmanageable balance of payments deficits that appeared to have become the order of the day. The new program was intended not only to cope with the acute foreign payments and inflation situation but also to bring an end to the etatist policies which had prevailed since the time of Atatürk and to replace those policies with pronounced market orientation. A period of profound institutional reform was to be initiated.

Institutional Reform

The reform program of January 1980 included institutional changes aimed at making policy formulation and implementation more effective; a devaluation of the lira against the dollar by 33 percent and the limitation of multiple exchange rate practices; greater liberalization of the trade and payments regimes; additional promotional measures for exports; substantial price increases for state-traded goods and abolition of price controls; increased competition for state economic enterprises and abolition of most government subsidies; higher interest rates; promotion of foreign investment; arrangements for consolidating Turkey's private commercial debt; and draft legislation for tax reform (*OECD Economic Survey, Turkey* 1980, p. 25). Incomes policy, in the form of constraints on union activities and collective agreements, was also on the agenda. The constitution of 1961 had legalized unionization and collective agreements which made strikes a weapon in industrial conflict; unionization had made considerable progress and was growing in militancy.

Increasing domestic political destabilization with massive, accelerating terrorism led then to a military takeover in September 1980. The mil-

Table 12-1. Macro Achievement and Policy Indicators, 1974–87

	Achievement indicator							Policy indicator		
	Real growth rate percent		Rate of unemployment (percent)	Rate of inflation (percent)	Share of GNP (percent)[c]			Budget deficit as a percent of GNP	Rate of increase of money supply (percent)[d]	Exchange rate (lira per dollar)
Year	GDP[a]	GNP[b]			Gross investment	Exports of goods and nonfactor services	Current account balance			
1974–76	8.8	8.7	7.1	20.7	23.8	6.3	-4.1	-0.1[e]	25.7	14.8
1977	5.1	4.1	7.6	24.5	25.4	4.8	-6.8	n.a.	33.9	18.0
1978	4.3	2.9	8.1	43.7	22.2	5.2	-2.5	n.a.	36.5	24.3
1979	-0.6	-0.4	9.4	71.1	21.1	4.3	-2.4	n.a.	61.7	31.1
1980	-0.5	-1.1	10.7	105.7	20.4	6.5	-5.5	-10.0	66.6	76.0
1981	3.6	4.1	11.2	41.9	19.8	10.6	-2.9	-5.4	89.0	111.2
1982	4.5	4.5	11.8	27.2	19.7	15.1	-1.5	-6.0	55.5	162.6
1983	3.9	3.3	12.4	28.0	19.0	15.8	-3.4	-5.2	28.7	225.6
1984	6.0	5.9	12.4	49.9	19.0	19.8	-2.6	-6.5	58.3	366.7
1985	4.2	5.1	12.6	43.6	20.7	21.1	-1.9	-4.9	57.1	522.0
1986	7.3	8.1	12.3	30.6	24.3	18.3	-2.7	-4.5	43.0	674.5
1987	6.5[f]	7.4[f]	12.0	37.1	n.a.	n.a.	n.a.	-8.3	38.9[f]	857.2

n.a. = Not available.
a. At factor cost.
b. At market price.
c. At current market price.
d. Money supply equals money plus quasi money.
e. For 1975.
f. Provisional data.
Sources: OECD, Economic Survey, Turkey, various years; World Bank (1988); IMF, International Financial Statistics, various years.

itary government endorsed the reform program and kept its engineer, Turgut Özal, in command of economic policy. Indicators of macro policies and achievements are shown in tables 12–1 and 12–2. Under the military government, budgetary deficits were reduced and with the decline in monetary expansion, the introduction of a ban on strikes, and the institution of an arbitration board to settle wage and other labor disputes, the rate of inflation was reduced from about 100 percent in 1980 to about 30 percent in 1983. Impressed by, certainly inspiring, perhaps even instigating the January 1980 program, the IBRD, the IMF, and the OECD consortium came up with a package of economic assistance of about $4 billion with a token contribution from Saudi Arabia. A reorganization of the state economic enterprises was initiated by the military in 1983. After the new constitution was adopted in 1982, general though somewhat restricted elections in 1983 gave Özal an absolute majority. A program to complete the economic reforms that had been announced in 1980 was proclaimed in December 1983. In addition to reinforcing the liberalization and market orientation of the 1980 program, it dealt seriously with social problems that had been ignored under the years of military rule. Trade to a considerable extent and capital movements to some extent were liberalized.

Both stabilization and liberalization proved to be a long-drawn-out process, developing by fits and starts from 1978. (A detailed description of financial aid and structural and stabilization measures is given by Kopits [1987, pp. 6–19]; for the first year of the reforms World Bank [1982] gives additional details.) The problem of inflation was not really tackled, despite stabilization programs and reforms. After the period of hyperinflation, with the rate of inflation exceeding 100 percent in 1980, inflation abated somewhat, but the rate reached 40 percent in 1985 and approached hyperinflation again in 1988. Behind the inflation is monetary expansion, fueled since 1975 by central bank financing of the budget deficit. Despite successful efforts to bring down the state economic enterprise deficits, the overall budget deficit, after a temporary improvement in 1981–83, remained high, partly hidden in special funds.

As early as 1974, the OECD *Economic Survey* (1974, pp. 48–49) pointed to the need for an incomes policy that would restrain wages and support price increases in agriculture. In 1978 the government committed itself to an incomes policy, and negotiations in public sector enterprises had already taken place in 1977 under a social compact between government and the Turk İş Labour Confederation (*OECD Economic Survey* 1978, pp. 11, 25). Although regular contacts were established under Ecevit between government, unions, and employers, little restraint appears to have resulted.[1] When a Price Control Commission was established in 1978 to regulate prices of all important product categories, incomes policy in effect meant price control without wage restraint. In

Table 12-2. Money, Prices, Interest Rates, and Real Effective Exchange Rate, 1978–85

| Year | Rate of increase (percent) | | | Interest rate (percent) | | | | Real effective exchange rate index[b] (1980=100) |
| | Money supply[a] | Prices | | Nominal | | Real, ex post | | |
		Wholesale	Consumer	Deposits	Lending	Deposits	Lending	
1978	37	53	53	7.3[c]	13.2[c]	−46[c]	−40[c]	116.3
1979	62	64	62	7.3	18.0	−57	−46	129.0
1980	67	109	110	10.0	25.7	−99	−83	100
1981	89	37	37	28.5	38.6	−8	2	95.7
1982	50	25	31	45.0	36.0	20	11	87.5
1983	29	31	33	45.3	35.5	14	5	87.6
1984	28	52	48	51.4	52.3	−1	0	83.0
1985	44	40	45	53.0	53.3	13	13	84.2

a. Money supply equals money plus quasi money.
b. Decline indicates real depreciation.
c. Conjecture.
Source: IMF, *International Financial Statistics*, various years; IMF data.

June 1980 a representative of the OECD is reported to have explained at a press conference that "it was imperative that wages should be frozen if the 24 January programme was to succeed" (Birand 1987, p. 127). The wage-price policy was completely reversed after the military takeover in 1980, with a ban on militant unions and the establishment of the Supreme Arbitration Board, which was authorized to settle all pending collective agreements and issue guidelines for future agreements. Strikes were declared illegal. These repressive measures were counterbalanced by restrictions on layoffs in manufacturing industry. The Demirel government prepared legislation to severely limit union activities but the legislation never reached Parliament. The Price Control Commission was at the same time abolished and state economic enterprises were instructed to adjust their prices to reflect actual costs. Only a few basic commodities (bread, sugar, coal, and fertilizer) remained subsidized. A market-oriented approach to agricultural support prices was adopted and subsequently implemented to make agricultural prices follow world prices. This system remained largely in force until 1985 when the role of the wage arbitration board was limited to areas where strikes were illegal and the collective bargaining process was liberalized; the ban on militant unions remained in force. In April 1987 the Arbitration Board was finally abolished.

Considerable real effective depreciation by 32 percent took place from 1979 to 1982. From 1982 to 1985 the additional depreciation was negligible, 4 percent (see figures 11–3 to 11–4). The real effective depreciation was engineered through nominal, discretionary depreciations against the dollar, undertaken with sufficient frequency and strength to neutralize both the depreciations of trade partners' currencies against the dollar during the years of the rising dollar and the inflation in Turkey that was in excess of her trade partners' inflation. This aspect of the program was successful although it may be questioned whether the oil price increase of 1979–80 and the related terms of trade loss did not require even stronger depreciation in 1979–82 and whether additional depreciation after 1982 would not have been appropriate. However, had real depreciation been measured by a REER (as an expression of domestic purchasing power) based on nominal wage rates rather than consumer prices, the real depreciation would have been stronger (see table 12–6).

Institutional interest rates were increased strongly from 1979 to 1982. With increasing inflation, real interest rates (ex post) had become negative and extremely low, in 1980 declining to −80 percent to −100 percent. Negative interest rates of such magnitude must have been a strong stimulant to private real investment and probably detrimental to private saving. In 1982 real interest rates again became positive (ex post) at a level of 11 percent and 20 percent for bank loans and deposits, respectively. Increasing inflation in 1983 and 1984 was not fully countered by increasing nominal interest rates, however, and in 1984 the real rates for both bank loans and deposits were down to zero. Upward adjustment of nominal interest rates in 1985 with a decline in the rate of inflation brought real interest rates up again to a level of 13 percent. Compared with the years before 1981, the government's interest policy was successful though the government's ability to control inflation and its flexibility in adjusting nominal interest rates to inflation left much to be desired. While private investment declined from 1974–78 to 1983–84 (table 11–5) as should be expected, there was no sign of increased private saving.

While both interest rates and exchange rates undoubtedly were brought closer to equilibrium in 1979–82, liberalization of trade took longer and mainly occurred somewhat later, at the end of 1983. While the stabilization program of 1978 was accompanied by the introduction of a stiff stamp duty of 25 percent and increased guarantee deposits on imports, from 1980 these were greatly reduced or abolished. Items were transferred from highly restrictive to less restrictive lists and import and export procedures were simplified between 1980 and 1983. From 1980, exporters were granted the right to import inputs free of duty; export incentives such as direct tax rebates for industrial goods were introduced ranging from 9 percent to 23 percent of the value of eligible exports. The incentives began to be cut back again in 1984, reaching a level of 8 percent in 1986. The percentage of imports on the liberalization list, the least restrictive category, increased steadily (Şenses 1984, table 5, p. 292).

	1978	1980	1983
Liberalization list	69.6	77.0	89.6
Quota list	17.0	12.0	1.8
Bilateral agreement	1.4	2.1	1.1
Other	12.0	8.9	7.5

The Özal program of 1983–84 classified imports as prohibited, approved, or liberalized, the latter being any imports neither prohibited nor requiring official approval. With the reclassification there was a strong increase in items on the liberalization list. A special list included once-prohibited imports that were now permitted against payment in dollar-equivalent liras set aside for a special housing fund. This was one of the few socially oriented features of the liberalization programs. Substantial reductions of tariff rates and production taxes were undertaken. It appears that tariff reductions mainly applied to capital and intermediate goods while consumer goods, particularly durables, actually may have experienced tariff and tax increases (Şenses 1984). Thus, import substitution policy was not entirely abolished. Bilateral trade, moreover, increased sharply with the increased trade with Middle East OPEC countries.

From the mid-1970s, progressive personal income taxation combined with strong inflation automatically increased marginal (and average) tax rates for employees in the formal sector where tax withholding was effective. Tax evasion and reduced incentives to work and to save allegedly resulted. More important was probably the incentive it gave for militant unions to push harder for money wage increases to keep real disposable wages increasing despite inflation and tax drift. Reforms of 1981 to 1985, adjusting tax brackets and marginal rates of taxation, and from 1984 introducing refunding in proportion to expenditure on basic needs, should therefore be seen as part and parcel of the incomes policy aimed at making the strong decline in pretax product wages palatable by keeping real disposable wages in line with consumer prices. It is claimed that while (presumably in terms of consumer goods) real wages before tax declined 3.4 percent annually from 1980 to 1986, real take-home pay increased by 2.8 percent annually (Kopits 1987, p. 23). To the extent that before the reforms increased taxation of wage earners' income through inflation drift was compensated for by higher negotiated wage increases and that existing price controls kept these wage increases from being shifted on to prices, the inflation drift in withheld income taxes in effect became a tax on profits. The reforms of wage income taxation with the policy of wage restraints and the abolishment of price controls after 1980 served then to remove this tax burden on enterprises without shifting it directly back to wage earners. Who paid the bill is not clear. Budget expenditure was reduced but the incidence of the expenditure cuts is not clear.

Before the reforms of 1981, small businesses and professions were virtually tax exempt, paying at most nominal lump sums. These were brought in line with inflation, with income below certain limits being taxed at 40 percent of assessed income. How this has worked is not clear. Unincorporated businesses, professionals, and farmers with higher income are required to file annual income declarations and to make payments in advance and tax collections generally have been speeded up.

Taxation of agricultural income was tightened. With the criteria of agricultural taxation redefined, the number of tax-exempt farmers should have been greatly reduced. Farmers must declare their income if they own more than one tractor, a harvester, or land of a certain size and have sales receipts above a certain limit. Moreover, a withholding tax of 5 percent is applied to all sales at official support prices. This, however, looks like a step backward to the old production (*uşr*) tax, abolished in 1925. Corporate income tax rates were unified in 1981 with rates adjusted slightly upward and state economic enterprises were subjected to income tax (economically mainly a bookkeeping reform). A value added tax of 10 percent, refunded at export, was introduced in 1985 to replace nine production taxes. With food exempted, this is not even a pure consumption tax. Although, as usual, supply-side effects do not appear to have materialized, the tax reforms with the incomes policy may have had important effects on the incidence of taxation.

Foreign exchange regulations related to capital movements were relaxed somewhat in December 1983. Residents and nonresidents were allowed to possess foreign currency and open foreign exchange accounts, with no restrictions on the use of such funds. Currency restrictions on tourists were relaxed and nonresidents were allowed, with permission, to invest in Turkey. Imports of Turkish financial assets kept abroad were given free. Residents were allowed to export up to $2 million in capital with permission of the Treasury, larger investments abroad requiring cabinet approval. Foreign credit could be used under certain conditions. Albeit a far cry from complete liberalization of capital movements, the new rules constituted a considerable relaxation of very rigid restrictions.

The liberalization process from 1978 to 1985 thus proceeded through depreciations, wage constraint with relaxation of price controls, domestic financial decontrol, liberalization of trade, tax reform, and finally some liberalization of capital movements, with too little done about inflation and the budget deficit.

Liberalization and Reform

The average GDP growth rate for the planning and import-substitution years 1961–63 to 1977–79 was quite high, 6.4 percent with GDP per capita growth at 3.9 percent. The average GNP growth rate per capita for middle-income countries (World Bank definition) was 3.7 percent for 1960–78. For 1973–76 Turkey's growth rate even exceeded 8.5 percent, with per capita growth about 6 percent. Severe drought in 1977 brought the GDP growth rate down to 5.1 percent (table 12–1). The foreign exchange crisis further reduced growth to 4.3 percent in 1978, and for 1979 and 1980 growth rates were negative at -0.4 percent and -1.1 percent, respectively, with per capita growth around -3 percent. For the years 1981–85 the economy was sluggish with a rather constant, low growth rate of 4.6 percent on average and per capita growth down to 2.4 percent. This is less than two-thirds of per capita growth for 1961–63 to 1977–79 and less than half that of the high growth years 1973–76. Partly because of favorable weather conditions the growth rate increased to about 8 percent in 1986 and a projected 6.5 percent for 1987. Even so, the growth rate was hardly better than under the import-substitution strategy.

The impact of liberalization and reform on employment is difficult to assess given the imperfect and incomplete labor market indicators. It is fairly clear that the national unemployment rate increased from about 3 percent in the late 1960s to about 12 percent by the mid-1980s. But there is much uncertainty about the path of unemployment before and after and in between these years and about its relation to early import-substitution policy, to the strong import-substitution policy of 1973–78, the foreign exchange crises around 1977–79, the stabilization efforts of 1978–80, and the reforms from 1980 onward. That a strong shift upward, possibly even the whole shift, took place from 1975 to 1980 seems indisputable. Part of the long-term increase may be voluntary unemployment related to improved education. Developments after the reforms are most uncertain. Urban labor force surveys point to increasing unemployment rates in 1982–85. Auxiliary placement office indicators point to improvement of the labor market situation after 1982, particularly after 1985 (Hansen 1989b, graph 1–1). The strong increase of registered unemployed during the 1980s should probably be ignored as being, partly at least, a consequence of new incentives for unemployed persons to register. Clearly the reforms and the associated fiscal-monetary and exchange policies were not able to reverse the employment trend and bring the unemployment rate back to the much more favorable level of the early period of inward-looking development strategy, but external conditions had become extremely difficult, with labor migration to Europe largely halted and terms of trade moving strongly against the country, at least until 1984.

The share of gross investment in GNP, which went up from 15.7 percent in 1962–63 to 21.7 percent in 1974–78, was down to 19.6 percent in 1983–84. Gross saving, which went up from 11.8 percent of GNP in 1962–63 to 17.2 percent in 1974–78, was down to 16.5 percent in 1983–84. Inflation was down from the hyperinflation rate of about 100 percent but continued at a rate of 40 percent in 1985, increasing to 80 percent in 1988. The country was still far from a controlled monetary situation. The total public sector budget deficit lingered at a level of 5 percent of GNP (1984–86). The balance of payments (table 12–3) showed a certain improvement with the current account deficit down from $2.2 billion for 1975–79 and $3.6 billion in 1980 to $1.9 billion for 1980–84 and $1.4 billion for 1984; this may have been the effect of the sluggishness of the economy more than liberalization and reform. However, while the balance of trade at current prices deteriorated from 1971–73 to 1980–84, at constant prices the balance of trade changed from deficit in 1962–70 to surplus in 1980–84 (see table 12–12). With a new balance of payments classification (*OECD Economic Survey,* 1986/87, table H[b]), slow continued improvement is discernible from 1981 to 1986. There is not sufficient information to make reliable statements about income distribution and poverty.

By and large the verdict would seem to be that expected benefits of reform and liberalization programs at best have materialized unevenly and rather slowly. However, the full effects of the new policy may not yet have shown up; long-term effects may not show up in half a decade.

Table 12-3. Balance of Payments, Annual Averages, in Millions of Dollars and as a Percentage of GDP, 1950–84

Category	1950–60 Percent of GDP	1950–60 Millions of dollars	1961–71 Percent of GDP	1961–71 Millions of dollars	1972–74 Percent of GDP	1972–74 Millions of dollars	1975–79 Percent of GDP	1975–79 Millions of dollars	1980–84 Percent of GDP	1980–84 Millions of dollars	1984 Percent of GDP	1984 Millions of dollars
Exports	4.0	323.3ᵃ	4.8	480.2ᵃ	7.6	1,691.7	5.2	2,762.6	13.8	7,177.8	19.4	9,538
Imports	-5.5	-437.2ᵃ	-7.2	-728.7ᵃ	-12.6	-2,800.3	-10.6	-5,629.6	-19.4	-10,092.4	-24.6	-12,097
Net exports	-1.4	-114.0ᵃ	-2.5	-248.5ᵃ	-5.0	-1,108.7	-5.4	-2,867.0	-5.6	-2,914.8	-5.2	-2,559
Interest, net	-0.2	-16.6	-0.4	-37.9	-0.3	-74.3	-0.9	-498.0	-2.3	-1,212.6	-2.8	-1,383
Profits	0.0	-2.0	-0.2	-18.0	-0.2	-47.0	-0.2	-83.6	-0.1	-44.4	-0.1	-50
Workers' remittances	n.a	n.a.	1.2	116.3	5.0	1,116.3	2.3	1,190.8	4.1	2,148.4	3.8	1,890
Net income from factor services	0.2	-18.6	0.6	60.4	4.5	995.0	1.2	609.0	1.7	891.4	0.9	457
Transfers	0.3	26.3	0.3	25.5	0.1	30.3	0.0	1.0	0	0	0	0
Other (tourism, travel, other)ᵇ	-0.2	-15.6	-0.1	-12.3	n.a.	n.a.	n.a.	n.a.	n.a.	n.a.	n.a.	n.a.

Current account balance	-1.5	-122.0[a]	-1.7	-174.7[a]	-0.4	-83.3	-4.2	-2,248.0	-3.9	-2,023.2	-4.3	-2,102
GDP at current market price (millions of lira)	23,930		98,525		312,454		1,100,560		9,821,758		18,214,777	
Official exchange rate (dollar per lira)	0.3347		0.1024		0.0710		0.0481		0.0053		0.0027	
GDP (millions of dollars)	8,009		10,089		22,184		52,988		52,055		49,180	

n.a. = Not available.

a. Not including nonfactor services.

b. Data from 1972–84 are included in exports and imports.

Source: World Bank (1975), table 3–1; World Bank (1982), table 3–1; World Bank data; IMF, *International Financial Statistics*, various years; Turkey, State Institute of Statistics and World Bank data.

Table 12-4. Value and Distribution of Exports, by Destination, 1962–84

Category	At current prices					At constant 1980 prices				
	LDCs	DCs	CPCs	Other	World	LDCs	DCs	CPCs	Other	World
Value (millions of dollars)										
1962	27.7	326.9	26.6	0	381.2	74.3	1,472.2	103.9	—	1,560.7
1965	34.7	355.2	69.0	0	458.9	111.9	1,571.8	218.9	—	1,840.0
1970	60.0	443.8	84.7	0	588.5	185.7	1,980.0	253.1	—	2,337.6
1975	280.1	997.0	124.0	0	1,401.1	384.8	1,863.0	198.0	—	2,424.8
1980	702.0	1,712.7	492.5	2.4	2,909.6	702.0	1,712.7	492.5	2.4	2,909.6
1984	3,048.3	3,777.3	307.9	0.1	7,133.6	4,086.7	4,188.0	381.0	—	8,689.4
Rate of increase (percent)										
1962–70	10.1	3.9	15.6	—	5.6	12.1	3.8	11.8	—	5.2
1970–80	27.9	14.5	19.3	—	17.3	14.2	-1.4	6.9	—	2.2
1980–84	44.4	21.9	-11.1	—	25.1	55.3	25.1	-6.2	—	31.5
Share of total (percent)										
1962	7.3	85.8	7.0	0	100	4.8	94.3	6.7	—	100
1965	7.6	77.4	15.0	0	100	6.1	85.4	11.9	—	100
1970	10.2	75.4	14.4	0	100	7.9	84.1	10.8	—	100
1975	20.0	71.2	8.9	0	100	15.9	76.8	8.1	—	100
1980	24.1	58.9	16.9	0.1	100	24.1	58.9	16.9	0.1	100
1984	42.7	53.0	4.3	0.0	100	47.0	48.2	4.4	—	100

LDCs = Less developed countries.
DCs = Developed countries.
CPCs = Centrally planned countries.
— = Not applicable.
Source: Computations by Edward F. Lucas, from UNCTAD tape of trade data.

Even disregarding the exceptional crops in 1986, it appears that in 1986–87 growth finally reached the same high rates as in 1962–77. Though interesting historically, the comparison between the achievements of planning and import substitution during 1972–77 and those of liberalization and reform during 1980–85 may be beside the point. The real question is what might have been achieved with continued planning and import substitution during 1977–85, assuming financing had been available, and with liberalization and reform during 1962–77. Both alternatives, I believe, would have failed miserably. Successful development has to begin with planning and import substitution and then shift into a policy of liberalization and reform. The question that remains is whether Turkey should have made the shift a decade earlier, for which there is much to be said. Reforms as well as fiscal and monetary policies could have been pushed more vigorously had politics permitted.

Despite its rather mixed achievements since 1980 in terms of growth, inflation, employment, and equity, Turkey has nonetheless been singled out as a particularly successful case of liberalization; a very strong increase in exports of manufactured goods is the main indicator of success. Measured as a percentage of GNP, exports of goods and services increased from 5.2 percent in 1975–79 to 13.8 percent in 1980–84 and 19.4 percent in 1984 alone. Of the total increase from 1971–73 to 1982–85, 75 percent originated in manufacturing industry. This is, indeed, remarkable.

Export Achievements

Turkish exports generally have been favorably influenced by the increase in import demand from Middle East OPEC countries that followed the oil price increases of 1973 and 1979. Table 12–4 presents a breakdown of Turkish export value from 1962 to 1984 by destination to developing, developed, and centrally planned countries. The OPEC countries are included in the broader category of developing countries (which they dominate) because this breakdown provides a cross-classification by commodity groups and a decomposition by price and volume changes that is necessary for detailed analysis. The striking feature of the table is the steady and dramatic increase in the developing countries' share of exports from 7 percent in 1962 to 43 percent in 1984, when the developed countries' share was declining steadily from 86 percent to 53 percent. The centrally planned economies' share fluctuated but was even lower in 1984 than in 1962, 4.3 percent against 7.0 percent. By far the largest part of the increase in the developing countries' share took place after 1970, yet half of it took place between 1980 and 1984. It stands to reason that although the oil price increases of 1973 and 1979 were important for increasing the share of developing countries, other

Table 12-5. Value and Distribution of Exports, by Commodity Group, 1962–84

Category	Total	Food and food products[a]	Agricultural raw materials	Mineral fuels	Minerals and metals	Semi-manufactures	Finished manufactures
Value (millions of dollars)[a]							
1962	381.2	255.4	90.2	6.2	25.1	4.0	0.4
1965	458.9	274.4	133.0	5.6	36.6	8.3	0.8
1970	588.5	290.0	197.6	3.7	47.7	40.9	8.6
1975	1,401.1	636.8	284.6	36.1	129.7	189.3	124.5
1980	2,909.6	1,486.0	395.4	41.5	232.3	509.5	244.9
1984	7,133.6	2,194.6	365.9	406.0	848.5	1,512.6	1,805.0
Share of total (percent)							
1962	100	67.0	23.7	1.6	6.6	1.0	0.1
1965	100	59.8	29.0	1.2	8.0	1.8	0.2
1970	100	49.3	33.6	0.6	8.1	6.9	1.5
1975	100	45.5	20.3	2.6	9.3	13.5	8.9
1980	100	51.1	13.6	1.4	8.0	17.5	8.4
1984	100	30.8	5.1	5.7	11.9	21.2	25.3

— = Not applicable.
a. At current prices.
Source: Same as for table 12–4.

factors played an important role. In real terms the shifts in export destination were even stronger, from 5 percent to 47 percent for developing countries and from 94 percent to 48 percent for developed countries. Throughout the period 1962–84 the rate of growth of both nominal and real exports to developing countries greatly exceeded that to developed countries which, on the other hand, fell short systematically of the growth rate of total exports.

Table 12–5 shows the composition of exports by commodity groups. The classification, from UNCTAD data tapes, is not ideal, for food and food products include manufactured food, while minerals and metals include iron and steel, and for Turkey mineral fuels are exclusively manufactured (refined) products. The table shows a strong change in composition of exports, agriculture-based exports (first two categories) going from 91 percent in 1962 to 36 percent in 1984, mining and quarrying-based exports (next two categories) from 8 percent to 18 percent, and semifinished and finished manufactures from 1 percent to 46 percent. About half the shift in commodity composition took place from 1980 to 1984, which again indicates that factors other than OPEC demand must have played a crucial role. Again it stands to reason that the factors at work must have been the liberalization policies in Turkey.

The cross-classification by both destination and commodity group in table 12–6 discloses that while the total increase in exports (values at current prices) was almost as large to developing as to developed countries, the distribution by commodity groups was entirely different for the two groups of countries. The increase of exports to developing countries was dominated by food and food products followed by semimanufactured goods and minerals and metals, in this order, while that to developed countries was dominated by finished manufactures, semimanufactures, and food and food products in this order. The increase of exports of food and food products to developing countries was almost double that to developed countries. The increase of finished manufactures to developed countries was more than three times that to developing countries. The increase of exports of semimanufactures was almost the same to the two groups of countries.

In real terms (1980 prices) relative increases in exports are quite different from those measured at current prices, as is clear from table 12–4. The shift toward developing countries is stronger in real terms. Turkey was faced with a systematic difference in the development of prices and volumes of exports to developed and developing countries. Throughout the period 1962–84, export prices to developed countries tended to increase more than did prices to developing countries, with the opposite tendency for export volumes, as is apparent in table 12–7. To emphasize this fact, table 12–8 shows the ratios between price and volume indexes for exports to developing and developed countries for the years 1970 and 1984.

Table 12–6. Value of Exports to Developing and Developed Countries, by Commodity Group, 1962–84
(millions of dollars)

Commodity and destination	Value of current prices				Value at 1980 prices			
	1962	1973	1984	Increase 1962–84	1962	1973	1984	Increase 1962–84
Food and food products								
Developing countries	23.4	83.5	1,226.9	1,203.5	58.5	145.3	1,761.4	1,702.9
Developed countries	214.9	495.8	820.1	605.2	852.8	1,403.3	1,109.0	256.2
Agricultural raw materials								
Developing countries	2.5	71.0	71.9	69.4	6.9	122.7	95.2	88.3
Developed countries	80.0	226.5	248.3	168.3	238.2	413.8	284.9	46.7
Minerals and metals								
Developing countries	0.0	7.4	542.4	542.4	n.a.	n.a.	n.a.	n.a.
Developed countries	23.9	50.3	249.9	226.0	139.0	184.1	282.4	143.3

Semimanufactures

Developing countries	0.2	25.3	731.6	731.4	0.3	45.7	1,052.2	1,051.9
Developed countries	3.1	105.7	737.8	734.7	14.7	229.3	659.3	644.6

Finished manufactures

Developing countries	0.1	10.3	409.5	409.4	0.2	17.1	455.1	455.4
Developed countries	0.3	59.7	1,380.3	1,380.0	1.8	158.3	1,246.3	1,244.5

Total[a]

Developing countries	27.7	201.3	3,048.3	3,020.6	74.3	379.0	4,086.7	4,012.4
Developed countries	326.9	983.2	3,777.4	3,450.5	1,472.2	2,750.4	4,188.0	2,715.8

n.a. = Not available.

a. Includes mineral fuels.

Source: Same as for table 12–4.

Table 12-7. Price and Volume Indexes of Exports to Developing and Developed Countries, by Commodity Group, 1962–84

Index, destination, and commodity	1962	1965	1970	1975	1980	1984
Price index, developing countries						
Food and food products	100	83.1	89.6	201.2	250.0	174.2
Agricultural raw materials	100	83.3	82.4	151.9	268.5	202.9
Minerals and metals	a	a	100.0	166.7	237.7	185.5
Semimanufactures	100	85.9	63.2	113.0	152.2	105.8
Finished manufactures	100	156.4	114.1	179.8	235.2	211.4
Total[b]	100	83.0	86.6	195.0	267.9	199.8
Price index, developed countries						
Food and food products	100	105.4	97.0	209.9	396.8	293.4
Agricultural raw materials	100	94.5	93.6	186.8	297.7	259.5
Minerals and metals	a	a	100.0	219.5	436.3	386.0
Semimanufactures	100	106.9	118.5	258.7	479.1	532.2
Finished manufactures	100	134.2	127.6	297.3	535.3	592.8
Total[b]	100	101.8	100.9	241.0	450.4	406.2
Volume index, developing countries						
Food and food products	100	123.2	136.4	251.2	645.2	3,012.9
Agricultural raw materials	100	410.8	945.8	1,528.2	664.3	1,388.9
Minerals and metals	a	a	100.0	462.2	704.1	16,625.4
Semimanufactures	100	302.5	6,395.5	27,732.8	47,598.6	369,631.1
Finished manufactures	100	103.0	2,154.0	18,782.2	40,097.4	215,238.6
Total[b]	100	150.7	250.0	518.0	945.1	5,502.1
Volume index, developed countries						
Food and food products	100	92.8	99.6	96.8	97.7	130.0
Agricultural raw materials	100	130.5	208.1	138.9	95.2	119.6
Minerals and metals	a	a	100.0	122.3	99.4	162.5
Semimanufactures	100	217.8	851.4	1,474.0	2,217.4	4,498.
Finished manufactures	100	141.3	1,421.1	9,288.7	8,092.0	69,088.8
Total[b]	100	106.8	134.5	126.5	116.3	284.5

Note: The indexes are chained Fisher indexes.

a. Data not available; 1970=100.

b. Includes mineral fuels.

Source: Same as for table 12–4.

This puzzling feature of Turkish export trade might be seen as in line with elementary demand and supply theory—the harder the quantities supplied are pushed, the lower prices will be. Such a conclusion, however, immediately raises the question why Turkish exporters should push hardest toward the markets of developing countries at the cost of a relative fall in prices. Indeed, if Turkish exporters were price takers and arbitrage were perfect, price developments would have to be the same everywhere, with relative quantities determined by price elasticities and other demand determinants such as income developments in the importing countries. Or, to look on the other side, the demand pull for Turkish exports from developing countries, which is dominated by oil-exporting countries, has undoubtedly been stronger than from developed countries, at least during the 1980s when much of the differences developed. This would easily explain the relatively strong increase in volume for developing countries but certainly not the weaker price developments.

It may be that this phenomenon is specific to Turkey. Similar indexes for a North-South country grouping show South-South export prices for 1970–82 declining 9 percent as compared with South-North export prices, with South-South export volumes increasing 37 percent more than South–North export volumes (Information from Edward F. Lucas). Although this tendency is the same as for Turkey, it is much weaker and the pattern is not uniform across commodity groups as it is for Turkey. Hence the phenomenon may not be universal.

Commodity composition may differ systematically between Turkish exports to developing (Middle East or oil-exporting) countries and the countries represented in table 12–8. To pursue this line of explanation further would require disaggregation which may not be practical for some of the commodity groups.

Competition may be imperfect in the sense that individual Turkish exporters perceive (differently) sloping foreign demand curves in separate markets; it is hard to see, however, why the result should be systematically relatively falling prices and increasing quantities in developing countries. Quotas for certain products in developed countries (textiles) might be part of the explanation, but since final products mainly went to developed countries and were not shifted toward developing countries, this cannot have been a major factor. For other products, interference from the side of the Turkish government may be the explanation (for cement, see below).

Thinking in terms of disequilibrium theory, it could be assumed that, at the beginning of the period, profit margins on exports to developing countries, particularly to Middle East oil-exporting countries, were excessive and served as an incentive for Turkish exporters to continue pushing harder in that direction despite a relative fall in prices. This could be related to the increase in oil prices, which in several countries

Table 12-8. Price and Volume of Exports to Developing Countries Relative to Exports to Developed Countries by Commodity Group and Region, 1970 and 1984 (annually chained Fisher indexes)

Category	By commodity group						By regions		
	Food and food products	Agricultural raw materials	Minerals and metals	Semi-manufactures	Finished manufactures	Total	Middle East	Oil exporters With capital surplus[a]	Other
Price									
1970	100	100	100	100	100	100	100	100	100
1984	64	89	48	38	40	58	56	70	51
Volume									
1970	100	100	100	100	100	100	100	100	100
1984	169	256	10,230	1,094	205	1,040	1,165	2,817	2,507

Does not include mineral fuels and commodities, not elsewhere stated.
a. United Arab Emirates, Libya, Kuwait, Saudi Arabia, and Brunei.
Source: Same as for table 12–4.

led to relaxation of import restrictions, assuming rents to have accrued to foreign suppliers rather than to domestic license holders (analogous perhaps, to Japanese car exports to the United States under the voluntary restraint arrangements). This situation, however, should have existed since 1962 and seems to require a market power that Turkish exporters may not have. The Islamic connection, with the fact that the expansion of Turkish exports to developing countries was concentrated on its two warring neighbors, Iran and Iraq, might, at least since 1980, help explain Turkish market power. The disequilibrium hypothesis could be tested through the computation of cross-country price indexes.

Turkish exporters may increasingly have exported low-quality products to developing countries and higher-quality products to developed countries. This would follow a classical export growth pattern. Germany and Japan before World War I and to some extent between the wars are reputed to have operated very successfully in export markets under the device of *billig und schlecht*. This might be a rational export policy in markets dominated by low-income customers. India did very well in cotton textile exports to China and Southeast Asia on the same principle before World War I (Morris 1983, chap. 7). All three cases are based on hearsay; testing such a hypothesis would be very difficult.

Finally, government behavior and interference could be the explanation. Turkish trade with the OPEC countries has mainly been bilateral which, incidentally, means that an increasing part of Turkish trade must have become bilateral after the reforms, a curious form of liberalization. With the OPEC countries, Iran and Iraq certainly given their predicaments, anxious to expand oil export and imports, always ready to cheat on their OPEC obligations through oil price discounts and similar devices, and with Turkey equally anxious to expand her exports and obtain relatively cheap oil, is it not conceivable that this particular game, involving two governments and considering the Islamic connection, may have led to relatively low prices on both sides? A detailed study of Turkish oil imports might give the answer. Such a study, if at all feasible, would have to consider in great detail both crude oil qualities and price policies of other relevant OPEC countries.

Although there is some uncertainty about the mechanisms behind the shift in Turkish exports toward developing countries, it seems that demand pull from these countries, particularly the oil-exporting countries, does not in itself suffice to explain the strong increase in Turkish exports generally and that the impact of the liberalization policy must have been very substantial.

Liberalization and the Structure of Trade

The full story of the impact of liberalization on trade is exceedingly complex and interesting. Table 12–9 breaks down for 1971–85, exports and

Table 12-9. Commodity Trade, by Sector of Origin, 1971–85
(millions of dollars)

Sector and trade	1971–73	1974–77	1978–79	1980–81	1982–85	Increase 1971–73 to 1982–85
Agricultural and Livestock						
Export	643.6	985.1	1,443.2	1,945.6	1,872.5	1,228.9
Import	55.6	175.3	43.6	87.4	276.7	221.1
Net export	588.0	809.8	1,399.6	1,858.2	1,595.9	1,007.9
Net export including processed products	660.1	787.5	1,447.6	1,904.2	1,945.9	1,285.8
Mining and quarrying based						
Export	39.0	105.3	128.3	192.2	212.0	173.0
Import	157.2	974.0	1,100.8	3,286.9	3,679.0	3,522.7
Net export	–118.2	–868.7	–972.5	–3,094.8	–3,467.9	–3,399.7
Net export including petroleum products	–118.7	967.8	–1,523.6	–3,787.4	–3,428.3	–3,309.6

Industry						
Export	277.0	571.2	703.2	1,668.8	4,556.8	4,279.8
Import	1,393.7	3,711.0	3,689.9	5,047.1	6,155.1	4,761.4
Net export	−1,116.7	−3,139.8	−2,986.7	−3,378.3	−1,598.3	−481.6
Net export excluding agricultural processed and petroleum products	−1,188.3	−3,018.4	−2,483.2	−2,731.7	−1,987.9	−899.6
All sectors						
Export	959.6	1,661.6	2,274.7	3,806.5	6,641.3	5,681.7
Import	1,606.5	4,860.3	4,834.2	8,421.4	10,111.9	8,505.4
Net export	−646.9	−3,198.7	−2,559.5	−4,614.9	−3,470.6	−2,823.7

Annual averages, at current prices.
Source: World Bank (1982), tables 3–2, 3–3; World Bank data; OECD, *Economic Surveys, Turkey* 1985.

imports by sectoral origin. The sectors are agriculture and livestock, mining and quarrying, and industry (manufacturing). Since classification by producing sector is somewhat ambiguous (are ginned and baled cotton and wheat flour agricultural or manufactured products?), the particularly important categories of agriculture-based processed products (food and beverages) and petroleum products are excluded from manufacturing industry and added to agriculture and mining, respectively, in separate calculations of net exports. This reclassification somewhat strengthens the conclusions but does not change them significantly. The periodization closely follows foreign exchange developments and the impact of liberalization and reform in 1982–85, when both were well on their way, compares well with that in 1971–73, when the foreign exchange situation was relatively easy and the lira may not have been overvalued. Comparison with 1974–77, the years of overheating, would reflect the impact of the change in demand management and obscure the impact of liberalization and reform per se. And comparison with the crisis years or the early years of liberalization would be appropriate only for short-term purposes. The years chosen for comparison are crucial for the conclusions drawn, however.

Turkey has traditionally been a net exporter of agricultural products, a net importer of mining and quarrying products (at least since oil became important), and a net importer of industrial products. From 1978–79 to 1982–85, exports of industrial products increased strongly with no less than $3,854 million from $703 million to $4,556 million. This is the basis for the success story. The interesting thing is, however, that the expansion of industrial exports was accompanied by an expansion in imports of industrial products. The comparison of figures for 1982–85 with 1971–73 (figures are not available for 1970 or earlier years) in table 12–9 shows a stronger expansion of imports than exports of industrial products, with an increase in net imports of industrial products. When agriculture-based processed products and petroleum products are reclassified to agriculture and mining, respectively, the conclusion is only strengthened.

The impact of the liberalization insofar as industrial products are concerned would thus seem to have been a large expansion of trade—exports as well as imports—rather than a net improvement of the balance of trade. This is, of course, partly an implication of the relatively high import content of Turkish industrial output and partly, presumably, the allocation improvement implied by the liberalization. The composition of total expenditure should tend to improve with a higher share of imported manufactured products, domestically produced manufactured products being sent abroad as payment. So-called "new" trade theory would predict this result (Dixit and Norman 1980; Krugman 1990, chs. 1 and 5).

Table 12–10. Production, Trade, and Domestic Use of Cement, 1977–83
(thousands of tons)

Year	Production	Exports	Imports	Domestic consumption plus stock changes[a]
1977	13,832	328	1	13,505
1978	15,340	1,240	0	14,100
1979	13,812	1,190	0	12,622
1980	12,875	736	1	12,140
1981	15,043	3,444	2	11,601
1982	15,577	4,124	2	11,455
1983	13,644	2,284	2	11,363

a. Production plus imports minus exports.
Source: World Bank data.

Had 1974–77 been compared with 1982–85, the increase in exports would have been stronger than the increase in imports of industrial products, with a contribution to improvement of the balance of trade. Part of the very strong increase in imports of industrial products from 1971–73 to 1974–77 may be the result of ongoing import substitution. Most of the increase did, however, take place between 1973 and 1975. It seems unlikely that import substitution in itself should lead to such an abrupt increase in industrial imports and more reasonable to see the explanation in demand overheating. Comparison with 1974–77 would be unfair to import substitution policy per se.

Microeconomic studies of individual industries and commodities will probably be required to fully understand these trade developments. For a relatively homogeneous commodity such as cement, the data in table 12–10 suggest that the very sharp increase in exports in 1981 must have been based on idle capacity in existing enterprises, related to the low level of investment in structures and the slow growth of the construction industry. Information about capacity utilization points to idle capacity in the cement industry on the order of 21 percent even in the year of maximum production (1982). Thus the *OECD Economic Survey* (1984, p. 17) claims that the decline in production and exports in 1983 was due to a shortage of electricity (related to drought). This indicates that the effective bottleneck may have been energy supply rather than capacity. In any case it seems that domestic consumption of cement (that is, construction) was on a downward trend from 1978 to 1983 and that exports served to keep capacity utilization higher than otherwise would have been the case. This would point toward a sluggish domestic economy as part of the explanation of the surge of industrial exports.

Cement is, on the other hand, a commodity for which competitive conditions do not exist within Turkey and for which both export prices and volumes appear to have been administered. A cartel of public and private producers fixed prices and allocated production mainly to protect the relatively inefficient public companies and prevent private producers from profiting from the situation. According to the World Bank study *Turkey, Industrialization and Trade Strategy* (1982, p. 271, note 2):

> Ex factory prices are uniform and a flat levy is imposed on all plants (at two rates depending on the age of the plant and its location). Proceeds of the levy are used to equalize clinker costs across Turkey, to provide finance of bulk cement handling facilities and to subsidize the difference between export and domestic prices. The provincial governors impose price ceilings on cement at construction sites or distribution points. Export prices are also controlled (by the Turkish Cement Producers Association) while export volumes are allocated by the Ministry of Industry and Technology. The system does allow individual producers to benefit from their efficiency, indeed to make excess profits in good times.

Practices such as these may explain the puzzling price and volume developments found above but doubt would then be thrown on the allocational benefits from export-led growth. It would appear that cement exports to a large extent were from Turkish Cement (one of the state economic enterprises).[2] Does that mean that public sector exports were in effect subsidized by private enterprise? A detailed price study of iron and steel exports might disclose similar practices; the iron and steel exports must also have been from publicly owned enterprises, unless it was a matter of transit trade to Iran and Iraq.

Table 12–11 shows the distribution of the increase of exports in millions of dollars from 1979 to 1985. For such comparison, choice of period, and classification of goods as usual gives rise to problems. While the increase in exports of agricultural products was by no means negligible (particularly if processed agricultural products were included), processed and manufactured products dominate completely in the increase from 1979 to 1985, both in absolute and in relative terms. Of the total increase by $5,697 million no less than $5,210 million was in processed and manufactured products ($4,714 manufactured). What is interesting from a microeconomic point of view is that at least 45 percent of the total increase in processed and manufactured products was in consumer goods (textiles and clothing, processed agricultural products, and hides and leather) from so-called light industries, which were systematically given low priority in the first four five-year plans. It may be significant, though, that during 1985 and 1986, exports of iron and steel, metal products and machinery, chemicals, and other intermediate and capital goods favored by the five-year plans were catching up while consumer goods exports appeared to be stagnating. Cement, on the other hand,

Table 12-11. Increase in Value of Exports, 1979-85

(millions of dollars)

Product	1979 value Amount	Increase in value, 1979-85 Amount	Shares percent
Agricultural	1,344	375	6.6
Mining and quarrying	132	112	2.0
Processed and manufactured	785	5,210	91.5
Processed agricultural	151	496	8.7
Manufactured	634	4,714	82.7
Textiles and clothing	378	1,412	24.8
Hides and leather	44	440	7.7
Forestry	2	104	1.8
Chemicals	23	243	4.3
Rubber and plastics	3	105	1.8
Petroleum	0	372	6.5
Glass and ceramics	37	153	2.7
Cement	45	-1	0.0
Iron and steel	31	938	16.5
Nonferrous metals	15	101	1.8
Metal products and machinery	18	432	7.6
Electrical equipment	4	115	2.0
Other	34	300	5.3
Total	2,261	5,697	100

Source: OECD, *Economic Surveys, Turkey,* 1986, table G.

was in 1985 down to the 1979 level. How much these recent developments are influenced by specific conditions in foreign markets (Arab and other OPEC countries, especially Iran and Iraq) and by domestic demand is difficult to say. Turkish construction contracts in these countries are part of the explanation of the increase in exports of iron and steel but a longer period of observation is needed before trends are clear.

Mining and quarrying products show a large increase in net imports, occurring in two big jumps, after 1973 and 1979, and the more so when petroleum products are included in the sector (table 12-9). Turkey's strong terms of trade losses, related among other things to the oil price increases, tend to show up in this sector. Preliminary data for 1986, when oil prices collapsed, indicate an improvement of terms of trade by some 16 percent in 1986, yet with terms of trade still considerably worse than in 1979.

Agricultural and livestock products show a strong increase in net exports, which is even more pronounced when agriculture-based processed goods are included in this sector. In the comparison with 1971–73 it is agricultural and not industrial net exports that have helped improve the balance of trade. The increase of agricultural net exports may not be an allocational effect but rather an effect of sluggish growth after 1977 with a deterioration of the distribution of income, combined with the strong increase in demand from the Middle East OPEC countries.

The UNCTAD data used in tables 12–4 through 12–8 permit commodities to be classed as agriculture based (food and food products and agricultural raw materials), mining and quarrying based (mineral fuels and minerals and metals), and other manufactures (semifinished and finished, not included in the other sectors). While the definition of manufactured commodities is narrow, the data not only cover the whole period 1962–84 but also offer a picture of exports and imports as well as net exports (trade surplus) by sector of origin at both current and constant prices.

In table 12–12 net exports (trade surplus) are shown at current prices and at constant 1962–70 prices for the periods 1962–70, 1971–73, and 1980–84. The development from 1971–73 to 1980–84 at current prices resembles much the one found in table 12–9 for the period from 1971–73 to 1982–85 with a strong increase in the agriculture-based surplus, a very strong increase in the deficit for mining and quarrying-

Table 12-12. Net Exports, by Sector of Origin and Price Terms, 1962–84

(millions of dollars)

				Increase	
Sector and Terms	1962–70	1971–73	1980–84	1962–70 to 1971–73	1971–73 to 1980–84
Agricultural					
At current prices	334.1	610.0	1,963.1	275.9	1,353.1
At 1962–70 prices	334.1	545.8	872.4	211.7	326.6
Mining and quarrying					
At current prices	−88.2	−293.2	−3,933.7	−205.0	−3,640.5
At 1962–70 prices	−88.2	−228.1	−501.4	−139.9	−273.3
Other manufactures					
At current prices	−464.7	−957.6	−1,694.4	−492.9	−736.8
At 1962–70 prices	−464.7	−850.1	−320.3	−284.7	529.8
Total trade					
At current prices	−218.8	−640.8	−3,655.0	−422.0	−3,014.2
At 1962–70 prices	−218.8	−501.0	50.7	−282.2	551.7

Source: Computations by Edward F. Lucas, from UNCTAD tape of trade data.

based trades, and a substantial increase in the deficit for other manufactured commodities. For 1962–70 to 1971–73 there is at current prices a doubling of the agricultural surplus and a somewhat larger increase in the deficit for other manufactured commodities, a result that is often thought to be the (paradoxical) consequence of import-substitution policies. At constant prices the 1962–70 to 1971–73 comparison gives results similar to the current price comparison. This is not surprising because prices in this period were relatively stable. In the 1971–73 to 1980–84 constant price comparison there is a moderate increase in the surplus for agricultural-based commodities with a similar increase in the deficit for mining and quarrying-based commodities. For the latter group the very strong increase in the current price deficit was, of course, largely caused by the oil price increases. For manufactures, however, current and constant price estimates give entirely different results. While the current price deficit increased substantially (as in table 12–9), the constant price deficit decreased; indeed, for total trade the deficit increased from $219 million during 1962–70 to $501 million during 1971–73 and changed into a small surplus for 1980–84.

It might be argued that the liberalization policies would have been highly successful insofar as the balance of trade is concerned had it not been for the deterioration of the terms of trade. Other things, however, might not have been equal because the deterioration of the terms of trade may have been a consequence in part of the export drive. These are the possible indirect costs of an export drive that should be taken into account in any evaluation of a change in development strategy from import substitution to export-led growth (see Derviş, de Melo, and Robinson [1982, chap.11]). The terms of trade loss on manufactures alone may have amounted to something like 2 percent of GNP. In any case, a successful balance of trade policy has to handle the trade deficit no matter whether it is related to volume or to price developments. Still, the constant price estimates indicate that Turkey was faced with unusually unfavorable external conditions for its reform policies.

Liberalization and the Structure of Production

The sectoral growth rates and sectoral contributions to growth for 1980–86 shown in table 12–13 are obviously strongly influenced by the fact that they describe an upswing from the stabilization recession in 1977–80. The leading growth sectors were industry and trade. The overall growth rate for 1980–86 was modest, 4.9 percent, and so were the growth rates for industry and trade, both about 7 percent. The two sectors are strong contributors to growth, 36.0 percent for industry and 19.9 percent for trade, so that together they account for almost 56 percent of total growth. Agriculture comes close to trade, contributing 15.5 percent to growth, the consequence of exceptionally good weather conditions in

Table 12–13. Growth Rates and Contributions to GDP Growth, by Sector, 1977–86
(percent)

Sector	Growth rate 1977–80	Growth rate 1980–86	Contribution to growth, 1980–86
Agriculture	2.4	3.3	15.5
Industry	–1.8	7.6	36.0
Construction	3.0	2.4	3.2
Trade, wholesale and retail	–0.3	6.7	19.9
Transport and communications	–0.9	3.9	7.5
Financial institutions	2.8	2.8	1.4
Dwellings	4.0	2.8	2.9
Professions and services	–0.4	5.5	5.6
Government, health, and education	5.4	3.9	8.4
Gross domestic product[a]	1.0	4.9	100.0

a. At factor cost, 1968 prices.
Source: OECD, *Economic Surveys, Turkey,* 1987, statistical annex, table A.

1986. It is natural to relate the very high contribution from trade to the expansion of foreign trade. Together with the even higher contribution from manufacturing, this may indicate that structural change was under way.

The second structural indicator is the distribution of imports by their use. Table 12–14 shows that from 1950–54 to 1974–77 the composition of imports shifted strongly from consumer goods to raw materials, with an unchanged share of machinery and equipment and a considerable

Table 12–14. Distribution of Imports, by Use, Selected Periods, 1950–85
(percent)

Goods	1950–54	1960–62	1974–77	1980–82	1985
Consumer	21.4	8.9	3.5	2.1	8.0
Machinery and equipment	35.7	41.4	35.0	21.9	20.5
Construction materials	13.2	5.9	4.7	2.1	2.5
Raw materials	29.8	43.7	56.7	73.9	69.1
Total	100	100	100	100	100

Source: Hershlag (1968), table 62; World Bank data.

decline in the share of construction materials. This is a standard pattern for countries pursuing import-substitution policies although increasing oil prices played a role. From 1974–77 to 1980–82 the share of consumer goods declined further to almost nothing (2.1 percent) and so did the share of construction materials. This might be a hangover from the old import-substitution policies but was probably a result in part of the early crisis policies. The share of machinery and equipment, however, declined strongly from 35 percent in 1974–77 to 22 percent in 1980–82 and further to 21 percent in 1985, with raw materials in those years increasing from 57 percent to 74 percent and then declining to 69 percent. These developments reflect, on the one hand, the fact that investment activities in industry suffered under the liberalization policies and that raw materials imports (for current production), on the other hand, recovered after the severe cutbacks under the crisis policies of 1978–79. The development of imports by this breakdown speaks against the interpretation of the liberalization policies as a policy of structural change in production.

Table 12–15 shows that gross fixed investment going into industries producing tradable goods and services increased from 7.2 percent in 1950–58 and 7.1 percent in 1963–70 to 9.1 percent in 1971–77 but then declined to 7.7 percent in 1980–84. The most adequate measure here may, however, be the total share of GDP allocated as investments in tradables and infrastructure. This share increased from 11–12 percent during 1950–58 and 1963–70 to 14.5 percent in 1971–77 where it remained in 1980–84. Apparently there was no major structural change after 1980 of investment away from domestic toward tradable goods and services or from capital-intensive toward labor-intensive technologies.

The aggregative investment data in these tables do not, of course, disclose whether investment in tradables in the 1980s was export or import oriented. In any case, it is probably a sound assumption that it was largely the industries existing at the time liberalization was initiated rather than newly established export industries that accomplished the strong increase in industrial exports. If so, the question is, of course, whether all of the old, inefficient import-substitution industries suddenly became models of efficiency. Had all of the infant industries built up from World War II to the time of the reforms in 1980 matured and become ready to compete for export markets? This, certainly, is one possible interpretation. Another, toward which I lean, is that the price system was adjusted to make the existing enterprises stand out as efficient export industries—which in one sense they are, but in another are not. The existing (industrial) production apparatus was largely built up behind strongly protective barriers. All serious observers agree that the production apparatus was adjusted to a highly distorted price system and was highly inefficient when viewed against the system of international prices and domestic shadow prices prevailing at that time. It is probably

**Table 12–15. Gross Fixed Investment as a Share of GDP,
by Tradable and Nontradable Goods and Services, 1950–84**
(percent)

Industries	1950–58	1963–70	1971–77	1978–79	1980–84
Tradable goods and services	7.2	7.1	9.1	8.0	7.7
Agriculture	3.5	2.4	2.5	1.8	2.1
Mining	0.2	0.7	0.8	0.9	1.1
Manufacturing	3.5	3.7	5.6	5.1	4.4
Tourism	n.a	0.3	0.2	0.2	0.1
Nontradable goods and services	8.8	10.0	11.1	14.2	12.1
Infrastructure (power, transport)	4.5	4.1	5.5	6.3	6.7
Other (housing, health, education, other)	4.3	5.9	5.6	7.9	5.4
Total tradable and nontradable	16.0	17.0	20.2	22.2	18.9
Public tradable and nontradable	7.2	9.1	10.5	10.9	11.3
Tradable as a share of total	44.4	41.8	45.0	36.0	40.6

n.a. = Not available.
Source: Hershlag (1968), table 23, p. 344; World Bank data.

also highly inefficient, though in a different way, when viewed against the background of an efficient price system. If Turkey were to build up her production apparatus from scratch today, making it fully efficient at current (and future) prices, it would probably look very different from the old, inherited system. In this sense the existing system was, is, and will continue to be inefficient until it is replaced completely. In another sense, however, this is beside the point. The existing apparatus is in place and cannot be replaced overnight or even in the span of another five-year plan. Bygones are bygone forever and within a reasonable horizon, efficiency means that for existing industries price should equal marginal costs in both domestic and international markets with no regard to rates of return to fixed capital already sunk in the production apparatus. That is what the foreign exchange rate and the incomes (wage) policies together have been aiming at; streamlining of tariffs and liberalization of import and export procedures have worked in the same direction. The financial liberalization with adjustment of interest rates and removal of credit rationing are probably less important from a short-term point of view.

Incomes policy, or, as I prefer to call it in analogy to the well-established expression "financial repression," labor market repression, is an OECD more than an IMF-IBRD philosophy. It seems to be the OECD rather than the IMF or the IBRD that tried to coerce Turkey into adopting an incomes policy. In any case, it is easy to demonstrate that the change in labor market policy in 1980 with a strong decline in product wages—that is, real wages in terms of manufacturing output (value added)—must have contributed significantly to the increase in the competitiveness of manufacturing industry in Turkey and perhaps even have been one of the most decisive factors. Table 12-16 shows GDP in manufacturing at constant 1968 factor cost per unit of labor input (number of employers), the nominal daily wage in manufacturing, and the nominal wage deflated by the GDP deflator for manufacturing. Real wage rates in this sense increased at a rate of 6.8 percent from 1965 to 1977 while labor productivity in terms of GDP increased at a rate of 4.7 percent. Everything else being equal, this must have contributed significantly to the erosion of competitiveness in Turkish manufacturing before 1977. During 1977–84, however, this development was radically reversed, with productivity increasing by 2.3 percent and the real (product) wage rate declining by 10.4 percent annually. In 1984 real wages in manufacturing in terms of GDP were thus practically speaking back to the level of 1965. For the whole period 1965–84, labor productivity increased by 3.8 percent annually while real product wages increased by 0.1 percent only.

From the first two columns of table 12–16 the nominal wage costs can be computed. They are combined with the NEER to obtain nominal wage costs per unit of GDP in trade partners' currencies and then compared with trade partners' WPI to express the relative labor cost position of Turkish manufacturing. Until 1979 the relative labor cost position shows much the same development as the general REER for Turkey, deteriorating slightly from 1965 to 1970, improving strongly after the devaluation of 1970, then steadily deteriorating until 1979. After 1979, however, the labor cost position improves much more dramatically than the REER, relative labor costs declining to almost one-third the 1979 value in 1984. Labor costs are not the whole story, of course; imported raw materials (oil, in particular) have to be taken into account.[3] Nonetheless, the decline in relative labor costs from 1977 must have helped to improve the competitive position of manufacturing substantially.

Wage costs as computed in table 12–16 are, of course, average wage costs. In relation to exports, however, marginal costs matter. The standard assumption that average and marginal costs tend to change proportionately (Cobb-Douglas) is in this case invalidated by restrictions on lay-offs. If these restrictions did amount to an effective ban on lay-offs, in a period of recession wage costs would tend to become a fixed cost

Table 12–16. Competitiveness of Manufacturing Industry, 1962–84

Year	GDP[a] per unit of labor (thousands of lira)[a]	Nominal wages (lira per day)[b]	Real wages in terms of GDP[a] (1965=100)	Nominal wage costs per unit of GDP[a] (1965=100)	NEER units of trade partners' currency per lira[c] (1980=100)	Wage costs per unit of GDP[a] in trade partners' currencies (1965=100)	Trade partners' WPI (1965=100)	Relative cost position of Turkish manufacturing (1965=100)	Wage bill (percent of GDP)[d]
1962	10.1	20.0	92.7	106.7	908.5	105.6	94.2	112.1	38.5
1963	11.3	18.7	83.9	88.7	902.0	87.1	95.2	91.5	32.5
1964	12.0	24.7	109.6	110.5	914.9	110.1	98.0	112.4	36.2
1965	12.9	24.0	100.0	100.0	918.3	100.0	100.0	100.0	36.8
1966	14.1	27.1	107.4	103.4	934.7	105.2	102.7	102.4	36.2
1967	14.7	30.5	117.4	111.2	975.7	118.8	104.4	113.8	38.0
1968	15.6	33.3	126.1	114.4	1,020.8	127.1	107.2	118.6	37.4
1969	16.7	n.a.	n.a.	n.a.	1,023.7	n.a.	111.9	n.a.	n.a.
1970	16.3	44.1	151.3	145.1	847.4	133.9	122.5	109.3	35.9
1971	16.9	54.5	153.6	173.2	594.7	112.3	123.8	90.7	34.9
1972	17.2	58.1	147.8	181.0	598.7	96.4	127.7	75.5	35.1

Year									
1973	18.4	63.7	136.3	185.5	576.2	116.4	147.9	78.7	34.4
1974	19.1	86.6	138.5	243.1	585.2	154.9	184.2	84.1	31.9
1975	20.0	114.6	164.3	306.7	569.7	190.3	196.9	96.7	37.5
1976	21.2	138.2	177.0	349.6	538.0	204.8	208.1	98.4	38.4
1977	22.3	205.4	212.9	493.9	466.3	250.8	221.1	113.4	44.7
1978	22.9	312.3	187.5	732.6	309.3	246.8	229.9	107.4	40.8
1979	22.2	537.8	170.6	1,299.1	237.9	336.6	253.1	133.0	38.4
1980	21.3	888.4	127.5	2,234.5	100.0	243.3	288.4	84.4	30.7
1981	22.5	1,276.5	132.0	3,039.6	77.1	255.3	317.5	80.4	29.6
1982	23.2	1,587.8	125.1	3,676.4	57.9	231.9	341.0	68.0	29.7
1983	24.3	2,083.4	124.9	4,649.3	46.8	237.2	366.2	64.8	24.3
1984	26.1	2,724.3	110.6	5,608.1	32.7	199.8	400.8	49.9	20.2

In this table GDP means GDP at factor cost in manufacturing.

n.a. = Not available.

a. Manufacturing, at 1968 factor cost.
b. Manufacturing, not including pension and social security contributions.
c. Nominal effective exchange rate = NEER.
d. Manufacturing, at current factor cost.

with marginal wage costs zero or at the least very low (covering sales costs and the like) for production shifted toward export markets.

The relative decline in labor costs shows up also in gross profits expressed as a percentage of GDP in table 12–16. The number of full workdays for employed workers in industry is assumed to be 300, unchanged from 1965 to 1984. Gross profits include contributions to social security and retirement funds. The share of profits net of depreciation at replacement value and contributions to social security and retirement funds should be considerably lower and tend to fluctuate more strongly. With this proviso accepted, the share of profit declined substantially from 1965 to 1970 after which it recovered completely (after the devaluation of 1970 and probably also as a consequence of an almost complete wage freeze under the military intervention of 1971–73 [Ataman Aksoy, in Özbudun and Ulusan 1980, p. 423]) in 1973 and 1974. It then fell to a low point of only 25 percent in 1977 after which it steadily climbed to reach a high of 70 percent in 1984. The conclusion can only be that it was changes in the price-wage structure and not in the physical production structure that made manufacturing industry competitive and profitable in exports in the 1980s. Price-wage structure adjusted to physical structure, not the other way around, not very much at least.

Labor market repression was thus an indispensable part of the Turkish reform policies achieved through a combination of economic liberalization and repressive measures. Presumably Turkish industrial workers would have had to suffer a considerable loss in real wages if a general liberalization policy were to be successful after the excessive real wage developments following the constitution of 1961 and its liberalization of the labor market. The labor market repression after 1980 may have been even more excessive, unless the high real wages in modern Turkish industry can be viewed as having roots that go back beyond the constitution of 1961, possibly even to the early etatism of the 1930s. Relative abundance of land at that time may be the explanation (see chapter 16).

From a production point of view, structural reform should presumably aim at increasing total factor productivity. Table 12–17 shows estimates of the increase in total factor productivity for the years 1973–87 for the economy as a whole, excluding only housing and general government. The methodology used in the computations is not clear; output seems to refer to GDP, and only two factor inputs seem to have been considered, labor and capital.

Uncertain estimates in chapter 11 point to a rate of increase in total factor productivity for 1958–75 of only 1.1 percent annually. The rate for 1973–87 in table 12–17 is only slightly higher, 1.4 percent. Since the latter estimate excludes general government, which by definition should have no increase in productivity, it would seem that productivity increase remained low and unchanged over the long term, unaffected by strategies and regimes. Comparison of the shorter periods, however,

Table 12-17. Annual Rate of Change in Total Factor Productivity, 1973-87

(percent)

Item	1973–76	1977–80	1981–84	1985–87	1973–87
Output	6.9	1.3	4.3	5.5	4.4
Factor input	5.1	3.1	1.7	2.1	3.1
Total factor productivity	1.8	–1.9	2.6	3.4	1.4
Labor productivity	1.2	–0.8	2.9	3.9	1.7
Capital productivity	2.4	–2.5	2.5	3.0	1.2

Source: OECD, *Economic Surveys, Turkey,* 1988.

conveys a different impression. While the subperiods 1977–80 and 1981–84 probably are entirely dominated by the stabilization recession and the following recovery, comparison of 1973–76 and 1985–87 indicates a certain improvement, from about 2.0 to about 3.5 percent. Increased capacity utilization and reduction in overstaffing may be part of the explanation but transfer of technology through liberalized imports of capital goods may also. It is, however, too early to judge.

Turkey around 1980 shifted from one distorted price system, promoting import substitution, to another distorted price system, promoting exports, given the existing production system. This may be efficient from a short-term point of view. From a long-term point of view the system as a whole is probably as inefficient as ever. This statement is made without regard to income distribution, a matter that I do not believe, however, can be handled as an afterthought without implications for resource allocation.

Distribution and Equity

For the years after 1973 there are no reliable surveys of income distribution. Extrapolations of the 1973 income survey (table 6–6) indicate little change through 1978 and 1983 but they are of low reliability. (The same is the case for the labor force surveys.) A slight increase in the Gini coefficients and a decline in the lowest quintile shares are hardly significant. The Kuznets K (table 6–13) increased slightly from 1980 to 1984 and returned to the level of 1970. A strong change in domestic terms of trade against agriculture with a strong decline in real wage rates and an equally strong change in functional distribution of nonagricultural income against wages, all from 1977 to 1984, would point toward a more unequal size distribution although tax reform tended to work in the opposite direction insofar as disposable income is concerned. Very high rates of inflation with financial liberalization and a strong increase in real rates of interest and increasing unemployment add to the uncertainties about the effects of strategy change and reforms on income distribution.

Notes

1. Information given by Ecevit at a seminar at the University of California at Berkeley, June 6, 1988.

2. World Bank (1982), p. 257, table 6–6, indicates that in 1980 exports from Turkish Cement were $103.1 million while OECD, *Economic Surveys, Turkey* (1986, table G), indicates that total exports from Turkey that year amounted to only $40 million. Something is wrong in the data.

3. Krueger and Tuncer (1980, table 2) report a share of purchased (produced) inputs in output for all manufacturing equal to 57 percent against only 1 percent for labor in 1968. The share of imports in total intermediate inputs varied according to Derviş, de Melo, and Robinson (1981, table 10–10) between 2 percent and 3 percent. For the economy as a whole this share was 15 percent. The share of direct plus indirect labor in total variable costs (labor plus raw materials) may thus easily have been one-half or more.

13 The Political Economy of Turkish Development

This chapter assesses the roles played by institutional and organizational factors, on the one hand, and political economy factors, on the other, for economic growth and equity in Turkey since the establishment of the republic.

Institutional and Organizational Developments

Profound institutional change has taken place in Turkey during the six decades since the establishment of the republic. Five rounds of institutional change can be distinguished.The first one included the replacement of the constitutional monarchy of 1876 and the caliphate with the republican constitution of 1924 and the following reforms of Atatürk, aimed at the modernization—Europeanization—of Turkey. It would be a great mistake to overlook the considerable modernization efforts pursued throughout the nineteenth century, particularly the Tanzimat, and those of the Young Turks in the early years of the twentieth century. Yet it was the reforms of Atatürk during the 1920s and 1930s that laid the foundation for modern Turkey and its economic development within the frame of an essentially capitalist economy. The reforms introduced civil, criminal, and commercial codes and a judiciary based on Swiss, Italian, and German models to replace Islamic law and courts as part of the secularization of society. Alphabetic and language reforms facilitated the establishment and expansion of a general, secular education system. The position of women was formally and, at least in the major cities, effectively Europeanized. A one-party system with benevolent autocracy prevailed to the late 1940s. Public development banks were established and legislation was enacted to promote industrialization. Tax reform created incentives to agricultural expansion but may have been inequitable. The forced replacement of minorities (Greeks and Armenians) with Muslim farmers may have been detrimental to the production of cash crops, trade, and some crafts. Generally, however, recovery from war conditions along with reform generated rapid economic growth during the 1920s.

421

A second round of change was related to the expiration of the Capitulations, which made possible the protectionist tariff reform of 1929, and to the simultaneous onset of the Great Depression. Turkey, like so many primary producers, was hit hard by the adverse terms of trade and the increasing autarky in traditional European markets. Bilateral agreements sprouted. Balance of payments controls followed and the inward-looking development strategy that, despite occasional relaxations, was to dominate Turkish development policy until 1980 was established. Shortly after, the policy of etatism was adopted with the establishment of a number of public development banks and large-scale, capital-intensive public enterprises. Though Turkey never aimed at replacing private entrepreneurship, the state was given a crucial, leading role in economic development. Five-year planning, with Soviet inspiration, was introduced. Large-scale distribution of public land to landless laborers and smallholders among the exchange population was instrumental in improving equity in land ownership and expanding the cultivated area. Conservative fiscal and monetary policies accompanied a remarkable expansion of production throughout the decade of the Great Depression. Despite an official policy emphasizing industrialization as the backbone of development, agriculture was the primary contributor to economic growth. As a result, Turkey experienced her first high-growth period.

With World War II and the mobilization for neutrality, Turkey became a substantial military power and after the war a NATO member with a large standing army, not without economic implications, inward and outward.

A third round of institutional change, initiated in 1946, saw the introduction of a multiparty system. The election of 1950 was lost by Atatürk's Republican People's party and brought Menderes's Democrat party to power, yet without threatening Kemalism. Turkey was now a democracy, supported by and ostensibly emphasizing agriculture, but in fact promoting industrialization. Inflation, which had grown strong during World War II, became rampant. With Menderes's autocratic leanings it triggered the military coup of 1960.

A fourth round of institutional change, codified in the new constitution of 1961, reestablished parliamentary democracy. Economically the constitution was important in attempting to block inflationary budget financing, requiring comprehensive planning, and making unionization a right of labor for the first time in the history of the country. The 1961 constitution thus provided the institutional conditions for continuation of the etatist, inward-looking development policy, which lasted until 1980. Investment volumes and patterns were determined by successive five-year plans, investment licensing, credit rationing, and import licensing, and Turkey experienced her second high-growth period, with inflation accelerating at the end.

A fifth round of institutional change, triggered by the debt crisis of 1978 and dismantling of the etatist framework established in the early 1930s, began in early 1980 with a reform program aimed at stabilizing and liberalizing the economy. The program was largely implemented during the years of military takeover 1980–83. It included liberalization of foreign trade and domestic financial markets, abolishment of most price controls, reform of public enterprises and taxation, and labor market repression in the form of compulsory arbitration and bans on militant unions. The inward-looking import-substitution strategy was partly replaced by an export-promotion strategy. The result was a huge expansion of foreign trade, of exports as well as imports, particularly in manufactured goods. Other benefits were slow to materialize. Deficits in the budget and the balance of payments continued at high levels and so did inflation. The economy was in recession several years after the stabilization program was implemented and not until 1986 and 1987 did growth rates again reach levels comparable to those of the decades of inward-looking development strategy. With this standard of comparison, by 1987 about 20–25 percent growth had been lost on the strategy change, a loss that can only be recovered by years of even higher growth. The change of strategy might have been less painful and more successful had it been undertaken ten years earlier, when import substitution was no longer easy and the foreign exchange situation was favorable. Though the loss may be no greater than that experienced by other countries that have adopted a stabilization program during a period of international recession, that does not make the case any better for Turkey. And though it can be argued that, given the international situation, the country would in any case have been in for a recession, the impact might have been very different if the policy chosen had been, say, like the Republic of Korea's export promotion with strong continued protection of domestic markets.

Apart from the impact of the general reforms, private sector production has not been subjected to profound institutional change from above. With an improved infrastructure, commercialization has expanded and subsistence farming has shrunk to almost nothing. Markets which for centuries, even millennia, have been efficient in coastal areas near the large ports and along traditional internal trading routes increasingly serve the interior of the country and include all goods and services. Development has benefited from the emphasis on elementary, secular education, and the army has played an important educational role for young men.

Economic Politics of Growth and Equity

Turkey experienced autocratic, one-party rule from 1923 to 1950. Since 1950, parliamentary democracy has prevailed, though it was temporarily suspended or controlled by military intervention in 1960–61, 1971–73, and 1980–83. The military establishment is, however, always breathing down the neck of parliamentary government. The etatist, inward-looking import-substitution strategy introduced by the Kemalists in the early 1930s survived under one-party rule, parliamentary democracy, and military rule. The outward-looking export strategy introduced in 1980 under parliamentary democracy found support under military rule as well as parliamentary democracy. During this long period of eight regimes (not counting the changes of government under democracy), there has been no simple relationship between governmental system, regime, and development strategy. What explains this apparent lack of correlation between political regime and economic policy?

Modern political economy views politics and government interference in the private sector as the outcome of a complex process of exchange among individuals in societies that "respect the individual value norm upon which a liberal social order is grounded," as the Nobel laureate James N. Buchanan (1987, p. 240) explains. In this political process of exchange, individuals may choose to operate on their own or in groups such as political parties, special interest groups, and economic organizations. The models of government as watchman with pressure groups, parties, and voters may be almost a truism for pluralistic societies—that is, democracies with a liberal social order (what else is a "liberal social order?")—and as such may apply to Turkey during its spells of parliamentary democracy, however imperfect. But it is far from obvious how to model the political economy of autocracies, dictatorships of all degrees and shades in which the individual value norm is not fully respected (if at all), a liberal order does not prevail, formation of groups may be banned or tightly controlled, and the ruler's discretionary and possibly arbitrary decisions are the law, which through coercion is imposed on the citizens. In the case of Turkey it is thus the political economy of Kemalism and military rule that requires modeling.

Hershlag, describing the economy of early modern Turkey, remarked that "the methods of Atatürk —the mixture of collectivism and individualism in his policies and legislation, the combination of dictatorship and democracy in the new regime—sometimes seem like a distant echo of Rousseau's 'general will' or Voltaire's 'enlightened and munificent prince'" (1968, pp. 37–38). If this characterization is correct, the widely held view that the platonic guardians model may best capture the basic features of Kemalism in 1923–50 and also of military intervention during later periods should be no surprise. "Indeed, the bureaucratic ruling tradition during the early republican period," Metin Heper writes, "recalls Plato's government by guardians who personified the essence of the public interest and the approved ideology and who were to be their devoted instrument. For the Turkish bureaucrats, the guiding ideology was a static version of Kemalism" (in Landau 1984, p. 93). And Udo Steinback notes that "the military coup of 27 May 1960 bore all the marks of an attempt at reinstating a Kemalist bureaucratic regime in the center of power" (in Landau 1984, p. 81).

If perhaps bureaucracy (the chambers of commerce, for instance) and military establishments were less platonic than Plato's guardians were supposed to be, the model nevertheless describes the bureaucrats' and officers' perceptions of themselves and their roles in society. This is not to say that no special interest groups were operating to benefit their own membership. Until 1946, political parties other than the Republican People's party were banned, as were labor unions, but generally the Kemalists did not destroy dissident groups (until 1960). These groups were not allowed to play a prominent role, however. Corruption does not seem to have been predominant either, probably because of the charismatic and principled leadership (guardianship) under both Atatürk and İnönü.

The social group or class orientation of the Kemalist revolutionary establishment is characterized thus by S.N. Eisenstadt:

> The revolution was undertaken by military officers ... [who] emerged from a modern educational setting and evinced strong ideological and intellectual tendencies. The ideology they carried was secular, rationalist, nationalist, anti-religious, and etatist, with relatively weak social orientation or themes. Consequently, they displayed a relatively low level of antagonism toward the upper and middle social classes, as distinct from the former [Ottoman] political and religious elites; however these classes were not allowed any autonomous access to the new center, just as they had been barred from the older one. The revolutionary groups had relatively little contact with the lower classes and the movements of the rebellion that flourished among them. (In Landau 1984, p. 14)

İlter Turan, in a general evaluation of the bureaucracy and armed forces after 1950, uses the same language:

> With the decline in economic and social status and in political importance, and the gradual loss of a sense of mission as the guardian of cultural modernization, the Turkish bureaucracy has moved from being a major actor in policy formulation and implementation to being an obstacle which governments have to contend with in formulating and implementing their own policies. A notable exception to this trend has been the armed forces. The Turkish Army has maintained its *esprit de corps* and its effectiveness. It has accepted "saving the Republic" (or "saving the state" in the Ottoman vernacular) as a fundamental mission, assuming political responsibility in cases where civilian politics is judged to have failed (In Landau 1984, p. 116)

Dankward A. Rustow emphasizes the role played by the military training schools since the time of the Tanzimat in the early nineteenth century:

> In this atmosphere, the officers' training schools increasingly became the seedbeds of constitutionalist sentiment. . . . Both in the schools and in the officer corps promotion depended far less on favoritism and intrigue than in the civilian bureaucracy. An army career thus combined the advantages of Westernized training with those of merit advancement and high social mobility. The cohesiveness and *esprit de corps* among the cadets and within the officers' corps furnished an essential prerequisite of political organization. (In Ward and Rustow 1964, pp. 359–60)

Political scientists generally view Kemalism as an elitist consensus ideology that was never approved or even understood by the Turkish masses. It was formalized in the 1924 constitution, which laid down the principle that supreme power can "in no way be left to any one individual, group or class" (Article 4); and in the RPP's famous "six arrows" of its program of 1930 (republicanism, nationalism, populism, revolutionism, secularism, etatism), this was precisely what was meant by populism. Populism was government for the people, not by the people. Society should be organized along occupational, not class characteristics, the ideal being a kind of corporate state in some ways similar to that of Mussolini. The evolution from Kemalist consensus ideology in the 1930s to democracy in the 1960s and 1970s with a wide range of competing ideologies and parties is seen by most scholars as driven by and accompanying the increasing modernization and diversification of Turkish society, economically, socially, and culturally.

A first blow to Kemalist consensus ideology came with the election victory of Menderes's Democrat party in 1950 and the accompanying "ruralization" and "de-elitization" (Mardin 1978) when the estrangement of the enlightened Kemalist elite from the broad, largely illiterate, largely rural masses, deeply rooted in traditional Islamic culture, came to the surface. The dissatisfaction of the emerging urban entrepreneurial class contributed. The beginning polarization was accentuated by the Kemalist-oriented military coup in 1960 and even further when in the mid-1960s after the election victory of Demirel's Justice party (a follower of Menderes's banned Democrat party) İnönü declared that Atatürk's old Republican People's party was left of center, thereby alienating both moderate liberal and conservative elements in the party. Ecevit's policies during the 1970s when the RPP again was in government and the reorganization of the RPP as a social democratic party, in the Western European style, with the emergence of extremist parties of various colors, completed the fragmentation and polarization of the Turkish political scene. Rapid unionization after the 1961 constitution, with increasing labor militancy, was another polarizing element. The accelerating terrorism from left and right, culminating in 1979–80 with some twenty assassinations, reported daily, has been seen as related partly to these domestic sociopolitical developments (Mardin 1978). The Islamic and Kurdic issues came to the surface later, around 1983–84.

Considering the debt crisis of 1978 with its severe cutback of imports, commodity shortages, and recession with hyperinflation and increasing, high unemployment, it is no wonder that government, political parties, and the elite looked for new strategies. Still, the Demirel government's announcement in January 1980 of a radical reform program, apparently without popular approval, was a remarkable political turnaround. Later, in September 1980 with military endorsement and implementation, the new military government combined hardfisted uprooting of terrorism (hereby allegedly violating human rights) with sweeping liberalization of the economy, labor market repression the major exception. Events like this severely test the models that political economists design.

One critically important aspect of political developments in 1980 was the introduction through the parliamentary political process of a program for radical change in development strategy and economic institutions. The new program did not have popular approval by the electorate in the fall of 1979 when Demirel's Justice party again came to power—the program was announced in January 1980 after the elections and came as a great surprise. Modern political economy is of little help in understanding this development. Formally, Turkey was still a liberal social order, but it was an order close to breakdown and free political exchange was threatened by terrorism and probably seriously circumscribed. The outcome of the 1979 Senate elections and political attitudes and opinions generally were, of course, profoundly influenced by the debt crisis and the following austerity policies. The debt crisis, however, was clearly caused by external developments and excessively expansionary, inflationary demand-management policies; it cannot possibly be seen as a collapse of the import-substitution strategy per se, however close to the end of the road this strategy may have been. Insofar as special interest groups are concerned, it is clear that private industry was badly hurt by shortages of raw materials and capital goods, and mercantile interests should always be favorable to liberalization of trade. Private enterprise should view reform of the state economic enterprises as well as the devaluations with sympathy. How the unions would look at the reforms is not obvious, among other things because the incomes policy (labor market repression) was not included in the Demirel's January 1980 program. In any case, dissatisfaction with the consequences of the stabilization programs of 1978 would not, I presume, automatically imply that the important special interest groups would support a dismantling of the protectionist systems with comprehensive liberalization of the economy.

Without a history of matters internal to the Justice party and the Demirel government from the fall of 1979 to August 1980, I am inclined to see the announcement of the reform program as a deliberate surprise move, aimed at a political breakthrough in a critical, even dangerous situation. It drew on and imitated successful experiences of other developing countries, combining recent academic advances in trade and development theory with intellectual fashion and ideology, and—not least—taking into account pressure from international organizations, donors, and creditors. I do not know whether the program was carefully calculated with special interest groups' responses in mind, but the omission of any mention of incomes policy that might alienate labor or agriculture indicates this might have been the case.

That raises once again the problem of the roles of elite groups and elitism in Turkish politics. A model of political economy that does not consider the role of the elite will not meet with approval from political scientists specializing on Turkey. Bringing in the elite is, of course, dangerously close to bringing in the platonic guardians, but as Turan explains:

> The structural pluralization of Turkish society and the ensuing decline in the power of the bureaucrats created a role crisis for which official ideology did not provide explicit solutions. The result has been a susceptibility to ideologies which more clearly provide for elite guidance of socio-economic change. The rapid spread of various socialist and extreme nationalist doctrines among bureaucrats in recent years [before 1980] can be attributed partly to the situation which can be summarized as an elite in search of an elitist ideology. (In Landau 1984, p.117)

Was export-led growth the missing ideology? Godsend!

Without the endorsement and implementation of the program by the military establishment after the takeover in September 1980, the fate of the program would have been very uncertain. How it would have fared in parliament cannot be known, but a considerable part of the legislation required would have been highly controversial. It is tempting once more to view the military as platonic guardians serving the public interest as they perceived it, putting the house in order, and stepping aside when the job was done—as so often before. That the platonic guardians this time only paid lip-service to old-time Kemalism, in fact adopted the reform program of the Justice party, and even let its chief architect, Özal, be in charge of the implementation with both Demirel and Ecevit in jail, does not mean that the military establishment did not continue to see itself as representing the public interest. Even platonic guardians in the guise of generals might honestly believe (and in this view they would have at least my support) that inward-looking import substitution with a large public sector and infant-industry policy is in the public interest in the early stages of economic development but would have to be replaced by market and export orientation at a later stage.

Still it is possible to argue that the military knowingly served special interest groups rather than a perceived public interest. The banning of left-leaning militant unions with the introduction of arbitration in wage disputes and the dramatic decline in product wages with the accompanying increase in industrial profits might be presented as circumstantial evidence. The terrorist connection should not be overlooked, however. Unions did, moreover, push wages excessively from 1962 to 1977 and were an important link in the inflationary process. The OECD for that reason pressed for an incomes policy and actually got a promise from the Ecevit government in 1978 of the introduction of such policy. The OECD clearly views incomes policy as being in the public interest and the military government may have followed up on the Ecevit government's earlier promises. It should not be overlooked that the military in 1980 had a problem of international respectability. If, finally, the platonic guardians of 1960–61 made a mistake in liberalizing the labor market without establishing an incomes policy, the guardians of 1980–83 should be entitled to rectify the mistake without necessarily being suspected of serving special interests.

The views of political scientists on the relation of the political process in Turkey to economic development strategy suggest that for the periods of autocracy, 1923–50, and military intervention, 1960–61, 1971–73, and 1980–83, the platonic guardians model may be more relevant than the model of voluntary political exchange. The latter model, on the other hand, seems to apply broadly to the periods of parliamentary democracy, 1950–60, 1961–71, 1973–80, and the period that began in 1983.

We have in this way no difficulties in understanding why the inward-looking strategy of the Kemalist autocracy should have continued under military rule in 1960–61 and military interference in 1971–73 and why the export strategy of the Demirel government of 1979–80 should have been continued by the military in 1980–83 and by parliamentary democracy thereafter. That, moreover, the Kemalists in the RPP under İnönü should continue their own old strategy during 1961–65 was only natural. The same can be said about the RPP under Ecevit between 1973 and 1979. That leaves the inward-looking policies of Menderes in the 1950s and of Demirel in the late 1960s and mid-1970s. Two factors enter the picture here. One is foreign exchange shortages and the reluctance to adjust the official exchange rate. Under a relatively easy foreign exchange situation 1950–53, Menderes did in fact continue a brief liberalization attempt started under İnönü, through relaxation of import licensing, yet with tariff protectionism unchanged, to please private industry. Conservatism and status considerations apart, the blame for the exchange rate policy should here be put squarely where it belongs—on the Bretton Woods philosophies and the policies of the IMF and the OEEC at that time. For the policies of Demirel in the late 1960s, similar considerations apply; additionally, the military was by then understood to monitor parliamentary government policies carefully and suspiciously to discover possible heresies. The easing of foreign exchange problems during 1971–73 again led to some relaxation of licensing, but with renewed tightening of exchange controls, the political situation in the mid-1970s was very much the same as during the second half of the 1960s, Turkish politicians responding very slowly to the breakdown of Bretton Woods.

Since World War II, inflation has, interrupted only by a few years of relative price stability around and after 1960, been endemic to the Turkish economy, ending with hyperinflation in 1980 and very high rates of inflation thereafter. Disregarding World War II inflation, during a time of full-scale mobilization with large budget deficits and foreign trade surpluses, the acceleration of inflation is clearly related to the poor functioning of parliamentary democracy after 1950 and possibly also to the relatively easy access as a high-priority member of NATO to concessionary foreign financing, organized through the OECD consortium. Agricultural interests and price support policies with rapidly increasing unionization and labor militancy after the adoption of the 1961 constitution were, however, important mechanisms of inflation. Turkish inflation has not been a purely monetary phenomenon; cost-push factors have been an important part of the inflationary picture. Hence the repeated appeals from the OECD for an incomes policy to control the two basic interest groups, agriculture and labor, and operating via agricultural prices and wages and salaries, appeals not responded to effectively until the military takeover in 1980. In relation to inflation, the military establishment has played an important stabilizing role, repeatedly calling politicians and parliament to order. The 1960 coup is, of course, the outstanding example.

Although I am inclined to be sympathetic toward the political scientists' view of the Turkish military as platonic guardians defending and pursuing the public interest, I have been careful to qualify that as the public interest "as perceived by the guardians." As an economist I know that the public interest in the sense of the maximization of a well-defined social welfare function for a particular group of individuals does not exist except under very special circumstances (this is the essence of Arrow's famous nonexistence theorem [1951]); dictatorship is one of them, however, and Plato's guardians, however benevolent, were indeed totalitarians. (Stone 1989, pp. 166-73). Our problem is how the military as a group perceived of what is called the public interest. Purists might point out that the military being so many individual (presumably higher) officers, there is by the same token no such thing as the military perception of the public interest. Strictly true as this is, it has to be admitted that the circumstances were very special, that the Turkish officer corps under Atatürk's charismatic leadership became an unusually ho-

mogeneous group in terms of preferences and ideology. This is one of
the special circumstances under which (in the limit) the public interest
may be well defined—by the dictator. How then Atatürk managed to
impose his preferences and ideology on the officer corps is a matter for
political scientists to explore. Harris, another political scientist, describes
the process:

... Marshall Fevzi Çakmak ran the military establishment on their
[Atatürk, İnönü, Özalp] behalf ... he took good care to keep the
armed forces out of day-to-day politics: in the 1930s, it was apparently even forbidden for the cadets to read daily newspapers in order
to make sure that in their formative years they were not stirred up by
political events. That was a futile gesture, of course, and it subsequently became clear that even communists on the left wing and Pan-
Turanists on the right had succeeded in assembling a tiny core of re-
cruits in these forbidden precincts. The regime's efforts to inculcate
the values of the Atatürk revolution, however, elicited far deeper response than did the competing attempts of those of left and right extremist persuasions; compulsory courses in the Turkish revolution
profoundly influenced the thinking of successive generations of officers. These officers were thus well prepared psychologically to carry
out the role Atatürk continually held up for them as the ultimate
guardians of the republic against enemies of the reform efforts as well
as against foreign foes. (1985, p. 156)

A typical example of the military in its role as platonic guardian are
the changes in the system of allocating import licenses and foreign exchange undertaken immediately after the coup in 1960 and again in
1971 (Ayşe Öncü, in Özbudun and Ulusan 1980, pp. 467–70). Against
the background of the widespread corruption and favoritism in the
Menderes administration in the 1950s, the military government in 1960
decided to authorize the Chambers of Industry to allocate licenses and
foreign exchange for industrial purposes. The Chambers of Industry
was a quasi-official organization established by law in 1950 (before the
elections) and administered by its membership of industrialists under
supervision of the government. Rent seeking and related corruption
nonetheless continued throughout the 1960s, and the organization's
powers were transferred to the Ministry of Commerce immediately after
the military intervention in 1971.

Like all other population groups, Turkish officers, no matter how
streamlined either by preference or by ideology, are presumably influenced by their own origin, background, and social environment, and a
careful sociological study of the composition of this group and its characteristics would probably be necessary to fully understand its perceptions of the public interest. I have come across no such study. Here it
shall only be pointed out that being in public service with pay levels and
conditions not unlike those of civil servants, officers could be expected

to have middle class attitudes and interests similar to those of other bureaucrats. The 1960 takeover as described by Harris, is instructive:

> The ground was prepared in the armed forces by the dramatic decline
> in status and prestige of military service as the Democrats courted the
> peasant masses rather than paying attention to the officers who were
> not even eligible to vote. . . . To emphasize the unimportance of the
> officers, the Democrat party administration allowed their pay to lag
> far behind the rapidly rising inflation, to the point where those in the
> lower ranks could no longer hope to lead a middle class existence. The
> contrast between this shabby treatment at the hands of a party that
> lacked traditional ties to the military establishment and the reinvigo-
> ration of that establishment by exposure to the political and economic
> norms of NATO countries where they were sent for training intensi-
> fied discontent among the officers. It provided them a new perspec-
> tive in which to see the failings of the government and to appreciate
> the gap between democratic practice in the West and in Turkey. (1985,
> p. 158)

The rather determined attitude of the Turkish military toward inflation and lax fiscal and monetary policies (even in 1980 they were able to
bring inflation down from over 100 percent to below 30 percent and
keep it down until 1983, when the civilian politicians returned) should
probably be seen as an expression of a group, certainly occupational,
perhaps even class interest rather than as a consequence of military discipline and specific military ideologies. A group with such economic interests should be in favor of stabilization programs of the IMF type. As a
group it would have everything to gain and nothing to lose, as long as
military programs were not cut back. With similar qualifications, all bureaucrats love stabilization programs. Thus group interests under
Atatürk were entirely compatible with his conservative fiscal and monetary policies.

The question consequently is not which special interest groups the
military is serving but what the military itself as a special interest group
with strongly ideological overtones represents. In the context of political
economy, a comparison with socialist-oriented labor unions would not
be farfetched. Even a comparison of a temporary military takeover with
a general strike might not be farfetched.

Exogenous Factors Influencing Growth and Equity

World War II and the accompanying mobilization had strong adverse effects on both growth and equity. Otherwise, the main exogenous factors
that have affected the Turkish economy are changes in terms of trade
and foreign financing as well as foreign demand for labor. (This ignores
cultural and technological change which, of course, mainly has come
from abroad.)

Fluctuations in the terms of trade have been strong and their effects considerable, directly through price changes, indirectly through economic policy responses. The agricultural crisis of the 1920s and the Great Depression and the accompanying terms of trade losses did great harm to agriculture and triggered the etatist policies. The end of the Korean War boom in the early 1950s and the oil price increase in 1973 both implied substantial terms of trade losses and after vain attempts by the governments to shelter the domestic economy led to stabilization programs and recessions in the economy. The 1979 oil price increase severely hampered the change in development strategy after 1980 although an indirect effect on exports and workers' migration in response to demand from OPEC countries, particularly Iran and Iraq, somewhat mitigated the effects.

The long-term trends of terms of trade are hard to discern in the violent short- and medium-term fluctuations but may perhaps be described as weakly upward before 1973 and thereafter strongly downward. Trends of growth and equity should be seen in the light of trends in the terms of trade. While the (possible) upward trend from 1923 to 1973 may have had little long-term impact on either growth or equity, the negative impact of the downward trend since 1973 has been considerable.

Demand for Turkish labor in Europe, particularly in Germany beginning in the mid-1960s, and a limited demand in the Middle East after the oil boom, had clearly beneficial effects on employment and probably on equity. Without the migration of workers, unemployment would have been much more serious and the foreign exchange situation more difficult, probably with negative effects on growth. The stagnation of migration from the mid-1970s, partly a consequence of ethnic prejudice, contributed to the foreign exchange and debt crisis in 1978 and the following stagnation of production.

III A Comparative Analysis

14 *The Setting*

Egypt and Turkey are countries of approximately equal population size at the lower, middle level of income and development; both are secularized Islamic countries; and both obtained independence in 1923. They also share the heyday of the Ottoman Empire as common history, present day Turkey having been the center and mainland of the empire from beginning to end, Egypt one among several provinces from 1517 to 1914. Center and provinces, however, were never completely streamlined into a common, uniform administrative and economic system, and the ability of the empire to rule and exploit its provinces declined dramatically from the sixteenth to the twentieth century.

Centralized govenment, imposed on Egypt immediately after the Ottoman conquest, was replaced by increasingly decentralized tax farming from the early seventeenth century. The mamelukes reestablished their old power and effectively ruled their fiefs and tax farms with little control from the Ottoman governor. Tribute payments to the Porte and the holy cities were substantially reduced and only made irregularly. With Mohammed Ali, Egypt virtually became an independent kingdom and a minor imperialistic power with highly centralized administration, the tribute fixed at a much reduced level. With the British conquest in 1882, Egypt continued nominally to be a province of the Ottoman Empire, formally ruled by descendants of Mohammed Ali but effectively an important link in the British Empire.

Present day Turkey was at the time of the Ottoman Empire governed directly from the center, the Porte. Here too centralized government was replaced during the seventeenth century by tax farming and decentralized administration. Attempts to centralize government during the nineteenth century were only partially successful until the last few years before World War I under the Young Turks (Richard L. Chambers, in Ward and Rustow 1964). Foreign influence increased but foreigners never gained the upper hand (Pamuk 1987).

Islamic law and tradition prevailed in most of the Ottoman Empire, a legacy of the Arab conquests of the seventh century. Efforts at secularization and modernization—that is, Europeanization—were parallel in the empire and Egypt with the former in the lead during the first, the latter during the second half of the nineteenth century and up to World War I. The mixed courts established in Istanbul in 1839 and in Egypt in 1875 with related law codes may serve as one example (Brinton 1968, pp. 6–12). Ownership rights to land were also introduced in the nineteenth century in both countries (Baer 1962, chap 1).

Some modern economic development took place in both Egypt and Turkey during the nineteenth and early twentieth centuries. Both countries were exposed to the strong expansion of exports of manufactured goods from Europe, particularly from the United Kingdom, and of grain from overseas. Though the process was painful and inequitable, it was probably beneficial in the long run, shifting labor toward agriculture and construction and away from such traditional handicrafts as spinning. Egypt, but never Turkey, became a one-crop exporter (but not a one-crop cultivator as is often claimed). Infrastructures were built up, cities Europeanized, and trade developed, largely financed by foreign capital. Apart from some processing of agricultural products, industrialization was almost absent. Central government played an important role in the modernization process in both countries.

A feature common to all parts of the empire was the Capitulations which, on the one hand, became a stimulus to Europeanization and, on the other, a constraint on both Ottoman (Turkish) and Egyptian economic development efforts. The common factor was not so much the empire as the Capitulary Powers, including most European countries and the United States. The Capitulations extended judiciary privileges to subjects of the Capitulary Powers and kept traditional domestic taxes (on land and buildings, in particular) at existing levels and taxation of foreign trade generally at low levels. With government monopolies ruled out through treaties with the individual powers after 1837 (in Egypt, after 1841), foreign trade was practically free from government control. Both Egypt and Turkey thus obtained independence in 1923 as virtually unprotected free trade countries without autonomy in matters of foreign trade until 1929–30.

While Egypt was neutral in World War I and came out in 1919 with a large exchange reserve and virtually no foreign net debt, the Ottoman Empire participated in and lost World War I as one of the Central Powers after having suffered serious defeats in the Balkan Wars of 1911–13 and yet was to fight a destructive albeit victorious War of Independence. At the time of independence Egypt was thus economically in fairly good shape while the remaining Turkey, consisting of Anatolia and Thrace only, stripped of all the provinces of the empire, ravaged by wars and massacres, disrupted by population exchanges, and saddled with considerable foreign debt, was economically in shambles.

Natural Resources

Nature has been kind to both Egypt and Turkey. Egypt's climate is uniform and stable. Apart from a narrow coastal strip with Mediterranean climate, desert climate prevails with mild, in the south even warm, winters and everywhere hot summers. In Turkey climate is unstable and varies extremely from Mediterranean in the south and west to harsh desert and mountain climates in the interior, and a mild climate on the Black Sea Coast.

Water is in Egypt almost exclusively supplied by the Nile. Before regulatory devices were constructed, beginning with the Delta Barrage (1846–91) and culminating with the Aswan High Dam (1959–71), water supplies were strongly fluctuating, with relatively regular seasonal patterns and erratic annual variations. With the major regulatory devices in place, water supply became almost constant and abundant, within and between years, and, in addition, water became an important source of hydroelectric power. Turkey depends entirely on rainfall that is very unevenly distributed over the country, strongly seasonal, and highly irregular between years. Rivers offer relatively little possibility for irrigation or generation of hydroelectric power.

Land in Egypt is available in two radically different, relatively uniform qualities: the alluvial and extremely fertile soil confined to the Nile Valley and Delta, and the stony, sandy, partly salty, and largely infertile expanses of the surrounding deserts. A further difference is that the Valley and Delta lands mostly are situated below the level of the Nile and above sealevel and thus allow for gravitational irrigation and drainage while the desert lands mostly are situated above the level of the Nile and thus require that water be lifted for irrigation. Economically agriculture is thus largely confined to Delta and Valley and most attempts to expand cultivation beyond that have been failures. Since about 1900 all economically cultivable lands have been cultivated.

Turkey is endowed with a much wider variety of land, from forbidding mountains to fertile coastal plains, from salty deserts to lush meadows and pastures. Cultivable land has been plentiful, with the economically cultivable margin not reached until around 1960. Even so, land remained much more abundant than in Egypt. Investment in transportation was required to open up the interior while irrigation investment has been of less consequence. Despite considerable deforestation throughout history, forests are extensive, particularly along the Black Sea Coast, and supply large quantities of timber and nuts.

Considering the natural conditions of water supply, climate, and soils, both Egypt and Turkey have excellent, albeit very different natural advantages in agriculture, horticulture, and, in the case of Turkey, forestry.

Oil and natural gas deposits are substantial in Egypt, sufficient to make the country an oil exporter of some consequence since the mid-1970s. Only minor deposits have been discovered in Turkey and the country is bound to be an oil importer.

Minerals in Egypt are limited to phosphate rock and some low-quality iron ore. Turkey is here much better endowed, with very substantial deposits of coal and lignite, copper, chromium, and iron ore.

Touristic attractions, natural and historical, are plentiful in both countries.

Location for both countries is a significant natural resource. The isthmus of Suez separates the Mediterranean and Indian oceans and the Suez Canal has provided Egypt with an exceptional transportation monopoly and opportunity to tax international maritime traffic, which is somewhat constrained by international convention. Turkey's corresponding command over the waterways of the Bosporus and Dardanelles is by international convention excluded from economic exploitation. Location, of course, also has political and military implications.

Population size and distribution by age and sex are roughly the same in the two countries. While population characteristics such as education and culture can be considered natural advantages or disadvantages, I address them as matters open to policy intervention. I abstain from speculating about national character and its relevance for development.

External Factors

External factors—anything that belongs to the international environment of a country—may affect the domestic economy through information, foreign trade and finance, factor movements, and international policy, including war and peace. Changes in the international environment constitute disturbances or even shocks to the domestic economy. These may take the form of random noise, unique events, or regular, predictable fluctuations and trends. They may or may not be exogenous from the viewpoint of the country. If they are considered responses to change in the domestic economy, they should be treated as endogenous in the analysis of the domestic economy. It is not always easy, however, to decide what external disturbances should be so treated. For theoretically small countries, the international environment is, of course, by definition given and one and the same. By this definition, however, few countries, are genuinely small. The conglomerate of countries, by economists called the world, is not atomistic. In political economy, any little island may matter for the world.

In analyzing external factors and disturbances, theoretical economists commonly start from the assumption that the world is in a perfectly competitive equilibrium and that the countries being analyzed are price takers in all international markets. Changes in taste and technology and economic policy abroad are then felt through the market system as price changes. International price changes are observable and it is a standard procedure (not without ambiguities) to measure terms of trade and finance and their direct effect on income. Terms of trade for Egypt and Turkey are depicted in figures 1–1,1–2, and 6–2. Estimates of direct income effects for Turkey, presented in tables 6–5, and 17–7 appear to be reasonably reliable. Estimates of direct income effects for Egypt, table 17–7, are not very reliable. Moreover, it is questionable whether terms of trade for either country should be treated as exogenous. Egypt and Turkey may theoretically be small from the import side for, practically speaking, all goods and services. It is not obvious that that is the case on the export side. Egypt did, from 1921 to 1932, pursue cotton export price policies, which were abandoned, allegedly as being unsuccessful; it is an open question, however, whether Egypt would not have been able, then and later, to pursue an optimum-tariff policy for her cotton. There seems to be general agreement that international demand for some important Turkish agricultural exports is less than perfectly elastic and even may be inelastic (Pamuk 1987, p.53; OECD, *Economic Survey, Turkey*, 1963, pp. 24-25). Without deliberately pursuing an optimum-tariff policy, Turkey did in fact operate supply-constraining export price policies in the 1950s (see chapter 10) and may have improved terms of trade in this way.

Whether exogenous or not, terms of trade did in fact develop quite similarly for Egypt and Turkey from the late 1920s to the end of the 1950s with a strong deterioration through the Great Depression, strong improvement after World War II culminating in and then collapsing with the Korean war boom. Throughout these three to four decades, terms of trade in both countries largely reflected the predominance of agriculture in their economies and the international terms of trade between agricultural and industrial products. About 1960, developments began to differ, Egypt possibly benefiting first as a Soviet client and then, after a short setback around 1973, gaining strongly as an oil exporter, and Turkey as an oil importer systematically losing on the terms of trade from 1973 to 1984. Oil is an external factor that favored Egypt and disfavored Turkey from the early 1970s, at least, with a reversal from 1984 onward.

World markets may not be in competitive equilibrium. Apart from organized commodity and financial markets possibly, they may never be. This aspect of trade is now being developed by so-called "new trade theory" (Dixit and Norman, 1980; Krugman, 1990). Moreover, during much of the period considered in this study, both Egypt and Turkey operated with direct controls (licensing) of trade and capital movements and price controls, including pegged exchange rates, thus creating domestic disequilibrium. In a disequilibrium environment, international disturbances make themselves felt not only through the price system but also through quantity effects at given prices, directly in the markets for goods and services as well as finance, indirectly through the availability of foreign exchange. In disequilibrium terms, international disturbances show up directly as fluctuations or trends in volumes of exports, and possibly in imports of goods and services and factor movements. Whether quantities are endogenous factors is, however, important for any country. To decompose changes in export and import volumes by external and domestic factors requires knowledge that is rarely available even for countries with an abundance of reliable data. Reliable disaggregated estimates of export and import functions would be difficult to produce for either Egypt or Turkey simply because both countries have lived with systems of quantitative controls during most of the period covered by this study. Any consideration of the impact of external, exogenous factors on prices and quantities of exports and imports would be no more than a series of highly subjective conjectures.

A special problem is the international transfer of technology and taste, including ideology. Changes in technology, taste, and ideology in most developing countries are based on imitation and imported from abroad, sometimes from other developing countries but usually from Europe and the United States, through information or experience. Contemporary Islamic fundamentalism, blue jeans, and computerization, all came to Egypt and Turkey as exogenous disturbances through other channels than the price system and all have had a strong impact. Quantification, however, is illusive even in an area so intensively studied as technology transfer where discussion must be limited to subjective conjectures. Twenty years of Soviet orientation in trade and aid, for instance, may have been a significant disadvantage for development in Egypt but evidence of that would at best be circumstantial.

Wars are shocking events and economists generally deal with them, whether aggressive or defensive, as exogenous shocks. Political economy, however, should not be allowed to escape so easily. More than 150 years ago, Karl von Clausewitz taught that "war should never be thought of as *something autonomous* but always as an *instrument of policy*" (1976, p. 88), "a continuation of political intercourse, carried on with other means" (1976, p. 87). For economics, Clausewitz's dictum might be narrowed down to "instruments of economic policy" and "economical-political intercourse." Accepting Clausewitz's views on war, however, a political economy worth the name may have to view war as an endogenous factor in the way it would other policy interventions, much as the choice and use of economic policy instruments are seen as endogenous factors by so-called modern political economy (Buchanan 1987; Lindbeck 1976). Marxist-Leninists have always faced this challenge, though unfortunately they have been misguided by poor theory and blinded by political biases and have produced little more than rhetoric. Modern political economy does not appear to have made major contributions to the subject either, which is deplorable because war and peace are an important part of the modern economic history of Egypt and Turkey.

Quite apart from World War I and its enormous consequences, which belong to the past and thus to the initial conditions in this study, both countries, like the rest of the world, of course, lived through World War II and both remained, in principle, nonparticipants. Turkish politicians, despite the determination of Atatürk to remain neutral in a future world war, must in their heart of hearts (if nowhere else) have contemplated the choice of entering the war on one side or the other and have answered the question, will it pay? Franz von Papen, German ambassador to Turkey from 1939 to 1945, is widely known for his efforts to prevent Turkey from joining the Allied camp. The fact that France at the outbreak of the war consented to Turkish annexation of Iskanderun from Syria suggests that Turkey's joining the Axis camp was not unthinkable.

Anwar Sadat did contemplate problems of the economic payoff in terms of trade and aid from Arabs, West and East before the 1973 war, as his postwar explanation of the motives for his decision to attack make clear:

> So that I can give you an idea of what the opening all is about, I must go back to the fourth of Ramadan of last year [October 1, 1973], six days before the battle. I invited to this same house in which we are now seated the members of the National Security Council consisting of the vice-president, the presidential assistants, the prime minister and deputy prime ministers, the minister of defence, the director of military intelligence, the national security advisor, and the minister of supply . . . and I laid before them the situation and asked them to advance their own opinions. . . . We debated for a long time. There were some who advocated fighting, and others who said we were not ready. . . . At the end I said that I wanted to tell them one thing only, that as of that day we had reached the "zero stage" economically (*marhalat al-sifr*) in every sense of the term. What this meant in concrete terms was that I could not have paid a penny toward our debt installments falling due on January 1 [1974]; nor could I have bought a grain of wheat in 1974. There wouldn't have been bread for the people, that's the least one can say. . . . But as soon as the battle of October 6 was over, our Arab brethren came to our aid with $500 million . . . and *this sum would never have come had we not taken effective action as regards the battle.* But despite these dollars, we are now in the same situation we were in a year ago, perhaps worse. (Sadat, *al-Usbu' al-Arabi*, October 9, 1974, quoted in Waterbury 1983, pp. 127–28; italics added.)

Sadat's later surprise visit to Jerusalem and Camp David should probably be seen in the same light. The chain of events from the Aswan Dam financing issue via the nationalization of the Suez Canal to the 1956 Suez War is another good topic in the political economy of war and peace (see Nutting 1972). Nasser's intervention in the Yemen War may have been an exogenous shock to Yemen but cannot possibly be considered exogenous from the viewpoint of Egypt; what the political economy of the case was is another matter.

The political economy of international alignments is yet another issue at stake in the case of Egypt and Turkey. Turkey was rewarded economically through the OECD consortium and otherwise for membership in John Foster Dulles's system of regional coalitions and NATO, while Egypt was correspondingly penalized economically by the United States and rewarded by the Soviet Union for taking position as a nonaligned nation. Both countries, however, had and did make a genuine choice and must have considered economic opportunities along with other more or less important matters. That Turkey was penalized economically for the invasion of Cyprus while Egypt was rewarded for its participation in the Camp David talks is equally indisputable. Likewise, political relations with Arab countries, Israel, and Greece have had strong economic overtones. Failure to treat these matters leaves a serious gap in a study of the political economy of both countries, but they go beyond the limits of this study.

15 *Political Institutions*

One means of comparing Egypt and Turkey is to examine the institutional and constitutional framework for economic policymaking as it has developed since independence in the two countries. The size of the public sector, in terms of resources absorbed and budgetary transactions, is in itself an institutional fact of relevance for growth and equity. Also, the larger the size of the state, the larger the bureaucracy. We next describe briefly the central bank systems through which monetary and foreign exchange policies normally are pursued. Thereafter we proceed to discuss political systems, Egypt being transformed from democracy to autocracy in 1952, Turkey from autocracy to democracy in 1950 (1946) in both cases with the military establishment a decisive part of the process.

The Public Sector and Fiscal Policy

The public sector in both countries has been given a special and central role in development strategies. In Turkey this was the essence of the policy of etatism, launched by Atatürk in 1932 and effectively adhered to until 1980. In Egypt, so-called Arab socialism from 1962 under Nasser and later rulers certainly amounted to big government.

Disclosing how large a part of the economy is in fact incorporated in and absorbed by the public sector is not easy, either conceptually or empirically. There is no way of measuring physical output of general government services and because they are not marketable, such services have no observable market price. Value added is correspondingly elusive. Standard procedure is to measure value added by primary factor (labor) input, thus ignoring the problem of productivity in general government and introducing a bias in the measured size and growth rates of gross domestic product (GDP) and gross national income (GNI). Public enterprises with a marketable output present a different measurement problem. In principle it should be possible to systematically separate private and public enterprises in all sectors although joint ownership might create problems. But official national accounts in Egypt and Turkey do not break down GDP by public and private sector (nor do they in any country, to the best of my knowledge). For Egypt, there is an unofficial estimate of GDP in the public and private sectors for 1945–54 (Abdel-Rahman 1959, quoted by Mead 1967, table 1-A-2) and for Turkey the manufacturing industry has been studied from this point of view (Krueger and Tuncer 1980) but no systematic, complete breakdowns of total GDP for the whole period are available. As an alternative to using the size and share of the total public sector in GDP or GNI, employment figures from the 1976 population census have been used to measure government in Egypt (Hansen 1985, app. 1). Of the total civilian, resident labor force fifteen years old and older, 25 percent were employed in general government and public enterprises. Thus measured, public employment outside of agriculture was slightly above 50 percent of civilian employment. I am aware of no other such attempt for either Egypt or Turkey and official labor force data do not operate systematically with this breakdown.

On the expenditure side, however, comparable breakdowns by public consumption and investment are given that add up to total final, public expenditure, which may be expressed as shares of GDP, GNI, or total final expenditure. Table 15–1 shows that as a share of GDP the public sector was slightly larger (relatively) in Turkey than in Egypt in 1952—20 percent against 18 percent. In 1982 the public sector had grown larger (relatively) in both countries with the proportions radically reversed, the public sector in Egypt now more than double that in Turkey, 45 percent against 22 percent of GNP. It is in particular the share of public investment that has grown strongly in Egypt, related to extensive sequestrations and nationalizations in the late 1950s and early 1960s. As to consumption, the difference is remarkable; in Egypt the share of public consumption increased by 50 percent, in Turkey it declined significantly.

Table 15–1. Final Public Expenditure as a Share of GNP, 1952 and 1982

(percent)

Category	1952		1982	
	Egypt	Turkey	Egypt	Turkey
Investment	3.2	6.1	23.6	10.8
Consumption	14.7	13.7	21.1	11.5
Total	17.9	19.9	44.7	22.3

At current prices.
Source: Hansen and Marzouk (1965, statistical appendix); World Bank data.

Table 15-2. Central Government Expenditure and Current Revenue as a Share of GNP, 1952-53 and 1985

(percent)

	1952–53		1985	
Category	*Egypt*	*Turkey*[a]	*Egypt*	*Turkey*[a]
Expenditure				
Defense	3.9	4.0	8.4	2.8
Education	2.6	1.7	5.1	2.6
Health	0.8	[b]	1.2	0.5
Housing, social security, other	3.2	12.2	6.9	2.8
Economic services	4.8	[b]	3.8	5.0
Other	7.1	[b]	22.7	13.9
Total	22.3	17.9	48.1	27.6
Revenue				
Taxes on income, etc.	2.9	2.7	6.0	6.8
Social Security contributions	0.1	2.2	5.4	3.2
Other taxes	1.7	0.2	2.6	1.8
Domestic taxes on goods	3.7	5.4	4.8	4.9
Taxes on international trade	8.4	3.8	6.2	1.4
Other	5.2	5.3	14.6	3.1
Total	21.9	19.6	39.4	21.2
Deficit	0.4	−1.7	10.4	6.4
Official development assistance, net disbursement	—	—	6.1	0.2

— = Not applicable.

a. Includes annexed budgets as well as budgets of social insurance institutions and government employees' retirement funds not included in World Bank data on government expenditure and revenue. Some double accounting arises that does not affect the deficit but makes both expenditure and revenue too large—about 0.5 percent of GNP for 1985 and probably the same for 1952–53. Data on social insurance and retirement funds under 1985 are for 1984.

b. Included under housing, social security, other.

c. Revenue and deficit do not add to total expenditure because data are from different sources.

Source: IMF, *Government Finance Statistics Yearbook;* World Bank, *World Development Report,* 1987, tables 23, 24; Turkey, *Statistical Yearbook,* 1985, tables 123, 129, 130, 132; Mead (1967), tables IV, E–3, 4; World Bank (1975), tables 5–1, 5–4, 5–5, 5–6, 5–18, 5–19.

Yet another way of measuring the size of the public sector is to express government expenditure and revenue as percentages of GNP. Table 15–2 does this, providing a measure of the relative size of government that gives an impression also of the distributive efforts of government.

Comparability is limited, between categories and countries as well as years. For 1952–53 shares for expenditure and revenue in the two countries are roughly the same—22 percent for Egypt, 18–20 percent for Turkey. In fact, if social security and pension contributions were added for Turkey in 1952, revenue would be 22 percent of GNP in both countries, with expenditure somewhat lower in Turkey than in Egypt. These shares are quite similar to those based on final expenditure in table 15–1. Including social security payments, Turkey would have an increase of expenditure to about 29 percent in 1985 with revenue increasing to about 22 percent and the deficit rising to 7½ percent of GNP as compared with a surplus of about 3½ percent in 1952–53. For Egypt the increase was even more dramatic, expenditure increasing to 48 percent of GNP with revenue increasing to 39 percent and a deficit of 10½ percent. The government sector thus measured was much larger in Egypt than in Turkey, again as in table 15–1. In both countries the deficit increased by 10–11 percent of GNP over the early 1950s experience, with roughly balanced budget in Egypt and even surpluses in Turkey. Relatively low revenue elasticity (buoyancy) is partly responsible for this result.

Central Banking and Monetary Policy

The central bank is, of course, part of the public sector and thus included in table 15–1 but it plays a special role in formulation and implementation of monetary and foreign exchange policy. Both countries now have central banks. Both countries, however, gained independence without having central banks, hence without the institution needed for pursuing independent modern monetary policy.

In Egypt a note-issuing bank, the National Bank of Egypt (NBE), was established in 1897. It was a private, mainly foreign-owned bank and did not serve as central bank until 1951. Before World War II, with capital movements entirely free and the sterling rate pegged at the parity from the time of the gold standard, Egypt simply had no independent monetary policy. The country was as much a part of the British credit market as, say, Scotland was. The supply of domestic money (Egyptian pounds) in this setting adjusted passively to domestic demand for money and the interest rate followed the London market with a declining risk margin over time. After 1951 private banks were requested to keep reserves with the NBE. Capital movements had been regulated since World War II and when the NBE began serving as lender of last resort, autonomously fixing its discount rate, the country finally had a monetary policy of its own despite continued pegging of the exchange rate. The domestic open capital market was thin, however, and the NBE was unable to make open market operations part of monetary policy. Monetary policy was thus limited to changes in discount and loan rates and reserve requirements. In 1960 the NBE was nationalized and divided into the Central Bank of Egypt (CBE) and a commercial bank that carried the old name NBE. With British and French banks sequestered from 1956 and the banking system as a whole soon to be nationalized, from 1961 monetary policy in the traditional sense of the word ceased to exist. The banking system now accepted deposits from the public at low fixed interest rates, gave loans to government and the private sector on a discretionary basis (the latter controlled by the CBE), and bought and sold foreign exchange at fixed rates on the basis of licenses issued by special authorities. Money supply changes were the passive outcome of these transactions. From 1973 a parallel own-exchange market, mainly based on migrant workers' remittances and with market-determined exchange rates, was allowed to develop. The system has been changed almost continuously but it remains in essence a U.S.-dollar-denominated system with own-exchange deposits, open for any resident or foreigner, at Eurodollar market interest rates, to be used freely for any payment, including payments for imports not explicitly requiring license, and foreign assets. With the exchange rate for licensed trade fixed at official rates, the country has had, practically speaking, no monetary policy, and fiscal policy has been the primary instrument for domestic demand-management policy.

Turkey established a central bank in 1930, which began operating in 1931. Until then exchange rates were floating but the situation was otherwise very similar to that in Egypt with, in effect, no monetary policy. The new central bank, Merkez Bankası, was authorized to issue currency, fix discount and interest rates, buy and sell foreign exchange at fixed rates, and regulate domestic credit. With foreign payments requiring license, the country now had a monetary policy of its own despite the fixed exchange rates. Domestic credit transactions did not take the form of open market operations (for the same reason as in Egypt) but rather took the form of direct loans to government, state banks, and the private sector. The situation remained much the same after World War II. Own-exchange deposits based on workers' remittances gained importance in the late 1960s but were not accompanied by the establishment of a free exchange market with free exchange rates. The years with crawling peg from the late 1970s saw strong depreciations but did not really change the situation institutionally although black market transactions increasingly gained importance.

Systems of Government

Over the six decades reviewed in this study both Egypt and Turkey lived about half the time under parliamentary democracy, half the time under autocracy. Here the similarity seems to end. The time sequence of the systems of government was reversed, Egypt moving from parliamentary democracy to autocracy, Turkey doing just the opposite. The roles played by the military establishments in both countries were crucial for the change in governmental systems but completely different, in Egypt destroying democracy, in Turkey establishing and repeatedly saving democracy. The problems faced by the two types of government were, moreover, very different. The disturbed times from the 1920s to the 1940s, including the international agricultural crisis, the Great Depression, and World War II and the following recovery were in Egypt a challenge to democracy, in Turkey to autocracy. The much more favorable international economic conditions of the post–World War II period were the background for the achievements of democracy in Turkey and of autocracy in Egypt; Turkey, however, remained largely untouched by the special problems of the Arab-Israeli confrontation but faced another set of special problems in her dispute with Greece over Cyprus.

It is impossible to say which governmental system was most conducive to growth and equity because surrounding circumstances were so different in the two countries and there are no lessons to be learned from a general comparison. Abstaining, as we presumably should, from drawing general lessons from the outcomes of singular, unique historical events, we may still ask more specific questions to which answers may be given and which may be of interest to students of the political economy of growth, equity, and poverty. The very general labels of democracy—even parliamentary democracy—and autocracy can obscure great differences in political systems, and the particular system existing at any given time in either of these countries could have generated different policies aimed at promoting growth and equity and eradicating poverty and neutralizing disturbances that threatened these political targets. Not only parliamentary democracy and autocracy but military establishments and bureaucracies are crucial factors in the evaluation.

First I compare Egyptian with Turkish democracy and Egyptian with Turkish autocracy despite the fact that both operated in different times and international environments. The military establishments and bureaucracies are thereafter compared separately. Then I compare contemporary Egyptian and Turkish government as they actually were in the interwar period despite the fact that one country had democracy, the other autocracy. I make the corresponding comparison for the years of World War II, and finally for the postwar period. I make no attempts to generalize my findings.

Parliamentary Democracy

Parliamentary government has been the preferred democratic system in both Egypt (1923–52) and Turkey (since 1950, with interruptions during periods of military interference), continental European parliamentary government the model. With the constitution of 1923, rather closely following the Ottoman constitution of 1876 and thus the Belgian prototype of 1831, Egypt established a constitutional monarchy with royal prerogatives far beyond those existing in what was considered modern parliamentary democracy during the interwar period. Universal manhood suffrage was instituted with indirect elections, financial and property requirements, and educational qualifications for electors and candidates, and (at least in the early 1930s) limits for the liberal professions to run for elections outside Cairo. The formation of parties was in principle free, but extremist and terrorist organizations (the Communist party and the Muslim Brotherhood) were banned. Few, if any, genuinely lower class representatives were ever elected to parliament. The system was set up to ensure conservative and at most moderately liberal policies. Powerful interest groups pressured the king and political parties on behalf of cotton grower, industrial, and foreign interests and the British reserved and occasionally made use of a right to interfere in the political process if the interests of the British Empire were deemed to so require.

Agricultural development efforts in Egypt continued along the lines of the old British model of "green revolution." The protectionist tariff reforms of 1930, supplemented with government subsidies in the form of cheap loans, the backbone of the import-substitution growth strategy for industry (still adhered to) and distributionally probably favoring capital, passed in parliament as a consensus policy with little opposition. Policies restricting cotton supply and stabilizing prices that had been pursued during the 1920s and early 1930s were abandoned by the semi-autocratic prime minister Sidky Pasha, apparently with the support of textile industrialization interests, he himself having been president of the Federation of Industry. Tax reforms proposed in 1937, aimed at taxing urban, hence foreign, business were hotly contended but passed with the support of landed interests. Equity, not between rich and poor but between foreigners resident in Egypt and Egyptian nationals, was here at stake. Only in this sense did parliamentary democracy in Egypt promote policies in favor of both growth and equity. Specific legislation to promote equity between poor and rich was negligible. Increased protection for cereals and sugar actually worked in the other direction. Land reform was never seriously considered during the time of democracy in Egypt despite the highly unequal distribution of land.

In Turkey parliamentary democracy has existed, with interruptions, since 1950. Universal suffrage actually prevailed even under the one-party system before 1946. Democratically elected governments until 1980 invariably pursued protectionist, import-substituting tariff policies with quantitative controls (licensing) waxing and waning with the foreign exchange situation, in this regard continuing the policies of Atatürk from the 1930s. These protectionist policies were accompanied by investment promotion through public enterprises on the one hand, and on the other through tax incentives and cheap financing, from abroad or from the central bank. The color of the government in power did not matter much. Interest groups have been strong and have mainly operated through the chambers of commerce and industry and the political parties. Unions were increasingly important from 1961 to 1980. Turkish governments during the times of parliamentary democracy in this way promoted growth systematically. With the elections of 1950 the rural population gained political clout, and agricultural price support policies at least until 1980 tended to favor agriculture, in this sense being conducive to equity. Whether the net outcome of protection was in favor of agriculture is another matter. In its effect on the cost of living, this policy might have been very harmful to real wages had it not been alleviated through sales of basic foods at prices below the support prices and a low-price policy for public enterprises, the subsidies largely financed through the central bank.

Liberalization of the labor market with the right to unionization, for the first time recognized in the 1961 constitution, more than compensated for the increase in the cost of living. Wage increases pushed by the unions were supported by minimum wage legislation. In this way parliamentary democracy in Turkey actually promoted growth as well as equity in the economic sense of the word. During this period a substantial social security and pension system was created. Education policies at the same time emphasized elementary education. That parliamentary democracy operated the politically cheap way, with inflationary central bank and foreign financing of investment and budget deficits, ultimately encountering a debt crisis and breakdown of the policy, is another matter. It only proves that parliamentary democracy, while respecting growth and equity targets, did not solve the problem of coexistence and simultaneous realization of these targets. In 1980 a dramatic change in development strategy from the old inward-looking to outward-looking export-led growth took place. It was largely implemented after the military takeover in September 1980.

The Autocrats

Comparing autocratic governments in Turkey and Egypt involves the almost incommensurable personalities of Atatürk and his chief lieutenant İnönü, on the one hand, and of Nasser and his followers Sadat and Mubarak, on the other. Both Atatürk and Nasser started governing on the assumption that economic development—more specifically industrialization—should be based on private ownership and entrepreneurship with incentives in the form of protection and subsidies. Both became "etatists" in responding to crises.

Atatürk was confronted with the breakdown of the international economy in the early 1930s. His response was a cautious, middle-of-the-road policy with general modernization and state economic enterprises to take the lead without replacing private entrepreneurship. His two five-year plans did not amount to comprehensive planning. His was never a socialist policy, and equity was never promoted through redistribution of private income and property. Distribution of public land to smallholders and landless labor, however, came to play an important role in connection with the extensive population exchanges and served not only to expand agricultural production but also to promote equity in rural areas, thus making land reform a secondary, elite issue. Atatürk's policies were continued by İnönü and other Kemalists who after World War II moved toward, and in 1946 deliberately introduced, parliamentary democracy. It is remarkable that the real costs of mobilizing for neutrality in World War II, with its serious setback in agriculture, were paid by cutting private consumption rather than investment. The autocrats here sacrificed political popularity for growth. Turkish autocracy thus clearly promoted growth, agricultural no less than industrial, equity being promoted mainly through modernization, elementary education, social security, and distribution of public land.

The first Egyptian land reforms in 1952 were perhaps mainly a political move against the royal family and the old land-owning aristocracy but were not otherwise directed against private ownership and entrepreneurship. By 1955, Nasser was confronted with international policy conflicts with serious economic implications for Egypt which culminated in the Suez War of 1956. That started the sweeping sequestrations and nationalization measures that from 1961 relegated private entrepreneurship outside agriculture to domestic, small-scale informal activities. Large-scale economic activities, including foreign trade in the hands of the government, and all private activities including agriculture were subjected to bureaucratic control under the label of Arab socialism. Growth policy under Nasser was devoted to Frisch-Tinbergen style planning, with emphasis on equity.

One constraint on Egyptian policy was the open warfare, from 1962 in Yemen and from 1967 against Israel, which meant that growth was largely sacrificed for military efforts, military expenditure being financed by Soviet and Arab aid and reduction of investment rather than private consumption. Furthermore, policies such as land reform, sequestration, nationalization, social security reform, and price and wage controls, however motivated, were blunted by administrative inefficiency and the spoils of the system. With political parties, organizations, and special interest groups banned or transformed into government entities, the political vacuum thus created was filled in by a partly military patron-client and crony system that quickly came to play an important, self-serving, albeit somewhat stochastic role in administration and even in the formulaton of policy (Springborg 1975; Waterbury 1983, pp. 346ff.).

Egyptian autocracy in Nasser's version was clearly growth and equity oriented, though national security concerns took the upper hand in the 1960s. It was largely concentrated in the public sector and thus difficult to evaluate in real terms, and its net impact on equity was mostly random and thus also difficult to evaluate.

Sadat's autocracy followed a different pattern. With the military back in the barracks, family connections and cronies dominated at the top. Private business activities, domestic as well as foreign, were given a role to play. Growth, greatly helped by external factors, was strongly promoted through both public and private investment as well as public consumption, of somewhat dubious value, however. Equity policy was strongly pursued through consumer goods subsidies financed partly through low agricultural output prices, partly through the budget. Because of the accompanying strong inflation, a bloated, inefficient, and self-serving administration, and discrimination against agriculture, the net impact of Sadat's policy on equity and poverty is as difficult to evaluate as that of Nasser.

Mubarak, who took power after the assassination of Sadat in 1981, has mainly continued Sadat's policies and sought to preserve a status quo with little reform or change of strategy. The private sector has, however, been allowed to expand in size and influence, the exploitation of agriculture seems to have been considerably reduced, and the military establishment has experienced a certain comeback with contacts to the private sector rather than to public enterprises as under Nasser. Lax budgetary policies, initiated under Sadat, have resulted in an unmanageable foreign debt, and growth has finally begun grinding to a halt, possibly with detrimental effects on equity.

Military Establishments

Egypt and Turkey have built up very large military establishments, the major expansion taking place in Egypt between the 1967 and 1973 wars, in Turkey at the beginning of World War II. Both countries have kept their armies at the maximum reached around 1972, about 450,000 men in Egypt, about 600,000 in Turkey, in both countries about 4 percent of the measured labor force. Even so, it might be asked why the military establishment should be singled out as a political force in its own right. Parliamentary democracy in Egypt was, of course, destroyed by a group of officers after a coup, but it is doubtful whether this small group of officers should be identified with the military establishment as such. In Turkey, parliamentary democracy has several times been suspended or controlled by military intervention, each time, however, with the military handing government back to an elected parliament. It is very much this special nature of the Turkish military takeovers and their economic consequences that makes the issue interesting. During the decades of democracy in Egypt, on the other hand, the military played no role worth talking about (until the coup in 1952, of course). All five autocrats—Atatürk and İnönü in Turkey, Nasser, Sadat, and Mubarak in Egypt—were military persons and it seems clear that they would not have been able to take over and remain in power without the support or approval of the military establishment. The nature of such support or approval and its economic implications are far from obvious and have, indeed, differed much in each case.

Kemal Atatürk, a military leader of the highest caliber with a brilliant military and political record, had little difficulty in imposing his authority on the military establishment after independence. A charismatic personality with explicit, original political philosophies, he had little difficulty either in indoctrinating the officer corps with his Kemalist ideology, emphasizing secularization and modernization—Europeanization—including democracy as an ultimate long-term goal. Beyond that he was anxious to shelter the military from politics; he did not want to see the army politicized and participating in day-to-day politics. The single political role assigned to the military was that of guardian for his modernization reforms and ultimately democracy. İsmet İnönü, also a military leader with an outstanding record and great popularity, continued Atatürk's policy, emphasizing and accelerating the move toward democracy; he introduced the multiparty system in 1946 and graciously handed over power to the winners of the first democratic election, in 1950. This ideology and tradition, which continues to govern the behavior of Turkish military leaders, explains the unusual role of the Turkish military as a guardian of democracy and, hence, against extremism to left and right (including religious fundamentalism).

It would be a mistake, however, to overlook the nature of the Turkish military as a political pressure group with typical middle-class characteristics and interests, such as price stabilization. On the other hand, it is a bureaucratic bloc with the normal interests of bureaucrats in expanding their budget and activities and contacts with NATO and the West. Through the military pension funds and their investment in private industry, something like a financial military-industrial complex has, it is claimed, in recent years begun to grow up. These characteristics taken together have to be considered to understand the Turkish military takeovers in 1960 and 1980 and the intervention in 1971, the strong military support to stabilization programs, and the subsequent handing back of power to civilian politicians.

The Egyptian military establishment has little in common with the Turkish. Since the feats of Mohammed Ali's armies under command of his son Ibrahim, who came close to conquering the Ottoman Empire, the Egyptian military record has been unimpressive and at times disastrous. No outstanding military leaders and ideologists have emerged with authority comparable to that of Atatürk and İnönü. Nasser's ideology,

Arab socialism, which was little more than a post hoc rationalization of his ad hoc measures, was never shared by a majority of the officer corps. Until 1967 the armed forces were under the direct command of Amer, appointed field marshal by Nasser. Amer, a middle-sized landowner, officially supported Nasser's nationalizations and sequestrations in 1961 and his Arab socialism which was spelled out in the Charter of 1962, but he resisted all attempts to politicize the army through penetration by the single party, the Arab Socialist Union. It is probably fair to say that the Egyptian army was never permeated by any particular political ideology, did not pursue any particular policies, and in this sense was not a special political force, even during the years of Nasser.[1] That officers played an important role in the patron-client system, hence in the civilian administrative system, is another matter. The politicizing military was the small group of Free Officers from which the junta emerged, followed by a small group of loyalists that supported Nasser when he outmaneuvered the other junta members and established autocratic power, though in cooperation with Amer insofar as the armed forces were concerned. For understanding the shallowness of Egyptian land reform, it may be worth noting that, apart from Nasser who continued deepening the land reforms until 1969, all junta members were middle-sized landowners.

Like any other group of public employees, the military in Egypt would presumably tend to act as an interest group, safeguarding its own salaries and fringe benefits in real terms, and, as a bureaucratic bloc, would seek to increase its budget or at least prevent budget cutbacks, an obvious possibility after Camp David.

Contemporary Government Comparison

During the interwar years after independence Egypt suffered parliamentary democracy, Turkey autocracy. Both countries faced similar unfavorable international economic developments, Egypt with reasonably favorable initial conditions, Turkey with tremendous recovery problems.

Under both types of government it was assumed that the tariff autonomy to be obtained in 1929 and 1930 should be used for tariff reform aiming at industrialization. Inward-looking import substitution on the successful nineteenth-century German model with higher tariffs for finished goods and lower tariffs for inputs (including capital goods) subsidized and financed through development banks was the chosen policy in both countries. From 1932, public enterprises in Turkey were given the leading role in the industrialization process, Atatürk's policy of etatism. In Egypt the emphasis was entirely on private entrepreneurship. In Egypt the single development bank was private with some government subsidization; in Turkey a system of state banks was established for development. In Egypt international transactions remained free from quantitative controls; in Turkey licensing of trade and capital movements prevailed after 1930. Egypt had no bilateral trade agreements; Turkey traded mainly on the basis of such agreements. The Egyptian currency was pegged to the pound sterling throughout the interwar period; the Turkish currency was by and large linked to gold (first through the French franc, then through the Reichsmark). As a result, Egypt experienced some real effective depreciation around 1931 when sterling went off the gold standard while in Turkey the real effective exchange rate, after some depreciation before 1930, slowly appreciated until World War II.

It would appear that the Turkish policies were much more successful than the Egyptian in terms of industrial growth despite the exchange rate policies which if anything should have led to the opposite result. High flexibility of factor prices in both countries may explain why exchange rate policies were inconsequential.

Agricultural growth in both countries was promoted through investment in the infrastructure, in Egypt in irrigation and drainage devices accompanied by the introduction of improved cotton varieties and strong expansion of input of chemical fertilizers, in Turkey in transportation opening up the interior. Turkey's policy was vastly superior, based as it was on the existence of surplus land.

Policies for equity did not include measures for redistributing income and property in either country. Such intervention was simply not on the agenda. Free elementary education was apparently pushed more strongly in Turkey than in Egypt. Distribution of public land in Turkey, mainly to the exchange population, took place on a large scale and as a byproduct probably served to make land distribution more equitable.

During World War II, Egypt continued in principle as a parliamentary democracy (with much interference from the Allied forces), Turkey as an autocracy. Both countries remained neutral, Turkey carrying the burden of mobilization for neutrality with some export surplus, Egypt carrying the burden of forced exports of goods and services to the Allied armies, including the Middle East Supply Centre with payments accumulated on low-interest sterling accounts in London, partially eroded through inflation. Both countries experienced strong inflation through central bank financing and in both the burden fell mainly on private consumption, probably with lower-income brackets and civil servants and other fixed-income families hardest hit. A capital tax in Turkey came close to confiscation of minority property. Industrialization in Egypt benefited from Allied demand, in Turkey from military demand and continued public investment. Agricultural production suffered in both countries, in Egypt through the forced change in crop composition (thus really an index problem) and shortage of fertilizers, in Turkey through drafting of men and animals.

Beginning about 1950–52 Egypt suffered autocracy, Turkey parliamentary democracy with intermezzos of military takeover. Both countries continued the inward-looking industrialization policies adopted around 1930, Egypt adding quantitative foreign payments controls to the picture, both countries from around 1960 operating on the basis of formal comprehensive planning of the Frisch-Tinbergen type. Otherwise, conditions and developments were very different.

From the mid–1950s a change in Egypt's international relations led to a gradual but radical shift of trade and aid from Western countries toward communist countries while open warfare in Yemen and against Israel shifted domestic expenditure toward military activities, away from investment, all of it with detrimental effects on growth from about 1965 to 1974. What a parliamentary democracy in Egypt would have done under those circumstances is impossible to say. It is interesting though that parliamentary democracy in Turkey, faced with a similar problem in relation to Cyprus, deliberately opted for a military approach with considerable economic consequences but without letting growth suffer. Following the Cyprus invasion in 1974, the U.S. Congress imposed an arms embargo on Turkey that was economically costly and threatened Turkey's membership in NATO. Unlike Egypt, Turkey did not turn to the Soviet Union for arms or aid but worked out a modus vivendi, culminating in a new Cooperation on Defense and Economy Agreement with the United States signed in 1980. Yet it is not farfetched to compare Turkey's situation in 1975 with Nasser's in 1955. Nor is it farfetched to ask whether and how the Turkish debt crisis of 1978 and its solution were related to the arms embargo crisis and its solution in the way Nasser's debt crisis of 1966 and its nonsolution were related to Egypt's arms problem and its solution.

Egypt under Nasser expanded public ownership greatly, both absolutely and relatively, through public investment activities on the one hand and sequestrations and nationalizations on the other. Turkey also expanded public enterprises absolutely under democracy but preserved by and large the fifty-fifty relationship between private and public ownership in manufacturing industry laid down in the Atatürk philosophies and explicitly upheld by Inönü as prime minister from 1961 to 1965. Turkey did undertake some nationalization of foreign enterprises both in the 1930s (transportation mostly) and in the 1960s (mining) but it was directed against foreign owners and they were fully compensated. The number of enterprises thus transferred to the public sector was small and never significantly changed the proportion of private to public ownership. Sequestrations without compensation were not practiced in Turkey as a policy instrument. And while Turkish etatism was seen as an instrument of growth policy, it did not aim at transforming society in a socialist direction.

The rural population gained clout under parliamentary democracy in Turkey. The leading political parties could not afford to ignore rural and agricultural interests and voters. In Egypt this did not happen, either under parliamentary democracy or under autocracy, before 1952 because large landowners had the upper hand in the political process both at the grassroots and at the top, after 1952 for obvious reasons. The systematic, direct exploitation of agriculture in favor of the urban population through low producer prices that in Egypt began under Nasser and reached a peak under Sadat could not happen under Turkish democracy. The need for weak Egyptian autocrats to seek if not popular support, then at least popular acquiescence—what has been called the social compact—led to absurd subsidization of basic consumer goods; the counterpart in Turkish democracy, as in any democracy, is political parties that have to appeal to the electorate. Democracies also may have social compacts that lock the political situation. The fact that both Egypt and Turkey went into accelerating budget deficits with central bank and foreign borrowing indicates that both countries had weak government, weak dictators in Egypt, poorly functioning democracy in Turkey; Turkey had the advantage of an ideologically motivated military establishment, prepared to step in for stabilization and rectification whenever democracy failed.

At the end of the 1970s both Egypt and Turkey faced serious foreign exchange problems with strong inflation. Both countries came under heavy pressure from international organizations and financiers to change strategy and seek export-led growth rather than continue the old import-substitution policies. Turkey did change strategy radically. The blueprints presented by Özal under the last parliamentary government in 1980 under the 1961 constitution were largely implemented by the military government, in 1980–83, which abandoned Kemalist etatism. Egypt depreciated strongly in early 1979 but in effect resisted a change of strategy, her foreign exchange situation easing temporarily with the oil price increase later in 1979 and her international political situation easing markedly with Camp David. Even after the oil price decline in 1984, the accompanying foreign exchange crisis, and the following IMF Accord of 1987 with renewed strong depreciation, Egypt in effect continued her reluctance to change strategy; Mubarak, the military establishment, and the civilian bureaucracy apparently were equally uninterested in fundamental policy reform and private sector producers were not interested in giving up protection of the domestic market. Under international pressure, agricultural price policies and, perhaps, strategy changed somewhat after 1980 in favor of agriculture.

Notes

1. Systematic studies of the social background of the Egyptian officer corps do not seem to exist. Binder (1978, pp. 3–4) refers to Vatikiotis (1961) and Abdel-Malek (1968) as agreeing on the "links between the military officers and the rural middle class" although Vatikiotis (1961, p. xiii) generally "suggests that

the army in the Arab states is not necessarily a class in the socio-economic sense, sharing similar social backgrounds and economic interests. It may not even be a professional group in the sense of the German, British, or American regular army officer class." Waterbury (1983, table 12–4) reports a study of the rural links of forty-nine Free Officers (not including Nasser, Sadat, Amer, and Zakareya Moheieldin) showing twelve sons of landowners, twelve sons of professionals who owned some land, fourteen "sons of professionals/businessmen w/o [without?] land," and ten with unclear background.

16 Trends of Endowments, Production, and Factor Prices

Standard theory suggests that before investigating the interrelationships of politics, growth, and distribution in Egypt and Turkey, it is appropriate to analyze the underlying trends in endowments and productivity of their economies. This chapter discusses hypothetical trends, assuming politics to be neutral. In countries dominated completely by agriculture, as these two were initially, endowments must at a minimum include land, capital, and labor; recent development modeling by Leamer (1987, 1984) as applied to Latin American countries by Lal (1987) does that. Conventional (two commodity–two factor Heckscher-Ohlin-Samuelson) theory or sector-specific endowments models like that of Jones may have theoretically convenient properties but they are not general enough to realistically cover the cases of Egypt and Turkey. Since even the Leamer model does not suffice to analyze Turkish developments before 1960, the Ricardo–von Thünen theory ought to be brought into the picture.

First I discuss factor endowments, their growth and productivity from 1923 to 1985, and I then try to characterize Egyptian and Turkish development patterns. The two cases are radically different, Egyptian development conditions being similar to those of East Asia, those of Turkey resembling Latin America, and both cases strongly influenced by policies of import substitution and etatism.

National Factor Endowments

National factor endowments and proportions are not known with any high degree of precision and even less is known about national factor productivity. Moreover, factor supplies may be sensitive to factor prices in real terms and thus may not be exogenously given.

The economically active population is enumerated by population censuses and labor force surveys, both of which suffer from serious deficiencies, particularly in the enumeration of unpaid family labor. Egypt strongly underenumerates unpaid females as compared with Turkey.

Both participation rates and working hours are known to be sensitive to real wages. It is thus preferable here to represent the national labor endowment by the total domestic population (and even that is not strictly exogenous over a sixty-year period).

Two measures of land are available—actually cultivated (including fallow) land and arable land. While actually cultivated land is fairly well defined and measured in both countries, arable land is not a well-defined concept. For Egypt arable land for the sixty-year period is identified with actually cultivated land in 1980. Considering the topography of Egypt and the failure to expand the area through reclamation, this is a reasonably good approximation. For Turkey arable land is defined as cultivated (including fallow) land plus land classified as pastures and meadows, not including forests. Considering that pastures and meadows could be and frequently are used for grazing livestock (including sheep and goats), this may not be an unreasonable approximation although some land classified as unproductive probably, if need be, could be used also for that purpose. Table 16–1 shows the land-labor ratios using these definitions.

The distinction between cultivated and arable area (as here defined) is of little consequence for Egypt. On both measures the land-labor ratio is very low and has declined steadily, by about one-third from 1927 to 1980. For Turkey the distinction is crucial. On both measures the land-labor ratio is much higher in Turkey than in Egypt and in relation to labor Turkey is on both measures much more land abundant than Egypt. Measured on arable land, the land-labor ratio in Turkey has declined steadily to less than one-third, as in Egypt. This is, of course, because arable land has been nearly constant in both countries while population for the period as a whole has grown at about the same rate. Measured on cultivated land, however, the land-labor ratio in Turkey increased by about 50 percent from 1927 to 1960 and in 1980, despite a decline from 1960, was still slightly higher than in 1927. While in Egypt throughout the whole period practically speaking all arable land was cultivated, in

Table 16–1. Ratios of Land to Labor, 1927, 1960, and 1980

(hectares per capita of total population)

Year	Egypt		Turkey		Turkey/Egypt	
	Cultivated	*Arable*	*Cultivated*	*Arable*	*Cultivated*	*Arable*
1927	0.16	0.19	0.61	4.10[a]	3.7	21.5
1960	0.09	0.10	0.91	1.94	9.8	18.9
1980	0.06	0.06	0.63	1.18	9.7	18.3

a. Conjecture.

Source: Turkey, *Statistical Yearbook;* Tezel (1975); Egypt, Ministry of Finance, *Annuaire statistique de l'Egypte;* Gardner and Parker (1985).

Turkey cultivated land increased from about one-seventh to more than one-half of all arable land. This is a consequence of the difference in land quality, both in fertility and location and in the movement of the cultivation margin toward the frontier (in the American sense of the word). Egypt reached the frontier in 1897. The increased share of cultivated land in Turkey is closely related to the increase in the stock of capital in transportation and mechanization and has been of crucial importance for the development of both GDP per capita and distribution. Here the ratio of arable land to labor is what matters. Table 16–1 shows that the land labor ratio was about twenty times higher in Turkey than in Egypt in 1927–80, Turkey in this sense being about twenty times more land abundant than Egypt, but then, of course, Turkish land is on balance much less fertile than that of Egypt.

I do not know of any reliable estimate of the national stock of capital in either Egypt or Turkey.[1] Measured on arable land, the capital-land ratios must have increased strongly in both countries, capital in this sense becoming increasingly abundant. The problem is how the capital-labor ratios developed. Estimates of the stock of capital in agriculture and industry for Egypt and indicators of the stock of capital in railways and in houses are shown in table 16–2. Assuming a 3.5 percent increase in the total number of houses from 1952 to 1966—certainly a minimum assumption—the stocks of capital in agriculture, industry, and houses all increased in relation to population from 1924 to 1966, and despite a relative decline in railways the national stock of capital undoubtedly increased more than population from 1924 to 1966. During the lean years 1966–74 with gross investment hardly exceeding normal depreciation and the Canal Zone with Port Said, Ismaileya, and Suez almost completely destroyed in Nasser's War of Attrition after 1967, the national stock of capital per capita probably declined. Comparing 1980 with 1966, it is doubtful whether the agricultural and housing stocks of capital per capita increased although the industrial stock of capital certainly did so. In railways the stock of capital per capita certainly continued de-

Table 16–2. Indexes of Population and Capital Stocks in Egypt, Selected Years, 1924–66

| Year | Population | Stock of capital | | | |
		Agriculture	Industry	Railways	Houses
1924	100	100	100	100	100
1952	155.4	206.8	270.9	126.1	211.3
1960	187.5	246.6	382.0	122.6	n.a.
1966	218.5	349.3	458.8	n.a.	n.a.

n.a. = Not available.
Source: table 2–1.

clining but motorcars and tractors may now have compensated for the decline in railway capital per capita. That the national stock of capital per capita should have increased faster than population between 1966 and 1980 is by no means a foregone conclusion. My best conjecture is that national capital per capita increased steadily from 1924 to 1966, declined from 1966 to 1974, and then increased from 1974 to 1980, when it possibly exceeded the 1966 level. The ratio of capital to arable land must have increased steadily from 1924 to 1980 with the possible exception of the years 1966–74.

For Turkey it appears justified to assume that the capital-labor ratio increased steadily over the whole period 1924–80. Leamer's estimates (1984) indicate a substantial increase from 1960 to 1975. Recent OECD estimates of total factor productivity seem to imply that capital per unit of labor increased by 0.5 percent annually in 1973–87 (*Economic Survey, Turkey*, 1987, table 3).

Figure 16–1 depicts these conjectures about factor endowments in the two countries, using Leamer's triangle of the endowment ratios of labor, capital, and land. Scales of measurement are nonlinear. Along a ray through one corner of the endowment triangle, every point has the same ratio of the other two factors and the ratio can be read off on the opposite edge. Conjectured paths of the endowment ratios for Egypt and Turkey from 1924 to 1980 are indicated. Egypt's land-labor ratio for the whole period is much lower than Turkey's. I assume that Egypt's capital-labor ratio was higher than Turkey's in 1924, considering the importance of the irrigation system in Egypt ever since antiquity and the destruction in Turkey during World War I and the Independence War, but that the two were about the same in 1980. The capital-land ratio I assume all the time to have been higher in Egypt than in Turkey.

Under standard assumptions, movement along a ray through a corner toward the opposite edge will imply an increase in the price of the factor in question. What happens to the factor price on a different ray is uncertain. The figure is drawn to show that in 1980 rent of land was higher in Egypt than in Turkey; it would seem likely that that was true in 1924, though it cannot be certain. It would in the same way appear likely though not certain, that returns to capital declined from 1924 to 1980 in both Turkey and Egypt. For labor and land the shift of ray for both Egypt and Turkey from 1924 to 1980 is so strong that even conjectures appear unwarranted. The capital-labor ratio increased strongly (with a reversal for Egypt in 1966–74) for both countries but the land-labor ratios declined strongly.

Factor Productivity

The estimates of total factor productivity in Egyptian agriculture for 1900–67 in table 4–12 show that productivity declined by 22 percent or

Figure 16-1. Endowment Ratio Triangle, 1924-80

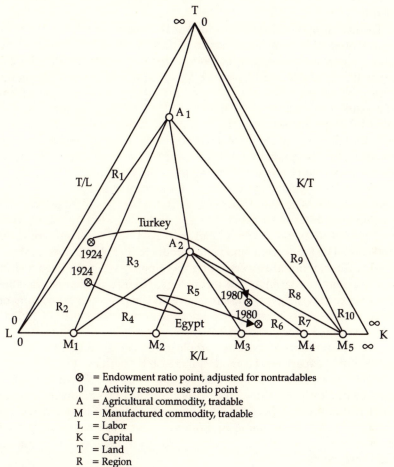

⊗ = Endowment ratio point, adjusted for nontradables
0 = Activity resource use ratio point
A = Agricultural commodity, tradable
M = Manufactured commodity, tradable
L = Labor
K = Capital
T = Land
R = Region

Source: Author's conjectures based on Lal (1987).

at a rate of 0.4 percent annually. The decline was, however, concentrated in the early part of the period, with a decline of 27 percent in 1900–20. From 1920 to 1967 a slight increase by 7 percent, or 0.1 percent annually, actually occurred. Uncertain information about the capital stock after 1967 indicates that the rate of increase in total factor productivity may have been of the same very low order from 1967 to 1981–82. Since independence, factor productivity in agriculture accordingly has, practically speaking, been constant with almost no residual. This is certainly a miserable performance. Agricultural factor productivity may even have been lower in 1981–82 than in 1900. Factor proportions in agriculture at the same time changed radically, land being almost constant, fixed capital increasing about three times, and labor increasing about one-third. There is something to indicate that technological change was land saving.

Disregarding the years of World War II (data being unreliable), total factor productivity in manufacturing (from table 4–14) increased by about 2 percent annually from 1945 to 1962 and then declined by 2.2 percent annually to 1970. From 1973 to 1981–82 there was a strong increase by 5.3 percent annually, in all probability partly recovery from the years with decline. For 1963 to 1981–82 the average increase was only 1.2 percent, down from the 2.0 percent during 1945–62. It is noticeable that the years of declining factor productivity in manufacturing coincided with the years of a declining ratio of national capital to labor. Factor proportions in manufacturing were almost constant from 1945 to 1981–82, labor (hours) increasing by 4.4 percent and capital by 4.3 percent annually. The slight increase in the labor-capital ratio was not caused by a shift toward labor-intensive technology but by overstaffing in 1963–64 to 1969–70 when labor increased by 8.0 percent annually and capital by 0.5 percent, and factor productivity fell by 2.2 percent annually. Considering the overstaffing there must even have been a shift toward more capital-intensive technology. No information is available on other sectors in Egypt. The strong overstaffing in general government must have been accompanied by a decline in factor productivity (whatever that means for government).

For the Egyptian economy as a whole my conjecture is that total factor productivity experienced a modest increase by perhaps 1/2–1 percent annually from 1923 to 1962, declined from 1962 to 1973, and then increased modestly. For the whole period 1923 to 1981–82 the increase in total factor productivity was insignificant. Capital formation had to compensate for the declining land-labor ratio and was hardly supported by increasing productivity in creating growth in the sense of increased GDP per capita.

For Turkey, total factor productivity in manufacturing increased 2.1 percent annually in the years 1963–76. My computation of the increase in total factor productivity for the national economy between the years 1958 and 1975 is presented in chapter 11; it is based on Leamer's definitions and figures for factor endowments in Turkey (1984, table B-1). His estimates for Egypt, unfortunately, cannot be used in the same way. The result for Turkey, for whatever it is worth, is a modest increase of total factor productivity in 1958–75 of 1.1 percent annually, hardly much better than the performance of Egypt. With an increase of 2.1 percent in manufacturing for 1963–76, factor productivity increase in agriculture must have been well below 1 percent, which is remarkably similar to Egypt's performance. For the years 1973–87 the OECD has estimated total factor productivity increase to be 1.4 percent annually (*Economic*

Surveys, Turkey, table 7–15), which is hardly any better than my conjecture for 1958–75.

For years before 1960, there are no estimates of factor productivity in Turkey. Probably, however, the strong increase of the cultivated area at given area of arable land dominates the situation. In real terms, GDP increased by 4.8 percent annually in 1924–60 (with a strong setback during World War II). Population increased by 2.1 percent. Arable land was, practically speaking, constant and the shares of both labor and land in total factor income were probably higher than those assumed for 1960–75. With a gross investment share of GDP on the order of 10 percent, capital formation must have been relatively modest. I would not be surprised if the residual was 2 percent or more for 1924–60, mostly because of the extension of the cultivation margin in agriculture, but partly because of investment in transportation. Although higher than for 1960–75 and 1973–87, even this is not an impressive residual.

Why has total factor productivity growth been so disappointing in both Egypt and Turkey since independence? Given the decline in the share of agriculture in GDP and the progress in education in both countries, particularly in Turkey (see chapter 17), it would be reasonable to expect a substantial residual. The explanation for both countries lies in the negative attitude of government to foreigners and in the negative aspects of etatism. Before independence, foreigners and foreign minorities in both countries played an important role in business, mainly in finance, commerce, and services but also in industry and to some extent even in agriculture; foreign participants and direct foreign investment accounted for much of the modernization of production that took place. The subsequent disappearance of foreigners and minorities from both Turkey (Greeks and Armenians especially) and Egypt (Europeans as well as Levantines) during the interwar and postwar years undoubtedly deprived both countries of an educated, knowledgeable, and dynamic element that probably would have been beneficial to productivity. The increasing obstacles to direct foreign investment and establishment of foreign-owned and -administered enterprises, until the 1970s in Egypt and the 1980s in Turkey, and the nationalization in Egypt of existing companies with sequestrations had similar effects.

In appraising the impact of etatism, a distinction should probably be made between quantity and quality. While there is little doubt that both in Egypt and in Turkey etatism led to an increase in the accumulation of real capital (volume of gross investment) as compared with what would have happened under private entrepreneurship, it is equally certain that productivity suffered under etatism.[2] The net effect is doubtful. My subjective judgment is that it was positive in its early years but subsequently became definitely negative. Although by no means unknown to Ottoman Turkey, modern etatism was introduced by Atatürk in the bleak 1930s when probably little industry would have developed without state intervention and initiative; inefficient industry may have been better than no industry. Interwar industrialization in Egypt was essentially based on private initiative, but agricultural investment in irrigation and drainage was as always planned and executed by government. After independence the Egyptian government continued British agricultural development policy, based on fixed investment in irrigation and drainage, and Egypt under Nasser continued the British policies. As T. W. Schultz (1964) has observed, after high returns in the beginning, this kind of policy yields rapidly declining returns. Large dam and barrage investments in the 1930s gave little agricultural return and the Aswan High Dam did no better. What was bold and rewarding investment planning on the part of government in the 1880s and 1890s became conservative and outdated policy in the 1930s and 1960s.

The positive side of British planning for agricultural development in Egypt between the wars (improved cotton varieties, increased fertilizer input, and improved drainage) was played down in the 1950s and 1960s in favor of land reclamation, and drainage was ignored. The blame for an almost nonexistent residual in Egyptian agriculture since 1900 should be put on misdirected and poorly conceived government policies long before, but accentuated under Nasser. Import-substitution policies should instantaneously tend to lower factor productivity but this should not be lasting if the decrease is assumed to be an infant-industry effect. Public ownership in industry has certainly not been conducive to productivity in either country, but Turkey has at least had the advantage that public ownership was not expanded relatively during the postwar period as it was in Egypt with the nationalizations and sequestrations under Nasser. Another major difference between Turkey and Egypt is that while organizational change in Turkey throughout the period since independence mainly has served to replace traditional with modern organization, in Egypt under autocracy since 1952 such change has mainly served to replace private with public organization and private entrepreneurship with bureaucracy. Egypt's radical though temporary shift from trade with Western Europe and the United States to communist countries during the years around 1960, which had no counterpart in Turkey, should tend to affect the growth rate negatively because of higher marginal capital-output ratios and less autonomous productivity increase in line with well-known inefficiencies of communist economies. The reversal of trade in the 1970s should, of course, tend to have the opposite effects but with the country now saddled with large, inefficient public industries the negative effects may linger for decades.

Hypothetical Development Paths, 1924–80

Because the residuals are so negligible, changes in total factor productivity have become of secondary significance, and changes in individual factor productivity have almost exclusively reflected changing factor proportions in both countries. To conjecture hypothetical development paths, following Leamer and Lal, requires operating with fixed coefficient activities, and for the fixed-coefficient analysis it is necessary to take into account resources absorbed in production of nontradable goods and services. Assuming agriculture and industry to be tradables-producing sectors and all others to be nontradables-producing sectors, both Egypt and Turkey produced around 1960 about 52 percent of GDP in the form of tradable goods and in 1983–84 about 46 percent. For Turkey this share was in 1924 about 55 percent. In 1984 about 58 percent of the labor force was employed in producing tradables in both countries, and in 1962 the share was 65 percent for Egypt and 81 percent for Turkey. In 1927 this share was 76 percent for Egypt. Nontradables are thus important. Land as measured here was, of course, exclusively employed in agriculture. Presumably urban land would have been used in the production of nontradables. Capital-intensive nontradables were housing, communications, and (modern) transportation. For nontradables the ratios of land to labor and of land to capital must have been moderate while the ratio of capital to labor must have been considerable. (Here I sidestep the problem of differential rent related to fertility and location, the latter including urbanization; Samuelson's approach to this problem treats land quality as continuously depending on distance from the center [1966, 31, appendix].) The endowment ratio point for nontradables must have been near the lower edge in the endowment ratio triangle (figure 16–1), probably moving upward (with urbanization) and toward the capital corner from 1924 to 1980. To find the endowment ratio point for tradables would require shifting the total endowment ratio point upward to the left or right, depending on whether the capital-labor ratios for nontradables were smaller or larger than those for total endowments in 1924 and 1980, respectively. For 1980 I see no reason why the ratios for the two countries should differ very much, considering the high degree of urbanization in both. For 1924 I would expect the capital-labor ratio to have been smallest in nontradables production. The implication would be that the endowment ratio path for Turkey would be steeper and even could be sloping positively. The Egyptian path would in principle also be steeper but it would in any case remain flat and it is inconceivable that it could change sign.

Next it is necessary to introduce a suitable array of linear activities to be represented by activity points in the endowment ratio triangle. Both Leamer and Lal operate with two agricultural activities, one based exclusively on land and labor with no capital inputs and another defined as capital intensive based on land T, labor L, and capital K. The former is not a reasonable representation of agricultural activities. Even the most primitive agriculture has a capital-output ratio of at least one (crops on the fields or in stores with animals and some land clearing and improvement). I operate with two agricultural technologies, using all three factors, the first one primitive with low ratios of capital to labor and to land, K/L and K/T, and a high ratio of land to labor, T/L; the second one more advanced with K/L and K/T higher and T/L lower and possibly producing a bundle of commodities with a larger share of industrial crops. For Egypt the more advanced technology describes the shift from basin to perennial irrigation with a simultaneous shift to multiple cropping and rotation, with increased production of cotton; with the area of arable land roughly given, this explains the simultaneous assumed change in the three ratios. For Turkey the more advanced technology assumes an expansion of mechanization and of the railway system, the latter considered agricultural capital. The cultivated area increases but arable area is unchanged and with easier marketing there is a shift toward dried fruits, cotton, and tobacco. That K/T increases and T/L falls is obvious. The increase in K/L is an assumption. For manufacturing I follow Leamer (1987), Lal (1987), and Krueger (1977) in assuming activities to require only labor and capital in varying proportions. I do this with no regrets because nontradables, including infrastructure, are assumed to use all three factors, including urban land. Figure 16–1 shows the activity points with the assumed diversification regions as determined by activities and international commodity prices (Leamer 1987). The agricultural activity points are A_1 and A_2, the latter having higher K/L and K/T and lower L/T ratios. The manufacturing activity points are M_1 to M_5, increasingly capital intensive in this order. The paths of the endowment ratio points, adjusted for nontradable activities and resource use, are assumed to be as drawn. Factors are never redundant. Within each diversification region R_1 to R_{10}, production of nontradables with tradables as indicated by the corners of the regions takes place—in region R_1, nontradables plus A_1 are produced; in R_4, nontradables plus A_2, M_1, and M_2; in R_9, nontradables plus A_2 and M_5; and so on. Within a region, factor prices are the same regardless of the combination of output and, except for regions R_9 and R_{10}, are determined exclusively by international commodity prices in line with Heckscher-Ohlin-Samuelson-theory; in R_1 and R_{10}, domestic demand is a codeterminant (based on Leamer 1987, p. 977). Relative regional prices of a given factor are found by sweeping a ray over the triangle around the relevant corner. The closer a region intersected by a ray is to the corner, the lower the factor price. Only qualitative changes and relations can be read off from the triangle.

Figure 16–1 suggests the development of output and factor prices in Egypt and Turkey. Needless to say, it has been cleverly drawn so as to produce the results desired. The results are extremely sensitive to particular features of the figure. Thus if the endowment ratio path for Turkey had passed below rather than above A_2, with the endowment ratio points for 1924 and 1980 unchanged, Egyptian and Turkish developments would have been (qualitatively) identical from 1924 to 1980.

The figure is drawn to show both countries starting from region R_2, producing both A_1 and M_1, labor-intensive products from agriculture and manufacturing industry. Historically this is a realistic characterization of the two countries, at least as far back as the midnineteenth century; Egypt produced and exported fine linen goods and cigarettes, Turkey carpets and cigarettes. Factor prices should be the same. Both countries move then into region R_3, adding capital-intensive agricultural commodity A_2 to their output baskets; real wages and rent of land increase while return to capital declines with factor prices remaining equal in Egypt and Turkey. Region R_3 may offer a better description of the two countries in 1924 than region R_2, and the diagram could be relabeled accordingly. For Egypt the actual development of factor prices in agriculture from around 1900 to the 1930s seems to correspond to the hypothetical development (Hansen 1989, table 9) from R_2 to R_3. The limited information about Turkish factor prices suggests that the development paths from R_2 into R_3 may not be counterfactual.

Beyond R_3, the hypothetical development paths of the two countries differ radically. Egypt moves into R_4 and R_5 with A_1 phased out; M_1 replaced by somewhat more capital intensive products, M_2 and M_3; real wages increasing; returns to capital declining; and rent of land increasing. After a temporary reversal in 1966–74 to R_4, the country should continue on the old track with manufacturing becoming increasingly capital intensive, real wages increasing, returns to capital declining, and rent of land increasing.

Turkey should move from region R_3 directly into R_8, with labor-intensive manufacturing, M_1, replaced by highly capital intensive manufacturing and both agricultural technologies in use. Thereafter the path leads into R_7 and R_6, with A_1 (the less capital intensive agricultural product) phased out and manufacturing shifting toward more and more labor intensive technologies. Real wages increase from R_3 to R_8 and decline then to R_6 yet remain higher than in R_2 and R_3. Returns to capital decline from R_3 to R_8 but increase then through R_7 and R_6 yet remain lower than in R_2 and R_3. Rent of land declines from R_3 to R_8 but increases then through R_7 and R_6. It is not possible to determine a priori whether rents of land in R_7 and R_6 are higher or lower than in R_3 and R_2.

Is this picture of the hypothetical development paths for Egypt and Turkey factual or counterfactual? The common development from R_2 into R_3 is historically realistic (factual), particularly when R_2 represents the nineteenth century and R_3 the twentieth century until the 1920s. The complete phasing out of labor-intensive manufactures, M_1, in R_5 and R_8, respectively, is, of course, counterfactual in the sense that even today both countries have substantial labor-intensive, small-scale industries in the informal sector. On the other hand, during the nineteenth century a large part of the existing traditional, labor-intensive, small-scale industry (spinning may be the most important example) was practically speaking wiped out by British competition. The diagram may be accepted as describing this phenomenon. I would have liked to see a development path for both countries preserving some labor-intensive industry alongside the new capital-intensive industries; I was not able to fix the diagram accordingly, although it does help to imagine M_2 and M_3 as being relatively labor intensive.

The development for Egypt from R_3 into R_4, R_5, and R_6 with more and more capital intensive manufacturing and A_1 phased out, with a temporary reversal to more labor intensive manufacturing in 1966–74 is factual, although the country probably moved into industry with much more capital intensive technology than justified by the factor endowments. The development is very nicely reflected in agricultural real wages which increased steadily from 1948 to 1984 apart from a serious temporary decline from 1964 to 1973 coinciding with the reversal of the development path (figure 16–2). This setback was not reflected in real wages in manufacturing, which were fixed by the government for reasons of political expediency and not by market forces as undoubtedly was the case for agricultural wages.

The movement of Turkey from R_3 directly into R_8 with M_1 replaced by highly capital intensive manufacturing is factual insofar as the industrialization policy of Atatürk and the Kemalists concentrated on capital-intensive manufacturing and mining. The diagram suggests that for Turkey the introduction of highly capital intensive industries in the 1930s may have been an optimal investment policy while the same policy simultaneously pursued in Egypt by Tala'at Harb and the Misr Group may not have been. Conventional wisdom has it that both countries invested in industries requiring too much capital. Turkey apparently should have gone into very capital intensive manufacturing while Egypt should have gone into much more labor intensive manufacturing than actually was the case.

The following hypothetical movements of Turkey into R_7 and R_6 are certainly counterfactual. If anything, the investment policies during the 1960s and 1970s led to increasingly capital intensive industries. No information is available on agricultural wages in Turkey but real wages in industry continued increasing sharply until 1977. Also in relation to real wages the hypothetical development of Turkey into R_7 and R_6 is counterfactual. The underlying assumption of full employment is also counterfactual. During the 1970s unemployment in Turkey seems to have increased strongly, possibly explained by the increasing real wages and the accompanying policy of capital-intensive commitments. It is interesting, though, that when in 1978 and 1979 the labor unions finally were unable to push money wages fast enough to compensate for inflation, and from 1980 when union activities were severely circumscribed by military government and wages were fixed through arbitration, real product wages fell to the level of the early 1960s, a movement the hypothetical development path suggests (see table 12–16 and figure 16–2). When the

Figure 16-2. Real Wages in Agriculture and Manufacturing, 1960-85

Index, log scale (1968 = 100)

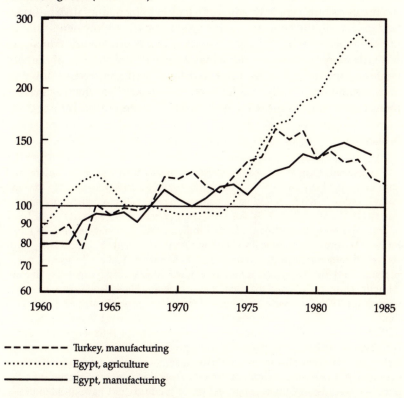

- – – – – – – Turkey, manufacturing
- ·············· Egypt, agriculture
- ——————— Egypt, manufacturing

Source: Egypt: CAPMAS and Ministry of Agriculture; Turkey: Census and Surveys, Manufacturing Industry, Hansen (1989).

decline in real wages from 1977 and the reforms of 1980–83 really began to take hold, the hypothetical path suggests that unemployment should decline and industry become more labor intensive. In 1985 there were some signs that that was happening.

Qualifying Remarks

The hypothetical development paths in Egypt and Turkey described in this chapter are mainly illustrative. They have the great advantage of operating with the three basic factors of production—land, labor, and capital—that any realistic analysis of the political economy of development in low-income countries must include. The analysis, however, has many limitations. It assumes perfect competition and full employment of factors with a possibility of redundancy at most. It ignores the demand side (nontraded goods being introduced indirectly only) and heterogeneity of factors (fertility and location of land being introduced implicitly only). The analysis runs in terms of fixed activity coefficients and its simplicity would evaporate the moment that substitution entered the picture in a significant way. Although it does bring quantitative information to bear on the choice of factor proportions in endowments and activities, it bears no resemblance whatever to modern empirical analysis. It is little more than a story, but it may help to demolish some of the conventional theoretical stereotypes that have predominated in development debate since World War II. It certainly makes clear that in development policy what is meat for one society may be poison for another.

Notes

1. I discount completely Leamer's resource endowment figures for capital and land in Egypt (1984, table B–1). The capital figure for 1960 is incredibly low and entirely out of touch with Radwan's painstaking estimates for agriculture and industry (1973, tables 2–8, 3–3). For 1960 Leamer has a GNP estimate of $4,103.2 million and a capital estimate of $545 million, less than one-seventh of GNP. Radwan's estimates for agriculture and industry, converted to U.S. dollars at official rate (Leamer's method) add up to $3,453.8 million. Adding for houses, transportation and the like (which are unknown) would probably result in a total capital figure close to GNP and that would make sense. This is also the result Leamer reaches for 1975. Leamer's land figure for Egypt is patently absurd. He gives a figure of 100 million hectares (more than India); the correct figure is about 2.5 million hectares. For Turkey Leamer's capital estimate for 1968 (but not for 1973) is rather low and his land figures do not agree with official data for either crop area (sown or sown plus fallow), cultivated area, or arable area. For both these countries and years, moreover, conversion to U.S. dollars at official rates is particularly dangerous. In conjecturing total factor productivity I have decided to use Leamer's endowment estimates for Turkey, assuming they are better than nothing. The national capital stock estimates used by the OECD in estimating total factor productivity 1973–87 (table 12–17) are not known to me.

2. It is sometimes argued that while obviously allocative distortion of resources should tend to affect the level of per capita income in a static sense, it is not obvious why and how it should affect the growth rate. My way of thinking is that if the growth rate g

$$g = \Delta GDP/GDP = (1+\pi)(GI/k)/GDP = (1+\pi)\ (1/k)\ (GI/GDP)$$

where k is the ratio of marginal capital to output and π is the autonomous productivity increase minus depreciation, etatism should tend to increase the ratio of gross investment GI to gross domestic product GDP while tending to increase k and lower π. The increase in k may partly be the result of static misallocation created by both import-substitution measures and bureaucracy in public enterprises. The decline in π should be ascribed to bureaucratic mismanagement of public enterprises.

17 Growth, Distribution, and Equity

This chapter compares and evaluates information about long-term achievements in growth, distribution, and equity in Egypt and Turkey. For the comparison of growth achievements, agriculture is the only sector for which comparisons covering the whole period 1923–85 are at all possible, and here World War II creates great problems in the case of Turkey. Agriculture is, however, one of the keys to understanding the relatively poor growth achievements of Egypt. Therefore, despite all difficulties, agricultural growth is compared for the whole period. The comparison of growth of gross domestic product (GDP) is split into the interwar years (with poor data), the post-World War II years (with much better data) of inward-looking growth strategy in both countries, and the years since Turkey's strategy change in 1980 (with conflicting data for Egypt).

Agricultural Growth, 1927–80

Tables 17–1 and 17–2 present basic data for Egyptian and Turkish agriculture from 1927 to 1980. The data on labor input are particularly unreliable and for Turkey there is no information on the total stock of capital in agriculture. The striking feature of the tables is the great similarity in agricultural growth rates in Egypt and Turkey from 1960 to 1980, with much higher growth in Turkey than in Egypt from 1927 to 1960.

During 1960–80, production increased in both countries by 2½–3 percent annually, slightly more in Turkey than in Egypt, at a slight increase in both countries of about ½ percent annually in cultivated area and an approximately unchanged labor force. Yields in the broad sense of production (GDP) per unit of land increased in both countries by 2–2½ percent annually while labor productivity (GDP per unit of labor) in both countries increased by almost 3 percent annually. Heavily regulated Egyptian farmers seem thus to have done about as well as free-wheeling, largely unregulated Turkish farmers. Both fertilizer consumption and the use of machinery (tractors) increased much faster in Turkey

Table 17-1. Indexes and Growth Rates of Agricultural Production and Inputs in Turkey, 1927–80

Measure and year	Production[a]	Cultivated area[b]	Labor[c]	Production per unit		Land-labor ratio[f]	Fertilizer consumption[g]	Tractors[h]
				Cultivated area[d]	Labor[e]			
Index (1960=100)								
1927	26.5	37.9	64.4	70.1	41.3	58.8	—	—
1935	39.9	48.3	73.4	82.5	54.3	65.8	—	—
1950	62.8	64.7	92.2	97.0	68.1	70.2	69.2	48.0
1960	100	100	100	100	100	100	100	100
1970	131.2	104.2	102.1	126.0	128.6	102.1	2,213.3	248.0
1980	178.8	109.3	101.4	163.5	176.3	107.8	7,466.7	1,036.3
Growth rate (percent)								
1927–60	4.1	3.0	1.3	1.1	2.7	1.6	—	—
1960–80	2.9	0.4	0.1	2.5	2.9	0.4	24.1	12.4
1927–80	3.7	2.0	0.9	1.6	2.8	1.1	—	—

— = Not applicable.

a. Three-year moving average of GDP at constant prices, $1,969 million absolute value in 1960 ($1 = LT2.80 before August 23, 1960, $1 = LT9.04 for imports and LT9.00 for exports after August 23).

b. Three-year moving average of area sown (*ekilen*), 15.3 million hectares in 1960.

c. Economically active labor force, 9.7 million workers in 1960.

d. In 1960, $127 per hectare.

e. In 1960, $202 per worker.

f. In 1960, 1.57 hectares per worker.

g. In 1960, 1.3 metric tons per 1,000 hectares.

h. In 1960, 2.8 per 1,000 hectares.

Source: Turkey, *Statistical Yearbook;* Tezel (1975); Bulutay, Tezel, and Yıeldırım (1974); World Bank data.

than in Egypt but then Turkey started at a much lower level in 1960 than Egypt, particularly in fertilizers.

While the levels of production per unit of labor were quite similar, production per unit of land was almost four times higher in Egypt than in Turkey. This, of course, (apart from the higher quality of land) reflects the much higher intensity of cultivation in Egypt in terms of labor and fertilizer, and, although data for Turkey are not available, certainly also in terms of capital (including canals, drains, and dams). The land-labor ratio in Turkey is about three times that in Egypt and despite the extraordinary increase in fertilizer consumption in Turkey, Egypt still consumes about three times as much fertilizer per unit of land as Turkey. In terms of machinery (tractors), however, cultivation had in 1980 become more intensive in Turkey. This was to be expected considering the scarcity of labor in relation to land in Turkey.

During 1927–60, on the other hand, agricultural production in Turkey increased about 4 percent annually against only about 1 percent in Egypt. Behind this very large difference in growth rates is an almost threefold increase in the cultivated area in Turkey and an almost unchanged area in Egypt. The land-labor ratio (thus defined) increased by 70 percent in Turkey but fell by 15 percent in Egypt. As a result, yields increased by about 1 percent annually in both countries while labor productivity increased by 2.7 percent annually in Turkey and only 0.6 percent in Egypt. That in Egypt the total stock of capital more than doubled while fertilizer input increased five times and that both factors were largely unchanged in Turkey did not suffice to reverse the impact of the different developments of the land-labor ratios.

Summing up, until about 1960 Turkey was a frontier country with rapid growth while Egypt had already reached the limits of cultivable land around 1900. When Turkey reached the frontier around 1960, the difference between agricultural growth in the two countries vanished and Turkey fell into the same mediocre pattern of growth that prevailed in Egypt.

GDP Growth in the Interwar Period, 1927–39

Turkey experienced rapid growth of its gross domestic product after independence was obtained. Immediately after 1923 much of the growth probably reflected recovery from the disastrous effects of World War I and the War of Independence. The period of interest here is the years of international agricultural crisis and the Great Depression, 1927–39. Both Turkey and Egypt were primarily agricultural economies, with two-thirds to three-quarters of their population living on agriculture. Since agriculture at that time grew much faster in Turkey than in Egypt, it is reasonable to expect GDP growth to have been faster in Turkey than in

Table 17-2. Indexes and Growth Rates of Agricultural Production and Inputs in Egypt, 1927–80

Measure and year	Production[a]	Cultivated area[b]	Labor[c]	Total capital stock[d]	Production per unit			Land-labor ratio[h]	Fertilizer consumption[i]	Tractors[j]
					Cultivated area[e]	Labor[f]	Capital[g]			
Index (1960=100)										
1927	66.9	93.7	80.3	42.6	71.4	83.3	157.0	116.7	16.4	—
1937	79.7	90.4	91.2	70.3	88.2	87.4	113.4	99.1	48.1	—
1947	77.3	97.9	92.8	84.6	78.9	83.4	91.4	105.6	35.3	—
1960	100	100	100	100	100	100	100	100	100	100
1970	129.7	100.7	115.4	147.0[k]	128.8	112.3	88.2	87.2	181.7	159.2
1976	148.6	98.5	110.8	—	150.9	134.3	—	88.9	242.1	—
1980	167.0	(97.0)	(95.3)	—	172.2	175.3	—	101.2	323.5	327.5

Growth rate (percent)										
1927–60	1.2	0.2	0.7	2.6	1.0	0.6	-1.36	-0.5	5.6	—
1960–80	2.6	0.5	-0.2	—	2.8	2.8	—	0.8	6.0	6.1
1927–80	1.7	0.3	0.3	—	1.7	1.4	—	-0.0	5.8	—

a. Three-year moving average of GDP at constant prices from 1960, based on $1,148 million value in 1960 (EL1 = $2.85); earlier years based on Wattleworth (1975) output index.

b. Three-year moving average of cultivated area, 2.6 million hectares in 1960.

c. Economically active labor force, 4.4 million workers in 1960 (women are probably grossly underenumerated).

d. In 1960, $714.6 per hectare.

e. In 1960, $447 per hectare.

f. In 1960, $260 per worker.

g. In 1960, 62.5 percent of capital value.

h. In 1960, 0.58 hectare per worker.

i. In 1960, 80 metric tons per 1,000 hectares.

j. In 1960, 4.3 per 1,000 hectares.

k. 1967.

Source: Wattleworth (1975); Egypt, Ministry of Finance, Annuaire statistique de l'Egypte; Egypt, CAPMAS (1964); Gardner and Parker (1985), table 11; Radwan (1973), table 2–8; FAO, *Production Yearbook,* various years.

Table 17-3. Growth Rate of GDP and Capital Formation for Turkey, 1927–39

Measure and period		Gross domestic product				Gross capital formation[a]
	Total	Agriculture	Industry	Agriculture plus industry	Non-agriculture	
Growth (percent)						
1927–33[b]	7.1	7.6	11.6	8.6	6.9	—
1933–39[c]	6.7	8.0	8.6	8.1	5.9	—
1927–39[d]	6.9	7.8	10.1	8.4	6.4	—
Capital-output ratio						
1927–33	1.6[e]	0[e]	n.a.	n.a.	2.6[e]	—
1933–39	1.5[e]	0[e]	2.0[e]	n.a.	3.0[e]	—
1927–39	1.6[e]	0[e]	n.a.	n.a.	2.8[e]	—
Value (millions of liras[f])						
1927	899.0	329.6	106.5	436.1	569.4	110
1933	1,359.7	511.2	205.3	716.5	848.5	119
1939	2,006.9	809.1	336.8	1,145.9	1,197.8	216
Increase in value (millions of liras[f])						
1927–33	460.7	181.6	98.8	280.4	279.1	732
1933–39	647.2	297.9	131.5	429.4	349.3	1,044[g]
1927–39	1,107.9	479.5	230.3	709.8	628.4	1,776

— = Not applicable.

n.a. = Not available.

a. Based on Bulutay, Tezel, Yıeldırım (1974).

b. Total population grew from 13.6 million to 15.4 million, at a rate of 2.1 percent a year.

c. Total population grew from 15.4 million to 17.4 million, at a rate of 2.0 percent a year.

d. Total population grew from 13.6 million to 17.4 million, at a rate of 2.1 percent a year.

e. Conjecture.

f. At constant 1938 market prices.

g. Alternative data (Hershlag 1967) indicate an increase of current prices of LT900 million, including LT135 million in public enterprises (industry component comprises mining and public utilities).

Source: Turkey, *Statistical Yearbook*; Bulutay, Tezel, and Yıeldırım (1974); Hershlag (1967).

Egypt. Uncertain indicators suggest that, in addition, industry in Turkey may have been growing at two to three times the rate in Egypt. Tables 17–3 and 17–4 (and figure 2–1) suggest that while in Turkey GDP during the years 1927–39 may have been growing at a rate of 7 percent an-

Table 17-4. Agricultural and Industrial Growth Rates for Egypt, 1927-39

Measure and period	Agriculture (three-year moving average)	Industry	Agriculture plus industry	Other sectors	Total
GDP growth (percent)					
1927-33[a]	0.9	5.4	2.1	n.a.	n.a.
1933-39[b]	1.8	2.3	1.9	n.a.	n.a.
1927-39[c]	1.4	3.8	2.0	n.a.	n.a.
GDP value (millions of Egyptian pounds[d])					
1927[e]	45.9	14.6	60.5	n.a.	n.a.
1933[e]	48.5	20.1	68.6	n.a.	n.a.
1939	54.0	23.0	77.0	101.0	178.0
Increase in value (millions of Egyptian pounds[d])					
1927-33	2.6	5.5	8.1	n.a.	n.a.
1933-39	5.5	2.9	8.4	n.a.	n.a.
1927-39	8.1	8.4	16.5	n.a.	n.a.

n.a. = Not available.

a. Total population grew from 14.3 million to 15.3 million, at a rate of 1.1 percent a year.

b. Total population grew from 15.3 million to 16.5 million, at a rate of 1.3 percent a year.

c. Total population grew from 14.3 million to 16.5 million, at a rate of 1.2 percent a year.

d. At constant 1939 prices.

e. Conjectures.

Source: Wattleworth (1975); Radwan (1973); Anis (1950).

nually and the population increasing 2.1 percent annually, in Egypt the GDP growth rate may have been about 2 percent annually with population growth 1.2 percent. There is no great difference between the two subperiods 1927-33 and 1933-39 in either country. From independence to World War II, Turkey was steadily on a high-growth path; Egypt was a stagnating economy.

Inward-looking Growth Strategies after World War II

Considering the politics of the case, I have chosen to compare the period 1951-53 to 1977-79 for Turkey with 1952-53 to 1981-82 for Egypt to consider periods when both were pursuing etatist policies with development strategies dominated by considerations of import substitution. Turkey gave up this strategy after 1980, so it seems natural for that country to use three-year moving averages, to smooth crop fluctuations, and let the period end in 1977–79. The period thus ends with the debt crisis of 1978 and the related stabilization policies; this, however, is as it should be because the point is to look at the ex post outcome of the policy, including its eventual collapse. Egypt has never seriously given up the inward-looking strategy, so the period for Egypt ends in 1981–82, the last year for which final, noncontroversial data are available. For 1981–82 to 1986–87 two conflicting estimates are available (see table 1–1); therefore, two sets of average growth rates for Egypt for 1952–53 to 1986–87 are given in tables 17–5. The difference in the average GDP growth rates for 1952–53 to 1986–87 thus obtained is not dramatic but not insignificant either, 5.6 percent against 5.2 percent. The beginning of the period for both countries is around 1952, which avoids the years of postwar recovery. Both countries experienced some trade liberalization around the Korean War boom, after which both introduced quantitative balance of payments controls which, in effect, amounted to import-substitution policies. Since formal planning was introduced by Egypt in 1959–60 and in Turkey in 1962, the period could have begun around 1960, which, however, would have done little to change the results. Problems in computing indexes from the constant-price estimates of the national accounts are significant. For both countries, but particularly Egypt, there are disturbing data problems. And for Egypt, classification of petroleum by productive sector introduces a serious problem (see appendix A).

Tables 17–5 and 17–6 decompose GDP growth by productive sector and by expenditure category. The two tables are arranged identically. In row 1 they show sectoral (category) shares of GDP, with row 2 showing sectoral (category) own rates of growth. In row 3 I have computed what could be called the marginal contribution to total GDP growth, defined as the increase in each sector as a percentage of the increase of total GDP. This is an informative way of pinpointing sources of growth in an ex post, accounting sense of the term.

Total GDP growth for the period as a whole was about the same in Turkey—5.8 percent annually—and in Egypt—5.4 percent. With population growth slightly higher in Egypt—2.8 percent—than in Turkey— 2.6 percent—GDP growth per capita was about ½ percent higher in Turkey—3.2 percent—than in Egypt—2.6 percent. For the period 1952–53 to 1986–87, per capita growth for Egypt becomes 2.8 percent or 2.4 percent, depending on the GDP estimate chosen. With the latter (probably realistic) choice, for the years of etatism per capita growth in Egypt was only three-quarters that of Turkey.

As would be expected the shares of agriculture declined dramatically in both countries, from 37 percent to 16½ percent in Egypt, from 47½ percent to 23 percent in Turkey. In both countries, agricultural shares thus declined to a little less than half, Turkey throughout the period re-

Table 17-5. Share in and Contribution to Growth of GDP, by Productive Sector, Selected Periods, 1952–82
(percent)

Category		Period	Agriculture	Industry, mining, electricity, etc.	Commerce, finance, other services[a]	Other	Total GDP
Egypt[b]							
Share of GDP		1952–53	37.0	14.3c	34.2	14.5	100
	A	1981–82	16.5	17.7	41.1	24.7	100
	B		16.4	23.6	40.8	19.3	100
Own rate of growth	A	1952–53 to 1981–82	2.5	6.3	6.1	7.2	5.4
	B			7.2		6.6	
Share of GDP growth	A	1952–53 to 1981–82	10.7	18.8	43.0	27.5	100
	B		10.6	26.0	42.6	20.8	100
Turkey[d]							
Share of GDP	B	1951–53	47.4	11.2	22.5	18.9	100
	B	1977–79	23.1	23.6	31.7	21.6	100
Own rate of growth	B	1951–53 to 1977–79	2.9	8.8	7.2	6.3	5.8
Share of GDP growth	B	1951–53 to 1977–79	15.7	27.3	34.6	22.4	100

A = Petroleum, 1974 to 1981–82, included in Other.
B = Petroleum, 1974 to 1981–82, included in Mining
a. Including government.
b. Price estimates at 1954 market prices, 1952–53 to 1960–61; at 1964–65 factor costs, 1960–61 to 1970–71; at 1970 factor costs, 1970–71 to 1974; at 1975 factor costs, 1979 to 1981–82 based on chained Fisher indexes.
c. Excluding petroleum about 13.3.
d. At 1968 factor costs.
Source: Hansen and Marzouk (1965), statistical app.; Ikram (1980), statistical app.; Turkey, Statistical Yearbook, various years; World Bank data.

Table 17-6. Share in and Contribution to (Absorption of) Growth of GDP, by Expenditure Category, Selected Periods, 1951–82

(percent)

Category	Period	Consumption		Fixed investment	Trade			GDP
		Private[a]	Public		Export	Import	Net	
Egypt[b]								
Share of GDP	1952	79.7	16.4	10.2	15.2	-21.6	-6.4	100
	1981–82	67.8	18.7	28.9	18.1	-33.6	-15.5	100
Own rate of growth	1952 to 1981–82	5.0	6.1	9.4	6.2	7.2	—	5.5
Share of GDP growth	1952 to 1981–82	64.8	19.2	33.6	18.9	-36.6	-17.8	100
Turkey[c]								
Share of GDP	1951–53	78.7	10.3	17.1	6.8	-12.8	-6.0	100
	1977–79	68.8	12.1	21.9	4.5	-7.2	-2.7	100
Own rate of growth	1951–53 to 1977–79	5.1	6.4	6.7	4.0	3.4	—	5.7
Share of GDP growth	1951–53 to 1977–79	65.7	12.7	23.4	3.7	-5.5	-1.8	100

— = Not applicable.

a. Includes change of inventories.

b. At constant 1965 market prices 1952–76; at constant 1978 market prices, 1976 to 1981–83; chaining based on Fisher indexes.

c. At constant 1968 market prices, all years.

Source: Same as for table 17–5.

maining somewhat more agriculturally oriented than Egypt. The own-growth rates were about the same.

The share of industry, including mining, electricity, and public utilities, more than doubled in Turkey. For Egypt, when petroleum is included in industry, the share increased from 14.3 percent to 23.6 percent, starting at a somewhat higher level than and ending at the same level as Turkey. Much of that increase for Egypt, however, came from petroleum (extraction and processing), which is an insignificant activity in Turkey. Since it is not possible to separate out manufacturing industry proper before 1974 for Egypt, table 17–5 shows two sets of figures for industry for Egypt, one excluding and the other including petroleum for 1974 to 1981–82. Since petroleum is included for Turkey for the whole period, comparability is not perfect (before 1974, petroleum does not seriously distort the picture). The progress of industrialization in Egypt was slow, moving from 13.3 percent to 17.7 percent of GDP as compared with Turkey's increase from 11.2 percent to 23.6 percent. On the same basis the own-growth rate of industry in Turkey was 8.8 percent against 6.8 percent in Egypt. This difference in industrialization is probably the major difference in the growth pictures of production in the two countries in the postwar period. This conclusion would remain valid even if industry in Egypt were defined properly as manufacturing only and the period for Egypt extended to 1986–87; the share for Egypt might then have increased from 14 to 19 (see appendix A).

Commerce, finance, and other services (including government) had by the beginning of the 1980s become the largest aggregative sector in both countries. Intangible services dominated in both countries, though much more so in Egypt than in Turkey. The sector's share increased from 34 percent to 41 percent in Egypt between 1952–53 and 1981–82 as compared with an increase from 22½ percent to 31½ percent in Turkey between 1951–53 and 1977–79. The own rate of growth of this sector, on the other hand, was slightly higher in Turkey, 7 percent, than the 6 percent rate in Egypt. It was not possible to separate out the government sector for Egypt, where the official national accounts lump together government with other services and reclassifications of other service sectors make it well nigh impossible to analyze these sectors. This is unfortunate because there are good reasons to believe that in both countries, but particularly in Egypt, the government sector includes considerable disguised unemployment.

The other sectors category includes construction, transportation, and housing. When petroleum is not included, the sector is relatively small for Egypt and the own-growth rates are about the same for both countries.

The share of GDP growth—the marginal contribution to growth—in table 17–5 shows much larger contributions from agriculture and industry for Turkey than for Egypt—in agriculture, 15½ percent of total growth against 10½ percent; in industry, 27½ percent against 19½ percent (excluding petroleum). Together, agriculture and industry contributed 43 percent of growth in Turkey against 30 percent in Egypt when petroleum is excluded and 36½ percent including petroleum. In Turkey growth was generated to a larger extent—and to a much larger extent when petroleum is disregarded—by sectors producing tradable goods and services than was the case in Egypt (even allowing for some contributions from the Suez Canal and tourism). Now, there is nothing wrong with petroleum in itself; it may be easy to produce, it is easy to trade, and it is a foreign exchange earner as good as any other tradable. Likewise, there is nothing wrong with nontradables in themselves if domestic demand marginally prefers nontradables to imports. The problems are only that price risks appear exceptionally large in the oil market, that oil extraction may not be a long-term option, and that nontradables actually produced may have little if any utility socially or privately.

Table 17–6, like table 17–5, is set up to facilitate the analysis of contributions to growth by expenditure categories, so-called absorption. Both data and index problems are even worse than in table 17–5 since the constant-price estimates in table 17–6 differ significantly from the current price estimates in table 15–1. Private consumption appears to have behaved very similarly in the two countries. The shares were 79–80 percent of GDP in 1952 and declined to 68–69 percent at the end of the period, with a slightly stronger decline in Egypt. The own rates of growth were almost the same, 5 percent. For the other categories, differences between the two countries are substantial. The shares of public consumption increased slightly in both countries but were about 50 percent higher in Egypt than Turkey both at the end and at the beginning of the period. Measured by consumption, the public sector in Egypt is relatively large as compared with Turkey and this apparently is not a new phenomenon. At current prices, the difference was much smaller in 1952 (table 15–1). The own rates of growth were approximately the same about 6 percent. The difference in the behavior of fixed investment is striking. At the beginning of the period the share in Egypt was much lower than in Turkey—10 percent against 17 percent. At the end it was much higher—29 percent against 22 percent, the own rate of growth being 9½ percent in Egypt against 6½ percent in Turkey.

The sum of all consumption and fixed investment—total domestic absorption—in Egypt increased from 106½ percent to 115½ percent of GDP, signifying a strong increase in the trade deficit from 6½ percent to 15½ percent. For Turkey, total domestic absorption declined from 106 percent to 102½ percent of GDP with a decline in the trade deficit from 6 percent to 2½ percent. Recall that the end point of the period in Turkey coincides with the debt crisis of 1978 and the accompanying stabilization program, including a savage administrative cutback of imports; in

Egypt rectifying policies were insufficient, unsystematic, and partial and rendered ineffective through continued inflationary financing of a huge budget deficit.

Part of the picture is the openness of the Egyptian economy compared to that of Turkey. The share of exports increased in Egypt from 15 percent to 18 percent of GDP but declined in Turkey from the already low level of 7 percent to only 4½ percent. Imports in Egypt increased at the same time from 21½ percent to 33½ percent but in Turkey declined from 13 percent to 7 percent. Own rates of growth of trade in Egypt were higher for both exports and imports, and imports grew faster than exports, 7 percent against 6 percent; in Turkey, exports grew faster than imports, by 4 percent against 3½ percent. This result, however, is again heavily dependent on the fact that for Turkey the end of the period examined coincides with the foreign exchange crisis and the following stabilization program.

In both Egypt and Turkey about two-thirds of GDP growth was geared to private consumption while contributions from both public consumption and fixed investment were about 50 percent higher in Egypt than in Turkey. Total marginal domestic absorption in this way amounted to 118 percent of GDP in Egypt against only 102 percent in Turkey, with marginal trade deficits of 18 percent and 2 percent, respectively. The much more open nature of the Egyptian economy also shows up marginally. While the marginal contribution to GDP growth from exports in Egypt was 19 percent against a drag (negative contribution) from imports of no less than 36½ percent, the corresponding figures for Turkey were 3½ percent and 5½ percent. Once more the choice of period for Turkey tends to exaggerate the result.

The description of growth contributions in tables 17–5 and 17–6 is based on data for the beginning and end of the periods considered and thus says nothing about the paths of growth followed during the periods. For some problems of growth, such as the accumulation of stocks, the paths of the flows are actually more important than the end points. Consider the contribution from investment—for Egypt, 33 percent of total GDP growth against 23 percent in Turkey. The own-growth rate of total GDP was at the same time a bit lower in Egypt than in Turkey. It does not follow, of course, that the ratio of capital to output was higher in Egypt or that Egyptian investment activities were less efficient in creating growth. If the increase in the share of investment from 10 percent to 29 percent actually took place at the end of the period, as much of it did, the capital-output ratio for Egypt may not have been particularly high. Net trade in relation to the stock of foreign debt presents a similar problem. Averages of shares for the period as a whole may be more informative than the differences between end-point shares.

Table 17–7 shows averages of shares of national income by expenditure categories at constant prices for periods similar to those in tables

Table 17-7. Shares of National Income, Selected Periods, 1930–84
(percent)

Category	Turkey 1930–39[a]	Turkey 1954–77[b]	Turkey 1978–84[b]	Egypt 1950 to 1981–82[c]
Consumption				
Private	76.4	72.3	80.0	68.8
Public	13.1	11.6	13.4	18.8
Total	89.5	83.9	83.4	87.6
Investment				
Fixed, gross	9.9	17.4	19.4	17.0
Inventories	n.a.	1.3	0.6	0.8
Total, gross	n.a.	18.7	20.0	17.7
Exports	8.3	4.8	7.3	16.3
Imports	7.0	7.8	6.8	23.9
Terms of trade effect[d]	–0.5	–0.3	–5.1	1.5
Net resource gap[d]	–0.5	2.6	2.0	5.8
National gross saving	10.5	16.1	16.6	12.4
Gross external liabilities	n.a.	n.a.	39.7[e]	70.2[e]

n.a. = Not available.
a. At constant 1938 prices.
b. At constant 1968 prices.
c. At constant 1965 prices for 1950–78; at constant 1978 prices for 1976 to 1981–82.
d. At constant import prices linked in 1976.
e. For 1984.
Source: Author's estimates; World Bank, *World Development Report,* 1986, tables 1, 15; World Bank data.

17–5 and 17–6 (the estimates are not comparable and the quality of the data in table 17–7 is less reliable than in tables 17–5 and 17–6). The data for Egypt in 1950 to 1981–82 and for Turkey in 1954–77, periods dominated by import-substitution strategies and etatism, show average investment shares of about 17 percent and GDP growth rates of about 6 percent in both countries. This obviously points to similar capital-output ratios in the two countries. Total consumption was somewhat higher in Egypt than in Turkey, 88 percent against 84 percent, with private consumption lower in Egypt than in Turkey, 69 percent against 72½ percent and public consumption much higher in Egypt, 19 percent against 11½ percent. Egypt gained slightly while Turkey lost on terms of trade over the whole period, with the losses concentrated after 1973. As a consequence, national saving ran at a considerably lower level in Egypt, 12½ percent against 16 percent in Turkey. The 3½ percent difference shows up on the balance of payments side with a deficit, imports minus exports, of 7½ percent in Egypt against 3 percent in Turkey, and in the net resource gap in terms of imports running at 6 percent in Egypt against 2½ percent in Turkey. There is an enormous difference between levels of trade under import substitution policies in the two countries, exports running at 16½ percent in Egypt and only 5 percent in Turkey, imports at 24 percent in Egypt and 8 percent in Turkey. The comparative size of trade was, however, radically changed with the shift of development strategy in Turkey, with exports increasing to 19 percent of GDP in 1984.

Under the import-substitution strategy, Turkey clearly did much better than Egypt in financing accumulation of real capital, something that is also reflected in the development of the national debt. At current prices and estimated in U.S. dollars (the snags here are legion), external liabilities had in 1984 reached a level of 70 percent of GNP in Egypt against only 40 percent in Turkey. If old military debts to the Soviet Union are added to Egypt's external debt, measured as a percentage of GNP, its debt may in 1984 have been about double that of Turkey. Total debt service in 1984 amounted to 32 percent of exports of goods and services in Egypt against 23 percent in Turkey, partly a consequence of the extraordinary expansion of exports from Turkey after the change of development strategy.

Aid has played an important role for both countries. The preponderance of concessionary loans and partly secret military aid makes quantification and comparison well-nigh impossible. Official assistance, with a substantial share in grants, has apparently covered most of the current account deficit in both countries.

Egypt and Turkey under Different Strategies, 1980–87

In 1980 Turkey shifted radically toward an export-led strategy while Egypt continued her policy of import substitution. Through a series of reforms Turkey steered away from while Egypt remained faithful to the policy of etatism that had originated in Atatürk's Turkey. Export promotion has in some spectacular cases (Japan, the Republic of Korea, and Taiwan) been accompanied by protection of the domestic market. Turkey's export-led growth was possibly a cleaner shift inasmuch as protection through tariffs and import restrictions was reduced, though somewhat unevenly, and the burden was carried by exchange rate policy.

Table 17-8. GDP Growth Rates, 1977–87

(percent)

| | Egypt | | |
Period	Ministry of Planning estimates	World Bank estimates	Turkey[a]
1977–81	8.6	8.5	1.7
1982–83	9.9	6.1	4.5
1983–84	8.0	5.2	4.0
1984–85	7.4	6.9	6.1
1985–86	4.8	1.9	4.2
1986–87	4.2	0.7	7.2
1987–88	n.a.	n.a.	6.5[b]

n.a. = Not available.
a. Calendar year.
b. Provisional.
Source: OECD, *Economic Surveys, Turkey,* 1987, table 1; Egypt, Ministry of Planning and International Cooperation (1987), table 2; World Bank (1988).

Export subsidies were increased, however. The shift in strategy was preceded by a stabilization program initiated in 1978. Nothing like that happened in Egypt which after the 1979 increase in oil prices felt safe.

As appears from table 17–8, the growth rate in Turkey suffered badly under the 1977–81 stabilization program while in Egypt growth continued at a high level. Turkey's growth rate then began to increase in 1982 and by 1986 and 1987 was finally back to the level of about 7 percent obtained in the mid-1970s. For Egypt the growth rate declined considerably, to 4 percent in 1986–87 by Ministry of Planning estimates, and by World Bank estimates dramatically, to less than 1 percent. According to the official estimates the decline was mainly caused by stagnation of value added in petroleum, Suez Canal and trade, the latter probably because of a decline in imports, all of it closely related to the deteriorating foreign exchange situation.

External factors were important in these developments; with the oil prices, terms of trade as usual moved in opposite directions and workers' remittances from the Gulf states followed the oil prices. The Gulf war, however, benefited Turkey more than Egypt. Bumper crops gave Turkey a strong boost in 1986. Domestic policies have been far from perfect in either country. It is difficult therefore to judge long-term trends. It stands to reason, however, that Turkey is benefiting slowly from its strategy change while Egypt remains locked in its cul-de-sac with increasing foreign exchange shortages and growth grinding to a halt.

Standard of Life Indicators

The indicators conventionally used to describe standards of life are presented in table 17–9. Most of the indicators cannot be carried back to the interwar years. Some of them may be of doubtful value as indicators of welfare (caloric intake above a certain level, urbanization in the form of shantytowns). Ambiguous though they are, the indicators support the impression given by GNP per capita that welfare generally has improved considerably in both countries and that the level of welfare in Turkey is superior to that in Egypt.

Summary of Growth Comparisons

- Population growth has accelerated in both countries, much more so in Egypt than in Turkey. During the interwar years, population increased in Turkey at a rate of 2.1 percent against 1.2 percent in Egypt. After 1950 the population growth rate in Egypt was 2.8 percent against 2.6 percent in Turkey. The population growth differential thus changed by about 1 percent in favor of Turkey.
- Total GDP during the interwar years grew at a rate of about 7 percent in Turkey against perhaps 2 percent in Egypt. During the postwar years of inward-looking, import-substitution strategy both countries experienced GDP growth on the order of 5½ percent, Turkey growing slightly faster than Egypt.

Table 17–9. Standard of Life Indicators, 1960 and 1985

Indicator	Egypt 1960	Egypt 1985	Turkey 1960	Turkey 1985
GNP per capita (in 1985 dollars)	275	610	570	1,080
Daily caloric supply (number per capita)	2,435	3,203	2,636	3,167
Life expectancy (years at birth)	46	61	51	64
Crude death rate (per thousand of population)	19	10	16	8
Infant mortality rate (per thousand live births)	109	93	194	84
Crude birth rate (per thousand of population)	44	36	43	30
Urbanization (percent of population)	38	46	30	46
Physicians (persons per physician)	2,560	760	3,000	1,530

Source: World Bank, *World Development Report.*

• Terms of trade have fluctuated strongly but have tended to favor Egypt, to penalize Turkey. For both countries the long-term effects have been small.

• In terms of per capita growth Turkey during the interwar years was a fast-growth country, with about 5 percent growth, while Egypt was almost stagnant. During the inward-looking, postwar years both countries grew at moderate rates, Turkey about 3¼ percent, Egypt about 2½ percent annually.

• Agriculture for the period since independence as a whole has grown in Turkey at a rate more than double that in Egypt, 3½ percent against 1½ percent annually, largely because Turkey before 1960 was still a frontier country with rapidly expanding cultivated area while in Egypt the frontier had been reached around 1900. Since 1960 agricultural growth has been only slightly higher in Turkey than in Egypt, 3 percent against 2½ percent annually.

• Industrial growth appears for the whole period since independence to have been considerably higher in Turkey than in Egypt. During the interwar period, industry in Turkey grew at a rate of 8 percent against perhaps 4 percent in Egypt. For the postwar years of inward-looking strategy the corresponding figures were 9 percent and 6½ percent, respectively.

• Industrialization as measured by the share of industry in GDP nonetheless did not advance in Turkey during the interwar years, mainly as a consequence of very rapid growth in agriculture. In this sense there may have been some industrialization in Egypt during the interwar years when agricultural growth was very feeble. For the postwar years of inward-looking strategy, Turkey industrialized rapidly while in Egypt industrialization, disregarding petroleum, made little progress.

• Agriculture and industry during the postwar years of inward-looking strategy contributed much more to growth of GDP in Turkey than in Egypt, 43.0 percent against 29.5 percent. Intangible services from commerce, finance, and other services, including government, contributed 43.0 percent of total GDP growth in Egypt against 35.0 percent in Turkey. The larger contribution in Egypt was not a result of faster own rate of growth, 6.1 percent against 7.2 percent in Turkey, but rather the larger initial share of GDP in Egypt, 34.0 percent against 22.5 percent in Turkey.

• The shortcoming of agricultural and industrial growth in Egypt has partly been compensated for by temporary growth in the petroleum sector. Substantial terms of trade gains in Egypt as compared with terms of trade losses in Turkey helped to compensate for low agricultural and industrial growth in Egypt.

• From the expenditure side, the contribution (absorption) from personal consumption has been very similar in the two countries.

• Public consumption and fixed investment contributed much more to expenditure growth in Egypt than in Turkey, 53 percent against 36 percent of total expenditure (GDP) growth. For public consumption this was the result of the high initial share in Egypt; own rates of growth were much the same. For fixed investment it was the result of a much higher own rate of growth in Egypt, 9½ percent against 6½ percent in Turkey, despite a much smaller initial share in Egypt.

• Marginally, domestic absorption measured on total GDP growth was about 118 percent in Egypt and 102 percent in Turkey for the period of inward-looking strategy, accompanied by an 18 percent trade deficit in Egypt against 2 percent in Turkey. The difference is partly the result of the stabilization program introduced in Turkey in 1978.

• In the period of import substitution after World War II, Egypt financed a much smaller share of her real capital accumulation through national saving than Turkey. Official assistance seems in both countries to have covered about half the current account deficit. As a consequence, the foreign debt and the foreign debt burden were in 1984 relatively much heavier in Egypt than Turkey; including military debts to the Soviet Union, the national debt may have amounted to about 80 percent of GNP in Egypt and 40 percent in Turkey, and debt service to 32 percent of exports in Egypt and 23 percent in Turkey.

• The ratios of capital to output appear to have been about the same for the two countries during the years of import-substitution strategy after World War II.

• In 1980 Turkey shifted from an inward-looking to an outward-looking development strategy. Egypt has no similar experience, having continued the import-substitution strategy. After seven years of, first, negative and then low growth rates from 1978 to 1985, Turkey reached growth rates of the same order as during the years of import substitution at a share of trade that compares well with that of Egypt.

Distribution and Equity

Information about distribution and equity is spotty for both Egypt and Turkey. Information on material wealth is limited to land distribution. For the interwar period, when both economies were largely agricultural, distribution of land would go a long way toward explaining income distribution. For the interwar period little solid information is available about income distribution, and only Egypt has statistics on land distribution. Comparisons of distribution must for that reason be largely limited to the period after World War II. The only indicator of income distribution stretching back into the interwar period is the so-called Kuznets *K*.

Table 17-10. Kuznets K Income Distribution Indicator, 1927-80

Year	Egypt	Turkey
1927	n.a.	5.42
1935	2.37[a]	7.08
1950	2.59	5.82
1960	3.07	4.43
1970	3.00	4.45
1980	2.60	4.40

n.a. = Not available.
a. For 1937.
Source: Author's calculations.

The Kuznets K

The Kuznets K is an emergency device adopted to indicate the distribution of income in Turkey (Kemal Derviş and Sherman Robinson, in Özbudun and Ulusan 1980; Pamuk 1985). It is defined as the ratio between GDP at current prices per unit of labor force in nonagricultural and agricultural activities. Because labor productivity is typically much lower in agriculture than in other activities, K is usually found to be well above 2. A decline in K and a decline in the share of agriculture should for that reason, everything else being equal, indicate a tendency for the distribution of national income by size to become more equitable. Needless to say, the Kuznets K is a very poor indicator of size distribution. The estimates of K in table 17-10 for years before 1950 are unreliable, particularly for Turkey where labor force developments are little more than conjectures. The Ks for Egypt are probably biased downward because of underenumeration of unpaid females in agriculture.

Even considering the downward bias, Egypt's Ks are relatively low, pointing to a relatively equitable distribution of income, with a tendency to declining equity from 1937 to 1960–70 and then increasing equity to 1980. This could be an example of Kuznet's U curve. The continuous decline in the share of agriculture should in addition tend to increase equity over the whole period. Whether this effect would dominate the tendency for K to increase from 1937 to 1960 is impossible to say.

For Turkey, K was consistently much higher than for Egypt, whose K remained at 2½ to 3. For Turkey it remained almost constant at a level of 4½ from 1960, with even higher values for earlier years. Internationally these are high values. The increase from 1927 to 1935 followed by decline through 1950 to 1960 might be seen as yet another example of the U curve. It could also be related to terms of trade developments. If so, it is difficult to see why Egypt should have a very low K in 1937, increasing to 1960.

Corresponding to the relatively high K for Turkey one might expect that the ratio between average household incomes in urban and rural areas would be higher for Turkey than for Egypt. For 1973 this ratio for Turkey was 1.5 (M. N. Danielson and Ruşen Keleş in Özbudun and Ulusan 1980, table 9–10, p. 279). For Egypt in 1974–75 the ratio, measured on expenditure, was also 1.5 (Ikram 1980, p. 83). Real diferences may, however, be larger. A lower rate of saving in Egypt, related to the lower level of income, and the higher proportion of nonagricultural income in rural Egypt might help explain this result. The Turkish data, however, may not be very reliable. The ratio between weighted, average household income in the three large cities (defined as the metropolitan region) of Turkey and in the predominantly rural regions in table 6–7 is 3.0 for 1968 against 1.6 for 1973. This difference between 1968 and 1973 is not credible. The expenditure and income surveys do not positively contradict the national account data (that the Ks are based on) but the support is weak at best.

Raising perhaps more questions than it answers, the Kuznets K thus indicates a more equitable distribution of income in Egypt than in Turkey, with a strong tendency for the latter country toward increased equity from interwar to postwar years. The behavior of K over time suggests the possible existence in both countries of Kuznets's U curve, naturally appearing earlier in Turkey than in Egypt, considering the relatively high per capita income and growth rate in Turkey during the interwar years.

Income and Expenditure Surveys

The data on Egypt in table 17–11 are based on relatively reliable national expenditure surveys, those on Turkey or relatively unreliable national income surveys. The surveys were taken in the two countries' years of inward-looking strategy.

To judge from the national Gini coefficients, there appears to have been a slight tendency in both countries for equity to increase. This would further support the U-curve hypothesis. No such tendency is apparent, however, in the Gini coefficients for rural and urban areas of Egypt or for agricultural and nonagricultural sectors of Turkey. Distribution thus does not show any clear tendency to change in either country in the years covered by table 17–11. Stability of income distribution is a phenomenon well known from highly developed countries. Egypt and Turkey seem to be no different.

Income distribution appears to have been more equitable in Egypt than in Turkey. This remains true even if the exclusion of saving from the expenditure survey is assumed to create a downward bias in the Egyptian Gini coefficients of perhaps 10 percent—that is, 0.03–0.04 points (Korayem 1982). The Gini coefficients thus (vaguely) tell the same story as the Kuznets Ks.

Table 17-11. Gini Coefficient Indicators of Expenditure and Income Distribution, Selected Years, 1958-82

Year	Egypt, expenditure			Turkey, income		
	Rural	Urban	National	Agricultural	Nonagricultural	National
1958-59	0.34	0.37	0.42	—	—	—
1963	—	—	—	0.43	0.59	0.56
1964-65	0.29	0.35	0.40	—	—	—
1968	—	—	—	0.59	n.a.	n.a.
1973	—	—	—	0.56	0.46	0.51
1974-75	0.36	0.37	0.38	—	—	—
1978-79	—	—	—	n.a.	0.40[a]	n.a.
1982	0.34	0.37	n.a.	—	—	—

— = Not applicable.
n.a. = Not available.
a. Urban income.
Source: Tables 1-8, 6-14.

In Egypt rural distribution appears to be slightly more equitable than urban distribution. The difference is small for most years and does not seem to have changed much from the end of the 1950s to the early 1980s. For Turkey the corresponding results appear contradictory. For 1963 agricultural distribution appears to be much more equitable than nonagricultural distribution. For 1973 (and perhaps 1968) the situation appears to have been just the opposite. It seems unlikely that distributional patterns should change so radically during a decade; the results probably bear witness to the poor quality of the Turkish surveys more than anything else. Thus it is important to attempt to infer the distribution of rural or agricultural income from distribution of land, for which data are available for both Egypt and Turkey.

A caveat is in order, however. The most that can be inferred from expenditure surveys is the distribution of disposable income—income after taxes minus subsidies. Income surveys for Turkey do report disposable income, so there is no problem of comparability with Egypt. Clearly, however, the information in table 17–11 tells nothing about the distribution of income before taxes and subsidies—about the impact of government transfers on income distribution. Such information is available for Egypt (see tables 4–34 and 4–35) but not, to my knowledge, for Turkey. There are serious methodological problems involved in such studies and the differences between the tax and social security systems in the two countries, both depending heavily on indirect taxation, are not so striking that the impact on distribution should be expected to be strikingly different. Food and energy subsidies, however, reached such proportions in Egypt during the 1970s and 1980s that, while they are

Table 17-12. Gini Coefficients for the Distribution of Land, Income, and Expenditure in Rural Areas or Agriculture, Selected Years, 1950-82

	Egypt				Turkey		
	Land		Rural households		Land		Agricultural income
Year	Holdings	Ownerships	Expenditure	Income	Holdings	Ownerships	
1950	0.68	··	··	··	··	··	··
1952	··	0.74	··	··	0.53	··	0.53
1956	0.70	··	··	··	··	··	··
1957	··	0.72	··	··	··	··	··
1958-59	··	··	0.34	··	··	··	··
1961	0.61	··	··	··	··	··	··
1963	··	··	··	··	0.59	0.53	0.43
1964-65	··	··	0.29	··	··	··	··
1965	0.53	··	··	··	··	··	··
1968	··	··	··	··	··	··	0.59
1970	··	··	··	··	0.60	··	··
1973	··	··	··	··	··	··	0.57[a]
1974-75	0.46	··	0.35	··	0.42[b]	0.54[b]	··
1977	0.47[c]	0.53[d]	··	0.39	··	··	··
1977-78	0.48	··	··	··	··	··	··
1980	··	··	··	··	0.58	0.57	··
1982	··	··	0.34	··	··	··	··

·· = Not available.
a. A simple average of five regions outside the three big cities was 0.51.
b. Selected provinces, Central Anatolia, mid-1970s (apparently not on family basis).
c. By rural families operating farms.
d. By rural families operating farms; other data indicate a coefficient of 0.66.
Source: Hansen and Marzouk (1965); Hansen and Radwan (1982); Radwan and Lee (1986); Adams (1985); Charles K. Mann in Özbudun and Ulusan (1980); Hirsch (1970); Aydin Ulusan in Özbudun and Ulusan (1980); author's computations.

not unknown in Turkey, they might be viewed as an economic policy with a significantly different impact on the distribution of real income in the two countries. I am inclined to believe that taking food and energy subsidies fully and adequately into account, the distribution of real disposable income in Egypt would appear even more equitable than that in Turkey during the 1970s, with probably a tendency to reversal in the 1980s.

Land and Income Distribution

Table 17-12 presents information on the distribution of land and income that is clearly far from perfect. The Gini coefficients for rural household expenditure for Egypt may be biased downward in relation to those for household income by about 10 percent. In a survey of rural income by the ILO for Egypt in 1977 (Radwan and Lee, 1986) the Gini coefficient was 0.39; the coefficient for rural expenditure in 1974–75 in table 17–12 is 0.35.

More troublesome is the distinction between rural and agricultural income. In Egypt the population census of 1976 classified 9.2 percent of the urban labor force as agricultural and 28.1 percent of the rural labor force as nonagricultural by main occupation (Hansen 1985). In Turkey in 1973 the urban agricultural population was 9.5 percent, and the rural nonagricultural population 12 percent (Kemal Derviş and Sherman Robinson, in Özbudun and Ulusan 1980, table 4–8). Even allowing for considerable definitional differences between the two countries, it seems clear that nonagricultural activities were much more important in rural Egypt than in rural Turkey, which might help in explaining a possible difference between the Gini coefficients for rural income in Egypt and agricultural income in Turkey. The ILO survey for 1977 for Egypt (Radwan and Lee 1986) provides a breakdown of rural income by source and although it is not capable of fully separating agricultural from other income accruing to rural households, it helps to answer the question whether the substantial incomes earned in rural areas from sources other than agriculture serve to lower the income Gini coefficient for rural Egypt as compared with agricultural Turkey. This does not seem to be the case. For incomes from wages from other farms, from family farms, and rents from land, equipment, and livestock, the Gini was 0.38 as compared with 0.39 for all income. That income from wages outside the village and from nonagricultural assets tends to increase average rural income and thus reduce inequality is another matter. A higher share of nonagricultural income should thus not be taken as the cause of a lower Gini coefficient in rural Egypt.

After increasing the Gini coefficients for expenditure in rural Egypt by 0.03–0.04 units, it should be safe to compare them with the Gini coefficients for agricultural income in Turkey. Even the 1963 survey would thus indicate a less equitable income distribution in rural Turkey. The problem remains whether rural distribution in Turkey is more or less equitable than urban distribution—that is, the 1963 versus the 1973 surveys. Here the distribution of land may help. The more unequal the distribution of land, the more unequal, presumably, the distribution of rural income would be. It would be natural, therefore, to seek the explanation for a higher, possibly much higher, rural (agricultural) income Gini coefficient for Turkey in a more unequal distribution of land. First it is necessary to distinguish between distribution of land by holdings and by ownerships and to decide for each country which is relevant for income distribution. A holding is a farm, a cultivation unit. The land cultivated by a farm may be owned by the cultivator, rented, or shared in some form of partnership. It may be consolidated in a single piece of

Table 17-13. Shares of Land by Quintiles of Holdings and Ownerships, Selected Years, 1950-80

	Egypt		Turkey	
Holdings	*1950*	*1977–78*	*1963*	*1980*
Share (percent)				
Lowest quintile	2	6	2	2
Middle quintiles	25	41	38	38
Highest quintile	73	53	60	60
Mean size (hectares)	2.6	0.8	5.2	5.8
Ownerships				
Share (percent)				
Lowest quintile	4[a]	5[b]	5	3
Middle quintiles	18[a]	25[b]	38	37
Highest quintile	78[a]	70[b]	57	60
Mean size (hectares)	0.9[a]	0.7[b]	5.4	5.4

a. For 1952.
b. For 1977.
Source: Author's computations.

land or fragmented in a number of locations. An ownership is an aggregate consisting of all land, no matter what its location or disposal, that is formally or informally the property of a particular owner. The owner may be an individual, a company (partnership), a nonprofit organization, or a public authority (the local community or the state). Each aggregate of land, thus defined, is counted as one ownership and the size of the ownership is the total area of the aggregate. The land in a particular ownership may be cultivated by one or several holdings (or, possibly, not cultivated at all). For Egypt the distinction between holding and ownership is crucial; for Turkey matters are uncertain. The difference between the two countries is related to the prevalence of land lease and sharing, widespread in Egypt but apparently not in Turkey. There are many data problems for both Turkey and Egypt.

From table 17–12 it appears that distribution by holdings around 1980 was more equal in Egypt than in Turkey. This may not have been the case earlier. For distribution by ownership, Turkey appears always to have been more egalitarian than Egypt. Land reform in Egypt did not change this distinctive difference between the two countries, raising the problem of which criterion to base the need for and effects of land reform on.

The distribution of land by quintiles of holders and owners in table 17–13 shows little difference for holdings and ownership in Turkey and little change from 1963 to 1980, the mean size of holdings increasing slightly. For Egypt the change for ownerships is remarkably modest, considering the extent of land reform. The share of the lowest quintile continued to be small and increased only marginally. The highest quintile suffered a moderate decline by about 10 percent of its share which continued to be very high, about 70 percent. The main gain was for medium-sized ownerships where the share increased by almost 40 percent. Notice that the average size of all ownerships declined little, from 0.9 hectares to 0.7 hectares. Egyptian land reform did not interfere deeply in ownership, being mainly an affair between the junta and the royal family.

The big—even revolutionary—change is in holdings in Egypt. The average holding size—2.6 hectares (6.2 feddan) in 1950—diminished to less than one-third—0.8 hectares (1.9 feddan)—in 1977. The number of holders (cultivators) increased from 1.0 million in 1950 to 3.0 million in 1977 at an approximately unchanged economically active population of about 4 million in agriculture. It is very difficult, both conceptually and numerically, to estimate the prevalence of landless labor in Egypt, but if the economically active, noncultivator population is accepted as a proxy for landless labor, the dramatic decline from 3 million to 1 million is a drop from 75 percent to 25 percent of the economically active population. The number of very small holdings, under 1 feddan, increased strongly from 0.21 million to 1.46 million. In this sense the land reform in Egypt went deep—if in fact this change can be ascribed to land reform. Moreover, the distribution of land by holdings around the dramatically lower mean became markedly more equal. The share of the highest quintile fell from about three-quarters to about one-half. The lowest quintile increased its share to three times the share in 1950 but the 1977 share of 6 percent is still very low. The big gains were made by the medium-sized holdings in the second to fourth quintiles. Whether this development will continue remains to be seen. The distribution actually became slightly more unequal from 1974–75 to 1977–78.

The smaller number of landless in Turkey, with the low incidence of lease and sharing, and the relatively equal distribution of land by ownership as well as holding are circumstances that help to explain why land reform never got off the ground in Turkey; by contrast, precisely the opposite conditions prevailed in Egypt where land reform with profound institutional change in agriculture did occur throughout the 1950s and 1960s. The differences between the distribution of land in Turkey and Egypt with the possibility that it was equalization of land distribution by holdings rather than by ownership that alleviated the land problem in Egypt reflect upon the apparent differences in income distribution and give rise to intriguing problems.

First, looking for a more unequal distribution of land in Turkey to explain the more unequal distribution of agricultural income, it must be distribution by holdings rather than by ownership that is decisive for income distribution. For it is the former that is relatively unequal in Turkey.

Second, the income Gini coefficients for rural Egypt remained quite stable from 1958–59 to 1982 despite land reform and increased equality of land distribution. Since it is distribution by holding much more than by ownership that has become more equal in Egypt, the suggestion is that it is distribution of land by ownership that matters for income distribution.

Standard theory tends to argue that it is distribution by ownership rather than by holdings that affects income distribution. In a perfectly competitive setting, with land and labor the only factors of production, with constant returns to scale, and all units of labor as well as land identical, no risk problems, no special reward for management, and equal access for everybody to input and output markets, it is easily understood that the size distribution of agricultural income must be determined exclusively by the distribution of land by ownership. No matter who cultivates the land, land rent will accrue to the landowner. Inequalities in income distribution can only arise from the distribution of land. There may be a long way from this competitive model for agriculture to the realities of rural areas in developing countries. The consensus seems nonetheless to be that it is distribution of land by ownership rather than by holdings that matters for rural income distribution.

With this model, land distribution does not help in explaining the relatively inequitable income distribution in rural (agricultural) Turkey. The measured national Gini coefficients for ownership distribution were higher for Egypt than for Turkey, the Egyptian individually based Gini coefficients, however, being biased in relation to the Turkish family-based Gini coefficients. Gini coefficients for rural ownership in Egypt may be more relevant for explaining differences in income distribution but there is only one such observation (from 1977); the comparability with the Turkish observation is not entirely clear, but the Egyptian Gini coefficient is clearly lower than the Turkish ones.

A basic question is, however, to what extent does the competitive model correctly describe the realities of Turkey and Egypt? Whatever may be said in favor of its applicability to Turkey, the model cannot be applied to Egypt without considering the restrictions on land lease and rents imposed by the land reform legislation of 1952 and later (discussed in chapter 4). These restrictions violate the competitive model and make distribution of land by holdings increasingly relevant for income distribution. The rent controls for agricultural land should tend to make increased equality in the distribution of holdings show up as increased equality of rural income distribution.

Regional Income Distribution

In the context of the Kuznets K it was found that the difference between urban and rural income for Egypt and Turkey might not be significant. This does not, however, exclude significant differences within urban and rural areas. For Egypt reliable regional studies do not seem to be available but Turkish data, presented in table 6–7, point to substantial differences in average income (per family) as well as Gini coefficients between regions, both most probably exceeding those in Egypt. The more trustworthy of the Turkish surveys, that of 1973, shows the average income of Ankara at a level of only 76 percent of Istanbul, and the Eastern region of Turkey 62 percent that of the Northern region, to compare the extremes. The latter, incidentally, also happens to be an ethnic comparison as the Kurdish population is concentrated in the Eastern region. In terms of Gini coefficients, however, regional differences appear relatively small, the poorest region, Eastern Turkey, having a Gini coefficient of 0.50 against 0.47 for the Western and 0.56 for the Southern region; for the cities, differences are larger, from 0.44 for Ankara against 0.52 for İzmir. Still, however, it stands to reason that relatively high regional inequality may be part of the explanation of high inequality for Turkey compared with Egypt. Public services are probably also more unequally distributed regionally in Turkey than in Egypt.

Functional Income Distribution

Comparison of the functional distribution of income has to be limited to nonagricultural GDP because for Turkey no breakdown of agricultural GDP by labor and other income is available. This may be a blessing because estimates of the share of labor in agriculture raise particularly difficult problems in imputing wages to owner and family labor. This is a smaller problem for nonagricultural income where it is the income of the self-employed that creates great difficulties. Table 17–14 presents functional distribution for nonagricultural income from the early 1960s to 1981–82 in Egypt and 1982–85 in Turkey.

For Egypt the share of labor in nonagricultural sectors edged slowly upward from the 1960–61 to 1964–65 period to the 1970–71 to 1974 period but then declined strongly to 1979 with a recovery by 1981–82, yet substantially below the level in the early 1960s. These developments are not at all reflected in the Gini coefficient for urban expenditure which remained at the same level from 1958–59 to 1982. Although there is a long way from functional to size distribution of income, one would expect the expenditure Gini coefficient to move in the opposite direction of the share of labor. The explanation is partly that a substantial part of profits accrues directly to government and thus does not affect the Gini coefficients, which reflects the distribution of income in the private sector. The share of labor is computed on total nonagricultural GDP at current prices. After 1973 when public sector revenues from oil and the Suez Canal increased strongly, the share of labor in nonagricultural GDP should, everything else being equal, tend to fall without necessar-

Table 17-14. Shares of Wages and Salaries in Nonagricultural GDP, 1960-85

(percent)

Period	Egypt	Turkey
1960–61 to 1964–65	53.7	39.1[a]
1965–66 to 1966–67	54.6	42.7
1967–68 to 1969–70	57.6	44.5
1970–71 to 1974	60.3	44.7
1975–76	52.2	46.9
1977–78	45.0	50.0
1979	36.9	43.3
1980	n.a.	35.1
1981–82	42.1	32.2
1983	n.a.	31.5
1984	n.a.	31.1
1985	n.a.	26.9

Note: At current factor costs.
a. For 1963–65.
n.a. = Not available.
Source: Ibrahim H. Issawi in Abdel-Khalek and Tignor (1982), table 4–4; World Bank data; Özmucur (1985, updated 1986).

ily any change in the distribution of income accruing to the private sector. Estimates of functional distribution of private sector income in Egypt in 1974–79 (table 1–7) show a considerable increase in the share of labor employed in nonagricultural sectors. Workers' remittances also affect expenditure and income distribution without having direct effects on functional distribution.

For Turkey the nonagricultural share of labor increased steadily from 39 percent in 1963–65 to 50 percent in 1977–78 and then declined steadily and dramatically to 27 percent in 1985. From 1963 to 1973 the Gini coefficient for nonagricultural income declined from 0.59 to 0.46 with, as should be expected, the share of labor increasing from 36½ percent to 44½ percent. Workers' remittances possibly worked in the same direction.

Notice that from the 1960–61 to 1964–65 period through 1975–76 the nonagricultural share of labor remained considerably higher in Egypt than in Turkey. This might explain the relatively high income Gini coefficient for nonagricultural Turkey as compared with urban Egypt. Had comparable functional distributions for agriculture been available, they might have explained the relatively high agricultural income Gini coefficient in Turkey. But then, of course, the problem remains of explaining the generally relatively low share of labor in Turkey.

Summary of Equity Comparisons

Indicators of distribution and equity are generally less reliable than indicators of growth, and more so for Turkey than for Egypt. The following statements should be qualified accordingly.

- For the period 1923–85 the experience of both countries appears to vaguely conform to Kuznets's U-curve hypothesis, the turnaround apparently being generated earlier in Turkey than in Egypt as a result of higher and faster-growing GDP per capita in Turkey.
- Throughout the whole period, inequality appears to have been more pronounced in Turkey than in Egypt. For years after World War II this seems to be the case for both urban and rural areas.
- Income per household and per capita for both countries is much lower in rural than in urban areas, the difference probably not being significantly larger in Turkey than in Egypt.
- Expenditure and probably income distribution appear in Egypt to be slightly more egalitarian in rural than in urban areas. Information for Turkey, pertaining to agricultural and nonagricultural sectors, is conflicting. Considering the relatively equal distribution of land ownership in Turkey, I am skeptical of the widely held view that distribution there should be more unequal in rural than in urban areas.
- Regional distribution is probably more unequal in Turkey than Egypt.
- Distribution of land, both by holdings and by ownership, has been extremely stable in Turkey. In Egypt distribution by ownership has, despite land reform, only become slightly more egalitarian while distribution by holdings has become much more egalitarian.
- Distribution of land by ownership, even after land reform in Egypt, is much more egalitarian in Turkey than in Egypt. Distribution by holdings, which immediately after World War II probably was more unequal in Egypt than in Turkey, is now much more equal in the former than in the latter country.
- The share of wages and salaries in nonagricultural GDP has for most of the postwar period been higher in Egypt than in Turkey, the exception being the years 1977–79. This is one factor that may help explain the generally more equitable distribution of income in Egypt than in Turkey. The higher share of government in profits and the larger workers' remittances in Egypt may, however, be part of the explanation.
- The share of wages in nonagricultural GDP has for both Egypt and Turkey moved in a long wave, increasing from 1960 to reach a peak, in Egypt around the period 1970–71 to 1974, in Turkey around 1977–78, and thereafter declining strongly. This wave was much stronger in Turkey than in Egypt.

Table 17–15. School Attendance and Literacy, 1960 and 1984

(percent)

	Number enrolled as share of corresponding age group									
	Primary education				Secondary education		Higher education		Literacy rate[a]	
	Male		Female							
Country	*1960*	*1984*	*1960*	*1984*	*1960*	*1984*	*1960*	*1984*	*1960*	*1976*
Egypt	80	94	52	72	16	58	5	21	26	44
Turkey	90	116	58	109	14	38	3	9	38	60

a. Read and write and formal education, fifteen years old and older.
Source: World Bank, *World Development Report*, 1980, 1987.

Educational Standards and Achievements

Education has implications for growth, equity, and poverty through its impact on productivity and opportunity. Education has a status (stock) and a development (rate of change) dimension. The two are closely related. Table 17–15 reveals significant differences in both status and development over time and between countries.

Poorly defined as it is and ambiguous as a measure of educational status, the adult literacy rate indicates a higher and more rapidly improving level of education in Turkey than in Egypt. In both countries the literacy rate was higher in 1976 than in 1960, and in both years higher in Turkey than in Egypt. The higher the enrollment ratio in primary education for a given group at a given time, the faster the increase in literacy, everything else being equal (especially the so-called read and write group). Turkey in fact had a higher enrollment ratio than Egypt in both 1960 and 1984 and the difference increased, absolutely as well as relatively. Educational status as measured by literacy rate must thus have improved faster in Turkey than in Egypt throughout the postwar period.

At any given time, the educational status of the adult population in countries that do not embark on adult education mainly reflects educational policies of the past. Changing that status is a matter of generations when, as in Egypt and Turkey, adult education is not pursued. Around 1980, for the schooling of the mature population (twenty-five years old and older), educational policies during and before the 1960s were decisive. Table 11–16 demonstrates strikingly the difference between Egyptian and Turkish policies during the interwar period and the early decades after World War II and their long-lingering effects on the educational situation. Circa 1980, only about one-seventh of the mature population in Egypt had schooling of any kind, against almost one-half in Turkey. In Egypt only 4½ percent of this population had

Table 17-16. Educational Status of Total Population, Twenty-five Years Old and Older

(percent)

Country and year	No schooling	Primary including noncompleted	Secondary entered	Post-secondary	Total
Egypt, 1976	86.3	4.7	5.7	3.4	100
Turkey, 1980	52.4	35.3	8.7	3.6	100

Source: UNESCO, *Statistical Yearbook*, 1987.

primary education, while almost the same percent, 3½, had postsecondary (academic) education, a truly absurd situation; for Turkey the corresponding figures were 35½ and 3½ percent.

Behind this situation we have modern educational traditions in Egypt that go back to the time of the British occupation when a university of considerable size and standards was established in Cairo while next to nothing was done about elementary education for the broad population. This tradition was by and large continued by parliamentary democracy before 1952, and even under Nasser and Sadat educational policy continued to be biased in favor of free higher education with almost a dozen new universities created in the late 1960s and 1970s while elementary education in rural areas left much to be desired. Turkey held back the admission to higher education and from the time of Atatürk emphasized elementary education. The difference between the two countries in emphasis on primary as opposed to higher education shows up also in the enrollment statistics in table 17-15. Enrollment in primary education has been higher in Turkey throughout the postwar period, in 1984 even exceeding 100 percent of the school-age population, while Egypt still has a long way to go until all school-age children are enrolled. For both secondary and higher education precisely the opposite is the case; Egypt has had much higher and faster growing enrollment rates than Turkey.

Enrollments in both countries are lower for females than for males although Turkey, practically speaking, has reached parity in primary education, with male enrollment at 116 percent and female at 109 percent. Egypt is still far from equality with female enrollment at only 72 percent and male at 94 percent. It is probably characteristic of the two countries that although Egypt has higher enrollment rates in secondary education for both males and females, the difference between males and females is also higher here for Egypt than for Turkey.

It is difficult to find comparable data for the educational status of urban and rural population and labor force. The data in table 17-16 come from a cross classification for Turkey of active population, twelve years old and older, by educational status and occupation, among which agriculture (including fishing, hunting, and forestry). For Egypt the data come from a cross classification of labor force by education and residence and from classification of education in a population census by both residence and occupation, the latter comparable to the Turkish census data apart from the age grouping. For Egypt the differences in age grouping appear unimportant and the rural, nonagricultural labor force appears to be much better educated than the agricultural labor force. The same may well be the case for Turkey. The comparison between the agricultural and nonagricultural labor force in Egypt and Turkey shows clearly that in Egypt the agricultural population until very recently was grossly ignored educationally as compared with Turkey. While in Egypt only 1½ percent, in Turkey no less than 42½ percent of the agricultural labor force had formal education in the mid-1970s. Moreover, the definition of formal education applied to Turkey is narrower than the one for Egypt and the Egyptian figures are strongly biased in favor of education because unpaid female family labor in the Egyptian statistics is grossly underenumerated as compared with Turkey.

The data on educational status in table 17–16 depict the situation in the mid-1970s; the picture must have improved in both countries by the mid-1980s, given the enrollment ratios in table 17–15. Preliminary results from the population census of 1986 in Egypt show that 73.8 percent of the population ten years old and older was without formal education, a disappointing decline from the 78.2 percent in 1976. Data for 1980 from the same sources as the 1977 data for Egypt in table 17–17 and the 1975 data for Turkey (with the exception that in 1980 unemployed job seekers are not included) give the following shares of the labor force with no formal education in 1980 and projected shares for 1985:

	Egypt			Turkey		
Year	Total	Rural	Urban	Total	Agriculture	Other
1980, actual	75.0	89.3	58.7	37.8	54.5	12.8
1985, projected	69.1	86.4	51.2	32.2	51.6	9.4

The 1985 projections assume the same rate of change of percentages for labor force with no formal education in 1980–85 as for 1975–80 in Turkey and for 1977–80 in Egypt. While more refined simulations could perhaps be made, this simple projection leaves no doubt that even by 1985 the educational status of the labor force in Turkey must have been much better than that in Egypt and that it will take decades for Egypt to catch up with Turkey.

It is difficult to find reasonable indicators of the quality of education. Student-teacher ratios are frequently used for this purpose, it being assumed, with some justification, that quality is inversely related to class size. Table 17–18 indicates that developments have been quite differ-

Table 17–17. Educational Status of Labor Force, 1970s

(percent)

Country and data characteristics	Sector	Formal education	No formal education[a]	Total
Egypt				
Labor force survey, 1977, ages 12–64	Rural	8.9	91.1	100
	Urban	36.3	63.7	100
	Total	21.2	78.8	100
Population census, 1976, ages 15 and older	Rural	8.2	91.8	100
	Urban	36.5	63.5	100
	Total	21.1	78.9	100
	Agriculture	1.5	98.5	100
	Other	36.1	63.9	100
	Total	21.1	78.9	100
Turkey				
Population census, 1975, ages 12 and older	Agriculture	42.4	57.6	100
	Other	82.6	17.4	100
	Total	55.6	44.4	100

a. For Egypt, illiterate plus read and write; for Turkey, illiterate plus literate without diploma.

Source: Egypt, CAPMAS, *Manpower Survey by Sample* (1979), table 4; Hansen (1985), appendix 1; Turkey, *Statistical Yearbook,* 1985, table 46.

Table 17–18. Student-Teacher Ratios in Primary and Secondary Education, Selected Years, 1937–85

(Number of students per teacher)

Year	Primary		Secondary	
	Egypt	Turkey	Egypt	Turkey
1937	n.a.	49	n.a.	24
1950	29	45	26[a]	14
1960	39	46	18	23
1970	38	38	27	33
1975	35	32	34	n.a.
1980	34[b]	27	27	20[b]
1985	31	31	21	21

n.a. = Not available.
a. For 1953.
b. For 1981.
Source: Hershlag (1968), app. table 66; UNESCO, *Statistical Yearbook,* various years.

ent for the two countries and for primary and secondary education. In primary education Turkey started out with many more students per teacher than Egypt, the ratio remaining steady until the end of the 1960s when a drop to about 30 in 1985 began. In Egypt the ratio increased to around 40 during the 1950s where it remained into the 1970s when a slow decline subsequently brought it down to the same level as in Turkey in 1985. For secondary education both countries experienced some increase in the student-teacher ratio during the 1970s but were in 1985 down to the same level of 21 students per teacher. While for primary education both countries still have a relatively high student-teacher ratio, for secondary education the ratio cannot be characterized as high. Quality of education, however, depends on many other factors and to characterize the educational situation in the two countries as equal and relatively satisfactory on the basis of this single indicator would be preposterous.

Since 1923, modern independent Turkey has, in terms of standard indicators, been much more successful than modern independent Egypt in creating a public education system and advancing the educational status of the broad population. Complete lack of formal education is even nowadays much more prevalent among the adult population of Egypt than of Turkey and in terms of actual outcome, policies in Egypt have been much more biased than in Turkey in favor of males, urban areas, and higher education. The bias in favor of males and urban areas inevitably means, everything else being equal, a selection of less talented youngsters which by its very nature is both inequitable and harmful to the growth process. This is a case of no conflict between growth and equity, both as conventionally defined and as measured. The bias in favor of higher education is also in its actual effects inequitable insofar as the subsidization implied by higher education in both countries tends to benefit offspring of higher-income families (Abdel-Fadil, in Abdel-Khalek and Tignor 1982; Özgediz, in Özbudun and Ulusan 1980). The impact on the growth process is a more complex matter. Micro data generally indicate higher returns to elementary than to higher education, which might be taken to imply more growth effect from elementary education although various externalities and complementarities of factors might alter that assumption. High-quality higher education may, on the other hand, have catalytic or Schumpeterian effects on the development process that no amount of elementary education could compete with. Even low-quality higher education may play a role in transfer and imitation of foreign technology. In Egypt, however, where the bias toward higher education since 1964 has been combined with an institutional mechanism—the public employment guarantee for graduates—that automatically allocates graduates of institutions of higher education to a sector with low, zero, or even negative marginal productivity, there is little doubt that the inequitable consequences of the bias are combined with sheer waste of resources.

The superior achievements of Turkey in the area of education are the more remarkable as Turkey throughout the postwar period has operated its educational system at a relatively lower level of public expenditure than Egypt (table 15–2).

Unemployment and Education

It is not possible to evaluate achievements in regard to poverty, equity, and growth without considering unemployment, one of the factors implicit in the indicators so far considered. Explicit indicators for unemployment are in any case useful. Opinions differ on the effect of unemployment on distribution and equity as measured by aggregative standard measures. Ideally, declining unemployment should be accompanied by higher growth rates and lower unemployment by higher per capita income and standard of living and less poverty. Educational achievements are, it would seem, a vital factor in understanding the unemployment problem.

Egypt has pursued policies with a strong expansion of and free access to higher education and with employment in the public sector (after a certain waiting period) guaranteed to all graduates of secondary and higher educational institutions. Since 1973, as a veterans' policy, discharged military draftees have had similar rights. These policies imply a strong bias toward higher education and have led to crowding and a declining quality of teaching in institutions of higher education and to overstaffing in the public sector. The policies were of little importance during the first years of their existence, but expansion of the system of higher education and the public sector during the 1970s made them a major factor in employment development, lowering open unemployment and increasing voluntary, "search" unemployment among students waiting for appointment. Elementary education, particularly in rural areas, has been somewhat neglected at the same time.

Turkey has pursued an education policy with emphasis on elementary education and with strict controls on admission to higher education. Enforced overstaffing in public enterprises has not been unknown but employment rights for graduates or discharged draftees do not exist and overstaffing in the public sector has never reached anything like Egyptian proportions.

Labor markets in Egypt and Turkey are difficult to compare because of differences both in employment institutions and policies and in the nature of existing unemployment. Table 17–19 summarizes information from labor force surveys (LFS) and population censuses (PCs) for both countries. Concentrating on the data on urban unemployment helps to sidestep two serious biases that would distort comparisons, but doing so leaves only 1969–70 and 1982–84 as the basis for comparison. Around 1969–70 both countries had relatively low urban unemployment, Egypt slightly more than Turkey, 4.2 percent and 3.3 percent, respectively. In 1982–84, both countries had relatively high urban unemployment, on average 9.2 percent and 11.6 percent, respectively. Both countries thus experienced a relatively strong increase in measured, comparable unemployment rates, Turkey's 252 percent against Egypt's 119 percent.

Around 1980, Turkey embarked on a serious and sincere stabilization program with reforms that had an impact on unemployment that can be compared to the simultaneous increase in unemployment in Egypt, where no comparable programs were undertaken. For Egypt an overwhelming share of measured unemployment in the LFSs since the early 1970s has consisted of workers who have had no work experience. The increase in unemployment, at least from 1973 to 1984, consisted almost exclusively of such labor, presumably to a large extent educated youngsters waiting for appointment in the public sector in line with the policy of guaranteed employment. Table 17–19 shows that the number of graduates signing up for public employment is large and increasing, and the waiting time has been increasing also. The LFSs in Egypt do not tabulate the unemployed by age or education, but the 1976 PC shows that the bulk of the unemployed were young and the incidence of unemployment was increasing with education. In this sense the increase in unemployment in Egypt may be seen as largely an increase in voluntary unemployment, educated youngsters preferring to wait for guaranteed public employment rather than taking employment in agriculture or the informal, private sector where the labor market probably clears and employment could be obtained—at a price (in lower wages).

Might similar tendencies to labor market segmentation prevail in Turkey and explain at least some of the increase in unemployment there? Turkey, of course, does not guarantee public employment for graduates, but education has generally expanded there more than in Egypt. In Turkey in 1985 (Hansen 1989b, table 1–9), almost two-thirds of the unemployed were single, almost two-thirds were less than twenty-five years old, almost two-thirds (excluding discouraged labor) had no work experience, and more than half had been unemployed for more than one year, facts that should not necessarily be taken to indicate that unemployment in Turkey tends to be voluntary. After all, the unemployed might be single and without work experience simply because they are long-time unemployed (which may make them rusty but cannot make them young). Nonetheless, labor market segmentation by education might exist also in Turkey. The fact that in Turkey the increase in unemployment from 1969 to 1985 seems (table 17–18) to consist largely of laborers without work experience, as in Egypt, is highly suggestive.

The comparison in table 17–20 of the incidence of unemployment by education in Egypt and Turkey is interesting. With a rate of total unemployment in Egypt in 1976 less than two-thirds that in Turkey in 1985, Egypt nonetheless had an incidence of unemployment for university-

Table 17-19. Unemployment Rates for the Civilian Labor Force, 1960–86
(Percent)

Year	From population censuses[a] Egypt	From population censuses[a] Turkey	Egypt[b] National Total	Egypt[b] National With work experience	Egypt[b] Urban[d]	Egypt[b] Rural[d]	Turkey[c] National Total	Turkey[c] National With work experience	Turkey[c] Urban Total	Turkey[c] Urban With work experience	Turkey[c] Rural[d]
1986	14.7	..	..	..	..	..	..	..	..	..	..
1985	..	..	..	..	..	..	12.3	3.4	14.8	..	(10.3)
1984	..	..	6.0	..	..	..	..	..	11.9	..	..
1983	..	..	6.6	0.6	(9.0)	(3.6)	..	..	12.1	..	..
1982	..	..	5.7	0.3	(9.9)	(4.0)	..	..	10.9	..	..
1981	..	..	5.4	0.3	(8.6)	(3.4)	..	..	..	..	..
1980	..	3.6	5.2	0.5	(8.1)	(3.2)	..	..	..	..	..
1979	..	..	4.6	0.3	7.7	3.0	..	..	..	..	..
1978	..	..	3.6	0.5	6.7	2.8	..	..	..	..	..
1977	..	..	3.1	0.3	5.7	1.9	..	..	..	..	..
1976	7.7	..	..	..	4.8	1.8	..	..	..	..	..

Year											
1975	..	1.6	2.5	0.3	4.4	..	..	..	..	..	..
1974	..	..	2.3	0.3	..	..	..	..	..	..	0.2ᵉ
1973	..	..	1.7	0.3	..	..	..	..	..	..	..
1972	..	..	1.5	..	..	..	..	..	..	..	..
1971	..	..	1.8	..	..	..	..	..	..	..	..
1970	..	..	2.4	..	4.2	..	..	3.3	..	2.3	..
1969	..	..	2.7	..	..	..	..	2.9	..	..	..
1968	..	..	3.1	..	..	..	..	2.8	..	..	..
1967	..	..	..	..	..	..	..	..	..	..	..
1966	..	..	..	..	..	..	..	..	..	..	..
1965	..	0.4	..	..	..	..	..	..	..	..	..
1961	..	..	3.2	..	7.0	..	..	..	..	..	..
1960	2.2	..	4.8	..	..	..	..	..	..	..	..

.. = Not available.
a. November, except Egypt 1960, September.
b. May.
c. November.
d. Percentages in parentheses are inferred.
e. Average of June and October 1973 and April 1974.
Source: Egypt, CAPMAS, *Manpower Survey by Sample;* Egypt, CAPMAS (1986); Turkey, *Statistical Yearbook;* Hanover (1989b).

Table 17–20. Incidence of Unemployment, by Educational Status, Egypt 1976 and Turkey 1985

(percent of labor force)

Educational status	Egypt 1976[a]	Turkey 1985[b]
Illiterate	2.5	8.8
Read and write[c]	n.a.	—
Primary	6.2	12.0
High school	20.6	22.5
Vocational[d]	—	15.4
University	11.3	7.0
Total	7.7	12.7

— =Not applicable.
n.a. = Not available.
a. Six years old and older; based on population census.
b. Twelve years old and older; based on labor force survey.
c. Data for Turkey 1985 are included in illiterate.
d. Data for Egypt 1976 are included in high school percentage.
Source: Egypt, CAPMAS *Manpower Survey by Sample;* Turkey, SIS, *Statistical Yearbook,* 1987.

educated members of the labor force two-thirds higher than that of Turkey and about the same incidence for those with an intermediate level of education. For laborers with primary education, on the other hand, Egypt's unemployment incidence was only half that of Turkey and for illiterates the incidence in Egypt was even smaller, absolutely and relatively. The labor market structure is very different in the two countries and the effect of guaranteed employment for graduates in Egypt is easy to spot. Turkey, however, also has a pronounced pattern of unemployment by education. The rate of unemployment is increasing up to and including high school education and is then declining. The low rate for university educated in Turkey probably reflects the rigid limits on admission to universities in Turkey in contrast with the free admission in Egypt. To understand this pattern, the breakdown in table 17–21 by urban and rural areas in Turkey is useful.

University educated have the same low incidence of unemployment in urban and rural areas of Turkey. For other levels of education, urban and rural areas differ radically. Urban areas have broadly the same incidence for other levels of education, 14–20 percent, with the consequence that while for university educated the share of unemployed is much lower than the share of the labor force, for other levels of education these shares are about the same. For rural areas the pattern is the same as at the national level. Indeed, it is the rural areas that form the national pattern (apart from university educated). In Turkey the LFSs as well as the

Table 17-21. Unemployment in Turkey, by Urban and Rural Areas and Completed Education, 1985
(percent)

Category	Unemployment rate	Share of unemployed	Share of labor force
National	(1)	(2)	(3)
No formal education	8.8	14.5	20.9
Primary	12.0	52.7	55.6
High school	22.5	24.4	13.8
Vocational	15.4	5.7	4.7
University	7.0	2.7	4.9
Total	12.7	100	100
Urban			
No formal education	19.8	13.2	10.2
Primary	14.0	45.7	49.9
High school	20.3	28.6	21.6
Vocational	14.5	7.9	8.4
University	7.1	4.6	9.9
Total	15.3	100	100
Rural[a]			
No formal education	5.8	16.0	29.4
Primary	10.7	60.5	60.1
High school	27.7	19.6	7.6
Vocational	18.6	3.3	1.9
University	6.1	0.6	1.0
Total	10.7	100	100

Both unemployed and economically active population including inactive unemployed, unemployed not seeking employment, and seasonal workers not seeking job.
a. Computed as difference between national LFS 1985 and urban places LFS 1985.
Source: Turkey, SIS, *Statistical Yearbook*, 1987, tables 137, 146.

PCs are taken in a slack agricultural season. The unemployment incidence for labor with no formal education is remarkably low, only 6 percent. This probably reflects mainly unskilled agricultural labor, and may indicate approximate market clearing in the agricultural labor market, particularly because the unemployed may be seeking employment in urban areas only at the time they are being counted as unemployed in rural areas. It is remarkable also that among workers without formal education the incidence of unemployment is only 6 percent in rural areas while in urban areas it is about 20 percent. For primary school educated, the unemployment pattern is similar though less extreme—11 percent in rural areas and 14 percent in urban areas. This is consistent with the predictions of Harris-Todaro theory. The situation is the opposite for high school and vocationally educated where rural unemployment rates are as high as 28 percent and 19 percent, respectively—both much higher than in urban areas. Again the rural unemployed may be seeking work in urban areas. The labor market segmentation may thus have several dimensions, educational as well as geographical. It is unfortunate that a geographical breakdown is not available for Egypt.

Everything considered, it would seem likely that the substantial improvement in the educational status of the Turkish rural labor force during the postwar period has indeed served to push the rate of unemployment up for the labor force as a whole. It is not possible to quantify this upward effect of education but it seems likely that, without it, the unemployment trend might have been definitely downward until the mid-1970s and from then on less strongly upward (see figure 11–1). Improved education, however, should not be able to explain the whole of the upward shift of the unemployment trend in Turkey from the mid-1970s as it might in Egypt. Despite the similarities of the statistical pictures, the underlying policy factors appear to have been entirely different in the two countries: in Egypt the guaranteed public employment for graduates, in Turkey the stabilization with reforms, with improved education in both cases possibly only a secondary factor. It would appear that while in Egypt the increase in unemployment may essentially be voluntary and the involuntary unemployment a secondary problem, in Turkey the opposite could be the case. It is an interesting question which of these non-first-best alternative policies is socially preferable.

A few comments on the major biases in the data may be in order. While the Egyptian LFSs systematically are taken in May, which since the closure of the Aswan High Dam in 1964 is the agricultural peak season, all Turkish LFSs for urban areas as well as the single national survey for 1985 were taken in November, a slack season in agriculture. In itself this circumstance should, even if agricultural labor markets clear instantaneously and completely around the year, tend to bias the measured unemployment rate for Egypt downward and for Turkey upward as compared with an annual average of monthly observations and to bias the measured rate in Egypt downward as compared with Turkey. The latter bias should of course be most pronounced for rural areas and less so at the national level but might spill over to urban areas. It is difficult to say how strong this bias is since no LFS data are available on seasonal variations in either country. For Turkey both LFSs and PCs are taken in November so that comparison of those data cannot disclose seasonal variations. For Egypt, however, comparison of data from the 1986 PC and the 1984 LFS suggests that the national, annual average unemployment rate might have been on the order of 10 percent by the mid-1980s, with perhaps 4 percent of a seasonal nature. With the Turkish national LFS of 1985 at 12.3 percent and biased upward, including an unknown amount of slack-season unemployment, the level of measured unemployment within the two countries might have been about the same in the mid-1980s; indeed, it could have been highest in Egypt. The comparison based on urban unemployment may after all have been biased, somewhat overestimating Turkish unemployment relatively.

Egyptian LFSs as well as PCs seem for various reasons to grossly underenumerate women in the labor force, particularly unpaid female family workers in rural areas (see chapter 4) while the Turkish LFSs, if anything, appear to do the opposite. With approximately equal population size and similar urbanization, Egypt counted 18,000 women as unpaid family labor in rural areas in 1980, Turkey 3.5 million in 1985. As a consequence not only female participation rates but also unemployment rates are biased upward in Egypt and possibly the opposite in Turkey. It is difficult to judge how strong the bias is, but it does tend to eliminate and may even dominate the seasonal bias. Its strength and effects are suggested by the computations of unemployment rates in table 17–22 (see also table 6–16).

In Egypt unemployment rates for rural areas are only one-half to one-third those for urban areas. This may partly be related to the timing of the LFS, taken at the peak season in May. For Turkey the rural LFSs are scanty and apparently conflicting. For 1985, national and urban LFSs together imply both absolutely and relatively high rural unemployment, about two-thirds the level of urban unemployment; the rural LFSs in 1973–74 indicate exactly the opposite. All these surveys were apparently taken in slack agricultural seasons. Both sets of results could, of course, be accurate, provided that rural unemployment had worsened more than urban unemployment over this decade. The dramatic reversal of rural-urban migration in Turkey, large before 1975 but negative from 1975 to 1980 (Hansen 1989b, tables 2–3, 2–4), could be the explanation.

Another significant difference between the two countries is in their social security systems. While Turkey has a system without unemployment insurance but with substantial severance pay and retirement pay, Egypt operates a system with virtual income security for permanent employees in the public sector, providing retirement and unemployment insurance and free health services. In both countries the system applies fully to the public sector but not to agriculture; in both there is uncertainty whether the system extends to the informal sector although, at least in Egypt, employees are becoming increasingly aware of their legal rights. Any detailed comparison of employment and unemployment should consider the effects of the social security systems. Clearly, unemployment benefits cannot be the explanation of a relatively high estimated unemployment in Turkey.

Poverty in Egypt and Turkey

In comparing achievements in Egypt and Turkey, this chapter has had little to say about poverty except by implication. Poverty has been stud-

Table 17-22. Unemployment Rates and Labor Force Participation, Egypt 1980 and Turkey 1985
(percent)

Category	Share of population in labor force		Unemployed in labor force[a]					
			Total		Excluding unpaid family labor		Excluding unpaid family labor, self-employed, and employers	
	Egypt[b]	Turkey[c]	Egypt	Turkey	Egypt	Turkey	Egypt	Turkey
Urban								
Male	40.1	36.9	5.6	11.7	5.9	12.2	8.0	20.9
Female	6.6	7.1	20.2	31.1	20.3	34.7	22.0	36.9
Total	46.7	44.0	7.7	14.8	8.0	15.6	10.3	21.1
Rural								
Male	51.6	33.0	2.6	13.2	3.3	16.6	5.7	32.7
Female	1.8	23.0	15.8	5.0	17.5	30.9	25.5	46.0
Total	53.3	56.0	3.0	10.3	3.8	19.1	6.6	35.7
Total								
Male	91.7	69.9	3.9	12.4	4.5	14.1	6.9	22.7
Female	8.3	30.1	19.2	12.0	19.8	35.5	22.6	41.1
Total	100.0	100.0	5.2	12.3	5.9	17.1	8.8	26.1

(Egypt, ages 12–64; Turkey, age 12 and above)
a. Excludes unemployed not seeking jobs and seasonal workers, seasonally unemployed and not seeking unseasonal jobs. In Egypt unpaid family workers are included only if they work more than one-third of full time during survey period.
b. Labor force of 10.3 million.
c. Labor force of 18.4 million.
Source: Egypt, CAPMAS, *Manpower Survey by Sample,* 1981; Turkey, *Statistical Yearbook,* 1987, tables 137, 138, 145, 146.

ied in both countries and the results were reviewed in parts I and II, in particular chapters 1 and 6. Well-known ambiguities of the very concept of poverty, and the incommensurability of attempts to quantify the phenomenon as reported here, prompted me not to extend the comparative discussion at this point beyond what can be inferred from measures of distribution, standard of living, and equity.

18 *The Politics of Growth, Distribution, and Equity*

Chapter 14 should make clear that initial conditions, endowments of natural resources, and external factors are responsible for both significant similarities and dissimilarities of development in Egypt and Turkey. Historical circumstances made independence and tariff autonomy almost simultaneous events in the two countries, with protectionist tariff reforms in 1929–30 the result. Turkey's agricultural frontier gave her a strong advantage in agricultural growth until the mid-1950s when Egyptian agriculture was almost stagnant. Wars cost Egypt dearly in terms of growth from 1963 to 1973. Availability of oil after 1974 gave Egypt a growth push, not experienced by Turkey, that petered out in 1984 and that was accentuated by an improvement in Egypt's terms of trade in 1976 and a deterioration in 1985, years in which Turkey experienced exactly the opposite terms of trade development. International political conflicts did much harm to Egypt after World War II while Turkey on balance benefited considerably on this account, but again the situation exactly reversed in the mid-1970s. This chapter assesses the influence that domestic politics had on these developments.

The Choice of Strategy

From a political economy point of view, one of the most interesting features of a comparison of Egypt and Turkey is the fact that both countries around 1930 adopted an industrialization policy based on inward-looking import substitution. Egypt has never given up the policy and Turkey continued it until 1980 despite radical differences and changes in the political regimes of the two countries over more than half a century.[1] Egypt's industrialization policy was adopted under parliamentary democracy and continued under three autocrats after 1952. In Turkey the policy was adopted under autocracy and continued after 1950 under parliamentary democracy and, occasionally, military government. Turkey changed her strategy in 1980 to export-led growth under a parliamentary democracy; the new strategy was implemented by a military government and later continued by a (temporarily constrained) parliamentary democracy. In these two countries there has been no simple relationship between political system and industrialization strategy. It might be claimed that underlying economic interests tend to rule the roost whatever the political system is. To support this view, it would be necessary to show which particular group(s) or in which well-defined sense something called the public interest would benefit from the inward-looking strategy and then to show how the particular group or public interest got to be served, no matter what the system was.

For Marxists there may not be a problem here. Both Egypt and Turkey might by Marxists be considered essentially capitalist countries with two classes, capitalists and workers, and economic policy always serving capitalist interests, with government (state) ultimately nothing but an instrument to exploit the working class and the superstructure nothing but a veil. This axiomatic approach is oversimplified, does not provide information about the economic and political mechanisms involved, and cannot be tested empirically. Substituting the word *bourgeoisie* for the word *capitalist* does not help.

Modern demand-supply theory (including so-called neoclassical, monetarist, and Keynesian theory) has the flexibility and the rigor required to analyze the problems involved and may be subjected to empirical testing. Its models, however, are no less oversimplified than the Marxist ones, and it cannot provide general answers to any question about policy effects. Two commodity-two factor, Heckscher-Ohlin-Samuelson, 2×2HOS, standard theory suggests that in countries with abundant labor and scarce capital, import-substitution policy should tend to favor capital and do harm to labor. For Egypt and Turkey, such a simplification is politically uninteresting and thus unacceptable for the purpose at hand. The moment, however, we just move to general 3x3 theory, not to speak of nxm theory, all such general conclusions collapse. The simplified 3x3 analysis ventured upon in chapter 16 leads to striking and interesting suggestions, but no more than that. A general equilibrium theory does not explain who benefits from what. Simulation, a useful analytical tool, does not help to answer empirical problems, even when based on so-called stylized facts.

Modern political economy of the Buchanan variety views economic policy as the outcome of a complex process of political exchange but applies at best only to societies with a liberal social order, protecting property and contractual rights. According to standard trade theory, those who benefit from protectionism should not be able, disregarding other distortions, from their benefits to compensate the losers. It might be asked how a voluntary process of political exchange should then come up with an import-substitution policy as the end result, at least under rational expectations and certainty. Both the theory of noncooperative games (the prisoner's dilemma) and the theory of public choice indicate that neither democracy nor benevolent dictatorship necessarily leads to efficient allocation of resources or decisionmaking (see for instance a recent review by Inman, 1987, pp. 692–739). That the political process does not lead to efficient solutions does not explain why so many different political processes lead to the same inefficient solution.

When the participants in the political exchange process have irrational perceptions, these would presumably have to be modeled explicitly. It would, for instance, be exceedingly interesting, perhaps in some environments even realistic, to develop a political exchange model in which labor unions perceive the real world through Marxist glasses (believing, say, that an increase in real wages would lead to a decline in unemployment) and employers are equipped with Chicago glasses and opposite perceptions (increased real wages lead to increased unemployment). With such perceptions it does not appear likely that the political exchange process would have a stable equilibrium solution. Other irrationalities might have to be introduced to make political exchange theory realistic in each particular case.

Moreover, the political exchange theory of Buchanan may not apply without serious modifications to a parliamentary democracy so imperfect as that of Egypt in 1923–52 or of Turkey in the late 1970s and the first years after 1983. If, for instance, rural labor was the loser from import-substitution policies and it effectively did not vote or participate and had no clout in the political process, the end result might well be import substitution although it is not an economically efficient solution and the majority might be the losers.

Even worse, the exchange theory of Buchanan does not apply to autocratic societies (including military government) and little other political economy theory exists for such societies. The benevolent dictator (Inman 1987) may be a rare find, if he exists at all. The platonic guardians model may have some relevance for Turkey and the predatory model is not entirely without relevance for Egypt. Still, these two models are at best tips of the iceberg. Neither explains why inward-looking import substitution is so frequently the outcome.

Since modern political economy seems to have difficulty explaining the choice of basic development strategy, more general models may help. Elite theory naturally enters the stage. When Imperial Germany in the last quarter of the nineteenth century emerged as the first serious challenger to British economic hegemony, the German (List) model with infant-industry protection and development bank financing came to be seen in much of the world, including many presentday developing countries, as the safe and fast road to economic independence and development and, in the long pull, even expansion into world markets. This generalization may have been no more justified than current generalizations about export-led growth on the basis of the experience of a handful of Asian countries. Be that as it may, in Egypt and Turkey spokesmen for modernization and national independence such as Tala'at Harb and Ziya Gökalp spread the List Gospel which became conventional wisdom amongst third world elite. Instead of accepting Buchanan's model of economic policy as the outcome of a process of political exchange, it may be best to look at policy as the outcome of elite-led games with the elite most often serving as imitators (rather than innovators), using coercion, even violence, and often basing their actions on irrational perceptions. The elite would include ideological and political leaders and their clients—planners, bureaucrats, and technocrats. This model of the political economy has the advantage of applying across political systems, autocracies as well as democracies and everything in between, and includes the Buchanan model as a very special case of a mild-mannered elite with rational perceptions and expectations. The elite model helps to explain the amazing lack of originality in national economic policies in a world where most countries seem to be copying others. Many developing countries worship or pay lip service to socialism; none of them invented the animal but all have development experts educated at Western universities and drilled in the latest intellectual fad. And communist elites have suddenly become idolators of market forces, not without some impact on their countries. The elite model thus helps to explain the similarity of development strategies across political systems.

The permanency of the inward-looking strategy in both Egypt and Turkey may suggest that elite-led policies governed the economies from the time of independence, with the shift in Turkey in 1980 led by an elite that was prodded and backed by an elite of World Bank, IMF, and OECD advisers (with financial clout, no doubt), and with the military accepting apparent elite consensus, whatever it is, as an expression of the public interest.

There is also a dynamic relationship between policies and interest groups. Policies may create interest groups that then start working for their own (further) benefit within the framework of the new policy. Examples are plentiful. Tariff reforms that are promoted by ideologists to start industrialization from scratch may, if successful, create industries with modern employers and employees who then organize and operate politically to preserve and expand the protectionist system. Unemployment benefits, introduced by political idealists or cynics when there is no unemployment, may create unemployment and hence a new interest group. Education may create educated people who push for public employment. These dynamics explain why governments tend to increase expenditures when groups are minuscule and then find it difficult to cut the expenditures as interest groups begin growing—in a vicious circle. Governments, of course, may destroy groups, as Stalin did the Kulaks, and Nasser did the big landowners. The economic theory of rent seeking may have little to contribute to the explanation of the introduction or change of basic strategy. Here the elite—ideologists and visionaries—may dominate completely, as they did in Egypt and Turkey around 1930 and in Turkey around 1980. Once the basic strategy and its institutions are in place, however, rent seeking begins.

Another feature of Egypt and Turkey's political systems since 1923 is the tendency for protection, especially quantitative controls, to vary inversely with the availability of foreign exchange. The extreme examples may be Egypt before World War II when quantitative trade and exchange controls were virtually nonexistent and exchange reserves abundant, and after Sadat's *infitah* when licensing was abrogated for own-exchange-financed imports not listed as requiring license and own exchange (in the form of remittances) was abundant. Turkey clearly shows the same pattern with relaxation of licensing in 1950–53 and 1970–73 when foreign exchange was relatively abundant. Rather than accepting this feature of economic policy as a change in long-term strategy, it should probably be seen as short-term foreign exchange policy with possible secondary effects on import substitution. Clearly it is a policy feature that is independent of political systems and groups.

Beyond industrialization as a target, there is the broader issue of national economic development, which sectors to emphasize, and particularly the role of agricultural development. Egypt's 1918 strategy called for balanced growth, with industrialization and agricultural growth to be pursued simultaneously and interdependently. Considering how slight the manufacturing industry sector was, the balanced strategy should probably be seen as a compromise between a dominating ideological, nationalistic, and visionary elite (Tala'at Harb) and hard-nosed interest groups (cotton growers and importers). In Turkey, industrialization was seen by the elite (Gökalp and Atatürk) as the driving force in economic modernization and development while agricultural development mainly was seen as a support to industrialization through the introduction of industrial crops and the provision of a market for industrial output. Ideologically, economic development was subsumed under Atatürk's "sixth arrow," which had little to say directly about agricultural development. Agricultural development policy grew out of the population exchanges and the related distribution of public land.

After World War II, economic development policy in both Egypt and Turkey came under the influence of international organizations. Initially the United Nations was the guide; its first development decade introduced the 7 percent growth target with an emphasis on planning and industrialization. Later the IMF and the World Bank sponsored export-led growth, with privatization and liberalization; they became influential in Turkey in 1980. Industrialization progressed much faster in Turkey than in Egypt, yet Turkey may have developed a problem of involuntary unemployment that Egypt apparently does not have.

Industrialization after World War II

Industrialization, measured by share in GDP, made little progress in either Egypt or Turkey until the 1950s. From 1952, on the other hand, the share of industry (including electricity, mining, with small amounts of oil) in Turkey increased from 11 percent to 24 percent in 1977–79, while in Egypt increasing from 14 percent (13 percent excluding petroleum) in 1952–53 to 21 percent in 1986–87 (but only about 18 percent excluding petroleum). The relatively poor industrialization record in Egypt does not appear to have been the consequence of investment policy ignoring industrialization. In this sense it is not a matter of so-called Dutch disease (see below). As a share of GDP, industrial investment in Egypt increased from 3.4 percent in 1952–59 to 6.9 percent in 1978–84, while in Turkey such investment increased from 3.7 percent in 1950–60 to 6 percent in 1978–79. In Egypt at the same time the share of total fixed investment increased from 13.9 percent to 28.5 percent, with total investment in Turkey increasing more modestly from 16.0 percent to 22.2 percent. The difference can almost completely be attributed to investment in the Suez Canal and petroleum in Egypt. It looks as if outside Suez Canal and petroleum Egypt had much less return to investments than Turkey. Deleting those two factors, the size and distribution of investment by sector was very similar in the two countries.

Crude estimates of incremental capital-output ratios (strictly the average ratios of gross investment to change in GDP) for industry defined as mining, manufacturing, and electricity, yield as 3.7 ratio for Egypt in 1952–53 to 1961–62 (Mead 1967, tables 1 A–7, 1 A–9, the data apparently including mining, at fixed 1954 prices, but not including Aswan Dam investments), and an 8.9 ratio in 1976 to 1980–81 (World Bank data, at fixed 1978 prices, not including petroleum). For Turkey the incremental ratios were 3.8 in 1963–72 (World Bank 1975, tables 2-1-A and -B, 2-3, at fixed 1971 prices) and 5.0 in 1972–77 (World Bank 1982, tables 2-2, 2-6, at fixed 1976 prices). Comparability is far from perfect. Periods and sectors have been chosen according to availability of data and policies pursued. Not surprisingly, in both countries incremental capital-output ratios appear to have been increasing over time. This is as expected for countries exhausting easy opportunities for import substitution. That Turkey should have a slightly higher ratio in 1963–72 than Egypt in 1952–53 to 1961–62 might be explained by the fact that Turkey's industry had a large share of state enterprises while Egyptian manufacturing was still based essentially on private enterprise. The much higher ratio for Egypt in 1976 to 1980–81 than for Turkey in 1972–77 could in the same way be explained by Egypt's now much larger share of public enterprises in manufacturing (60 percent against 37 percent, when measured by employment). The whole interpretation thus depends upon the assumption of relatively low efficiency in public enterprises, with import substitution being a strategy with declining efficiency.

For Egypt, however, Sadat's *infitah* with its extensive import liberalization may be part of the explanation of the very high incremental capital-output ratio for 1976 to 1980–81. Despite attempts by the government to protect public sector enterprises from the competitive onslaught by limiting own-exchange imports through special lists for commodities requiring license, serious competition may nonetheless have been inflicted on both old and new public sector enterprises, with low utilization of capacity the result. Considering the devaluation of 1979 it is not clear, however, why public and, for that matter, private enterprises did not begin to shift toward exports. Once more Egypt's bloated bureaucracy and relative overstaffing may be the culprit in the public sector, but this explanation hardly applies to the private sector where the free foreign exchange market should have opened up possibilities. The explanation may be that the lists of commodities requiring licenses for imports were drawn up so as to protect not only public enterprises but also influential private industries against competition from own-exchange imports. In the shoe industry, for example (Springborg 1989, chap. 3), production is mainly private and mainly small scale, yet dominated by a relatively small number of oligopolists who obviously have financial clout and are probably capable of wielding (rent-seeking) influence on the bureaucrats who draw up the lists. Certainly there appears to be no competition in Egypt's domestic shoe market from Spanish, Brazilian, and other successful shoe exporters in newly industrialized countries. It may be that the *infitah* did not permit any really competitive own-exchange imports. Compared with the Turkish reforms of 1980, the Egyptian *infitah* may thus have been nothing but surface.

Did Egypt and Turkey Suffer Dutch Disease?

It has become almost a tenet of political economy doctrine that countries experiencing large windfalls such as improvements in their terms of trade through sharp increases in export prices (of oil, gas, phosphate, and bauxite, for example) tend to be afflicted by Dutch disease through the market forces or frivolous fiscal-monetary and exchange rate policies (the literature is not precise on the nature of the doctrine). Events like these create large income effects that tend to drive up prices on nontraded goods and services, labor, and land (assuming free capital movements) that, because of market imperfections, may prevail after the reversal of the initial windfall or may lead to deficits in the public sector that may be politically irreversible. If the windfalls were forever, there would be no special problems; however, they do not last. The irreversibility of both factor prices and public spending may be a fact of life, not over the very long term, but certainly in the short term and possibly in the middle term.

Egypt has been suspected of being a clear case of Dutch disease. Having recovered her oilfields after Israeli annexation and exploitation and having discovered new oil and gas deposits, Egypt became a net oil exporter in 1976, enjoying the benefits of the oil price increases of 1973 and 1979 and of a huge inflow of remittances from workers who migrated to Arab OPEC countries. Turkey enjoyed large-scale migration of its workers to European countries, especially to West Germany, from the mid-1960s, and their remittances increased to substantial proportions in the late 1960s. Again the issue of Dutch disease has been raised, though Turkey's case differs because it suffered terms of trade losses in 1973 and 1979 parallel to the gains that Egypt enjoyed. A priori it would thus seem more likely that Dutch disease should be found in Egypt than in Turkey.

The ratio between indexes of prices of traded and nontraded goods and services might serve as direct evidence. But how such price indexes should be formulated and weighted is a problem; in any case no such indexes are readily available. The implicit value-added deflators in table 18–1 are a primitive proxy; alternative A represents all sectors producing tradables and nontradables, and alternative B excludes petroleum from the tradables sector in Egypt and government from the nontradables sector in both countries; the data are ratios between the implicit deflators for tradables and nontradables. Price controls have played a role in both countries and for Egypt an attempt has been made to take such controls into account by excluding electricity and public utilities, housing, transport, and communications from nontradables producing sectors so that for Egypt these include only construction and trade and finance. Taken at face value, the data in table 18–1 indicate Dutch disease for Egypt but not for Turkey, a priori a credible result. The indications for Egypt are weak, however, and they are influenced by price controls and price interference in both agriculture and industry that tend to keep deflators in both sectors down. For Turkey, if anything, the indication for 1975 is the opposite of Dutch disease, and for 1970 and 1982 the indications are insignificant.

Computations for Egypt based on the consumer price index gave results similar to those in alternative B. Agricultural wages (available for Egypt but not for Turkey) might also be used as an indicator of nontradable prices. The very strong increase in such wages after 1974 (figure 16–2) would probably again support the diagnosis of Dutch disease in Egypt. Finally, the so-called accounting ratios for Egypt, reported in table 4–19 with a breakdown of tradables and nontradables, point to Dutch disease in a comparison of medians, but the unweighted means yield contradictory results, against Dutch disease.

Table 18-1. Price Relatives for Tradables and Nontradables, Ratios between Implicit Deflators for Selected Sectors, Selected Years, 1965-84

	Egypt			Turkey			
Item	1975	1980–81	1983–84	1965	1970	1975	1982
Alternative A	1.00	1.59	1.17	1.00	0.97	1.06	1.02
B	1.00	0.92	0.89	1.00	0.99	1.11	0.98

Alternative A = All sectors included. Tradables for Egypt include agriculture, manufacturing and mining, petroleum, Suez Canal, and tourism; for Turkey, agriculture, industry and mining. All other sectors in nontradables.

Alternative B = Tradables for Egypt include agriculture, manufacturing and mining, Suez Canal, and tourism; for Turkey agriculture, industry, and mining. Nontradables for Egypt include construction and trade and finance; for Turkey, all other sectors except government.

Source: World Bank data.

Quite apart from problems of price controls and other interference, the large public sectors and direct public interference in the allocation of resources, especially through investment, are powerful forces in these two countries. No matter how prices have developed, they may not have served to direct the allocation of resources simply because government investment decisions have ignored considerations of social and even private profitability and efficiency. For that reason it may be preferable to look directly at the allocation of investment between tradable and nontradable sectors (shown in tables 4–11 and 12–15). Table 18–2 shows that in sectors producing tradable goods other than petroleum, there was little change in either country in tradables investment measured as a percentage of GDP. In both countries this percentage stayed rather constantly at 8–9 percent, a little lower in Turkey than in Egypt. There is nothing here to indicate Dutch disease in the two countries. On the other hand, the percentage of total investment represented by investment in sectors producing tradables other than petroleum for Egypt shows a dramatic decline from 48.4 percent in 1960–61 to 1964–65 to 32.7 percent in 1980–81 to 1983–84, which could be interpreted as a strong indicator of Dutch disease. For Turkey that percentage is about the same for 1963–70 and 1980–84 and slightly higher for 1971–77, a result that conforms remarkably well with the finding from the comparison of implicit-deflator ratios.

Policies Affecting Agricultural and Industrial Prices

Price and wage policies have a bearing on growth and distribution. In both Egypt and Turkey, government has intervened actively in price and

Table 18-2. Gross Investment in Petroleum, Other Tradable and Nontradable Goods and Services, Selected Periods, 1960–84

Sector	Egypt			Turkey		
	1960–61 to 1964–65	1974–79	1980–81 to 1983–84	1963–70	1971–77	1980–84
Total investment						
(percent of GDP)	17.6	25.0	28.5	17.0	20.2	18.9
Petroleum[a]	0.6	2.6	3.7	—	—	—
Other tradables	8.5	10.3	9.2	7.1	9.1	7.7
Nontradables	8.5	12.1	15.4	10.0	11.1	12.1
Other tradables as a						
percent of total	48.4	41.2	32.7	41.8	45.0	40.6

— = Not applicable.

a. Included in other tradables for Turkey; petroleum was negligible.

Source: Hansen, in Vatikiotis (1968); World Bank data.

wage developments ever since independence, and especially since World War II. The effects of policies that influence relative prices of agriculture and industry have been estimated for both countries. The ratio between the GDP deflators for agriculture and industry—sometimes called the internal terms of trade—are shown in table 18–3.

Prices apparently developed more favorably toward agriculture in Turkey than in Egypt from 1945 until 1980–81 when again they were approximately the same. This would indicate a shift in favor of agriculture in Turkey before 1950 to be lost during the 1970s, with, if anything, the opposite happening in Egypt. During the 1980s, agricultural terms of trade improved strongly in Egypt, the opposite happening in Turkey.

Estimates of relative protection for manufacturing and agriculture, respectively, in Egypt and Turkey at the end of the 1970s point in the same

Table 18-3. Ratio between Price Deflators Agriculture and Industry, Selected Years, 1945–87

Year	Egypt	Turkey
1945	100	100
1952–53	91.2	115.9
1960–61	101.1	113.3
1970–71	96.1	114.8
1980–81	106.0	107.9
1986–87	177.7	95.6

Source: Hansen and Marzouk (1965); Ikram (1980); World Bank data; World Bank, *World Tables 1987.*

direction. In Egypt, traded manufactured goods had on balance an accounting ratio (AR) between shadow price and market price of 1.03 against 1.57 for agricultural outputs and inputs (table 4–19). The ratio between the two ARs was 1.52. For Turkey the effective rates of protection for industry were 1.75 (general tariff) and 1.58 (European Community tariff) against 1.40 for agriculture (see chapter 9). The ratio between the two was 1.25 (general tariff) and 1.13 (EC tariff), considerably lower than the AR ratio for Egypt.

The estimates of transfers to and from agriculture through price and other forms of intervention, are derived from two conceptually different analyses (table 18–4). The nominal results are essentially based on partial analysis of transfers to and from agriculture; they measure the effects of the protection (positive or negative) of agriculture viewed in isolation. The real results take into account the protection enjoyed by the rest of the economy, mainly industry, and thus measure the relative protection of agriculture. In a national context, positive protection for one sector is negative protection for the rest of the economy, assuming a zero-sum game (which, of course, is not the case). If both agriculture and industry enjoy protection, viewed in isolation, but industry is more strongly protected than agriculture, then the latter may even suffer negative absolute, net protection (see Dethier 1989; World Bank data).

Price intervention covers all measures that make producer (ex-farm) prices of tradables differ from border prices (plus domestic transportation and the like). The difference between "direct" and "total" effects of price intervention is the effect of so-called "indirect" intervention, which largely corresponds to over- or undervaluation of the currency. In fact, this difference is negative for both countries for all periods, since both suffered overvaluation of the currency because of exchange rate and trade controls throughout the years considered (at least according to the study that presented estimates). The estimates of transfers caused by price intervention take into account supply and demand responses, considering also procurement and rationing, but they do not include all repercussions through the economy. Factor price responses, for instance, are not considered. Methods are at some points—particularly in the estimates of equilibrium exchange rates, which are crucial for gauging indirect effects—simplistic and may for Egypt systematically underestimate the impact of overvaluation after 1975, especially in 1981–84 when trade partners depreciated strongly while Egypt kept the official U.S. dollar exchange rate constant. Methods are, on the other hand, uniform; results are reasonably comparable, and may indicate orders of magnitude realistically.

Other intervention, added to price intervention to obtain "overall" intervention, includes such measures as public investment and current public expenditure in agriculture. For Turkey, credit subsidies (data available only for 1981–83) are left out; they are substantial and the

Table 18-4. Transfers to Agriculture as a Result of Intervention, Selected Years, 1961-85

(percent of total GDP)

	Price intervention		Overall intervention	
Country and period	Direct	Total	Direct	Total
Nominal results				
Egypt, 1965–81	−6.5	−11.7	−4.0	−10.0
Turkey, 1961–80	1.3	−3.8	2.5	−2.7
Egypt, 1982–85	−1.1	−5.3	1.1	−3.2
Turkey, 1981–83	−1.7	−5.1	−1.4	4.8
Real results				
Egypt, 1974–81	−4.6	−7.9	−4.9	−10.6
Turkey, 1961–80	−0.4	−2.9	0.7	−1.1
Egypt, 1982–85	−0.7	−3.2	0.4[a]	−2.9[a]
Turkey, 1981–83	−0.1	−0.1	0.2	0.2

a. For 1982–84.

Source: Dethier (1989), tables 9–5, 9–8, 9–9, 1–3; World Bank data.

omission tends to bias the support to agriculture for Turkey downward for the whole period.

The full period for Egypt has been divided to mark the takeover by Mubarak after the assassination of Sadat; for Turkey the division marks the adoption of the reforms of 1980 and the following military takeover. Including 1981 for Egypt and 1980 for Turkey in the second period would have yielded roughly the same results—a radical change in agricultural support policy, which in Egypt was in favor of agriculture and in Turkey was in nominal terms against but in real terms in favor of agriculture.

In the long periods in Egypt under Nasser and Sadat, 1965–81, and under parliamentary etatism in Turkey, 1961–80, there was no visible trend of change in agricultural support policy in either country, although in individual years composition by crops and distribution by output-input might deviate considerably from the averages. By any measure, nominal or real, price or overall intervention, direct or total impact, Egyptian agriculture in this period suffered strong negative support—that is, taxation or exploitation in favor of the rest of the economy, particularly the urban population. Real support, however, was systematically less negative than nominal support. The explanation is the simultaneous tendency for (modern) industry also to be discriminated against through price controls, forced production, and the like.

For Turkey, the picture is more complex. The direct, nominal impact of both price intervention and overall intervention was favorable to agriculture. However, agriculture was hit in the back, partly by the overvaluation which made total, nominal effects strongly negative, partly through the strong effective protection of industry which made real direct effects less favorable, even negative, and real total effects substantially negative, though less so than nominal total effects.

Comparing total, real effects of overall intervention (in the last column of table 18–4), both Egyptian and Turkish agriculture apparently suffered negative support, Egyptian much more so, however, than Turkish agriculture. Everything considered, including indirect intervention and support to industry, it helps agriculture to have political clout as was the case in Turkey.

In the years under Mubarak in Egypt, 1982–85, and under military government in Turkey, 1981–83, agricultural support policies changed dramatically within and between countries. That agricultural policies should change in Turkey was to be expected; this was partly what the much advertised reforms were about—market orientation was the key term. Egypt's low-key approach, however, apparently concealed a more radical change in agricultural price discrimination. Again, the total, real effects of overall intervention, in the last column of table 18–3, show transfers from Egyptian agriculture going down from 10.6 percent to 2.9 percent of total GDP, with transfers from Turkish agriculture down from a modest 1.1 percent of total GDP to a slight transfer to agriculture of 0.2 percent. The shift in Egypt amounts thus to 7.7 percent of total GDP against only 1.3 percent in Turkey, the relative improvement for Egyptian agriculture by far exceeding that for Turkey.

Political Power and the Price Structure

The weak price position of Egyptian agriculture from the early 1950s to the late 1970s as compared with that of Turkey probably reflects the changes in the political power structure of the two countries over the six decades of their existence as independent nations. The shift from autocracy to parliamentary democracy in Turkey, in time coinciding with the opposite shift and the destruction of the big and middle-sized landowner classes in Egypt, tilted the relative political balance in Turkey in favor of agriculture and in Egypt in favor of urban society. The shifts were reflected in the relative price structures until around 1980 when agricultural price policies were reversed in both countries, in Turkey as part of a profound reform, in Egypt more quietly.

In Egypt in the 1920s big landowners, with support of the palace but apparently not of the British, managed to dominate the parliamentary political process and push through policies aimed at stabilizing and supporting cotton prices through supply restrictions. Within agriculture the possible gains would be biased in favor of large and middle-sized land-owners and in favor of land as compared with labor because cotton was a relatively labor-intensive crop (capital was mainly publicly owned). But agriculture as a whole and hence the rural population as a whole would stand to gain in relation to the urban population. The big land-owners should not be identified exclusively with cotton. Big owner-cultivators would tend to choose a three-year rotation, with cotton grown only every third year, and such owners would have a keen interest in all agricultural prices. The protection of wheat from 1932 was pushed by the big growers. With the government of Sidky Pasha around 1930, the power balance swung in favor of the industrialization forces, partly supported by the cotton growers, who (irrationally) had become interested in the development of the domestic cotton textiles industry as a response to the agricultural crisis. With the tariff reform of 1930 and abrogation of the cotton price-support policies after 1932, price policies on balance favored the nonagricultural urban population and probably favored capital over land and labor.

After the land reforms of 1952 and later and the accompanying destruction of landowner power, and Nasser's emergence as autocrat, agriculture not only was on the defense as during the 1930s but became the exploited underdog. With the big and middle-sized landlords eliminated, agriculture was left without any political clout because Marx's "bag of potatoes," the peasantry, was never given any serious political role under Nasser. For a weak dictator in need of placating the urban population, the temptation was overwhelming and price policies shifted strongly against agriculture. While thus, beyond all dispute, small farmers gained instantaneously from the redistribution of land, over time agriculture as a whole, including small farmers and landless labor, tended to lose from the destruction of the big and middle-sized landowner classes. Their function as a vehicle of technical progress, which had worked well during the interwar period in promoting "green revolution" (chemical fertilizers and new cotton varieties), was not replaced by adequate institutions such as sufficient rural elementary education and efficient extension services, the cooperatives being nothing but another huge bureaucratic machine serving mainly as an employment outlet for incompetent graduates.

Neither Nasser's occasional political rallies nor Sadat's theatrical performances could hide the fact that agriculture had no politically powerful spokesman at the national level after the big landowners were eliminated. Under Mubarak's "exclusionary" policies the process was completed (Springborg 1989). That middle-sized farmers may have dominated in local administration and politics under Nasser and Sadat (Binder 1978; Waterbury 1983; chapter 4, above) as well as under Mubarak (Springborg 1989) does not mean that they had an impact at the national policy level, particularly in relation to pricing. The net impact of agricultural price policies continued largely unchanged under Sadat as initiated under Nasser. It was left to Mubarak, under strong international pressure, to reverse the situation, which was done for supply-side and growth effects rather than to shift distribution in favor of agriculture, although that happened as a by-product.

The crux of the argument here is that the big and middle-sized landowning classes were something more than just "feudal" parasites, as the mythology (official and leftist) termed them. They were also an entrepreneurial class with entrepreneurial functions in the growth process and clout in the political process. In conformity with neoclassical thinking, one could assume that landowners always act rationally to promote their own interests, with the hidden hand serving to make the situation one of Pareto optimality, a model that may be no better or worse than in other contexts. Or the well-known line of Marxist thinking would lead to the assumption that capitalism and capitalists have a "historical mission" in promoting production and that the premature destruction of capitalists and capitalism may do more harm than good to the working classes.

In sum, considering the inability of autocracy in Egypt after 1952 to replace the progressive features of big landownership—technological progress and political promotion of agriculture, with extension services and elementary education for the peasantry—and leaving the peasantry more than ever a political "bag of potatoes," the decline and final destruction of the class of big and middle-sized landowners may have been harmful to agriculture in particular and generally to both growth and distribution in Egypt. When around 1981 internal terms of trade finally moved in favor of agriculture, it was probably pressure from donors and international organizations that caused the change. With the decline in oil prices from 1981–82, Egypt became entirely dependent on international financing. To what extent the shift in policy is lasting remains therefore to be seen.

Long-term structural developments in Turkey have in this regard been almost the opposite of those in Egypt. Large landowners and landless labor never dominated the scene as they did in Egypt before 1952. The futile attempts at land reform in the sense of redistributing land never seriously threatened big landowners and were never pushed by landless labor. The expansion of agricultural production until the end of the 1950s was a frontier phenomenon based on abundance of land, improved transportation, tractorization, and population growth. Elementary education in rural areas and extension services, while far from satisfactory, may have worked better in Turkey than in Egypt. Last but not least, compared with the decades of autocracy in Turkey before 1950, parliamentary democracy gave clout to agriculture and rural population through the popular vote. The competition for the rural vote since the

1950s has been reflected in relatively favorable support price policies for agricultural outputs and subsidization of inputs.

If the estimates of transfers to or from agriculture for Turkey shown in table 18-3 can be trusted, they give rise to interesting political economy problems both for the situation prevailing in 1961–80 and for the policy reversal after 1980 (see Krueger, Schiff, and Valdes 1988). If participants in the policy process were equipped with rational perceptions and expectations, they would presumably ultimately be concerned with and operate on the basis of total, real effects of overall policy interference. For the period 1980–83, military government was the decisionmaker. If it heeded international advice and pressure, it should have pursued an approximately neutral policy toward agriculture, with approximately zero net real transfers. With total, real effects of overall interference down to 0.2 percent of GDP, agriculture came close to being right on target. It is hard to believe that the military government could have been equipped with the rationality and foresight to accomplish that (assuming that table 18-3 represents truth); on the other hand, both the policy of market orientation for agricultural prices and the exchange rate depreciations to reduce overvaluations together should lead in this direction. Considering the debt situation, the international organizations had clout. Before 1980, however, parliamentary government prevailed. If Buchanan-type political exchange theory is applied to the period 1961–80 and agriculture is acknowledged as a participant in the political process, the contrast between positive direct support in nominal terms and negative total support, whether in nominal or real terms, is puzzling. If agriculture were aware of the negative total effects prevailing over two decades, it is difficult to perceive of the political exchange process as converging on an equilibrium. If, on the other hand, agriculture concentrated its attention on the positive direct, nominal effects, it would either appear as being irrational or as having incomplete information. It may appear inconceivable that this state of affairs could last for two decades.

The explanation may be that while agriculture in Turkey was politically powerful enough to influence special policies directly related to and affecting agriculture, it may not have been sufficiently powerful to have much impact on national, aggregative policies (general budgetary and monetary policies, choice of general development strategy, and so forth) or special policies directly related to and affecting other sectors. Moreover, agriculture may have been aware of its own limited policy clout and thus have been perfectly rational in concentrating its political efforts on specific agricultural support policies, assuming that other policies were outside its reach. Agriculture might thus be a "policy taker" insofar as aggregative and nonagricultural specific policies are concerned but one among many "policy setters" (players) insofar as agriculture-specific policies are concerned. Agriculture in developed countries is certainly frequently in this kind of position; the same may be the case in Turkey. Given overvaluation, budget deficit, protection to industry, and the like, agriculture should, rationally, concentrate on direct effects from agricultural price policy, agricultural investment, and the like. This may have been the case in the 1970s and the 1980s. In the 1950s and the 1960s agriculture was the swing vote and was probably very much aware of that.

Real Wage Developments and Unemployment

Scattered information on Egypt indicates that during the interwar period agricultural wages were market determined, with the agricultural labor market clearing but not perfectly competitive. There is no reason to believe that the agricultural labor market in Turkey should have been any different. Next to nothing is known about wages in the urban small-scale private sector in either country. Unions were banned in Turkey, and in Egypt while agreements between unions (in 1951 total membership was 150,000 or 5 percent of the nonagricultural labor force and 25 percent of employment in manufacturing) and enterprises were possible, they were not enforceable in court.

After World War II the situation reversed. In Egypt, compulsory arbitration applied generally from 1952 and the unions were soon effectively transformed into government organizations (as was the most important employer organization, the Federation of Industry). In Turkey unionization was made a constitutional right under military government in 1961. Legislation was passed in parliament in 1963 and unionization rapidly gained importance throughout the 1960s and 1970s, the number of unionized workers increasing to 2.2 million in 1977, or 15 percent of the total labor force, 37 percent of all wage earners, and 46 percent of wage earners legally entitled to unionize (Maksut Mumcuoğlu, in Özbudun and Ulusan 1980, pp. 379, 404). Statutory minimum wages were introduced in the late 1960s. Civil servants were the most important group not entitled to unionize. In 1980 several militant unions were banned by the military government and compulsory arbitration then prevailed to 1985. In Egypt agricultural wages continued to be market determined; statutory minimum wages were not complied with and no attempts were ever made to enforce them.

The real wage developments depicted in figure 16–2 indicate that long-term trends for industry are quite similar in Egypt and Turkey despite the apparently entirely different labor market institutions. In the short term, however, fluctuations around the trend are much stronger in Turkey than in Egypt, apparently reflecting changes in the political-institutional situation much more than changes in the labor market. Real wage developments in agriculture in Egypt bear little resemblance to those of industry.

For Egypt since 1962, perhaps even since 1952, it is safe to assume that wages in manufacturing have been a political price, decreed by the government for public enterprises (which in 1979 accounted for about 60 percent of total manufacturing, measured by employment) and applied to the relatively few large private enterprises through collective agreements between the equally government controlled labor unions and Federation of Industry. As actually decreed by government, increases in money wages tended to compensate for cost-of-living increases, at least until 1981; they bore little relation to labor demand and supply conditions either in the short or the medium term. Neither Phillips relation nor marginal value productivity theory helps to explain industrial wage developments (Hansen 1985, 1986 app. table B). The fact that white-collar workers' salaries have lagged far behind both the cost of living and blue collar workers' wages (Zaitoun 1988, tables 13, 15) could be interpreted as government's acknowledgment of the long-term labor-supply effects of its own educational policies. With a relative increase in educated labor has to go a relative fall in its remuneration, if not directly through market forces then through budgetary considerations. Government compliance with the so-called social compact and political expediency determine overall real wage developments in the public sector.

In Turkey since 1961 (1963) free unions have stood against enterprises—in substantial part, public enterprises (in 1980, about 37 percent of the manufacturing sector, measured by employment). These were, practically speaking, fully unionized. Private enterprises, partly organized in employers' associations, are less unionized than public enterprises, unionization declining with size of enterprise and locality. Guild-like associations of craftsmen and artisans play an unknown role in price and wage setting. In rural areas unionization is largely absent apart from local public enterprises (in mining and steel, for instance; see Roy 1977) and public works. Negotiations and agreements are decentralized and wage formation in public and private enterprises appears to be rather different.

Econometric estimates with questionable specifications (Ataman Aksoy, in Özbudun and Ulusan 1980, pp. 421–29) suggest that in public enterprises, money wage increases have tended to fully compensate for cost-of-living increases, with an autonomous annual increase nearly equal to the average annual increase in labor productivity in 1950–75. Aksoy made no attempt to estimate Phillips relations with the rate of change of wage rates depending on the unemployment rate or some other excess supply indicator. He argues that the necessary data are not available and that in any case unemployment does not affect wages in underdeveloped countries. An attempt to establish Phillips relations for

Turkey (Hansen 1989b) seems to support this view, at least for 1962–85, though in part for other reasons; labor militancy, however, appeared as a powerful explanatory variable. An apparently more successful study, using unemployment rates in a setting of nonaccelerating inflation (OECD *Economic Survey, Turkey,* 1987, annex 1) suffers, unfortunately, from serious data and specification problems.

Altogether, the evidence is not convincing but it would seem that market forces do not significantly influence money wages in Turkish manufacturing; that unionization has increased wages in Turkey, union wages being estimated to be "30 percent higher than comparable non-union wages" (Aksoy, in Özbudun and Ulusan 1980, p. 435); and that union militancy has strongly influenced wage increases. It appears that wages tended to accelerate before military intervention in both 1971 and 1980, after which the military put paid to further wage acceleration.

Although freedom to unionize was introduced under military government in 1961, wages were effectively restrained and real wages declined substantially under the military interference in 1971–73. The relatively strong increase from 1973 to 1977 may partly be seen as a delayed union response after the lifting of martial law but may also reflect the general increase of political militancy after 1973. The collapse of real wages from 1978 through 1980, however, calls for explanation. As a consequence of compulsory arbitration and the banning of strikes and some militant unions from September 1980, employees were not compensated fully for cost-of-living increases in 1980 despite the ongoing hyperinflation, and after 1980 real wages declined very substantially. This, however, does not help to explain the earlier decline in real wages in 1978 and 1979. In connection with the debt crisis of 1978 and under pressure from the OECD and its consortium, the Ecevit government committed itself to an incomes policy; the wage negotiations in 1978 between the state economic enterprises and unions are reported by the OECD (and confirmed privately by Ecevit) to have taken place under a social compact. Despite increased union militancy, the combined impact of the stabilization program and the mounting recession with increasing inflation apparently created a situation in which unions were unable to catch up with inflation and lost the real wage gains from previous years. Nothing like that happened in Egypt, despite the fact that Egypt was under pressure from the IMF and did devalue strongly in 1979. But then, incomes policy is an OECD rather than an IMF specialty and the difference in the two countries' international positions at that time—particularly with regard to the United States Congress after the invasion of Cyprus for Turkey, and after Camp David for Egypt—undoubtedly helps explain Egypt's softer treatment. The Greek and Jewish lobbies in Washington did their job.

That agricultural wages fared much better than wages in manufacturing may have been the result of underlying short- and long-term market forces and only indirectly of government policy. Agricultural real wages in Egypt increased, with substantial fluctuations, from 1948 to 1964, declined steadily to 1974, and then increased strongly to the middle of the 1980s. Over the period 1948–82 agricultural real wages in Egypt increased by 3 percent annually against 2.5 percent in manufacturing (Hansen 1986, p. 5). Nominal agricultural wages appear during the same period to have been closely geared to nominal value added in agriculture, in line with marginal value-productivity theory (figure 4–1 above; Hansen 1986, p. 14). Figures 16–1 and 16–2 relate these developments to national factor proportions, the real wage decline in 1964–74 reflecting the reversal of the capital-labor ratio during this period of open warfare and a low level of gross investment. Explaining agricultural wages by agricultural value added goes hand in hand with the factor proportions approach and brings into the picture both agricultural price policies and migration in and out of agriculture, the latter again related to the wartime slack in domestic civilian construction activities and their surge after 1974 with the strong increase in domestic investment and migration to Arab OPEC countries after 1973.

If market forces do not directly affect wages in the public sector and the organized private sector in either Egypt or Turkey, wage developments do have an impact on the market and may help explain unemployment. With the survey and comparison of unemployment in the two countries and the possible impact of educational and social security policies on unemployment in chapter 17, combined with the survey and comparison of wage policies and developments, it is possible to appraise unemployment in the two countries. Because data on both countries are so unsatisfactory, as is the state of the art of macroeconomics generally, the appraisal is bound to be qualitative and intuitive.

In countries with unrestricted imports, estimates of the competitiveness of tradables production (agriculture, mining, and industry, particularly) should indicate the possibility of wage costs exerting a negative influence on employment, hence tending to create involuntary unemployment. For both countries, measured unemployment increased from the early 1970s to the early 1980s (see figures 1–3 and 11–1 and table 17–18). The estimates in tables 4–22, 4–23, and 12–16 show that competitiveness declined significantly in Egypt (both in industry and in agriculture) in 1974 to 1981–82 and in Turkey (in industry) during the late 1960s and again in 1975–79 after an interval of improved competitiveness in 1970–74.

In Egypt, 1974 to 1981–82 was the heyday of Sadat's *infitah*, with liberalization of own-exchange imports and a strong increase of such imports. The liberalization of own-exchange imports was, however, circumscribed by official lists of commodities for which import licensing continued to apply; moreover, for license-free imports the free exchange rate applied while the estimates of competitiveness in tables 4–22 and 4–23 are based on average, hence lower, exchange rates estimated by the

IMF. It is not clear how much direct competition to domestic production the own-exchange imports really represented. The private shoe industry, for example, continued to be sheltered completely against foreign competition (Springborg 1989). Unemployment created by the own-exchange imports may have been limited and may represent a minor part of the increase in unemployment in these years. For Egypt the policy of guaranteed public employment for graduates and its increased waiting periods, combined with seasonal unemployment outside the agricultural peak season, stands out as the major cause of the increase in unemployment.

In Turkey the early 1970s experienced a brief period of some import liberalization followed, however, by tightened, quantitative import controls after 1974. In Turkey therefore during both the 1960s and the 1970s the changes in competitiveness were more or less compensated for by neutralizing changes in import controls; the impact of excessive wage increases during the years of increased union militancy on unemployment may thus have been only a secondary factor in creating unemployment. The increase of unemployment during the five years before the stabilization program of 1978 may have been caused by the stagnation of migration to Europe in 1973–74 and the general effects of education and urbanization. Why unemployment did not decline significantly after 1980, when there was a strong increase in competitiveness of industry and exports of manufactured products, remains a problem. It may be that education and its ability to create labor market segmentation and accompanying unemployment play a role. The unemployment situation appears to be complex, with significant involuntary and voluntary unemployment existing simultaneously; the U.S. labor force survey model as applied in Turkey unfortunately cannot distinguish clearly between these two forms of unemployment when combined with preferences for rural-urban migration and migration abroad. In rural areas, educated youngsters, unwilling to enter the clearing rural labor markets but unable to obtain employment in the nonclearing urban markets, may remain in the rural labor force, enumerated there as unemployed seeking work. Both unionization and enforcement of minimum wage legislation are unevenly distributed over rural and urban areas and probably also over informal and formal sectors, with labor market clearing highly asymmetric.

Nominal and Real Rates of Interest

Egypt and Turkey have a long history of interest control related to religious doctrine. Islamic doctrine in principle bans all interest on financial capital as usury, and Christian doctrines of *justum pretium* and usury, while less categorically, have tended to require low rates of interest. In Marxist doctrine, interest is exploitation. In modern Egypt and Turkey all doctrines, particularly the Islamic one, spill over into populist opinion and create resistance to high interest rates. Maximum and legal interest rates have traditionally been fixed in law, by decree or by courts. Before 1882 the contractual maximum was 12 percent in Egypt. It was then lowered to 9 percent, with legal rates declining to 5 percent in civil and 7 percent in commercial cases (Hansen 1983). In modern banking, interest rates tended to adjust to international levels within the limits of the law until controls with capital movements entered the picture, in Turkey in the 1930s, in Egypt during World War II. Both in Egypt and in Turkey institutional rates of interest were kept artificially low despite considerable inflation, and real interest rates tended to be negative. Under strong pressure from international organizations during the 1970s, institutional nominal rates in both countries were adjusted upward sufficiently to make real rates positive in Turkey, but probably not in Egypt. Islamic fundamentalists exert pressure to make the two countries adhere to Islamic principles, which may partly be the reason for the smaller increase in Egypt. In both countries, however, developmental and distributional considerations play a role.

Policies of Land Taxation

Until World War II, direct taxation was in both Egypt and Turkey largely limited to agricultural land and urban property (buildings) taxes. In Egypt the land tax remained a significant part of the revenue system until 1952. It gradually lost importance, mainly as a consequence of land reform and inflation without corresponding reassessments. In Turkey the basic land tax (*uşr*) was abolished in 1925 but temporarily reintroduced during World War II. In neither country was the land tax ever effectively replaced by other forms of direct taxation of agriculture except perhaps in Turkey after the reforms of 1980. In both countries direct taxation of agriculture has differed radically from that of the rest of the economy, and social security does not extend to agriculture in either country.

Land taxes in both countries have their roots in antiquity. In Egypt the land tax is in principle levied as a fixed percentage of the assessed rental value of land, nowadays with extensive exemptions. This principle of land taxation was put into effect, in terms of collection, from 1905 under the British occupation. The need for land tax reform had been realized in 1878–79 by the foreign debt commissioners (Lord Cromer, then Evelyn Baring, was the representative for the British bondholders) after the bankruptcy of Ismail. Nothing was done about reform until 1895 when commissions were appointed (under Willcocks as director general) with the instruction "to assess the rental value of all lands in the country, on which fixed rates of tax were being paid, with a view of obtaining a basis for a more equal distribution of the total amount" of taxation (*Egypt*, 1

[1900], p. 11). Cromer emphasized "the very unequal incidence of the land-tax . . . as a blot on the fiscal system of Egypt" and "without being too sanguine as to the possibility of ever attaining theoretical perfection in the incidence of taxation" he found existing "glaring inequalities" "wholly incapable of justification." It is clear that to Cromer the ideal land tax was a fixed, proportional tax based on market rental value. There is no doubt that this is the Ricardian land tax. Cromer might have encountered Ricardo in public school, at the Royal Military Academy, or at the Staff College for officers, but it is more likely that this was one of the lessons of his experience as secretary to the viceroy and as colonial administrator in India in 1872–77 and 1880–83. It is generally recognized (although the leading economic historian, Roger Owen, in his detailed discussion [1968] of this matter does not take up the land tax as an example) that in formulating policy in Egypt, Cromer drew heavily on British experience in India. It is conceivable that James Mill's attempts, first as assistant, later as head examiner of the India Correspondance, to persuade the East India Company to institute the Ricardian land tax in India were known to Cromer.

Mill argued, like all "British political economists who addressed these issues in the first half of the nineteenth century," that for the sake of the empire "the British connection should advance the well-being of the Indian people" and "stimulate growth in the Indian economy" (Barber 1975, p. 143). This then was what required the institution of the Ricardian land tax. "Malthus was the first to link differential rent theory with the Indian problems and to transmit it to India's future 'guardians'. The same insights reached the headquarters of the East India Company via another route. In the formulation of rent theory, Malthus and Ricardo had shared the honours. It was primarily through Ricardo's influence on James Mill that the doctrine was appropriated to build a new official model for economic policy in India" (Barber 1975, p. 155). "India's backwardness, as Malthus saw it, derived primarily from the fact that . . . the traditional practice—in which a proportion of the gross product of the land was transferred to the state—produced major distortions in the economy" (Barber 1975, p. 152). "The stagnation of pre-British India was now persuasively interpretable in economic terms. Though the cultural condition of the people (to which James Mill had attached such importance in his *History*) made a contribution to the total explanation, the main burden fell on the unfortunate distortions in the economic structure which flowed from taxation of gross (rather than net) agricultural product" (Barber 1975, p. 154). Mill argued in public hearing that "what is collected by the *zemindar* from the *ryots* is a full rent; there is reason to apprehend that it is more" (Barber 1975, p. 161). The remedy was obvious: a tax levied on rental value (the net product) at a low fixed rate.[2]

One apparently successful criticism of the Mill policy came from J. R. McCullogh, a Scottish economist of some standing, who argued that the "ryots should have access to land 'at such a reduced rent as they may be able to pay without difficulty'" (Barber 1975, p. 184). This is the distribution argument, but McCullough overlooked the fact that the Ricardian land tax cannot be shifted by the owner to the tenant. Richard Jones (Barber 1975, chap. 12) argued that the competitive market conditions assumed by Ricardian differential rent theory were not at hand in India and that the Ricardian theory for that reason was inapplicable; Jones's own theory of rent was akin to Marx's later theory of absolute rent that permits taxation beyond the (coexisting) differential rent without distortive effects.

How much of this was known to and understood by Cromer is not clear to me. Since, however, for a number of years Mill's policy with its "scientific tax," as he happily called it, was in fact practiced by the East India Company and intensely debated publicly, it would be strange if Cromer had not heard about it and did not know the main arguments for and against.

Cromer was concerned with both equity and growth. He was not aiming at an egalitarian tax policy in Egypt. His concern was equity in the formal sense that a dollar is a dollar is a dollar and should be taxed equally no matter who earns or owns the dollar. Practically, the big equity problem was related to the distinction between 'ushuriya land on which only a tithe ('ushr) was levied and kharajiya land on which a tribute (kharaj) was levied, both apparently assessed at fixed levels with the possibility of exemption (sharaki) in case of low flood. On balance, the tithe was much more lenient than the tribute and since 'ushuriya land largely was in possession of privileged families close to the palace, the tax reform was for Cromer a matter of eradicating economic privilege and not a matter of economic equality. However, those privileged were "persons of wealth and importance" (Cromer 1908, 1, pp. 114–15) and thus probably in the upper income and wealth brackets. Since the Ricardian land tax was in effect a progressive tax on income, Cromer's tax reform of 1905, whatever the intentions were, did promote equity not only in the formal sense but also in the economic sense of shifting income distribution in a more egalitarian direction. It is more doubtful whether the incentive effects of the new tax were better than those of the old taxes, which appear to have been fixed taxes. But the new tax was also a fixed tax, for assessments were to be kept unchanged for thirty years, and to be changed only in case of improvements in the public irrigation system. Fixed taxes should have no incentive effects.

Cromer's land tax reform probably helped to alienate the privileged, large landowners who were the losers and push them into the nationalistic anti-British camp. Cromer is very difficult to fit into Marxian or dependency-theoretical models of imperialism. He belonged to the enlightened elite of the colonial bureaucracy and behaved accordingly.

In Turkey the abolishment of the tithe (*uşr*) in 1925 happened at a time when the negative, distortive effects of a tithe had become, a century after Malthus, conventional wisdom. Being an old tax, it may, in practice, have become a fixed tax with limited distortive but pronounced distributive effects, discriminating against agriculture, the largest and poorest sector of the economy. Considering Atatürk's policy of seeking support from large landowners, it is not surprising that the tithe was abolished very early.

Taxation of land, measured as a percentage of agricultural GDP, developed as follows from 1924–25 to 1982–83:

	1924–25	1937–39	1950–51	1982–83
Egypt	4.0	6.3	4.1	0.7
Turkey	6.5	<1.0	0	0

For Turkey landed property tax revenue is included and so is the livestock tax (Hershlag 1968, tables IV, V). Including a temporary doubling of the land tax in Egypt during the Korean War boom, 1949–52, the incidence of the Egyptian land tax remained, practically speaking, unchanged from 1924–25 to 1950–51, at 4 percent of agricultural GDP (Egypt, Ministry of Finance, *Annuaire statistique de l'Egypte*; data from IMF); taxation of land in Turkey, practically speaking, disappeared during the same period.

To understand the incidence in relation to GDP in agriculture, assessments, tax rates, and agricultural price developments must be taken into account. By law, assessments in Egypt were to be unchanged until the end of the 1930s, and by agreement with the Capitulary Powers, the Egyptian government at the time of the land tax reform in 1905 had committed itself not to lower the land tax revenues below LE 4.2 million until the public debt was repaid. The Capitulations, on the other hand, prevented an increase in land tax on foreign owners. These stipulations effectively locked assessments, tax rate, and nominal revenue until the end of the 1930s. Despite parliamentary democracy from 1923, with landowners playing an important role, nothing could be done about the tax. In 1897 the incidence of the land tax was about 13 percent of agricultural GDP. Inflation reduced the incidence to about 4 percent in 1924 but with the deflation of the Great Depression, the incidence went above 6 percent in 1937–39. By law of 1939 the tax rate was reduced from 26 percent to 14 percent. Wartime inflation, despite reassessment in 1949, would have brought the incidence down to about 2 percent had it not been for a temporary doubling by law of 1951 for the years 1949–52 undertaken because of price increases related to the Korean

War boom. The land reforms of 1952 then reversed the relation between rental and tax by fixing rentals at seven times the tax assessments of 1949. Legal rentals and actual tax remained at this level (with exemptions for smallholders) until the mid-1970s when a slight increase took place. Even so, the incidence of the land tax was down to 0.7 percent in 1982–83. Considering the combination of agricultural price policies and rent control, what happened during the 1960s and 1970s was in effect the replacement of Cromer's enlightened Ricardian land tax by an unintelligent "tithe." Egypt would have benefited from combining the agricultural price adjustments under Mubarak with a strong revival of the land tax (Hansen and Radwan 1982, pp. 224–25).

For Turkey the abolishment of the *uşr* sent down the incidence of the remaining land property and livestock taxes to less than 1 percent from 6.5 percent in 1924–25 and although the Great Depression somewhat increased the incidence during the 1930s, World War II inflation reduced the incidence to almost nothing in 1950–51. Agriculture being the swing vote in 1950, land tax was no longer on the agenda, a point that Nicholas Kaldor did not understand when in 1962, as a consultant, he made suggestions that the Ricardian land tax be applied to Turkey (1980).

Development Financing

Development financing is part of the general development strategy but has little direct relationship to the issue of inward- and outward-looking strategy. Financing is more a matter of time perspective. This is an area where ex antes and ex posts differ wildly, where there is, of course, only one ex post although it may be difficult to pinpoint because of data deficiencies and complexities, not to speak of defaults and rescheduling. Unfortunately, there are many layers of ex ante, not only because sincerity and honesty of governments may leave something to be desired but also because the ex ante may be used, internally and externally, as a device for political and financial negotiations. For all these reasons, I abstain from comparing plans and outcome. Another reason for not doing so is that comprehensive five-year planning was not adopted by Egypt until 1960–61 to 1964–65 and Turkey until 1963–67 and such planning was suspended temporarily by both countries when they encountered serious financial difficulties, Egypt in 1965–66 to 1975 and Turkey in 1978–79. Hence the comparison in table 18–5 is limited to annual averages of national net borrowing—planning or no planning.

Egypt has relied much more on foreign financing than Turkey— measured on GNP, no less than three times more. While Turkish borrowing has by no means been negligible, Egypt's has by all standards been very large. In Egypt the national net debt in 1984 had reached a size almost equal to that of GNP against 40 percent of GNP in Turkey.

Table 18-5. National Net Borrowing, by Domestic Sector, Current Account, and Capital Account, 1960–84

(percent of GNP)

Borrowing category	Egypt, 1960–61 to 1983–84	Turkey, 1962–84
Domestic sectors	7.3	2.5
Public	13.7	8.9
From central bank	6.1[a]	4.1[a]
Private	−6.4	−6.4
Current account		
Goods and services deficit	9.1[b]	4.0
Factor payments abroad, net	−1.8[b]	−1.9
Interest and dividends	2.7[b]	0.3
Migrant workers' remittances	−4.5	−2.2
Capital account		
Official assistance	5.9	2.3
Other capital inflows, net	1.4	0.2

Averages.

a. Conjecture.

b. For 1965–66 to 1981–82.

Source: Tables 4–24, 4–28, 11–5, 11–8; OECD, *Development Cooperation*, 1987.

In both countries the private sector has been a net lender, by 6.4 percent of GNP; in other words, private saving has exceeded private investment to that extent. Since private savers and investors to some extent are different persons or companies, it is, of course, fortuitous that private net lending in the two countries has been exactly the same size. There is nothing in the macro policies pursued that should lead to this result and since private saving is derived as a statistical residual, there is little to say about it beyond stating the fact. The relatively larger national net borrowing in Egypt is thus located in the public sector, to some extent probably a natural consequence of that country's relatively larger public sector but probably also indicating a more frivolous budgetary policy than in Turkey, compounded by relatively larger central bank financing in Egypt.

In the current account, the goods and services deficit accounts for, practically speaking, the entire difference between national net borrowing in the two countries. Much larger workers' remittances in Egypt than in Turkey have been swallowed up by much larger interest and dividend payments, net, which is natural for a country with a relatively larger debt.

It is difficult to break down national net borrowing by official assistance and other net capital inflow. Official assistance for Turkey has been computed as the sum of project and program credits plus the Turkish lira value of grain imports and grants (under the U.S. Public Law 480 program), with no deductions for repayment of such loans. For Egypt the information seems also to pertain to gross assistance until 1975, after which the net inflow of official development assistance (ODA) has been used. Other capital inflow net, obtained as a residual for both countries, thus does take into account some repayment of official assistance, the net of which must have been smaller for both countries than what appears from table 18–4. For the years 1974–84 comparable OECD data on average official development assistance measured by GDP show for Egypt 8.7 percent against only 1.5 percent for Turkey. The current account deficits for the same period amounted to 10.9 percent and 3.8 percent, respectively, indicating relatively much larger official assistance to Egypt than to Turkey since 1974.

These results may look surprising, considering the way Egypt repeatedly has been penalized in her international zigzagging. However, there has always been an "other side" for Egypt that has been prepared to pick up the tag. Egypt's client games with the United States, the Soviet Union, and the Arab OPEC countries, played by Nasser, Sadat, and Mubarak, have apparently paid off in terms of official assistance. Turkey's systematically Western-oriented policies, the country once (in the Cyprus invasion) having been penalized for her foreign policy with nobody to pick up the tab, have on balance given less return in this form. Until 1977 about half the official assistance to Egypt came from Arab OPEC countries and funds and 18 percent from communist countries (not including military aid). Since World War II Turkey has received almost nothing from these sources. In 1960–84 Egypt and Turkey received about the same official assistance from the West in relative terms.

Notes

1. Both countries, responding to political pressure from special-interest groups, also adopted an export-promotion strategy for agriculture. Turkey never gave up the policy but Egypt replaced hers with import substitution and a so-called basic-need strategy in the 1970s.

2. Marshall's neoclassical criticism of "Ricardo Doctrine as to Taxes and Improvements in Agriculture" (1938, app. L) assumes a closed economy which then requires analysis of the demand for agricultural products, something Ricardo did not venture on. In the present context it is appropriate to assume an open economy with commodity prices given from abroad. Marshall's objections to the Ricardian doctrine are then irrelevant.

Bibliography

The word "processed" describes informally produced works that may not be commonly available through libraries.

Abdel-Fadil, Mahmoud. 1975. *Development, Income Distribution, and Social Change in Rural Egypt.* Cambridge, U.K.: Cambridge University Press.

Abdel-Khalek, Gouda, and Robert Tignor, eds. 1982. *The Political Economy of Income Distribution in Egypt.* New York: Holmes and Meier Publishers.

Adbel-Malek, A. 1968. *Egypt: Military Society.* New York: Random House.

Abdel-Rahman, S. H. 1959. *A Survey of Foreign Trade of Egypt in the Post-war Period.* Ph.D. diss., Cairo University, Faculty of Commerce.

Abdel Wahab, Ahmed. 1930. *Memorandum on the bases of a stable cotton policy.* Submitted to the Minister of Finance. Cairo: Government Press.

Adams, Richard H., Jr. 1985. "Development and Structural Change in Rural Egypt, 1952–1982." *World Development* 13 (6): 705–23.

_____. 1986. *Development and Social Change in Egypt.* Syracuse, N.Y.: Syracuse University Press.

_____. 1988. "Worker Remittances and Inequality in Rural Egypt." Washington, D.C.: International Food Policy Research Institute.

Alderman, Harold, and Joachim von Braun. 1984. *The Effects of the Egyptian Food Ration and Subsidy System on Income Distribution and Consumption.* Washington, D.C.: International Food Policy Research Institute.

Al-Sayed-Marsot, A. L. 1977. *Egypt's Liberal Experiment: 1922–1936.* Berkeley: University of California Press.

Anis, M. Amin. 1950. "A Study of National Income of Egypt." *l'Egypte Contemporaine* (Cairo) 261–62: 659–926.

Arrow, Kenneth J. 1963. *Social Choice and Individual Values.* 2nd ed. New York: John Wiley and Sons.

Baer, Gabriel. 1962. *A History of Landownership in Modern Egypt, 1850–1950.* London: Oxford University Press.

Barber, William J. 1975. *British Economic Thought and India, 1600–1858.* Oxford: Clarendon Press.

Behrman, Jerre R. 1976. *Foreign Trade Regimes and Economic Development: Chile.* New York: Columbia University Press for National Bureau of Economic Research.

Berger, Morroe. 1957. *Bureaucracy and Society in Modern Egypt.* Princeton, N.J.: Princeton University Press.

Bhagwati, J., and R. A. Brecher. 1980. "National Welfare in an Open Economy in the Presence of Foreign Owned Factors of Production." *Journal of International Economics* 10 (1): 103–16.

Bhagwati, J., and T. N. Srinivasan. 1975. *Foreign Trade Regimes and Economic Development: India.* New York: Columbia University Press for National Bureau of Economic Research.

Binder, Leonard. 1978. *In a Moment of Enthusiasm.* Chicago: University of Chicago Press.

Birand, Mehmet Ali. 1987. *The Generals' Coup in Turkey: The Inside Story of Twelve September 1980.* London: Brassey's Defence Publishers.

Birge, J. K. 1944. "Turkey Between Two World Wars." *Foreign Policy Reports.* New York: Foreign Policy Association.

Birnberg, T. B., and S. A. Resnick. 1975. *Colonial Development: An Econometric Study.* New Haven: Yale University Press.

Boratav, Korkut. 1966. "Türkiye'de Kisisel Gelir Dağılımı ve Planlama Teş'kilatının Araştırması." *Journal of the Faculty of Political Sciences* (Ankara) 20.

von Braun, Joachim, and Hartwig de Haen. 1983. *The Effects of Food Prices and Subsidy Policies on Egyptian Agriculture.* Washington, D.C.: International Food Policy Research Institute.

Bresciani-Turroni, E. 1930. "Relations entre la récolte et la prix du coton égyptien." *l'Egypte Contemporaine* (Cairo) 21 (124): 633–89.

Brinton, Jasper Y. 1968. *The Mixed Courts of Egypt.* Rev. ed. New Haven: Yale University Press.

Brown, C. H. 1955. *Egyptian Cotton.* London: Leonard Hill Books.

Buchanan, James N. 1987. "The Constitution of Economic Policy." *American Economic Review* 77(3): 243–50.

Bulutay, Tuncer, Yahya S. Tezel, and Nuri, Yıldırım. 1974. *Türkiye Milli Geliri, 1923–1948.* Ankara: University of Ankara Publications.

Bulutay, Tuncer, Serim Timur, and Hasan Ersel. 1971. *Türkiye'de Gelir Dağımılı.* Ankara: University of Ankara Publications.

Butzer, Karl W. 1976. *Early Hydraulic Civilization in Egypt: A Study in Cultural Ecology.* Chicago: University of Chicago Press.

Celasun, Merih. 1983. *Sources of Industrial Growth and Structural Change: The Case of Turkey.* World Bank Staff Working Paper 614. Washington, D.C.

———. 1986. "Income Distribution and Domestic Terms of Trade in Turkey, 1978–1983." *METU Studies in Development.* (Ankara) 13(1–2): 193–216.

Chen, John-ren. 1970. *Der Weltbaumwollmarkt.* Berlin: Duncker and Humbolt.

Chenery, Hollis, Sherman Robinson, and Moshe Syrquin. 1986. *Industrialization and Growth: A Comparative Study.* New York: Oxford University Press.

Chenery, Hollis, and Moshe Syrquin. 1975. *Patterns of Development, 1950–1970.* New York: Oxford University Press.

von Clausewitz, K. 1976. *On War.* Princeton, N.J.: Princeton University Press.

Cleland, Wendell. 1936. *The Population Problem in Egypt.* Lancaster, Penn.

Coe, David T. 1985. "Nominal Wages, the NAIRU and Wage Flexibility." *OECD Economic Studies* 5: 87–126.

Collier, Paul, and Deepak Lal. 1986. *Labour and Poverty in Kenya, 1900–1980.* Oxford: Clarendon Press.

Commander, S., and A. A. Hadhoud. 1986. *Employment, the Labour Market, and the Choice of Technology in Egyptian Agriculture.* Cairo: Ford Foundation, and London: Overseas Development Administration.

Cromer, Earl of. 1908. *Modern Egypt.* 2 vols. London: Macmillan and Co.

Crouchley, A. E. 1936. *The Investment of Foreign Capital in Egyptian Companies and Public Debt.* Cairo: Ministry of Finance.

———. 1938. *The Economic Development of Modern Egypt.* London: Longman Green and Co.

Cuddihy, William. 1980. *Agricultural Price Management in Egypt.* World Bank Staff Working Paper 388. Washington, D.C.

Denison, Edward F., and William K. Chung. 1976. *How Japan's Economy Grew So Fast.* Washington, D.C.: Brookings Institution.

Derviş, Kemal, Jaime de Melo, and Sherman Robinson. 1981. *General Equilibrium Models for Development Policy.* Cambridge: Cambridge University Press.

Derviş, Kemal, and Sherman Robinson. 1982. "A General Equilibrium Analysis of the Causes of a Foreign Exchange Crisis: The Case of Turkey." *Weltwirtschaftliches Archiv* 118: 259–79.

Dethier, Jean-Jacques. 1989. *Trade, Exchange Rate, and Agricultural Pricing Policies in Egypt.* 2 vols. World Bank Country Study. Washington, D.C.

Dixit, Avinash and Victor Norman. 1980. *Theory of International Trade. A Dual, General Equilibrium Approach.* Cambridge: Cambridge University Press.

Economic Surveys, Turkey, OECD, Paris.

Egypt, CAPMAS. 1987. *Population, Housing, and Establishment Census 1986. Preliminary Results.* Cairo.

———. *Manpower Survey by Sample in Egypt.* Various years. Cairo.

———. *Statistical Yearbook.* Various years. Cairo.

Egypt, Information Department. 1962. *The Charter, 21 May 1962.* Cairo.

Egypt, Ministry of Finance. *Annuaire statistique de l'Egypte.* Various years. Cairo.

Egypt, Ministry of Planning and International Cooperation. 1987. *Egypt's Second Five-Year Plan for Socio-Economic Development (1987/88–1991/92) With Plan for Year One (1987/88).* Vol. 1: *Primary Components.* Translated by Ronald G. Wolfe. Cairo: Professional Business Services.

Egypt, National Bank of Egypt. 1948. *National Bank of Egypt, 1898–1948.* Cairo.

Eldem, Vedat. 1970. *Osmanlı imparatorluğunun iktisadi Şartları Hakkında Bir Tetkik.* Istanbul: İş Bankası Yayınları.

El Imam, M. A. 1962. "A Production Function for Egyptian Agriculture, 1913–1955." Memo 259. Cairo: INP.

FAO (Food and Agriculture Organisation). *Food Balance Sheet.* Various years. Rome.

————. *Production Yearbook.* Various years. Rome.

Fisher, Irving. 1927. *The Making of Index Numbers.* 3rd ed. Boston: Houghton Mifflin.

Forte, David F. 1978. "Egyptian Land Law: An Evaluation." *American Journal of Comparative Law* 26: 273–78.

Friedman, Milton. 1968. "The Role of Monetary Policy." *American Economic Review* 58(1): 1–17.

Friedman, Milton, and Anna J. Schwartz. 1982. *Monetary Trends in the United States and the United Kingdom—Their Relation to Income, Prices, and Interest Rates, 1867–1975.* Chicago: University of Chicago Press for National Bureau of Economic Research.

Fry, Maxwell. 1972. *Finance and Development Planning in Turkey.* Leiden: E. J. Brill.

Gaathon, A. L. 1971. *Economic Productivity in Israel.* New York: Praeger.

Gaitskell, Arthur. 1959. *Gezira: A Story of Development in the Sudan.* London: Faber and Faber.

Gardner, George R., and John B. Parker. 1985. *Agricultural Statistics of Egypt, 1970–84.* Statistical Bulletin 732. Washington, D.C.: U.S. Department of Agriculture.

Goldberg, Ellis. 1986. *Tinker, Taylor, and Textile Worker: Class and Politics in Egypt, 1930–1952.* Berkeley: University of California Press.

Hale, William M. 1981. *The Political and Economic Development of Modern Turkey.* New York: Croom Helm.

Handoussa, Heba. 1988a. "The Impact of Foreign Aid on Egypt's Economic Development: 1952–1986." Paper presented to Conference on Aid, Capital Flows, and Development, September 13-14, 1987. Sponsored by the World Bank and the International Center for Economic Growth, Talloires, France.

————. 1988b. *Reform Policies for Egypt's Manufacturing Industry.* Cairo: sponsored by International Labour Organisation.

Hansen, Bent. 1967. *Long- and Short-Term Planning in Underdeveloped Countries.* Amsterdam: North-Holland.

————. 1969. "Employment and Wages in Rural Egypt." *American Economic Review* 59(1): 298–313.

————. 1975. "The Demand for American and Egyptian Cotton, 1889–1913, and 1920–38." Working Paper 35. University of California at Berkeley, Department of Economics.

————. 1979. "Income and Consumption in Egypt, 1886–87 to 1937." *International Journal of Middle East Studies* 10: 27–47.

————. 1981. "Trade Position, Domestic and International Prices: Wheat in Egypt, 1884–1913." Working Paper 154. University of California at Berkeley, Department of Economics.

————. 1983. "Interest Rates and Foreign Capital in Egypt under British Occupation." *Journal of Economic History* 63 (4): 867–84.

———. 1985. "The Egyptian Labor Market: An Overview." DRD Discussion Paper 160. Washington, D.C.: World Bank, Development and Research Department.

———. 1986. "A Full Employment Economy and Its Responses to External Shocks: The Labor Market in Egypt from World War II." DRD Discussion Paper 253. Washington, D.C.: World Bank, Development Research Department.

———. 1989a. "Factor Prices in Egypt from 1900 to World War II with International Comparisons." Working Paper 89–113. University of California at Berkeley, Department of Economics.

———. 1989b. "Unemployment, Migration, and Wages in Turkey, 1962–1985." PPR Working Paper 230. Washington, D.C.: World Bank, Policy, Planning, and Research Department.

Hansen, Bent, with C. Kerr and A.S. Becker. 1970. *The Economics and Politics of the Middle East*. New York: Elsevier.

Hansen, Bent, and Edward F. Lucas. 1978. "Egyptian Foreign Trade, 1885–1961: A New Set of Trade Indices." *Journal of European Economic History* 7 (2–3): 429–60.

Hansen, Bent, and G. A. Marzouk. 1965. *Development and Economic Policy in the U.A.R. (Egypt)*. Amsterdam: North-Holland.

Hansen, Bent, and Donald Mead. 1963. "The National Income of the UAR (Egypt), 1939–1962." Cairo: Memo 355. Cairo: INP.

Hansen, Bent, and Karim Nashashibi. 1975. *Foreign Trade Regimes and Economic Development: Egypt*. New York: Columbia University Press for National Bureau of Economic Research.

Hansen, Bent, and Samir Radwan. 1982. *Employment Opportunities and Equity in a Changing Economy: Egypt in the 1980s*. Geneva: International Labour Organisation.

Hansen, Bent, and Khairy Tourk. 1976. "The Profitability of the Suez Canal as a Private Enterprise, 1859–1956." *Journal of Economic History* 38 (4): 938–58.

Harris, George S. 1985. *Turkey: Coping with Crisis*. Boulder, Colo.: Westview Press.

Hershlag, Z. Y. 1968. *Turkey: The Challenge of Growth*. Leiden: E. J. Brill.

Hicks, J.R. 1979. *Causality in Economics*. Oxford: Basil Blackwell.

Hirsch, Eva. 1970. *Poverty and Plenty on the Turkish Farm: A Study of Income Distribution in Turkish Agriculture*. New York: Columbia University Press.

Hirsch, Eva, and Abraham Hirsch. 1963. "Changes in Agricultural Output per Capita of Rural Population in Turkey." *Economic Development and Cultural Change* 11 (4): 372–94.

———. 1966. "Tax Reform and the Burden of Direct Taxation in Turkey." *Public Finance* 21 (3): 337–63.

Hoffmann, Walter G. 1965. *Das Wachstum des deutschen Wirtschaft seit der Mitte der 19. Jahrhundert*. Berlin, Heidelberg, and New York: Springer-Verlag.

Ikram, Khalid. 1980. *Egypt: Economic Management in a Period of Transition*. Baltimore: Johns Hopkins University Press.

ILO (International Labour Organisation). 1985. *The Cost of Social Security.* Various years. Geneva.

———. *Yearbook of Labour Statistics.* Various years. Geneva.

IMF (International Monetary Fund). *Balance of Payments Yearbook.* Various issues. Washington, D.C.

———. *Government Finance Statistics Yearbook.* Various years. Washington, D.C.

———. *International Financial Statistics.* Various issues. Washington, D.C.

Inman, Robert. 1987. "Markets, Government, and the 'New' Political Economy." In A. J. Auerbach and M. Feldstein, eds. *Handbook of Public Economics.* Amsterdam: North-Holland.

Issawi, Charles. 1961. "Egypt since 1800: A Study in Lopsided Development." *Journal of Economic History* 21: 1–25.

———. 1980. *The Economic History of Turkey, 1800–1914.* Chicago: University of Chicago Press.

Kaldor, Nicholas. 1980. *Reports on Taxation.* London: Duckworth.

Keynes, J. M. 1930. *A Treatise on Money.* 2 vols. London: Macmillan.

Kopits, George. 1987. *Structural Reform, Stabilization, and Growth in Turkey.* Washington, D.C.: International Monetary Fund.

Korayem, Karima. 1982. Estimation of the Disposable Income Distribution in the Urban and Rural Sectors of Egypt", in *Cairo Papers in Social Science.* Vol. 5. Cairo: American University.

——— 1987. *The Impact of Economic Adjustment Policies on the Vulnerable Families and Children in Egypt,* Report for Third World Forum and UNICEF, Cairo.

Krueger, Anne O. 1974a. "The Political Economy of the Rent-seeking Society." *American Economic Review* 64 (3): 291–303.

———. 1974b. *Foreign Trade Regimes and Economic Development: Turkey.* New York: Columbia University Press for National Bureau of Economic Research.

———. 1977. *Growth, Distortions, and the Patterns of Trade among Many Countries.* Princeton Studies of International Finance. Princeton, N.J.

———. 1987. "The Importance of Economic Policy in Development: Contrasts Between Korea and Turkey." Working Paper 2195. Cambridge, Mass.: National Bureau of Economic Research.

Krueger, Anne O., Maurice Schiff, and Alberto Valdés. 1988. "Agricultural Incentives in Developing Countries: Measuring the Effect of Sectoral and Economywide Policies." *World Bank Economic Review* 2 (September): 255–71.

Krueger, Anne O., and Baran Tuncer. 1980. "Estimating Total Factor Productivity Growth in a Developing Economy." World Bank Staff Working Paper 422. Washington, D.C.

Krugman, Paul R. 1990. *Rethinking International Trade.* Cambridge, Mass.: MIT Press.

Lal, Deepak. 1987. "After the Debt Crisis: Modes of Development for the Long Run in Latin America." Processed.

Landau, Jacob M., ed. 1984. *Atatürk and the Modernization of Turkey.* Boulder, Colo.: Westview Press.

Landes, D. S. 1969. *Bankers and Pashas*. New York: Harper and Row.

Leamer, Edward E. 1984. *Sources of International Comparative Advantage*. Cambridge, Mass.: MIT Press.

————. 1987. "Paths of Development in the Three-factor, n-Good General Equilibrium Model." *Journal of Political Economy* 95 (5) 961–99.

Leibenstein, H. 1957. *Economic Backwardness and Economic Growth: Studies in the Theory of Economic Development*. New York: Wiley.

Leith, J. Clark. 1975. *Foreign Trade Regimes and Economic Development: Ghana*. New York: Columbia University Press for National Bureau of Economic Research.

Lindbeck, Assar. 1976. "Stabilization in Open Economies with Endogenous Politicians." *American Economic Review* 66 (2): 1–19.

Mabro, Robert, and Samir Radwan. 1976. *The Industrialization of Egypt, 1939–1973*. Oxford: Clarendon Press.

McCarthy, Justin. 1983. *Muslims and Minorities in the Population of Ottoman Anatolia at the End of the Empire*. New York: New York University Press.

Maddison, Angus. 1985. *Two Crises: Latin America and Asia, 1929–38 and 1973–83*. Paris: Organisation for Economic Co-operation and Development.

Mardin, Şerif. 1978. "Youth and Violence in Turkey." *Archives européenes de sociologie* 19 (2): 229–54.

Marshall, Alfred. 1938. *Principles of Economics*. 8th ed. London: Macmillan.

Martin, Germain, and I. G. Levi. 1910. "Le marché egyptien et l'utilité de la publication des mercuriales." *l'Egypte Contemporaine* (Cairo) 1 (January).

Mead, Donald C. 1967. *Growth and Structural Change in the Egyptian Economy*. Homewood, Ill.: Richard D. Irwin.

————. 1982. "Small Industries in Egypt: An Exploration of the Economies of Small Furniture Producers." *International Journal of Middle East Studies* 14: 159–71.

Metha, S. D. 1953. *The Indian Cotton Textiles Industry: An Economic Analysis*. Bombay.

Michaely, Michael. 1975. *Foreign Trade Regimes and Economic Development: Israel*. New York: Columbia University Press for National Bureau of Economic Research.

Milner, Alfred. 1907. *England in Egypt*. London: Edward Arnold.

Mitchell, B. R. 1974. *European Historical Statistics*. New York: Columbia University Press.

Moheieldin, Amer. 1979. "The Role of the Construction Sector in the Egyptian Economy." Cairo University and M.I.T., Technological Adaptation Program. Processed.

Morris, D. Morris. 1983. "The Growth of Large Scale Industry to 1947." In D. Kumar and M. Desai, eds. *The Cambridge Economic History of India*. Cambridge, U.K. Cambridge University Press.

Mundell, Robert A. 1963. "Capital Mobility and Stabilization Policy under Fixed and Flexible Exchange Rates." *Canadian Journal of Economics and Political Science* 29 (4): 475–85.

Nour El Din, S. S. 1959. *A Statistical Analysis of Some Aspects of Cotton Production and Marketing with Special Reference to USA and Egypt.* Ph.D. diss. London: London University.

Nutting, Anthony. 1972. *Nasser.* London: Constable.

O'Brien, Patrick. 1966. *The Revolution in Egypt's Economic System.* London: Oxford University Press.

Odekon, Mehmet. 1977. "The Impact of Education on the Size Distribution of Earnings in Turkey." Ph.D. diss., State University of New York at Albany.

OECD (Organisation for Economic Cooperation and Development). *Development Cooperation.* Various years. Paris.

_____. *Economic Surveys, Turkey.* Various years. Paris.

OEEC (Organisation for European Economic Co-operation). 1957. *Statistical Summary of Agricultural Production and Food Consumption in the OEEC Countries,* Paris.

Ökçün, Gündüz. 1970. *Osmanlı Sanayii, 1913. 1915 Yılları Sanayi İstatistiki.* Ankara: University of Ankara Publications.

Owen, Roger, E.R.G. 1969. *Cotton and the Egyptian Economy, 1820–1914.* London: Oxford University Press.

_____. 1968. "The Influence of Lord Cromer's Indian Experience on British Policy in Egypt, 1883–1907." *St. Antony's Papers* (Oxford) 17: 109–39.

_____. 1981. "The Development of Agricultural Production in Nineteenth Century Egypt." In A.L. Udovitch, ed. *The Islamic Middle East, 700–1900, Studies in Economic and Social History.* Princeton, N.J.: The Darwin Press, Inc.

Özbudun, Ergun, and Aydin Ulusan, eds. 1980.*The Political Economy of Income Distribution in Turkey.* New York: Holmes and Meier Publishers.

Özmucur, Süleyman. 1985–86. "Gelirin Fonksiyonal Dağılımı, 1963–84." Ankara. Processed.

Pacific Consultants. 1980. *New Lands Productivity in Egypt: Technical and Economic Feasibility,* Washington, D.C.

Paine, Suzanne. 1974. *Exporting Workers–The Turkish Case.* Department of Applied Economics, Occasional Papers 41, London: Cambridge University Press.

Paldam, M., and S. Jorgensen. 1986. "The Real Exchange Rates of Eight Latin American Countries, 1946–1985." Washington, D.C.: World Bank. Processed.

Pamuk, Şevket. 1986. "Income Distribution in Turkey, 1963–1985." Processed.

_____. 1987. *The Ottoman Empire and European Capitalism, 1820–1913: Trade, Investment and Production.* Cambridge, U.K.: Cambridge University Press.

Radwan, Samir. 1973. *Capital Formation in Egyptian Industry and Agriculture, 1882–1967.* Ph.D. diss., University of London.

Radwan, Samir, and E. Lee. 1986. *Agrarian Change in Egypt: An Anatomy of Rural Poverty.* London: Croom Helm.

Ricci, Umberto. 1932. "Die Nachfrage nach Ägyptischer Baumwolle und ihre Elastizität." *Weltwirtschaftliches Archiv* 35 (1): 250–61.

Richards, Alan. 1982. *Egypt's Agricultural Development, 1800–1980: Technical and Social Change.* Boulder, Colo.: Westview Press.

Richards, Alan, and P. L. Martin, eds. 1983. *Migration, Mechanization and Agricultural Labor Markets in Egypt.* Boulder, Colo.: Westview Press.

Rivlin, Paul. 1985. *Dynamics of Economic Policy Making in Egypt.* New York: Praeger.

Rostovtzeff, Michael. 1922. *A Large Estate in Egypt in the Third Century B.C.* University of Wisconsin Studies 23: Social Sciences and History 6. Madison, Wisc.

Roy, Delwin A. 1977. "Labor and Trade Unionism in Turkey: The Ereğli Coalmines." In E. Kedourie, ed., *The Middle Eastern Economy, Studies in Economics and Economic History.* London: Cass & Co.

――――. 1980. "The Egyptian Economy: Conversation on Social Contract, Economic Development, and Policy Alternatives." Processed.

Saab, Gabriel, 1967, *The Egyptian Agrarian Reform, 1952–1962.* London: Oxford University Press.

Said, Abdel Moghny. 1972. *Arab Socialism.* New York: Harper and Row.

Salacuse, Jeswald W. 1980. "Back to Contract: Implications of Peace and Openness for Egypt's Legal System." *American Journal of Comparative Law* 28: 315–33.

Salop, S. C. 1979. "A Model of the Natural Rate of Unemployment." *American Economic Review* 69 (1): 117–25.

Samuelson, P. A. 1959. "A Modern Treatment of the Ricardian Economy: I. The Pricing of Goods and of Labor and Land Services. Appendix, Theory of Differential Rent." *Quarterly Journal of Economics* 73 (2): 1–35.

Schultz, T. W. 1964. *Transforming Traditional Agriculture.* New Haven: Yale University Press.

Şenses, Fikret. 1984. "An Assessment of Turkey's Liberalization Attempts since 1980 against the Background of Its Stabilization Program." *METU Studies in Development* (Ankara) 10 (3): 271–321.

Springborg, Robert, 1975. "Patterns of Association in the Egyptian Political Elite." In George Lenczowski, ed. *Political Elites in the Middle East.* Washington, D.C.: American Enterprise Institute.

――――. 1979. "Patrimonialism and Policy Making in Egypt: Nasser, and Sadat, and Tenure Policy for Reclaimed Land", *Middle Eastern Studies* (January): 49–67.

――――. 1982. *Family, Power, and Politics in Egypt.* Philadelphia: University of Pennsylvania Press.

――――. 1989a. *Mubarak's Egypt: Fragmentation of the Political Order.* Boulder, Colo., and London: Westview Press.

――――. 1989b. "Rolling Back Agrarian Reforms in Egypt." Working Paper. North Ryde, New South Wales: Macquarie University.

Stone, I.F., 1989. *The Trial of Socrates.* New York: Doubleday.

Tezel, Yahya S. 1975. "Turkish Economic Development, 1923–50: Policy and Achievements." Ph.D. diss., Cambridge University.

Tignor, Robert L. 1966. *Modernization and British Colonial Rule in Egypt, 1892–1914.* Princeton, N.J.: Princeton University Press.

————. 1984. *State, Private Enterprise and Economic Change in Egypt, 1918–1952.* Princeton, N.J.: Princeton University Press.

Todd, John A. 1934. *The Marketing of Cotton.* London: Sir Isaac Pitman and Sons.

Turkey, SIS (State Institute of Statistics). 1980. *Report, 1980 Agricultural Census.* Ankara.

————. 1988. *Household Labour Force Survey Results 1985.* Ankara.

————. *Statistical Yearbook of Turkey.* Various years. Ankara.

Udovitch, A. L., ed. 1981. *The Islamic Middle East, 700–1900: Studies in Economic and Social History.* Princeton, N.J.: Darwin Press.

UNESCO (United Nations Educational, Scientific, and Cultural Organisation). *Statistical Yearbook.* Various years. Paris.

UNIDO. 1972. *Guidelines for Project Evaluation.* New York.

United Nations. *Demographic Yearbook.* Various years. New York.

United States, Bureau of the Census. 1975. *Historical Statistics of the United States, Colonial Times to 1970.* 2 parts. Washington, D.C.

Vatikiotis, P. J. 1961. *The Egyptian Army in Politics.* Bloomington: Indiana University Press.

————. 1969. *The Modern History of Egypt.* London: Weidenfeld and Nicolson.

Vatikiotis, P. J., ed. 1968. *Egypt since the Revolution.* London: George Allen and Unwin.

Ward, R. E., and D. A. Rustow, eds. 1964. *Political Modernization in Japan and Turkey.* Princeton, N.J.: Princeton University Press.

Waterbury, John. 1977. "An Attempt to Put Patrons and Clients in Place." In E. Gellner and J. Waterbury, eds., *Patrons and Clients in Mediterranean Societies.* London: Duckworth.

————. 1983. *The Egypt of Nasser and Sadat: The Political Economy of Two Regimes.* Princeton, N.J.: Princeton University Press.

Wattleworth, Michael. 1975. "Report on the Construction of Agricultural Indexes for Egypt, 1887–1968." Institute of International Studies, University of California at Berkeley. Processed.

Willcocks, W. 1899. *Egyptian Irrigation.* 2nd ed. London: E. and F. N. Spon.

————. 1935. *Sixty Years in the East.* London: W. Blackwood and Sons.

Willcocks, W., and J. I. Craig. 1913. *Egyptian Irrigation.* 3rd ed. 2 vols. London: Spon, and New York: Spon and Chamberlain.

World Bank. 1975. *Turkey: Prospects and Problems of an Expanding Economy.* World Bank Country Economic Report. Washington, D.C.

————. 1982. *Turkey: Industrialization and Trade Strategy.* World Bank Country Study. Washington, D.C.

————. 1988. *World Tables 1987.* 4th ed. Washington, D.C.

————. *World Debt Tables.* Various years. Washington, D.C.

————. *World Development Report.* Various years. Washington, D.C.

Zaitoun, Mohaya A. 1988. *Earnings, Subsidies, and Cost of Living: An Analysis of*

Recent Developments in the Egyptian Economy. Working Paper. Geneva: International Labour Organisation.

Ziadeh, Farhat J. 1978. "Law and Property in Egypt: Real Rights." *The American Journal of Comperative Law* 26: 239–71.

Index

Land (Turkey): abundance of, 258; as factor of production, 462–63; as natural resource, 439; the frontier, 257–58, 263, 267, 280
Landau, Jacob M., 425, 428
Land Code (1858) in Ottoman Empire, 297
Land distribution in Egypt, 47–49, 67, 497; in Turkey, 334, 457, 497. *See also* Land Distribution Law (1946) in Turkey; Land Reform Law (1952) in Egypt
Land Distribution Law (1946) in Turkey, 341
Landes, D. S., 50, 56
Land ownership (Egypt): by foreign nationals, 67; private, urban, 127–28; redistribution (1952), 118; by royal family, 67; unequal distribution of, 105
Land ownership in Ottoman Empire, 298–99
Land ownership in Turkey, 257–58, 280
Land Reform Law (1952) in Egypt, 67, 118, 120, 124, 244, 453
Lausanne Peace Treaty (1923), 310–11, 312–14, 320
Law for the Encouragement of Industry (1909, 1915), 293, 314, 317
Leamer, Edward E., 356, 461, 464, 466, 469, 470, 474 n1
Lee, E., 33, 136, 498
Legal system in Egypt, 50–51
Leibenstein, H., 280
Leith, J. Clark, 239 n8
Levi, I. G., 53, 243
Lewis, Arthur W., 27
LFSs. *See* Labor force surveys (LFSs)
Liberal party in Turkey, 322
Liberation Rally party in Egypt, 111
Life expectancy in Egypt, 41, 234; in Turkey, 282
Lindbeck, Assar, 442
List, Friedrich, 312, 522–23
Literacy rate in Egypt, 505; in Turkey, 505
Lucas, Edward F., 10, 12, 401
Lutfi, Ahmad, 61

Mabro, R., 87, 96, 99, 160
McCarthy, Justin, 295, 318
McCullogh, J. R., 543
MacDonald Report (1920) in Egypt, 90
Maddison, Angus, 319
Mahdi rebellion, 90
Mahmoud, Mohammed, 64
Malthus, T. R., 542

Manufacturing sector (Egypt): government determination of wages in, 185; employment in, 131; total factor productivity in, 160–62, 466
Manufacturing sector (Turkey): performance in etatist period of, 325; performance of, 266–67, 270, 316, 321, 330, 357; total factor productivity in, 355–56, 466
Mardin, Şerif, 426, 427
Marei, Sayed, 120–23, 124–25, 155
Marginal productivity theory in Egypt, 136
Marshall, Alfred, 547 n2
Martin, Germain, 53, 243
Martin, P. L., 56, 184
Marx, Karl, 543
Marxism-Leninism in Egypt, 115
Marxists-Leninists, 442
Marzouk, G. A., 5, 48, 97, 99, 102, 120, 188, 211
Mead, Donald C., 62 n4, 185, 446, 525
Menderes, Adnan, 338, 339, 340, 354, 422, 426
Merkez Bankası (central bank) in Turkey, 449
Metha, S. D., 108 n4
Middle East Supply Centre, 96, 242, 457
Migration (Egypt): as constitutional right, 251; to Arab OPEC countries, 28, 131, 180, 251, 254; effect on labor force statistics of, 131, 135; seasonal agriculture, 55–56
Migration in Ottoman Empire, 295
Migration (Turkey): from rural to urban areas, 288, 342; of workers to Europe, 267, 289
Military assistance in Egypt, 204
Military establishments, 454–56
Military government (1980–83) in Turkey: economic policies of, 385, 387, 423, 427, 452; impact of public interest on policy of, 428–32; role of, 450
Military power in Egypt, 450; in Turkey, 422
Military takeovers in Egypt, 457–58; in Turkey, 257, 352, 383, 422, 424, 426, 455, 457–58
Mill, James, 542
Milner, Alfred, 62 n5
Mining sector in Egypt, 14, 33–35; in Turkey, 267
Ministry of Agrarian Reform in Egypt, 121–22
Ministry of Industry in Egypt, 126–27, 159

Anwar
Social compact in Turkey, 385
Social mobility in Turkey, 288–89; in
 Egypt, 30–31
Social security organization in Ottoman
 Empire, 349
Social security system in Egypt, 223–26,
 517; in Turkey, 349, 351, 368–69, 517
Social structure in Egypt, 30–31
Soviet Union: assists in Tahrir reclama-
 tion, 122; economic assistance from,
 198; effect of aid and advice of, 160;
 as Egypt's trading partner, 99–100,
 144, 212; influence on agriculture and
 state farm development of, 155, 245;
 involvement in Egypt's War of Attri-
 tion, 123; participation in Aswan High
 Dam construction, 154; supports
 Kemalists, 312
SPO. *See* State Planning Organization
 (SPO) in Turkey
Springborg, Robert, 110, 112–14, 117,
 120, 155, 238 n1, 240 n12, 248, 251,
 453, 526, 533, 540
Srinivasan, T. N., 239 n8, 357
Standard of living in Ottoman Empire, 294
State economic enterprises (SEEs). *See*
 State-owned enterprises
State-owned enterprises (Egypt), 243–44;
 effect on investment and savings of,
 193–95; as form of government inter-
 vention, 171–74
State-owned enterprises (Turkey), 257–
 58, 270; deficits of, 344–45; as monop-
 olies, 314, 323; role in industrialization
 of, 456
State Planning Organization (SPO) in
 Turkey, 352–54, 360–61
Steinback, Udo, 425
Subsidies in Egypt, 26, 226–28
Sudan, 90
Suez Canal: investment in, 525; nationa-
 lization of, 14, 19, 40–41, 99; revenues
 from, 14–15, 19, 40–41, 99, 130
Suez War (1956), 99, 253, 453
Sümer Bank in Turkey, 314
Supreme Arbitration Board in Turkey, 387
Syndicate of Agricultural Engineers,
 122–24
Syrquin, Moshe, 355, 358, 365

Tahrir project in Egypt, 120–21
Tanzimat Decree (1839): impact of, 292–
 93, 421

Tariff reform (Egypt) (1930): 65, 81, 87–
 88, 99, 107, 246, 451; (Turkey) (1929),
 320, 422
Tax farming in Ottoman Empire, 299; in
 Turkey, 315
Tax system (Egypt): historical, 92–93;
 policy under Capitulations of, 59–60,
 247; reform of, 64–65, 67, 93–94
Tax system in Ottoman Empire, 299
Tax system (Turkey): effect of increased
 rates of (1970s), 389; reform in 1935
 for, 337; reforms for (1981–85), 389–
 90; revision of Ottoman, 315–16
Taylor, 30
Technical efficiency measurement in
 Egypt, 162–63
Terms of trade in Egypt, 10–12; in Tur-
 key, 265–66, 272, 319, 332
Textile industry (Egypt): Bank Misr
 Group control in, 126; cotton textiles
 in, 89
Textile industry in Ottoman Empire, 301
Thornburg, M. W., 338
Tignor, Robert, 65, 78, 79, 81, 83, 90,
 103, 108 n1, 112, 238 n1, 246, 509
Tinbergen, Jan, 352–53, 360–61
Todd, John A., 52
Tourism industry in Egypt, 130, 200
Tourk, Khairy, 62 n3
Trade policy (Egypt): bilateral, 144; of
 Capitulations, 3, 87; for cotton exports
 (1921–32), 83–86; government control
 with nationalization, 200; liberalization
 under Sadat regime of, 526; no controls in pre-World War II period, 79;
 since 1918, 136–45. *See also* Tariff reform
Trade policy (Turkey): bilateral agreements as, 457; liberalization of, 388–
 89, 403–11, 423. *See also* Tariff reform
Trade sector (Egypt): bilateral trade since
 World War II, 144; data inconsistencies
 for, 137, 142–44; effect of other country policy on, 254; impact of treaties
 on protection levels, 87; lack of bilateral agreements for (1930s), 79, 144,
 457; levels of growth for, 15, 19, 22; licensing in, 100, 243–44; quantitative
 controls in, 243; shift toward communist countries of, 144–45, 254; terms of
 trade trend and fluctuation of, 10–13,
 82–83, 441. *See also* Effective rate of
 protection (ERP) in Egypt; Protection
 levels in Egypt
Trade sector (Ottoman Empire): expan-